SOCIOLOGICAL STUDIES IN ROMAN HISTORY

Keith Hopkins was a sociologist and Professor of Ancient History at Cambridge from 1985 to 2001. He is widely recognised as one of the most radical, innovative and influential Roman historians of his generation. This volume presents fourteen of Hopkins' essays on an impressive range of subjects: contraception, demography, economic history, slavery, literacy, imperial power, Roman religion, early Christianity, and the social and political structures of the ancient world. The papers have been re-edited and revised with accompanying essays by Hopkins' colleagues, friends and former students. This volume brings Hopkins' work up to date. It sets his distinctive and pioneering use of sociological approaches in a wider intellectual context and explores his lasting impact on the ways ancient history is now written. This volume will interest all those fascinated by Rome and its empire, and particularly those eager to experience challenging and controversial ways of understanding the past.

Christopher Kelly is Professor of Classics and Ancient History at the University of Cambridge and President of Corpus Christi College. His books include *Ruling the Later Roman Empire* (2004), *The End of Empire: Attila the Hun and the Fall of Rome* (2009) and *Theodosius II: Rethinking the Roman Empire in Late Antiquity* (Cambridge, 2013). He is editor of the *Journal of Roman Studies*. He owes a great deal of his fascination with power and the workings of institutions to Keith Hopkins who supervised his doctoral thesis on 'Bureaucracy and corruption in the later Roman empire'.

CAMBRIDGE CLASSICAL STUDIES

SOCIOLOGICAL STUDIES IN ROMAN HISTORY

KEITH HOPKINS
University of Cambridge

Edited by
CHRISTOPHER KELLY
University of Cambridge

Shaftesbury Road, Cambridge CB2 8EA, United Kingdom

One Liberty Plaza, 20th Floor, New York, NY 10006, USA

477 Williamstown Road, Port Melbourne, VIC 3207, Australia

314–321, 3rd Floor, Plot 3, Splendor Forum, Jasola District Centre, New Delhi – 110025, India

103 Penang Road, #05–06/07, Visioncrest Commercial, Singapore 238467

Cambridge University Press is part of Cambridge University Press & Assessment, a department of the University of Cambridge.

We share the University's mission to contribute to society through the pursuit of education, learning and research at the highest international levels of excellence.

www.cambridge.org
Information on this title: www.cambridge.org/9781009353786

DOI: 10.1017/ 9781139093552

First published 2018
First paperback edition 2022

A catalogue record for this publication is available from the British Library

ISBN 978-1-107-01891-4 Hardback
ISBN 978-1-009-35378-6 Paperback

CONTENTS

FIGURES

TABLES

CONTRIBUTORS

Peter Fibiger Bang is Associate Professor at the Saxo Institute in the University of Copenhagen. H. asked to supervise the second year of his Ph.D. in Cambridge and made it one of intellectual play and expanding horizons. Trying to stay true to this lesson, his work is located at a crossroads of Roman, comparative and world history and has sought to tackle a variety of themes ranging from the economy to imperial culture. He is the author of *The Roman Bazaar: A Comparative Study of Trade and Markets in a Tributary Empire* (2008), and co-editor of a number of books, among others, *Tributary Empires in Global History* (2011), *Universal Empire: A Comparative Approach to Imperial Culture and Representation in Eurasian History* (2012) and *The Oxford Handbook of the State in the Ancient Near East and Mediterranean* (2013).

Mary Beard is Professor of Classics at the University of Cambridge. Her books include *The Roman Triumph* (2007), *Laughter in Ancient Rome: On Joking, Tickling, and Cracking up* (2014), *SPQR: A History of Ancient Rome* (2015) and *The Colosseum* (2005), written jointly with H. She was a friend and colleague of H. from 1979 until his death. They shared many lunches, but never exchanged letters.

Keith Bradley is the Eli J. and Helen Shaheen Professor Emeritus of Classics at the University of Notre Dame and Adjunct Professor in the Department of Greek and Roman Studies at the University of Victoria. The beneficiary of a long friendship with H., he remains grateful for the challenging example and encouragement H. constantly offered to understand and recover Roman historical experience. He is the author most recently of *Apuleius and Antonine Rome: Historical Essays* (2012).

Kate Cooper is Professor of History at the University of London and Head of Department at Royal Holloway. She writes and teaches on the world of the Mediterranean in the Roman period, with a special interest in gender and the household, and the interconnected problems of religion, resistance movements and violence. Her recent books include *Band of Angels: The Forgotten World of Early Christian Women* (2013) and *The Fall of the Roman Household* (2007). Her path crossed briefly with H.'s during her first year as a young scholar in the UK from overseas many years ago – which is a big part of how she met all the most interesting people.

Catharine Edwards is Professor of Classics and Ancient History at Birkbeck, University of London. Her first book, *The Politics of Immorality in Ancient Rome* (1993), was based on a Ph.D. thesis supervised by H. With Greg Woolf, she co-edited a stealth Festschrift for H., *Rome the Cosmopolis* (2003). Her other books include *Death in Ancient Rome* (2007). She is currently working on Seneca.

Jaś Elsner is Professor of Late Antique Art at the University of Oxford and Humfry Payne Senior Research Fellow in Classical Art and Archaeology at Corpus Christi College. He is also Visiting Professor of Art and Religion at the University of Chicago. He apologises for his Oxonian affiliation: H. once opened a seminar with the comment that: 'there is a subject called psychology, which in Oxford is mainly conducted by experiments on rats'. His current project is an international exhibition at the Ashmolean Museum – Empires of Faith – comprising a Leverhulme Trust funded collaboration between the British Museum and Wolfson College, Oxford concerning the birth of the visual cultures in the world religions.

William Harris is Shepherd Professor of History at Columbia University and Director of the University's Center for the Ancient Mediterranean. His *Roman Power: A Thousand Years of Empire* was published last year by Cambridge, and a volume he edited, *Popular Medicine in Graeco-Roman Antiquity: Explorations* also came out in 2016 (in the series Columbia Studies in the Classical Tradition). He memorialised H. in the *Proceedings of the British Academy* 2005.

Mamoru Ikeguchi is Associate Professor at Kurume University (Fukuoka, Japan). Two of the central chapters of his Cambridge doctoral thesis, 'The dynamics of agricultural locations in Roman Italy', were supervised by H. in his final two years as Professor of Ancient History. His economic/geographical approach – exemplified in 'Settlement patterns in Italy and transport costs in the Mediterranean' (*Kodai* 13/14 2003–4: 239–49) – is a result of encouragement by H. – 'H. always had an insight into what I wanted to do.'

Willem Jongman is Reader in Economic and Social History at the University of Groningen. His *The Economy and Society of Pompeii* (1988, now an ACLS Humanities E-Book), begun while a research fellow at King's College Cambridge, owed much to H.'s inspiration, criticism and friendship. His work is often characterised by a combination of economic (and sociological) theory and method and archaeological data. In autumn 2016, he gave a series of public lectures at the Collège de France on the archaeology of Roman economic performance.

Christopher Kelly is Professor of Classics and Ancient History at the University of Cambridge and President of Corpus Christi College. His books include *Ruling the Later Roman Empire* (2004), *The End of Empire: Attila the Hun and the Fall of Rome* (2009) and *Theodosius II: Rethinking the Roman Empire in Late Antiquity* (2013). He owes a great deal of his fascination with power – its use and abuse – and the workings of institutions to H. who supervised his doctoral thesis on 'Bureaucracy and corruption in the later Roman empire' and taught him college politics, wine and gardening (in equal measure). He is H.'s literary executor.

Neville Morley is Professor of Classics and Ancient History at the University of Exeter. He works on different themes within ancient economic history, historical theory and the modern reception of the ancient world. His recent books include *Antiquity and Modernity* (2009) and *Thucydides and the Idea of History* (2014). He was supervised briefly by H. at Cambridge, and has continued to engage with different aspects of his work, especially in relation to historical methodology and the influence of social science on ancient history.

Walter Scheidel is Dickason Professor in the Humanities, Professor of Classics and History, and Kennedy-Grossman Fellow in Human Biology at Stanford University. He has published on ancient social and economic history, historical demography and the comparative history of labour, sex and state formation. He cherishes the memory of co-teaching 'Ancient History: Problems and Methods' with H. back in the late 1990s, and stubbornly believes that *Crocodile Mummy* would have been the best title for the present volume.

Caroline Vout is Reader in Classics at the University of Cambridge. She is a historian and art historian with a particular interest in the literary and visual cultures of the Roman imperial period and their reception. Her last book is titled *Sex on Show: Seeing the Erotic in Greece and Rome* (2013). Her next one, *Classical Art: A Life History from Antiquity to the Present*, will be published in 2018. Her doctoral dissertation was supervised, in part, by H. – usually over a lengthy lunch.

Greg Woolf is Director of the Institute of Classical Studies at the School of Advanced Study in London. His recent books include *Tales of the Barbarians* (2011) and *Rome, An Empire's Story* (2012). He was taught by H. in the 1980s at Cambridge and has since written on cultural change, literacy, the economy, urbanism and religion, often in the shadow of H. Rereading some of H.'s essays for this volume reminded Greg not only how sharp his argumentation was but also how much fun his conversation (and footnotes) could be.

PREFACE

As Keith Hopkins' students we learned early the importance of being able to justify our labours and always to have ready an answer, ideally both elegant and plausible, to the implied question So what?

C. Edwards and G. Woolf, 'Cosmopolis: Rome as world city', in their (eds), *Rome the Cosmopolis*, 2003.[1]

This volume collects a selection of fourteen essays by the Roman historian and sociologist Keith Hopkins (1934–2004), Professor of Ancient History in the University of Cambridge (1985–2001) and Fellow of King's College (1963–7 and 1985–2004). It is not – and this should be stressed at once – a biographical memoir. That task has been handsomely and sympathetically discharged by William Harris on behalf of the British Academy (and in more modest compass by Robin Osborne for *Past & Present*).[2] It is also fair to say that H. himself would have been wary of any attempt to monumentalise his work between hard covers, reluctant to see his essays pressed and preserved like some anthology of dried flowers.

In reply to H.'s (still echoing) 'So what?', it should be said – and with confidence – that the essays included in this volume are worth reprinting, not because they represent the final or conclusive word on an impressive range of subjects, but rather because they still provoke the careful and critical reader to further thought, and because, taken together, these fourteen pieces represent a highly original and innovative approach to

[1] Edwards and Woolf 2003b: 18.

[2] Osborne 2004a; Harris 2005; see too the obituaries in *The Guardian*, 29 March 2004 (Graham Burton); *The Telegraph*, 17 March 2004; *The Times*, 25 March 2004; *The Independent*, 23 March 2004 (Christopher Kelly); *The New York Times*, 15 March 2004 (Campbell Robertson); and *King's College Cambridge Annual Report* (2004) 42–7.

ancient history-writing which still commands – and demands – attention. It is with the continued importance and relevance of H.'s work in mind that each essay in this volume is followed by an "Afterword" written by one of H.'s friends and/or colleagues and/or former graduate students. These brief interventions set each essay in its wider context, offer an assessment of its impact on the field and (most importantly) reflect on why it is still an enjoyable, stimulating and rewarding read.

Of course (and unashamedly) there is an element of celebration in this volume. For H.'s former graduate students, solidly represented here, thinking about this project provided an opportunity to recall H.'s professorial seminars on Tuesday afternoons in his magnificent rooms in King's. Two agonistic hours were followed by an escape across King's Parade to a newly opened vegan café for carrot cake and curious teas. Of course, looking back, it is clear that this was no escape at all: continued spirited discussion, and lasting camaraderie, was precisely what H. had hoped would result. For H.'s friends and colleagues (here happily overlapping categories), this project allowed them to remember H.'s wit, his passion for gardening, his convivial dinner parties and his impressive private cellar. H. was capable of being extraordinarily good fun. To quote William Harris' assessment:

> Keith Hopkins' public persona was the unembarrassed hedonist, who sought pleasure with fine wines, at table (he was an outstanding cook), in gardens, in far-off places, and in the company of women. These pleasures were, obviously, quite genuine, and it was an added pleasure that they sometimes scandalised his staider colleagues. He unstintingly gave great pleasure to others too, and was a profoundly sociable being.[3]

But in this volume, pleasant personal reminiscence is deliberately shouldered into the background. The focus is firmly on H.'s work. It is hoped that this tactic might have appealed to H. who treated biography as (at best) a pallid form of history. He always doubted (here commenting on St Paul) 'that knowing the man and his context will explain his thoughts – as

[3] Harris 2005: 104; obit. in the *King's College Cambridge Annual Report* (2004) 46–7.

though knowing that Beethoven was short, deaf and lived in Vienna from the age of 22 helps us to understand his music. I suppose it does, but only at the 5 per cent level.'[4]

This volume is (self-evidently) the work of many hands. I am particularly grateful to the thirteen friends and colleagues who (readily) agreed to write the Afterwords; for their enthusiasm for this project from its inception and their patience during its completion; and to the journals and publishing houses who responded so kindly and enthusiastically when informed of this project and its intention to reprint some of H.'s essays in a completely revised format. Especial thanks are due to a gang of four graduate editorial assistants – Richard Flower, Robin Whelan, Luke Gardiner and Graham Andrews – who all tirelessly chased down references and bibliography in Cambridge, Oxford, Chicago and Manchester; to Richard Flower who discharged with peerless proficiency the task of re-formatting the texts after they had been scanned; to Graham Andrews for expertly compiling an intelligent and helpful index; to Alessandro Launaro who first suggested the fine jacket illustration from the *agrimensores*; to Robin Osborne and Michael Sharp, for much useful advice and help; and to Martha T. Roth (former Dean of Humanities, University of Chicago) and Brenda L. Johnson (Library Director and University Librarian, University of Chicago), and her staff at the Regenstein Library, whose unfailing courtesy and assistance made it possible for this project to be completed in America.

Editorial assistance for the preparation of this volume was generously supported by the Henry Arthur Thomas Fund in the Faculty of Classics and the Newton Trust Small Research Grant Scheme in the School of Arts and Humanities, University of Cambridge.

[4] Hopkins 1997a: 15.

EDITORIAL NOTE

The fourteen essays reprinted in this volume have all been re-edited: that is, rather than being presented in the widely diverse formats of the originals, they now confirm to a single set of editorial and bibliographical conventions. It should also be noted – and with all due delicacy – that the various, and not infrequent, slips and errors in the footnotes have, as far as possible, been identified and (silently) amended. No new secondary bibliography has been added, but (where it seemed helpful or appropriate) additional information on texts and translations has been offered. This material has been placed in the footnotes ⟨between angled brackets⟩. From that point of view, the essays in this volume are best regarded as 'corrected reprints'. That said, for ease of reference, in citations the page number of the original publication is always given first, followed by the page number of this volume [between square brackets]. The bibliography serves two simultaneous purposes: it gathers together all the items cited by H. in thirteen of the fourteen essays presented here (allowing the reader to form some impression of H.'s library);[1] but it also includes the items cited in the Introduction, Afterwords and the occasional ⟨bracketed⟩ additions to the footnotes. Save for H.'s own works, these latter are, in each case, marked by an asterisk (*).

1 The exception is the posthumously published, 'The political economy of the Roman empire' (Hopkins 2009 = essay 13) for which almost all of the footnotes and bibliographical references were supplied by Walter Scheidel in April 2006. Only the references in the main text and elements of footnotes 21, 47–9, 57, 66–7, 71, 76–8, 83, 87 and 89 are derived from H.'s own manuscript of a paper first given in Stanford in 2000, and lightly revised by H. in 2002; see explanatory note at [488 n. **] and Woolf [527 n. 1].

BIOGRAPHICAL NOTE

(Morris) Keith Hopkins was born in Sutton, Surrey on 20 June 1934 and died in Cambridge on 9 March 2004. He is buried in the churchyard of St John the Baptist, Finchingfield, Essex. He was educated at Brentwood School. After two years of National Service (learning Russian in the Royal Navy's language programme and qualifying as a Service Interpreter in February 1955), H. went up to Cambridge to read Classics as a scholar at King's College, Cambridge. He graduated with first-class honours in 1958. The following year he began doctoral work under the supervision of A. H. M. Jones. From 1961 to 1963, he was assistant lecturer in Sociology at the University of Leicester; assistant lecturer and then lecturer in Sociology at the LSE from 1963 to 1972 (held concurrently with a research fellowship at King's College from 1963 to 1967); on secondment to the University of Hong Kong as Professor of Sociology from 1967 to 1969; and Professor of Sociology and Social Anthropology at Brunel University from 1972 to 1985 (Dean of the Faculty of Social Sciences from 1981). He spent 1969–70 and 1974–5 at the Institute for Advanced Study at Princeton. He was elected a Fellow of the British Academy in 1984. From 1985 to 2001, he was Professor of Ancient History in the University of Cambridge and a Fellow of King's College, and Vice-Provost from 2000 until his death. In addition to scholarly articles (fourteen of the most important are reprinted in this volume), H. published one edited volume, *Hong Kong: The Industrial Colony* (Hong Kong/London, 1971); two collections of essays, *Conquerors and Slaves* (Sociological Studies in Roman History 1) (Cambridge, 1978) and *Death and Renewal* (Sociological Studies in Roman History 2) (Cambridge, 1983); and one monograph, *A World Full of Gods: Pagans, Jews and Christians in the Roman Empire* (London, 1999).

INTRODUCTION

KEITH HOPKINS: SIGHTING SHOTS

Building the Wigwam

> Much research is a waste of time; the marginal productivity of each extra footnote is low. Besides, time spent on detail stops one from doing something more useful.
>
> 'Some sociological approaches to Roman history' (1974)[1]

Such provocative openings are at best only half-truths. They are gadfly aphorisms deliberately intended to sting a late-afternoon graduate seminar into sharp response (here Oxford in January 1974). Keith Hopkins delighted, like any skilled soapbox rhetorician, in wittily, repeatedly and unrepentantly overstating his case. His target was a perceived lack of intellectual enterprise amongst his fellow ancient historians (and, of course, only amongst *some* ancient historians – but this is polemic).[2] In reviewing the third edition of the *Oxford Classical Dictionary* for the *Times Literary Supplement* in February 1997, H. offered qualified praise for 'the inclusion of several hundred synoptic or analytical pieces', singling out a handful of new contributions for their 'exemplary clarity, intellectual economy and interest. … They provided the necessary information, but subordinated incidental facts to general problems.' But he also fretted about the growth in the number of entries which he dismissed as 'unnecessary fillers of insignificant omissions made in the previous editions: yet more rarely mentioned Greek colonies, minor characters from Roman Republican and imperial history, forgettable towns in the Roman imperial provinces'. He noted, for example, that the articles on the thirteen successive Hellenistic

[1] 1974a: 1; see too 1990: 624–5; Hopkins and Burton 1983b: 132 caption to table 3.2.

[2] For an approved list, see 1978b: 252 (a tactic not later repeated).

kings of Cappadocia all named Ariarathes or Ariobarzanes – 'about whom we know very little' – occupied two columns: taking up '1/1600 of the whole classical world'.[3]

For H., the *Oxford Classical Dictionary* unhappily exemplified what he found least attractive about the priorities of many of his colleagues: an obsessive interest in detail ('perhaps that is the masochism of our profession'[4]); a privileging of proper nouns (delightfully damned as 'the upper-case mentality of so many British classicists'[5]); and an involuted concentration on a limited cache of evidence only interrupted by fits of donnish excitement about occasional new discoveries which helped 'foster the illusion of academic progress'.[6] In H.'s sharply drawn caricature, classics was an inward-looking discipline in which too many scholars were so enamoured of each other's ability to extract data from often technically difficult and refractory texts (in long-dead languages in which there was a steadily shrinking competence) that they neglected to interrogate the contexts in which that information was embedded. 'For too many ancient historians history is an account of the "evidence", not of the humans or of the society in which the evidence was created.'[7]

There was nothing strikingly new in this critique. Thirty-five years before H.'s provocative graduate seminar, the historian, philosopher and archaeologist R. G. Collingwood had recalled in his *Autobiography* that, as an undergraduate in Oxford before the First World War, he had experienced Roman history in the process of transformation (his heroes were Haverfield and Mommsen), but that Greek history 'was left high and dry by the tide of new methods'. Shunned by the cleverest students, classical Greece remained the dull preserve of 'the scissors-and-paste man'.

At bottom, his business was to know what 'the authorities' had said about the subject he was interested in, and to his authorities' statements he was tied by the

3 1997b.

4 Hopkins 1987: 121 [essay 4: 146]; see too 1978c: 185.

5 1997b; see too 1972a: 356, 1978c: 185; Hopkins and Burton 1983a: 41 n. 16.

6 1994a.

7 1978c: 186; and see especially the critique in 1972a and the 'Sieve syndrome – or a fixation on pebbles' in 1990: 623–5.

leg, however long the rope and however flowery the turf over which it allowed him to circle. If his interest led him towards a subject on which there were no authorities, it led him into a desert where nothing was except the sands of ignorance and the mirage of imagination.[8]

H. – an enthusiastic quoter of Collingwood[9] – did not echo his optimistic view of any continuing improvement in the state of Roman history: 'alas, scissors-and-paste people still dominate the ancient history profession, and some even pride themselves for it'.[10]

To be sure, neither Collingwood nor H. was simply dismissive of facts or 'authorities'. Rather, H.'s anxieties are best illustrated by the sharp contrast (drawn in a number of essays in this volume) between induction and deduction. On the inductivist side stand historians whose sedimentary understanding of the ancient world consists of a careful and continuous accumulation of data. 'In this view, the ancient sources provide our major authority for the description and interpretation of events; description of the evidence should therefore be comprehensive, and discrepancies in the evidence resolved.'[11] For H., the result was a too frequently misplaced confidence in an understanding of the past unruffled by a stifling preponderance of texts written by and for a narrow, highly educated élite (and, in turn, refracted by the sometimes frankly eccentric preoccupations of monk-librarians in medieval scriptoria). 'Credit goes to the ancient historian who makes the best pattern out of the largest number of pieces and cites the most obscure sources relevantly.'[12] Ancient history was still tightly tied by the leg: constructed and constrained by the surviving ancient evidence (as though 'the sources by and large faithfully reported the world in which they lived'[13]), and dangerously prone to glib overgeneralisation ('the Romans thought', 'the Jews believed')

[8] Collingwood 1939: 79–80, see too 82–3.
[9] 1978c: 182–3, 1995–6: 44, 1998: 191 n. 10 [essay 12: 439 n. 10].
[10] 1995–6: 65 n. 8.
[11] 1972a: 355; see too 1983b: p. xiii.
[12] 1978c: 182.
[13] 1978c: 183.

on the basis of a slight handful of supposedly authenticating citations.[14]

By contrast, deductivists (with H. as their self-appointed poster boy) emphasised the importance of working out patterns which might help more broadly to contextualise the ancient data. For H. (who rightly prided himself on his own culinary abilities), this was a difference in approach which separated 'a pre-packed meal from a factory' and 'a crafted confection from a chef. The ingredients are partly the same, the results significantly different.'[15] In 'On the probable age structure of the Roman population' (1966) [essay 3] and its reprise 'Graveyards for historians' (1987) [essay 4], H. used the recently available United Nations model life tables (an aggregate of a vast amount of census data from a wide range of developing countries) to argue that a reconstruction of the Roman population based on the age of death given in funerary inscriptions – 43,000 examples in the western half of the empire[16] – resulted in a distribution of age and mortality unrecognisable in any other pre-industrial society. 'It is inconceivable that the *pattern* of Roman mortality should be so unlike that of all other known populations.'[17] As Walter Scheidel makes clear in his thoughtful response to these two essays:

> H. did not simply seek to answer an empirical question: instead, his contribution focuses on the feasibility of exploring Roman population history – on the nature of the evidence itself. His studies are as much an exercise in applied epistemology as demographic analysis.[18]

Tested by reference to an external standard[19] (the UN model life tables), recorded ages on Roman funerary inscriptions were 'demographically ludicrous'.[20] 'Instead, and this point seems worth stressing, Roman tombstones provide us with a biased

[14] 1964–5: 311, 1978c: 183–5, 1983b: 8 n. 13 (quoted below p. 36), 1983d, 1991a: 482 n. 14, 484 n. 18 [essay 8: 318 n. 14 and 321 n. 18], 1993: 8 n. 8 [essay 11: 403 n. 8], 2000a: 5; Hopkins and Burton 1983b: 156 n. 49; and see below n. 57.

[15] 1998: 191 [essay 12: 439].

[16] 1987: 113 [essay 4: 135].

[17] 1966a: 255 [essay 3: 121].

[18] [154].

[19] To follow H.'s carefully chosen language at 1966a: 264 [essay 3: 134].

[20] 1987: 119 [essay 4: 143].

set of commemorations. Commemorative practice is useful for analysing Roman commemorative practice … useless for understanding Roman patterns of death.'[21]

H.'s concern with pattern and plausibility is elegantly exemplified by 'Christian number and its implications' (1998) [essay 12]. Selecting the end-point was straightforward: an acceptance of the conventional estimate of the number of Christians in the Roman empire at the beginning of the fourth century AD (at the time of the Emperor Constantine's public profession of Christianity) at around 6 million – roughly 7–10 per cent of the empire's population.[22] But early Christianity had started small. The number of 'first' Christians in AD 40 (soon after the crucifixion) was set at 1,000. On the assumption of a constant growth rate between 40 and 300, there were then only 7,400 Christians in 100, 100,000 by 180 and 1 million by the mid-third century.[23] H.'s utter lack of commitment to any of these arbitrary figures is crucial. They are neither necessarily correct nor true.[24] For a start, there is no compelling reason to assume that Christianity grew at a constant rate. Perhaps it advanced rapidly in its early decades: but then it must have slowed later. Perhaps growth fluctuated or sometimes even declined. 'Drawing a single path of consistent growth is merely an intellectual economy in the face of competing probabilities, and in the absence of reliable data.'[25] Rather than provide any definite answer, H.'s calculations aimed to circumscribe a problem.

This approach to evidence and argumentation is perhaps at its clearest in 'Taxes and trade in the Roman empire (200 BC–AD 400)' (1980) [essay 6], which explored the relationship between the flow of taxes and trade in a unified and increasingly

[21] 1987: 115 [essay 4: 137].

[22] 1998: 191–2 [essay 12: 439–40].

[23] 1998: 193 fig. 1 [essay 12: 441 fig. 12.1]. Straight-line growth between 40 and 6,000,000 over 250 years works out at 3.35 per cent (compounded) per annum.

[24] 1983a: 85 [essay 7: 272]: 'Without any commitment as to its truth, let us tentatively estimate … '

[25] 1998: 194 [essay 12: 442]; for a useful parallel, see the discussion of coin loss in 1980a: 107 [essay 6: 226]: 'I should stress that assuming a constant rate of loss is a heuristic device, not a description of reality', and 1995–6: 53.

monetised Mediterranean world. 'For the sake of clarity, I have canvassed several probabilities in the form of propositions, but the evidence is so sparse that it is difficult to *prove* that each proposition is right.'[26] It might be more helpful to say that not all of the seven propositions advanced were equally persuasive. While H. – revisiting the arguments in 'Rome, taxes, rents and trade' (1995–6) and 'Rent, taxes, trade and the city of Rome' (2000) – was eager to defend, modify and improve individual propositions, he remained chiefly concerned with the overall pattern. His objective was to establish a framework (like the steady-line growth of Christianity) 'against which the fragments of evidence can be tested, or around which they can be fitted'.[27] H. was (ruefully) aware that the piecemeal evidence would only support each proposition more or less convincingly than the others. Hence the emphasis on achieving plausible coherence: 'all these arguments, and the evidence from which they are derived, are partial, but they draw strength from their inter-relationship. They back each other up. ... This is what I have called a wigwam argument, in which weak arguments prop each other up.'[28]

It seems a fair claim that the style and shape of H.'s arguments are (in his own formulation) 'distinctively different from the norm'[29] – at least it is a claim put to the test by the essays collected in this volume and those published by H. (some the result of collaboration) in *Conquerors and Slaves* (Sociological Studies in Roman History 1) (1978) and *Death and Renewal* (Sociological Studies in Roman History 2) (1983).[30] But to

[26] 1980a: 101 [essay 6: 213].

[27] 1998: 194 [essay 12: 442] and see below pp. 15–16.

[28] 1980a: 116 and n. 43 [essay 6: 241 and n. 43] with B. D. Shaw 1982: 23 and Jongman [264]. See too the formulation in 1978b: 19–20: 'Unfortunately there is hardly any sound evidence with which this generalisation can be validated; yet it seems more attractive than any alternative I can think of. There are several pieces of evidence, each insufficient or untrustworthy in itself, which seem collectively to confirm it. I call this the wigwam argument: each pole would fall down by itself, but together the poles stand up, by leaning on each other'; and 1995–6: 42 (quoted below p. 15).

[29] 1995–6: 42.

[30] *Conquerors and Slaves* (1978b) consisted of five essays: (1) 'Conquerors and slaves: the impact of conquering an empire on the political economy of Italy'; (2) 'The growth and practice of slavery in Roman times'; (3) 'Between slavery and freedom: on freeing slaves at Delphi' (in collaboration with P. J. Roscoe); (4) 'The

insist on viewing his argumentative strategies, as H. frequently demanded, as taking sides in a methodological tug-of-war between inductive and deductive approaches to ancient history-writing is ultimately unprofitable. Perhaps (and more kindly) it should be understood instead as a deliberately swashbuckling stance which, to plunder H.'s own phrases, offered a convenient 'simplification of a complex reality'[31] – a handy 'intellectual economy in the face of competing probabilities'.[32] But simplicity and economy have their costs. In wittily ridiculing the perceived deficiencies of conventional scholarship, H. risked trivialising his own close commitment to the ancient evidence. As Wim Jongman rightly remarks (in his commentary on 'Taxes and trade in the Roman empire (200 BC–AD 400)' [essay 6]): 'if there is one thing that characterises H.'s work, it is precisely the passion for facts and empirical detail.'[33] For example, the fulcrum of 'On the probable age structure of the Roman population' [essay 3] was a study of seven thousand funerary inscriptions from Rome, Italy and North Africa.[34] The third essay in *Conquerors and Slaves* (written in collaboration with P. J. Roscoe) – 'Between slavery and freedom: on freeing slaves at Delphi' – analysed inscriptions which recorded twelve hundred legally binding acts of slave manumission executed between 201 BC and AD 100.[35] One of the most persuasive propositions in 'Taxes and trade in the Roman empire' [essay 6] (proposition 6: 'the integration of the monetary economy in the high empire') was supported by 'the analysis of over 90,000 silver coins found in five regions of the Roman empire: southern Germany, northern Italy,

political power of eunuchs' (a lightly revised version of 1963a); (5) 'Divine emperors or the symbolic unity of the Roman empire'. *Death and Renewal* (1983b) was made up of four essays (two co-authored with Graham Burton): (1) 'Murderous games'; (2) 'Political succession in the late Republic (249–50 BC)' (= Hopkins and Burton 1983a); (3) 'Ambition and withdrawal: the senatorial aristocracy under the emperors' (= Hopkins and Burton 1983b); (4) 'Death in Rome' (in collaboration with Melinda Letts).

[31] 1995–6: 41.

[32] 1998: 194 [essay 12: 442].

[33] Jongman [267]; see too Woolf [528–9].

[34] 1966a: 259 n. 22 [essay 3: 124 n. 20].

[35] 1978b: 133–71 with the data conveniently summarised at 140 table 3.1.

Britain and Gaul, the Balkans and a garrison town in Syria'.[36] The lengthy and detailed demographic analysis of senatorial career-patterns in the late Republic and early empire in *Death and Renewal* (co-authored with Graham Burton) was based on the close study of five hundred men elected (or appointed) to the consulship.[37] A final example: one of the central arguments in 'The political economy of the Roman empire' (2009) [essay 13] was driven by H.'s own enthusiasm for new scientific research on deep-drilled core-samples from Greenland, glacial lakes in Sweden and Swiss peat bogs. (By measuring a marked rise in windborne pollutants, especially lead, in the first and second centuries AD – and to levels not reached again until the eighteenth century – these ice-cores could be argued to capture the atmospheric results of a surge in the production of silver in the Roman mines in Spain. For H., the increased availability of silver, mostly for the imperial mint, was an index both of the prosperity that came with empire and of the importance of monetisation in the development of a more integrated Mediterranean-wide economy.[38]) To this scatter of illustrations of close engagement with ancient data, add, for good measure, H.'s learned excursions into the heavily fortified technical fields of textual criticism ('A textual emendation in a fragment of Musonius Rufus: a note on contraception' (1965) [essay 2]), papyrology ('Conquest by book' (1991) [essay 10]) and epigraphy.[39]

Softening (but not conceding) his position in 'Rome, taxes, rents and trade', H. offered 'a slightly shame-faced, perhaps also two-faced apologia'.

Actually, there is ample room for both compromise and overlap between model-builders and inductivists; their positions are more complementary than opposed. After all, deduction like induction is partly a rhetorical pose. The

[36] 1980a: 112 [essay 6: 235]; see too 1978a: 39–40 n. 11 [essay 5: 165–6 n. 11].

[37] Hopkins and Burton 1983a and b; see particularly 1983b: 130–3 on the research design.

[38] 2009: 197–8 [essay 13: 518–20] with Woolf [528]; see too 2004: p. xix.

[39] See, for example, 1978a: 41–2 n. 13 [essay 5: 167 n. 13], 1980a: 105 n. 16 [essay 6: 222 n. 16], 1983a: 108 n. 34 [essay 7: 295 n. 34] on *IG* XII suppl. 348; or 1995–6: 55 on Hyginus. H. as expert is cleverly assessed in Morley 2006: 30–2.

> model-builder, if he/she is going to have any chance of success, has to know much of what the sources tell us. The pure inductivist, if he/she is going to be understood outside a narrow range of committed specialists, has to think through what the implications are of his detailed arguments.[40]

The shift in language is also important. To be sure, H.'s ancient history-writing was, first and foremost, propositional and problem driven. He described this approach as 'matrix thinking'[41] (a term used once, and swiftly discarded) or, more satisfactorily, as model-building. What mattered most was the 'fall' of the data; that is (as 'On the probable age structure of the Roman population' [essay 3] exemplifies), H. was chiefly concerned to plot the ancient evidence against a wider set of possibilities – or, perhaps better, probabilities. 'Models allow us to construct whole pictures, into which the surviving fragments of ancient source material can be plausibly fitted.'[42] From that point of view, H.'s Roman history was at base as inescapably anchored to a bedrock of traditional source-citation as the ancient history-writing to which he objected.[43] Whatever the distinctive difference of his preferred style of argument, H. shared with his colleagues a steadfast concern to understand the often poor and patchy evidence for the ancient world by testing its strengths, deficiencies and limitations.

One key concern was to establish the field of play. That is most clearly illustrated by the use of UN model life tables in 'On the probable age structure of the Roman population' [essay 3] or the initial postulate of straight-line growth in 'Christian number and its implications' [essay 12]: 'the straight line ... is like a set of goal posts in a game of football; arbitrarily placed, but good to measure the game against'.[44] It was equally important to establish the boundary conditions – the parameters – of any proposition. This might usefully be done by a series of 'crude and speculative' calculations. 'My

[40] 1995–6: 41–2; see also 1998: 186 n. 2, 194 [essay 12: 433 n. 2, 442–3] and the optimism (later abandoned) of 1972a: 356. Note too the comments of Harris 2005: 99.

[41] 1995–6: 66 n. 14.

[42] 1995–6: 41; see too 1983a: 95 [essay 7: 287–8], 1998: 194 [essay 12: 442] quoted above p. 6.

[43] Millar 1979: 170; B. D. Shaw 1982: 30, 49–50; Osborne 2004a: 7; Harris 2005: 93.

[44] 1998: 194 [essay 12: 443].

objective here is not accuracy, but a rough order of magnitude to tease out implications which might remain obscured without rough figures.'[45] In 'Taxes and trade' [essay 6], H.'s estimate of the gross domestic product of the Roman empire started with a benchmark proposition: 'we can make a *minimum* estimate by multiplying the size of the population by the amount of food necessary to keep that population at the minimum level of subsistence'.[46] These 'sighting shots'[47] – 'a first fix',[48] 'guesstimates',[49] 'a crude guess',[50] 'provisional, simplifying calculations',[51] 'closer to guesses than to fact'[52] – were the building blocks of H.'s parametric reasoning. 'We make a simplifying assumption, to see where it leads us, without facing up initially to all the complexities of the real world. It is as though, in order to guess the weight of an elephant, you first imagine it to be a solid cube.'[53]

This pattern of reasoning was also important on a smaller scale. H. was always wary of validating the exceptional because widely scattered data when averaged yielded a plausible result (that 'is like confirming reports about giants and pygmies by reference to average height in England'[54]); or of being too quick to allow an outlier to defeat a general proposition ('I call this the Mt Everest gambit'[55] or the 'Irish dwarf syndrome'[56]). Above all, H. was always reluctant to assume (at least as a starting-point) that the Roman empire had broken loose from the broad material constraints faced by any pre-modern

45 1983a: 88 [essay 7: 276–7]; see too 1978b: 32 n. 41, 56, 110 n. 23, 1991b: 134 [essay 10: 364].

46 1980a: 117–18 [essay 6: 244].

47 1983a: 100 [essay 7: 296], 1991b: 134 [essay 10: 364], 1978b: 3 n. 6.

48 1983a: 85 [essay 7: 271].

49 1995–6: 73 n. 73, 1998: 193 n. 17 [essay 12: 442 n. 17].

50 1978b: 69*p*.

51 1995–6: 45.

52 1983a: 95 [essay 7: 288].

53 1995–6: 42, 1998: 192 [essay 12: 440].

54 1966a: 251 [essay 3: 114]; see too the careful explanation (for classicists) of mode and median in 1964–5: 309 n. 1; also 1966a: 249 [essay 3: 110]; but not always: 'variance explained is the correlation coefficient squared', 1980a: 111 [essay 6: 230] with Morley 2006: 31 n. 18.

55 1995–6: 65 n. 5; see too Hopkins and Burton 1983a: 41.

56 1990: 625; dwarves are repurposed in 1995–6: 43.

society. Reviewing A. N. Wilson, *Paul: The Mind of the Apostle* (1996), H. listed a number of Wilson's errors:

By error I mean opinions with which I disagree. For example, I very much doubt that … the hyper-sophisticated Philo popularised anything, let alone a Neoplatonic way of reading the Bible; or that 'all Jews believe' one thing in particular (that is surely a Christianising formulation) … [or that] the city of Rome had a population of two million (twice the size of London in 1800).[57]

Similarly, reflecting on Roger Bagnall and Bruce Frier, *The Demography of Roman Egypt* (1994), H. questioned their high estimates for urbanisation at 'three times the levels found in Europe in 1800'.[58] Likewise, Roman census figures for Italy in the early third century BC: 'the transmitted figures … are unbelievable: they give an average density of 111 persons per km^2 in Roman territory, which is several times the figure for the agricultural population in Italy in 1936'.[59] It is important to stress that these critical observations signalled the beginning of a debate: they were 'invitations to argument and discussion'.[60] What was principally at stake for H. was plausibility. For example, on Roman demography:

It seems to me that the burden of proof is firmly on those who wish to assert that the Roman population in general had a lower mortality than other pre-industrial populations with similar technical achievements or towns; they must show that there were present in the Roman empire factors which could have led to a general diminution of mortality.[61]

So too the population of the city of Rome. In truth, H. had not played A. N. Wilson entirely fair. Although H.'s preferred estimate at between 800,000 and 1 million was half Wilson's figure, that still meant that Rome in the first century AD (as H. noted elsewhere) 'was as large as London in 1800, when London was the largest city in the world'.[62] H. was

57 1997a: 15.
58 1995–6: 64–5 n. 4 with Bagnall and Frier 1994: 56.
59 1978b: 20 n. 26; see too 69*k*, 1980a: 116 n. 45 [essay 6: 242 n. 45], 1983b: 237 n. 48, 243 n. 56.
60 1983a: 95 [essay 7: 288].
61 1966a: 264 [essay 3: 133].
62 1995–6: 58; see too 2000b: 261, 2004: p. xiii, 2009: 190 [essay 13: 507–8], and the flicker of doubt in 1978a: 38 n. 7 [essay 5: 163 n. 7].

reluctant to discard this apparent outlier. As he concluded in a closely argued appendix to the first essay in *Conquerors and Slaves*: ('On the probable size of the population of the city of Rome'): 'all the recorded numbers indicate a very large city by pre-industrial European standards ... Precision is impossible. But all the figures cited suggest that the city of Rome had a very large population.'[63] The exception demanded explanation. Rome's size – the largest city in Europe for seventeen hundred years and 'by far the largest and wealthiest single market'[64] in the ancient Mediterranean world – was a topic to which H. repeatedly returned as an important element in constructing an overall understanding of the political economy of the Roman empire.[65]

As Neville Morley stresses in his assessment of 'Economic growth and towns in classical antiquity' (1978) [essay 5], 'what really matters in this style of argument is the coherence and plausibility of the overall interpretation and its underlying assumptions, the extent to which this account is more

[63] 1978b: 96–8, quoting 97 and 98.

[64] 1983a: 88 [essay 7: 277].

[65] 1978a: 37–8 [essay 5: 163–4], 1978b: 1–2, 1983a: 88 [essay 7: 276–7], 1995–6: 58–9, 2000b: 260–2, 2004: pp. xii–xiv, 2009: 190–2 [essay 13: 507–11]; see too, helpfully, Jongman 2003c: especially 100–3. For a useful parallel, see the comments in B. D. Shaw 1982: 29–30 suggesting that in 'Contraception in the Roman empire' (1965a) [essay 1] H. may have been too swift to accept the silence of the Roman evidence in dismissing the use of coitus interruptus; see too Parkin 1992: 193 n. 159. But note that this was only done after a careful survey of comparative evidence which H. accepted, but did not find wholly persuasive: see especially the marked uncertainties in the discussion at 1965a: 148 [essay 1: 88–9]. H. also accepted that Roman Egypt had been utterly exceptional in the incidence of brother-sister marriage: a practice 'not known to have been common amongst ordinary people in any other human society' (1980b: 303, 1994b: 79–80, 91). The evidence was over one hundred household returns from the census held every fourteen years from the first to the mid-third centuries AD. These showed that 'brother-sister marriages account for between 15 and 21 percent of all ongoing marriages' (1980b: 304). In 'Brother-sister marriage in Roman Egypt', H. advanced a series of sophisticated anthropological, demographic, social and economic arguments in an attempt to understand the practice and its persistence; and again with some nervous uncertainty, see 1980b: 327 (quoted below n. 92). See now the suggestion of Sabine Huebner that the declaration of 'brother-sister' marriages in the Egyptian census returns should more plausibly and economically be explained as the result of the adoption of a son-in-law by his wife's parents (who did not themselves have a surviving biological son); the married couple continuing to live with the wife's parents: Huebner 2007, 2013: 187–96; with the objections of Remijsen and Clarysse 2008; and Rowlandson and Takahashi 2009.

persuasive than the alternatives'.[66] For H., it was working out the room for manoeuvre that mattered most. Readers (or perhaps potential reviewers) of *Conquerors and Slaves* were issued a sharp challenge: 'If you do not agree with these values, please consider the implication of changing each of them up or down'.[67] In 'Taxes and trade', a key element in a series of parametric calculations was the suggestion that the annual budget of the Roman state in the early first century AD was not much larger than 800 million sestertii[68] – a figure in part derived by calculating the rough cost of the standing army at over 350 million sestertii and treating military expenditure as 'a very large element in the total state budget – this is the anchor of our calculations'.[69] On H.'s 'hypothetical and tentative'[70] estimates (the detailed working out is most conveniently deferred to the essay itself[71]) this indicated an effective government tax-take of 10 per cent of gross domestic product. As H. insisted, it is not the figures themselves that mattered ('they are better treated as metaphors, than as reliable statistics'[72]), but how the set of propositions they suggested were most plausibly to be fitted together.

> Given the estimated cost of the army, at over 350 million sestertii per year, and its dominance in the state budget, there is not a great deal of room for manoeuvre. Double the population, and you must halve the effective tax rate or claim that the cost of the army was only a minor element in the state budget. Claim that most people were producing at twice the level of minimum subsistence, or double the price of wheat, then you must halve the effective tax rate, if the army dominated the state budget.[73]

[66] Morley [209]; see too B. D. Shaw 1982: 22–3.
[67] 1978b: 56 n. 79; see too 1995–6: 53.
[68] To give some very approximate sense of scale: these amounts 'are expressed in the standard unit of Roman currency, the sesterce. Five hundred sesterces was sufficient to feed a peasant family on minimum subsistence for a year; 2000 sesterces was the notional price of an unskilled slave. 1 million sesterces was the amount of wealth necessary to qualify for senatorial rank' (Hopkins and Beard: 2005: 90).
[69] 1980a: 119 [essay 6: 248].
[70] 1980a: 119 [essay 6: 247].
[71] 1980a: 116–20 [essay 6: 240–9].
[72] 1995–6: 46; see too 54, 59, 1998: 195, 212 [essay 12: 443, 463–4].
[73] 1980a: 119 [essay 6: 247–8]; see too 1995–6: 47–8; and, for further examples, 71 n. 50, 1983a: 95–6 [essay 7: 288–9], 2000b: 257–9.

In (crude) summary, the more prosperous or populous or fertile the Roman empire, the less effective imperial government would then seem to be in one of its central activities: tax collection. (Or, to play the game, estimates of imperial government expenditure would need significant upward revision.[74]) In turn – to move in just one direction – how these various factors are coordinated has ramifications for understanding the relationship between government and élites as public and private competitors for the surplus wealth of empire: emperors with an overriding interest in collecting tax and landowners with an overriding interest in collecting rents. While H. (carefully adjusting the statistical metaphor) was later to suggest a tax-take of 5–7 per cent,[75] pitching as low as 3–4 per cent of actual GDP risked, in his view, exaggerating the weakness of Roman government.

> One way round this difficulty would be to argue that government revenues were so low, and could not be raised, because of the obstructive power of the aristocracy who depended on rents. I too think that rents and taxes were competitors for a limited surplus, but see the emperors in the first two centuries A.D. as having an edge over the aristocracy. But such perceptions are matters of judgement and of competing probabilities.[76]

H.'s distinctively different approach to Roman history-writing is perhaps clearest in this critical insistence on the importance of building an understanding – 'elegant and economical in its construction'[77] – by fitting together competing probabilities. To quote again Wim Jongman's Afterword on 'Taxes and trade in the Roman empire' [essay 6]:

[74] See too the discussion in 1995–6: 46 in the light of Duncan-Jones' (1994: 33–46) estimate of an annual government expenditure of 670–804 million sestertii in the mid-first century AD. On the room for manoeuvre, see usefully Lo Cascio 2007: 622–5; Scheidel and Friesen 2009; and especially Bang 2008: 79–93; Scheidel 2015: 156–63 and Jongman [264–6] who all cleverly play the parametric game. For a useful parallel, see the comments of Bang and Ikeguchi [306–12] on H.'s discussion in 'Models, ships and staples' (1983) [essay 7] of the scale of inter-regional trade, the size of merchant ships and the costs of transport.

[75] 1995–6: 47; 2009: 183 [essay 13: 497].

[76] 1995–6: 67 n. 23 with the discussion at 48–50; see too 1965c: 19–24, 1983b: pp. xii–xiii, 1996a: 225–8, 2000b: 254–5, 2009: 187–90 [essay 13: 503–7]; Hopkins and Burton 1983b: 171–93.

[77] 1995–6: 43.

It was characteristic of the modus operandi in much of H.'s work on economic and social history that rather than come up with a traditional continuous narrative dotted with selective quotations from written sources, he would give a discontinuous analytical account, operationalising variables in such a way that he could measure them, and then create a 'bitty' account from such in-depth, exhaustive analyses, using his incisive rhetoric to glue the bits together.[78]

And as H. would be ever eager to emphasise, 'this method cannot establish which answers are right, but the matrix of probabilities makes one aware of the implications of choice'.[79] The wigwam again. 'The area circumscribed by the arguments considered as a set should cover and account for much of the surviving relevant evidence … the imperfect, but complementary arguments prop each other up; the principle of construction is similar to a Red Indian wigwam.'[80]

This style of 'co-ordinate thinking'[81] is neatly illustrated by returning briefly to 'Christian number and its implications' [essay 12] for a snapshot of the argument. Importantly (as noted above), 'it is quite possible to think of the implications without knowing the exact size of the Christian population'. If, for example, early Christians usually met in private houses, then the more Christians there were, the more house cult-groups.[82] And this, in turn, has an impact on how the history of the Church as an institution should be written (that is, any account of the establishment of a wider and more unified community of believers under the control of bishops and clergy). Similar thinking shapes an understanding of the size and distribution of Christian communities in the late second century. To begin again with the arbitrary straight-line figure for AD 180: 100,000 Christians empire-wide. How should this be distributed? If, for example, the number of attested Christian communities in the late second century is doubled to two hundred (arbitrarily: 'simply to see where it leads us'[83]) that would allow for an average membership of five hundred persons in each

[78] Jongman [267].
[79] 1980a: 119 [essay 6: 248].
[80] 1995–6: 42.
[81] 1995–6: 45.
[82] 1998: 192 n. 15 [essay 12: 441 n. 15].
[83] 1980a: 118 [essay 6: 245]; see too 119 [247], 1995–6: 42.

community. But, in turn, that would still mean that around 90 per cent (1,800 out of roughly 2,000) cities in the Roman empire had no Christian community at all. Or perhaps 'dispersed smallness, with a handful of exceptionally large metropolitan communities', is to be preferred?[84] Or perhaps a much larger Christian population at the end of the second century? But to allow that would be to accept a lower overall growth rate for Christianity in the third century. Or perhaps suggest (the most radical revision of all) that conventional estimates of the number of Christians at the time of Constantine's public profession of faith should be substantially raised. That last option has never been seriously advocated, and would push hard against contemporary Christian accounts. The rough-and-ready guesstimate of 6 million Christians at the beginning of the fourth century (like a set of goal posts in a game of football) still provides 'an arbitrary boundary against which to test other conclusions'.[85] And so on. A sense of how a history of the growth of early Christianity might be written called for close attention to a set of interconnections – and how they could be jigsawed together. (The wider implications of these number games are explored by Kate Cooper in her thoughtful response to H.'s speculations.[86]) 'Actually, not a lot hangs on the exact numbers either at the beginning or the end … Our primary purpose … is to think through the implications of Christian growth, not to measure it precisely (that is impossible), nor even to explain it.'[87]

So too, thinking about the wealth of the Roman world in 'Taxes and trade' required teasing out the probable relationships between a network of often quite technical economic arguments (monetisation, coin circulation, agricultural yield, volume of demand, long-distance seaborne trade), but it also demanded a 'neatness of fit' between understandings of the Roman economy, Roman society, the play of imperial politics and the impact of empire. For H., this remained 'not so much

84 1998: 202–3 [essay 12: 452].
85 1998: 192 [essay 12: 440].
86 Cooper [485–6].
87 1998: 192 [essay 12: 440–1].

a problem of fact and evidence, but rather a problem of preference, of a general sense of how the Roman world worked, and of the balance of probabilities and plausibilities'.[88] As William Harris exposes in his discussion of 'Conquest by book' [essay 10], it is that 'general sense of how the Roman world worked' that shapes H.'s understanding of the scattered data on literacy and his approach to the typicality of the Egyptian evidence, or the ability of soldiers and small farmers to deal with the demands of Roman government, or the emergence of Coptic as 'a script of protest'.[89]

And it is precisely this same problem of preference that precipitated one of the most striking methodological confessions in any of the essays collected in this volume. H. concluded 'From violence to blessing: symbols and rituals in ancient Rome' (1991) [essay 8] by freely admitting to an impasse. His chief tactic (rapidly summarised) had been to describe the complex of political mass participation rituals central to the Roman Republic (the military levy, the census and popular assemblies) in order to explore their success, as H. saw it, in establishing legitimacy, loyalty, hierarchy and communal identity. 'This common culture ... drew together people with different interests and helped propel them toward common actions.'[90] But it was these same political rituals which were degutted at end of the first century BC by the Emperor Augustus who 'revolutionised Roman political life by superimposing monarchy on traditional republican forms', creating a 'ritual vacuum'[91] not filled (in H.'s view) until Constantine's public adoption of Christianity. In a final footnote, H. squared up to the difficulties that this too quick and easy formulation attempted to side-step.

> I face a problem here which I cannot easily or satisfactorily resolve. The more important I claim political rituals to have been in the political and social life of the Republic, the more problematic their abolition or transformation under the emperors becomes. My claim ... that the abolition of ritual created a vacuum,

[88] 1995–6: 60; see too 1968: 71, 1983a: 96 [essay 7: 288].
[89] 1991b: 146 [essay 10: 377] with Harris [392 n. 3].
[90] 1991a: 488 [essay 8: 326]; and see below pp. 24–5.
[91] 1991a: 497 [essay 8: 338–9].

only filled centuries later by the invasion of Christianity, puts too much weight on a metaphor, and telescopes time uncomfortably.[92]

In other words, what mattered above all else in establishing the plausibility of a set of linked propositions was working out the room to manoeuvre in building any argument: 'not only do our choices constrain each other, but the final results must also be compatible with whatever else we want to believe'.[93] This 'tactic of intellectual discovery'[94] is the key to understanding H.'s strikingly innovative approach to Roman history-writing (and his frustrations with too narrowly based inductive reasoning). As 'From violence to blessing' neatly exposes, constructing the wigwam was only the first step in a complex and critical process. For H., the real challenge – to mess with the metaphor – was to keep it standing.

Sociological Studies in Roman History

> This is a book about the Roman empire. It is not a narrative history, but an attempt to analyse a changing social structure and to evoke a lost world. It is also an attempt to apply some modern sociological concepts and techniques to Roman history.
>
> *Conquerors and Slaves*, Sociological Studies in Roman History 1, 1978[95]

> After a long divorce, there are several signs that history and sociology will be reconciled. Of course, by no means everyone wants a reconciliation. Many ancient historians look on sociology as a mass of illegitimate generalizations, as far too abstract, barely respectable as an academic subject … Sociologists on the other hand … cheerfully sneer at the ancient world as 'irrelevant' and dismiss classicists as pedants or fact-grubbers. Obviously these hostile stereotypes constitute one important barrier to a rapprochement.
>
> 'Classicists and sociologists' (1972)[96]

Keith Hopkins (at least as an academic author) was carefully staged. His style – certainly compared to the prevailing

[92] 1991a: 498 n. 36 [essay 8: 339 n. 36] with the humane critique of Elsner [340–5]; see too 1980b: 327: 'Let me confess straight away that the end of this article is disappointing. I do not have an explanation.'

[93] 1980a: 117 [essay 6: 244]; see too 1995–6: 43, 1978b: 2–3 n. 4.

[94] 1983a: 95 [essay 7: 288].

[95] 1978b: p. ix.

[96] 1972a: 355.

conventions of ancient-history-writing, even in the last twenty years – remains distinctive and recognisable. In great part, it is driven by his self-portrayal as a solitary scholar (like a lonely knight errant) battling to make sense of a fragmentary and recalcitrant past, and with a friendly concern to coopt the sympathy of the reader at each stage on a lengthy and difficult quest. To repurpose (and only slightly) Neville Morley's observation:

> [H.] seeks to exemplify the exciting possibilities of an alternative approach to historiography, dramatising the thought-processes of the theoretically self-conscious historian. Interpretation and argument are presented almost as a high-wire act, emphasising the constant risk of failure or frustration as well as the potential rewards.[97]

H.'s rhetorical track is perhaps most easily followed (and it is hoped without any fresh bloom of cynicism for it having been pointed out) in 'Taxes and trade in the Roman empire (200 BC–AD 400)' [essay 6] or 'Rome, taxes, rents and trade' (1995–6) or 'Christian number and its implications' [essay 12]. The stylistic way-markers will swiftly become familiar; so too the finely calibrated hesitations and sudden courageous advances, often carefully juxtaposing footnotes and main text.[98] 'I shall try, rather rashly, to estimate';[99] 'can we estimate the gross product of the Roman empire? At first sight it seems hopeless. But ...';[100] 'we are now in a position to move to the next stage of our argument. Let us guess ...';[101] 'I had a flash of revelation';[102] 'my methods are frankly speculative and exploratory';[103] 'if I had been a hungry, wandering Christian beggar-missionary in search of success and food ...';[104] 'I hope this does not sound too

[97] Morley 2006: 33.

[98] Morley 2006: 31–3. I have learnt much from Morley's engagement with 'Taxes and trade'. As H. could charmingly remark: 'I would not have spotted it, or thought of it, by myself' (1991b: 138 n. 11 [essay 10: 369 n. 11]).

[99] 1980a: 104 [essay 6: 220].

[100] 1980a: 117 [essay 6: 244].

[101] 1995–6: 45.

[102] 1995–6: 54.

[103] 1998: 185 [essay 12: 432].

[104] 1998: 214 [essay 12: 466].

reductionist';[105] 'this is a bit complex to work out';[106] 'do other people argue like this?'[107]

But the past was not the only peril to be faced. As the first part of this introduction makes clear, H. was (again to follow Neville Morley) 'at least as much interested ... in questioning historians' assumptions about how arguments should be put forward and how they can be supported'.[108] In these skirmishes (like well rehearsed fight scenes), H.'s preferred pose was as an heroic outsider struggling – and, it is to be assumed, successfully – against the suffocating strictures of complacent convention. The reader is invited to take sides: 'it will not have escaped you that I am behaving rather like an early Christian in pagan society, trying to upset fellow scholars by non-conformity'.[109] Against the 'dominant orthodoxy among traditional ancient historians',[110] H. is the self-proclaimed 'scholarly iconoclast and mischief-maker' (quoting Morley, not H.[111]), the impenitent preacher of academic 'heresy' (this time H.[112]). It is perhaps then no surprise that H. had a certain fondness for strands of early Christian belief later rejected by a more firmly established Church. He remained a devotee of second-century Gnosticism. The notion that the creation of the world was the unhappy result of a cosmic sexual misdemeanour (the illicit love of Wisdom for Profundity) appealed to H., as did the tropical profusion of Gnostic theology and hermeneutics.

> It is sad and salutary to remember that the hierarchical rigidities of orthodox Christianity helped preserve its coherence; while the inventive open-mindedness of Gnostics to various interpretations ... subverted hierarchy, and made effective organization and orthodoxy impracticable. The moral rigidity and simple narrative of orthodoxy beat the fanciful flexibility of Gnostics. Gnostics remained speculative and marginal outsiders.[113]

105 1998: 219 n. 69 [essay 12: 471 n. 69].
106 1998: 220 n. 70 [essay 12: 472 n. 70].
107 1998: 205 n. 41 [essay 12: 455 n. 41].
108 Morley 2006: 32.
109 1998: 194 [essay 12: 443].
110 1995–6: 41; see too 1983a: 85 [essay 7: 270].
111 Morley 2006: 33.
112 1995–6: 41, 1987: 115 [essay 4: 138].
113 1991c: 3; see too 1999: 264. H. also approved of the disagreements amongst Jewish rabbis: 'truth for them ... came to lie in, or was represented as, a balance of

At first blush, much of H.'s own *curriculum vitae* did not support his self-presentation as an outsider: minor public school educated (senior NCO of the cadets, captain of the chess team, head of house and senior prefect), an undergraduate scholar at King's College, Cambridge (graduating with first-class honours in Classics in 1958), briefly a postgraduate and then (research) fellow (1963–7), and, from 1985 to 2001, Professor of Ancient History at Cambridge, again a fellow of King's and the college's Vice-Provost from 2000 to his death in March 2004. But the intervening years make a stronger claim: for more than two decades H. was – at least, professionally – neither a classicist nor a historian, but a sociologist: at the University of Leicester (1961–3), at the LSE (1963–72), as reviews editor for the *British Journal of Sociology* (1964–6), on secondment to the University of Hong Kong (1967–9) and as Professor of Sociology and Social Anthropology at Brunel University (1972–85) and Dean of the Faculty of Social Sciences (1981–5).[114] There can be no doubt that this prolonged exposure to the social sciences was fundamental in shaping H.'s engagement with the ancient world. It is evident in some of his approaches – although there is no particular reason to view his concern with cohesion or plausibility, or with elegant and economical argumentation, as somehow particularly 'sociological'. (As H.'s invocation of Collingwood suggests, all this could equally well be presented as a debate about historical methodology.) That said, a number of the pieces collected in this volume – in particular, 'Economic growth and towns in classical antiquity' (1978) [essay 5], 'Models, ships and staples' (1983) [essay 7], 'Slavery in classical antiquity' (1967) [essay 9] and 'The political economy of the Roman empire' (2009) [essay 13] – clearly reflect the priorities of some of the best (in H.'s judgement) historical sociology written in the 1960s and 1970s.

competing opinions' (1998: 217 [essay 12: 469]); see too 1999: 82–3 and 237–8 with Harris 2005: 102).

114 The details are carefully set out in Harris 2005: especially 83–7. King's generously permitted H. to hold his research fellowship concurrently with his post at the LSE. For the formal notice of election, see University of Cambridge *Reporter*, 20 March 1963 (no. 4343), p. 1145.

Most important (as the Afterwords to each of these essays explore) was a shared interest in social structures as a first step in understanding social development and change. 'Structures are those coral reefs of human relations which have a stable existence over relatively long periods of time. But structures too are born, develop, and die'[115] – from the opening paragraph of Immanuel Wallerstein, *The Modern World-System*, vol. 1: *Capitalist Agriculture and the Origins of the European World-Economy in the Sixteenth Century* (1974). Wallerstein likely topped the bibliography suggested to new doctoral students at their first meeting with H.[116] It was followed closely by S. N. Eisenstadt, *The Political Systems of Empires* (1963), Perry Anderson, *Lineages of the Absolutist State* (1974) and Karl Wittfogel, *Oriental Despotism: A Comparative Study of Total Power* (1957).[117] Those graduates who completed their reading assignment could easily appreciate the importance of this intellectual itinerary for H.'s ancient history-writing. As Greg Woolf points out (in his assessment of the contribution of sociology to H.'s thinking in 'The political economy of the Roman empire' [essay 13]), it is the emphasis on a 'total approach' to the empire as a system that is most striking.

> Thinking of the Roman empire as a system … was not an ancient historical issue until H. put it on the agenda. Indeed, H.'s opening remarks on the significance of writing, money and iron technology have become such commonplaces, that it is almost necessary to open up issues of journals published in the 1970s to remind oneself how unusual it then was to start by standing *outside the frame* of Greco-Roman antiquity.[118]

From that point of view, it makes sense (as Neville Morley observes) that in H.'s essay on 'Economic growth and towns in classical antiquity' [essay 5], the discussion of towns should be displaced to the final pages of a long piece, deliberately deferred by H. in favour of 'the most extended summary in his published works of his view of the Roman economy as

[115] Wallerstein 1974: 3.

[116] See Woolf [530]; Wallerstein's introduction also offers a close model for H.'s own highly personalised academic style.

[117] 1968: 63, 1978b: 197 n. 1, 253, 2005: 72 [essay 14: 534].

[118] Woolf [530].

a whole'[119] which also embraced – in summary form – the 'sketch' (H.'s own term[120]) of the political economy of the Roman Republic set out in the opening essay in *Conquerors and Slaves*.[121] It was only within this expansive context that towns could properly be understood. With an even broader remit, 'Slavery in classical antiquity' [essay 9], first given in April 1966 at an international symposium in London on caste segregation and racist ideologies, was intended (to quote Keith Bradley) 'to provide a statement on the slave-owning character of the ancient Mediterranean world for comparison with statements on human oppression and prejudice in later ages and other regions'.[122] H. insisted that slavery needed to be discussed, not in polemical isolation, but as 'only one of the many methods used in the ancient world for extracting surplus production to feed the urban population and to support the distinctive lifestyle of the rich'.[123]

That push 'to bridge the gap between modern concepts and ancient sources'[124] is again evident in H.'s approach to social anthropology. In his essay on the symbolic power of Roman emperors (the closing piece in *Conquerors and Slaves*), H. credited his recognition of the significance of imperial processions and other icons of royal authority to a conversation with Clifford Geertz and subsequent reading of Geertz's then unpublished 'Centers, kings and charisma'.[125] H.'s lengthier treatment of Roman grief (in the fourth essay in *Death and Renewal*) was presented in the context of a survey of contrasting positions (knowingly) crudely divided between cultural relativists ('culture and material conditions significantly change both the expression and the experience of grief') and ethological humanists ('evolutionary development and culture may alter surface expressions of grief, but behind the astonishing

119 Morley [209].
120 1978b: 15.
121 1978a: 59–64 [essay 5: 187–91] summarising 1978b: 1–74.
122 Bradley [357–8].
123 1967: 175 [essay 9: 355].
124 1978b: p. ix.
125 1978b: 219 n. 30; Geertz 1977.

variety of cultural expressions, much is constant'). H. was not concerned to contribute to, or choose between, these approaches; rather he preferred to discuss some of the issues in dispute as starting-points for thinking about Roman society. 'Without taking a specific position in this debate, I think that these modern observations suggest interpretations of Roman evidence.'[126]

H. was rarely so revealing of what he had learned from his wide reading in sociology and anthropology. In 'From violence to blessing: symbols and rituals in ancient Rome' [essay 8], he signalled in two brief footnotes the importance in formulating his argument of Maurice Bloch, *From Blessing to Violence: History and Ideology in the Circumcision Ritual of the Merina of Madagascar* (1986).[127] H.'s use of various strands of social anthropology is anatomised by Jaś Elsner in his Afterword to this essay.[128] H. does not indicate in any detail what he reckoned he owed to Bloch. Certainly, H.'s concern to capture the ordered complexity of Roman political rituals in terms familiar to modern readers ('like an orchestra, with each ritual standing for a single instrument', 'like a stately eighteenth-century dance, such as a gavotte or pavane'[129]) parallels Bloch's more theoretically burdened decision to use 'language that recalls our own culture' in order to establish 'a continuity' of understanding from subject to author/observer to reader.[130] H. again: 'Each ritual was a public performance. … [At the Roman republican military levy] the plump knight had to lead his aging horse through the forum in front of the censors. Cold constitutionality had a sweating face, set in a potentially jeering crowd.'[131] Both

[126] 1983b: 217–26, quoting 222, 223, 223–4.

[127] Bloch 1986 cited in Hopkins 1991a: 479 n. 1 ('a brilliant study of the changing meaning and functions of circumcision rituals among the Merina of Madagascar') and 482 n. 13 ('the best discussion which I have read about how rituals should be interpreted'); see also the brief reference at 479 n. 4 to the presence of Christians at the Merina circumcision ritual [essay 8: 313 n. 1, 317 n. 13, 314 n. 4].

[128] Elsner [342]; see too Edwards [427 n. 7].

[129] 1991a: 485 and 487 [essay 8: 322 and 324].

[130] Bloch 1986: 2.

[131] 1991a: 486 [essay 8: 323–4].

Bloch and H. are centrally concerned with the ways rituals can establish legitimacy and confirm communal solidarity, and with the negotiation of order and violence. But such tenuous connections – itself a rather heavy-handed term – are too delicate for conventional citation in footnotes. (And, of course, as might now be expected, H. offered no commentary on Bloch's distinctive approach to social anthropology.) Rather, H.'s tactical debt to Bloch for informing – underwriting, inspiring, initiating – some of the most original propositions of 'From violence to blessing' was handsomely discharged in the graceful inversion of *From Blessing to Violence*.[132]

H.'s engagement – another too definite a term – with Bloch is part of a wider pattern of important difference between H.'s approach to ancient history-writing and his recommended reading in sociology and social anthropology. First, and perhaps in a conscious attempt to win over classicists, he was always careful to ensure his arguments were neither 'crushed by jargon'[133] nor freighted with lengthy theoretical discussions which he regarded as 'even more arid than empiricism'.[134] (H. presented his project in the preface to *Conquerors and Slaves* in recognisably conventional terms: 'This is not the place to embark on a long discussion about methods. That requires an abstract language of its own.'[135]) Secondly, H.'s history-writing – in clear contrast to Marxists such as Perry Anderson – was offered without any explicitly enunciated political or ideological agenda. H., for example, despite his extensive treatment of Roman society, declined to intervene directly in important methodological debates on 'class' and

[132] Elsner [342]. See too H.'s invocation of Clifford Geertz, 'Deep play: notes on the Balinese cockfight' (1972) in the first footnote of 'Murderous games' (the opening essay in *Death and Renewal*) where H.'s claim of a degree of 'direct imitation' (1983b: 1 n. 1) seems somewhat strained (although his debt to Geertz's approach, and especially his concluding arguments, is clear). Note too H.'s referencing of Stephen Greenblatt, *Shakespearian Negotiations: The Circulation of Social Energy in Renaissance England* (1988) in the first footnote to 'Novel evidence for Roman slavery' (1993: 3 n. 1 [essay 11: 398 n. 1]) with Edwards [428 n. 8].

[133] 1978b: 253.

[134] 1972a: 356.

[135] 1978b: p. x, see too 89; contrast, for example, the foreword in Anderson 1974: 7–11.

'status'.[136] Thirdly (and perhaps the greatest contrast with much of the sociology he most admired), H.'s interests were tightly circumscribed. His focus was on the impact of conquest on the social structures and political economy – in the broadest sense – of the Roman empire across four hundred years (roughly 200 BC to AD 200). It was not H.'s chief purpose to deploy Roman economic or social history to develop or refine a general understanding of pre-industrial society. He cited, but never discussed (to choose one possible starting-point) Max Weber's 'Die sozialen Gründe des Untergangs der antiken Kultur' (1896)[137] or his 'Agrarverhälnisse im Altertum' (1909).[138] Indeed, while greatly admiring Weber's emphasis on model-building, H. remained wary of one of Weber's most influential contributions to sociology: the 'ideal type'. 'The weakness of the ideal type, in spite of the intentions of its creators, is that it replaces complexity with oversimplification.'[139]

Similar doubts caused H. to shy away from the large-scale comparative projects of Eisenstadt and Wittfogel and their attempts to construct broad explanatory frameworks for the study of 'historical bureaucratic empires'.[140] Eisenstadt was clear in setting out his project: 'its main objective is the comparative analysis of a certain common type of political system that can be found in different societies'.[141] Reviewing a collection of Eisenstadt's essays for the *British Journal of Sociology* in September 1966, H. praised their sophistication and their richness of abstraction, but worried that they were not sufficiently grounded in an 'interplay of theory and hard information'.

This simple but productive set of hypotheses has been repeatedly elaborated as it is placed in a wider or different institutional context. If this were done at an empirical level, each elaboration would represent some sort of advance, but as

[136] B. D. Shaw: 1982: 31–6; Woolf [531]; but see too, in the following year, Hopkins 1983c: pp. xiii–xiv – a brief, but spirited, defence of Finley's emphasis on status in 1973: 35–61.

[137] 1967: 170 [essay 9: 350], 1978b: 109 n. 20.

[138] 1972a: 355; 1978b: 252.

[139] 1978a: 72–5, quoting 75 [essay 5: 200–4, quoting 204] with Morley [211–12].

[140] Eisenstadt's term: 1963: 3, fleetingly glossed by H. in the title of 1968.

[141] Eisenstadt 1963: p. viii.

it is done at an abstract level it is worth asking whether Eisenstadt's technique is cumulatively profitable.[142]

Again, H.'s aims were more firmly bounded. He preferred to deploy his impressive knowledge of other societies (notably imperial China and pre-modern Europe) to set plausible limits for understanding the Roman world[143] or to emphasise that certain key features of the Roman empire (settled agriculture, urbanisation, long-distance trade, monetisation, literacy) represented clear advances over earlier Mediterranean societies.[144]

Above all, for H., finding the right – the most elegant, the most plausible – argument was the key to writing good history. Crucially, this was a two-way process: the explanatory framework was informed (tested, refined, rejected) by the available data and, in turn, helped to give some ordered sense – itself, a convenient intellectual economy – to the complexity of the past. For H., the seduction of sociology was that it treated 'concepts and methods of analysis' with the kind of 'critical acumen' that traditional classicists reserved for texts.[145] But (as noted above) H. did not seek to include antiquity as another case study in some wider enterprise. He was not interested in the Roman world as part of a broadly based comparative project nor in investigating the (arguably) common structural features of pre-modern societies or world empires. H.'s aims – at least when viewed by some sociologists – were much more modest and more openly (and cheerfully) parasitic: at stake 'is rather what can be borrowed from sociology and adapted to the purposes of ancient history'.[146] From that point of view,

142 1966b: 326; see too 1965d: 197.

143 1964–5: 311–12, 1974b: 77, 1995–6: 64 n. 3, 2000b: 254 n. 2. Good examples in 1965a: 134–5 [essay 1: 69–70] with Vout [100], 1978b: 6–7 n. 12, 11 n. 19, 1980a: 102 n. 4, 120 n. 56, 121 n. 60, 124 n. 72 [essay 6: 215 n. 4, 248–9 n. 56 and table 6.1, 252 n. 60, 257 n. 72], 1983a: 90 and 91 table 1, 95–6, 100–1 [essay 7: 279 and 280 table 7.1, 288, 296–7], 1987: 115–16 [essay 4: 138]; Hopkins and Burton 1983a: 70–3, 100–2, 1983b: 145, 186; and see above p. 4. Contrast, for example, Eisenstadt's approach: 1963: 8–10.

144 1978a: 37–41 [essay 5: 163–6], 1991b: 135 [essay 10: 365]; crystallised in H.'s arguments for modest economic growth in 1983c: pp. xiv–xxi, 2009: 195–202 [essay 13: 515–26].

145 1972a: 356; see too 1983b: 52 n. 33.

146 1972a: 356; see too 1978b: p. x.

ideas incubated in sociology or social anthropology might enable the open-minded ancient historian more effectively or efficiently to define a research problem (rather than provide handy, ready-made solutions), or suggest ways in which an argument might be more persuasively or plausibly articulated. It is this coalition – or, perhaps better, coordination – between his approaches to sociology and ancient history that H. sought to capture in sub-titling his two collections of essays (*Conquerors and Slaves* and *Death and Renewal*), 'Sociological Studies in Roman History'. This neat formulation both underscores H.'s significant methodological innovations in ancient history-writing and his debt to sociology. But there is also a deliberate (and admirable) ambiguity in its cautious interdisciplinary claim. Certainly, H. always appeared to many ancient historians to be a sociologist (and enjoyed playing up that subversive role) – but from the point of view of many sociologists he must have seemed still very much an ancient historian.

Being There

> To be sure, historians should master the evidence, but they should also, I think, in some sense transform and perhaps even transcend the originals and so build something which is both trustworthy in its derivation and recognizably different from the sources themselves.
>
> 'Rules of evidence' (1978)[147]

> I wondered, and still wonder what it was like to be there.
>
> *Death and Renewal*, Sociological Studies in Roman History 2, 1983[148]

> I'm far too inhibited an academic to make things up.
>
> *A World Full of Gods: Pagans, Jews and Christians in the Roman Empire*, 1999[149]

Keith Hopkins was not always a 'historical sociologist' (his professional self-definition in a review for *Social Sciences Information/Information sur les sciences sociales* in December

[147] 1978c: 185.
[148] 1983b: 203; see too Beard [553].
[149] 1999: 3.

1965) with a focus on the ancient world.[150] In 1966 (then in post at the LSE), he published a careful account of 'Civil-military relations in developing countries' in the *British Journal of Sociology*. He opened by questioning the approach of previous research on the military in these societies which had (in his view) been too focused on *coups d'état*: 'In this sense coups are like convicted criminals to the criminologist, the visible part of the iceberg, but an iceberg of unknown size; they can provide a useful set of statistics but they may not be a fair sample of crime, let alone of deviance.'[151] H. based his discussion on a much wider data-set which compared army strength and military expenditure in fifty countries against a variety of other factors (for example, national budget, GDP, urban population, literacy),[152] focusing on military ideology, internal rivalries and cohesion, and the problems faced by army officers tasked with civilian administration. A junta 'is torn between the Scylla of delegation and the Charybdis of civilianizing itself which raises the problem of controlling the military'.[153] H.'s sharpest criticism was reserved for claims that outsized armed forces (and inflated military expenditure) in developing countries could, in part, be justified by the key role soldiers played in modernisation, education and construction. 'But surely teachers are better educators and engineers better builders; why put them into military uniform? Secondly, the military consumes a large amount of skill and imported equipment whose only visible product is shell smoke and craters in training areas.'[154]

The following year (1967), H. accepted, on secondment from the LSE, the chair of sociology at the University of Hong Kong. For the next two years, the ancient world was displaced by the demands of supervising a fieldwork project on public housing.[155] In brief: in the late 1960s, the British colonial

[150] 1965d: 197.
[151] 1966c: 165–6.
[152] 1966c: 166–8 tables 1–3.
[153] 1966c: 179.
[154] 1966c: 181.
[155] Part of the Squatter Research Project financed by the Centre of Asian Studies at the University of Hong Kong (1971b: 330–1 n. 5, 1972b: 204).

administration could lay claim to one of the most successful public housing policies in the non-communist world: of a population of just under 4 million, almost 40 per cent lived in some form of government-funded accommodation. This large-scale building programme was, in part, a response to a fourfold rise in Hong Kong's population following the communist revolution in China (from an estimated 600,000 in 1945 to 2,360,000 in 1950) and the resulting growth of large squatter settlements, with an estimated 300,000 squatters in the early 1950s. The proximate cause of increased government expenditure on public housing was a large fire in a squatter camp on Christmas Day 1953 that made more than 50,000 people homeless: 'it took a slum fire to singe Government's conscience'.[156] By 1969, more than 1 million squatters had been permanently resettled, with another 500,000 in various forms of low cost public housing. Resettlement was an achievement only made possible by the rapid construction of H-shaped, six- or seven-storey concrete buildings with minimal amenity (without electricity or provision for cooking space) and an assumption of communal living that allocated each adult a floor space of only twenty-four square feet – 'twice the area of a grave'.[157] To continue quoting from H.'s inaugural lecture delivered on 6 March 1969:

> In general, then, the Resettlement programme has been a very great success both as a building programme and as an administrative process for moving squatters into new housing. As a design for living, however, the success of the programme is questionable. … I deprecate overcrowding which involves, for example, the sharing of one or two bunks by large families and the lack of private space for individuals … Government has for too long sacrificed reasonable ideals of housing to expedience and economy.[158]

156 1969a: 3. The role of the fire in the Shek Kip Mei squatter settlement in the formation of government policy is carefully examined in Smart 2006: especially 181–90.

157 1969a: 1, 1971b: 297, 1973: 18. This description is of Resettlement blocks built before 1964. The space allocation was raised to thirty-five square feet per adult by the Hong Kong Housing Board in 1966; the first building conforming to these new standards was occupied in 1969 (1969a: 1 n. 4 and 3 n. 16, 1972b: 213 n. 16).

158 1969a: 4. This thumbnail sketch is based on H.'s own account of the origin, and his critique of the achievements, of the Resettlement programme (the statistics are drawn from Hong Kong government reports); see in particular 1969a: 1–4, 1971b: 275–7, 295–300 and 1972b: 200–4 (the last originally given as a paper at

H.'s fieldwork in 1968 and 1969 aimed to assess the impact of the public housing programme (particularly resettlement) on the living standards of the poor. (At the time, despite resettling 1 million squatters, squatter settlements – to considerable government frustration – were larger than when the resettlement programme had begun.[159]) The fieldwork undertaken in 1968 included 1,650 interviews conducted by second-year students in the Department of Sociology (and concentrated on Resettlement estates and squatter settlements); the following year, a further 3,000 interviews also surveyed other forms of housing, including privately rented tenement blocks.[160] H.'s conclusions from this mass of new data characteristically challenged conventional assumptions. A quick selection: the resettlement of squatters did not result in a rise in average household income, nor in the proportion of children attending primary or secondary school, nor a reduction in the average number of children working under the age of 15. The only significant difference was that families in Resettlement estates were much more likely to own consumer durables such as televisions, telephones and refrigerators.[161] Nor did overcrowding in Resettlement blocks mean a sharp decline in standards of hygiene or infant care or a steep rise in crime.[162] H. also undermined the common claim that squatters were chiefly recent immigrants attracted by Hong Kong's prosperous economy: in fact, a substantial number had moved to squatter settlements rather than pay rent for slum-standard accommodation in privately rented tenements.[163]

an international conference on 'The city as a centre of change in Asia', held at the University of Hong Kong in June 1969).

159 The *Annual Reports* of the Commissioner of Resettlement estimated 300,000 squatters in 1953 and 443,000 in 1968 (1969a: 9 with table 9, 1971b: 279 with table 7.1, 1972b: 204).

160 1969a: 4 and 12 on the 1968 survey; 1971b: 331 n. 5 on the 1969 survey.

161 1969a: 4–7 with tables 1–7, 1971b: 314–17.

162 1973: 16.

163 1971b: 284–6, 1972b: 204–5. H. matched the radical conclusions of his research with equally innovative policy proposals which he set out both in his inaugural lecture and in a companion article for the *Far Eastern Economic Review* (1969b). H. argued that one significant problem to be faced by the colony's administration was a likely further steep increase in demand for housing principally driven

It is important to emphasise that H. was personally involved in collecting the data on which these conclusions rest. Like his second-year sociology students, H. (with a Chinese interpreter) conducted interviews, measured rooms and counted refrigerators, televisions, washing machines and electric rice cookers. Indeed, one of the quiet pleasures of reading H.'s main account of his research – 'Housing the poor', his contribution to *Hong Kong: The Industrial Colony* (1971), a volume which he also edited[164] – is to follow the newly arrived, Cambridge-educated, thirty-something professor of sociology into squatter settlements (where he was menaced by vicious dogs[165]) and private tenement blocks (where he was, by turns, embarrassed by the lack of privacy and his own Western prudery).

by population growth: 'it is surely acknowledged that Government is in a fix. It has become direct landlord of more than one and a half million people, most of whom are young, many of whom will be shortly married. It has stepped on a treadmill, and cannot step off' (1969a: 11 = 1969b: 310). In 1966, just over half of Hong Kong's population was under 20 years old (1971b: 277). H.'s solution to increase government funding for public housing was to raise the low fixed rents in Resettlement estates. His research indicated that the overwhelming majority of households could afford to pay (1969: 12). This was a proposal made against the low taxation policies in Hong Kong – an income tax of 15 per cent or less, and regressive: lower on income above about US$15,000 equivalent (1971b: 299). 'I could advocate progressive taxation with moral conviction, but without much hope of success. … In the circumstances, it seems reasonable and expedient to raise money for future housing development partly from those who are benefiting from present public housing' (1969a: 11 = 1969b: 310). H. also recognised that raising rents for 1 million government tenants might risk provoking riots (1969a: 11 = 1969b: 310). Whatever the merits of H.'s proposals (somewhat muted two years later in 1971b: 299), they had little impact on government policies: rents (as a proportion of household income) remained low; see, for example, the discussions in Hui and Wong 2003: 169–71 and Yung 2008: 88–91, striking in their repetition of some of H.'s proposals (H. is not cited). H.'s recommendation that the housing problem would be alleviated by the provision of greater amenity (garbage collection, water supply, covered drainage, public latrines, electricity) to squatter settlements was rejected out of hand (1969a: 8 = 1969b: 308, 1971b: 290–5, 1973: 19). The colonial administration did not shift from its unwillingness to pursue policies that might be seen as countenancing the legitimacy of illegal occupation of Crown land; see the overview in Wong 1978, especially 227–32, noting H.'s recommendation at 230. For a rebuttal of H.'s proposals by D. J. Dwyer, H.'s professorial colleague at the University of Hong Kong (in the Department of Geography), see Dwyer 1972b: 174–7 (in the same volume, edited by Dwyer, which included Hopkins 1972b).

164 1971a, 1971b.

165 1971b: 280.

One of the worst tenements which I saw was owned by a famous charity. The building occupies a block and is approached by a narrow flight of dirty and crumbling stairs. … Men were lounging in their pyjamas on their beds, while some women were preparing food outside. I was rather shy at intruding, but my guide was bolder and asked whether we might look around, for the purpose of a study we were doing at the University. … [The chief tenant] occupied the front cubicle which was light and airy … there was another cubicle at the front on the other side of the passage, occupied by two unmarried workers, and behind them the saddest sight of all, four bed spaces, in two bunks, each 6 ft. long, about 3 ft. wide and only 4 ft. high. Here on a neat and hard bed board, three single persons and a couple slept surrounded by their few neatly folded possessions. … What struck me particularly about this visit was the freedom I was given to look in on people as they lay in bed or sat around – was it because I was a foreigner, or because they have already lived in public for so much of their lives?[166]

Of course, like any good story, it is impossible to know how much has (inescapably) been sharpened in the retelling – here in the tranquil and spacious surroundings of the Institute for Advanced Study in Princeton where this essay, and the editorial work on *Hong Kong: The Industrial Colony*, was completed in early 1970.[167] But – as H. would be the first to suggest – the accuracy of this story is not what really matters.[168] Far more interesting is the decision to include these frankly personal accounts alongside the more conventional tabular presentation of the fine-grained information derived from 5,000 interviews. H. opted to offer 'a patchwork of data … from a variety of sources and … of varying reliability'.[169] Alongside official reports ('usually concerned to defend present policies rather than to reveal the discussions which preceded decisions'[170]) he included 'my visits to and impressions of many homes … discussions with students and colleagues, and my own beliefs'. All these 'have been pressed into service in that difficult but inevitable process of deciding what to include and what to leave out'.[171]

166 1971b: 322–3.
167 1971c: p. xv, 1971b: 330 n. 1, 1978b: p. xi; Harris 2005: 90.
168 1983b: 28–9, 1978b: 198, quoted below p. 38.
169 1971b: 274.
170 1971b: 274–5.
171 1971b: 275.

There are – and perhaps unsurprisingly – almost no explicit links between H.'s two years in Hong Kong and his Roman history-writing. One exception is his observation in defence of a high estimate for the population of the city of Rome.[172] If, H. argued, the area inside the third-century AD city walls (1,373 hectares) corresponded roughly with the size of the city under the Emperor Augustus, then for a population of 1 million that would yield an average density of 730 persons per hectare. 'This was certainly possible … And I myself have seen squatter settlements in Hong Kong, comprising one- or two-storey ramshackle huts, built of bamboo and tin-sheeting, with densities considerably higher (up to 2,500 per hectare).'[173] More significant than such rare reminiscences is a clear continuity of concern with the fall of data and its presentation. As explored in the first part of this introduction, the wigwam argument, with its focus on parametric propositions, was a strikingly innovative way of suggesting how 'the inevitable partiality and distortions of the ancient evidence'[174] might be understood within a broader matrix of probabilities. In part, this was an attempt to give ancient history an (albeit still pallid) equivalent to the full flush of data taken for granted in other fields, and enjoyed by H. in his work on housing in Hong Kong or on civil-military relations in developing countries. But there were limits.

> We are not suggesting that history should normally cover what is not known, let alone what did not happen and what might have been. … if probabilities are finite or if the size of the universe is known or can be estimated … it is worthwhile systematically analysing what our sources did not report and what the Romans did not do.[175]

Yet for all its clear gains, for example in suggesting plausible demographic constraints on the Roman world, H. (in the same graduate seminar in Oxford in January 1974 with which this introduction opened) worried that 'one obvious disadvantage' of his own emphasis on model-building was 'the

[172] Above pp. 11–12.
[173] 1978b: 97.
[174] 1974b: 78.
[175] 1983b: p. xiv; and see Hopkins and Burton 1983a: 42.

depersonalization of history'.[176] The danger was a too bloodless account of Roman society. Neglecting 'conflict, passion and violence ... it leaves out the sympathetic understanding of feeling and fears, of ambiguities and ambivalence'.[177]

H. answered his own challenge – perhaps even more pressing after another decade focused on economic and social structures – with the two essays which bookend *Death and Renewal* (1983).

> They are both heavily dependant on direct citation of classical sources, and present in effect a collage of quotation and interpretation, in the hope of arousing the reader's empathetic imagination. ... In tacking these questions, we are exploring the limits of the value of empathy as a tactic of historical analysis.[178]

With deliberate and disarming honesty, H. admitted that assembling 'a collage of quotation and interpretation' pushed him hard back against his own acerbic criticisms of scissors-and-paste history.

> The limitations and dangers of this method are considerable. Interpretations are subjective, translations into English unavoidably reflect English, not Roman culture, excerpts are necessarily cited out of context, the criteria for the selection of each quotation cannot be made explicit.[179]

'Murderous games' and 'Death in Rome' are brilliant attempts to have it both ways. At first sight, the main text in 'Murderous games' (which opens *Death and Renewal*) is a magisterial display of the virtues of the conventional classicist. Here is an impressive parade of erudition: fascinating fragments of information culled from a wide range of literary texts, inscriptions and graffiti, archaeological reports and museum collections (some viewed under trying circumstances[180]). On the surface, H. plays – and plays extremely well – a very traditional game: 'credit goes to the ancient historian who makes the best pattern out of the largest number of pieces and cites the most obscure sources relevantly'.[181] But this is an enterprise

[176] 1974a: 2.
[177] 1978c: 180 and 183.
[178] 1983b: pp. xiv and xv.
[179] 1983b: p. xv; see too 221 (quoted below p. 37), 1978c: 180, 1999: 2.
[180] 1983b: 22 n. 32 on his adventures in the *gabinetto segreto* of the Naples Archaeological Museum.
[181] 1978c: 182, quoted above p. 3.

expressly undermined by the footnotes. A brief selection: 'as always, it is difficult to deduce frequency of practice from frequency of mention in our surviving sources'; 'the dangers of such a tactic are obvious. But then a historical method, which uses excerpts from fragmentary surviving texts not merely as illustration, but more often as alleged authentication of arguments, is fraught with dangers'; 'This figure is often cited, but should it be believed?'; 'This story has an implausible ring to it'; 'I have no idea how many Romans believed in or thought of these interpretations'.[182]

The challenge to the reader is to move between two mismatched parallel accounts: text and footnotes. The intellectual reward of this productive tension – in open defiance of the established conventions of history-writing – is in tracing the repeated, and sometimes witty, failure of the references to support the argument. Even so, and despite some clear hits (which underscored the partial and problematic nature of the ancient evidence), the hollowing out of the main text by a persistent methodological fretting in the footnotes was a difficult tactic to sustain across a thirty-page essay. After all, as H. was all too well aware, not every element in a carefully layered account could be unpicked or its context interrogated. He had to trust the readers to do some of the hard interpretative work themselves: 'the total impact is probably as much or more the product of each reader's perceptions as it is of the author's intentions'.[183]

'Death in Rome' (the final essay in *Death and Renewal*, written in collaboration with Melinda Letts) set out to confront the cursory reader who had only paid attention to the main text of 'Murderous games'. Rather than sweep the difficult issues of evidence and its interpretation into the footnotes, H. left them as jagged obstacles in the main text. Again a brief selection: 'the best we can hope for is an impressionistic sketch, a collage … an artificial, almost timeless composite, inset with illustrative vignettes'; 'posing this problem is not the same as finding a

[182] 1983b: 1 n. 2, 8 n. 13, 8 n. 12, 23 n. 34, 22 n. 31.
[183] 1983b: p. xv.

solution to it'; 'the trouble with subjective judgement is that it is liable to error, all the more so since we are translating from one language to another'; 'nagging doubts remain'.[184] From that point of view, 'Death in Rome' is close in its concerns to those essays explored in the first part of this introduction ('On the probable age structure of the Roman population' [essay 3], 'Taxes and trade in the Roman empire (200 BC–AD 200)' [essay 6], 'Christian number and its implications' [essay 12]) which insisted that the reader follow carefully the construction of a complex argument and explore its strengths and limitations. Like functionalist architecture, it is important to these essays that their workings are clearly on view. Hence it is no surprise (as noted above) that 'Death in Rome' should offer H.'s most detailed engagement with social anthropology: a discussion of cultural relativist and ethological humanist approaches to grief and how that debate could 'suggest interpretations of Roman evidence'.[185] And, as might also be expected, H. was eager to put on display the limitations of the surviving material. He offered a compassionate and beautifully written account of Roman bereavement, quoting moving confessions of sorrow and touching epitaphs: 'Everything in me that you used to love has died.' 'I have lost my wife. Why should I stay longer now? … I am gripped by grief, alive when my wife is dead.'[186] But H. did not allow these emotions – which he himself had aroused – to cloud the reader's judgement. He immediately interjected.

> Understanding grief is difficult. The main problem lies in the gap between expression and experience … modern English may infuse Latin words with feelings which were not intended. And in any case, a poet writing odes, however evocative, is not necessarily heart-broken, while she who mourns silently or expresses her grief conventionally on a tombstone may nevertheless be truly grief-stricken.[187]

Again, as in 'Murderous games', this tight juxtaposition between evidence and problematised interpretation was

[184] 1983b: 203, 205, 221, 225.
[185] 1983b: 217–26, quoting 224; see above pp. 23–4.
[186] 1983b: 220–1, quoting Cic. *Att.* 12.14 and *CIL* VI 15546.
[187] 1983b: 221; see too Hopkins and Burton 1983a: 86.

difficult to sustain – for both author and reader. The methodological warnings in the main text fade away in the second half of the piece (which, unusually for H., ends suddenly without any attempt at more general conclusions) – or perhaps now H. had confidence in his readers to unpick his text themselves with only the occasional footnoted reminder?[188] Certainly, at its best, 'Death in Rome' is a provocative, intelligent and explicit exploration of the problems of writing an empathetic history of grief in a society whose life expectancy and (resulting) frequent experience of death, especially of infants, is so radically different from our own. 'That is the kernel of our problem. What were their feelings? What is the connection between the experience of feelings and their expression? Needless to say, I have no satisfactory answer to such questions.'[189]

H. revisited the difficulties of empathetic (or 'evocative'[190]) history-writing in 'Novel evidence for Roman slavery' (1993) [essay 11] which built on the two essays in *Death and Renewal* and on an earlier piece, 'Divine emperors or the symbolic unity of the Roman empire' (the final essay in *Conquerors and Slaves*), which had emphasised the importance of stories and story-telling in the construction of imperial ideology. 'Stories circulated. They were the currency of the political system, just as coins were the currency of the fiscal system. Their truth or untruth is only a secondary problem.'[191] 'Novel evidence' is 'built around a single source':[192] the unapologetically fictional *Life of Aesop*, an anonymous, composite work most likely, at least in its finished form, from first-century AD Egypt. H. devotes much space (enjoyably, scurrilously) to anthologising the tale: Aesop's grotesque ugliness; the accident of his purchase by his thrifty new master, Xanthus; Aesop's repeated outwitting of Xanthus (a provincial philosophy professor, and so all the more amusing – especially to H. who particularly appreciated the jibes at academic pedantry); Aesop's attempts

188 1983b: 236 n. 45, 237–8 n. 48, 241–2 n. 53, 243 n. 56, 254 n. 76.
189 1983b: 204.
190 1993: 26 [essay 11: 423].
191 1978b: 198; see too 1983b: 28–9.
192 1993: 3 [essay 11: 398].

to get Xanthus to grant him his freedom; and Aesop's athletic sexual prowess with Xanthus' wife. But the details are best left to the essay itself. After all, it would be a petulant introduction that spoiled a good story.

H.'s chief concern is to trace the fault lines in the text exposed by its comic inversions of hierarchy, order, obedience and propriety. (His cultural parallels are Robin Hood, Rumpelstiltskin, David and Goliath, and stories about American summer camp and '*au pairs* in modern British families'.[193]) 'Aesop is a projection of repressed emotions; he is potent, cunning and vengeful. He is what we desire, envy and fear.'[194] H. is careful to note that his readings represent only one set of interpretative responses from a plurality of possibilities available to ancient listeners[195] – and Catharine Edwards' insightful Afterword explores further the sexual politics and gender polarities of the tale.[196] In the opening pages of this essay, H. quickly surveys a handful of anecdotes – excised from the historians Tacitus, Suetonius and Cassius Dio and a treatise by the second-century court physician Galen, *On the Affections and Errors of the Soul* – and their variously problematic contexts. These brief extracts are a reminder (particularly given the concerns prominent in the running methodological commentaries on 'Murderous games' and the first part of 'Death in Rome') that there are other master–slave stories surviving from antiquity.[197] The bulk of 'Novel evidence' (true to its title) is focused on the *Life of Aesop*. For H., this text – the only extended narrative surviving from antiquity told from a slave's point of view[198] – offers a clear and persuasive illustration of 'the basic argument of this article ... that fiction provides a usable and trustworthy representation of Roman culture ... a mirror of Roman thinking and feelings'.[199] Indeed the particular pleasure

[193] 1993: 16, 18–19 and 21, quoting 21 [essay 11: 411–12, 414–15 and 417–18, quoting 417].
[194] 1993: 22 [essay 11: 418].
[195] 1993: 6–7, 10 n. 13, 14 n. 19, 19 n. 30 [essay 11: 401–2, 406 n. 13, 409 n. 19, 415 n. 30].
[196] Edwards [428–31].
[197] 1993: 4–5 and 7–10 [essay 11: 399–400 and 402–6].
[198] 1993: 3 and 10 [essay 11: 398 and 406].
[199] 1993: 4 n. 3 [essay 11: 399 n. 3].

of this essay, to quote Edwards, is to admire the ways in which 'H. weaves evocative history out of the flagrantly fictional'.[200] The *Life of Aesop* is 'good to think with'[201] (for both ancient slave-owner and modern cultural historian) precisely because it exploits well-worn stereotypes to expose the mutual anxieties of the master–slave relationship: an ugly, clever subordinate pitted against a second-rate superior, both trapped by their interdependence. This 'fictional biography runs along the raw nerves of slavery'.[202] For H., these conflicts (amusing, admonitory, advisory) are 'structural and symptomatic, not personal and idiosyncratic'.[203]

> Roman masters needed slaves in order to be masters, and they needed stories about slaves in order to work through and recreate some of the problems which their own social superiority inevitably caused. In these stories, the anti-hero, the ugly hunchback dwarf slave … is socially despised, but symbolically central. He is created from a repertoire of social images, whose appeal lies in the tension they generate between underpinning and undermining the dominant culture.[204]

H. wonders what it might have been like for a slave-owner and his family to have the *Life of Aesop* read aloud to them by an educated slave. 'Humour camouflages, but does not fully hide, the lines of battle in the unceasing guerrilla warfare between master and slave.'[205] Who here had the last laugh?

Despite pioneering an inventive approach to the cultural history of Roman slavery, H. was not committed to a linguistic turn.[206] Rather he favoured an approach which, in his view, represented an even sharper, and more disruptive, break with the expectations of conventional history-writing. H.'s last book, *A World Full of Gods: Pagans, Jews and Christians in the Roman Empire* (1999)[207] had its genesis in a collaborative research project on 'Early Christianity' (with four postdoctoral

200 Edwards [431].
201 1993: 21 [essay 11: 417].
202 1993: 12 [essay 11: 408].
203 1993: 18 [essay 11: 414].
204 1993: 21–2 [essay 11: 418].
205 1993: 19 [essay 11: 415].
206 Harris 2005: 105.
207 Published the following year in the USA under the title, *A World Full of Gods: The Strange Triumph of Christianity*.

research fellows and H. as the principal investigator) funded from 1992 to 1996 by the Research Centre at King's College, Cambridge.[208] In discussions, seminars and reading groups (there was never any joint publication), H. became convinced that a history of early Christianity needed to be set firmly in its Roman and Jewish contexts and, above all, should seek to recover the profusion of alternative 'Christianities' which were suppressed or demonised by a triumphant orthodoxy tightly bound to an emergent institutional Church.

The core of *A World Full of Gods* is a careful unpicking of the canonical foundation narratives of early Christianity: most effectively in a set of brief and thoughtful discussions on 'the feverish imagination' of Gnosticism, the apocryphal *Acts of Thomas* and the complex construction of the Gospel texts.[209] The most interesting intervention – which exploited the central tactic of 'Novel evidence for Roman slavery' – sketched out an original approach to reading early Christian martyr acts. H.'s focus was the account of the arrest, trial and execution of Polycarp, bishop of Smyrna in the second century. This was presented as a worked example of the 'structured series of ingredients' which he suggested was typical of martyr acts.[210] H. argued that these highly charged narratives of political confrontation and religious affirmation were popular precisely because they enabled their 'readers (or listeners) vicariously to act out the effrontery of opposition with impunity'.[211] They were powerful and inspiring substitutes for the real thing. 'Christians read about martyrs, instead of being one.'[212]

H. was eager to emphasise that his history of early Christianity was founded in the interpretation – rereading, retelling – of stories about the divine and miraculous. (H. told and retold stories about martyrs, monks, ascetics, bishops, holy men, gods, angels, demons and their mundane intermediaries.)

208 1999: 2; Harris 2005: 100; obit. in the *King's College Cambridge Annual Report* (2004) 46.
209 1999: 156–72, 252–65, quoting 252, 301–21.
210 1999: 111–23, quoting 115.
211 1999: 114.
212 1999: 115.

'Story-telling used to be the stuff of history.'[213] Of course, and certainly by the late 1990s, the close genetic relationship between story-telling and history-writing was a methodological commonplace. But for H. (aside from a small handful of exceptions), ancient historians had been slow to recognise the importance of stories in understanding the past, and, more particularly, to accept that stories were the main surviving evidence for Roman religion – and the principal means of persuasion or conversion. In *A World Full of Gods*, the problematic relationship between history-writing and story-telling is foregrounded by the inclusion of (blatantly, wittily) fabricated texts, some of which lurch between the ancient and the modern. The ideals of the Qumran community – rigorist, messianic, millenarian, all-male, celibate – were replayed in a televison script (presented as part of a pitch to the Co-ordinator of Religious Programmes at Channel 4) in which a modern production crew, with presenter and director, time-travelled to late first-century Rome to interview 'talking-heads' for a prospective documentary: *Judaism, Then and Now*. With a further disregard for chronology, they recorded a debate – which they also provoked – between an aged extremist, Isaac (who had avoided the Roman massacre of the Qumran community during the Jewish revolt of AD 66–73) and Justin (the mid-second-century controversialist and Christian martyr).[214] In another fake, the disagreements between Macarius, a recent Christian convert, Isidorus/Simon, a hellenising Jew, and Crispus, a prosperous pagan, were rehearsed in a detailed account of their dinner-party conversation which H. alleged had been preserved in 'two previously unpublished third-century letters'.[215] A final example: the death-bed confessions of Augustine – the most influential Christian thinker in antiquity after Paul – which H. claimed had been discovered in a cache of documents buried under the floor of the saint's library in Hippo (on the North African coast) before the city's capture by Vandals in 431.[216]

[213] 1999: 4.
[214] 1999: 53–77.
[215] 1999: 208–44, quoting 208; see too 369 n. 47.
[216] 1999: 287–9; see too 375 n. 82.

For H., the repeated retelling of stories – which comprised the bulk of the book – was a key strategy in the attempt 'to re-experience the thoughts, feelings, practices and images of religious life in the Roman empire, in which orthodox Christianity emerged in all its vibrant variety'.[217] After all, it was not possible to follow Maurice Bloch amongst the Merina in Madagascar or a younger H. amongst the tenement blocks in Hong Kong and conduct fieldwork in the ancient world. Except that *A World Full of Gods* also set out to remedy that deficiency. H. included two reports from Martha and James, who were dispatched as time-travellers to Pompeii (arriving just before the eruption of Vesuvius) and to Egypt (Tebtunis in the Fayum), Syria and Ephesus.[218] In Pompeii, James and Martha are menaced by vicious dogs (a distant reminiscence of H.'s own visits to squatter settlements),[219] purchase a slave, visit the baths, join a procession in honour of Isis and are guests at a wedding.

> We were shit scared … [but] … no one ever believed that we had actually broken through time-barriers, and had gone to ancient Rome and back. Some friends did ask us about it all, with a sort of amused tolerance, but their staying power was five minutes max, as though we were talking about a package holiday on the Costa Brava.[220]

A World Full of Gods was meant to be fun (even if H. sometimes strained to find a convincing colloquial idiom). Equally importantly, the careful juxtaposition of knowingly 'naive fiction' with 'different methods of historical reportage, description and analysis'[221] was intended to be read as a serious reflection on the limits of modern knowledge of the ancient world, and on the delights and difficulties of writing a history of Roman religion based largely on stories. And (as might now be expected) the stories were painstakingly constructed. H. prided himself on the inclusion of 'real' ancient material in his fictional accounts. Thus, for example, in the script

[217] 1999: 6.
[218] 1999: 7–42, 179–207.
[219] 1999: 11.
[220] 1999: 9.
[221] 1999: 5 and 3.

of the television documentary, most of Isaac's responses are skilful pastiches of prayers, community rules and apocalyptic predictions from the Dead Sea Scrolls. Justin self-quotes extensively from his own *Dialogue with Trypho*.[222] At the pagan Crispus' dinner-party, Macarius' Christian views (and most of his interlocutors' objections to his new religion) are a mash-up of second-century apologists, including Athanagoras and Minucius Felix, and Origen's *Contra Celsum*.[223] Augustine's death-bed confessions are a collage of quotations excerpted from a wide range of his surviving writings, including the (real) *Confessions*, *On the Grace of Christ* and *On Original Sin*.[224] The account of the time-travellers' first adventure draws on Apuleius' *Metamorphoses*, the *Life of Aesop* and a close knowledge of Pompeii. James and Martha stay at the inn of Hermes, visit the Suburban Baths and are guests at the Casa degli Amorini dorati (House of the Gilded Cupids). The wedding takes place at the House of the Vetti.[225] Specialists will immediately spot (at least some of) the literary and archaeological references; for non-specialists, the answers are at the back of book. In the endnotes, H. notes his own research trips to Pompeii.[226] He cites an impressive range of ancient texts, excavation reports and modern scholarship in English, French, German and Italian.

In fact, if you, dear reader, actually read all that stuff, including this note, congratulations. Quotations from the ancient texts are meant to give the genuine ancient experience. They don't? Well.[227]

The juxtaposition of H.'s deliberately over-referenced notes and the time-travellers' jocular reportage amusingly explores the unstable boundary between fact and fiction. 'Time-travellers stand for one version of history, fictionalised in order to expose the difficulties which all historians face in

[222] 1999: 342–5.
[223] 1999: 367 n. 1.
[224] 1999: 376 n. 85.
[225] 1999: 337 nn. 14–15 and 19, 338 n. 40, 339 nn. 46–7.
[226] 1999: 338 n. 40; see too 339 n. 47.
[227] 1999: 343 n. 33.

recreating the past. But time-travellers have a restricted view; they can only report what we already know.'[228] Martha and James' text provides – to return to a familiar theme – another provocative commentary on the hazards, as H. saw them, of inductive history-writing based on, or principally authorised by, the careful citation of ancient sources. 'Credit goes to the ancient historian who makes the best pattern out of the largest number of pieces and cites the most obscure sources relevantly.' The endnotes (a kind of deferred academic pleasure) transform the time-travellers' reports into H.'s ironic attempt at scissors-and-paste history. After all, what difference does it make if the reader – finally thumbing the endnotes – belatedly knows that James had accurately described the delicately patterned red and gold wall-painting in Cubiculum I of the Casa degli Amorini dorati, or that Martha's lingering eye for detail in her account of the erotic paintings in the changing-room of a bath-house is confirmed by the standard scholarly publication of the Suburban Baths (reviewed by H. in the *Times Literary Supplement*)?[229]

A World Full of Gods is also a book ever eager to tell its own story. One of H.'s most striking tactics is the inclusion (interleaved in seven of the eight chapters) of letters drawn from a portfolio of correspondence with colleagues who offer encouragement as well as a critique of the project as it developed. Mary (a fellow ancient historian in Cambridge and fellow of New Hall) in reply to a letter from H. set out some objections to the time-travellers' narrative, doubting whether it offered any serious supplement to more standard forms of history-writing.

> One trouble is that your time-travellers only see what they see, and what they see is inevitably selective. … But the main difficulty is that your scholarly (sic!) inhibitions prevent you from allowing your time-travellers to see/hear significantly more than what modern scholars already know, while your style of presentation allows you to present only a small fraction of that knowledge. … Your

[228] 1999: 3.

[229] 1999: 30, 338 n. 40 and plate 4 with Seiler 1992: 50 and plate 321; Hopkins 1999: 17–18, 337 nn. 14–15 with Jacobelli 1995: especially 32–60 with plates II–IX, reviewed in Hopkins 1996b.

account is halfway between the pure Roman and modern scholarship, and has the advantages of neither.[230]

And for those readers who had somehow missed the main methodological point, there was an extensive exchange with Hartmut in Heidelberg.

My dear Keith,

Thank you for sending me your brief manuscript. I assume that it is part of larger project, since as it stands it violates most of the sensible rules of ordinary history … history, as I should not have to tell you, is concerned with fact, and if possible with truth. … My colleagues here in Heidelberg would not have to be told all this. … And I do realise that we pay the penalty of our own commitment to truth, thoroughness and accuracy. Not many people read our books.[231]

But – as should now come as no surprise – these letters are (at sympathetic best) distant echoes of now irrecoverable encounters with colleagues. Most likely they are complete forgeries as Mary Beard emphasises in her Afterword to the final essay in this volume.[232] Perhaps the first give-away is the correspondents' phoney bonhomie: 'Could we talk about it over a boozy lunch?'; 'Sure, you're on for lunch, I hope you're paying.'[233] Or perhaps it is the contrived stereotypes: Hartmut the unimaginative German traditionalist from the Theologische Fakultät in Heidelberg; Avi the religiously observant scholar from the Jewish Theological Seminary in New York; Josh the theoretically adept social anthropologist from H.'s old department at Brunel; Mary the clever, but difficult, colleague in Cambridge; Angela the liberal Anglican priest in an unremarkable English town. Or perhaps it is simply that all the letters read as if they had been written by H., too closely capturing his own priorities, concerns and sensitivities, and occasionally recycling his own published research.[234] Or perhaps it

230 1999: 44.

231 1999: 151.

232 Beard [553–4].

233 1999: 43, 45.

234 Most egregiously, Avi recycles 'Christian number and its implications': 1998: 217–18 n. 67 [essay 12: 470 n. 67] with 1999: 237–8; and the summary of the main argument with matching observations on Herodian: 1998: 196 [essay 12: 444] with 1999: 243.

is because the advice they contain is for the most part simply (and cheerfully) discarded.[235] In short, the letters are just too good to be true. Of course, a degree of playfulness remains. Some senior professors are, in fact, convivial lunch companions. The apparent stereotyping might be an unintended result of H.'s laudable concern to preserve his correspondents' anonymity.[236] Judgements on academic style and proclivities are always subjective. Taking advice from friends and colleagues (no matter how well meaning) can be difficult. The final determination rests with the reader – who is warmly welcome to collude with the fiction that the letters are independent scholarly interventions. For H., what mattered was that the letters could plausibly be taken as another inventive example, in a book overflowing with teasing illustrations, of the blurring of story-telling and history-writing (and writing about history-writing), and of their overlapping tactics and methods. Read as genuine or fake, the letters are yet more stories in a world full of stories.[237]

'How to be a Roman emperor: an autobiography' (2005) [essay 14] continues the key methodological concerns of *A World Full of Gods*. The framework is familiar: a fabricated text and an exchange of letters between H. and Martha, an academic friend (and seemingly not the time-traveller[238]). H. claims to be offering the first draft of a translation from Latin (the provenance of the original manuscript is confidential) of the *post mortem* reflections, channelled from the afterlife, of the late second-/early third-century emperor, Septimius Severus.[239] The

235 Most blatantly at 1999: 156.
236 1999: 359 n. 30.
237 Letters as a critical foil had been used before, and to sharp methodological effect, in the writing of early Christian history. H. was aware of the precedent: Gerd Theißen, *Der Schattern des Galiläers. Historische Jesusforschung in erzählender Form* (1986). It is (of course) pointed out by Hartmut: 1999: 359 n. 30. H. cleverly elaborated Theißen's model. Theißen had only one correspondent ('Dr Kratzinger', whose conventional views mark him out as a close literary relative of Hartmut) and openly admitted in an epilogue that the correspondence was no more than a convenient fiction: Theißen 1986: 259. H. refused to give the game away so easily.
238 But see Beard [553].
239 2005: 72 [essay 14: 534].

choice was, in part, inspired by seeing Severus' heroic naked bronze statue in the Cyprus Museum in Nicosia.[240] 'How to be a Roman emperor' was included in a slim volume edited by Roger Tomlin which also presented the published versions of five other lectures given at Wolfson College, Oxford in early 2003 to mark the centenary of the birth of Sir Ronald Syme (arguably the most innovative and influential Roman historian of the mid-twentieth century). And Syme was a scholar, as Mary Beard makes clear in her witty reaction to this essay, whose open preference for grand political history was used by H. (and not always fairly) as a foil to his own approach.[241]

Certainly, H. rises to this anniversary occasion. His text – a lightly revised transcript of his lecture[242] – is offered without references (neither footnotes nor endnotes). Perhaps H. enjoyed placing his readers in the same situation as his scholarly audience in Oxford, unpicking the text as it was presented (or, perhaps, worrying that some allusion had slipped past unidentified). H.'s scissors-and-paste – or, better, papier mâché – emperor offers his thoughts on previous imperial colleagues, domestic life, court intrigue, family rivalries and his victory in a bloody and hard-fought civil war.

> Of course, you do not have to be emperor for long to realise the huge gap between apparent omnipotence and real power. You are omnipotent only in subjects' imagination ... To take a trivial example: when you were feeling peckish and ordered a hot snack, it took simply ages for anything to arrive, and when it did it was usually cold.[243]

Martha's responses – she had clearly read H.'s correspondence with Mary in *A World Full of Gods* – are pointed and predictable (the papier mâché quip is hers[244]), chiefly concerned with the restrictions imposed by the concentration on a single imperial point of view and with the limitations of H.'s method: 'Inevitably, because your vision is blinkered by scholarly conventions, you stick by and large to the

240 McCann 1968: 133–4 no. 11 and plate C; Soechting 1972: 140 no. 15.

241 Beard [550–1].

242 Tomlin 2005b: 10.

243 2005: 74 [essay 14: 536–7].

244 2005: 83 [essay 14: 546].

sources – Herodian, Dio, with bits of Tacitus and Philo – and you gain considerably by taking a fresh look and inverting their perspective ... but it is a single tactic ploy, say, like playing Beethoven backwards'.[245] There is no surprise either in H.'s courteous response to Martha's advice – 'thank you very much for taking the time and trouble to send me such thoughtful and constructive criticisms' – or in his charming assurance: 'I will certainly rewrite this before I publish it.'[246]

On the face of it, such an amusing *pièce d'occasion* (H.'s own description[247]) – and, more broadly, his emphasis on empathetic imagination – represented a divergence in method and style from his essays on political, economic and social structures. But that contrast is easily overdrawn. It masks a close continuity of concern with a set of interlocking issues explored in the first part of this introduction: the arc of an argument (its articulation, plausibility, economy), the fall of data (especially a dislike of inductive reasoning) and a recognition of the gaps and biases in the fragmentary record of the Roman empire. For H., the shortfall was alarming. He observed that if the fifty known Christian communities in the Roman empire around AD 100 are reckoned to have written on average just two letters a year between AD 50 and 150 (to opt for a deliberately low level of inter-community correspondence) 'then in this period, 10,000 letters were written, of which barely fifty survive'.[248] Another telling example:

> Consider the following: the Romans conducted seventeen censuses of the Egyptian population by households at fourteen-year intervals between AD 19 and 257. If the average household size was five persons, and the population is deliberately estimated low at 3.5 million, and we have less than one thousand surviving census returns, the survival ratio is c. 1:12,000.[249]

The most memorable cautionary tales are H.'s fabricated texts themselves. 'How to be a Roman emperor' is a stark and bitter reminder of what has *not* been saved from the ancient world.

[245] 2005: 83 [essay 14: 546].
[246] 2005: 84 and 85 [essay 14: 547 and 548].
[247] 2005: 84 [essay 14: 547].
[248] 1998: 200 [essay 12: 449].
[249] 1991b: 133 n. 2 [essay 10: 363–4 n. 2].

Aside from a scattered handful of quotations, Augustus' public record of his *Achievements*, Marcus Aurelius' *Meditations* and some embarrassingly poor poetry by the Emperor Hadrian, there are no personal writings preserved from over twenty emperors in two hundred years. There are no surviving imperial archives.

It is this profound sense of loss, and the working out of strategies to cope with it, that underpins much of H.'s work in Roman history. In his first published essay (to begin again right back at the beginning), H. had invoked the surviving correspondence of Ausonius (a fourth-century poet and teacher of rhetoric from Bordeaux) as a reliable guide to contemporary provincial society: 'there is no reason to suppose that the picture he gives is untypical of life in the provinces'.[250] H. held to his claim, although he admitted that Ausonius' exceptional political and social success was founded on the rare chance of an intimate imperial connection as tutor to the future Emperor Gratian.[251] In 'Contraception in the Roman empire' (1965) [essay 1], H. attempted to assess the importance of various forms of contraception and abortifacients by tabulating their frequency of mention in the surviving work of twenty-six ancient medical writers. Those writers whose gynaecological and obstetric works had survived – such as the Περὶ γυναικείων παθῶν (*On the Diseases of Women*) by the late first/second-century AD physician, Soranus – assumed a due, and perhaps unsurprising, prominence.[252] H.'s method seems (at least in retrospect) somewhat naive, as does the caveat: 'It may be that frequency of mention is more a function of ineffectiveness than of concern with a problem.'[253]

H. did not pursue either of these tactics.[254] (He was later pointedly to remark that he doubted most doctors in antiquity had ever read Soranus.[255]) Rather, as surveyed in

[250] 1961: 239.
[251] 1961: 245.
[252] 1965a: 132–4 with 'Table of medical writers consulted' [essay 1: 65–8 with table 1.1].
[253] 1965a: 132 [essay 1: 66].
[254] Although traces remain: see, for example, the defensive remarks at 1983b: 8 n. 13.
[255] 1990: 629.

the first part of this introduction, H. developed a distinctive and highly original parametric/propositional approach, drawing freely on the language and model-building methods of the social sciences, as a means of constructing a much broader and more complex understanding of the Roman world than the skewed and sketchy surviving information might at first sight seem to allow. This important and innovative work, spanning a wide range of interests in demography, economics, and social and political structures, is represented by the majority of the essays in this volume. It remains H.'s most admired intellectual achievement. Yet as the two chapters which bookend *Death and Renewal* ('Murderous games' and 'Death in Rome') make clear, he was also concerned 'to understand, and to develop ways of expressing, Roman experience'.[256] In this collection, H.'s concern with 'arousing the reader's empathetic imagination'[257] is exemplified by three essays: 'From violence to blessing: symbols and rituals in ancient Rome' [essay 8], 'Novel evidence for Roman slavery' [essay 11] and 'How to be a Roman emperor: an autobiography' [essay 14].

For H., the pitfalls of empathy were clear. Some (as explored in the discussion above) were inescapable: history is written in a modern language and reflects modern sensibilities and experiences. 'We cannot reproduce antiquity.'[258] Ancient texts never simply speak for themselves. They are always and inevitably out of context. Nor – as H.'s fabricated dialogues, death-bed confessions and imperial memoirs underscore – can these patchy and piecemeal survivals offer anything approaching a wide-angled view of the Roman past. But that does not absolve the ancient historian from trying. As H. insisted in 'From violence to blessing', despite 'the dangers and limitations', if we want to understand how the Romans experienced their world, 'then we have to recapture the excitement … the cheering, jeering crowds voting death with their thumbs down at the gladiatorial

[256] 1983b: p. xv.
[257] 1983b: p. xiv.
[258] 1999: 2.

games, the pious prayers of worshippers seeking victory in war or helplessly hoping to escape an epidemic'.[259]

This too was a long-standing concern. To follow Caroline Vout's lead in her comments on the opening essay in this volume, 'Contraception in the Roman empire' (1965):

> H.'s anxiety about how to handle the gap between his own, and the Roman, conceptualisation of the world weighs heavy throughout. … Thirty-five years on, this anxiety would still drive him to experiment with how to write history and explore everyday life in Pompeii with the help of a time machine.[260]

A World Full of Gods – in all its chaotic inventiveness and tediously repetitive story-telling – is a good case overstated. In the end, it was perhaps just too much to ask one text (or its readers) to orchestrate 'empathetic wonder, knowledge, pseudo-objective analysis, ignorance, competing assumptions and disagreements'.[261] But, as Vout shrewdly suggests, the break with H.'s earlier work (at least in methodological terms) should not be exaggerated. Arguably, *A World Full of Gods* represents the working out of an approach to history-writing first enunciated three decades before in his account of his fieldwork on resettlement housing in Hong Kong. Then H. had strikingly declined to base his conclusions solely on the mass of detailed information derived from 5,000 interviews, the careful measurement of rooms and the census of consumer durables. For H., those generalisations – even when backed by more hard data than could ever be imagined for the ancient world – were insufficient to convey a full understanding of housing in Hong Kong, particularly from the perspective of the poor in squatter settlements or tenement slums. Instead, as noted above, H. chose to present 'a patchwork of data … from a variety of sources and … of varying reliability'[262] and to include his own experiences, personal impressions and beliefs.

H.'s brief experience as a sociologist in the field informed his practice as an ancient historian. Hong Kong foreshadowed

[259] 1991a: 484 [essay 8: 320].
[260] Vout [99]; see too Beard [552–3].
[261] 1999: 2.
[262] 1971b: 274, quoted above p. 33.

Rome. In his own work, H. continued to aim at a productive tension between imperfect data, a sophisticated understanding of social, political and economic structures, empathetic imagination, and an acute sense of the author's own modernity and active presence in the text, selecting from the surviving material and shaping the argument. It was a tough and demanding ask – not least for his graduate students and the distinguished speakers invited to address the weekly ancient history seminar in Cambridge.[263] And H. himself did not always find a convincing or workable balance. But – most importantly – confronting these competing concerns was at the heart of the ancient history he most wanted to write.

> One useful guide may be to see the historian as holding a balance between a least four protagonists: first, the actors, their acts, beliefs, values, intentions and justifications ... secondly, the social structure which reflects, restricts and also shapes the actors' acts, thoughts and feelings; thirdly, the sources ... and finally, the audience of readers to whom the historian with his own biases must interpret a dead culture. I realize that such a specification makes history writing difficult; it can also make it exciting.[264]

* * *

The essays collected in this volume (and the reflective Afterwords by friends, colleagues and former graduate students) together demonstrate the significant impact of Keith Hopkins' work on the way ancient history is written – and continues to be written. H.'s methodological interests and incisive innovations, and his disarming frankness about the problems of understanding the classical past, challenge – and continue to challenge – the complacent primacy of much conventional scholarship. H., of course, would be the first to dam this incipient flow of praise. There was no harsher critic of H. than H. himself.[265] Indeed, there is no reason to think that he would wish readers of the essays collected in this volume to be any less severe – provided that they were also prepared to scrutinise their own historical

[263] Harris 2005: 97; obit. in the *King's College Cambridge Annual Report* (2004) 45; Elsner [340 n. 1]; Beard [554].

[264] 1978c: 183.

[265] Osborne 2004a: 6; Harris 2005: 104–5; Jongman [264 n. 14]; Beard [553].

practice with an equal rigour and to recognise 'the sheer difficulty of writing history and the vulnerability of each solution.'[266] Simply put, H. wished other ancient historians (and especially his graduate students) to share both his own perfectionism and his passionate excitement at the 'elegant' – his rare and most precious complement – architecture of a well constructed essay.

But an argument can always be improved. H.'s dissertation – 'The later Roman aristocracy: a demographic profile' – which he submitted in his late twenties to King's College, Cambridge (and which secured his election to a research fellowship in 1963) opens with a brief discussion: 'The subject, the problem and the method'. It offers a recognisable early formulation of what was to develop into the wigwam argument.

> The model is not a lofty structure, in which the whole case stands or falls by the acceptance of each successive stage of the argument, or where the final conclusion is the lowest common denominator of uncertainty. Here rather each separate argument is on the same level; in so far as they interlock, or have a mutual coherence, they circumscribe the area of probability.[267]

In the copy of this fellowship dissertation which H. gave me a few weeks before his death (in March 2004), the faded typescript quoted above has been marked in black ink by an older H. who in the margin confronts, in distinctively gaunt handwriting, his younger self, curtly asking: 'Do you live up to this?' This stinging injunction crystallises H.'s restless and dissatisfied attitude to his own ancient history-writing, and hints at how he might have approached this volume. It is a painfully honest moment of still lingering self-doubt – and one (for the reader, at least) now perhaps most profitably resolved by a critical and empathetic engagement with the fourteen essays which follow.

266 2001.
267 1963b: 4.

I

CONTRACEPTION IN THE ROMAN EMPIRE*

It has long been recognised that upper-class Romans in their desire for small families practised abortion on a large scale. What is not well known is the extent to which these same upper-class Romans were concerned with contraception. Some of the methods advocated by Greek and Roman doctors could have been very effective, and aspects of ancient contraceptive theory were as advanced as any modern theory before the middle of the nineteenth century. Such contraceptive theory was part of a lively literary medical tradition, appearing first in Aristotle and in the Hippocratic Corpus; its repeated appearance in our fragmentary sources, when considered together with the organisation of doctors' training, argues for its significance in medical practice, at least among the upper class. Nonetheless, the total effect of contraception upon fertility in Rome cannot be seen only in these terms.[1] For many other ancient contraceptive methods were ineffective; indeed, the rudimentary character of some Romans' knowledge of this subject is highlighted by what seems to be an interesting and surprising confusion of contraception with abortion, both in method and conceptualisation. Nor can we necessarily assume that Romans who wished to limit their families had recourse to what might seem to be an obvious and effective solution, namely the practice of coitus interruptus. It is possible that some Romans practised it. But knowledge of coitus interruptus is by no means universal and is even unknown in societies in which other methods of family limitation are used.

* First published in *Comparative Studies in Society and History* 8 (1965) 124–51 (= Hopkins 1965a).

1 Fertility is not used in any biological sense, but refers to the rate at which births actually occur in a particular group of people. Where fertility in the biological sense is meant, fecundity (the ability to bring about a pregnancy) is used.

Finally, on general theoretical grounds I shall argue that the practice of all forms of contraception declined in the later empire.

* * *

I shall deal mainly with those methods of birth control which Romans of the upper classes used intentionally in order to prevent conception. I have left out those practices which in fact limited fertility but which were not undertaken with that end primarily in view (e.g. religious celibacy, homosexuality). The lower classes are left out because so little is known about them. Abortion and infanticide are also left out (they would require an article each), except in so far as Romans confused abortion with contraception.

This confusion of abortion with contraception and the problems of deciding whether the Romans practised coitus interruptus both raise and provide an opportunity to examine some wider methodological considerations. To the modern the concepts contraception and abortion are obviously distinct. In ancient Rome, as I hope to show, this was not always the case. Yet as moderns and as historians we have no alternative but to use our own concepts and categories to describe and explain other societies. Even if the inhabitants of the societies we describe used quite different concepts and categories to make patterns out of the external environment, we can explain their behaviour only in our own terms. Yet the existence of differences between our own and the Roman conceptualisation of the external world poses problems. We have to ask what are the limitations of using categories to describe and explain behaviour which was not conceived by the actors themselves in those terms. Certainly, the difficulties are not solved merely by becoming aware of the problem – though this awareness certainly prompts questions and even suggests answers. Some systematic investigation of the differences or similarities in conceptualisation is surely necessary, and it is surprising that so little of the efforts of ancient historians has been directed to this end.

Ancient historians have mostly been content with assuming that Romans in all significant ways thought, perceived and attached meaning to their actions in a manner roughly comparable to their own – be they French, English, Italian or German of the eighteenth, nineteenth or twentieth centuries. This may be justifiable in straight political history; it is certainly less justifiable in social history – and in both cases it would be better, if systematically and openly justified. The confusion of abortion and contraception provides one example of how our concepts differ from the Romans; the problem of coitus interruptus raises another related issue. If we can assume some harmony between the conceptualisation of total environment on the one hand and personality on the other, differences in conceptualisation would lead one to expect differences in personality. Romans might typically be significantly different from modern Westerners. This difference is obviously difficult to assess, but at least per contra it seems illegitimate for historians to assume that human nature (as in 'Naturally ...') or 'reasonable' behaviour can be used as constant elements in their explanations of historical acts. Human 'nature', if it is to be used at all, may more reasonably be seen as variable, not constant, and this degree of variability is a proper subject for investigation not assumption. But such issues are too grand to receive any adequate treatment in an article on birth control. Yet they are germane; I began by wondering how aristocratic Romans kept their families small and I found that only by touching upon these wider questions could I come to terms with the subject.

It is also beyond the scope of this article to establish, delimit and document the extent, intensity and causes of the motives which led the upper classes to limit the size of their families. Yet one of the most important aspects of contraception is that conscious motivation is a key to its success. The intensity of the desire not to beget or not to conceive is an important factor in increasing the efficiency of most contraceptive methods, from the most hazardous to the potentially most efficient. A general fall in fertility is a product of will plus technique, but the will is prior, if not to the discovery of contraceptives, at least to their use.[2]

Nevertheless for current purposes it is enough to refer to what is well known: the legislation of the Emperor Augustus (18 BC and AD 9) designed to increase fertility; the complaints of low fertility and references to the unashamed practice of abortion which abound in the literature of the first centuries before and after Christ; the re-enactment of Augustus' laws in the second and third centuries AD and similar legislation in the middle of the fifth century AD. Let us assume that these complaints had some substantial foundation in reality, at least among the upper classes; let us assume that the birthrate was, in fact, low; that a significant number of upper-class families had fewer than three children born to them, since this was the target set by the Augustan laws.[3]

Roman girls married young; half of their first marriages would have lasted about eighteen years.[4] If they had regular and frequent intercourse we should expect many more than three children from most marriages. Some have claimed that the low fertility of Romans can be explained by racial decline, either through racial mixture or through selective breeding of the weakest (e.g. Seeck's 'Die Ausrottung der Besten').[5] There is little serious evidence in favour of either argument. In all societies in which it has been observed, fall of fertility has been too swift to be accounted for by biological changes. There

[2] Ariès 1949: 469; Kiser 1950: 272.

[3] For example: Gell. *NA* 1.6; Prop. 2.7; Plin. *HN* 14.5; Augustus' laws: Suet. *Aug.* 34, 89; *Dig.* 35.1.64.1 (Terentius Clemens); their re-enactment: *Fragmenta Vaticana* 168, 247; cf. *CIL* XI 6354; and in the third century: *Dig.* 50.5.2 (Ulpian); *CJ* 5.66.1 (AD 203); these laws were formally annulled by Constantine, *CTh* 8.16 (AD 320), though something of it lingered: cf. *CTh* 9.42.9 (AD 380) and 8.17.1–3 (AD 396 and 410). Majorian re-enacted penalties for childless women in AD 458 (Maj. *Nov.* 6.5). The evidence for small families among the upper class in the early empire is legion; I have collected some of the evidence from the later empire in my unpublished fellowship dissertation, 'The later Roman aristocracy: a demographic profile' (Hopkins 1963b: 28–37).

[4] For this calculation I have used UN model life tables, level 10, with an expectation of life at birth for both sexes of 25: see United Nations 1956: 74–6. The median duration of first marriages, with no account taken of divorce, but only of one or both partners' death, is based for purposes of illustration on a couple married at 15 (female) and 25 (male); cf. Hopkins 1964–5: 325.

[5] Seeck 1920–2: I 269–307; cf. also the similar, if much qualified, views of Last 1947.

is in modern studies some backing to be found for Galton's theory that 'only' children (Galton's heiresses) are sub-fertile (and sub-fecund); but only to a limited degree. It has yet to be shown that a significant number of fecund aristocrats married the only daughters of rich bourgeois; and it has yet to be shown that these 'heiresses' were 'only' children because of the hereditary sub-fecundity of their parents, rather than through the earlier death of siblings or parents.[6] Secondly, it might be argued that Romans avoided large families by being unfaithful to their wives. There was in Rome little or no ideal of the faithful husband. Courtesans were extolled in the literature and presumably visited.[7] But, on the other hand, adultery among equals, affairs between mistresses and slaves, were also, if the literature reflects reality, common enough, morally condemned but often condoned. Besides, even discounting the wife's infidelity, occasional or repeated infidelity by the husband alone might be insufficient to account for the widespread achievement of less than three children over the total length of married life; that would require not occasional infidelity but considerable periods of continence. This may have occurred but all in all it seems reasonable to assume that, in general, low fertility among upper-class Romans was achieved by some means of family limitation.

Thus, I assume that Roman women of the upper classes had a median married life (first marriage) of eighteen years, significant exposure to the risk of pregnancy (whether marital or extra-marital), as high a fecundity as is to be found in comparable pre-industrial populations and a low fertility. Since motivation and achievement are closely related, it is possible to deduce from this a high level of motivation to limit family size. The question remains; how was this low fertility achieved? We

[6] Galton 1869: 130–40; R. A. Fisher's elaboration in Fisher 1930; Hollingsworth 1957–8: 23–4.

[7] E.g.: uxor legitimus debet quasi census amari: nec censum uellem semper amare meum ⟨a wife should be loved like wealth acquired legitimately; but I wouldn't want to love my wealth forever⟩ (Meyer 1835: I no. 147) ⟨see also E. Baehrens (ed.) *Poetae Latini Minores*, 5 vols, Leipzig, 1879–83, IV no. 78 = D. R. Shackleton-Bailey (ed.) *Anthologiae Latinae*, Stuttgart, 1982, no. 466: uxor, legis onus, debet quasi census …⟩. For prostitution, cf. Herter 1960. (This article is not sociological.)

know that Romans practised abortion with little or no sense of shame.[8] There is some evidence that they practised infanticide, but it is by no means agreed that this was common among the upper classes.[9] What we are concerned with is to discover whether upper-class Romans, highly motivated as they were to limit their families, extended the logic of infanticide and abortion; did they use contraceptives and were these contraceptives efficient? Some advantages of contraception are apparent; it is an extra line of defence against the unwanted child; it saves the mother the pain and danger of childbirth and abortion; it saves interruption of love life; it avoids the disruption and tension which surround the responsibility of killing one's own child.

We may perhaps guess that Romans used contraceptives – or say that it is likely that they did – but can we know? Representatively, Professor Syme has answered that we do not know, that there is no evidence.[10] And to be sure the evidence is slight – but some at least does exist, and we shall see if something can be made of it.[11]

The Medical Tradition

A major part of Roman medicine was derived from Greek medicine, and indeed many of the famous doctors who practised in Rome were Greek-speaking and trained in Greek 'universities'. Greek medicine in the Roman empire rested upon a long-established and voluminous literary tradition. As Drabkin wrote: 'Though many a doctor must have been trained with few

[8] Cf. Hähnel 1936; J. H. Waszink, *RAC* I: 55–60, s.v. 'Abtreibung'.

[9] Kaser 1955–9: II 143–4 and the literature cited there. I agree, of course that the lower classes also killed or sold their children, though the usual economic causes cited need qualification. For infanticide by the rich, cf. Longus 4.35; Suet. *Aug.* 65.4, *Claud.* 27; Tert. *Apol.* 9.1–8; Musonius Rufus, frag. 15b (ed. O. Hense, Leipzig, 1905) ⟨= Stobaeus 4.664–6 (ed. C. Wachsmuth and O. Hense, Berlin, 1909) = Stobaeus, *Flor.* 84.21; trans. Inwood and Gerson 2008: 184; C. King 2011: 63–4⟩; Firm. Mat. *Math.* 7.2 ⟨ed. P. Monat, Paris, 1997; trans. Bram 1975⟩.

[10] Syme 1960: 324–5.

[11] Two scholars in particular have blazed the trail: Himes 1936: especially 79–101; he was not a classicist and relied upon translations, which in one or two instances were misleading, and in others incomplete. The other is Diepgen 1937, which gives a fuller, but somewhat fragmented account and is concerned with the knowledge, rather than with the use, of contraceptives.

or no books, it is, nevertheless, the literary tradition that is all important for the significant development of Greek medicine, and its transmission to later ages … Great as is the bulk of ancient medical writings, much greater than that of any other field of ancient literature, by far the greatest part has failed to survive.'[12] The surviving writings however amply illustrate the liveliness of the literary tradition; for writers frequently expressed their indebtedness to previous medical scholars. Soranus, for example, cited thirty-nine medical authorities in his 152 pages on gynaecology. But over and beyond literary doctors the very structure of medical training and practice must have reinforced the significance of the central core of ancient medical learning. True, there were many uneducated doctors, and many slave doctors, but there were also famous centres of medical training such as Alexandria, Smyrna, Pergamum and Rome; the state and the municipalities paid for the establishment of chairs of medicine, gave privileges and tax immunities to doctors throughout the empire, and from the second century AD provided positions for a number of salaried doctors according to the importance of the town. In the later empire, especially, doctors were highly honoured.[13] All these arrangements are likely to have encouraged the employment of doctors trained at one of the famous universities. In Ephesus, for example, there was a competition organised by the local medical association with prizes for achievements during the previous year in surgery and for medical knowledge. In Rome during the fourth century, state doctors had to be chosen by at least seven other doctors.[14] Taking all these factors together

[12] Drabkin 1944: 350.

[13] In general, cf. Allbutt 1921: especially 443–74, on the public medical service, and Diepgen 1949: 151. Scribonius Largus laments that anyone can become a doctor ⟨*Compositiones, Epistula dedicatoria* 10⟩ (ed. G. Helmreich, Leipzig, 1887) ⟨ed. S. Sconocchia, Leipzig, 1983; German trans. K. Brodersen, *Scribonius Largus. Der gute Arzt/Compositiones*, Wiesbaden, 2016⟩. On public payment and privileges given to doctors: cf. Suet. *Iul.* 42.1, *Aug.* 42.3; Cass. Dio 53.30.3; *Dig.* 27.1.6.2 (Modestinus); *CTh* 13.3 (AD 333); Strabo 4.1.5. On public lectures and medical schools: Gal. *Libr. Propr.* 3.12–15 (ed. D. Kühn, *Opera Omnia*, vol. 19, Leipzig, 1830) ⟨ed. V. Boudon-Millot, Paris, 2007; trans. P. N. Singer, Oxford, 1997⟩ and Oehler 1909: 14–15.

[14] On the Ephesus medical association, cf. Friedländer and Wissowa 1921–3: I 192; for others, cf. the epitaphs to a *tabularius scholae medicorum* (Orelli 1828–56: II

it is reasonable to suppose that general medical precepts and contraceptive advice which survive and are found repeatedly in ancient medical writings had a fairly wide circulation; in particular those doctors who served the well-to-do are likely to have had access either to 'university' training or to the written tradition; or to both.

While the influence of Greek medicine on Roman medicine is well documented for the early empire, its continuing influence during the later empire (from the fourth century onwards) is perhaps less well known and deserves illustration. This I shall give with especial reference to the gynaecological literature with which we shall be dealing later. The works of Vindicianus (c. AD 370), Theodorus Priscianus (c. AD 400) and Cassius Felix (c. AD 440) all show traces of earlier Greek writings. Theodorus Priscianus wrote his medical treatise, the *Euporiston*, first in Greek, then both shortened it and translated it into Latin. Both Vindicianus and Cassius Felix were highly indebted to Greek sources and both were intent on spreading Greek knowledge. From the fifth century, there also survives the translation by Caelius Aurelianus of Soranus' lengthy work *On Acute and Chronic Diseases* and especially important for our present subject is his recently discovered translation of Soranus' *Gynaecia*.[15] Oribasius, a medical encyclopaedist and court physician to the Emperor Julian (AD 361–3), cited Soranus as well as Galen, to name but two of his many sources. In the sixth century, Mustio, possibly an African, and Aëtius of Amida, as well as Mustio's later Byzantine translator,

no. 4226) and set up by a *scriba medicorum* (*CIL* VI 9566). On the selection of municipal doctors ⟨in Rome⟩, *CTh* 13.3.9 (AD 370).

15 Some of Vindicianus' work, including a *Gynaecia*, survives in fragmentary form (ed., with the works of Theodorus Priscianus, V. Rose, Leipzig, 1894). He was a teacher of Priscianus, and one of his main purposes was to make Greek works available in Latin, so K. Deichgräber, *RE* 9A.1: 29–36, s.v. 'Vindicianus 2', at 36. ⟨See also *PLRE* I 967.⟩ Theodorus Priscianus also wrote a *Gynaecia*, which shows the influence of Soranus, whether direct or indirect, cf. K. Deichgräber, *RE* 5A.2: 1866–8, s.v. 'Theodoros 46'. ⟨See also *PLRE* I 728.⟩ The *De medicina* of Cassius Felix was written in AD 447 and has in the manuscript (Cod. Parisianus Latinus 6114) the subtitle: *medicinae logicae sectae de graeco in latinum liber translatus*. It was based particularly upon Galen. ⟨See also *PLRE* II 461; ed. A. Fraisse, Paris, 2002.⟩ Caelius Aurelianus was also an African; his *Gynaecia* was first published in Drabkin and Drabkin 1951. ⟨See also *PLRE* II 201.⟩

preserved the gynaecological work of Soranus.[16] According to Cassiodorus, translations of Hippocrates, Dioscorides and Galen, as well as Caelius' translation of Soranus, were being read in Italy in the sixth century. Marcellus of Bordeaux at the beginning of the fifth century seems to have relied almost completely on such Latin translations and adaptations of Greek knowledge.[17]

The opinion of Cassiodorus and the internal evidence of the nine medical writers, cited above, provide evidence of the lively and derivative medical tradition during the later empire. Thus the writings of the earlier Greek doctors should not be seen as single contributions, fixed to the time of their composition. They were repeatedly read, learned, revised, translated; more than that they were part and parcel of day-to-day medical practice.

The tradition of effective contraceptive knowledge is part of this wider medical tradition. Our knowledge of it stems, as with so much else, from the Hippocratic Corpus and Aristotle.[18] It

[16] The influence of Soranus may be seen in Oribasius, *Collectiones* 24.31 (ed. J. Raeder, *CMG* VI.2.1, Leipzig, 1931; ed. U. C. Bussemaker and C. Daremberg, Paris, 6 vols, 1851–76: III 369–78); cf. Ilberg 1910: 27–33. Soranus is drawn on by Tert. *De anim.* 6.6 and praised by Aug. *Contra Julianum* 5.14.51 (*PL* 44: 813) ⟨trans. R. J. Teske, *Answer to the Pelagians II,* The Works of St Augustine: A Translation for the 21st Century I/24, New York, 1998⟩. Aëtius was physician at the court of Justinian I in Constantinople ⟨but see now *PLRE* II 20; Scarborough 2013⟩; he was strongly influenced by Soranus, cf. his *Libri medicianales,* book 16 (ed. S. Zervos, Leipzig, 1901) ⟨on the incomplete and problematic editions of this text, see helpfully Scarborough 2013: 744 nn. 6–7⟩. Mustio translated and adapted Soranus' *Gynaecia*; his work was edited by V. Rose under the title *Sorani Gynaeciorum vetus translatio Latina* (Leipzig, 1882); it had been retranslated into Greek and attributed to Moschion (ed. F. O. Dewez, Vienna, 1793), who was long thought to be a different man; but their identity is shown by Ilberg 1910: 6, 9, 74–114. ⟨On Mustio, see also *PLRE* II 769; trans. A. Prenner, *Mustione traduttore di Sorano di Efeso. L'ostetrica, la donna, la gestazione*, Naples, 2012.⟩ A brief account of the influence of Soranus on later gynaecology is given by Temkin 1956: pp. xliv–xlv.

[17] Cassiod. *Inst.* 1.31 ⟨trans. J. W. Halporn, Translated Texts for Historians 42, Liverpool, 2004⟩; Marcellus Empiricus or Burdigalensis (ed. G. Helmreich, Leipzig, 1889; M. Niedermann, *CML* V, Lepizig, 1916 ⟨revised edn, E. Liechtenhan, Berlin, 1968 with German trans.⟩) wrote in a letter ⟨prefaced to his *De medicamentis*⟩, addressed to the sons of the Emperor Theodosius I, of his Latin sources (*Prol.* 5–6; *CML* V 4); also cf. E. Kind, *RE* 14.2: 1498–503, s.v. 'Marcellus 58' ⟨and *PLRE* I 551–2⟩.

[18] Arist. *Hist. an.* 583a ⟨= 9(7).3 (ed. D. M. Balme and A. Gotthelf, Cambridge Classical Texts and Commentaries 38, Cambridge, 2002)⟩, recommends that a woman who does not want to conceive should before intercourse smear her genitals with cedar oil, white lead or frankincense. [Hippoc.] *Nat. mul.* 98 (ed. E. Littré,

can thereafter be traced faintly in Pliny the Elder;[19] and certainly in Dioscorides in the first century AD.[20] In the beginning of the second century AD, the great doctor Soranus, a Greek who practised in Rome, advanced in his *Gynaecia* both

Paris, 10 vols, 1839–61: VII 414) ⟨ed. F. Bourbon, Paris, 2008⟩ and *Mul.* 1.76 (ed. Littré VIII 170) recommends that the woman should drink misy, which is possibly copper sulphate. In *Genit.* 5 (ed. Littré VII 476) ⟨ed. R. Joly, Paris, 1970⟩, the author mentions the practice of women who do not want to conceive, but the wording is so vague that it is difficult to know what is meant; it seems to be either coitus interruptus or some method of getting the semen out of the vagina after coitus; such methods are often found elsewhere (cf. Himes 1936: 26, 82): Ἐπὴν δὲ μιχθῇ ἡ γυνή, ἢν μὲν μὴ μέλλῃ λήψεσθαι πρὸς ἑωυτήν, πρὸς τῷ ἔθει χωρεῖ ἔξω ἡ γονὴ ⟨ἡ⟩ ἀπ' ἀμφοτέρων, ὁκόταν ἡ γυνὴ ἐθελήσῃ· – 'When the woman has intercourse, if she does not intend to conceive, the semen from both customarily falls outside, when the woman wishes it', cf. *Nat. pue.* 13 (ed. Littré VII 490) ⟨ed. R. Joly, Paris, 1970⟩. ⟨On the various tracts in the Hippocratic corpus, see now usefully Craik 2015.⟩

19 Certainly if it is there at all in Pliny it is distorted. Plin. *HN* 24.18: 'Gossip records a miracle: that to rub it [cedar gum] all over the male part before coition prevents conception', cf. below [73] and n. 39. Not only is it a distortion of Aristotle's prescription, it is also unlikely to be effective. There are many other references to contraceptives in Pliny's *Natural History*, but most of them are cautionary: e.g. fern, or asplenon, is good for such and such, but it should not be taken by women because it causes sterility or abortion (27.80, 27.34, and similarly 20.114, 20.142–3, 20.147–8). He also positively recommended some antaphrodisiacs and medicines designed to cause impotence (for use against third parties?); these are purely magical (28.122, 28.256) and herbal (22.91). In another passage Pliny states his attitude towards the use of contraceptives (29.85): 'There is also a third type of *phalangium*, a hairy spider with an enormous head. When this is cut open, there are said to be found inside two little worms, which, tied in deerskin as an amulet on women before sunrise, act as a contraceptive (*ne concipiant*), as Caecilius has told us in his *Commentarii*. They retain this property for a year. Of all such preventives (*atocio*) this only would it be right for me to mention, to help those women who are so prolific that they stand in need of such a respite', cf. Tosefta, *Yevamot* 8.4.

20 Pedanius Dioscorides came from Cilicia and served in the Roman army. He wrote *De materia medica*, one of the most important ancient pharmacological and botanical treatises. It had great influence in later times and after the invention of printing went through seventy editions in many European countries (cf. Himes 1936: 85–6). There survives from antiquity a sixth-century manuscript of it with fine drawings of many plants; these have been published in Gunther 1934. The references here are to the text ed. M. Wellmann, 3 vols, Berlin, 1906–14; his enumeration differs slightly from Gunther's ⟨trans. L. Y. Beck, Altertumswissenschaftliche Text und Studien 38, 2nd edn, Hildesheim, 2011⟩. I have not been able to consult I. Fischer 1927, nor to translate Lachs 1949. Dioscorides has at least twenty prescriptions for childlessness: (a) only four of these are cautionary (2.179.3, 4.20.2, 4.185, 5.146); (b) three are magical (e.g. asparagus as an amulet and its decoction drunk, 2.125, considered spurious by Wellmann; and also 2.79.2, 3.134.2); (c) seven are ineffectual potions (e.g. willow leaves with water, 1.104; and also 1.81, 2.19, 2.75.1, 4.19, 5.80.1); (d) two are ineffectual pessaries (to be applied to the genitals) one after coitus (2.75.2, 2.159.3); (e) only the last four are possibly effective; they consist of pessaries or sticky substances to be applied to the genitals before coitus (peppermint (?) + honey + water, 3.34.2; cedar (?) gum, 1.77.2; axe-weed with honey, 3.130; alum, 5.106.6).

technique and theory to a level surpassed only in the last hundred years.[21] After him, the tradition is to be found partially in Oribasius, and more fully in the work of Caelius Aurelianus in the fifth century AD and of Aëtius in the sixth.[22] It is of considerable significance that this tradition can, given the gaps in our sources, be traced so far. But for the recent discovery of the translation of Soranus' *Gynaecia* by Caelius Aurelianus, we might have been faced with large gaps between Soranus, Oribasius and Aëtius. For in the gynaecological writings of Theodorus Priscianus who shows the influence of Soranus, in the fragmentary Vindicianus and in Mustio's translation of Soranus there is no mention of contraception. The fact that translators and adapters of Soranus omitted his sections on contraception calls for investigation. It may be that in the fourth and sixth centuries after Christ some writers thought that married people were no longer interested in contraception. I shall return to this later.

Meanwhile, we must establish the importance of the ancient evidence on contraception. In order to do this, I looked at the work of twenty-six ancient medical writers; their work comprises the bulk of published ancient medical writings; the principle of their selection was their easy availability in standard texts.[23] These works cover general medical texts, books on herbs, simples, gynaecology, chronic and acute diseases, etc. I excluded the work of four writers from the following

[21] Himes 1936: 88; Soranus, *Gynaecia* 2.44 ⟨ed. J. Ilberg, *CMG* IV, Leipzig, 1927; P. Burguière, D. Gourevitch and Y. Malinas, 4 vols, Paris, 1988–2000; trans. Temkin 1956⟩; *Suda* s.v. Σωρανός ⟨ed. A. Adler, 5 vols, Leipzig, 1928–38, IV Σ851⟩.

[22] Oribasius, *Euporiston* 4.116 (ed. U. C. Bussemaker and C. Daremberg, Paris, 6 vols, 1851–76: V 777–8; Latin version: VI 623) gave essentially the same advice as Dioscorides in three prescriptions, of which only one is possibly useful (a pessary of axe-weed to be applied before coitus), added a further useless pessary (of cabbage) to be applied after intercourse and converted what was to Dioscorides an ingredient in a possibly effective prescription into a sole and useless ointment for the male genitals (peppermint). Caelius Aurelianus, *Gynaecia* 1.83 (Drabkin and Drabkin 1951: 29) follows Soranus and, except for recommending that the woman should hold her breath on receiving the semen, proposes possibly effective methods. Aëtius at his best closely follows Soranus; he added brine and vinegar (⟨a 'vegetable astringent' is suggested⟩ in Knowlton 1880: 48 ⟨for this text, see below n. 27⟩), but he added also magical recipes (*Libri medicianales* 16.16–17).

[23] Teubner and the Corpus of Greek and Latin medical writers.

discussion, because the nature of their subject matter (e.g. kidneys, lungs, poisonous animals) made it unreasonable to expect contraceptive information. Of the remaining twenty-two, eleven suggested contraceptive methods, while a further writer, Galen, mentions the practice of preventing conception, without actually suggesting means.[24] Of those nine writers with specifically gynaecological works or sections five mention contraceptive methods (three at length); three of the four who do not mention contraceptive methods come from the Christian West during the fourth and fifth centuries. Of these same twenty-two writers, eighteen mention methods of aiding conception, but then there is more reason why the medical profession should see sterility as pathological. Eighteen writers also mention abortion, of whom fifteen give methods. But in fact, and in spite of the Hippocratic oath which forbids abortion, abortifacients figure more frequently than either aids to conception or contraceptives.[25] Among the simples of Paulus of Aegineta, for example, there are ten abortifacients, one remedy for sterility and one contraceptive. In Sextus Placitus there are six remedies for sterility and nine contraceptives; and in Dioscorides' first two books (of five), twenty-six out of over four hundred herbs, plants etc. are said to be abortifacients, only two are remedies for sterility, while nine are contraceptives. It may be that frequency of mention is more a function of ineffectiveness than of concern with a problem; but I do not think so. Nevertheless one could not claim any preoccupation with contraception; neither it nor abortion occurs as frequently as toothache or gout; but the fact that eleven out of twenty-two medical writers suggest contraceptive methods is surely important.

[24] Gal. *In Hippocratis epidemiarum librum II commentaria* V (trans. from the Arabic by F. Pfaff, *CMG* V.10.1, Leipzig, 1934, 221) ⟨and see n. 39 below⟩. The exact references to contraception in these eleven authors are given elsewhere below, except for Paulus Aegineta 7.3 ⟨ed. J. L. Heiberg, *CMG* IX.2, Leipzig, 1924⟩ and Ps.-Apuleius Platonicus, *Herbarius* appendix 90 (ed. E. Howald and H. E. Sigerist, *CML* IV, Leipzig, 1927).

[25] Soranus, *Gynaecia* 1.60.

Table 1.1. *Table of medical writers consulted.*

Name and century	Nature and length of work	Abortifacients detailed	Aids to conception detailed	Contraceptive methods detailed
Aëtius (6 cent.)	General medicine; * long	Yes	Yes	Yes
Aristotle (4 cent. BC)	* voluminous	Yes	Yes	Yes
Caelius Aurelianus (5 cent.)	Gynaecology; * short	Yes	Yes	Yes
Cassius Felix (5 cent.)	General medicine; medium	No	No	No
Celsus (1 cent.)	General handbook; long	Yes	Yes	No
Dioscorides (1 cent.)	Herbal; long	Yes	Yes	Yes
Galen (2 cent.)	General medicine; * voluminous	Yes	Yes	practice but not method
Hippocratic Corpus (from 5 cent. BC)	General medicine; voluminous	Yes	Yes	Yes
Marcellus (4 cent.)	General medicine; long	No	No	No
Mustio (and Moschion) (6 cent.)	Gynaecology; * short	Yes	Yes	No
Oribasius (4 cent.)	General medical encyclopaedia; long	Yes	Yes	Yes
Paulus Aegineta (7 cent.)	General medicine; long	Yes	Yes	Yes
Pliny (1 cent.)	General encyclopaedia; voluminous	Yes	Yes	Yes

(*continued*)

Table 1.1. (*cont.*)

Name and century	Nature and length of work	Abortifacients detailed	Aids to conception detailed	Contraceptive methods detailed
S. Placitus Papyriensis (?5 cent.)	Herbal etc.; short	Yes	Yes	Yes
Ps. A. Musa (well after 1 cent.)	Herbal; short	No	No	No
Ps.-Apuleius Platonicus (4 cent.)	Herbal; long	Yes	Yes	Yes
Scribonius Largus (1 cent.)	Simples; medium	No	No	No
Q. Serenus (3 or 4 cent.)	Medical handbook in verse; 600 lines	No	Yes	No
Soranus (2 cent.)	Gynaecology; * medium	Yes	Yes	Yes
Theodorus Priscianus (4 cent.)	General medicine; * long	Yes	Yes	No
Vindicianus (4 cent.)	Gynaecology; * fragmentary	No	Yes	No
Antidotarium Bruxellense (?)	200 folk recipes	No	Yes	No
	Excluded because of subject			
Alexander Tralles (6 cent.)	Kidneys, lungs, ears etc.; long			
Aretaeus (2 cent.)	Acute and chronic diseases; Medium			
Philumenus (?2 cent.)	Poisonous animals; short			
Rufus (2 cent.)	Bladder, kidneys; fragmentary			

Short = <100 pp. text; Long = >200 pp. text; * = with special gynaecological section.

Effective and Ineffective Methods

The contraceptive methods which Greek and Roman doctors suggested include the application before coitus of cedar gum, vinegar, brine or olive oil to the vagina or male genitals and a gamut of vaginal plugs and occlusive pessaries, mostly with wool base soaked in honey, alum, white lead or olive oil.

Ancient attitudes to the problems of efficient contraception, partly scientific, partly unverified theory and partly superstition but in no way authoritarian or religious, may be seen at their best in one passage of Soranus, He wrote:[26]

> For if it is much more advantageous not to conceive than to destroy the embryo, one must consequently beware of having sexual intercourse at those periods which we said were suitable for conception.[27] And during the sexual act, at the critical moment of coitus when the man is about to discharge the seed, the woman must hold her breath and draw herself away a little, so that the seed may not be hurled too deep into the cavity of the uterus. And getting up immediately and squatting down she should induce sneezing and carefully wipe the vagina all round; she might even drink something cold.
>
> It also aids in preventing conception to smear the orifice of the uterus all over before with old olive oil or honey or cedar resin or juice of the balsam tree, alone or together with white lead; or before the act with moist alum, or with galbanum together with wine; or just to put a lock of fine wool into the orifice of the uterus; or before sexual relations to use vaginal suppositories which have the power to contract and to condense. For such as these things as are styptic, clogging and cooling cause the orifice of the uterus to shut before the time of coitus and do not let the seed pass into its fundus.

Several other contraceptive prescriptions follow.

Many of these methods could have been effective, and were still being used in western countries in the last thirty years. M. Stopes was still advocating the use of olive oil in 1931. In

[26] *Gynaecia* 1.61; trans. Temkin 1956: 63–4. The passage by Aëtius is similar: *Libri medicianales* 16.16–17.

[27] *Gynaecia*, 1.36: 'when urge and appetite for intercourse are present' at the time after menstruation. This idea was still current among Western doctors in the nineteenth century, e.g. Knowlton 1880: 38. (Charles Knowlton, *Fruits of Philosophy: The Private Companion of Young Married People* was first published anonymously in January 1832 in New York, and under the author's name the following year in London. The second edition (entitled *Fruits of Philosophy: An Essay on the Population Question*) is cited here. For a publication history of the first edition and the unsuccessful attempts to suppress it though the courts, see Chandrasekhar 1981: 21–54.)

1947, E. L. Koos, reporting on his investigations in New York City, found that some members of the lower classes were using douches of water with vinegar, lemon juice or alum. Alum, vinegar and brine are all highly spermicidal and were recommended by Stopes in 1927.[28] Olive oil and the sticky substances recommended by the ancient authors, besides blocking the os of the uterus, would reduce the motility of the sperm and so diminish the chances of conception. If Roman aristocrats acted upon recommendations such as these at all consistently, the effect upon their fertility would have been considerable.

But this would have been difficult for them. Just as Soranus suggested sneezing, almost in the same breath as he recommended the blocking of the cervix, many medical writers at Rome indiscriminately mixed the effective with the ineffective or magical. Isolation of methods which are or can be efficient distorts the issue. Soranus remonstrated against amulets, but from what we know of Roman superstitions by no means all Roman aristocrats, or for that matter all fashionable Roman doctors, can be credited with the same critical and scientific attitudes.

There are in fact some writings of the later empire extant (e.g. the *Liber medicinae ex animalibus pecoribus et bestiis uel auibus* of Sextus Placitus Papyriensis[29]), which consist entirely of ineffective medicines. All nine of Placitus' contraceptive recipes are useless, so that it may have been as well that he gave his followers so many alternatives. Even Aëtius, whose passage on contraception is, after Soranus', the most rational and complete, recommended the following charms against conception:

> Wear the liver of a cat in a tube on the left foot ... or else wear part of the womb of a lioness in a tube of ivory. This is very effective.[30]

[28] Stopes 1927: 119–21, 124–5; Stopes 1931: 359; Himes 1936: 96; Koos 1947. J. T. Noonan, the typescript of whose book I have been privileged to see, cites some recent research which suggests that some potions used by primitive peoples do have a temporary contraceptive effect ⟨Noonan 1965: 11–12⟩; these researches do not tell us whether any specific ancient medicines were effective, only that some potions may be effective or partially effective. Cf. de Laszlo and Henshaw 1954; Jackson 1959.

[29] Ed. E. Howald and H. Sigerist, *CML* IV, Leipzig, 1927. The work dates from the fourth or fifth century AD.

[30] Aëtius, *Libri medicianales* 16.17. To the contraceptive methods noted there may perhaps be added the first intimations of a condom: see the curious story in Antoninus

Similar recipes are to be found in Pliny and Dioscorides.

Yet some of the methods recommended were more effective; the wealthy had access to those doctors who could and probably did read the writers who recommended, inter alia, effective contraceptives. Sometimes, by luck rather than by judgement, they must have hit upon them.

The Use of Contraceptives and the Confusion of Contraception with Abortion

Yet in one respect both effective and magical methods of contraception point in the same direction. Both point to the existence of motives to limit family size. These motives taken together with the consistent and repetitive tradition of contraceptive prescriptions constitute a *prima facie* argument that contraceptives (even if many were useless) were recommended, available and used.

As evidence that contraceptives were used, the existing medical writings leave a lot to be desired. But the very existence of contraceptive prescriptions from each century of the Roman empire prompts us at the very least to turn to the question with which we started. If contraceptives were known, readily available (olive oil and wool, rather than wombs of lionesses) and used, why do we not hear more of their use?

To some extent we can say that the subject is not one which appealed to Roman litterateurs;[31] Juvenal perhaps, but only perhaps, refers to contraceptives; after him satire declined, and we have to wait for the next wave of social criticism, to be found in the sermons of Christian priests. But although these will yield a thin harvest, the problem goes deeper than that. There was, I think, a basic lack of clarity about the

Liberalis, *Metamorphoses* 41.5 (ed. E. Martin in *Mythographi Graeci* II, Leipzig, 1896, 124–5) (ed. M. Papathomopoulos, Paris, 1968, and trans. F. Celoria, London, 1992). A kind of condom made from a goat's bladder is described, but its use seems to have been less contraceptive than prophylactic; cf. Richter 1911: 35; Himes 1936: 187–8.

[31] Juv. 6.595–7: 'So powerful are her arts and medicines that she makes women sterile and brings about the killing of humans in the womb' (tantum artes huius, tantum

concept 'contraception' even in the most educated circles. Contraception was in some ways confused with, or at least not distinguished from, abortion, surprising as that may seem; the same confusion has been found in Japan and India recently, in English professional medical writings at the end of the nineteenth century and in French literary writings of the sixteenth and seventeenth centuries.[32]

To be sure, Soranus made the distinction with some firmness, indeed with sufficient emphasis to make it clear that there were still people to persuade that the distinction was valid. 'A contraceptive differs from an abortive, for the first does not let the conception take place, while the latter destroys what has been conceived. Let us, therefore, call the one "abortive" (*phthorion*) and the other "contraceptive" (*atokion*). And an "expulsive" (*ekbolion*) some people say is synonymous with an abortive.'[33] Others were not so clear headed. St John Chrysostom talked in a sermon of *atókia*, contraceptives, but confessed he did not know what to call them and then ambiguously described what they are for. 'Indeed something worse than murder. I do not know what to call it. For it does not only destroy what is conceived but prevents it from being conceived.'[34]

Moreover some of the medicaments recommended by doctors as contraceptives were also considered abortifacients.[35]

medicamina possunt, / quae steriles facit atque homines in uentre necandos / conducit). *Steriles* may refer to contraceptives, but it may also refer to abortion. The desire for childlessness is again mentioned by Juvenal together with the means to achieve it: Juv. 6.366–8: sunt quas eunuchi inbelles ac mollia semper / oscula delectent … / et quod abortiuo non est opus. ⟨There are those whom unwarlike eunuchs and their soft kisses always delight … and the fact that abortion/contraception is not required.⟩ But this use of eunuchs cannot have been very common, although the same accusation is found in the fifth century: Cyril of Alexandria *Sermo contra eunuchos* (*PG* 77: 1109B) ⟨= *Georgii Monachi Chronicon,* ed. C. de Boor, 2 vols, Leipzig, 1904, II 654⟩.

32 Ariès 1953: 468–9; Taeuber 1958: 272; Dandekar 1962: 8; Peel 1964: 136.

33 Soranus, *Gynaecia* 1.60 (trans. Temkin 1956: 62); cf. Aëtius, *Libri medicianales* 16.16.

34 Joh. Chrys. *Hom. in Rom.* 24.4 (*PG* 60: 626). cf. also *Hom. in Matt.* 28.5 (*PG* 57: 357) which may refer to abortion, but probably refers to contraception.

35 Some were in fact abortifacients: Diepgen 1937: 301. Perhaps in the same confusion the lawyer Marcian wrote (*Dig.* 48.8.3.2): 'By senatorial decree a woman is to be exiled if, without malice, but setting a bad example, she gives a medicine (*ad conceptionem*) (?against) for conception, from which the recipient dies.' Noonan ⟨1965: 26–7⟩ thinks this *ad conceptionem* might refer to contraception, rather

Soranus listed some of them and warned his readers against them: 'These medicines not only prevent conception but also destroy its product. According to our opinion the damage caused by them is considerable.'[36] Soranus was, as we have seen, clear about the distinction between abortion and contraception, but it is difficult to think how he conceptualised the workings of these dual prescriptions. Dioscorides considered pepper an abortifacient, unless applied after coitus; then it was a contraceptive (*atókion*); he explicitly makes this distinction; but why after coitus?[37] Again it is hard to envisage his conceptualisation. He mentioned another plant – *Pteris aquilina* – and said it caused both childlessness and abortions; it was the same herb which Pliny considered antaphrodisiac as well as abortifacient and contraceptive (its effects lasted for twelve days).[38] Such evidence is circumstantial perhaps and justifies raising the question rather than calling it settled. But in the following passage of Pliny, surely the confusion between contraception and abortion is unambiguous? About cedar he wrote: *portentum est quod tradunt abortiuum fieri in uenere ante perfusa uirilitate.* W. H. S. Jones, in the Loeb edition, translated this: 'Gossip records a miracle: that to rub it all over the male part before coition prevents conception.' This certainly conveys some of Pliny's intention, but Jones rationalises and imposes the clarity of modern concepts on Pliny's obvious confusion between *ante* (before coition) and *abortiuum.*[39]

This confusion by some writers was no doubt facilitated by the fact that ancient doctors (and presumably laymen) neither found it easy to tell when pregnancy had begun nor were

than conception. Certainly an abortifacient seems more likely to kill; but contra Mommsen 1899: 637.

36 *Gynaecia* 1.63.

37 *De materia medica* 2.159.3.

38 *De materia medica* 4.185; it is the nymphaea (pteris) of Plin. *HN* 25.75, and cf. also 27.80, 20.142–3.

39 Plin. *HN* 24.18 (trans. W. H. S. Jones 1956: 17). Another interesting passage, which to my mind is only explicable in terms of a confusion between abortion and contraception, is to be found in the German translation of an Arabic text of Gal. *In Hippocratis epidemiarum librum II commentaria* V (F. Pfaff, *CMG* V.10.1, Leipzig, 1934, 221) ⟨and see above n. 24⟩.

they agreed about the length of gestation. According to Aulus Gellius, for example, a child could be born after seven, nine or ten months, but not eight.[40] He lived, it is clear, amid an upper class which was not interested in testing the reality of these myths. An accurate reckoning of the time of conception was made more difficult – and the confusion with abortifacients was helped, since very early abortions can pass easily, almost unnoticed. Indeed, in Latin, the uncommonness of the distinction between the two is illustrated by the absence of any abstract word to express contraception. For abortion there was *abortio*; for contraception, the verbal clauses, *ne concipiat* or *ut non concipiat* (sic) were used.[41]

It would be reasonable to assume that such unclarity about the concept and the unavailability of a single word in Latin restricted the frequency with which authors mentioned the practice. But such unclarity probably is symptomatic of difficulties in applying contraception. If Romans found difficulty in timing conception to the nearest month and confused abortion with contraception in practice and concept, it would hardly be surprising if they found it difficult to isolate those contraceptives which were likely to be efficient from those which were magical. Abortion and infanticide are methods of family limitation whose success or failure can be seen very quickly; magical remedies are more likely to be discountenanced. Moreover, both involve less inconvenience for the man than for the woman. But contraceptives, besides involving the inconvenience, forethought and persistent effort of the

[40] E.g. on signs of pregnancy, cf. Soranus, *Gynaecia* 1.44; Caelius Aurelianus, *Gynaecia* 1.55 (ed. Drabkin and Drabkin 1951: 18). The difficulties of diagnosing pregnancy must also have been increased by the prevalence of amenorrhea; I think it must have been prevalent because of the very large number of remedies given for it. Gell. *NA* 3.10.8, 3.16; the discussion of the seven-month child has a long history, stretching back to Aristotle and Hippocrates. Oribasius, *Collectiones* 22.5 (ed. Bussemaker and Daremberg III 63–5) cites Aristotle who held that eight-month babies do survive though they are smaller than seven- or nine-month babies and that Greeks only think that they do not exist from a preconception that it is impossible.

[41] *ne concipiat*: Plin. *HN* 29.85 where he uses the Greek *atocium* also; *ut non concipiat*: Placitus, *Liber medicinae ex animalibus* ⟨1.β14, 14.12, 15.1–4, 17.4, 17.18, 21.2; ed. E. Howald and H. Sigerist, *CML* IV, Leipzig, 1927⟩; *inhibeatur conceptio*: Caelius Aurelianus, *Gynaecia* 1.83 (ed. Drabkin and Drabkin 1951: 29).

man and/or woman cannot be immediately gauged according to their effectiveness. Far from it – for the task of convincing someone of the efficiency of a technique is massively complicated by factors some of which are to this day not widely known; for example, the chances of conception from coitus at different times and frequencies, the fecundity of the husband, the fecundity of the wife, the incidence of sterility, the recall of the consistency with which a particular practice has been used.

Many of these shortcomings can be overcome by the sharp intellectual perception of the factors most germane to conception – and therefore of those most germane to contraception. But even in those ancient medical writers who perceived what was germane, we also find some irrelevant or marginal suggestions, such as sneezing. It is exactly this situation in which there is no culturally dominant perception of the most important factors in conception, which opens the way for the use of magical as well as non-magical contraceptives. For in such a society a man who has used an efficient contraceptive once, but had a child as a result of subsequent intercourse, can be outfaced by another, who is sub-fecund, but who has successfully used an ivory tube on his ankle.[42] In such general circumstances, prevalent in most pre-industrial societies, abortion and infanticide have preceded and precluded contraception.

This confusion of abortion with contraception, and the failure to make the distinction between them explicit, may colour all our evidence. Actual use of contraceptives may be lost in general references to means of remaining childless or to abortifacients. Alternatively of course the near silence of the literary sources may reflect the infrequency of the use of contraceptives. We cannot tell. In any case it is certain that references to wilful abortion and abortifacients and to infanticide are many times more frequent than references to contraception.

[42] For this same syndrome, Hasanat 1945: 111. Several passages of this book seem aimed at readers not much different from those envisaged by ancient doctors, for example 106–11; the same amulets are described by Soranus, *Gynaecia* 1.63.

But the sources are not completely silent. Augustine, bishop of Hippo in the early fifth century, spoke of *sterilitatis uenena,* used by married couples who did not want children; abortion was a second line of defence, if the poisons were unsuccessful.[43] Jerome, in the late fourth century, accused some women of drinking potions to achieve sterility and of murdering 'unsown humans' (*necdum sati hominis homicidium*).[44] Caesarius, bishop of Arles in the early sixth century, accused land- and slave-owning wives of taking deadly poisons in order not to conceive.[45] Perhaps his accusations were justified, even if poisons are more readily associated with abortifacients than with contraceptives. At least this may be evidence of the use of contraceptives if not of their efficiency.

Augustine, in his *Confessions*, obviously had doubts about the efficiency of contraceptives when he recalled his relations with his concubine:

> ... with her I discovered by my own experience what a great difference there is between the restraint of the marriage bond contracted with a view to having children and the compact of a lustful love, where the children are born against the parents' will.[46]

Not that Augustine could complain, since from thirteen years' cohabitation with this one concubine, and from his other affairs, he had (for all we know, and the *Confessions* are fulsome) only one son. It would be tempting to think that this was achieved by his use of some contraceptive device; but apart from coitus interruptus, to which we shall return later, the only practice which Augustine mentioned, and for

43 Aug. *De nuptiis et concupiscentia* 1.17 (ed. C. F. Urba and J. Zycha, *CSEL* 42, Vienna, 1902) ⟨trans. R. J. Teske, *Answer to the Pelagians II,* The Works of St Augustine: A Translation for the 21st Century I/24, New York, 1998⟩. Ambrose's two accusations against the rich – in utero proprios negant fetus et parricidalibus sucis in ipso genitali aluo pignera sui uentris extinguunt: *Hexameron* 5.18.58 (ed. C. Schenkl, *CSEL* 32.1, Vienna, 1896) ⟨'they repudiate their own offspring *in utero* and with murderous potions in the depths of their own genitals destroy the promise of their womb'⟩ – probably both refer to abortion.

44 Jerome, *Ep.* 22.13.2 ⟨ed. I. Hilberg, *CSEL* 54, Vienna, 1910; 2nd edn, 1996⟩.

45 Caesarius, *Serm.* 44.2 (ed. G. Morin, *CCSL* 103, Turnhout, 1953) ⟨ed. M.-J. Delage, *SC* 243, Paris, 1978⟩.

46 Aug. *Conf.* 4.2; echoed perhaps by Caesarius, *Serm.* 42.4, 44.3.

which he castigated the Manichaeans, was continence during the time at which women were most likely to conceive. This would of course have reduced the chances of conception but for the fact that the time Augustine thought most fecund was immediately after menstruation. This was also the opinion of many ancient doctors.[47] If continence then was compensated by pleasures taken later, the chances of conception would have been increased rather than diminished.

As against this, the pagan and Christian objectors accused people of achieving childlessness, so that some of the methods used may have been effective. Hippolytus, priest at Rome in the early third century, wrote of Christian women of good birth who used 'medicines of childlessness' and abortive techniques in their relations with slaves.[48] Epiphanius, bishop of a town in Cyprus in the fourth century, in his old age recalled the sexual perversions of the heretical Gnostics whom he had visited, seen or heard of in his youth. They practised, he said, abortion, homosexuality, masturbation and coitus interruptus. 'They have intercourse yet forbid the begetting of children. Their corruption has run riot not for children but for pleasure.' Augustine makes similar accusations against the Manichaeans – and especially of interest to us, he accused them of practising coitus interruptus – once in general and on the other occasion in what seem to be ritual orgies.[49] These are

[47] Aug. *De moribus Manichaeorum* 65 (*PL* 32: 1373) ⟨ed. J. B. Bauer, *CSEL* 90, Vienna, 1992; trans. R. J. Teske, *The Manichean Debate*, The Works of St Augustine: A Translation for the 21st Century I/19, New York, 2006⟩; *c. Faust.* 15.7 (ed. J. Zycha, *CSEL* 25, Vienna, 1891) ⟨trans. R. J. Teske, *Answer to Faustus, a Manichean*, The Works of St Augustine: A Translation for the 21st Century I/20, New York, 2007⟩. Soranus, *Gynaecia* 1.36; Caelius Aurelianus, *Gynaecia* 1.46 (ed. Drabkin and Drabkin 1951: 14); Mustio, *Gynaecia* 1.33 ⟨above n. 16⟩; Oribasius, *Collectiones* 22.3 (ed. Bussemaker and Daremberg III 54) citing Galen; also before menstruation suitable, but rarely, Oribasius, *Collectiones* 22.7 (ed. Bussemaker and Daremberg III 69).

[48] Hippol. *Haer.* 9.12.25: ἀτοκίοις φαρμάκοις ⟨ed. M. Marcovich, Patristische Texte und Studien 25, Berlin, 1986⟩; again these medicines of childlessness might refer to abortion and/or to contraception – but given the Greek ἀτόκιον (contraceptive) Hippolytus may have had contraceptives in mind.

[49] Epiph. *Panarion* 26.5.2 (ed. K. Holl, *GCS* 25, Leipzig, 1915) ⟨2nd edn, ed. C.-F. Collatz and M. Bergermann, *GCS* (NF) 10/1–2, Berlin, 2013; trans. F. Williams, Nag Hammadi and Manichaean Studies 63, 2nd edn, Leiden, 2009⟩; Aug. *c. Faust.* 22.30; Aug. *De haer.* 46.13 (*PL* 42: 36) ⟨ed. R. Vander Plaetse and C. Beukers, *CCSL*

almost the only Greco-Roman references to coitus interruptus and it is interesting to find it numbered among the sexual perversions of heretics who came from the East.

Not all contraceptive practices, however, are known to us only because they were condemned by Christians. In the works of Methodius (third century) there appears that strange phenomenon, the mention by a Christian father of contraceptive practice without condemnation.[50] And on a papyrus from the fourth century we have a Greek spell or charm advertising its contraceptive powers and boldly declaring its uniqueness: 'Contraceptive, the only one in the wide world'.[51] It would be idle to think that such a claim won no followers.

The earliest explicit evidence for the use (as opposed to the recommendation) of contraceptives in the Roman empire is to be found in a secular condemnation by the Stoic Musonius Rufus in the first century AD, at least if an emendation of the text which I have recently proposed is accepted. The emended passage is translated:

> The rulers forbade women to abort and attached a penalty to those who disobeyed; secondly they forbade them to use contraceptives on themselves and to prevent pregnancy; finally they established honours for both men and women who had many children and made childlessness punishable.

It is impossible to say with certainty to what if any historical reality a philosophic writer like Musonius was referring. It could perhaps have been a reference to Augustus' legislation. But however that may be, it cannot be pure fantasy; Musonius, and the rulers he refers to, thought that people used contraceptives, and it is therefore probable that they did. Moreover there

46, Turnhout, 1969; trans. R. J. Teske, *Arianism and Other Heresies*, The Works of St Augustine: A Translation for the 21st Century I/18, New York, 1995⟩; cf. Titus, *Adversus Manichaeos* 2.33 (*PG* 18: 1197).

50 Methodius, *Symposium* 4.3 (ed. G. N. Bonwetsch, *GCS* 27, Lepizig, 1917) ⟨ed. H. Musurillo, *SC* 95, Paris, 1963⟩.

51 Ἀσύλληπτον, τὸ μόνον ἐν κόσμῳ in *P. Oslo* I 1 line 321. This is probably aimed beyond the upper classes, and so is in a way outside my scope, as are contraceptive precautions taken by prostitutes – but even these are mentioned very seldom; cf. Lucr. 4.1274–5; Aug. *Contra Secundinum* 21 (ed. J. Zycha, CSEL 25, Vienna, 1892) ⟨trans. R. J. Teske, *The Manichean Debate*, The Works of St Augustine: A Translation for the 21st Century I/19, New York, 2006⟩.

is the implication that, together with abortion, contraception could prolong childlessness.[52]

It is not by chance that most of the references to contraceptives which are found in non-medical writings condemn it. Both Romans and Christians had an ideal of marriage as an institution for the procreation of children (*liberorum procreandorum causa*). Yet it is clear that many people did not live up to this ideal; else there would have been no need for moralists, Stoic philosophers and Christian priests to preach against those who had intercourse without desire for children. Yet it is remarkable that in these condemnatory passages we find so few explicit references to contraception. In one passage, for example, Clement of Alexandria, a leading Christian thinker of the very early third century, condemned the waste of semen; he instanced adultery and intercourse during menstruation and pregnancy, but not contraception. In yet another passage Lactantius, who wrote in the early fourth century, preached that a Christian who is too poor to have a family must be continent; abortion, he said, and infanticide and exposure are wrong, but he made no mention of contraception.[53]

It is clear that many people, in spite of some moral and even perhaps legal condemnation, did limit their families. But did they do it by contraception? The moral and legal condemnation would not I think have had much effect – indeed the very difficulty which the modern scholar has in discovering an early Christian viewpoint on contraception reveals that it was to them only a peripheral issue. Tacitus refers to the inefficacy of the laws.[54] Some doctors, Soranus says, condemned the use of

[52] Musonius, frag. 15a (ed. O Hense, Leipzig, 1905) in Stobaeus 4.605–6 (ed. C. Wachsmuth and O. Hense, Berlin, 1909) ⟨= Stobaeus, *Flor.* 75.15⟩. Hopkins 1965b [essay 2]: the impossible ἀτοκία in the manuscript has been converted in the standard texts to an awkward ἀτοκίᾳ; I suggest moving the accent to read ἀτόκια.

[53] Clem. Al. *Paedagogus* 2.10.91–2.10.93.1 (ed. O. Stählin, *GCS* 12, Leipzig, 1905) ⟨revised 3rd edn, ed. U. Treu, Berlin, 1972; see now ed. M. Marcovich, *Vigiliae Christianae* supplement 61, Leiden, 2002⟩; Lactant. *Div. inst.* 6.20.18–25 (ed. S. Brandt, *CSEL* 19, Vienna, 1890) ⟨ed. C. Ingremeau, *SC* 509, Paris, 2007; trans. A. J. Bowen and P. Garnsey, Translated Texts for Historians 40, Liverpool, 2003⟩.

[54] Musonius, frag. 15a ⟨above n. 52⟩; Hopkins 1965b [essay 2]; above n. 35; Tac. *Germ.* 19.

contraceptives as well as of abortifacients.[55] Yet others did not, and many Roman doctors were not in a sufficiently secure professional position to withstand the demands of their wealthy clients.

All in all, the evidence on the use of contraceptives in Rome is slight, and I have brought forward all that I have been able to find. Several qualifications may be made; contraception is unlikely to be mentioned much in the type of literature that survives; its confusion with abortion might lead to an underestimate of its commonness. Nevertheless the very infrequency of references to contraception when compared with abortion and infanticide, and the silence about it in passages where one might expect it, lead me to doubt that contraception played a major role in family limitation in Rome. However, that said, there is an obverse side; adequate and sound knowledge on contraception was available in the medical writings; the use of that knowledge is referred to, though seldom, in the literature. It would therefore be rash to claim that the effect of contraception on Roman family limitation was negligible.

A Note on the Talmudic Tradition[56]

In the Talmudic tradition, we find two forms of contraception which are completely or almost completely absent from the Greco-Roman tradition. No doubt the rabbinical writings were not widely read by Romans; but on the other hand, even before the destruction of Jerusalem (AD 70) Jews were by no means confined to their homeland. In so far as contraception arises from a life situation, rather than from a literary tradition, we may well argue that Jewish knowledge may have been relevant to some Roman lives, and may have spread from one culture to the other.

[55] Soranus, *Gynaecia* 1.60.

[56] I have in this section followed Himes 1936: 70–5; Noonan (1965: 49–53) has a fuller treatment.

In the Tosephta, *Niddah* (which dates from AD 230, though the tradition is older), a spongy substance is suggested as an occlusive contraceptive:

There are three women that must cohabit with a sponge: a minor, a pregnant woman and one that nurses her child – a minor, because she might become pregnant and die; a pregnant woman, because the foetus might become a foetus compressus; one that nurses her child, because she might kill her child.[57]

Secondly there was coitus interruptus. The story of Onan is well known. According to later Catholic theologians the sin lay exclusively in the practice of coitus interruptus, though this is very rarely noted in ancient commentaries.[58] Jewish rabbis stressed rather his punishment for refusing to perform the levirate marriage. Some rabbis however did condemn coitus interruptus, others merely refused to recommend it. Still others recommended it in some circumstances; for example, Rabbi Eliezer (AD 80–100) recommended its use for nursing mothers[59]

Coitus Interruptus

It is then the Talmudic tradition which draws our attention to coitus interruptus. This may be surprising; one might imagine that it was the obvious remedy for the Romans' unwanted fertility. It would compensate for the shortcomings of all the other contraceptive methods, whether mechanical, herbal or chemical. Yet there are difficulties in accepting this view.

Apart from the Jewish writers and two ambiguous passages in the Hippocratic Corpus,[60] no ancient author before

[57] Tosefta, *Niddah* 2.6.

[58] Noonan ⟨1965: 101⟩ cites Epiphanius (fourth century) as the first important Church father to interpret the story of Onan in terms of condemning coitus interruptus: *Panarion* 26.11.10–11 ⟨above n. 49⟩; but in the immediate context the contraceptive purpose of coitus interruptus is not mentioned. Noonan ⟨1965: 137–8⟩ also cites Aug. *De adulterinis coniugiis* 2.12.12 (ed. J. Zycha, *CSEL* 41, Vienna, 1900) ⟨trans. R. Kearney, *Marriage and Virginity*, The Works of St Augustine: A Translation for the 21st Century I/9, New York, 1999⟩; in contrast he cites several passages in which one would expect, but does not find, this interpretation.

[59] Babylonian Talmud, *Yevamot* 34b; *Niddah* 31a (third century); cf. Rabbi Meir (AD 150), Tosefta, *Niddah* 2.6.

[60] [Hippoc.] *Genit.* 5 and *Nat. pue.* 13 (above n. 18); Lucr. 4.1268–77 does not seem to be referring to coitus interruptus. The phrase coitus interruptus is not of classical origin.

the fourth century AD mentions coitus interruptus. In the fourth and fifth centuries, it is twice mentioned by Epiphanius and Augustine in the restricted context of orgies attributed to Gnostic and Manichaean heretics. On another occasion Augustine accused the Manichaeans in general of practising it; and on yet another he said that it was shameful to have intercourse 'where the conception of offspring is avoided. This is what Onan the son of Juda did and God killed him for it.'[61] This reference to Onan may be an illustration only, with no imputation that coitus interruptus was practised frequently

It is of course possible that by this time the practice had spread. Coitus interruptus is mentioned by the Talmudic writers, and Christianity did after all unite the Hebraic with the Greco-Roman tradition. Nonetheless the complete silence of all previous classical writers on this subject is surely a little puzzling. By itself of course the silence proves nothing. On the one hand, one could argue how extraordinary it is that a writer like Soranus, for example, who dealt at length with the subject of how not to have a child, said nothing about coitus interruptus; but on the other hand, one could argue that he was concerned with medicinal contraceptives only, that he took coitus interruptus for granted. Besides, whether or not coitus interruptus appeared in medical textbooks may not be all that important. Many people may have practised it without having learnt it from a book.

We must examine such arguments as these for assumptions. There can be no doubt of the efficacy of coitus interruptus as a contraceptive practice. Obviously its efficiency varies according to the consistency, thoroughness and accuracy with which it is performed; these would in turn depend upon knowledge and motivation which are very difficult to measure accurately. We do know, however, that coitus interruptus has been used by large sectors of modern populations over long periods as the

[61] These references I owe to Noonan (1965: 95–7, 119–26), although my interpretation of them is different. For Epiphanius and Augustine cf. above n. 49 and Aug. *De adulterinis coniugiis* 2.12.12 (above n. 58). Noonan (1965: 107–39) has shown that most Christian references to Onan in these times do not mention coitus interruptus – so little, perhaps, did it matter to them.

sole or a major contraceptive method. Its efficiency bears comparison with other contraceptive methods, and its use has had considerable effect upon the birthrate.[62] On the other hand, there are several populations, in which there is a desire to limit fertility, and in which abortions and infanticide and even other forms of contraception are practised, but not coitus interruptus.[63] The problem may thus be recast; we should try to isolate some of the factors which may account for the use of coitus interruptus in some societies, but not in others. We may then see if these can be applied to Rome.

The important point that strikes one on reading contemporary Indian reports, and the earliest English and American tracts on birth control which date from the beginning of the nineteenth century, is that the effective use of coitus interruptus as a method of family limitation has to be learnt. It is quite wrong to assume that, given the knowledge that ejaculation of the sperm into the vagina is a necessary condition of conception, coitus interruptus automatically follows. Far from it. This can be amply illustrated. Indian propagandists of birth control point out that there is 'almost complete ignorance regarding the possibility of family planning and limitation'.[64] In

[62] French historical demographers at least seem agreed that coitus interruptus was primarily responsible for the fall in the birthrate in the eighteenth and nineteenth centuries; cf. Ariès 1948: 496–7. The comparative and varied effectiveness of coitus interruptus may be seen from table 1.2. The extent of the consistent and successful use of coitus interruptus may be seen in England (1946–7, nationwide sample). Of married couples with any contraceptive experience, 43 per cent used coitus interruptus only, and this figure rose to 61 per cent among unskilled manual workers. The pregnancy rates per one hundred years of exposure were twelve in the first five years of marriage, nine in the second five years and five in the third. Coitus interruptus was slightly less efficient than appliance methods in the first ten years. See Lewis-Faning 1949: 132 table 91.

[63] Many writers have assumed that the knowledge of coitus interruptus is elementary and have therefore guessed at its existence among most tribes (e.g. Himes 1936: 183–4). Nag 1956 tabulates the following information. In nineteen out of forty-seven simple societies, coitus interruptus was practised; it was however frequently practised in only three of these societies and in only one practised commonly by the married outside the post partum period, (Nag 1956: 130–1, 214–18 table 70). Its most general use is pre-maritally and post partum. In eleven out of forty-one simple societies there was frequent recourse to abortion; in three out of these eleven there was no practice of coitus interruptus recorded, and in a further one almost none (219–21 table 73). The accuracy of such data is, however, doubtful.

[64] Dandekar 1962: 8.

Table 1.2. *Pregnancy rates per one hundred years of exposure with different contraceptive methods in three surveys.*

	Indianapolis 1927–42 (data collected 1941–2 by recall)	Princeton study 1950–6	Calcutta 1956–7 Social Class:		
			1	2	3
Diaphragm	4.5	14.9	–	–	–
Condom	7.0	15.0	11.9	25.4	32.1
Coitus interruptus	9.3	16.0	9.3	10.7	15.2
Douche	19.3	37.8	–	–	–
Rhythm	–	34.5	13.1	18.7	25.0
Other methods	10.8	28.9	19.9	27.3	61.7

Based on Tietze 1962: 365 table 5 and Poti, Chakraborti and Malaker 1962: 64 table 6.

particular, 'coitus interruptus as a method of family planning required great effort on the part of the field workers to convince the villagers of its practicability'.[65] A primer on family planning, written in 1945, indeed treated coitus interruptus as obvious: 'The method is apparently simple, and suggests itself to couples. No tutoring seems necessary … Simply stated the method of "withdrawal" consists in …', and the explanation follows.[66] Other campaigns to induce Indians to practise birth control treat coitus interruptus as something to be taught.

The evidence of the early English and American tracts has a different timbre. Here we have no sociological or demographic reports but only the propaganda of enthusiasts encouraging and cajoling the ignorant. The evidence is therefore much more patchy (in this respect it is similar to much Roman evidence), nevertheless it is revealing. Knowlton, the first major advocate of the douche, saw the greatest obstacle to the acceptance of his proposals in the multiplicity of erroneous beliefs about the process of conception. For this reason, he thought that people would have no confidence in his ideas. He also explained coitus interruptus and insisted that partial withdrawal was wrongly relied upon, through a false idea of the process of conception.[67] Owen, who advocated coitus interruptus above all other methods of contraception, appealed to honour, to the customs of France and to man's duty to the fair sex; but above all, he explained what coitus interruptus was and persuaded his readers of its possibility. Owen cited a case in point. A trusted acquaintance of his had practised coitus interruptus and had spoken to his relatives about it, 'one or two of whom, he knew, had profited by his advice, and afterwards expressed to him their gratitude for the important information'.[68] Richard Carlile, again, explained coitus interruptus; he averred that it was commonly practised on the Continent, and offered an inefficient and mystical variation of it to his

[65] Mathen 1962: 41.

[66] Hasanat 1945: 125.

[67] Knowlton 1880: especially 47.

[68] Owen 1831: 61–5, quoting 64.

readers, and also admitted that given the various theories of conception, experience alone must decide whether complete or partial withdrawal was more suitable to particular persons.[69]

Individual instances could no doubt be multiplied by further searches into the literature; but I shall cite only two cases more. M. Stopes cites a letter written in 1868 in which a distinguished doctor wrote that he had 'explained' coitus interruptus to a clergyman.[70] In the Place Collection, in the British Museum, there is a manuscript letter initialled 'by I.C.H.', attributed by Stopes to Francis Place but perhaps wrongly (it can be dated to 1823 or thereabouts), which observes:

> It now remains to suggest a more simple method; it is little known to the English, who are full of the coarsest and most vulgar prejudices on these subjects. … This expedient is sometimes called la Chamade, the Retreat, but most commonly by the softer name of la Prudence, or la Discrétion …

The writer goes on to explain what seems to be coitus interruptus. And then says:

> Those to whom this is made known for the first time always object that 'I do not perceive the moment, and if I did, it would be impossible to escape.'[71]

Thus there are many people in pre-industrial and industrialising societies who presumably know the connection between the ejaculation of sperm into the vagina and conception, but who remain nevertheless unaware of coitus interruptus. Not only do they have to be taught how to practise coitus interruptus, but they have to be convinced of its practicability. They have to be persuaded of its effectiveness. Why? Surely once the connection between the ejaculation of the sperm into the vagina and conception is known, the knowledge of coitus interruptus can be assumed to follow. Logically perhaps, but the stubborn facts provide evidence to the contrary. The early English and American writers on the subject argued that the fault lay in the multiplicity of theories of conception. Drelincourt, mentioned by Knowlton, 'is said to have collected

[69] Carlile 1828: 40–2.

[70] Stopes 1927: 325.

[71] British Museum, Place Collection, vol. 68, 103 (manuscript); Stopes 1927: 321.

260 hypotheses of generation'.[72] Carlile wrote: 'The theories of conception are various. The precise process is as much unknown to modern anatomists and physiologists, as it was to Aristotle, Hippocrates, or Galen. Hitherto, it has eluded all research, and there is scarcely a hope of discovering it, since women are not anatomists, and since their own experience is not equal to an explanation.'[73]

But only part of the blame can be placed here, for to isolate the physiological factors is misleading. As a result of modern scientific discoveries and the modern revolution of rationality, we can isolate those factors which are relevant to conception. It is not that every member of modern industrial nations is knowledgeable about the process of conception itself, but rather that by and large he has been accustomed to exclude metaphysical beliefs and fortuitous contemporary occurrences from his explanation of it; but we should be wrong to transpose the clarity of our own concepts upon pre-industrial or industrialising populations. The contemporary recipients of Indian propaganda on birth control and the recipients of early English and American leaflets (and most Romans), if the authors of the propaganda judged their audience at all correctly, must have conflated the magical, metaphysical and physical worlds so that the fact that a mother was breast feeding, for example, or the fact that a piece of ivory was worn on the left ankle, or a fatalistic belief that the incidence of children is beyond human control, or the belief that the spacing of children is peculiarly innate to every woman seemed relevant to conception.

Thus, although the Romans, just as the Indians now and the Americans and English in the early nineteenth century, knew about the process of conception and knew the relevant role of the ejaculation of sperm into the vagina in the process of conception, they knew much more besides, they knew the relevance of heat, God, breast feeding, homeopathy etc. We do violence to historical imagination, if we seek to transpose upon them our own analytical categories based upon physiological factors

72 Knowlton 1880: 26.
73 Carlile 1828: 41.

alone; we are surprised that coitus interruptus was not known, seemed impracticable or ineffective, only if we expect others to have shared in what is, after all, the fruit of a revolution in rationality, a revolution viable because of our control of physical nature and because of the growth of the custom of testing hypotheses experimentally.

We must now see how these conclusions may be applied to Rome. Basically, we do not know whether the Romans practised coitus interruptus or not, but we can examine the circumstantial evidence and make some deductions. We cannot theorise with certainty, because even in societies about which we know much more, no one has established an adequate theory to explain the rise of motives which led to the demographic revolution of the nineteenth century. But there are several factors which make the practice of contraception more or less likely.

The demographer Ariès noted that modern populations in industrial countries were the first in which coitus interruptus was practised on a wide scale. He related the conscious self-control necessary for the efficient practice of coitus interruptus to the growth of modern rationalism; the widespread use of coitus interruptus was possible only when the body and the self were identified and separated as interesting objects of study; the practice of coitus interruptus required, he claimed, a conscious separation of sex for pleasure and sex for procreation.[74]

This is an ingenious theory; but it is clearly based upon European experience alone and it depends upon Ariès' intuitive selection of what he thinks important from among the many and complex factors at work. But there is also some evidence which cannot be fitted easily into his theory. According to some ethnographers coitus interruptus is practised among some primitive tribes. It is best attested among the Tikopia, Kgatla, Nupe and Masai.[75] Such tribes as these cannot be called rational in Ariès' sense. Besides it is clear from modern societies that rationality can be compartmentalised, that ends-means efficiency can arise in one particular sector of society

[74] Ariès 1948: 494–8, 514–21.
[75] Nag 1956: 214–18 table 70.

alone, or, for that matter, that irrationality may survive in a society whose dominant ideal is technical rationality. A scientific astronomer may still look at his stars.

Of course the citation of contrary examples does not invalidate Ariès' theory, but his theory is certainly incomplete as it stands. The practice of coitus interruptus in these tribes may possibly be explained by the conflict to be found there between the relative sexual freedom particularly of adolescents and the strong social pressures against pregnancy. This relative sexual freedom might minimise mythmaking about sex and thus allow people to test their fantasies against reality, to isolate relevant variables in the process of conception in order to prevent pregnancy. This formulation which refers to the difficulty of isolating relevant variables in the process of conception is preferable I think, to Ariès' body/self, pleasure/procreation dichotomies; although I do think that they are closely related to each other. What seems valuable in Ariès' theory is the proposition that will, rationally and conscious self-control are all variable, that they change, and that their change may be, or rather is, related to social institutions.

The precise pattern of this relationship must await fuller studies, more information and an overriding theory, but for the present we can hypothesise that efficient contraception in general, and coitus interruptus in particular, are more likely to occur in a society which displays to a high degree some or all of the following characteristics:

1. Religion and common beliefs do not block the perception that the incidence of children may be controlled by man rather than by God.
2. The individual family/couple is sufficiently isolated to promote its own advantage; and/or the extended family or state has an interest in limiting fertility.
3. Rational scientific attitudes in non-sexual activities predominate.
4. Sexual activity is sufficiently uninhibited, but pregnancy is sufficiently feared to promote the conceptual isolation of the process of conception.
5. The married or sexually involved female has high social power and is reluctant either to abort or to have children.
6. Contraception is differentiated from abortion.

According to these criteria, the structure of Roman institutions was more favourable to the extensive use of contraception during the late Republic and early empire (c.200 BC–AD 200) than in the early Republic or later empire. The late Republic and early empire saw, in the upper class at least, the growth of rationalism, scepticism, individualism, high status for women and sexual freedom for women after marriage. We have had enough difficulty in establishing the use of contraceptives in the Roman empire at all, and it would be absurd to try to use this same evidence to measure the comparative extent of contraceptive practice at different times. We must therefore resort to hypothesis. It is reasonable to suppose that the evidence we have for the use of contraceptives during the early empire does not also apply to the time of the Kings or to the early Republic (before 200 BC). The use of contraceptives must have begun at some time; and it is reasonable to place this beginning in the second century BC when the Roman upper classes first became very wealthy, urbanised and less religious. By the same token the use of contraceptives must have ended at some time; for we have next to no further evidence for the use of contraceptives in Europe outside the circles of prostitutes, before the seventeenth century. Ariès has argued for the virtual absence of contraception during the Middle Ages except among prostitutes.[76] When did contraception stop? A lot of our evidence for the use of contraceptives in the Roman empire came from the later empire. Yet I cannot help feeling that this is fortuitous and reflects more the survival of the later literature than social reality. The fourth century AD is the best documented century of the whole of classical antiquity. Besides, the fourth and fifth centuries AD saw a growth in irrationalism, a lowering in the status of women, a reconflation of the physical and metaphysical worlds and a decline in experiment. Dissection for example, was forbidden; and in the West, two translations and adaptations of Soranus' *Gynaecology* omitted the sections

[76] Ariès 1948: 496–9 and 1953: 465: 'On admet sans discussion que les procédés contraceptifs n'étaient pas pratiqués dans les sociétés occidentales, du Moyen Age jusqu'au XVIIe siècle.'

on contraception.[77] It was a period, which, according to the hypothesis we have outlined above, was likely to have seen a decline in the use of contraceptives.

Conclusions

The Romans did have available some useful and some useless contraceptive techniques. Soranus, the greatest Greek gynaecologist, and his later followers perceived clearly the relevant parts of the process of conception and devised means to prevent it. But even in Soranus' work there are ineffectual suggestions. The majority of doctors and laymen must have inextricably confused the effective and the ineffective, and one can only suggest that in the majority of cases, the habit of trying everything, which stands out in the herbals and medical books, might have had some limiting effect upon the fertility of the Romans.

There was in the literature an interesting confusion between abortion and contraception, a confusion which is paralleled in other societies. It highlights the difficulties of isolating relevant factors in the complex process of conception and contraception and warns us against the naive transposition of our categories upon the Romans. The same difficulties arose with coitus interruptus. There is no Roman evidence for its use and comparative evidence shows that there is no ground for assuming its use. But its incidence may vary, as may the incidence of contraception in general, with the development of social institutions. There is no adequate tested theory of this relationship, but certain criteria are suggested. By these criteria it

[77] On dissection, see Vindicianus 429–30 ⟨above n. 15⟩. The elimination of contraceptive knowledge in the Middle Ages can be traced in the transmission of Dioscorides' herbal. Paulus Aegineta in the seventh century ⟨above n. 24⟩ leant heavily upon Dioscorides, mentioning many of the same herbs; but he cited only one as contraceptive, as against over twenty cited by Dioscorides. In the late thirteenth-century herbal of Rufinus, which also depends heavily upon Dioscorides, there is again only one contraceptive recipe: Thorndike 1946: 187, 404. Add to these the omission by Theodorus Priscianus and Mustio (or by their copyists) ⟨above nn. 15–16⟩ of the contraceptive passages in their adaptations of Soranus' *Gynaecology* and we have at least some evidence of the decline of contraceptive knowledge in and after the fourth century AD.

seems more likely that contraception was practised more intensively in the early empire than in the later empire; but there is no direct evidence for this.

Two points emerge. As is obvious with analytical categories like class, race and liberty, one cannot transpose them to Rome without some investigation of how they match the subjective feelings of the Romans; or at least, they become blunt instruments unless this is done. The confusion between contraception and abortion, and the assumed relevance to conception of amulets, for example, worn around the left ankle, reveal that the conflation by the Romans of the physical and the metaphysical worlds makes categories like abortion or contraception difficult to apply – rather, that unless this inapplicability is realised, wrong questions are asked or wrong answers assumed. We might assume that, once the correct elements in the process of conception are recognised, given the motivation to limit families, coitus interruptus automatically follows. But this would be to neglect the Roman conflation of the physical and metaphysical, and secondly it would probably be based upon an assumption on the constancy of rationality and will. Ariès and Elias have pointed out that these factors vary, and this has to be borne in mind, as does the probability that they vary in a specific relation (as yet unknown) to given social institutions.[78] Too often ancient historians treat rationality and will as constants, as part of human nature, and they use them as the intervening factor between historical facts and their explanation.[79]

[78] Elias 1939, a brilliant treatment of the growth of modern rationality and self-control.

[79] I should like to thank Professor A. H. M. Jones for much teaching and advice; it was under his supervision that I first began this work; I should also like to thank Mr J. A. Crook, Dr M. I. Finley, Professor D. V. Glass and Dr A. N. Little for their helpful criticisms.

2

A TEXTUAL EMENDATION IN A FRAGMENT OF MUSONIUS RUFUS: A NOTE ON CONTRACEPTION*

In the fourth book of Stobaeus' *Anthologium*, in a section entitled, 'The Virtue of Having Children', Ὅτι καλὸν τὸ ἔχειν παῖδας, there is preserved a passage from the writings of the first-century Roman knight and Stoic, Musonius Rufus. This passage is headed: 'Whether all children born should be raised', ἐκ τοῦ εἰ πάντα τὰ γινόμενα τέκνα θρεπτέον.

The sentence with which we are now concerned reads (Meineke, vol. III, p. 74; Wachsmuth-Hense, vol. IV, pp. 605–6; Musonius Rufus, ed. Hense, frag. 15a, pp. 77–8): τοῦτο μὲν γὰρ ἀμβλίσκειν ἀπεῖπον ταῖς γυναιξὶ καὶ ταῖς ἀπειθούσαις ζημίαν ἐπέθεσαν, τοῦτο δὲ †ἀτοκία† προστίθεσθαι καὶ τὴν κύησιν εἴργειν ἀπηγόρευσαν αὐταῖς, τοῦτο δὲ πολυπαιδίας ἔταξαν γέρα καὶ ἀνδρὶ καὶ γυναικί, καὶ τὴν ἀπαιδίαν ἐπιζήμιον κατέστησαν. The impossible ἀτοκία has been emended by the above editors into ἀτοκίᾳ.[1] They were probably led to the abstract ἀτοκίᾳ by the presence of the other three abstracts in the sentence (κύησιν, πολυπαιδίας, ἀπαιδίαν), and perhaps through ignorance of the medical technicalities of contraceptive practice in the ancient world. The result is a sentence awkward in its phrasing and illogical in its sequence of thought.

* First published in *Classical Quarterly* 15 (1965) 72–4 (= Hopkins 1965b).

[1] ⟨= Stobaeus, *Flor.* 75.15; *Ioannis Stobaei, Florilegium*, ed. A. Meineke, vol. III, Leipzig, 1856; *Ioannis Stobaei, Anthologium*, ed. C. Wachsmuth and O. Hense, vol. IV, Berlin, 1909; *C. Musonii Rufi, Reliquae*, ed. O. Hense, Leipzig, 1905.⟩ The manuscript reading is given by Wachsmuth and Hense: 'ἀτοκία sed alterum α rescripsit A2'. The editors' reading was also accepted by Powell 1937: 175–6 when he completed the fragmentary *P.Harr.* I; nor was this commented upon by Körte 1939: 112. ⟨Recent modern translations have continued to follow this text: 'Because they thought this, they forbade women from inducing miscarriages and established punishment for those who disobeyed, they forbade women from agreeing to be childless and from preventing contraception, they honored married couples who had a lot of children, and they punished those who were childless' – C. King 2011: 62.⟩

However, one should not be misled by the other abstracts in the sentence. πολυπαιδίας and ἀπαιδίαν form an opposition which is self-contained; and as far as the structure of the sentence is concerned they have nothing to do with the preceding words. Further, an abstract ἀτοκίᾳ is embarrassingly tautological in view of the later ἀπαιδίαν, if not indeed in view of the κύησιν εἵργειν which follows immediately: 'they forbade them to "engage in" childlessness and to prevent conception, ... and they made childlessness punishable'. Finally, the metaphor ἀτοκίᾳ προστίθεσθαι 'to side with ἀτοκία' (cf. LSJ, s.v. προστίθημι, B.I) used in order to express the idea of 'indulging in (practices causing)' ἀτοκία would be very strained.

All these difficulties are resolved if we simply read ἀτόκια – 'contraceptives'. The accentuation ἀτοκία instead of ἀτόκια in the manuscript tradition may be due to confusion, through itacism, with a *Nebenform* of ἀτόκιον, namely ἀτοκεῖον. The word ἀτόκιον is well attested in near contemporaries of Musonius, the doctors Dioscorides and Soranus.[2] The latter details various ἀτόκια, many of them occlusive pessaries or vaginal suppositories.[3] This is important in that προστίθεμαι is used in medical writings with βαλάνον – 'suppository'.[4] Further, while the second half of the sentence contains the balance of πολυπαιδίας and ἀπαιδίαν, which has already been noted, the first half contains the balance of the practical methods of achieving childlessness which are forbidden: on the one hand, abortion, on the other, contraception. The phrase τὴν κύησιν εἵργειν, formerly awkward, can now be justified in that it makes explicit the result of using ἀτόκια. That such enlargement might have been necessary in antiquity is suggested by comparative studies. Both in Japan among the general population even recently and among the literary classes in France during the sixteenth

2 Dioscorides, *De materia medica* 1.77.2, 3.130, 3.134.2 (ed. M. Wellmann, 3 vols, Berlin, 1906–14; trans. L. Y. Beck, Altertumswissenschaftliche Text und Studien 38, 2nd edn, Hildesheim, 2011); Soranus, *Gynaecia* 1.60 (ed. J. Ilberg, *CMG* IV, Leipzig, 1927; see now P. Burguière, D. Gourevitch and Y. Malinas, 4 vols, Paris, 1988–2000; trans. Temkin 1956).

3 Soranus, *Gynaecia* 1.61–2.

4 Hippoc. *Epid.* 1.26 α΄.

and seventeenth centuries, the function of contraceptives as distinct from abortifacients remained obscure.[5] This is corroborated by the fact that St John Chrysostom confessed his lack of understanding of the difference between them, and by the fact that some contraceptives advocated by ancient doctors were, in fact, abortifacients.[6] In this case the use of ἀμβλίσκειν in the first clause logically precludes the attribution of the meaning of pregnancy to κύησιν: it has in this context its primary meaning, conception. We have then a good logical sequence, well expressed. They forbade (a) abortion, (b) contraception; they rewarded high fertility and punished childlessness.[*]

It is difficult to identify the lawgivers, ⟨'those god-like and divinely favoured men'⟩ (νομοθέται, θεῖοι καὶ θεόφιλοι ἄνδρες) who were, according to Musonius, responsible for these prohibitions. It is possible that Musonius might have been indulging in a general and timeless philosophical discourse on the benefits of having children, and on the strong ties of brotherhood.[7] He might on the other hand have been referring to one historical situation or to an amalgam of many. Philosophers were not much troubled by an historical conscience. Yet it would be tempting to think that his remarks bore some relation to the contemporary or recent situation at Rome.

Augustus in his laws, the *lex Julia de maritandis ordinibus* and the *lex Papia Poppaea,* had tried to stimulate the birthrate. Presumably he did this because he thought it was low, because a significant number of married couples were having less than three children. This low birthrate must have been achieved by artificial control, whether by infanticide, abortion or contraception. The literature of the first century AD abounds with

[5] Taeuber 1958: 272; Ariès 1953: 469.

[6] Joh. Chrys. *Hom. in Rom.* 24.4 (*PG* 60: 626); Diepgen 1937: 301.

[*] ⟨H. offered a translation of the amended text in 1965a: 141 [essay 1: 78]: 'The rulers forbade women to abort and attached a penalty to those who disobeyed; secondly they forbade them to use contraceptives on themselves and to prevent pregnancy; finally they established honours for both men and women who had many children and made childlessness punishable.'⟩

[7] Musonius Rufus, frag. 15b (ed. O. Hense, Leipzig, 1905) ⟨= Stobaeus 4.664–6 (ed. C. Wachsmuth and O. Hense, Berlin, 1909) = Stobaeus, *Flor.* 84.21; trans. Inwood and Gerson 2008: 184; C. King 2011: 63–4⟩.

references to the reluctance of women to have children and to the fashionable acceptance of abortion.[8] The measures chosen by Augustus to counteract the low birthrate (e.g. rewards for three children, and the restriction of legacies among the childless) together with the opposition which these measures provoked among the senatorial and equestrian orders, are strong evidence that these laws applied to and affected these high social groups.[9] Musonius himself was an equestrian; and it is possible that the passage cited refers to the Roman situation with which Augustus tried to deal.

But there are objections to this view. In the Roman law of the *Digest* there is no prohibition of abortion as such.[10] In a law of Septimius Severus, which penalised a wife who aborted in deceit of her husband, it was the deceit, not the abortion, which was unlawful; another law penalised the sale of abortifacients, but grouped them with aphrodisiacs under the law of poisons.[11] In Roman law the foetus had neither individuality nor soul: its destruction could not be murder.[12] Another objection might be that a Roman emperor would hardly forbid actions which are so hard to discover. But a casual look at the Roman law codes, let alone the concept of *lex imperfecta* (to say nothing of contemporary British law) rapidly disposes of this objection. Laws were often unenforceable.

It is again possible that Musonius was referring in general to Augustan Rome, where 'rewards were set up for man and wife for having many children [three] and childlessness was penalised', while the specific prohibition of abortion and contraception was Musonius' own historically unjustified rhetorical enlargement on this theme. On the other hand is it not

[8] E.g. Sen. *Helv.* 16.3; and, in general, cf. Hähnel 1936.

[9] Cass. Dio 54.16, 56.1–10; Suet. *Aug.* 89.

[10] *Dig.* 48.8.8 is an interpolation, cf. Biondi 1952–4: III 487–8.

[11] *Dig.* 47.11.4 (Marcian); cf. 48.19.39 (Tryphoninus); and *Dig.* 48.19.38.5 (Paul); cf. 48.8.3.2 (Marcian).

[12] *Dig.* 25.4.1.1 (Ulpian): partus enim antequam edatur, mulieris portio est uel uiscerum ⟨for a child before it is born is part of the woman or, better, of her insides⟩; 35.2.9.1 (Papinian): partus nondum editus homo non recte fuisse dicitur ⟨a child as yet unborn connot correctly be said to be a person⟩. Cf. *Dig.* 38.8.1.8 (Ulpian); 37.9.7 (Ulpian); 28.6.10.1 (Ulpian).

possible that there was such an explicit law against abortion and contraception at Rome? Tertullian refers to a law against infanticide which he claims was universally flouted, even by members of the governing class.[13] This law is not known from the *Digest* or any other source; the absence from the *Digest* of the law against abortion and contraception, and the silence of the surviving classical authors is not necessarily a clinching argument. Moreover, the silence may not be complete. Tacitus says in a well-known passage of the *Germania*:

> numerum liberorum finire aut quemquam ex agnatis necare flagitium habetur, plusque ibi boni mores ualent quam alibi bonae leges.[14]

Tacitus implies that the Romans by contrast with the Germans both limited the number of their children and killed their late-born children and were not prevented from doing this by good laws. This could mean that there was a law in Rome against artificial limitations of the family. Such a law would be an easy corollary to the Augustan laws on the birthrate, but in the present state of knowledge it must remain unproven.

What does stand out from the textual emendation I have suggested (if it is accepted) is the use of contraceptives. From Aristotle, Pliny and Soranus, who practised as a doctor in Rome under Trajan, we know only that contraceptive techniques were known, and efficient ones at that.[15] From this reading and from its context, and on the principle that practice precedes prohibition, it emerges that prior to Musonius Rufus (or Lucius[16]) contraceptives were used. The passage indicates that contraceptive techniques were significant enough, at least putatively, to be considered on equal terms with abortion as

[13] Tert. *Ad. nat.* 1.15.3 ⟨ed. J. W. P. Borleffs, *CCSL* 1, Turnhout, 1954⟩, see also *Apol.* 9.6; Musonius Rufus, frag. 15b ⟨above n. 7⟩.

[14] Tac. *Ger.* 19: ⟨to limit the number of one's children or to kill any children after the father has drawn up a will is seen as an abomination, and good morals have greater force there than good laws do elsewhere⟩.

[15] Arist. *Hist. an.* 583a ⟨= 9(7).3 (ed. D. M. Balme and A. Gotthelf, Cambridge Classical Texts and Commentaries 38, Cambridge, 2002)⟩; Plin. *HN* 24.11; Soranus, *Gynaecia* 1.61–2.

[16] On the authenticity and authorship of the fragments of Musonius Rufus, cf. K. von Fritz, *RE* 16.1: 893–7, s.v. 'Musonius 1'.

a means to childlessness. Whether they were used singly, or together, much evidence from the first century AD suggests that among the Roman upper classes they had a significant effect upon the size of families.[17]

[17] I should like to thank Dr G. Giangrande of King's College, Cambridge, and Professor A. Wasserstein of Leicester for their help and encouragement.

AFTERWORD

CONTRACEPTION IN THE ROMAN EMPIRE

A TEXTUAL EMENDATION IN A FRAGMENT OF MUSONIUS RUFUS: A NOTE ON CONTRACEPTION

CAROLINE VOUT

'Contraception in the Roman empire' is part of a palette of papers which Keith Hopkins produced in the 1960s at the London School of Economics – a palette of demographic studies which was to prove seminal in applying the data and models of population history to ancient history. The influence of medieval historian, Philippe Ariès, is writ large throughout, not only in the references to his work on contraception in France, but in the disconnect, which he had famously underlined in the uncited *L'enfant et la vie familiale sous l'ancien régime* (1960), between the modern Western family and earlier structures of social organisation. H.'s anxiety about how to handle the gap between his own, and the Roman, conceptualisation of the world weighs heavy throughout: 'We do violence to historical imagination, if we seek to transpose upon them our own analytical categories based upon physiological factors alone' (1965a: 147 [essay 1: 87–8]). Thirty-five years on, this anxiety would still drive him to experiment with how to write history and explore everyday life in Pompeii with the help of a time machine.[1]

If all of this already hints at the trail-blazing nature of H.'s research, the companion piece, on a fragment of the Stoic philosopher, Gaius Musonius Rufus (born sometime before AD 30), is evidence of his training in classics, with the emphasis on philology which that then implied. I wonder what amused him more, playing at textual critic and moving the accent on the emended ἀτοκίᾳ (ἀτοκία meaning 'barrenness'/'childlessness') to ἀτόκια (contraceptives), or cramming his footnotes with evidence for potions and pessaries? The two activities are

[1] Hopkins 1999: 7–45.

not unrelated: the fragment's revised testimony about lawgivers (presumably meant to be the Emperor Augustus and his legislators) forbidding women from using contraceptives and from preventing conception may constitute a misreading on Musonius' part of the Julian laws on marriage, but it is the earliest explicit evidence that any of these substances might actually have been used in the Roman empire.

H.'s work on contraception in the Roman empire builds on the assumption that the élite took active measures to ensure small families, and uses evidence from ancient authors like Musonius, together with comparative sociological data, to determine the extent to which contraception, coitus interruptus included, was an important part of this limiting imperative. His desire to prove Ronald Syme wrong (1965a: 128 [essay 1: 60]) and to provide an affirmative answer is palpable: pages are spent on establishing the seriousness and circulation of the works of Greek and Roman medical writers. The works of twenty-two of these writers are sieved for mention of contraception and its methods, and the results tabulated. Yet for all the cedar gum, olive oil and vaginal plugs listed, and the fact that olive oil was still a recommended contraceptive in England in 1931 (1965a: 134 [essay 1: 69]), the conclusion can seem a little underwhelming – that although contraception probably did not play a major role in family limitation in Rome, its effect was probably not negligible (1965a: 142 [essay 1: 80]), at least not until the later empire, when, on general theoretical grounds, H. argues that its use is likely to have declined. His problem is working out how theory translated into practice. Musonius aside, literary authors have frustratingly little to say about contraception and, beyond the Jewish tradition, even less about coitus interruptus. H. is forced to come clean – even if the élite used these methods, and with the aim of limiting their offspring, this does not mean that they were effective.

Few scholars enjoy an *absence* of evidence as much as H. The section on coitus interruptus sees him at his most propositional, drawing on tracts on birth control produced in Britain and America in the nineteenth century, and on statistics from modern population studies to decide how best to read the silence. This was H. at his most innovative, highlighting patterns which might then determine how likely it was for ancient Romans to have done x or y. This hypothesising showed him that the structure of Roman institutions was more susceptible to the use of contraception in the late Republic and early empire than at other times, due to 'the growth of rationalism, scepticism, individualism, high status for women and sexual freedom for women after marriage' (1965a: 149 [essay 1: 90]) – a bold statement which goes a long way towards alleviating the *ennui* of the above conclusion, and was to become central to *Death and Renewal* (1983). Although H.'s judiciousness still has him admit that we do not know how many Romans saw the world as he imagines, or indeed limited the size of their families by a combination of contraception, abortion and infanticide,[2] these measures make sense in an aristocratic culture where it was politically advantageous to conserve family wealth by keeping it in the hands of a small number of children.

'Contraception in the Roman empire' was written pre-Foucault and Laqueur, prior to the flourishing of feminist scholarship and related works on the history of science, prior to the publication of Jack Goody, *The Development of the Family and Marriage in Europe* (1983) and to Bagnall and Frier's careful analysis of Roman Egypt's census returns (1994).[3] We live in a different world. H.'s surprise at the Roman confusion of contraception and abortion ('to the modern the concepts … are obviously distinct' (1965a: 125 [essay 1: 56]) sounds naïve in the light of pro-life arguments concerning RU486 or 'the morning after pill'. But by 1983, and the publication of *Death and Renewal*, it was already a different world: H.'s (with Graham Burton) brief nod to female status and sexual freedom had become a 'movement towards competitive sexuality and

[2] Hopkins and Burton 1983a: 97.

[3] Foucault 1976–84 and Laqueur 1990. Musonius Rufus' own 'feminist' stance has also been debated: see Nussbaum 2002; Engel 2003; Reydams-Schils 2004. Scheidel 2001a is excellent in its summary both of the state of research into ancient demography and of systematic surveys of the ancient material beyond Bagnall and Frier 1994.

emancipated pleasure-seeking'. Women in the late Republic/early empire were accorded their own agency – they act to maintain their status as well as that of their families, 'some remarried for love or pleasure', and the most fashionable of them are 'reluctant to spoil their figures with a large number of children'. It is 'mostly women who executed the decision to restrict fertility', even if partly in response to male and other pressures.[4]

Over fifteen years ago, Helen King drew attention to the problems of pushing this line of argument to the limit: the identification of contraception as a women's concern 'is a feminist reading creating Greek women in the image of women of the post-Pill era, able to exercise – preferably without men's knowledge – their "right to choose"'.[5] It is an assessment aimed not at H. but mainly at the historian, John Riddle, whose *Contraception and Abortion from the Ancient World to the Renaissance* (1992) and *Eve's Herbs: A History of Contraception and Abortion in the West* (1997) argue for the existence in antiquity and throughout the Middle Ages of databanks of 'women's wisdom' about contraceptive remedies. In contrast to H.'s meticulous building of a case, Riddle throws historical acumen to the wind to claim that not only were the kinds of herbal remedies detailed in H.'s footnotes routinely used; they worked. Critics have not been shy in coming forward. As King also highlights,[6] even the term 'contraception' is potentially anachronistic (might an ἀτόκιος substance not be more accurately translated as an 'infertility agent'[7])? Conception was seen as a gradual, lengthy process, and the most fertile time of the month, just after a menstrual period.[8]

The reaction to Riddle's books has rather detracted from H.'s foray.[9] Interestingly, neither of H.'s articles feature in the bibliography of Rebecca Flemming's *Medicine and the Making*

[4] Hopkins and Burton 1983a, quoting 94 and 97.
[5] H. King 1998: 141.
[6] H. King 1998: 133–5.
[7] Flemming 2000: 164.
[8] As H. himself acknowledges at 1965a: 140 [essay 1: 77].
[9] See e.g. the review by Flemming 1999.

of Roman Women: Gender, Nature, and Authority from Celsus to Galen (2000). Amongst scholars of ancient demography, however, he is still a hero, and the question of whether the population of the Roman empire practised forms of family limitation that led to demographic contraction, a live issue. First, as Bruce Frier and others have pointed out, the assumption that family limitation and birth control are one and the same phenomenon is again distinctly modern: even if the Romans routinely used 'infertility agents', they might have done so to space out their families or for the sake of extra-marital sex.[10] Second, the proliferation of new data (census returns, bigger databases of funerary inscriptions, etc.) notwithstanding, Roman fertility rates are not directly attested: as Walter Scheidel notes, 'even eminent aristocratic families are not sufficiently well documented for us to calculate the mean number of children per couple who survived to maturity, let alone total rates of marital fertility'.[11] Rather, fertility rates are estimated, as H. estimated them, from likely levels of mortality and mean age at first marriage. Whereas H. calculated that, on average, girls were married for the first time between the ages of 12 and 15, this has slowly risen, to a figure closer to 20 years old, which narrows the window.[12] How confident are we in the notion of any kind of decline, even among the upper classes; that upper-class families dying out was evidence of more than a high risk of mortality and near natural fertility?[13] Key to H.'s evidence was the Augustan legislation on marriage of 18 BC and AD 9, but as he was forever telling his students, laws are prescriptive, not descriptive.

Despite the advances in demographic theory, we are no nearer to proving that even the élite significantly restricted

[10] Frier 1994: 332–3.

[11] Scheidel 1999: 278.

[12] Hopkins 1964–5 with B. D. Shaw 1987, 2001 and Saller 1994: 25–42; although note the uncertainty maintained by Parkin 1992: 124.

[13] There has been a shift in recent years away from an emphasis on family limitation in Rome – extended by Brunt (1971a: 140–54) to encompass not just the élite, but all Italians – to examining the value of children, 'the more, the merrier' (Hin 2011, quoting 116). Bibliography is growing all the time, but particularly influential is Caldwell 2004.

fertility. Rather our increased reliance on databases makes this lack of proof seem more worrying. But this is to make too little of H.'s influence: for his hypothesis seems no less likely today than it did in the 1960s. As he himself admits: 'to be sure the evidence is slight – but some at least does exist, and we shall see if something can be made of it' (1965a: 128 [essay 1: 60]).[14]

[14] I hope Keith will forgive me for attempting this Afterword: I am neither social historian nor textual critic, and never experienced the 1960s when these pieces were written. I trust that I prove as good at demography as he was at visual analysis. I thank the Trustees of The Leverhulme Trust for awarding me a Philip Leverhulme Prize which gave me the space in 2011 to revisit and engage with Keith's work, and Rebecca Flemming, Robin Osborne and Walter Scheidel for their reading.

3

ON THE PROBABLE AGE STRUCTURE OF THE ROMAN POPULATION*

Argument

It has long been thought possible to use the ages of death given on Roman tombstones in order to calculate the average age at death of Roman men and women; and from this, on the assumption of a stationary population, to estimate the expectation of life at birth and subsequent ages. Such reckonings can be used for a variety of purposes; for example, to understand the insecurity of life and the frequency of death in the ancient world, to calculate the chances of young magistrates or bureaucrats surviving to compete for high office or to estimate the average number of children needed in order to maintain the size of an élite group or of the total population. In fact, the existing findings have been under-exploited for such purposes. Yet in general the work of scholars such as Beloch, Macdonell and Burn on the expectation of life in the Roman empire has gained a general, if guarded, acceptance.[1] And this has been reasonable in that the results have themselves seemed reasonable and demographically probable. They can be summarised in terms of an average expectation of life at birth of between twenty and thirty years.[2]

What has escaped sufficient comment is the distributional pattern of the ages at death, as recorded on tombstones. Nearly everyone acknowledges that the deaths of infants (under one year old) are seriously under-represented; and most imply the same about the deaths of children (aged 1–9), but often, as I shall show, mistakenly; still others have taken

* First published in *Population Studies* 20 (1966) 245–64 (= Hopkins 1966a).

[1] Beloch 1886: 41–54; Macdonell 1913; Burn 1953: summarised at 25, and more recently in his review of Nordberg 1963 (= Burn 1965).

[2] Étienne 1959: 418; Moretti 1959: 77; Hombert and Préaux 1945: 143–5.

into consideration the clear overstatement of very old ages.[3] Although several scholars have realised that the demographic patterns of the ancient world are likely to be similar to those of historical European patterns, or of underdeveloped countries before these came under the impact of modern medicine, they have nevertheless lacked any means of testing the reliability of the Roman data against a sample of comparative data. This can now tentatively be done by using the UN model life tables.[4] And by means of such calculations I have found that the pattern of ages at death, derived from Roman tombstones, even between the ages of 10 and 60, is mostly demographically impossible and always highly improbable. This has escaped notice, I think, because in summary form the average of the improbable and the real are very close. It is the pattern of distribution which shows the shortcomings of the ancient data.

Moreover, some aspects of this curious pattern can be relatively simply explained by reference to the customs of commemoration. The universe of tombstone inscriptions can be divided into several categories: (a) fragments, honorary inscriptions, those set up by living persons to themselves and tombstones with just the name of the deceased and nothing else; (b) those which give only the age at death; (c) those which give the age at death and a named relationship (e.g. to my son aged 9 years); (d) those which give only a named relationship.[5] Previous studies of Roman ages at death have indiscriminately combined figures from categories (b) and (c). However, a study of categories (b), (c) and (d) reveals that the Roman custom of commemoration makes the ages at death anything but a random or representative sample of those dying. Not only are infants under-represented, but children aged 1–9 and youths aged 10–19, commemorated by their parents, are very much over-represented. Whereas it has been generally accepted that Roman women died relatively young, I shall argue that young wives were commemorated disproportionately often, not so

[3] Cf. Burn 1953.

[4] Durand 1959–60; United Nations 1956: especially 74–5.

[5] To this last category may be added those inscriptions set up by spouses which give no age at death, but only a length of marriage.

much because more of them died young, but because the younger they died the more chance there was of having husbands still surviving to commemorate them. And husbands tended to put the age at death of their wives on the tombstone, whereas children who often commemorated their parents only rarely did so. Nor is this merely a matter of intuitive interpretation; the rise of mortality among Roman women in early adulthood as shown by tombstones can be measured and shown to be very improbable, if not impossible.

Unfortunately, therefore, the argument of this article is negative, for there is no means at our disposal for correcting the distortions due to habits of commemoration. The only conclusion possible is that, even on the assumption of a stationary population, which is in itself fragile, ages at death derived from Roman tombstones cannot be used to estimate expectation of life at birth or at subsequent ages.

The Evidence

There are huge numbers of inscriptions collected by modern scholars according to city, province, religion (i.e. pagan or Christian), language (Latin or Greek) or more recently by date of discovery. Most were set up in the first three centuries AD. Nearly all inscriptions came from towns; there is practically no record of rural mortality, which on comparative grounds is likely to have been lower than urban. On the other hand, there is likely to have been a heavier mortality in a large metropolis like Rome than in much smaller towns. To some extent, the evidence bears this out.

There is, also, a serious class bias. Inscribed tombstones were not cheap. Even cheap ones may have cost roughly the equivalent of three months' wages of unskilled labour.[6] Although

[6] Duncan-Jones 1962: 90–1 lists the prices of thirty-eight slabs and stelai, ranging in price from 96 to 5,000 sestertii; twenty-five of these cost 1,000 to 2,000 sestertii. Two bases of statues and a marble vat cost 500, 400 and 200 sestertii (Duncan-Jones 1962: 106). Although a price of 96 sestertii is recorded, it stands alone; prices of 400 sestertii and above are much more common. There is little evidence of wage rates. Estimates vary from 200 sestertii per annum by Duncan-Jones 1963: 171, to 87.5–100 sestertii per month by Szilágyi 1963a: 348. It is highly probable that the dead

some members of the lower class joined burial clubs, it is generally agreed that tombstones represent the *respectable classes* – a suitably vague term by which I want to convey something like small shopkeepers and above – disproportionately often. Macdonell has given a breakdown by social class of persons whose age at death is recorded – but these represent only 5 per cent of his total.[7] It is to be noted that slaves and ex-slaves were quite often commemorated. First, there were a lot of slaves; secondly, although slaves were juridically at the bottom of the social scale, they were sometimes relatively well-to-do; this was true especially, for example, of the slaves and ex-slaves of the emperor.

Average Age at Death – Alleged Regional Variations

Since there are so many recorded ages at death surviving from different provinces, scholars have sought some means of condensing the data in order to compare the results. Unhappily they have generally used the average age at death, which they have equated with the average duration of life. For example, Moretti analysing Macdonell (probably at second hand), Moretti alone, Étienne and Harkness gave the following expectations of life at birth (table 3.1).[8]

However, it is by no means certain that such a summary of ages at death given by inscriptions is well founded. As I have said, it is universally agreed that infant mortality is seriously

were commemorated not by tombstones only, but also by inscriptions on wood which would be unlikely to survive, or by uninscribed markers of stone or other material; and it is certain that they were sometimes commemorated by painted epitaphs or by epitaphs incised on perishable material such as stucco, whose survival rate is very low. For an inscription on wood (not, however, an epitaph) cf. *RIB* I 1935, and for a painted epitaph cf. Goodchild and Reynolds 1962: 41–6, especially 42. I owe these last comments and references to Miss J. M. Reynolds. The collections I am dealing with consist of incised pillars and slabs of stone.

7 Macdonell 1913: 368.

8 Harkness 1896: 66; Étienne 1959: 418; Moretti 1959: 60, 61, 70. In fact Macdonell did divide his data by each year of death, and by sex (*pace* Moretti 1959: 63), and thus his work on inscriptions from Rome, Spain and Africa represents the fullest and most usable analysis of ages at death: Macdonell 1913: especially 378–9.

Table 3.1. *Average ages at death in four Roman regions, according to different scholars.*

	Macdonell Moretti	Moretti[a] & Étienne[b]			Harkness
	Both sexes	m.	f.	Both sexes	Both sexes
Rome	21.65	22.07[a]	19.72[a]	21.16[a]	22.3
Spain	37.4	37.7[b]	34.0[b]	36.2[b]	
Africa	46.7	47.4[b]	44.1[b]	45.2[b]	
Bordeaux		37.2[b]	34.6[b]	35.7[b]	

under-represented in these inscriptions. Does the same apply to the mortality of early childhood? This is indeed a question which has puzzled ancient historians; they have unwittingly come to contradictory solutions. De Marchi and Degrassi, for example, claimed that Romans had a penchant for recording early deaths, while Burn obviously thought that the deaths of children under 10 years of age were under-represented.[9] But it is not much use saying that too few children's deaths were recorded, unless we have a standard by which this understatement can be judged, or better still, measured. What we need is some independent measure, some estimate of what sort of mortality one could reasonably expect at these times. The use of comparative evidence seems more profitable than naked assertion. To this I shall return later.

For the moment let us follow Harkness and Burn in leaving out deaths before the age of 10.

The most striking part of these results is the wide divergence between average age at death in different parts of the empire, particularly between Rome and Africa. Average age at death in Rome was about 21 or 22, and 29.3 years for those surviving to 10 years of age, while in Africa it was about 45 or 46 and 53.3 respectively.

[9] de Marchi 1903: 1027; Degrassi 1964: 91–8. His eight samples (tables 1–8) vary in size from 70 to 318 ⟨Burn 1953: 4–5⟩.

Table 3.2. *Average age at death of those surviving to age 10, both sexes.*

Rome	29.3	England	36.5
Latium	29.6	Asia, Greece	36.8
Cisalpine Gaul	32.1	Aemilia, Etruria, Umbria	37.1
Brutii, Lucania, Campania, Sicily, Sardinia	33.7	Spain	37.8
Calabria, Apulia, Samnium	34.8	Africa	53.3

Source: Harkness 1896: 67, based on *CIL* II, III, V–XI and XIV.

It may be thought that these differences can be adequately explained by the appalling sanitary conditions probably prevalent in metropolitan Rome (but can we ignore the evidence from Latium, Cisalpine Gaul, etc.?); Étienne thought longevity in Africa could be explained by 'l'air pur, la vie à la campagne' in the African uplands. For Sallust wrote about Africa: 'a healthy breed of men who are quick and endure toils well; many die in old age, unless killed by the sword or wild beasts; disease rarely kills anyone, but there are lots of dangerous animals'.[10]

Of course, mortality in metropolitan Rome is likely to have been very high. But even the African inscriptions come predominantly from towns; and it is hard to account for the apparent result that African towns had a low 'post-industrial' mortality, while not only Rome but also Italian towns exhibited the high mortality of pre-industrial societies. One is at least tempted to look for alternative explanations.

To some extent, an explanation can be found in the misleading use of the concept average. Averages are useful for summarising data when the data are distributed normally, evenly or reliably. But in the African inscriptions the dispersion is very skewed. Of 10,697 African ages at death collected by Macdonell there are 27 of more than 120, 290 of 100–19, and 400 from 90 to 99, a total of 7 per cent; from Rome, of 8,067

[10] Étienne 1959: 419. Genus hominum salubri corpore, uelox, patiens laborum; plurosque senectus dissoluit, nisi qui ferro aut bestiis interiere, nam morbus haud saepe quemquam superat; ad hoc malefici generis plurima animalia: Sall. *Iug.* 17.6.

ages, there are none over 120, 7 between 100 and 119, and 45 of 90–9, a total of less than 1 per cent. Altogether ages at death over 70 are 24.8 per cent of the total in Africa and 2.8 per cent in Rome. The discrepancy is so marked that it is difficult to believe that it is only due to longevity in Africa; and the large number of late deaths in Africa give a marked skew to the average. Further, the number of claimed centenarians in a population can often be considered a function of illiteracy rather than of longevity. Calculations on the British census of 1901–11 showed that old people claimed a growth in their ages at the rate of 17 years per decade.[11] No modern population has 3 per cent of its population as centenarians. It may be difficult to assert that there was more illiteracy in Africa than in Rome; but rather than claim a unique longevity for Africa, it seems more economical to suppose that the Africans were less accurate and more boastful about their age than urban Romans or Italians.

The Median Length of Life – Alleged Regional Variations – a Critique of Burn

Once again it was Burn who sought to avoid the bias brought about by using the average. Instead he chose the median, i.e. the age by which 50 per cent of his population (in this case, those surviving to 15) had died. Whilst this method did not avoid the relatively large numbers of old men recorded in African inscriptions, it did at least avoid the bias caused by the exaggeration of their ages at death.

Burn's data are clearly very interesting. He supplemented the table reproduced here (table 3.3) by other tables which gave the absolute number and percentage of those who survived to successive ages, having survived to the age of 10. These could be very useful, for example, to estimate the number of soldiers who would survive to receive their pensions, or to estimate the chances of promotion in the imperial bureaucracy. He also drew graphs

[11] McWhirter and McWhirter 1964: 11: 'the correlation between the claimed density of centenarians in a country and its national illiteracy is 0.83 ± 0.03'.

Table 3.3. *Ages by which one-half of those surviving to the age of 15 would have died, by area and social group.*

Province and social group	Males	*n* at 15	Females	*n* at 15
African Provinces				
(a) N.-W. Africa	48	398	44	325
(b) Carthage; slaves and freedmen	38	331	33	229
(c) Lambaesis (a garrison town)	45	549	38	415
(d) Egypt (after Hombert and Préaux 1945)	36*	641*		
(e) N. Africa Christians (4th–6th centuries)	52	146	47	96
Europe				
(a) Bordeaux, Brindisi and Merida (Spain)	44	284	36	229
(b) Danubian provinces	40	667	33	378
(c) Britain (mostly military districts)	40	108	37	47
(d) North Italy (Christian period)	52	79	40	66
India (census of 1931)	48		43	

* Both sexes.
Source: this table follows Burn 1953: 16 table 1.

in which he compared the pattern of survival in various social groups and provinces; the first graph represents the survival of the two groups with extreme patterns of survival, if slaves and Christians (fourth–sixth centuries) are excepted as non-typical groups. The pattern of survival in India 1901–10 fits quite neatly in the middle of these two Roman curves (figure 3.1). The design is striking and has won followers. A. H. M. Jones, for example, used it to illustrate the probable pattern of mortality in Athens.[12]

[12] A. H. M. Jones 1957: 82–3. I agree with the rough comparability of Athenian and Roman mortality, that is with Jones' general conclusions; what I am criticising is his and Burn's method. Moreover, the data from Britain comprise only 113 inscriptions.

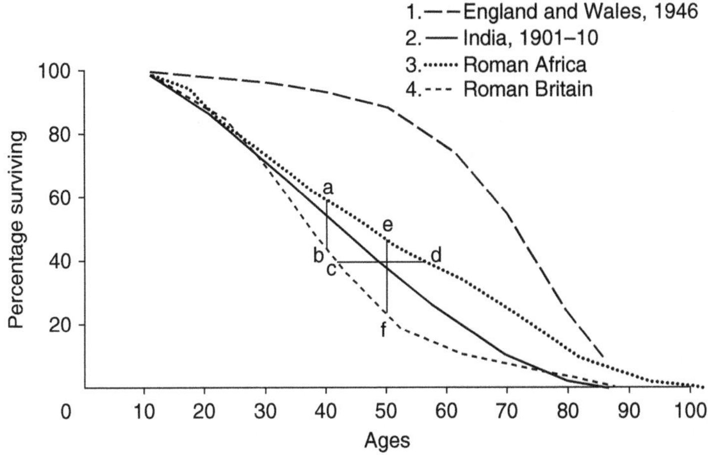

Figure 3.1. Ancient and modern populations compared (males only). The graph shows the percentages of those alive at age 10 who remain alive at successive ages up to the age of 100 (alleged). (1) Showing a population living throughout under conditions of 1946. (3) Excludes (a) Egypt and (b) slaves at Carthage. (4) All known inscriptions.
Source: Burn 1953: 25 graph A.

Burn's article, with the exception of Durand's more recent article and a note by L. Henry, is by far the most sophisticated and serious discussion of Roman mortality.[13] Nevertheless, I think his method and his presentation of data are open to grave objections. There are three major questions to be asked. First, are his samples from Africa, Spain, Bordeaux, the Danubian provinces and Britain representative? He has missed Rome out on quite spurious grounds and gives no data from Italy in pagan times.[14] Analysis of Macdonell's data shows that 50 per cent of males surviving to 15 in Rome died by the age of 29 (survivors at 15 = 2,535); in Spain the same median is 39

[13] Durand 1959–60; Henry 1957, *inter alia* a critique of Étienne's work, which the latter has regrettably ignored. I should perhaps add Willcox 1938 and Hombert and Préaux 1945, and cf. below n. 30.

[14] The grounds are given in Burn 1953: 4–5 and expanded in Burn 1965: 257. First, Romans set up stones to themselves while still alive; true, but these stones can easily be excluded. Secondly, the governing classes did not give their age at death. It may be true of aristocrats; so what? Thirdly, the old are under-represented, and even when commemorated their ages are not given; this Burn explains, inadequately, by their poverty or neglect.

(survivors at 15 = 998); in Africa 51 (survivors at 15 = 5,508). There is, in other words, considerable discrepancy between Burn's medians, which range from 38 to 52 (or if we exclude the special groups of slaves, and Christians) from 40 to 48, and those gained from a fuller study of Rome, Africa and Spain, which range from 29 to 51.[15]

The next question to ask is what is the significance of the difference between 29 or 39 and 51, or between 40 and 48, as median figures of survival for those surviving to 15. Are these differences minor or great, are they the sort of differences which we should expect to find in pre-industrial populations? The third question is somewhat similar and relates in particular to the acceptability of the graph (figure 3.1). Independently of Burn's summary (i.e. the medians at 40 and 48), are the levels of mortality in each age group 15–100 (a) reliable, (b) internally consistent? For example, when looking at Burn's graph we should note that though the curves are near each other at ages 10–25 and partly again at 75, the slope or rate of dying and the *horizontal* and *vertical* distances are widely divergent (lines ab, cd, ef). What we need, again, is some objective measure to see whether the data collected by Burn are demographically possible or probable. As we shall see later, the Indian data which he uses and whose curve fits so neatly between Roman Britain and Africa are merely a bridge between two improbables; in method at least Burn's presentation is like confirming reports about giants and pygmies by reference to average height in England.

Tests of Consistency

We have seen that Roman tombstones do not provide as simple a clue to the incidence of mortality as has usually been assumed. It is now necessary to examine the internal consistency of the recorded deaths, especially between ages 1 and 70.

[15] I am not sure what other bias there is in Burn's data; as in this case some of the data he analyses refer to specific social groups, e.g. slaves, military cantonments and nearby settlements, Christians. The graph of deaths in Roman Britain is built on only 113 cases. Cf. below n. 19.

Scholars have often made such comparisons, but have usually chosen as their reference point the contemporary data of their own countries or, equally arbitrarily, data from one or two countries which confirmed their findings.

We are fortunate in having available the UN model life tables, which summarise demographic data from a wide variety of countries. They are subject to considerable error since they are often based on the unreliable census data of countries with high illiteracy rates, but nevertheless they are the best we have, and can be very useful since they tabulate high probabilities about the sequence of mortality. For example, a population is unlikely to suffer very high mortality compared with other countries in the age group 35–9, but relatively low mortality in the age group 40–4. The chances are that age-specific mortality will follow a pattern which is internally consistent, within limits. This is in fact what happens, and it is this test which we shall apply to the Roman data.

These model life tables are divided by sex, are then grouped according to expectation of life at birth (20, 22.5, 25, etc.) and deathrates in successive age groups (0–1, 1–4, 5–9, 10–14, etc.). Thus, each column shows deathrates in each age group given a life expectation at birth of 20, 22½, 25, etc., up to over 70 years. In general we should expect the deathrates of a real population to stay fairly near a particular model life table; a variation of more than 7½ years in expectation of life at birth would cause some surprise.

In tables 3.4 and 3.5 and in figures 3.2 and 3.3 I have analysed two large collections of ages at death from inscriptions found in four areas of the Roman empire: the city of Rome itself, Italy excluding Rome, Spain and North Africa. Armini published his data on Italy in five-yearly groups (n = 5,343), while Macdonell gave the frequencies of death in each year (n = 20,758).[16] Thus in the latter case it was possible to smooth out bias caused by the large number of ages divisible by five, especially at ages over 20. After that age the proportion of ages divisible by five does not rise or differ significantly between sexes

[16] Armini 1916: especially 93. Macdonell 1913: 378–9.

Table 3.4. *Male chances of death and expectation of life at birth in the corresponding UN model life table according to tombstone inscriptions from four areas of the Roman empire.*

	Rome					Italians,† but not Romans			
a	*b*	*c*	*d*	*e*	*f*	*b*	*c*	*d*	*e*
Age	Survivors at beginning of age interval	No. of deaths recorded	$\frac{c}{b}$ (as %)	Corresponding expectation of life at birth	% dying when e_o=20 in UN model life table	Survivors at beginning of age interval	No. of deaths recorded	$\frac{c}{b}$ (as %)	Corresponding expectation of life at birth
0–1	4,575	74	1.6	73.9	33.2	3,269*	129* }	11.6	much >73.9
1–4	4,501	788	17.5	30.0	26.8	3,140*	249* }		
5–9	3,713	759	20.4	much <20.0	8.9	2,891	352	12.2	much <20.0
10–14	2,954	419	14.2	much <20.0	5.6	2,539	253	10.0	much <20.0
15–19	2,535	529	20.9	much <20.0	6.8	2,286	358	15.7	much <20.0
20–4	2,006	450	22.4	much <20.0	8.6	1,928	341	17.7	much <20.0
25–9	1,556	333	21.4	much <20.0	10.0	1,587	259	16.3	much <20.0
30–4	1,223	264	21.6	much <20.0	12.0	1,328	212	16.0	much <20.0
35–9	959	224	23.4	much <20.0	14.7	1,116	203	18.2	much <20.0
40–4	735	165	22.4	much <20.0	18.5	913	190	20.8	20.0
45–9	570	101	17.7	25.0	22.4	723	122	16.9	25.0
50–4	469	81	17.3	30.0	25.7	601	149	24.8	20.0
55–9	388	69	17.8	35.0	30.3	452	90	19.9	32.5
60–4	319	85	26.6	30.0	35.0	362	104	28.7	27.5
65–9	234	49	20.9			258	39	15.1	70.2
70+	185					219			

* 0–2
2–4

†After Armini 1916; the data are not rounded off at numbers divisible by five.

	Spain					Africa			
a	*b*	*c*	*d*	*e*	*f*	*b*	*c*	*d*	*e*
Age	Survivors at beginning of age interval	No. of deaths recorded	$\frac{c}{b}$ (as %)	Corresponding expectation of life at birth	% dying when e_o=20 in UN model life table	Survivors at beginning of age interval	No. of deaths recorded	$\frac{c}{b}$ (as %)	Corresponding expectation of life at birth
0–1	1,111	4	0.36	much >73.9	33.2	6,238	32	0.5	much >73.9
1–4	1,107	31	2.8	63.2	26.8	6,206	228	3.7	57.6
5–9	1,076	31	2.9	42.5	8.9	5,978	219	3.7	37.5
10–14	1,045	47	4.5	25.0	5.6	5,759	247	4.3	25.0
15–19	998	112	11.2	much <20.0	6.8	5,512	363	6.6	20.0
20–4	886	133	15.0	much <20.0	8.6	5,149	443	8.6	20.0
25–9	753	110	14.6	much <20.0	10.0	4,706	408	8.7	25.0
30–4	643	89	13.8	much <20.0	12.0	4,298	394	9.2	27.5
35–9	554	69	12.5	22.5	14.7	3,904	349	8.9	32.5
40–4	485	67	13.8	25.0	18.5	3,555	336	9.5	35.0
45–9	418	55	13.2	32.5	22.4	3,219	295	9.2	40.0
50–4	363	58	16.0	32.5	25.7	2,924	334	11.4	40.0
55–9	305	57	18.7	35.0	30.3	2,590	297	11.5	47.5
60–4	248	61	24.6	32.5	35.0	2,293	340	14.8	52.5
65–9	187	42	22.5	50.0		1,953	307	15.7	
70+	145					1,646			
(100)	6					(177)			

or social groups (e.g. ex-slaves), nor is there a much greater proportion of ages divisible by ten, except over the age of 70.[17] It has usually been assumed, at least with reference to middle age, that the margin of error implicit in this practice is less than five years; that is, that people recorded ages to the nearest number divisible by five. This can be shown to be untrue of very late ages, and on comparative grounds it is questionable that in general adults had an exact idea of their ages.

Explanation of Tables 3.4 and 3.5

The first figure in column *b* is the total of all inscriptions collected, which I treat as a population who were born and then died at successive ages. The other figures in the column show the number who survived at successive ages, e.g. at 1, 5, 10. Column *c* gives the number of deaths recorded in each age interval marked in column *a*, e.g. 788 males died in Rome between the ages of 1 and 4. Column *d* gives a rate of those dying as a percentage of the survivors at the beginning of the age interval. Column *f* gives the comparable percentage given in the UN model life table for an expectation of life at birth of 20, which is the highest mortality given in the UN tables and the highest likely to be found in a stationary population. But Roman mortality, as revealed by inscriptions, is often very much higher than that shown in any UN table; for example, the highest UN mortality at 10–14 is 5.6 per cent of survivors to 10; in the city of Rome it appears from the tombstones to be 14.2 per cent. In column *e* I have given the expectation of life at birth which most

[17] For a full analysis of this aspect, cf. Levison 1898: especially 22–6: some, but not all, groups of soldiers were less prone to putting ages at death divisible by five. Analysis of Macdonell's data for males and females from Rome and Africa (n = 18,762) shows in most age groups over 30 a range of 60–75 per cent of all ages divisible by five, and 35–50 per cent divisible by ten. By contrast, under 20 numbers divisible by five or ten occur little above random. I smoothed Macdonell's, but not Armini's, data by averaging the frequencies of death at the two ages on either side of numbers divisible by five (e.g. sum of deaths occurring at 44, 45 and 46 divided by 3) and attributed the product to each age. The effect can be roughly gauged by comparing the curves from Armini's data (Italy outside Rome) with the other curves in figs 3.2 and 3.3.

Table 3.5. *Female chances of death and expectation of life at birth in the corresponding UN model life table according to tombstone inscriptions from four areas of the Roman empire.*

	Rome					Italians,† but not Romans			
a	*b*	*c*	*d*	*e*	*f*	*b*	*c*	*d*	*e*
Age	Survivors at beginning of age interval	No. of deaths recorded	$\frac{c}{b}$ (as %)	Corresponding expectation of life at birth	% dying when e_o=20 in UN model life table	Survivors at beginning of age interval	No. of deaths recorded	$\frac{c}{b}$ (as %)	Corresponding expectation of life at birth
0–1	3,490	46	1.3	much >73.9	30.7	2,074*	73*	3.5 }	60.4
1–4	3,444	470	13.6	35.0	27.3	2,001*	165*	8.2 }	
5–9	2,974	456	15.3	much <20.0	9.3	1,836	183	10.0	<20.0
10–14	2,518	330	13.1	much <20.0	6.3	1,653	181	10.9	much <20.0
15–19	2,188	520	23.8	much <20.0	7.7	1,472	298	20.2	much <20.0
20–4	1,668	506	30.3	much <20.0	9.5	1,174	291	24.8	much <20.0
25–9	1,162	398	34.3	much <20.0	11.3	883	222	25.1	much <20.0
30–4	764	242	31.7	much <20.0	13.2	661	151	22.8	much <20.0
35–9	522	156	28.9	much <20.0	15.3	510	101	19.8	much <20.0
40–4	366	95	26.0	much <20.0	17.0	409	93	22.7	much <20.0
45–9	271	70	25.8	much <20.0	19.1	316	57	18.0	22.5
50–4	201	44	21.9	20.0	21.9	259	56	21.6	20.0
55–9	157	30	19.1	27.5	25.3	203	33	16.2	32.5
60–4	127	33	26.0	25.0	26.0	170	52	30.6	20.0
65–9	94	25	26.6	37.5	38.0	118	26	22.0	42.5
70+	69					19			
(100+)	(2)					(4)			

* 0–2
2–4

†After Armini 1916; the data are not rounded off at numbers divisible by five.

	Spain					Africa			
a	*b*	*c*	*d*	*e*	*f*	*b*	*c*	*d*	*e*
Age	Survivors at beginning of age interval	No. of deaths recorded	$\frac{c}{b}$ (as %)	Corresponding expectation of life at birth	% dying when e_0=20 in UN model life table	Survivors at beginning of age interval	No. of deaths recorded	$\frac{c}{b}$ (as %)	Corresponding expectation of life at birth
0–1	885	2	0.22	73.9	30.7	4,459	16	0.35	much >73.9
1–4	883	21	2.4	63.2	27.3	4,443	170	3.8	57.6
5–9	862	40	4.6	32.5	9.3	4,273	158	3.7	37.5
10–14	822	42	5.1	22.5	6.3	4,115	172	4.2	27.5
15–19	780	107	13.7	much <20.0	7.7	3,943	292	7.4	20.0
20–4	673	118	17.5	much <20.0	9.5	3,651	338	9.3	20.0
25–9	555	122	22.0	much <20.0	11.3	3,313	365	11.0	20.0
30–4	433	80	18.5	much <20.0	13.2	2,948	341	11.6	22.5
35–9	353	64	18.1	20.0	15.3	2,607	302	11.6	25.0
40–4	289	52	18.0	20.0	17.0	2,305	269	11.7	27.5
45–9	237	40	16.9	25.0	19.1	2,036	187	9.2	35.0
50–4	197	51	26.0	20.0	21.9	1,849	203	11.0	37.5
55–9	146	36	24.7	25.0	25.3	1,646	194	11.8	42.5
60–4	110	33	30.0	25.0	26.0	1,452	244	16.8	40.0
65–9	77	18	23.4	47.5	38.0	1,208	199	16.5	55.0
70+	59					1,009			
(100+)	(4)					(140)			

nearly corresponds in the UN tables to the figure given in column *d*. Thus, mortality at ages 1–4 in the city of Rome corresponds to an expectation of life of 30 years at birth, but at ages 5–9 to an expectation of grotesquely less than 20. The whole improbable pattern of the Roman data can be seen in figures 3.2 and 3.3.

Both the tables and the graphs highlight the unreliability of the Roman tombstones as a basis for the estimate of Roman mortality. It is inconceivable that the *pattern* of Roman mortality should be so unlike that of all other known populations. And it is the *pattern* of recorded mortality that we should look at just as much as at the recorded *levels* of mortality. It is not much use taking, for example, the recorded levels of African male mortality at each age level separately. Separately, the levels in this area are at least demographically possible; as a pattern they are demographically inconceivable in a stationary population (see table 3.4, col. *e*). In the other three areas both the levels and the patterns are mostly impossible. By the same token, *pace* Durand, it is of no great use to take particular age groups as being least susceptible to bias.[18] For how and on what grounds can particular groups be chosen?

Burn's data show similar distortions when they are recast in this way, that is by taking the number of recorded deaths in each age group and expressing them as a percentage of survivors to the beginning of the age group. There is again an exception from Africa. His data from the garrison town of Lambaesis (n = 1,112) from the age of 15–49 fluctuate only between levels corresponding to an expectation of life at birth of 20 to 25. As I shall argue later on general grounds this presents no problem; moreover, the portion of my sample from the same town (n = 1,000) gave the distorted result found elsewhere. Nevertheless, it seemed a curious result, worth further examination. Figure 3.4 illustrates the explanation. An almost equal number of military personnel and civilians, each with equally improbable but opposite recorded demographic

[18] Durand 1959–60: 370.

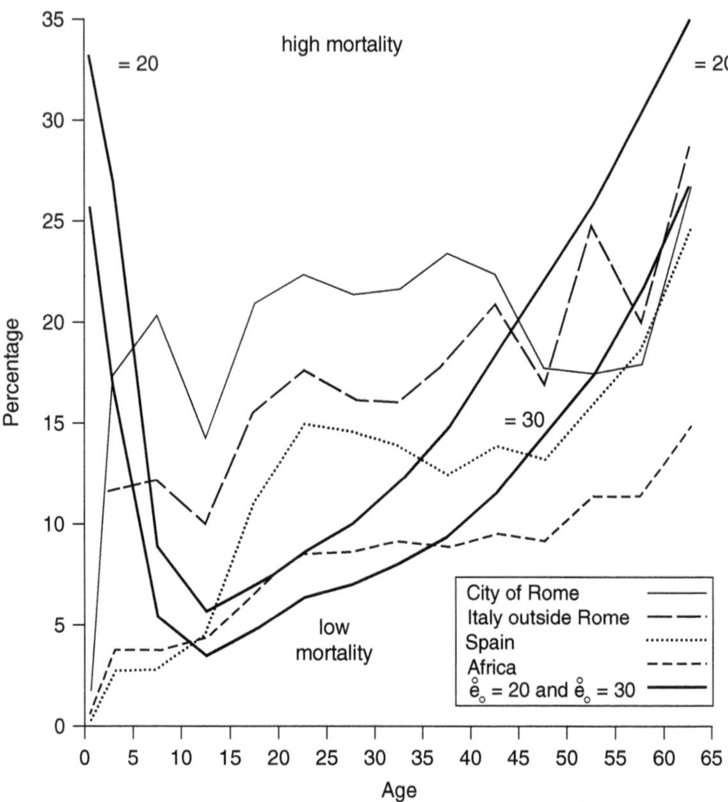

Figure 3.2. Graph showing males dying in successive age groups as percentage of those surviving to the beginning of that age group in two UN model life tables ($\mathring{e}_0$ = 20 and 36) and from inscriptions from four areas of the Roman empire.

characteristics, have been amalgamated to make an average, which on first sight appears reasonable.[19]

These mortality patterns present a problem: how did they arise? Part of the answer lies in the bias which comes from studying ages at death alone, and from ignoring what was inscribed on tombstones, other than the age at death. For

[19] Burn's data from Roman Britain give for all age groups over 15 a life expectation of below 20. His North African data give a range of expectation of life at birth from 40 at 10–14 to less than 20 at ages 15–24, and then again up to 47.5 at age 60–4. See fig. 3.4 [p. 124], the graph is based on the data from Burn 1953 in table 3.6 [p. 125].

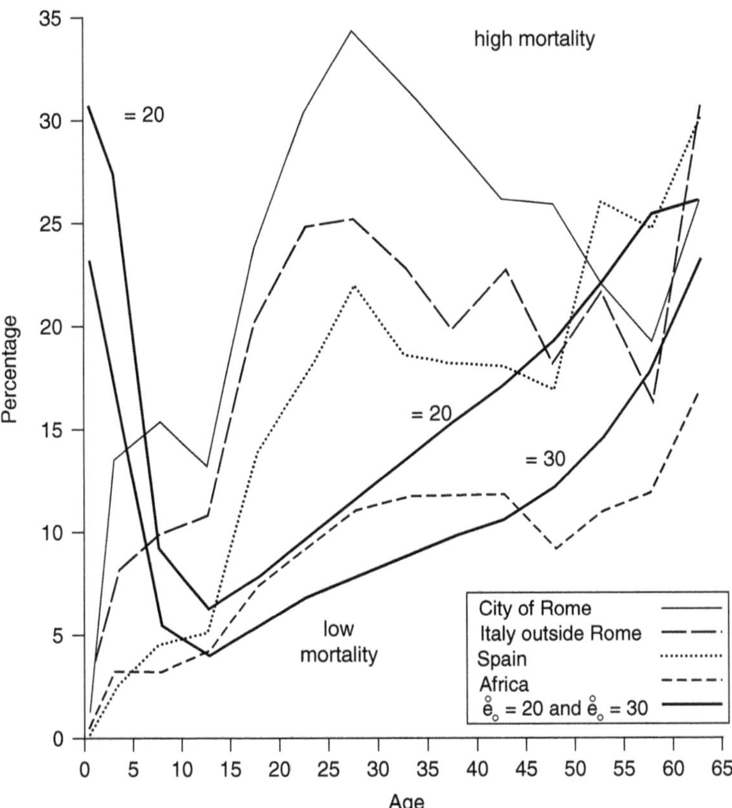

Figure 3.3. Graph showing females dying in successive age groups as percentage of those surviving to the beginning of that age group in two UN model life tables ($\mathring{e}_0$ = 20 and 30) and from inscriptions from four areas of the Roman empire.

some epitaphs give just the age at death, others name relationships as well as ages at death, others name relationships only, and still others set up to spouses give the length of marriage, occasionally with an age at death but more frequently without. In order to study the implications of these commemorative habits, I took a sample of 7,000 inscriptions, 2,000 from the city of Rome, 2,000 from Italian towns, 2,000 from African towns and 1,000 from the African garrison town of Lambaesis. In addition, I have used some of the results of my

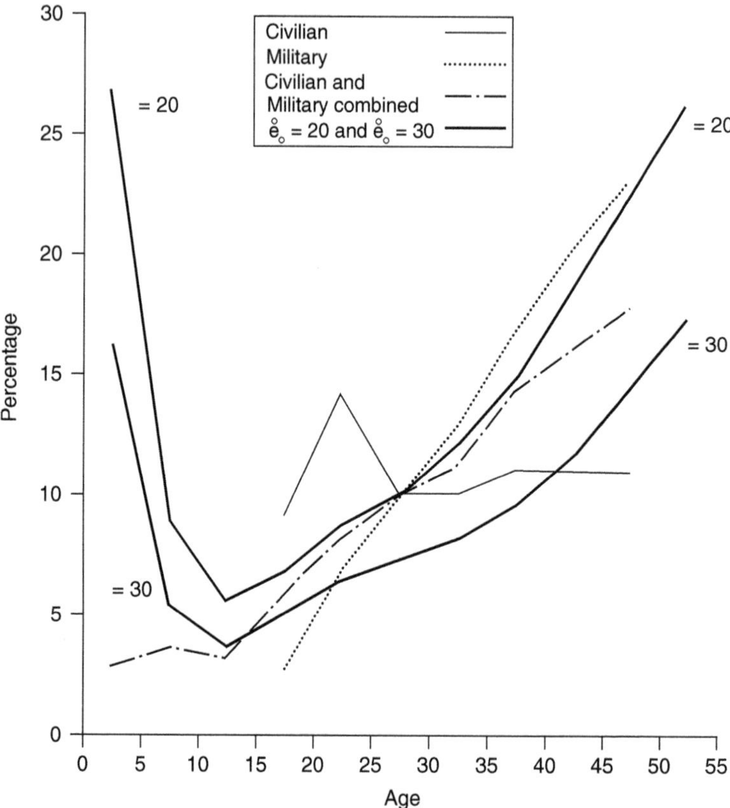

Figure 3.4. Graph showing males dying in successive age groups (1–55) as a percentage of those surviving to the beginning of each age group in two UN model life tables ($\mathring{e}_0$ = 20 and 30) and in a civilian and military population in Roman North Africa, considered separately and together, based on Burn's data.

previous research on inscriptions from the city of Rome (*CIL* VI 1–30,000), which was undertaken for a different purpose.[20] Once fragmentary and honorary inscriptions and those set up to the living and those giving neither age nor relationship

[20] Hopkins 1964–5. The present sample of 7,000 inscriptions was made up of *CIL* VI 20001–22000; IX 1538–2044; X 2001–400; XI 1601–700, 2101–593, 4191–340, 4361–560, 4847–996; VIII 301–500, 11551–650 ⟨Amaedra⟩; 1901–2200, 16551–750 ⟨Thevestae⟩; 27851–28050 ⟨Cirta⟩; 7175–412, 12591–790, 13216–375 ⟨Carthage⟩; and Lambaesis: *CIL* VIII 3293–4180, 18281–392.

Table 3.6. *Tabulation of data for figure 3.4 from UN model life tables and from Burn 1953 for a civilian and military population in Roman North Africa.*

	$\mathring{e}_0=20$	$\mathring{e}_0=30$	Civilian	Military	Civilian and Military		$\mathring{e}_0=20$	$\mathring{e}_0=30$	Civilian	Military	Civilian and Military
1–4	26.8	16.4	–	–	2.8	30–4	12.0	8.0	10.0	12.6	11.2
5–9	8.9	5.3	–	–	3.6	35–9	14.7	9.4	11.0	16.7	14.3
10–14	5.6	3.5	–	–	3.2	40–4	18.4	11.5	11.0	20.0	16.0
15–19	6.8	4.8	9.2	2.7	5.8	45–9	22.4	14.2	10.8	22.9	17.6
20–4	8.6	6.4	14.3	6.8	8.3	50–4	26.0	17.2	–	–	–
25–9	10.0	7.1	10.0	9.9	9.9						

⟨Note: e_0 is the *curate* life expectancy for a person at birth; technically different from $\mathring{e}_0$ the *complete* life expectancy. This is a distinction of interest principally to actuaries (since few people die precisely on their birthday). Aside from these early papers on demography, H. was usually content with e_0 as a convenient shorthand for life expectancy at birth.⟩

Source: Burn 1953.

Table 3.7. *Numbers of inscriptions giving age and relationships (sample of 7,000 inscriptions).*

Inscriptions excluded		Inscriptions remaining			
	No. of inscriptions		No. of inscriptions		No. of inscriptions
Fragmentary	2,094	Age at death only	1,176	Age	2,919
Honorary and *inter vivos*	361	Age and relationship	1,743	Relationship	2,985
Giving neither age nor relationship	384	Relationship only	1,242		
	2,839		4,161		

Table 3.8. *Numbers of ages and relationships recorded, by types of relationships.*

Relations commemorated	No. of named relationships	No. of ages at death and relationship	No. of relationships only
Spouses	1,172	604	568
Children	782	612	170
Parents	556	301	255
Siblings	233	143	90
Others	527	209	318
	3,270*	1,869	1,401

* These numbers do not match the number of inscriptions given in table 3.7 because some inscriptions name more than one relationship.

(just the name) have all been excluded, the remaining inscriptions can be further analysed along the lines already set out (see tables 3.7 and 3.8).

I cannot embark at this stage on a detailed analysis of the results of this enquiry into ages at death and relationships recorded on inscriptions. There are considerable regional variations in commemoration, which complicate exposition and are difficult to explain. In Rome and Italy there is a greater tendency to name a relationship than to record the age at death, and noticeably fewer parents are commemorated. This difference does not justify Burn's exclusion of Roman and Italian data from his calculations, nor his complementary reliance on African data on the grounds of their fullness. The African data give age and relationship more often, but are the deaths representative of the population? Two examples of bias, which arise from the habits of commemoration, must suffice.

The Length of Marriage

In the sample a large number of inscriptions were set up by spouses. It was common to record the death of a spouse and not to give his or her age at death. In the city of Rome and in Italy (but very rarely in Africa) some inscriptions gave the length of marriage, usually in place of the age at death. But such inscriptions have been neglected in calculations of the average age at death; how serious this is can be judged from the following data. In the sample, 85 Roman and Italian inscriptions gave the length of marriage, of which only 21 gave the age at death as well; these should be set against the 199 Roman and Italian inscriptions recording a spouse's age at death. On the basis of previous research we can say that over 50 per cent of Roman girls of the *respectable classes* would have married by the age of 15. In the sample, median age at death of Roman women surviving to 15 is 25; the median and average ages at death of Roman wives are 27 and 29.6 (n = 82). Thus, on the basis of this evidence, the median and average length of married life in the city of Rome were roughly between 10 and 14.6 years. But the average length of marriage where the marriage was broken by the death of the wife, in the city of Rome was 26 (n = 27).[21] It seems clear that length of marriage was recorded if it was something to be proud of. But neither set of inscriptions taken by itself can serve as a representative basis for the calculation of life expectancy; nor can one feel particularly optimistic about an amalgamation of the two (which in this case would add more than two years to the wives' average age at death) unless more is known about the habits of commemoration.

The Imputed Early Death of Women

A second probable error may be found in the recorded sex ratio of those commemorated and in the relatively high mortality of young women, which is universally imputed by modern scholars.

We know that in most populations the sex ratio at birth is between 102 and 106 males per 100 females. In populations with a high mortality this sex difference is likely to be much diminished

[21] Similar findings based on a much larger number of inscriptions are analysed in Hopkins 1964–5: 322–3. There the average age at death of Roman wives was 29.8 (n = 379) and the average length of marriage 22.8 years (n = 259).

Table 3.9. *Recorded sex ratio (men per 100 women) at death, by age.*

(*n* = 11,924 m.; 8,834 f.)			
Years	Ratio	Years	Ratio
0–4	159	45–59	157
5–14	144	60–99	173
15–29	104	100+	129
30–44	123	all ages	135

Based on data in Macdonell 1913.

or to have disappeared by the end of the first year (provided there is no extensive practice of female infanticide or relative neglect of female children). In the inscriptions of the Roman empire which give age at death, the sex ratio is 135 males per 100 females (table 3.9). No one has argued seriously that such a ratio actually existed; for how could the age-specific fluctuations be explained? The sex ratio can be rejected as impossible and can be satisfactorily explained by the relatively low social estimation of females among those who set up tombstones.

But there are difficulties, for, as Burn noted, the numbers of female deaths in different age groups vary widely. He saw that relatively more women died in the reproductive ages and that wives were commemorated more often than husbands. He used this and comparative evidence to bolster his argument that women in the Roman empire died earlier than men. He explained this high mortality, in an amusing but unconvincing passage, by referring to the dangers of (a) early marriage and (b) childbirth, (c) overwork: 'primitive mankind has always essayed … to combine in one organism the functions of the milch-cow and the draught-ox'.[22] These last remarks may well apply to many women in peasant societies, but are unlikely to be true of the relatively well-to-do women who were commemorated on tombstones.

But did women die sooner than men, or rather, how far can we deduce this from the inscriptions? To be sure, relatively more women were commemorated at the ages of 15–29 than

[22] Burn 1953: 12, citing Burns 1942: 186.

before or after (see table 3.9), but is this solely a function of their increased mortality? Just as the low proportion of females commemorated at early ages is assumed to be a matter of their social standing, not of their low mortality, it may also be possible to explain the increased commemoration of women by their heightened social estimation, for at this age (15–29) they would be wives as well as daughters; their deaths could be commemorated by husbands as well as by parents. The lowering of the sex ratio may then be a function of increased social importance as well as of increased mortality.

I am not, of course, denying that relatively more women die during the reproductive period than immediately before it. Yet, the rate of deaths in childbirth or in the reproductive period in general should not be overestimated. The figures from the Roman empire for the age group 15–29 compared with the previous age group (10–14) show a decrease of over 20 per cent in the sex ratio at death (men per 100 women), whereas at these ages according to the UN model life tables, a population with very high mortality shows, if anything, a slight increase in the sex ratio at death. It looks as though we shall find the major explanation of this increased commemoration in social custom rather than in mortality.

This argument will have more force if we can discover some validating measurement. As we have seen, the ages of women at death were in general recorded much less often than men – 135 men per 100 women. Daughters were commemorated by their parents even less often, at the rate of 149 sons:100 daughters (age + relationship 157:100). Wives, on the other hand, were commemorated by husbands at the rate of only 63 husbands:100 wives (age + relationship 56:100).[23] This is, I think, surprising – the change is too drastic to be explained by a rise in mortality. It is too drastic to be explained by a rise in the status of women. Both probably contributed, but it is impossible to claim that wives were more highly regarded than husbands.

A possible explanation is as follows: tombstones giving the age at death of women have previously been regarded as the

[23] Based on my sample of 7,000.

index of female mortality. This is obviously true, but it is only half the truth. For tombstones are a function not only of the mortality of the commemorated, but also of the survival of the commemorator. A wife will be commemorated by her husband only if her husband is still alive to commemorate her. Therefore, one could reasonably expect that disproportionately more tombstones would commemorate the deaths of wives who died young enough to be survived by their husbands. Moreover, husbands were typically nine years older than their wives and would therefore tend to predecease them.[24] At successive ages, therefore, there would be fewer and fewer husbands alive to commemorate the deaths of their wives. Wives who died young had a greater chance of being commemorated. This would explain the very steep rise in the sex ratio of commemorations at ages 15–29, but it also has this corollary: the recorded mortality of Roman wives is not a good index of female mortality. It is far too dependent upon custom and the availability of a commemorator.

Some corroborative evidence for this general assertion can be found in Henry's analysis of a graveyard in France, dating from 1833 to 1834.[25] The mortality given by these tombstones can be measured against general mortality known from other records (official death registers) for 1831–5 which are more likely to be accurate. He found a serious under-representation of deaths under 15; in the graveyard they accounted for under 10 per cent of all deaths; in the population over 40 per cent. Among adults he found an exaggeration of deaths among young women by over 50 per cent between the ages of 15 and 34; and an exaggeration of male deaths between ages 35 and 75 by 15 per cent. Here, too, the cultural patterns of commemoration have led to a serious bias.

I have argued that customs of commemoration are an important and hitherto underestimated source of bias in our surviving records of ages at death. First, a considerable body of commemorators recorded the length of their marriage, rather than the age of their spouses' death; secondly, women in

[24] So Hopkins 1964–5: 325.
[25] Henry 1959.

general were under-enumerated, especially daughters. Wives, on the other hand, especially at ages 15–29, were more frequently recorded than their husbands. First, their deathrate increases at these ages, but this factor has been overestimated; in any case it certainly would not account for the rise in commemoration shown by the inscriptions (see figure 3.3). But chiefly, I suggested that the cause of this apparent rise in the mortality of wives was the relative availability of live husbands to commemorate their wives, if wives died young.

If wives died later there was less chance of their being commemorated and of having their ages recorded. For, from the sample, in the city of Rome and in Italy 225 parents were commemorated, but the ages of only 34 were given. Habits were different in Africa; there 331 parents were commemorated, 267 with their ages. This could account for the somewhat more even pattern of deaths in Africa, but caution is required against assuming that parents so commemorated are representative. In Africa the median age of mothers was 60, but of fathers 75. This seems too old to be true.

In general, the pattern of male deaths fluctuates less than that of women. This can be partly explained by two factors. First, sons were commemorated by their parents, both more frequently and until much later ages than daughters, a joint reflection of their later age at marriage and their continued importance in 'patrilineal' families.[26] Secondly, husbands were typically older than wives and therefore tended to predecease their wives at later ages. Wives commemorated husbands at much later ages than husbands commemorated wives. In the sample the median age of death of all wives was 34; of husbands, 46.5.

It is thus apparent that data derived from inscriptions contain elements which are mutually inconsistent, improbable and just plain wrong. Some of these we can allow for or even correct within fairly narrow limits (e.g. the sex ratio); but other factors, age-specific mortality, for example, are irremediably obfuscated by the patterns of commemoration. Unfortunately, therefore, my main conclusion is that ancient inscriptions cannot be used as

[26] Hopkins 1964–5: 324 fig. 2.

the basis for calculations of mortality, absolutely or even relatively. For we cannot tell how much the longevity recorded in African inscriptions is the product of commemoration or of actual longevity.

Yet this does not mean that there is nothing we can say about ancient mortality. Our rejection of the recorded sex ratio, or of the recorded infant mortality, was based explicitly on an external comparative standard, summarised conveniently in the UN model life tables. We rejected the pattern of mortality derived from Roman tombstones on the grounds that it was unlike that of any known population; conversely, we argued that the Roman population is likely to have conformed to known demographic patterns. On the assumption of a stationary population, the expectation of life at birth must have been above 20, because otherwise the difficulties of self-replacement are too great. Life expectancy at birth was also probably under 30, with infant mortality above 200 per 1,000; for this has been generally true of pre-industrial populations and correlates with the predominance of agriculture, low average income and scarcity of doctors and of useful medical knowledge, which together distinguish the Roman empire and other pre-industrial societies from modern industrial societies.[27] This upper limit of life expectation is, however, tentative, in the sense that the determinants of the demographic revolution in Western Europe are even now only dimly understood.[28] Nevertheless it seems to me that the burden of proof is firmly on those who wish to assert that the Roman population in general had a lower mortality than other pre-industrial populations with similar technical achievements or towns; they must show that there were present in the Roman empire factors which could have led to a general diminution of mortality.

In the absence of any such significant factors, it seems reasonable to hypothesise on these general grounds that the Roman population probably had an expectation of life at birth of 20 to 30 years. But by the same token that we rejected the

[27] United Nations 1953: 49.
[28] Cf. Glass 1965.

evidence of the inscriptions, we cannot use them now as corroboration. For if we rejected evidence which does not conform to the hypothesis on the ground that it does not conform (e.g. the under-representation of infant mortality), we cannot usefully accept evidence which confirms the hypothesis merely because it confirms it. For example, we cannot accept the evidence of Africa on the sole ground that it yields levels of mortality at particular ages similar to those we have hypothesised, but reject the evidence of the city of Rome because it is different. We have to show instead some other grounds for its validity; for example, that in Africa all people who died were commemorated, hence the reasonable demographic levels of mortality at certain ages. But clearly we do not have enough evidence for such an assertion.

The most important aspect of this argument is that the 'truth' of the inscriptional evidence is 'tested' by reference to the external standard of the UN model life tables.[29] Our attention therefore should no longer be directed to different aspects of inscriptions,[30] but rather to a more general assessment of the applicability of these model life tables and to an analysis of the determinants of mortality, both in Rome in particular, and in general. To do this more accurately and sensitively we need life tables based on the total range of existing historical material and the critical construction of theories explaining population growth.[31]

[29] The same should be done with Ulpian's 'Life Table' cited in *Dig.* 35.2.68.*pr.* (Aemilius Macer). Beloch 1886: 44 thought it empirically based, and others have followed him in this, noting differences between Ulpian's table and their findings or modern data, but never analysing the significance of the differences. In fact, Ulpian's table is neither empirically based – how could it be? – nor is it demographically possible. M. Greenwood's critique (1940) was already sufficient; he saw Ulpian's life values as intelligent interpolations between the legal maximum value of any usufruct (30 years) and the practice by which valuation had been nil at age 60.

[30] There does exist a quite different source of evidence, based on tax census data of living persons from Egypt (c. AD 34–258; $n = 503$). The major outlines are clear and demographically possible; combining both sexes, the age groups 10–29, 30–49 and 50+ fit the UN model life table at $e_0 = 27.5$. Cf. Hombert and Préaux 1952: 40–1, 159–60.

[31] I should like to thank Dr M. I. Finley, Professor D. V. Glass, Mr J. Hajnal and Professor A. H. M. Jones for their advice and help. I am also grateful to my research assistant Mrs C. J. Rowe for her careful work on the sample and to the Social Research Division of the London School of Economics for financial support.

4

GRAVEYARDS FOR HISTORIANS*

In this paper, I shall be pessimistic, even gloomy. My raw material is the 180,000 epitaphs chiselled on tombstones surviving from the western half of the Roman empire. The texts of these epitaphs have been carefully reproduced over the last century, mostly in the massive volumes of the *Corpus of Latin Inscriptions*. These tombstones record some 43,000 ages at death.[1]

My problem is simple. Can the ages at death, recorded on Roman tombstones, be used fruitfully as a sound basis for calculating the ages at death of Roman men, women and children in different periods and in different regions of the Roman empire?

If the answer is yes, then we can turn the pages of demographic history back several centuries to Roman times. If the answer is no, and if the evidence from Roman tombstones is demographically unreliable, then many scholars have wasted much of their own and of their readers' time.

* * *

Unfortunately, the answer to my question is no. The main reason can be simply stated: the ages at death recorded on Roman tombstones are a biased sample of all deaths, and the bias cannot, in my opinion, be corrected.

* First published in F. Hinard (ed.) *La mort, les morts et l'au-delà dans le monde romain. Actes du colloque de Caen, 20–22 novembre 1985*, Caen: Centre de publications de l'Université de Caen, 1987, 113–26 (= Hopkins 1987).

[1] The ages of death recorded on Roman tombstones are tabulated in immense detail by Szilágyi 1961, 1963b, 1965, 1967. The literature is very large. Listing it would not be helpful. See in particular the sceptical accounts by Éry 1969 and Hopkins 1966a [essay 3], which contains an earlier version of the arguments presented here. Two notable recent discussions are by Frier 1982 and Saller and Shaw 1984.

Some aspects of this uncorrectable bias are well enough known. First, urban bias. Tombstones have been found principally on urban sites. The rural population, who constituted the great mass of the inhabitants of the Roman empire, is therefore under-represented in surviving inscriptions. Secondly, class bias. Inscribed gravestones cost money, though not necessarily a lot of money; but in all the ceremonies and expenses surrounding death, inscribed tombstones were only one element in all the costs to be borne by the bereaved. By no means could everyone afford an inscribed tombstone. By no means was everyone thought to deserve an inscribed tombstone. Even among those decently buried, many were not commemorated by name. We know from archaeological excavations that the urban poor were often buried in simple clay wine jars, and even in common pits.[2] And so, the surviving inscribed tombstones significantly under-represent the poor. These biases are uncorrectable, but could be circumvented. We could limit our demographic conclusions to a predominantly urban, relatively prosperous but variegated social stratum, comprising those with sufficient funds and a desire to erect an inscribed tombstone.

The third bias, the bias of commemorative practice, is the most serious. Tombstone inscriptions were a by-product of family relationships. And some relatives were commemorated more often than others.[3] For example young sons were commemorated more often than young daughters, and wives were commemorated more often than husbands. In Italy, parents were often commemorated by their children, but without their ages at death. These biases in the sex ratios of the recorded dead, and in the decisions which commemorators made whether or not to report ages at death, cannot be corrected from Roman sources.

[2] See Lanciani 1888: 64–7; Calza 1940: 45 fig. 9; Hopkins 1983b: 205–11. Thorough archaeological excavations of Roman cemeteries often reveal decent individual burials with grave goods, but with only rare commemoration by name: see e.g. Capitanio 1974.

[3] Hopkins 1966a: 259 table 7 [essay 3: 127 table 3.8]; Saller and Shaw 1984: 147–55.

Finally, age bias. Some age groups, such as infants (under one year old) and young children are systematically under-represented in surviving Roman tombstone inscriptions. That has been frequently acknowledged.[4] But its implication has been under-exploited. We know that infant deaths were under-represented only because we know roughly what to expect. We set recorded age-specific patterns of death over against the age-specific patterns of death which we expect and then find that the recorded pattern of death is distorted. Put another way, the critical test of the acceptability of the demographic evidence from Roman tombstones lies in their compatibility with what we expect, i.e. with what we know about demographic patterns from other historically comparable societies. That is the logical implication of the phrase; 'infants are under-represented'. But more of that in a moment.

Altogether, Roman tombstone inscriptions do not provide us with a good random sample of ages at death. Instead, and this point seems worth stressing, Roman tombstones provide us with a biased set of commemorations. Commemorative practice is useful for analysing Roman commemorative practice; it may or may not also be useful for analysing the relative importance of relationships with the Roman family, or for testing the existence of the extended family at Rome.[5] But commemorative practice is, I maintain, useless for understanding Roman patterns of death.

The outline of my argument is now, I hope, clear. I reject the utility of ages at death recorded on Roman tombstones for analysing the ages of actual death on two main grounds First, irremediable bias; and secondly, the logic of procedure.

4 Burn 1953 has been influential. The sophisticated accounts by two distinguished demographers have not been given the weight they deserve: Durand 1959–60; Henry 1957. The discussion by Patlagean 1977: 95–101 is flawed by demographic ignorance and enthusiasm for the available testimony, as is Lassère 1977: 519–63.

5 Saller and Shaw 1984. Their conclusion that tombstone inscriptions provide no evidence for the Roman co-residential extended family is entirely convincing. But further arguments about the relationship between commemorative practice and the strength, weakness or absence of affective ties tread much more delicate ground. Simply because more husbands commemorated wives than wives commemorated husbands, for example, one could not deduce that husbands loved wives more than wives loved husbands.

If the test of the acceptability of Roman testimony is an external demographic standard, then given the extent of the irremediable bias, we might as well jettison the Roman testimony and simply apply the external demographic standard. Let me elaborate, illustrate and justify this heresy.

* * *

In general, all large pre-industrial societies have suffered high deathrates and have had high birthrates.[6] To be sure, in response to fluctuating harvest, famines and epidemic diseases, there have been considerable oscillations and variations both over time and in different localities within each large society. Even so, oscillations by themselves do not defeat generalisation; conceptually, at least, it is easy enough to envisage an average line drawn through a series of short-term oscillations. Our problem, for the Roman world, is to know or to guess where that line should be drawn.

In general and in the long run, large pre-industrial populations have an average expectation of life at birth of between 20 and 40 years. This is not a law, but it is a regularity observed in societies for which we have good demographic evidence. An average expectation of life at birth of less than 20 years poses considerable problems of reproduction. An average expectation of life at birth of more than 40 years is difficult to achieve without significant advances in the practice of medicine and in average standards of living. This limit was consistently exceeded in England, France, the USA, Holland and Scandinavia only in the nineteenth century. The average expectation of life at birth in Italy and Spain in the eighteenth century was still only about 27 years.[7] I therefore surmise that average expectation of life at birth in the Roman empire as a whole was in the bottom half of our range of expectations, namely 20 to 30 years.

6 This is now the conventional wisdom. See e.g. Heer 1975: 11.

7 Wrigley 1969: 171; Wrigley and Schofield 1981: 230. For eighteenth-century Italy, see Del Panta and Livi Bacci 1980: 105; for eighteenth-century Spain, see Livi Bacci 1968: 88–93.

The convention of expressing patterns of death summarily in terms of an average expectation of life at birth may be misleading. The problem is that mortality in all pre-industrial populations is highest amongst infants and small children. Therefore, the average expectation of life for those who survive the first year of life is significantly higher than for newborn babies. For example, in a population with an average expectation of life at birth of 24 years, average life expectation at age one year is a further 34 years. At the same level of mortality, life for males aged 20 years is a further 29 years.[8] And then, as adults get older, the chances of dying increase; for example, again in a population with an average expectation of life at birth of 24 years, only 14 per cent of 40-year-olds would die within the next five years; this proportion rises to 20 per cent for 50-year-olds and to 31 per cent for 60-year-olds.

These figures are derived from model life tables, which are mathematical extrapolations, derived from all available historical and modern populations with good demographic statistics.[9] The model life tables provide figures to several decimal places, but it is important not to be overimpressed by what is for Roman historians spurious accuracy. The model life tables are the best demographic tools we have, but they can provide only rough orders of magnitude, or broad bands of probability, within which Roman demographic experience probably fell. They also provide a benchmark by which we can measure the trustworthiness of the testimony derived from Roman tombstones.

The model life tables show that, although deathrates varied considerably by place and period, the pattern of age-specific

[8] Coale and Demeny 1983: 43.

[9] The most recently developed model life tables allow one to see the demographic impact of steady growth and steady decline; they also envisage different paths of age-specific mortality within broad bands of probability. But such sophistication is of little use to Roman historians, except to remind them of diverse probabilities, since we cannot be sure whether or how much population growth/decline occurred in the Roman empire, let alone which pattern of age-specific mortality (labelled seductively North, South, East and West by Coale) applied. For our purposes, therefore, any one well constructed model of a stationary population is as probable as another. For variations, see United Nations 1956: 74–5; Ledermann 1969; Coale and Demeny 1983.

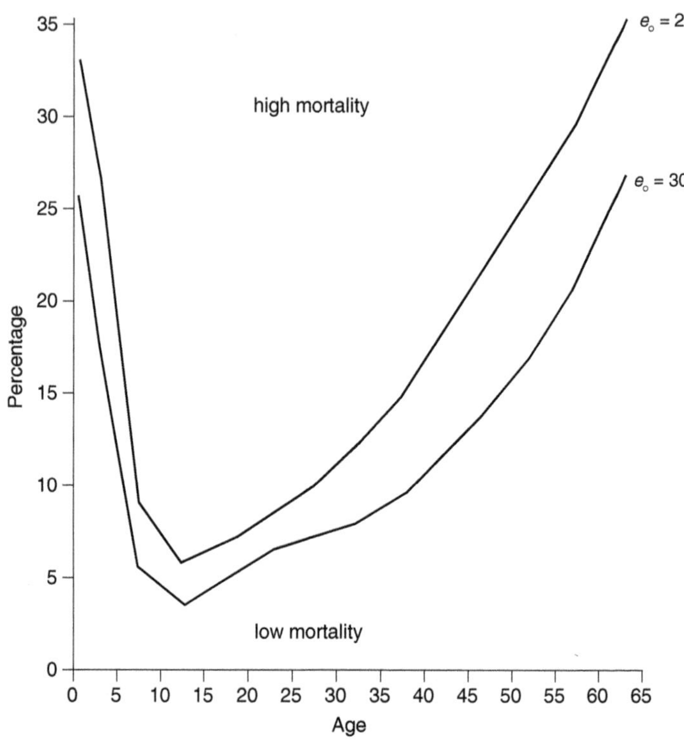

Figure 4.1. The pattern of deaths in large pre-industrial populations.

deathrates is similar in shape in all pre-industrial populations. Mortality is highest among infants and children, lowest among youths, and then steadily increases amongst ageing adults. This pattern of deaths in large pre-industrial populations is set out in figure 4.1. Put crudely it is like the letter V. But the ages of death recorded on Roman tombstones are quite different, and sometimes even form a pattern shaped like an inverted letter V (see especially figure 4.3*). These demographically improbable patterns, unlike those found in any human population, are the product of the biases in recording ages at death on Roman tombstones, which I have already summarised.

* ⟨Fig. 4.3 = Hopkins 1966a: 257 fig. 3 [essay 3: 123 fig. 3.3].⟩

There is a complication. The deaths recorded on Roman tombstones yield average ages at death (that is an average expectation of life at birth), which at first sight may seem reasonable. If we ignore the *pattern* of deaths, the average derived from a V-shaped curve is similar to an average derived from a curve shaped like a V upside-down; some averages thereby achieve a specious plausibility. I have listed some of these findings in table 4.1. The average expectation of life at birth worked out from tombstones found in the city of Rome was 24 years for males and 21 years for women. In Italy outside Rome, the average was 29 years for males and 25 years for females. The average rises in the provinces, and is highest of all in North Africa, where it reaches 49 years for males and 47 years for females. The sex ratios (males per 100 females) throughout table 4.1 seem improbable.

This mass of testimony has proved irresistible. The consistently lower recorded average expectation of life for females has been used as indicative of women's underprivileged status in antiquity, and of their frequent death in childbirth. The adverse sex ratio has been used as confirmation of female infanticide.[10] The low expectation of life recorded for the city of Rome has been taken as an index of appalling sanitary conditions in the metropolis; the interprovincial comparisons have seduced nationalistically minded historians, while the high recorded average expectation of life in Africa bears out the opinion of Sallust, who described North Africans as 'a healthy breed of men ... many die in old age, unless killed by the sword or wild beasts; disease rarely kills anyone' (*Jugurthan War* 17.6).

But can we really believe that populations reproduced themselves in ancient conditions of mortality with a sex ratio of 150

[10] E.g. Burn 1953: 10–13; Lassère 1977: 560–2; so also Kajanto 1968, in spite of his scepticism about the utility of African tombstones for estimating life expectancy; cf. Hombert and Préaux 1952: 156, 160. But recent research in France and England suggests strongly that maternal deaths in childbirth in pre-industrial societies may have been grossly exaggerated. Maternal deaths in and immediately after parturition totalled only about 1 per cent per birth in eighteenth-century England, France and Sweden; see Gutierrez and Houdaille 1983; Schofield 1986.

Table 4.1. *Average recorded ages at death from Roman tombstones (western provinces).**

	Average recorded age at death		Sex ratio m.:f.100	Number of cases
	Males	Females		
	(years)			
City of Rome	24.0	20.8	151	9,980
Italy (outside Rome)	28.7	25.2	159	5,960
Gaul	30.7	26.9	147	1,204
Germany	33.3	29.4	475	546
Britain	34.6	27.9	220	221
Danubian provinces	35.7	31.0	170	4,074
Spain/Portugal	38.8	34.3	129	2,388
North Africa	48.7	46.6	136	18,056
Total			148	42,429

* These figures were calculated from the tables published by Szilágyi 1961: 128–42; 1963b: 131–78; 1965: 309–21; 1967: 25–31.

males for every 100 females, or that life expectancy in Roman North Africa was twice that in the city of Rome, and higher for both men and women than it was in north-west Europe and the USA in 1880? As before, I think that these figures reflect different tendencies in commemorative practice, not real differences in mortality.

At first sight, this argument may seem disappointing. In table 4.2, I present data on the recorded ages at death from the city of Rome over six centuries. They have never before been published in this form as a single series. Their implications are serious. They show unequivocally that as the Roman empire in the West fell, the mean recorded age at death consistently rose. Once again, tombstone commemorations present us with demographically ludicrous conclusions. To be sure, the number of cases which form the basis of this conclusion is slight. But that would be a minor problem, if the sample had been randomly drawn, and if the results made sense. The basic problem is that the results do not make sense. Put another way, the test of the acceptability of these statistics lies outside the statistics themselves. And in these circumstances, there seems no difficulty in thinking that the results can be explained away as the result of a change in commemorative practices.

* * *

In spite of all these difficulties, repeated attempts have been made in recent years either to use ages at death recorded on tombstones indiscriminately as fruitful demographic data or to rescue particular fragments from the general debris and to treat them as special and reliable. I thought it would be worthwhile to deal briefly with three arguments proposed by Frier in two recent and sophisticated articles.[11] Put summarily, he argued that the tombstone evidence on ages at death from Roman Africa was so full and unselective that it was at least in part reliable. He also argued that archaeological evidence of skeletons from cemeteries in Pannonia corroborated his other demographic conclusions and that further archaeological

[11] Frier 1982, 1983.

Table 4.2. *The average age at death in the city of Rome rose as the Roman empire fell.**

	Average age at death		Number of cases	
	Males	Females	Males	Females
	(years)	(years)		
First and second centuries AD	23.9	22.2	4,420	2,711
Third to sixth centuries AD (mostly pagan)	24.0	17.8	1,588	1,261
Fourth century (Christian)	29.1	24.3	172	170
Fifth century (Christian)	31.2	30.8	90	63
Sixth century (Christian)	39.1	34.4	54	30

* Based on data tabulated by Szilágyi 1963b: 131–2 and by Nordberg 1963: 39.

investigations of cemeteries would be demographically invaluable; and finally, he argued for the demographic plausibility of the provisions made by Roman lawyers in the early third century AD, in Ulpian's so-called Life Table (*Dig.* 35.2.68.*pr.*). This legal ruling involved calculating the total value of an annuity by reference to the beneficiary's current age. This problem arose, for example, when someone left a legacy to a friend in the form of say: 'let her be paid 123 denarii each year until her death'. In order to assess the tax liability of the dead person's estate the capital value of this legacy had to be calculated; in doing this, the friend's age, and by implication her life expectancy, was taken into account. Frier argued that the lawyers' calculation was demographically consonant with the evidence derived from both tombstone ages and excavated skeletons.

I am sceptical about all three arguments. Let me deal briefly first with the last argument about Ulpian's so-called Life Table, because it is both novel and extreme. At the beginning of the third century, Ulpian (or his advisers) revised the conventions by which the total value of an annuity was calculated for the purposes of tax on the dead person's estate. Previously, the maximum capital value of an annuity was reckoned to be thirty times the annual payment to the beneficiary, with some reductions made according to the beneficiary's age. Ulpian introduced a new scheme, in which the capital value of the annuity was reduced by a series of eight steps, from thirty times the annual payment when the beneficiary was aged 20 years, to five times the annual payment when the beneficiary was aged 60 years. The English statistician Greenwood thought that Ulpian was merely interpolating intermediate values crudely between the two extremes, reducing the capital value of the annuity according to the beneficiary's age.[12] After all, the Romans knew that young adults had a higher expectation of life than old adults. I agree with Greenwood. Frier smoothed the eight steps, and found that the resulting curve roughly coincided with a life table found in Mauritius in 1942–6. The novel element in Frier's argument is that he alleges

[12] Greenwood 1940; ⟨see too Hopkins 1966a: 264 n. 32 [essay 3: 134 n. 29]⟩.

sophisticated demographic consciousness among the Romans. Frier's hypothesis about Ulpian's Life Table presupposes that Ulpian (or his advisers) in some rough sense knew how many more years people typically had left to live at successive ages, and presupposes that they took this demographic knowledge rationally into account in creating a tax law. I myself cannot believe that. I see no sign that Romans thought analytically about population statistics. In my opinion, the coincidence of Ulpian's interpolations with a modern life table is both approximate and adventitious.

Secondly, my objections to the archaeological analysis of skeletons from Roman cemeteries for demographic purposes are similar to the objections which have already been made.[13] The ratio of hard work to intellectual reward is lamentably meagre. Perhaps that is the masochism of our profession. The problems of selective burial, of differential survival of bones by age and sex, and of measurement error in allocating ages to bones are well known. The result will always be on too small a scale relative to the knowledge, which we need about long periods, complete provinces or about the Roman empire as a whole. In the Roman empire, indeed in large provinces, death-rates fluctuated over long periods, oscillated considerably in short periods and varied widely by locality. Single cemeteries, even large ones, are therefore a poor basis for generalisation. And for all the modesty and specificity of their explicit presentation (for example, a cemetery containing 120 skeletons in Keszthely-Dobogó, Hungary, in the fourth century AD), the implications made or drawn are always about a much larger population or period, such as the fall of the Roman empire or the barbarian invasions. The acceptability of the archaeological results from cemeteries will be determined (as they are with tombstones) by demographic criteria, generated outside cemeteries, in other comparable historical societies with better

[13] For a contrary view, see in general Ubelaker 1978 and several papers in this collection (= Hinard 1987); see also Acsádi and Nemeskéri 1970: 215–34, which contains a brief section on the Roman empire, for a different intellectual tradition. Weiss 1973 develops techniques for creating model life tables for very small populations of excavated skeletons. Russell 1985 is indiscriminately enthusiastic.

demographic data. It is pious to say that more archaeological excavations of skeletons will be demographically useful. It is also unrealistic.

* * *

Finally, let us turn back now to ages at death recorded on tombstones. At first sight, the pattern of ages at death which emerges from Roman North African tombstones looks attractive. Figures 4.2 and 4.3 ⟨below [pp. 148–9][*]⟩ show that death-rates computed from Roman North African tombstones, among both men and women, were at realistic levels for a considerable range of ages: 10–39 for males, 10–44 for females. I have two objections.

The first is the familiar objection to the logic of procedure. Of course, it must seem churlish to reject apparently corroborative evidence. But on what grounds can we accept the tombstone evidence on recorded ages at death from Roman North Africa as reliable, simply because it yields a level of mortality similar to what we expected, if at the same time we reject tombstone evidence from elsewhere, because it yields unexpected levels of mortality and unexpected patterns of death? We can argue properly in this way only if we can isolate a reason for accepting the African tombstone data, and for rejecting the data from the city of Rome, which is other than the results which they yield.

My second objection to privileging tombstone data from Roman Africa depends upon some detailed investigation of the figures. It is not reassuring. For example, the number of old people commemorated is too large. The corpus of North African epitaphs comprises 636 alleged centenarians; and over one quarter (28 per cent) of all recorded deaths allegedly occurred over the ages of 70 years. Such longevity was first achieved in England, France and the USA in the early twentieth century as a result of unprecedented prosperity and medical care.[14]

* ⟨Fig. 4.2 = Hopkins 1966a: 256 fig. 2 [essay 3: 122 fig. 3.2]; fig. 4.3 = Hopkins 1966a: 257 fig. 3 [essay 3: 123 fig. 3.3].⟩

[14] Keyfitz and Flieger 1968: 142, 322, 528.

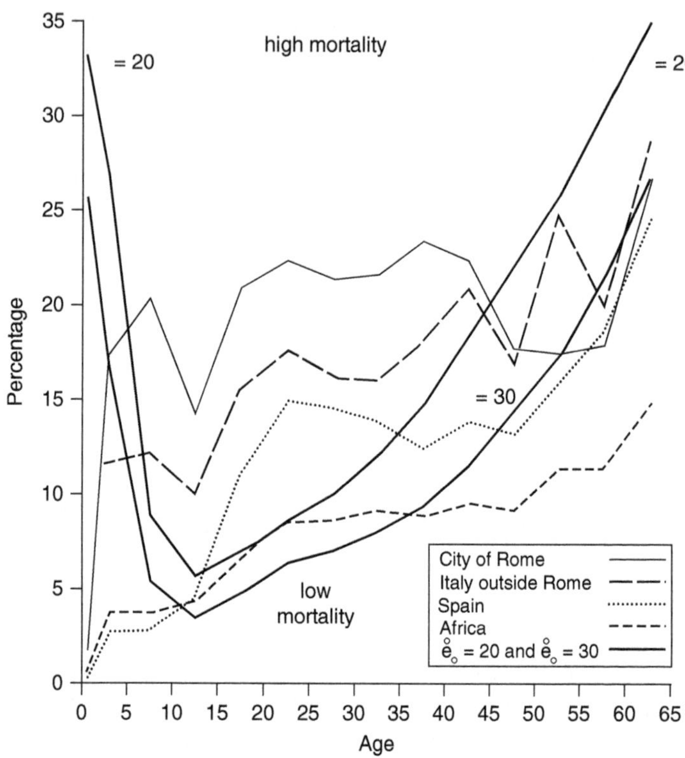

Figure 4.2. Graph showing males dying in successive age groups as percentage of those surviving to the beginning of that age group in two UN model life tables ($\mathring{e}_0$ = 20 and 36) and from inscriptions from four areas of the Roman empire.

It is absurd to assume that such a high proportion of North Africans lived so long in Roman times. To be sure, we can get round this exaggeration by taking the median instead of the average age of recorded deaths, just as we can get round the under-representation of infant deaths by considering only the life expectancy of adults.[15] But this massage of the data is only cosmetic; massaging slightly improves their looks without removing the basic flaws.

[15] Burn, 1953: 14 followed, for example, with some adaptations by Patlagean 1977: 95–6.

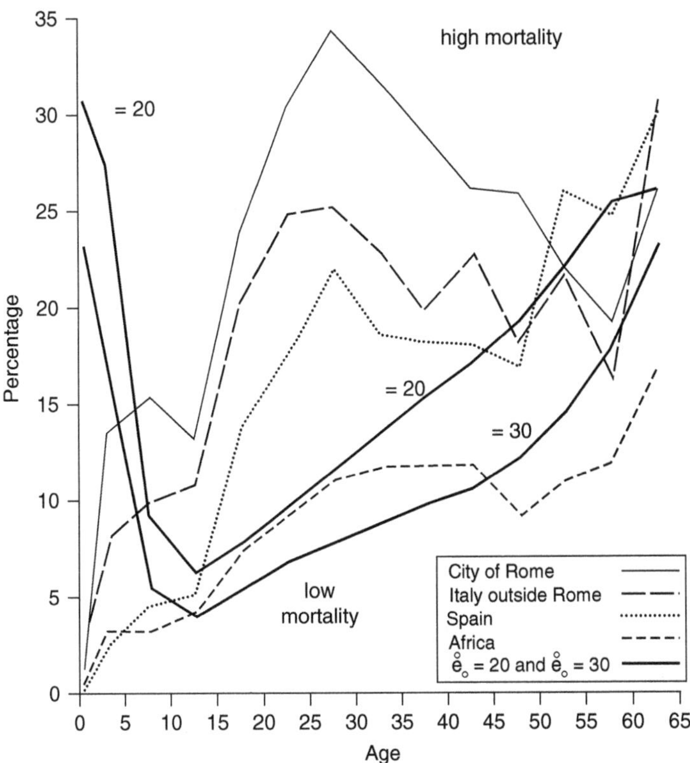

Figure 4.3. Graph showing females dying in successive age groups as percentage of those surviving to the beginning of that age group in two UN model life tables ($\mathring{e}_0$ = 20 and 30) and from inscriptions from four areas of the Roman empire.

Paradoxically, the plausible level of recorded ages at death derived from North African tombstones is an unintended by-product of the methods of measurement which I have used. The curves drawn in figures 4.1–4.3 are created by dividing the number of people dying in any one age interval by the total number of survivors to the beginning of the age interval, so those dying at age 40–4 are divided by all survivors to age 40. And so, a disproportionate number of old survivors brings the whole curve down to seemingly realistic levels. Our problem here is not only that Africans exaggerated their old

Table 4.3. *The old are over-represented in epitaphs from Roman Africa.**

Proportions dying aged	Tombstones		Model population	
	Males	Females	Males $e_0 = 23$	Females $e_0 = 25$
	%	%	%	%
10–39	36	40	39	39
40–59	22	21	34	28
60+	43	39	27	33

* Sources: cf. table 4.1 and Coale and Demeny 1983: 43.

people's age at death, but also that they disproportionately commemorated and gave tombstones to old people. Some illustrative figures comparing North African tombstones with a model population are set out in table 4.3: roughly speaking the tombstones commemorated a third more old people than we should have expected. If we turn our attention away from the level of mortality and look instead at the patterns of mortality, i.e. at the ratios of recorded deaths in one interval to the recorded deaths in the next interval, then we can see that the pattern of death recorded in Roman Africa, even in central age groups among youths and young adults, was very different from the pattern of death found in model populations. Under close scrutiny, the flaws in the data derived from African tombstones becomes easily visible.

Further examination of relationships between the commemorators and the recorded dead reveals further demographic flaws. Tombstone commemorations were the product of a relationship, usually of a close family relationship. Father, mother or both parents together commemorated the death of a child; husband or wife commemorated the death of a spouse; a child commemorated the death of a parent. Most distant relatives (grandparents/grandchildren, brothers/sisters) account for only a small minority of those inscriptions in which a relationship was recorded.[16] I cannot stress enough that we are dealing

[16] Saller and Shaw 1984: 134, 147–55.

with the statistics of commemoration and not with the statistics of mortality.

The role which a dead person occupied within his or her family strongly affected their chances of receiving a tombstone commemoration. We have already noted that overall males were commemorated more often than females. The sex ratio in North African tombstones is 136 males:100 females (see table 4.1). At this point, we face a difficulty. In the course of a lifetime, most men passed from being son to husband to father, and most women changed from being daughter to wife to mother. Some occupied all three roles at the same time. This amalgamation of roles makes it practically impossible for us to follow the previous tack of setting what we find against what we would expect. We do not know the probable proportion of fathers, husbands or sons whom we expect to find as either commemorators or commemorated.

Three related but inseparable factors probably influenced commemorative practice:

(a) the statistical frequency with which people died in the role of son, husband or father;
(b) the relative perceived importance of family roles;
(c) the capacity of survivors to set up inscribed memorials;
(d) social values, such as the perceived untimeliness of the death of children and of young wives, and the high evaluation of longevity.

We cannot study these factors separately, but we can glimpse their impact by considering commemorations of matched pairs of relatives: sons and daughters, husbands and wives, fathers and mothers.

The unequal ratios of commemoration within these matched pairs reinforce the conclusion that the recorded ages at death were biased by commemorative practice. Let us begin with sons and daughters. At early ages, sons were much more favoured than daughters. From age 0–9, the ratio in African inscriptions was 130 sons to 100 daughters (see table 4.4); but from age 10–14, perhaps because daughters were approaching marriageable age, the ratio changed to 89 sons:100 daughters. From ages 15–19, if we amalgamate sons with husbands, and more importantly daughters with young wives, the sex ratio is 77 males:100 females. Overall, wives were commemorated much more often than husbands; the ratio is 54 husbands:100 wives (see table 4.4). I suspect the reason is that wives dying young typically predeceased their older husbands and so had a greater chance of being commemorated than either young husbands who had only poor widows to remember them or young widows who died before their children were grown up enough to commemorate them. The number of fathers and mothers commemorated was roughly equal (99 fathers:100 mothers), but the median age at death of mothers was 60 years and the median age of fathers at death was 75 years. By that advanced age, parents had children who were old enough to command the resources necessary to commemorate a dead parent. Enough of detailed analysis. It is clear that tombstones tell us more about social and economic relationships within the family than about typical life expectancy.

The basic problem is an intellectual one. Roman historians, in this field as in others, have spent too much care and trouble on listing and on relisting the surviving evidence from

Table 4.4. *Matched pairs of commemorated relationships illustrate statistical bias in epitaphs from Roman Africa.**

Ages	Sons	Daughters
0–9	130	100
10–14	89	100
15–19	77**	100**
	Fathers	Mothers
	99***	100***
	Husbands	Wives
	54	100

* Reworked from a sample of 3,000 inscriptions, detailed in Hopkins 1966a: 259 n. 22 [essay 3: 124 n. 20].

** In this age group, husbands are included under sons and wives under daughters.

*** Median age: mothers 60 years; fathers 75 years.

tombstones, without thinking enough about the universe from which the testimony comes. The African evidence, for example, is never so good that we can confidently assert that Roman mortality over several centuries followed a particular line within the broad band of probability. All that work, all that labour of collection and tabulation, and the end result is a conclusion that Romans in North Africa for a limited segment of adult life experienced a level of mortality such as we find in other pre-industrial societies. Surely we could have made that assertion confidently enough without reading any tombstone inscriptions at all.[17]

[17] I should like to thank Dr Mary Beard and Mr Greg Woolf for critical advice.

AFTERWORD

ON THE PROBABLE AGE STRUCTURE OF THE ROMAN POPULATION

GRAVEYARDS FOR HISTORIANS

WALTER SCHEIDEL

In his classic piece of 1966 [essay 3], Keith Hopkins addresses a key problem of Roman history: life expectancy matters because it is a highly informative measure of human well-being.[1] How can we tell, in the famous Monty Python phrase, 'what have the Romans ever done for us?' (or rather, for themselves and their subjects) if we cannot measure the impact of Roman power on the human body and compare the Roman experience to that of other periods?[2] In the 1960s, this was clearly a desideratum, as Moses Finley was in the process of reviving the debate about the nature of ancient economies, just as it is today, as we witness growing interest in the causes, scale and consequences of Roman economic performance. Human well-being is also relevant for assessments of the character of empire, Roman and otherwise. Life expectancy and age structure are therefore issues of great significance far beyond the technical concerns of demographers. Yet H. did not simply seek to answer an empirical question: instead, his contribution focuses on the feasibility of exploring Roman population history – on the nature of the evidence itself. His studies are as much an exercise in applied epistemology as demographic analysis.

Inquiries into Roman age structure need not appear hopeless from the outset: if usable Chinese sources reach back two

[1] Next to GDP and literacy, longevity is one of the three principal components of the UN Human Development Index.

[2] For a survey of existing findings (and some pessimistic conclusions), see Scheidel 2012c.

millennia, why should the rich Roman record fail us?[3] By far the largest body of quantifiable data consists of ages at death reported on Roman funerary inscriptions, and had long been mined for demographic insights. H. showed that this effort was utterly futile. He was not the first to do so. Several years earlier, in the late 1950s, the French demographer Louis Henry and the American demographer John Durand had pioneered the use of model life tables in identifying demographically impossible patterns and striking commemorative biases in Roman epigraphic age records.[4] Nor was he to be the last.[5] H.'s own contribution lay in presenting a comprehensive analysis that was painstakingly crafted to leave no room for reasonable doubt. Employing model life tables as an external standard against which to evaluate the demographic implications of the epigraphic data, he affirmed and reinforced the emerging understanding of these data as a record of cultural preferences rather than of actual demographic conditions.[6]

For anyone who would listen, this study firmly shut the door to further attempts to derive Roman life expectancies or

3 Cf. Zhao 1997.

4 Henry 1957 had been the first to apply the then brand–new UN model life tables to a set of Roman epitaphs and argue for the over-representation of young women. In Henry 1959, he observed analogous bias in French tombstones from the early nineteenth century. Durand 1959–60 independently performed a more elaborate comparison of Roman data and model life tables; his tables 3 and 4 provided the template for tables 3.4 and 3.5 in essay 3. Durand likewise (at 368) ascribed the prominence of female deaths at certain ages at least in part to the efforts of surviving husbands. Repeated lack of formal acknowledgement in essay 3 obscures H.'s very considerable debt to the highly original contributions of Henry 1957 and Durand 1959–60.

5 Clauss 1973 offers a rich survey; see also Salmon 1987; Parkin 1992: 5–19. In a particularly striking illustration of commemorative bias, Éry 1969: 60 observes that recorded ages in Greek–language epitaphs in the city of Rome imply a mean life expectancy more than twice as high than those found on the capital's Latin tombstone inscriptions.

6 It is true that the predictive value of model life tables (which for very low levels of life expectancy are not directly grounded in historical statistics) should not be over-rated: see Scheidel 2001d: 3–11. In essay 4, H. upgraded from the UN model life tables of 1955–6, that had he used in essay 3, to the revised Coale and Demeny models of 1983, with similar results. The models more recently developed by Woods 2007 may be more suitable for high-mortality populations. However, the distortions of the epigraphically attested age patterns are so extreme that checks on their plausibility remain unaffected by the limitations of demographic model projections.

age distributions from epitaphs.[7] Yet although H. convinced most of his colleagues, demographic readings of Roman tombstones refused to die and, as many an implausibly resilient movie villain, kept staggering back, however battered and bloodied. Most of these flare-ups were simply born of blithe refusal to engage with the substance of H's argument and may safely be discarded without further discussion.[8] As H. himself acknowledged, the sole exception was Bruce Frier's technically sophisticated attempt in the early 1980s to salvage certain epigraphic age records for demographic analysis, an attempt which provoked the restatement of his own original argument [essay 4]. Frier noted that the distribution of ages at death for 5–45 or 55-year-olds in a large North African sample of Roman epitaphs corresponded to that found in Mauritius in the 1940s (chosen for its exceptionally low adult life expectancies) and was therefore at least 'demographically possible', a point reiterated on a later occasion – in no less authoritative a forum than the revised *Cambridge Ancient History* – by observing a match between Roman African records from ages 10–54 and a model life table associated with a mean life expectancy at birth of 22.5 years that made the former seem 'credible'.[9] This procedure, however, failed to come to terms with H.'s compelling methodological premise that 'we cannot accept the evidence of Africa on the sole ground that it yields levels of mortality at particular ages similar to [model predictions] ... we have to show instead some other grounds for its validity' (1966a: 264 [essay 3: 134]). In this case, not only are no such grounds apparent, but H. offered two separate but congruent reasons for rejecting this superficially appealing data-set.[10] Circuitous

[7] Cf. B. D. Shaw 1982: 24–8 for an earlier discussion of essay 3.

[8] There is no point listing them here. The resolutely curious may wish to consult Scheidel 2012a: 119 n. 86 for pertinent references.

[9] Frier 1982: 231, 235–8, 2000: 791–2.

[10] In 1966a [essay 3], a breakdown of the African material into civilian and military samples highlighted the improbable make–up of the overall data-set; but it was not until 1987 [essay 4] that H. recognised that massive epigraphic over-representation of the elderly depressed adult mortality levels to speciously plausible levels. See also Scheidel 2001b: 17–19.

'picking and choosing'[11] for the sake of making at least *some* data, somewhere, match demographic predictions remains a dead end.

But that is only part of the story. H.'s deconstruction has proved alarmingly corrosive well beyond the study of Latin epitaphs. Equivalent commemorative bias can be observed in funerary records from Roman Egypt.[12] A combination of ancient selective practices of interment and technical obstacles to the ageing of adult bones appears to account for comparably striking distortions of the overall age distribution of skeletons recovered from Roman cemeteries.[13] Reporting preferences likewise detract from the demographic value of a body of data that H. had at least initially judged more generously: those preserved in the census returns of Roman Egypt.[14] Ostensibly recording the demographic properties of an actual population, these census records have repeatedly been used to reconstruct the age structure of the residents of (mostly Middle) Egypt in the first three centuries AD.[15] This material is made to bear a lot of weight: the most ambitious study to date seeks to derive specific levels of life expectancy and even rates of population growth from the precise configuration of documented ages.[16] Yet closer inspection reveals that the census data suffer from some of the same problems that H. and others had identified in the epigraphic record. Reporting was selective: while urban residents commonly passed over female children, villagers habitually concealed teenagers as they approached an age threshold for tax liability. Twins are much more numerous than expected, a possible artefact of cultural preference. Implied sex ratios reflect the heightened appreciation for young adult women that is also visible in

[11] Parkin 1992: 166 n. 51.

[12] Boyaval 1976: 242–3.

[13] See Hopkins 1987: 121, 124 [essay 4: 146–7, 150–1], and, for example, Parkin 1992: 41–58 and the references in Scheidel 2001b: 19 n. 66.

[14] Hopkins 1966a: 264 n. 33 [essay 3: 134 n. 30]. Cf. also his later reliance on this evidence, coupled with the suspicion 'that there is something seriously wrong with the ages recorded' therein, in Hopkins 1980b, quoting 320.

[15] Hombert and Préaux 1952; Bagnall and Frier 1994.

[16] Bagnall and Frier 1994: 81–90.

Latin tombstone inscriptions.[17] Even if some of these distortions are more muted in these official documents than in private dedications, they are structurally similar. Shaped as they are by cultural practice, the Roman Egyptian census data can take us only halfway from H.'s minimalist position of using model life tables instead of ancient sources to the historian's goal of being able to replace the models with superior empirical data. Although the census records very broadly corroborate model projections in a way funerary inscriptions could never do, they are insufficiently reliable to supersede them or narrow our estimates of Roman life expectancy beyond the probabilistic range advocated by H.[18]

Going a step further, H.'s scepticism concerning the demographic value of epigraphic evidence may also be directed against his own work. In a prequel to his article on Roman age structure, he drew on the fairly small number of Roman epitaphs that mention both age at death and length of marriage to determine the typical age of first marriage of Roman women. Uncharacteristically electing to take the record at face value, he argued in favour of relatively early marriage concentrated between the ages of 12 and 15.[19] Two decades later, Brent Shaw's investigation of much larger epigraphic data-sets that inferred a significantly later modal marriage age from changes in the identity of commemorators (with husbands replacing parents as the commemorated entered marital unions) cast serious doubt on H.'s conclusion. Taking a leaf from H.'s own book, Shaw argued that the exact same habit of epigraphic over-representation of young women in Roman epitaphs that had been critical to H.'s rejection of demographic readings of age-at-death records also happened to skew epigraphic reports of length of marriage in favour of women who had married at unusually young ages, thereby undermining the representative character of this sample.[20] Yet

[17] See Scheidel 1996a, 2001c: 142–62, 2012a: 118.

[18] Thus, Scheidel 2001c: 172–80. If anything, H.'s range of 20 to 30 years (1966a: 264 [essay 3: 133]) may well be too restrictive: cf. Scheidel 2001d: 25–6.

[19] Hopkins 1964–5: 319–23.

[20] B. D. Shaw 1987: 32–6, especially at 35.

Shaw's and Richard Saller's innovative method of estimating typical marriage ages from age-specific commemorative shifts from parents to spouses is by no means immune to doubts about the representative nature of their own findings.[21] It is also increasingly doubtful whether Latin epitaphs are able to shed any light on Roman household structure.[22]

All this shows that H. put his finger on a defining characteristic of the evidence: seemingly 'neutral' records of life and death were so pervasively shaped by varied cultural preferences that we would be ill-advised to take them at face value.[23] Nearly half a century after H.'s opening salvo, the shockwaves keep expanding, shaking our confidence in the use of *any* Roman records for demographic purposes. The key lesson of his contributions – never to let our guard down – is as fresh and challenging as ever.

[21] For the method, see B. D. Shaw 1987; Saller 1987, 1994: 25–41. Whether, or to what extent, the late age of male first marriage conjectured with the help of this approach is representative of general Roman practice or merely of the urban environment that produced most of the epigraphic record remains an important question: see Scheidel 2007a, with reference (at 400–1) to delayed male marriage in late medieval Florence that did not occur in the surrounding countryside.

[22] Saller and Shaw 1984 argue for the centrality of the nuclear family in Roman society based on the predominance of funerary dedications within that unit (accepted and taken as relevant for our understanding of actual household composition by H. (1987: 115 n. 5 [essay 4: 137 n. 5]), an understanding shared by B. D. Shaw 1984). While such texts may well reflect the prevailing scope of affective ties, Huebner 2011 shows that in Roman Egypt, similarly narrow commemorative preferences (as documented on tombstones) coincided with a strong presence of extended and complex households (as attested in the census returns).

[23] Even the very foundations of H.'s own essay on brother–sister marriage in Roman Egypt (Hopkins 1980b), are now put in question by the intriguing – if highly controversial – thesis that such couples may not have been made up of biological siblings at all: thus Huebner 2007, rejected by Remijsen and Clarysse 2008; Rowlandson and Takahashi 2009.

5

ECONOMIC GROWTH AND TOWNS IN CLASSICAL ANTIQUITY*

Was there economic growth in classical antiquity? If we take the Bronze Age at the end of the second millennium BC as our base line, the answer is definitely yes. In the early Homeric world, weapons and sacrificial ornaments were usually made of bronze; iron was an object of treasure, and so it remained in north-western Europe until much later.[1] Greek myths of the world's evolution from the Age of Gold to the Ages of Silver, Bronze and finally Iron reflected real changes in the material base of culture. But by the beginning of the last millennium BC, the transition to iron as a cutting edge had begun; among Greek weapons found by archaeologists, the great majority were made of iron not bronze.[2] Over the next thousand years, the Athenians, Macedonians and Romans successively conquered empires with the cutting edge of iron swords and increased the productivity of land by tilling it with iron-shod ploughs. It was this increase in agricultural productivity which made the growth of towns possible.

But if we ask whether there was economic growth between Periclean Athens at the end of the fifth century BC and the age of the Antonines in the second century AD in the Roman empire, then the answer is more complicated. We take Periclean Athens as our base because it represented the peak of economic development in the classical city-state. Let us first exploit the

* First published in P. Abrams and E. A. Wrigley (eds) *Towns in Societies: Essays in Economic History and Historical Sociology*, Cambridge: Cambridge University Press, 1978, 35–77 (= Hopkins 1978a).

1 Archaeologists have found hoards of hundreds of iron bars in Britain (Tylecote 1962: 206–7). In Gaul, iron bars were used as currency, which suggests rarity (Caes. *B. Gall.* 5.12).

2 Snodgrass 1965: 231 found that of 88 surviving cutting weapons and knives from northern Greece datable to 1050–900 BC, 77 were made of iron and only 11 of bronze.

distinction between *aggregate* and *per capita* growth.[3] If we take the whole Mediterranean basin, or the Roman empire at its largest extent, as the area of our study, then the growth in aggregate produce is again beyond doubt. The gross product of the whole Roman empire significantly exceeded the gross product of the hundreds of tribes and city-states which existed in the same area in the fifth century BC. Settled agriculture, flourishing towns, impressive monuments, the whole panoply of classical culture and of archaeological evidence from North Africa to the north of Britain provide convincing demonstration that a sizeable surplus was being produced and consumed throughout the Roman empire and that the average standard of living was higher over a wider area than ever before. But if we compare *per capita* product in classical Athens with *per capita* product in any prosperous provincial town in the Roman empire, then the differences (which may have existed) are extremely difficult to trace.

Our overriding problem here is of course shortage of data; we know a huge amount about the ancient world, especially in the realm of ideas and culture, but rarely enough to give sophisticated answers to problems of economic history. The historian or social scientist who wants to trace economic developments back to an earlier age will find to his dismay either uncoordinated details of archaeological finds, fragments from historical sources or theories of economic growth retrospectively applied. The rest of this paper is devoted to a discussion of the role of towns in economic development. Inevitably it ranges beyond towns, because their contribution to economic change can be understood only in the context of the political system in which they existed, and of the rural hinterland on which they depended. I shall concentrate on the Roman empire, because that is what I know most about.

My first main point has already been implied: major changes in aggregate product in the Mediterranean basin in the centuries

3 My discussion at this point owes a lot to Gould 1972; I found Hicks 1969 provocative, though often wondered how far his model coincided with historical realities. Throughout this essay I am in repeated debt to, and continuous debate with, Finley 1973: especially 123–49.

close to the birth of Christ occurred as a result of the diffusion of productive techniques and of political organisation in the wake of conquest. Techniques of agricultural production and of manufacturing spread roughly along the axis south-east to north-west, that is from the Middle East to Greece to Italy and north-western Europe. Or put another way, changes in the size of the surplus were a function of changes in political organisation as well as of technical innovation. By innovation, I mean the adoption of techniques previously invented. Historians of technology, bedevilled by romantic notions of originality, have concentrated on inventions, on the problem of who discovered what first. In doing this, they have neglected the process of innovation and have underestimated the difficulty of getting inventions accepted and used over a wide area. But that is what matters for economic development. In this sense, classical antiquity was not a period of important inventions but of widespread innovations, spread by conquest.

Conquest by the Greeks, particularly under Alexander the Great, by the Carthaginians and finally by the Romans created larger and larger states. Indeed, one of the most striking changes in the Mediterranean basin during classical antiquity, that is from about 1000 BC to AD 400, was the growth in the size of political units. At the beginning of this period, in the world of Homer, warring Achaean chiefs formed an uneasy alliance in a piratical expedition to Troy. Egypt was the only kingdom of any size and consequence; Italy, Spain and north-western Europe were a mêlée of warring tribes with a low level of material culture.[4] By the end of the period, the Roman empire stretched from the north of England to the Red Sea and had a population which is conventionally estimated at 50 to 60 million, roughly the same as China at the same time; each had about one-fifth or one-sixth of the world population.[5]

[4] This statement appears to coincide thoughtlessly with an outdated stereotype, according to which barbarians, such as Celts or Iberians, produced very little before they were conquered by the Romans. I realise that archaeologists have long admired the artefacts of the Celts and that their iron works, for example, were as advanced as those of the Romans. That said, I still think that their general level of production was lower than in Roman times.

[5] Beloch 1886: 507; Heer 1968: 2.

A Homeric visitor to the Roman world would have been amazed by the extent of settled agriculture; arable land had replaced large areas of woodland, scrub and pasture. It supported a correspondingly larger population. And a significant proportion of this population (perhaps 10 per cent, though that is only a guess) fed off the surplus produce and lived in towns. The visitor would have been struck by the frequency, size and similarity of these towns.[6] But if he had visited the city of Rome, he would have been overawed, as even ancients were, by its size and by the splendour of its public monuments. It had a population which is best estimated at about 1 million; the city of Rome in the first century AD was as large as London in 1800.[7] The Colosseum to take but one example is still admired today for its size and boldness. But the less spectacular system of public aqueducts (nine aqueducts brought water to Rome from up to 91 kilometres away), fountains, baths and drains were more useful and made it possible for a large population to live together in one city without them all succumbing to infectious diseases.[8] To be sure, the city of Rome was a special case; but most cities worthy of the name also had baths and aqueducts; some had mains drainage; the cities of Alexandria, Antioch and Carthage each had a population of two to three hundred thousand and so were

[6] Pausanias, writing in the second century AD, dismissed the claims of a town to be a *polis*, that is a true 'city', because it had 'no public buildings, no gymnasium, no theatre, no market-square, no water conducted to a fountain' (Paus. 10.4). Like the rectangular layout, these public buildings became the expected uniform of Roman towns.

[7] The best account of the ancient evidence on Rome's population is still that of Beloch: 392–412, though Kahrstedt 1921 adds something. The estimated population is based on the recorded number of male citizens who received free wheat doles (320,000 when Julius Caesar held power); to these we should add women, children and slaves. We also know the area of the city (1,373 hectares), the number of houses listed in a fourth-century topography ⟨*Libellus de regionibus urbis Romae*, ed. A. Nordh, Skrifter utgivna av Svenska Institutet i Rom 3, Lund, 1949⟩ and unreliable figures on the amount of wheat consumed in the city. Even when all these are taken into account, we still have to guess: but the best guesses are at the level of 800,000 to 1,000,000 inhabitants. It does seem very large. ⟨See Hopkins 1978b: 96–8, 1983a: 88 [essay 7: 276–7], 2009: 190–2 [essay 13: 507–11].⟩

[8] Frontin. *Aq.* 1.1 and 4 ⟨ed. R. H. Rodgers, Cambridge Classical Texts and Commentaries 42, Cambridge, 2004⟩; Frontinus boasted of the usefulness of aqueducts, compared to the idle pyramids or the inert but famous works of art of the Greeks (1.16). By no means did all Roman towns have aqueducts or drains.

as large as any European town except London before the nineteenth century.[9]

Our Homeric visitor would have been amazed by two other great advances which had taken place in the last millennium BC: the spread of literacy and the invention of coinage. We do not know how literate the masses were in the Roman empire. The Greek-speaking East remained largely impermeable to Latin, except among the upper classes, and local languages, such as Syriac, Aramaic, Punic and Celtic, everywhere survived centuries of Roman rule.[10] But in the West, Latin eventually permeated popular speech and so helped mould modern French, Spanish and Romanian. Evidence from Pompeii, schoolboy exercises scribbled on walls, election slogans and advertisements for gladiatorial games daubed on stucco walls, price lists displayed in common taverns, all show that the capacity to read extended well beyond the élite. The success of Christianity, a dogmatic religion based upon holy writings and on their orthodox interpretation from one end of the empire to the other, in circles outside the ruling élite, provides yet further evidence of the revolution in literacy which the Roman empire had fostered. The word pagans (*pagani*) means countrymen; the orthodoxy of Christianity spread first between towns and among townspeople.

The diffusion of coined money as a general medium of exchange (after its invention in western Asia Minor in the seventh century BC) made possible the unification of the whole Roman empire into a single monetary economy. Figure 5.1[*] shows that an increase in the volume of money in any one province was accompanied by a rise in the volume of money in

[9] On the size of smaller towns see Duncan-Jones 1974: 259–77, which goes through the ancient evidence but draws some questionable comparisons and conclusions. However, the free population of Alexandria at 300,000 (Diod. Sic. 17.52.6), and the similar size of Antioch (Strabo 16.2.5) and of Carthage, though at a later date (Herodian 7.6.1 and 4.3.7), are quite well attested, even if somewhat vague ⟨see too Hopkins 1983a: 89 [essay 7: 277–9] ⟩. But the number of slaves deduced from the single passing reference in Galen, *De propriorum animi* 9.13 (ed. D. Kühn, *Opera Omnia*, vol. 5, Leipzig, 1823 ⟨ed. W. de Boer, *CMG* 5.4.1.1, Leipzig, 1937; trans. P. N. Singer, Oxford, 1997; and see below n. 72⟩) is very doubtful.

[10] On vernacular languages see Brunt 1976: 170–2.

[*] ⟨Fig. 5.1 = Hopkins 1980a: 113 fig. 4 [essay 6: 236 fig. 6.4].⟩

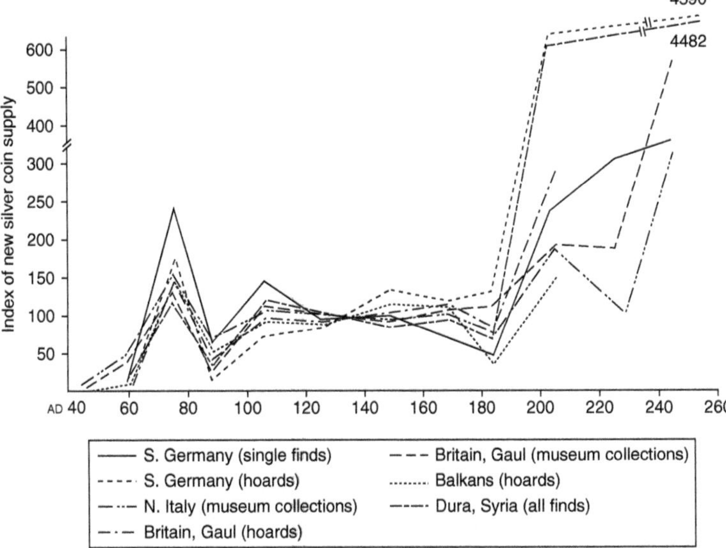

Figure 5.1. Fluctuations in the numbers of silver coins found, by date of minting and by region of find.

other regions of the empire within the same short period.[11] It is based upon the analysis of over 90,000 dated silver coins found in five regions of the Roman empire.

[11] Fig. 5.1 has been drawn so that each line on the graph represents the volume of silver coins found in a region. Some of these regions are very large, and the lines presented here comprise several strands from sub-regions, such as Britain, northern Gaul and southern Gaul. Where possible I have checked before compression to make sure that I was not mixing markedly different patterns; the patterns which I found in the sub-types seemed sufficiently similar to justify compression. I have kept hoards (strictly twenty or more coins found together) and other excavated coins separate as far as possible, because hoards may have been collected over long periods with a bias towards better coins and therefore may not correctly represent the coins in people's purses. The coins from museum collections, surveyed by Reece, may have been collected over long periods and their provenance is uncertain. It is extremely interesting that the singly found coins, carefully listed in modern German sources, produce a line which is similar to the line from the same region based on hoards. The graph is based on a ratio scale. The base (100) is the number of coins from each region and of each type (singly found, hoards) dated AD 96–180, divided by 84 years. This period was the most stable period in the Roman economy. The average number of coins per year found in any one regnal period (e.g. AD 96–117, 193–217, 217–38) for each line was then expressed as a ratio of this base. For example,

The prime cause of this monetary unification of the empire was the complementary flow of taxes and trade. Some of the richest provinces of the empire (Spain, Syria, Greece, southern Gaul, Asia Minor) paid taxes in money, most of which were exported and spent, either in Italy or in the frontier provinces where the armies were stationed. The rich core provinces then had to gain their tax money back, by selling food or goods to the tax-importing regions. Towns in this network of taxes and trade acted as (1) intermediate markets for collecting staple foods (grain, wine, oil) and (2) as processors of primary products (wool, flax, hides) which, through the activities of townsmen, could be transformed into goods of higher value but lower volume (cloth, leather, dies, ropes, etc.) for sale in the chief markets of the empire. Thus the prime stimulus to long-distance trade in the Roman empire was the tax demands of the central government and the distance between where most producers (taxpayers) worked and where most of the government's dependants (soldiers and officials) were stationed.

The unity of the Roman market also depended on the fact that the inhabitants of the Roman empire could treat the Mediterranean as their own internal sea, free from pirates, from rivalries between competing states, indeed free from the magical dangers which for so long obstructed Odysseus' reunion with Penelope. The Homeric visitor would have been amazed at the size of the largest Roman ships (as indeed some ancients were).[12] But even the average merchant ship had

of 3,812 singly found silver coins from southern Germany, an average of 5.3 were minted per year in the period AD 96–180; 5.3 therefore equals 100; in the period AD 117–38, the average number of coins found per year was 4.9 (= 92).The sources for this figure, about which I shall publish more in due course ⟨Hopkins 1980a: 112–16 [essay 6: 233–40]⟩, were Reece 1973 (Dr Reece very kindly reworked some of his data, so that I could split the reign of Domitian from Vespasian and Titus); Bolin 1958: 335–57; Bellinger 1949; *FMRD* (*Die Fundmünzen der römischen Zeit in Deutschland*) volumes on the Saar (III), Pfalz (IV.2), Schwaben (I.7), Oberbayern (I.1), Südbaden (II.2) and Südwürttemberg (II.3). ⟨See Hopkins 1980a: 113 n. 35 [essay 6: 235 n. 35].⟩

[12] The classic description of a large ship is by the Greek satirist Lucian in his essay *The Ship*, which some scholars have taken too seriously, but see the sceptical account of Rougé 1966: 66–71. For an apologistic account, Casson 1971: 186–8. ⟨See Hopkins 1983a: 99 [essay 7: 293–4].⟩

increased significantly in size over the last millennium BC.[13] These larger ships carried both the increased volume of trade and the taxes levied in wheat which fed the city of Rome. The increased security of the seas helped shipowners risk owning bigger ships, as did the system of partnerships and maritime loans known from classical Athens and Rome, which split the risk of loss among participating investors. Improvements in steering and in rigging also helped bigger ships arrive at their intended destination.[14] From the first century AD, Roman ships regularly sailed with the monsoon almost 2,000 sea-miles from the Red Sea ports directly across the Indian Ocean to southern India. Accurate estimates of the earth's circumference (by Eratosthenes in the third century BC), maps, gazetteers, astronomical sophistication all bear witness to the slow accumulation of intellectual knowledge and its percolation from the élite to the level of practical seamanship.[15] That said, the size of ancient ships, the seamanship, the rigging all fell short of what was achieved in Europe by the fifteenth century. Ancient ships had no magnetic compass, no stern rudders, and big ships to a great extent relied on square (instead of fore and aft) rigging which limited manoeuvrability; they always had difficulty in tacking against a wind. The recent growth of underwater archaeology owes its success to Roman ships' frequent failure. From fear of sinking, Roman merchantships did not as a rule set sail during four winter months, from November to March.

[13] We have no accurate evidence on the average size of Roman merchant ships. The minimum tonnage which would give a shipowner tax immunity for bringing wheat to the city of Rome was 325 tonnes burden, but that could be split among several ships, provided none was less than 65 tonnes burden (*Dig.* 50.5.3 (Scaevola)). This gives an idea of ship size on the empire's biggest supply route. Casson's assertions (1971: 170–3, 183–90) about the normal size of ancient sea-going ships are mainly based on an inscription (*IG* XII suppl. 348), which has been both doubtfully restored and mistranslated (but see Launey 1933: 394–401). ⟨See Hopkins 1980a: 105 n. 16 [essay 6: 222 n. 16], 1983a: 97–102, 108 n. 34 [essay 7: 291–9, 295 n. 34].⟩

[14] Rougé 1966: 47–65. Roman ships had rudders near the front of the ship and it now seems agreed that such steering was quite effective, although the projecting protective covers would have impeded a ship's progress.

[15] Thomson 1948: 176–7, 298–300; E. G. R. Taylor 1956: 52–64; and the anonymous *Circumnavigation of the Red Sea* (translated in Schoff 1912) ⟨see now L. Casson, *The Periplus Maris Erythrae: Text with Introduction, Translation, and Commentary*, Princeton, 1989⟩. See also Plin. *HN* 6.101–6.

During this long winter, sea trade was at a standstill, and state post usually went round the Mediterranean coast by road.*

Roman roads are impressive monuments to the Roman empire. Within Pompeii or on the outskirts of Rome itself, one can still see whole stretches of road paved with great flat stones. In Britain, the line of Roman roads is still visible especially in aerial photographs, running straight as a die through the countryside. According to some estimates, there were 90,000 kilometres of main paved roads in the Roman empire.[16] A fourth-century pilgrim has left a record of his journey from Bordeaux to Jerusalem via Milan and Constantinople, a distance of about 5,000 kilometres; the roads he travelled were equipped with regular state posting-stations and rest-houses; he passed through three hundred of them on his journey.[17] The foundations of Roman roads, discovered by archaeological cross-sections and described in Roman literature,[18] were deep (deeper than for many modern roads) and correspondingly expensive. In Britain, roads were often raised on causeways 1–1½ metres above the level of the surrounding country. One gets some further idea of the scale of Roman road-building from the fact that the Alps were pierced by seventeen roads; great efforts were apparently made to keep the gradient less than one in six. Rivers were bridged in wood or stone; obstacles were overcome by tunnels, embankments or by retaining walls. As monuments then Roman roads remain very impressive. But was the cost of their construction justified by the traffic they carried? Politically, the answer must surely be yes. Straight high roads grandiosely demonstrated Roman dominance and, as in other pre-industrial empires, the roads and the horses in

* ⟨See now Beresford 2013.⟩

16 On Roman roads, see Forbes 1934, 1955–64: II 145–55. (Forbes' work should be treated with caution); Margary 1955–7; Goodchild and Forbes 1956: 500–8.

17 The normal distance between posting stations was between 7 and 20 kilometres; these distances had apparently been reduced since the second century AD. See the itineraries of different date in *Itineraria Romana* (ed. O. Cuntz, Leipzig, 1929). On the Bordeaux pilgrim's route ⟨*Itinerarium Burdigalense*⟩, by my count there were 67 towns, 77 large posting stations and 164 relay stations (*mutationes*).

18 Stat. *Silv.* 4.3.40–60.

the post-stations enabled messages of state to be transmitted swiftly from the edges of the empire to the capital. But the cost of maintenance must have been huge.

From a commercial point of view, Roman paved roads were less useful. The current orthodoxy makes great play of the high cost of ancient road transport and of the high ratio of cost between land, river and sea transport.[19] The surviving ancient evidence is thin. The Emperor Diocletian's Edict on Maximum Prices (AD 301) made a land journey by ox-cart for 1 kilometre cost the same as transporting the same weight 57 kilometres by sea on a long voyage, for example, from Syria to Spain.[20] From such evidence we can deduce rough price ratios per tonne/kilometre of about 600 price units for land transport, 60 for river transport and 10 units for sea transport per tonne/kilometre, with considerable variation around these figures. These price ratios are roughly concordant with the price ratios for transport found in other pre-industrial societies.[21] That is exactly the point I wish to make: the cost of Roman land transport was not significantly higher than in many other pre-industrial societies. But in medieval Europe, significant amounts of goods were moved from one region to another by road. And so they were in the Roman empire.

[19] A. H. M. Jones 1964: II 841–2; Finley 1973: 126–7. These two are the authors of what I shall call the new orthodoxy, as distinct from the previous modernising orthodoxy of Rostovtzeff 1957.

[20] ⟨Price Edict 17.3 (for ox-cart); 35.15 (for sea transport).⟩ For Diocletian's Edict the convenient text and English translation in Frank 1933–40: V 305–421 is now seriously incomplete. Even Lauffer 1971 is outdated by recent discoveries ⟨see now Giacchero 1974⟩. I follow Duncan-Jones 1976a in taking the military *modius* as equal to 1½ ordinary *modii* (each of 6.5 kg wheat). The prices given for sea transport in the Price Edict varied considerably (per tonne/km) and were particularly inaccurate in the western Mediterranean. Apparently the Byzantine administrator who fixed the prices was working from an old map or gazetteer and took no account of winds or traffic on routes. Therefore these legally fixed prices can be used only as very rough guides to actual practice. The price ratios between sea, river and land differ slightly from those given by Duncan-Jones 1974: 368.

[21] A list of comparative data can be found in Clark and Haswell 1970: 196–8 table 47. The use of well-fed and well-bred and economically harnessed draught horses in the eighteenth century in north-western Europe along improved roads eventually made land transport costs much lower than comparable costs on Roman roads by ox-cart. Pack-mules and donkeys were cheaper than ox-carts, faster, and did not need roads. ⟨See Hopkins 1983a: 102–4 [essay 7: 299–302] with discussion in Bang and Ikeguchi [311 n. 16].⟩

Land transport was important for trade in the Roman empire; the truth of this proposition can be illustrated but not proved. Let us take pottery as an example; but first some words of caution. The sheer survival of pottery has sometimes tempted archaeologists and economic historians of the ancient world to exaggerate its importance in the ancient economy. The most noted case is the rise and decline of Arezzo as the centre of manufacture of medium-priced tableware in the last century BC and the early part of the first century AD. Rostovtzeff put Arezzo among 'the large industrial centres of the ancient world', and then, when the manufacture of such pottery was moved to southern Gaul, he commented on the decentralisation of Italian industry and took it as symptomatic of Italy's economic decline. It is this view which M. I. Finley has so effectively quashed.[22]

The point which I want to make is different. Arezzo lies deep inland, 100 kilometres from the sea and, although it is fairly near the headwaters of the Tiber and near a tributary of the Arno, it is not near a sizeable navigable river. Yet Arretine pots have been found all over the Roman empire, and as far away as India. The inconvenience of Arezzo's inland location was overcome. When Arezzo declined, its place was taken by potteries at La Graufesenque, on a tributary of the Garonne which flows into the Atlantic Ocean. Yet La Graufesenque's main markets were the Roman army on the Rhine and Danube and in Italy. For these, its riverside location was of little use. Most of its pots, which were bulky, heavy and not particularly valuable, must have been taken by road to other river heads. The volume of production was very large: we know the names of several thousand potters and have lists of products, some of which run to over 700,000 items.[23] My point here is not that the Roman economy depended on the manufacture of pots, but

[22] Rostovtzeff 1957: 36, 172–5; Finley 1973: 137, 'as for Lezoux and La Graufesenque, they flourish only in archaeological manuals', beautifully but unfairly dismissive.

[23] Hermet 1934: I 291–353; Stanfield and Simpson 1958. Another example of the volume of production and trade involved can be cited; dredging work at Chalon on the river Saône in 1869 revealed 24,000 wine amphorae from southern Gaul discarded near the river port (Déchelette 1913: 156).

that, as the Greek geographer Strabo stated,[24] a considerable volume of goods (of which pottery is but one example) was transported by land, between rivers or from sea port to river port, for considerable distances; for example, from the Rhone to the Loire, a distance of about 140 kilometres, and from Aquileia, near modern Trieste, through the Alps to Nauportus on a tributary of the river Save (75 kilometres).[25]

Distance overland was not then a decisive determinant of all trade or choice of route. Two further examples may be useful. First, lead ingots. The distribution of lead ingots from Roman Britain shows that lead mined in Derbyshire was taken sometimes to Brough-on-Humber, a nearby seaport, but at other times was taken long distances overland to Southampton.[26] The second example is at the opposite extreme: medium-quality pottery cups found in the Roman military fort at Usk in south Wales and dating from the middle of the first century AD. These cups came from seven different regions of the Roman empire, stretching from the lower Rhine, which was the nearest of these sources, to southern Italy. The great majority of the cups (82 per cent, $n = 214$) came not from the most convenient source, but from Lyons, in spite of the cost and inconvenience of long transport by road, river and sea.[27] Obviously, the trade in cups was of negligible importance to the economy of the whole empire; but cups have survived and can reasonably stand proxy for all the more perishable items of medium value which were traded throughout the Roman empire for considerable distances even overland, in spite of the cost of transport.

Up to now, we have been dealing with manufactured articles; let us now deal with staples. It was impossible to move large quantities of cereals for long distances overland, unless the transport was organised by the government and the cost imposed on taxpayers. If there was a famine in an inland district, there was little that anyone could do to relieve it and the

[24] Strabo 4.1.14.
[25] Strabo 4.6.10.
[26] Tylecote 1962: 87.
[27] Greene 1973.

central government seldom intervened. Two classic cases illustrate this point. The first concerns the town of Caesarea in central Asia Minor, which is about 350 kilometres by road from the nearest Mediterranean port and considerably further by river from the Black Sea. The following account is given by Gregory of Nazianzus, a fourth-century divine:

There was a famine, the most terrible in the memory of man. The city languished but there was no help from any part, no remedy for the calamity. Cities on the seacoast easily endure a shortage of this kind, importing by sea the things of which they are short. But we who live far from the sea profit nothing from our surplus, nor can we produce what we are short of, since we are able neither to export what we have nor import what we lack.[28]

The second case is a famous famine in Antioch in AD 362–3, which was relieved by the Emperor Julian when he came there. He had 2,600 tons of wheat, about 6,700 cartloads, brought by road from two towns 80 and 160 kilometres distant where there was a surplus. Private entrepreneurs had been unable to draw upon the same source, probably because they could not command transport (oxen and donkeys) on that scale, over those distances. But the cost of land transport was probably not the main obstacle, since at known transport prices, the cost of bringing wheat 160 kilometres would have raised its price only by about 50 per cent, which is well within the range of wheat prices charged at Antioch during that year.[29]

The arguments which I have just advanced, namely that there was a significant volume of inter-regional trade, much of it overland, diverge from the current orthodoxy.[30] This new orthodoxy, if I may call it that, runs somewhat as follows. Because most regions of the Mediterranean basin have a similar climate, in Roman times they grew the same produce. What was not grown locally, the masses of peasants and townsfolk could not afford.

[28] Greg. Naz. *Or.* 43.34 (*PG* 36: 541C–544A) ⟨ed. J. Bernardi, *SC* 384, Paris, 1992⟩.

[29] See Finley 1973: 126–7 for the contrary view; see A. H. M. Jones 1964: I 446, II 844 and Liebeschuetz 1972: 126–32 for a discussion of the evidence. Julian fixed the price for wheat brought overland at 10 *modii* per solidus, and for wheat brought later from Egypt at 15 *modii* per solidus. Normal prices, in spite of Julian's claims, were substantially lower elsewhere.

[30] See above n. 19.

Therefore there was no large-scale inter-regional trade in staple foods (wheat, barley, wine and olive oil). To be sure, there were exceptions. The capital cities of Rome and later Constantinople, and perhaps the other great cities of the empire, Alexandria, Antioch and Carthage, were too large to be fed from their immediate hinterlands. But all large ancient cities were near the sea and/or on rivers. The armies of the high empire (300,000-men strong) also received some of their supplies from a distance; for reasons of supply as much as for defence, most of them were stationed in garrisons along rivers (Rhine, Danube and Euphrates). In any case, the army and the capital cities were largely fed by taxes, levied in wheat, so that their supply was not part of a pattern of exchange, but of taxation.

Local self-sufficiency in agriculture went hand in hand with self-sufficiency in manufacture. The Romans never developed systems of manufacture which substantially cut the costs of production through economies of scale or capital investment in equipment. The units of production were small. The largest recorded factory was a shield factory worked by 120 slaves in classical Athens; some forty government arms factories established in the fourth century AD may also have been large.[31] But as far as we know the concentration of workers in these factories did not apparently involve any sophisticated division of labour. In the arms factories, for example, each armourer was responsible for the whole process of making helmets and cheek pieces. In general, then, provided there were local supplies of raw materials, goods could be made in small quantities for each local market as cheaply as they could be made in large quantities at a single centre of production, from which transport costs had also to be paid. In other words, there were no effective economies of scale. Conditions differed only when a particular town had better access to raw materials, or had a monopoly of skilled craftsmen or had a marketable reputation for certain goods (ropes from Capua, linen from Tarsus, women's clothes from Scythopolis).[32] These premium goods, like

[31] A. H. M. Jones 1957: 14, 1964: II 834–5.

[32] See Cato, *Agr.* 135; Price Edict 26.

fine wines or other prized agricultural produce, fetched premium prices, and so were bought only by the élite; and therefore, since the élite was small, trade in premium goods involved only a low volume of transport.

This orthodoxy, which I have oversimplified, deserves some qualifications. First, the size of the cereal harvest varied each year, but the demand for food was relatively steady. Even in modern times, in spite of all the help from fertilisers and from mechanically pumped water, the mean inter-annual variation in the size of wheat crops in the fourteen nations which are the successor states to the Roman empire was 28 per cent (unadjusted mean of means, 1921–30).[33] These are national figures. In Roman times, the inter-annual variation in crop size in small self-sufficient districts, in the rural areas around each town, must have been considerably larger. To some extent, one year's surplus could have been stored against the next year's deficit, particularly by rich men. But these stores were often not large enough. Local shortages, even famines, recurred. These local shortages and the complementary gluts elsewhere stimulated sizeable flows of trade.

Bringing food from elsewhere cost money. In some towns, emergency supplies were paid for by regularly appointed local officials (*sitonai*) or by private benefactors (the central government usually concerned itself only with the city of Rome itself).[34] The volume of private or municipal help was usually small in each town in relation to the need and, as we have seen, nothing much could be done to relieve famine in towns deep inland. But the aggregate volume of all such relief brought by trade or benefaction must have been large. The main difference between ancient and modern marketing systems lay in the absence of any regular routes of large-scale exchange between

[33] The national figures on wheat harvests are taken from the *International Yearbook of Agricultural Statistics, 1922–1938* (International Institute of Agriculture, Rome). The median annual variation round the mean for a decade was 14 per cent ⟨see Hopkins 1983a: 91 table 1 [essay 7: 280 table 7.1]⟩.

[34] See A. H. M. Jones 1940: 218; he cites two cases in which benefactors provided enough money or wheat to feed up to 5,000 people for a month.

regions specialising in the production of an agricultural surplus and regions specialising in the production of manufactures. The lines of trade in staples produced by local gluts and shortages were unpredictable.

The second qualification relates to luxuries, which have always held considerable fascination for economic historians. Some Romans dressed in wool from Asia Minor, in Egyptian linen or Chinese silks; women wore Indian pearls and diamonds, and beautified themselves with Arabian cosmetics; at table, they used Spanish silverware and Syrian glass and ate eastern spices; they decorated their houses with African ivory and Greek marbles.[35] Yet there were very few such people.

Two questions arise: was the luxury trade important in its aggregate value, or was it only a small stream directed primarily at the Roman élite in Italy? As in other pre-industrial empires, the rich were very rich; Roman senators in the high empire commonly had annual incomes two thousand times higher than the levels of minimum subsistence of a peasant family.[36] But there were only six hundred senators and only a few thousand Roman knights. If the luxury trade was important, it must have penetrated well down the social scale and have concerned prosperous landowners in provincial towns throughout the empire. Luxuries allowed the élites, at metropolitan and provincial levels, to enhance their status and by ostentatious consumption to dramatise their differences from common folk. Even well-to-do peasants or prosperous merchants were sometimes involved. In a good year, some of them probably bought a trinket or a new cloak, or stored away some gold or a jewel for the family chest or their daughter's dowry. Thus, in my view, although the élite at Rome constituted

[35] *Dig.* 39.4.16.7 (Marcianus).

[36] This ratio is given in an attempt to invest ancient money figures with some meaning and is based on the following coordinates. A senatorial fortune at 20 million sestertii yields an annual income of 1.2 million sestertii at a 6 per cent return on capital. The minimum subsistence for a family is taken as 1,000 kg wheat which would cost approximately 450 sestertii per year (wheat at 3 sestertii per *modius* of 6.5 kg). Several of these figures are disputable, but the suggested ratio of senatorial to poor peasant income seems of the right order of magnitude. On senatorial fortunes, see Duncan-Jones 1974: 17–32, 343–4.

the single largest market for luxuries, the luxury trade was important both in economic and social terms, because it reflected stratification throughout the empire; in sum, it was widespread.

Two figures from ancient sources confirm this view. Pliny wrote that imports from China, India and Arabia cost the Romans 100 million sestertii each year.[37] Of course such large round numbers in ancient sources make one sceptical (it equals 7 tonnes of gold) and there is only a remote chance that Pliny gleaned this figure from state records of customs dues. But it is reasonable to conclude that imports from the East were on a large scale. The geographer Strabo is more reliable, because he himself visited Upper Egypt with its then governor in the reign of Augustus: he wrote that the trade with India had grown considerably and that in his time 120 ships set sail every year from the Red Sea port of Myos Hormos to India.[38] The trade in foreign luxuries was clearly substantial and probably grew in the first century AD. I am not refurbishing the old argument that foreign trade in luxuries ruined Rome; rather I am arguing that luxury trade on this scale helped provide a living for thousands of merchants, traders and other intermediaries, such as boat builders and hauliers, most of them living in towns. Nor should we forget the luxuries, manufactured within the Mediterranean basin. If we interpret luxuries loosely to include such items as fine linens, papyri and unguents, then Roman luxuries probably exceeded eastern goods in value and volume.

Finally, we should take into account the huge variety of goods consumed in the ancient economy. No ancient source discusses this, except the encyclopaedist Pliny in his *Natural History*; but we are not concerned here with evidence for the existence of varied trade goods but with their importance. Even the plentiful surviving Egyptian papyri do not help us, because they came from the countryside and so give only fragmentary information about trade. In the absence of data from

[37] Plin. *HN* 12.84.
[38] Strabo 2.5.12.

the Roman period, we can perhaps legitimately use later evidence, such as the Genizeh papyri from Cairo in the period AD 950–1250 to give us insights on classical trade.[39] It seems likely that the items traded, as distinct from the trading conditions, were very much the same as in Roman times. Even so, we still have to deal with fragments; we have no summary figures on trade.

Most of the items traded were natural products in the raw state or at only a slight remove from the raw state (olive oil, wax, onyx), but some products such as chemicals were won from the earth only at the cost of considerable labour and were besides important for transforming natural produce elsewhere (alum and alkali for cloth, pitch for storing wine, dies for glazing pots). Few of the goods were manufactured in the sense of being the composites of several raw products; this reflects the underdeveloped state of manufactures and of the market. That said, the large total demand in the market is reflected in the wide variety of and distance between provenances and destinations, and in the value and volume of throughput. The following list sets out the items traded by one large general merchant:*

1. Flax (sent from Egypt to Tunisia and Sicily)
2. Silk (sent from Spain and Sicily); other fabrics, including cotton from Syria, felt from North Africa and all types of garments, such as robes and bed covers
3. Olive oil, soap, wax (from Tunisia, Syria and Palestine)
4. Spices, such as pepper, cinnamon, cloves
5. Dies and tanning materials, such as indigo, lacquer, sumac, gallnuts and saffron
6. Metals, such as copper, iron, lead, mercury, tin, silver (sent from the West)
7. Books
8. Aromatics, perfumes and gums, such as aloe, ambergris, camphor, frankincense, musk and betel leaves
9. Jewels and semi-precious stones, such as pearls, cornelians, turquoises, onyx
10. Ornaments, such as coral, cowries, tortoiseshell

[39] Goitein 1967; an exciting set of documents.
* ⟨For the products listed, see Goitein 1967: 154.⟩

11. Chemicals, such as alkali, alum, antimony, arsenic, borax, naphtha, sulphur, starch, vitriol
12. Hides, leather including shoes
13. Pitch.

This list by no means exhausts the items recorded in the Genizeh documents, but that does not matter. The Genizeh papyri reassure the classical historian by giving us a lively picture of the relationships between, on the one hand, small, fragmented units of production and mostly small-time traders and, on the other hand, the movement of large quantities of medium- and high-value goods along and across the Mediterranean, even when those lands were subjected to a diversity of competing rulers.

Textiles and Metals

Two products deserve special mention: textiles and metals. Any economic history of medieval Europe takes the cloth trade seriously; several towns in England, France, Flanders and Italy owed their prosperity in great measure to their capacity to make and sell large quantities of cloth. By contrast, few modern historians of the ancient world (A. H. M. Jones is an honourable exception[40]) have taken the ancient cloth trade seriously, partly because very little ancient cloth has survived and partly because no surviving ancient source tells us much about it.

The cloth trade in classical times must have been important. Townspeople living in the cramped multi-storey blocks in the city of Rome or Ostia, or in the cramped two-storey houses in Pompeii, had no room for the complex process of scouring, combing, weaving, fulling and dyeing which turned raw wool into cloth. They may have spun at home, but spinning enough yarn for your clothes required more than casual labour. Moeller's recent study of wool-making at Pompeii shows that in a town with a population of about 20,000, there were at least forty establishments devoted to the manufacture of cloth or

[40] A. H. M. Jones 1960.

felt, some of them quite large and employing perhaps twenty workers.[41] Even in Egyptian villages, there were professional weavers, organised in guilds, making cloth for local consumption and apparently for delivery to army units in central Asia Minor and Palestine.[42]

A. H. M. Jones argued that army units in central Asia Minor or Palestine would not have ordered clothing in dribs and drabs (four cloaks and a tunic from one village, nineteen cloaks and five tunics from another) if single large suppliers had been available. Nor did the government help the development of large-scale production by levying tax in cloth and so opting out of the market. Later, in the fourth century, the central government did set up large wool and linen weaving establishments to supply the army. These were probably conglomerates of piece workers, all working together under a single roof; we know very little about them. And we know of only a handful of large or middling privately owned manufacturies engaged in making cloth. All their owners seem to have been primarily interested in other activities, as landowners or officials.[43] So far as I know, no fortunes in the ancient world were based on cloth-making, even if textiles contributed to some fortunes.

Too much is often made of the small scale of manufacturing units. Of course, most manufacturing units in a pre-industrial

[41] Moeller 1976. Some of his conclusions seem speculative, but the double furnaces and large vats in some establishments can still be seen.

[42] The four papyri, cited by A. H. M. Jones 1960: 186–7, are *BGU* VII 1564 and 1572 and *P.Ryl.* II 94 and 189. All date from the second century AD.

[43] The evidence for two of these largish units is discussed by Wipszycka 1965: 81–90, 1961: 185–90. The official Apollonius of the second century AD clearly had considerable landholdings, was personally involved in his textile business (choosing dyes, cut, etc.) and integrated the activities of outworkers. Another Egyptian was said to have employed 'many workmen in his workshop' making linen (*P.Oxy.* XXII 2340). A municipal magistrate in a small North African town was a weaver who sat down to dinner with his workmen (Optatus, A*gainst the Donatists,* appendix 2 §8 ⟨ed. C. Ziwsa, *CSEL* 26, Vienna, 1893; see too J.-L. Maier, *Le dossier du Donatisme*, vol. 1, Texte und Untersuchungen zur Geschichte der altchristlichen Literatur 134, Berlin, 1987, 171–87 at 182 and trans. M. J. Edwards, *Optatus: Against the Donatists*, Translated Texts for Historians 27, Liverpool, 1997, 170–80 at 176⟩). The house of L. Veranius Hypsaeus, a town magistrate at Pompeii, was equipped with large-scale fulling equipment (della Corte 1954: 46).

economy are small; so they were still in Germany and France at the beginning of the twentieth century.[44] What matters are the number and size of the exceptions and whether there was any system by which a host of small producers, each engaged in one stage of production, was integrated by the activities of capitalistic entrepreneurs, who took a share of the profits in return for their effort and capital risk. There is only slight evidence that such integration did take place in the Roman world and it seems probable that in textiles, as in other handicrafts, the roles and institutions of integrating fragmented piece workers were never highly developed.[45]

The small scale of most weaving establishments and their obvious lack of capital, the general poverty of the populace and the high cost of transport have all been used, in my opinion wrongly, to buttress the proposition that inter-regional trade in cloth was of low volume and of low aggregate value because only the élite could afford to buy. But the poverty of individual peasants should not be confused with their aggregate demand; even if 50 million people or even 10 million people buy cloth or clothes once in a decade, their aggregate demand is still enormous. Even in the Egyptian villages mentioned above, there were several weavers (eight or twelve in one, seven in another); this suggests that many rustics bought rather than made their own clothes. The cloth trade did not serve only the élite. This is confirmed by Diocletian's Edict on Maximum Prices, which listed linens 'fit for the use of commoners or slaves' (Edict 26.10). The regular purchase of cloth even of the lowest quality by poor peasants or for slaves in local markets created a nexus of exchange. Consumers of cloth

[44] 95 per cent of all manufacturing and mining units in Germany and 98 per cent in France employed fewer than ten persons in 1906–7 (Gerschenkron 1962: 64).

[45] See e.g. Wipszycka 1965: 81. Of 328 tradesman mentioned on tombstone inscriptions in the graveyard at Kōrykos in Rough Cilicia, four were *ergodotēs*, putters out. The existence of the word argues the frequency of the role. From Goitein's study ⟨1967: 169–79⟩ of the Genizeh papyri I should expect to find sleeping partners in small businesses in the Roman world, though the evidence is, I think, slight; but see, for example, the interesting papyrus *P. Vindob. G.* 19792, published in Casson 1957 ⟨= *SB* VI 9571; and see now Casson 1986⟩, which shows active banking investment in trade.

had to sell their produce on the market to get money to pay clothiers, just as clothiers paid a longish line of associates (fullers, spinners, dyers) for their help and peasants for their food. This is a process which medieval historians take for granted. But for the Roman world, especially for rural areas, the emergence, persistence and importance of a monetary exchange economy between peasants and artisans still has to be argued.

But was the inter-regional cloth trade exclusively concerned with the élite? The evidence of Diocletian's Edict on Maximum Prices shows decisively that it was not. The Edict was composed in the eastern capital of the empire (Nicomedia in Asia Minor). Yet the provenances of the raw wool and of the woollen garments named were spread throughout the whole empire (from Britain, northern Gaul, Spain, Italy, Africa, Greece and the Balkans). This implies a far-reaching trade. And the value of raw wool, let alone of made-up cloth, was so high in relation to volume that long-distance transport, whether by road, river or sea, would have added only marginally to costs. Even the very cheapest wool was priced at seven and a half times the price of wheat (per unit of weight; Edict 1.1, 25.9), so that a journey by mule of 300 kilometres would have added only 10 per cent to the cost price (Edict 17.5). Of course, the most costly cloths, wool, linen or silk, were for the very rich, but the Edict fixed a wide range of intermediate prices. We can see this best with linens, since that part of the inscription is best preserved: different prices were given for three distinct qualities of linen made in each of five towns, all of them in the eastern half of the empire. To be sure, linen was made elsewhere also; but these five towns were famous for linen and presumably were sizeable centres of production, and not just for the élite. Prices for shirts, for example, ranged from 7,000 to 2,000 denarii in the named qualities and then from 1,500 to 500 denarii in the qualities for soldiers, commoners and slaves (Edict 26.13–33). The wide range of price and provenance and the availability of knowledge about them all in the capital indicate a firm market pattern, in which cloth from different regions competed.

Perhaps one problem is that we split the population of the empire into only two strata: a tiny élite and the broad mass of peasants and proletarians, who lived near the level of minimum subsistence. But the aggregate demand from a middling stratum must have been quite large: best clothes for brides and grooms, or for rich peasants or prosperous traders to wear at festivals or in street parades, or ordinary clothes for respectable school teachers or doctors or for middling landlords; all these added up to a varied, significant and sophisticated market.

Metals

Two aspects of metal production in the ancient world deserve emphasis: first, the difficulty and cost of their extraction, which required a large labour force and, in some cases, huge capital investment; secondly, the importance of metals as items of trade, in the manufacture of implements (swords, saucepans, mirrors, water pipes) and as money. The monetisation of the Roman economy was possible only because the Romans mined vast quantities of precious metal, just as the effective defence of Roman frontiers by large armies, equipped with iron swords and breastplates, depended upon large-scale supplies from Roman iron mines.

Some idea of scale may be useful. A reliable source, the Greek historian Polybius, tells us that in the mid-second century BC, the silver mines near Cartagena in Spain were worked by 40,000 slaves and yielded 25,000 drachmae per day in government revenues.[46] If these figures are roughly right, government revenues from these mines alone equalled 35 tonnes of silver a year, to which we should add entrepreneurial profit. Let us consider what that meant. According to Patterson, the production of one tonne of silver in ancient conditions involved 500–1,000 man-work years.[47] It involved digging up roughly 100,000 tonnes of rock with iron and stone picks, hammers,

[46] Cited in Strabo 3.2.10.

[47] C. C. Patterson 1972: 231. Dr Patterson's article and figures are obviously speculative and as he himself emphasises should be treated with some caution. They provide only rough orders of magnitude. I have no competence to judge the plausibility of most of them. Those I have checked with friendly metal-minded archaeologists were thought probable.

chisels and gads or by fire-setting; this rock had to be dragged to the surface in baskets by ropes and human muscle. In deep workings, and some Roman workings in the Spanish silver mines were 250 metres underground, this labour would involve the use of tonnes of illuminating oil. Once the ore was brought to the surface, it was broken up by hammers, picked over by hand, ground and washed. Ten thousand tonnes of trees provided enough charcoal (between 500 and 2,000 tonnes) to smelt the ore at the necessary temperature (1,000° C). The by-product was 400 tonnes of lead and lots of slag which had to be carted away. Often the silver was still impure and had to be washed and remelted to produce refined silver. All this was necessary to produce one tonne of silver. I thought it worthwhile going into such detail, in order to indicate the ramifications of large-scale silver production, in terms of investment, equipment, fuel and organisation.

Other evidence from Spain shows the huge scale of Roman workings.[48] In southern Spain, the Rio Tinto and Tarsis mines each had an estimated volume of 20–30 million tonnes of slag. Tarín calculated that the ancient slag at Rio Tinto and Tarsis (neither of which was worked between late antiquity and the early modern period) would have involved 5,000 workmen for 300 years.[49] The workings go deep underground and there are several kilometres of underground galleries, usually only one metre high. This prevented the use of haulage animals, or animal-powered waterwheels, which were apparently unknown in antiquity. Drainage was achieved by cutting long transverse channels and by banks of man-operated Archimedian screws or waterwheels, each of which painfully raised the water by only two metres. In the same region at Sotiel, there was an

[48] The gold workings in north-western Spain, for example, are estimated to have involved moving more than 70,000,000 tonnes of earth, some of it washed away by water brought in aqueducts, in one case some 50 km long. See O. Davies 1935: 99–103; Lewis and Jones 1970: 175–6; Jones and Bird 1972. ⟨See Hopkins 2009: 197 [essay 13: 518–20].⟩

[49] ⟨J. Gonzalo y Tarín, *Descripción física, geológica y minera de la provincia de Huelva*, 2 vols, Madrid, 1886–8, II 57⟩ cited as an intelligent source by Nash 1904: 19. See also O. Davies 1935: 126–31; Rickard 1932: I 428–30; and Avery 1974, a history of the Rio Tinto mine.

abortive exploratory mine which yielded nothing but 30,000 tonnes of rock. The scale of working, on exploration and on profitable and unprofitable exploitation, makes it clear that private entrepreneurs (for these were not state mines) spent very considerable sums on capital investment.

Silver and gold mining (together with salt mining and tax farming) were the four activities in which it was legal for Romans to form corporations with a collective legal persona.[50] The Romans did not develop a concept of limited liability nor a public market in shares; some corporations may have been broken up on the death of their president; but in spite of their transience and inflexibility, these corporations obviously provided an effective mechanism for raising private capital and for sharing risks in very large mining enterprises. Strabo tells us that Cadiz was a very prosperous town and that in a census of his own time there were five hundred men from Cadiz registered as knights, a number equalled in Italy only by Rome and Padua.[51] Their presence reflected the agricultural wealth of the valley of the Guadalquivir, the mineral wealth nearby and the importance of long-distance trade.[52]

Up to now we have been dealing with the integration of the Roman economy and with the volume of trade. These are obviously germane to the function of towns in the economy, but they are no substitute for looking at the towns themselves and at the conditions under which they grew. However, before we do that, perhaps it would be sensible to review quickly two of the main arguments advanced and to enter some qualifications. I have argued (cf. figure 5.1) that the Roman economy was heavily

[50] *Dig.* 3.4.1.1 (Gaius). Iron was apparently worked at a much larger number of sites than silver or gold. Measurement of ancient slag at iron mines is often difficult because of subsequent working at the same site. But some idea of scale can be gained from local studies. From a careful study of the volume of slag and its metal content at six out of thirty sites in the east Weald in southern England, Cleere (1976) has conservatively estimated production at these six sites as averaging 550 tonnes per year from AD 120 to 240. The six sites would have kept about five to seven hundred men at work. Production at the iron mines in Noricum was obviously greater.

[51] Strabo 3.5.3.

[52] 'These are the men', wrote Strabo of the people of Cadiz, 'who fit out the most and the largest ships both for our sea and for the sea outside' (3.5.3).

monetised and constituted a single entity in which sizeable sums of money flowed between provinces. But most produce stood outside the money economy. Most produce was consumed by the peasants who produced it; each peasant and his family produced most of what he and his family consumed; the market was not involved. This was very important both at the economic and at the political level. The monetised economy was a thin veneer stretched over and at some remove from the subsistence economy; it was attached to that stable base by the tendons of tax, rent and exchange. At the political level, the prevalence of peasant self-sufficiency helps explain the stolidity of pre-industrial empires; they can survive crises, partly because the superstructure is only marginally relevant to the way most of the population live; the superstructure can be split asunder by civil wars and by regional fragmentation, as it was in the Roman empire in the third century and repeatedly in Chinese history, and can then be swiftly reunited. The peasant base and the élite superstructure belonged to separate, encapsulated worlds.

The second main argument was that taxation can be considered as the prime mover, creating a high volume of interregional trade. This occurred because money taxes were typically spent at some distance from the taxpayers. The taxpayers then had to buy back their money by the export and sale of goods. This model posits that a large volume of goods, equal in value to the exported tax, were transformed in towns from simple natural produce into higher value, lower volume transportable exports. The main routes of this trade were from the rich core provinces of their empire, on the one side, to Italy and the frontier provinces where the armies were stationed, on the other side. Distribution maps of durable exports, principally pottery tableware and wine jars, corroborate this model, if we can safely regard pots as proxy for perishable but economically more important exports, such as wooden barrels of wine, cloth and leather.[53] But no short list of 'important' items of trade can do justice to the variety of goods which passed

[53] I am very grateful to Dr M. J. Fulford for guidance on this point. There is no handy compendium of distribution maps, which archaeologists are just beginning to draw.

often each in small quantities along the trade routes of the empire. Most of the inhabitants of the empire were poor, but even they bought something which they did not produce. The sum of their demands, and the demands from the prosperous non-gentry and from the élite, all added up to a significant trade in non-subsistence goods.

Three qualifications seem to be necessary. First, not all trade was the reciprocal of taxation (although a significant part was similarly the reciprocal of rents paid to absentee landowners resident in regional centres or in the metropolis). But some trade, and a significant part of the whole, represented the exchange of produce between town and country and between specialist producers and consumers. Secondly, this model takes the existence of taxation as given. But taxation was a result of conquest, an advance, for both parties, over piracy and plunder. The imposition of taxes helped increase the productivity of subject peoples. In order to pay their taxes, peasants had to grow a surplus which they previously had not grown and they had to sell this surplus on a market so that they could get money to pay taxes. This process occurred first in the eastern Mediterranean in the states and kingdoms which were formed before the Roman conquest (in the case of Egypt long before). It happened in the western Mediterranean and Balkans, largely under Roman influence. As Strabo wrote of the 'barbarians' in the back country behind Marseilles: 'they have become civilised, and instead of making war, they have turned to civic life and to settled agriculture, because of Roman rule'.[54] Thus taxation increased productivity, threw extra produce onto the market and helped the growth of towns, as this produce was transformed by urban artisans into goods exported in order to buy money to pay their taxes with. Thirdly, not all taxes were levied in money: those levied in kind obviously stood outside these market relationships. In the later empire, that is in the fourth century, most taxes were levied in kind, and there was apparently a downturn in trade and in the prosperity of many towns. This fits with, indeed it corroborates, our model.

[54] Strabo 4.1.5.

Conquest and the Growth of Towns

The growth of towns was a function of conquest. We know most about this process in Italy during the last centuries before Christ, that is during the period of Rome's greatest expansion.[55] The Romans acquired their huge empire by a fanatical dedication to fighting wars. It is difficult to find a single index of their militarism; perhaps the award of triumphs can serve: Roman generals were awarded triumphs only if they had secured victories over 'worthy enemies' and if at least 5,000 of the enemy had been killed in a single battle. The scale of Roman slaughter is reflected in the fact that in the two centuries to 50 BC over seventy triumphs were awarded. The profits of empire, booty, treasure, taxes and slaves poured into Italy. The privileged benefited most; that was one advantage of being privileged, at once a token of high status and a means of reinforcing it. Throughout the last two centuries BC, the rich grew steadily richer and their style of living became more luxuriously ostentatious. The grandest town house in the city of Rome in 78 BC was not even among the top hundred town houses a generation later;[56] this observation and the competition it implies reflect the growth of wealth inside the Roman élite.

For reasons of status and tradition, Roman aristocrats and knights invested most of their new wealth in Italian land. It was not only respectable and safe, it was almost the only large-scale form of long-term investment available. Poor peasants were bought out or forced off their land; their farms were amalgamated and were worked more efficiently by slaves, more efficiently in the sense that the surplus produced on the farms cultivated by slaves was (net of subsistence) considerably larger than the surplus produced on small family farms. An arable farm of 50 hectares could be cultivated, according

[55] This is a much shortened version of the discussion given in my forthcoming book, *Conquerors and Slaves* ⟨= Hopkins 1978b: 1–132⟩. See fig. 5.2 [190] ⟨= Hopkins 1978b: 12 fig. 1.1⟩, where the interaction of several important factors is schematically portrayed.

[56] Plin. *HN* 36.109.

to the Roman agricultural writer Columella, by eight male slaves with one supervisor and his wife (only the supervisor was allowed a wife).[57] In the second century BC, the same area (50 hectares) would have provided farms for between four and twenty colonists and their families.[58] The gain to the landowner from replacing free peasants with slaves was clear.

The dispossessed citizen peasants migrated to the city of Rome and to other Italian towns where they helped constitute a new market for the surplus grown on the estates of the rich, or they went to the newly formed colonies like Bologna and Piacenza in northern Italy, or they went into the army and so captured still more booty and slaves both for themselves and for their leaders. In this way, conquest materially, if indirectly, fed the growth of towns by stimulating migration from the countryside and by providing a replacement agricultural labour force of slaves in the countryside.

Some idea of scale may help; according to the ancient figures and by conservative estimates, it seems likely that in the last two centuries BC over 2 million slaves were imported into Italy; it is difficult to know, but it is possible to estimate that somewhat more than half these new slaves went into the countryside and the rest went to work for their new masters in towns.[59] One consequence of their immigration was an acute and recurrent shortage of agricultural land in Italy; the crises were repeatedly 'solved' by allocating land to ex-soldiers, but only at the cost of dispossessing a fresh set of peasants. The final solution reached under Julius Caesar and the first

57 Columella, *Rust.* 2.12.7.

58 Details of colonial allotments are conveniently given in Frank 1933–40: I 122–3. Some of the colonial allotments at the beginning of the second century were so small that they could not have supported a family. To preserve the analogy, I have disregarded the smallest allotments and have included only those of 10 *iugera* (2.5 ha.) and above.

59 These figures are only very approximate. Their implications and the conclusions cited here are elaborated in my forthcoming book (see above n. 55). I follow Beloch: 418, 435–6 rather than Brunt 1971a: 124, who thought in terms of 3 million slaves in Italy about the time of Christ. The difference between these careful scholarly estimates gives some idea of the inadequacy of the data. Of course, the sum of slave imports over two centuries far exceeded the number of slaves living at any one time.

emperor, Augustus, was the settlement of over 200,000 adult male citizens overseas.[60] In all, I estimate, on Professor Brunt's figures, that nearly 400,000 adult male free Italians, that is a third of Italy's free population, were resettled by direct state intervention in colonies sited in Italy or in the provinces during the second half of the last century BC. This removal of large numbers of free citizens from central Italy reduced the demand for Italian land and so formed one important economic foundation for the Augustan settlement.

We have then a nexus of interrelated factors: continuous wars, the import of booty and of a massive number of slaves, the extrusion of free peasants, the growth of large estates, the creation of a large surplus and the growth of towns both in Italy and in the provinces. The interaction of these factors is set out in figure 5.2.* The growth of Italian towns was made possible, I think, by the very uneven distribution of profits from war, which in turn forced investment in land and increases in farm size and made possible economies of scale. The same forces simultaneously created a new surplus (grown on farms worked by slaves) and a new market, which consisted of imported urban slaves and the former peasants who had been extruded from their smallholdings and who had migrated to the city of Rome and to other Italian towns.

Urbanisation also depended upon an increase in inequality; the rich grew much richer and the poor became relatively poorer, and in many cases absolutely poorer, if they lost their farms and then became urban pensioners of the state. Let us discuss these developments. Much of the stored wealth of the Mediterranean basin was suddenly heaped into Italy. The wealth of the Roman élite grew commensurately with the growth of Rome's political power. Only a small part of this huge influx could be profitably invested in production; much of it was spent on importing slaves. Some of the provincial

60 These figures are derived from those given by Brunt 1971a: 234–65. The gross figures for all migrations inside Italy and out of Italy are amazingly high; but even halved, for which there would be no justification, they would still be significant.

* ⟨= Hopkins 1978b: 12 fig. 1.1.⟩

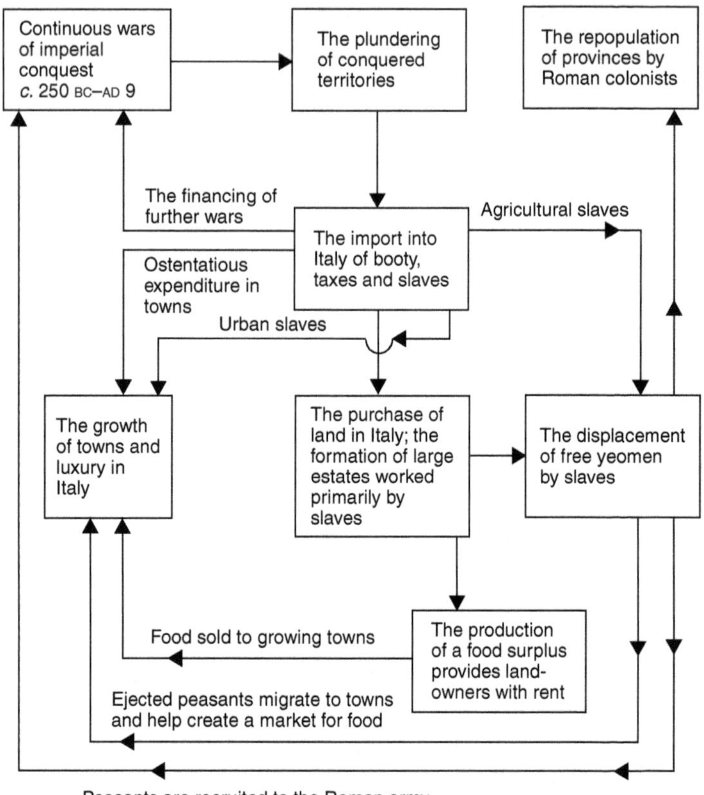

Figure 5.2. The growth of towns in Roman Italy – a scheme of interdependence.

profits were lent back to provincial taxpayers at usurious rates of interest. Rich men also spent lavishly in the city of Rome. We know from dozens of references in our sources that the whole lifestyle of the Roman élite was transformed by the wealth of conquest. Nobles ate from silver, instead of from wooden platters. Their wives bought jewellery and silks. Sumptuary laws which attempted to hold expenditure down at traditional levels were repeatedly passed and repeatedly ignored.

The stratification pyramid not only grew in height, but also thickened out at the top to incorporate new skills. Some were necessary for the administration of an increasingly complex empire, and some reflected the growing luxury of the élite. For example, advocates, consultant lawyers, doctors, architects, rhetoricians, poets, playwrights, school teachers, secretaries, even bankers were all unknown as distinct occupations in Roman society before its imperial expansion overseas. Some of these new workers helped create and inculcate a new integrative culture common to the élite throughout the empire; others helped the élite govern; others simply helped the élite spend its money in ostentatious consumption.

Expenditure by the rich percolated through the economy. Nobles kept and fed slaves, built palaces, commandeered services; in short, they spent money, which by its multiplier effects gave lots of people living in the city of Rome enough, or nearly enough, money to buy food, clothing and shelter. Without this expansion of the market and population in the city of Rome and a similar expansion in other Italian towns, nobles' investment in agriculture would have been fruitless.

The purchasing power of the urban proletariat must often have been in doubt. But its political power at Rome was strong enough to secure from state resources substantial distributions, at first (from 123/122 BC) of subsidised, and then (from 58 BC) of free wheat. The number of recipients (adult male citizens resident in the city of Rome) rose to 320,000 in 46 BC, and was 250,000 in 29 BC. These distributions of wheat must have encouraged urban immigration. They also underwrote with state funds the capacity of the poor to purchase the surplus food grown on the estates of the rich. A third function was to hold down the cost of services provided by the free poor to the rich. The economic cost of keeping a population of close on a million people in the city of Rome was disguised by transferring a substantial part of the cost to the state budget. Yet even if this helps explain away the huge size of Rome in a pre-industrial epoch, the size of Antioch, Carthage and Alexandria remains remarkable and unexplained.

One question seems outstanding and important: how significant was slavery in these developments? Slavery as a major productive force, mass slavery, has been extremely rare in human history. By mass slavery, I mean that about 20 per cent or more of the labour force were slaves.[61] Only five such slave societies are known in human history: three American societies (Brazil, the Caribbean islands and the southern states of the USA) and two from classical antiquity (Greece and Roman Italy). All these slave societies were closely associated with large-scale imperial conquests and with a shortage of easily exploitable labour. The rarity of known slave societies should take the edge out of the old Marxist contention that slavery was a universal stage in social development. Clearly it has not been. Even in the Roman empire, slavery was concentrated in Italy, although significant pockets of slaves persisted in Greece and in Greek cities in western Asia Minor; but there too, the majority of both rural and urban workers was always free. In the rest of the Roman empire, slavery was of little importance in production, although the ownership of domestic slaves was always a symbol of high status.

Slavery had three main economic functions. First, it secured the long-distance mobility of labour in a society in which there was no effective labour market. By defining humans as property at the disposal of the purchaser, slavery allowed conquering Romans to import an underclass of exploitable aliens. Without slaves, how could rich Romans have exploited their wealth? But slavery was not the only agent of migration; indeed in the process of conquest, slavery can be seen as the reciprocal of military movements and of colonisation. Conquered slaves were brought from the provinces so that they could work for their new masters, while conquering soldiers, recruited from their farms and dispossessed of their lands by members of their own élite, eventually settled in huge numbers in colonies on the land of the conquered. Needless to say, the switch between imported slaves and exported peasant soldiers sounds neater than it was in reality. Moreover, imported slaves included large numbers of

[61] The exact proportion of slaves is clearly arbitrary, but there does seem to be a real discontinuity. The number of slave societies would not be increased by changing the proportion to 15 per cent or even 10 per cent. And if slaves are a very small minority (less than 10 per cent) it is difficult to see how they can colour all exploitative relationships in a society.

educated Greeks who upgraded the conquerors' administrative services; rather like the import of American technology into a modern underdeveloped economy, they partly deformed, partly improved the efficiency of the native culture.

Secondly, by the mass import of exploitable aliens, slavery made possible a rise in the height of the stratification pyramid, without forcing citizens into directly exploited roles, except in their traditional role as soldiers. In other words, slavery allowed the myth of notional equality among Roman citizens and of citizen rights to survive a tremendous increase in inequality. Indeed, slavery defined even poor free citizens as belonging to a superior stratum. And so in élite culture and sometimes in Roman law, certain relationships of exploitation, such as working long term for another free person, came to be regarded as slave-like. For example, free men resident as workers in the household of their employers were regarded in law as being like slaves (*loco servorum*).[62] This degradation did not prevent some poor free men working in this way; presumably they had little choice. But, in general, the existence of mass slavery at the critical time of Roman economic expansion precluded the use of wage labour as an alternative means of aggregating free men under the exploitation of single entrepreneurs.

This brings us to the third economic function of slavery. Slavery did allow the coordination of several workers under the domination of a single owner. Indeed slavery allowed, or even demanded, a greater degree of exploitation than free men were used to. Whereas free peasants on a largish subsistence plot could achieve more than minimum subsistence with only one hundred man-workdays per year, by my reckoning the normal price of an agricultural slave implied a working year for slaves of at least two hundred man-days per year.[63] There

[62] *Dig.* 43.16.1.18 (Ulpian). See the commentary by de Robertis 1963: 121–42 and the corrective remarks by Nörr 1965: 90–3.

[63] Such calculations are difficult and fraught with possible error. But if the normal price of an adult unskilled male slave was 500 denarii (see *CIL* VIII 23956 and A. H. M. Jones 1956: 193–4), and if that price were amortised over twenty years (a longish period) at 6 per cent per year (a minimum rate), and if maintenance including clothing and housing is reckoned at 400 kg wheat equivalent per year, then the annual cost of a slave equalled 750 kg per year. A free labourer according to Diocletian's Edict on Maximum Prices (7.1a) cost 2.5 kg wheat per day plus

is little surprising in that. Slaves were forced to work harder than free peasants. In this way slavery brought an increase in labour productivity in agriculture. Theoretically wage-labour might have been more efficient, but that was not a path open to Roman landowners in the Roman political culture.

Did slavery hold back economic development? Much debate on this problem has been doctrinaire.[64] We have seen that the massive import of slaves into Italy precipitated an increase in agricultural productivity, which in turn made possible an increase in the size of towns. Many of the imported slaves were skilled and there is no evidence from the classical world, as there apparently is from the southern states of the USA, that slaves were entrusted only with unbreakable and therefore clumsily inefficient working tools. Slaves did cost a lot of money and so perhaps diverted money away from more productive investment; but slavery expanded fastest when conquering Romans had at their disposal booty, unattached free-floating resources from an expanding empire, for which there was a shortage of potential investments. The rich in a sense wasted capital on the purchase of lifelong labour, but it is difficult to think how else they could have used their capital more productively. Finally, it is argued that slavery restricted the size of the consumer market, because slaves were kept poor. But the majority of workers in town and countryside were always free. I cannot see that slavery was a critical factor in fixing consumer demand.

Up to now we have concentrated on the impact of conquest on economic development in Italy, with special reference to the import of slaves and the growth of the city of Rome. But the reciprocal flows of migration, the export of soldier colonists and some urban proletarians from central Italy, contributed significantly to urban growth in the rest of Italy and in the provinces. Bologna, Genoa, Modena, Parma and Turin, for example, were all colonial foundations or refoundations. But the greatest

maintenance (a low price, but possible by the standards of underdeveloped economies; see Clark and Haswell 1970: 139–51). Let us put the total cost at about 3.5 kg wheat equivalent per day. Then the slave would have to work 200 man-days per year or more to rival free wage labour.

[64] Kiechle 1969: 1–7 reviews the varied views on this point.

impact of colonisation was in the provinces: Julius Caesar and Augustus arranged for the foundation of over one hundred colonies scattered throughout the Mediterranean basin.[65] As we have seen, one of the main functions of these colonies was that they helped transfer some of the surplus free population out of Italy, so that more land was available there for occupation by the rich. In addition they allowed poor Romans some share in the fruits of conquest, without obliging the state to transfer extra taxes all the way from the provinces to Italy. In a low-level economy, it was more economical to move the conquerors out to occupy provincial land, where they created their own surplus on sequestrated farms, than to transport taxes and pay the conquerors a subsidy at home. Finally, of course, colonies overseas served as bastions of Romanisation and as garrison towns in the inner provinces. On the frontiers large towns grew up around legionary encampments, such as Cologne, Mainz and Strasbourg on the Rhine, Vienna and Belgrade on the Danube. Legionaries were paid twice as much as was necessary to maintain a peasant family at the level of minimum subsistence.[66] They therefore constituted new consumer markets, replete with cash, a situation rare in a pre-industrial economy.

Such urbanisation (colonies and garrison towns) was a direct result of conquest. So too, perhaps, was the development of administrative towns, shaped by Roman strategies of government. Roman administration of the provinces depended upon the cooperation of town councillors (decurions) who were responsible probably for the allocation, and almost certainly for the collection, of taxes. Conquest by Rome seems therefore to have stimulated the development of tribal towns, especially in the western provinces;[67] the predominant pattern visible in the list of towns given, for example, in Ptolemy's *Geography* was that each tribe had just one town ('beyond them, the

[65] Brunt 1971a: 589–601.

[66] Legionary pay in the first century AD was 900 sestertii per year; if wheat cost 3 sestertii per *modius* of 6.5 kg, this pay equalled almost two tonnes of wheat equivalent. I reckon minimum subsistence for an average peasant family of four persons at one tonne wheat equivalent per year.

[67] See e.g. Rivet 1964: 72–6.

Parisii and the town Lucotecia, beyond them the Tricasii and the town Augustobona and beyond them across the Loire, the Turonii and their town Caesorodunum'[68]). In Gaul, Spain and Britain, some hilltop forts were dismantled and the population was resettled in a more accessible, less defensible site below.[69] We know of several cases, particularly in the eastern provinces, in which towns vied with each other in the magnificence of their public buildings – temples, arcades, theatres, baths. Equipping towns with the appropriate urban adornments was an expensive business. In Italy itself, in the last century BC, village populations were sometimes synoecised, perhaps forcibly, into towns; and much money from provincial booty was spent on providing these towns with walls, a forum, paved streets and fountains.[70] This was not just a question of aesthetics, but of political status; to have local autonomy, one's own magistrates, local laws (and tax collectors), a place had to look like a real town. This was the prime stimulus to competitive expenditure.

Turning villages into agro-towns probably contributed little of itself to economic growth. Initially public building and municipal works may have offered temporary employment opportunities for rural workers, and even marginal gains made a difference to poor populations. But just as towns ostentatiously competed with other towns, so perhaps did local landowners compete with each other within towns. Towns gave them a stage: the forum, the porticoed arcades, the large town houses, in which they could show off their wealth. Perhaps competitive expenditure by local notables made them increase rents, just as conquest increased taxation. Certainly, the gradual integration of the Mediterranean economy, and the consequent growth of absentee landlordism (as large landlords owned property in several townships), must have forced tenants to earn back exported rents, just as taxpayers had to earn back exported taxes. In this process, towns played a vital role as transformers of local produce into exportable items of trade.

68 Ptol. *Geog.* 2.8.13–14.

69 See e.g. Grenier 1934: II 665–726, especially 669–79.

70 Gabba 1972.

The Level of Urbanisation and the Functions of Towns

The level of urbanisation in the Roman empire was not equalled or surpassed for at least a millennium.[71] That is a plausible claim and even probable; but how does one demonstrate that it is true? There are several indices which can be used: the size of the urban population, the inhabited area of towns, the area enclosed by walls, the sheer number of towns, the splendour of public monuments, the size of public benefactions, the sophistication of artefacts found by archaeologists, the known division of labour. Each index has its shortcomings, but all the indices seem to point in a similar direction, that is to a high level of urbanisation.

Let us quickly review the evidence and then discuss the functions of towns in the Roman economy. The size of the populations of the four or five largest Roman towns has already been mentioned. We have very little information on the size of other lesser towns. We have to rely on passing remarks and on stray bits of possibly inaccurate information. From these we gather, for example, that three cities in the eastern Mediterranean (Apamea, Ephesus, Pergamum) may have had free populations in excess of 100,000 – figures which by medieval or early modern European standards are substantial.[72] But the ancient figures may include the population of the rural area around the town.[73] Archaeological surveys have revealed the built-up area

[71] See Finley 1977. I am very grateful to Professor Finley for letting me see this article before its publication. I have been much influenced by it, without always agreeing with it.

[72] The evidence is found in Dessau *ILS* 2683, a census figure of Augustan date; Keil 1930: 57–8 ⟨= *IEph.* 951⟩; and a passing remark by Galen (see above n. 9) about a rich man, which I cite in full because it has been taken as concrete evidence: 'if our citizens number about four myriads, and if you add women and slaves, you will find yourself undoubtedly richer than twelve myriads of humans'. From this, having added children, Duncan-Jones deduces that the proportion of slaves in Italian towns was 22 per cent. I do not think it can properly bear that weight, but see his essay on 'Size of cities' in Duncan-Jones 1974: 259–87, which contains a careful review of all the ancient evidence, somewhat vitiated by misleading comparisons between Roman towns and modern populations (Italy in 1951), large industrial cities (Berlin in 1890) and the density of whole countries including large tracts of desert (Tunisia in 1966).

[73] Even if these figures included the rural population, it seems that the urban population would have been sizeable. Most of Duncan-Jones' figures (Duncan-Jones 1974: 273) are for citizens, that is for all adult males living in the area; one apparently urban figure, about 16,000 for Comum, is again large by post-medieval standards.

of Roman towns: for example, Leptis Magna covered an area of 120 hectares; Timgad 50 hectares; Thugga 20 hectares; Ostia 69 hectares; Pompeii 65 hectares. As with the areas enclosed by walls, such figures mean little unless we also know the density of buildings, their height and their rate of occupancy. Yet compared with towns, for example, in the late medieval period, these ancient urban areas seem sizeable and may indicate large urban populations.[74] The sheer number of Roman towns also seems large: nine hundred in the eastern provinces, over three hundred along the North African littoral, excluding Egypt, and a similar number in the Iberian peninsula and in Italy.[75] Once again such an index is far from perfect; the distinction between large village and town is arbitrary and was sometimes unclear in the ancient world.[76] The frequency of towns in an area might reflect its past political fragmentation, as in central Greece, or the administrative policy of rulers, as in Britain, as much as economic prosperity.

The monumental ruins of classical towns, even of quite small towns, seem very impressive. Paved streets, life-size statues, shady colonnades, temples, gymnasia, public baths, fountains, theatres, amphitheatres and aqueducts all give the impression of urban prosperity. Yet once again interpretation of this evidence is ambiguous. First, if we cost a typical set of urban public buildings, and then spread this total cost over two or three centuries, the annual investment, even making allowances for maintenance, seems quite modest.[77] In any case, ostentatious expenditure on public buildings represents as much a cultural as an economic phenomenon; for example, it could have resulted from decisions to spend money on permanent public

74 All these examples are given by Duncan-Jones (Duncan-Jones 1974: 264 n. 4, 276 n. 7). Data for Britain and Gaul are set out, rather more systematically than the evidence deserves I suspect, by Pounds 1969: 152–3: but enclosed area is not an accurate guide to relative importance. For later towns, see for example, but with caution, Russell 1972.

75 A list of Roman towns in the eastern empire is given by A. H. M. Jones 1971: 522–52 appendix 4. For the western empire, the best list is by Ptolemy in his *Geography*, from which this count was made.

76 Strabo 3.4.13.

77 This ingenious test was made by MacMullen 1974: 142–5.

buildings rather than on transient rituals. Buildings may also reflect the degree to which the poor were exploited by rentiers as much as a general rise in prosperity. Of course, prosperity and exploitation are by no means mutually exclusive. Since we cannot be sure, I prefer to remain cautiously sceptical rather than to assume *a priori* that grand public buildings, from palaces to basilicas, reflected widespread increases in urban wealth.

Is there then any safe way of getting at general levels of prosperity in ancient towns? We do not know wage rates, we have no surviving census returns from towns.[78] The first temptation may be to give up in despair. But perhaps two indices hold out some hope. The first is the stratified archaeological findings which in western provinces repeatedly show a higher concentration of artefacts at Roman compared to pre-Roman levels: more coins, pots, lamps, iron tools, carved stones, ornaments; in short a higher standard of living than was common in the pre-Roman population occupying the same sites.[79] The second index is the division of labour. Tombstones from the city of Rome show the existence of over two hundred named trades and occupations. An astrological handbook mentioned 264 occupations. This compares with about 350 trades listed in Campbell's *London Tradesmen* published in the mid-eighteenth century.[80] Such lists obviously

[78] In about AD 300 the population of the city of Autun in Gaul was taxed at 25,000 heads as against 32,000 previously (*Pan. Lat.* 5.11), but that was the taxable population of the district, not specifically of the town (see now Nixon and Rodgers 1994: 280–1 n. 46). Besides, the government had little interest in an exact head count. They were interested in the relative capacity of towns to pay tax. I imagine that even if originally tax units related to heads, they were not regularly or efficiently re-examined, whatever the government intended.

[79] To an outsider, archaeological reports seem hopelessly fragmented. Archaeologists seem more interested in doing another dig and writing up last year's finds than in making sense of the last generation's advances. I can therefore cite only incidental studies of individual sites which make a passing reference to comparisons between Roman and pre-Roman levels: Schulten 1933: 153–5; Kraeling 1962: 8–10, 93–4, 115–16; Morel 1965: 108–11; Clavel 1970: 331–3.

[80] *CIL* VI.2 pp. vii–viii; Firm. Mat. *Mathesis* with Bram 1975: 315–22 Index of occupations; Bücher 1904: 286–7 stresses that the division of labour has different implications according to whether it implies division of production (spinner, fuller, weaver), specialisation of trade (e.g. nailsmith, who turns raw product into finished article) or subdivision of labour (one man makes nail head, another the shaft). Each has different economic implications. The ancient division was obviously more of the first two types than the third.

have to be used with caution (probably none is complete), but I think they reflect the fact that by the eighteenth century London and other large northern European towns had reached a level of economic sophistication such as classical Rome never reached.

Complete lists of trades from other classical towns are difficult to get, either because trades were not written on tombstones or because only few tombstones survive from each town. However, there is one set of tombstones, perhaps dating from the third to the sixth centuries AD, from Kōrykos, a small and insignificant town in Rough Cilicia in south-eastern Asia Minor.[81] Over half of the males commemorated ($n = 702$) there had their occupations named, and these cover 110 different trades, probably not all present at one time. Extremely poor tradesmen were probably under-represented, but less than usual, since the tombs were reused and the inscriptions were both short and simple. Some of the trades mentioned were very humble, including woodcutters, beggars, clothes menders and cooked-food sellers. Overall the distribution of tradesmen corroborates the view expressed above that luxury trades (13 per cent) and textiles (18 per cent) were important and it reinforces the idea that urban markets even in small towns met a complex of needs (pottery manufacturing 10 per cent, shipping 8 per cent, smithying 5 per cent, building 5 per cent, food sales 15 per cent – $n = 328$). The plausibility of this apparently large number of trades is confirmed by the eighty-five trades attested from Pompeii, a town with a population of about 20,000.[82]

What then was the function of ancient towns? One powerful view is that they were primarily centres of consumption; this is the definition given by Sombart: 'By a consumption city (*Konsumptionsstadt*) I mean one which pays for its

[81] These are to be found in *MAMA* III 200–768. I have listed trades for males only, since females were markedly under-represented.

[82] The occupations from Pompeii are mostly attested in election posters daubed on stucco walls. They are to be found in the indices to *CIL* IV and in della Corte 1954: 422–4 index 4. But when della Corte deduced an occupation without corroboration, it has not been included.

maintenance ... not with its own products, because it does not need to. It derives its maintenance rather on the basis of a legal claim (*Rechtstitel*) such as taxes or rents, without having to deliver return values.'[83] Now that is an ideal type; an ideal type according to Weber is formed by the one-sided accentuation of a particular point of view and by the synthesis of several discrete and diffuse phenomena 'into a unified analytical construct (*Gedankenbild*) ... this mental construct cannot be found empirically anywhere in reality. It is a utopia. Historical research faces the task of determining in each individual case, the extent to which this ideal-construct approximates to or diverges from reality.'[84]

The idea of a consumer city is brilliant. But it does not imply that only consumers lived in ancient towns; a considerable number of townsmen were obviously petty commodity producers. But in the 'consumer city', the producers were subsidiary to the consumers, and their 'existence was determined by the share of the consumption fund allowed to them by the consumption class'.[85]

The value of an ideal type does not lie in its precision, or in the exactness of its fit with 'historical reality', but in its isolation of a vital difference from alternative ideal types, such as the garrison town, the administrative city and the village, and above all the manufacturing or commercial town of northern Europe in the post-medieval period. In the commercial city, the burghers were primarily interested in trade or manufacture, and they had some political independence from a rural aristocracy; they could set their own pace and could develop their own ethical and legal standards. By contrast, one of the prime strengths and limitations of the ancient city was that it coalesced the rural and urban population into a single autarchic autonomous unit, in which agricultural landowners set the tone. Roman

83 In this and the following pages I am much indebted to, although I diverge from, the stimulating article by Finley 1977. The quotation is from Sombart 1916–27: I 142 and is cited by Finley 1977: 317.

84 ⟨Weber 1904: 65⟩ trans. Shils and Finch 1949: 90.

85 Sombart 1916–27: I 143.

conquest penetrated that autarchy but never separated the town from its countryside.

Were ancient cities consumer cities? The answer must be yes. Great landowners lived in towns. They drew the bulk of their income from their estates, whether by direct exploitation through bailiffs or from rents. Landowners were the wealthiest urban residents. The money they spent in towns was largely drawn from outside the towns. In that sense, ancient towns were parasitical on the surrounding countryside. Towns were centres of consumption in which landowners spent profits derived from rural property and from the hard work of dependent peasants.

From early times in the classical world, town and countryside had been integrated into single city-states. Landowners were citizens. This organisation persisted even when city-states became the administrative units of empire. Therefore, there was no political organisation specific to the town, which excluded the surrounding countryside. There were no institutions which fostered specifically urban, commercial or manufacturing activity and gave traders or manufacturers a status independent of, or parallel to, the traditional status of landowners. In this way, ancient towns differed, as I understand it, from those post-medieval European towns which grew up in the interstices of feudal baronies, and whose burghers had only very limited opportunities to become members of the landed aristocracy. Dutch or Hanseatic burghers concentrated therefore on the acquisition of commercial wealth and elaborated an ethos which morally elevated their own activities. In the ancient world, however, successful merchants sought respectability and safety by reinvesting their commercial profits in the ownership of land. I suspect that this was only a difference of degree, since we find the same phenomenon of gentrification by the acquisition of land among English merchants. But Roman financiers, tax farmers and public contractors were always required to give land as security for the performance of their duties. It was thus extremely rare in the Roman world for a man to be wealthy without being a landowner.

I do not mean by all this that Romans despised trade. Of course, some members of the literary élite, whose writings have survived, affected to despise trade, at least if it was on a small scale; philosophers despised trade because haggling over prices involved deception. Yet numerous monuments set up in the Greek and Roman world depict tradesmen and artisans at work; these monuments show in a convincing way that among the working classes, and even among the prosperous commercial classes, there was nothing demeaning about work.[86] But trade was less prestigious than owning land. And no prosperous, high-prestige stratum or corporation of urban merchants, as distinct from landowners, ever emerged in Roman society.

In the current orthodoxy, the contribution of manufactures to the urban economy in the Roman world is considered to have been negligible.[87] And it is true that most manufacturing and trading units were small; only a few can have employed slaves or apprentices or wage-labourers. Petty commodity production and a bazaar economy of fragmented services predominated. But the small scale of most units of production should not be taken as evidence of their aggregate unimportance. Indeed these small units of non-agricultural production elevated the average standard of living in the Roman empire above, even if only slightly above, the average standard of living in most preceding states.

The Roman empire was borne on the backs of its peasants, and much of the taxes and rents which they paid were spent in towns, for the benefit of townsmen. But it is wrong to assume that peasants got nothing in return. They got law, protection, peace, rituals, ceremonies and medical advice, even surgery. Towns gave independent peasants and free tenants opportunity to buy extra food and services, necessities and luxuries (tools, pots, clothes, seeds, pastries). Moreover, the towns

[86] See numerous examples in Esperandieu 1907–28: III especially 82–4 nos 1881–4. The Pompeian wall paintings depict several manufacturing scenes: see Mau 1899: 376–7.

[87] 'In most of the cities of the empire, trade and industry played a minor role … Trade and manufacture played a very minor part in the economy of the Roman empire. The basic industry was agriculture' (A. H. M. Jones 1954: 168–9).

themselves generated economic activity. Urban artisans had to be serviced, housed; they bought goods. The list of tradesmen from Kōrykos, the small town in Rough Cilicia (see [200] above), shows that most tradesmen were engaged in making useful things. The very size of Roman towns indicates the volume of demand which they generated. Much of that demand required urban produce.

In sum, the ideal type of the consumer city has much to recommend it; it largely fits the towns of the ancient world, providing we realise that, in reality, ancient towns also served other functions: they were administrative centres, they were garrison towns, they were centres of exchange both as between towns and regions, and between townsmen and the surrounding countryside. All these functions were important. The weakness of the ideal type, in spite of the intentions of its creators, is that it replaces complexity with oversimplification: all too easily, the 'consumer city' becomes the parasitical city, consisting exclusively of idle consumers, fed from the countryside and giving nothing in return.

In the ancient economy, agriculture was clearly pre-eminent; most adults in the Roman world worked in the fields; most wealth was based on landownership. This was because the institution of tenancy allowed rich Romans to aggregate the activities of tens, even hundreds of agricultural workers, with little managerial cost. Land could therefore be the prime focus of rich men's investments. If we want to find economic growth in the ancient world, we should look for it in agriculture, not in towns. Average yields of cereals at four or more times seed in Italy and at ten times seed in Egypt were apparently well above early medieval levels. Conquest brought improved productivity and forced up yields through taxation. The Roman conquest of Britain, for example, induced the extension of settled agriculture and the introduction of new crops such as beans, cabbage and peas which had a profound (and lasting) effect on British diets.[88] Further increases in

[88] See Applebaum 1972: 108–21. Other imports under Roman influence include the turnip, cherry, mustard and radish. There was also a considerable and important improvement in the shape of the plough.

peasants' productivity were limited partly by the technical inadequacy of agriculture, but even more by poor peasants' chronic underemployment. Their access to more land was restricted by the rich. Small farms kept peasants underworked, while their low consumption demands held down urban productivity, so that only about one family in ten lived away from the land.

The arena for strictly urban economic development was thus very limited. There was no urban institution which rivalled tenancy as a medium of exploitation. Slavery was expensive and important but as a form of production only a transient function of conquest. Tenancies of urban property were important only in the city of Rome. Partnerships in trade, both active and sleeping, were known but were usually on a small scale. Shared risks in sea-loans, on ships and their cargoes, helped investment in a risky branch of trade. But private corporations investing in tax farming, in mining and in contracts for public works were probably the only productive non-agricultural outlet for large sums of capital.

These corporations are especially interesting because they seem to foreshadow developments which were of great importance in later European banking. In post-medieval Europe, kings borrowed from private bankers, who often protected their credit and their lives by living in other countries. Thus the fragmentation of Europe into rival nations and city-states afforded, even encouraged, developments which the overarching size of the Roman empire precluded. Roman emperors never borrowed from private citizens; indeed, the emperors, in the interests of efficiency or good government, slowly strangled the private tax farming corporations. When they were in need of money, emperors either raised taxes, or confiscated the property of the rich or debased the currency.

In some respects, Rome was a victim of its own success. In other societies, heavy state expenditure on war has stimulated economic growth; the competitive drive to win has promoted creative investment and the military has constituted a very large market for arms, supplies and ships. This also occurred in the Roman empire, in that the exaction of taxes to pay troops was a major stimulus to long-distance trade. But

Roman armies never faced an enemy which was significantly superior in equipment, so that war did not act as a spur to imitation or invention. Indeed, because of state power, military demands eventually restricted economic growth. In the late empire, military supplies and taxes were removed from the market; military supplies were demanded as taxes in kind; for a time, money taxes were virtually abolished. The response to increased external pressure from barbarians was thus not invention but a tightening of the screws of state repression. The standing army was doubled in size from about 300,000 to about 600,000 men; the army was already, by my reckoning, the largest occupational subset after the peasantry. This was both a reflection of the limits of economic and urban sophistication in the Roman empire and of the considerable resources that were used to preserve the safety of the state. Huge pre-industrial empires accumulate huge resources; they spend a large part of that accumulated surplus on self-preservation, not on economic growth.[89]

[89] I should like to thank Chester Starr, Mark Hassall and John North for advice and help.

AFTERWORD

ECONOMIC GROWTH AND TOWNS IN CLASSICAL ANTIQUITY

NEVILLE MORLEY

This essay, and the volume in which it was originally published (P. Abrams and E. A. Wrigley (eds), *Towns in Societies: Essays in Economic History and Historical Sociology*, Cambridge, 1978), stemmed from the 1975 conference of the Past and Present Society on the theme of 'Towns and Economic Growth', which set out to explore the long-standing assumption in historical studies of a clear link between urbanisation and economic growth. In ancient history, this approach was found in the works of historians such as M. I. Rostovtzeff, who took it entirely for granted that towns and cities in the Hellenistic and Roman worlds were centres of industry and trade, dominated by a merchant class or bourgeoisie that was quite separate from the traditional landed aristocracy.[1] A more recent example was Walter Moeller's *The Wool Trade of Ancient Pompeii* (1976), cited by Hopkins (52 [178–9]), which surveyed the archaeological and epigraphic evidence for cloth production in the city, and concluded both that the Pompeian economy was founded on the production and export of textiles, and that 'wool interests' played a significant role in local society and politics.[2] However, these 'modernising' views of the ancient (especially the Roman) economy – seeing it as essentially comparable to early modern Europe in its nature and level of development – were never universally accepted. Back in the nineteenth century, economists like Karl Bücher had insisted that antiquity was thoroughly pre-modern and pre-capitalist in its organisation, while early twentieth-century sociologists like Max Weber and Werner Sombart saw the ancient city as quite different from the late medieval and early

[1] E.g. Rostovtzeff 1941, 1957.
[2] Jongman 1988: 155–86 offers a detailed critique of Moeller 1976.

modern European cities that provided (it was widely agreed) the paradigm for the dynamic, economically productive urban centre acting as a stimulus on the rest of society. As H. was writing this essay, Moses Finley was working on a similar theme, reviewing earlier attempts at characterising the ancient city (in particular those of Sombart and Weber) in order to show that it was best understood as a 'consumer' rather than a 'producer', dominated by the landowning élite rather than any new merchant class, and reflecting the undeveloped and static nature of the ancient economy.[3] Over the following two decades, the question of whether the ancient city is best characterised as a producer or consumer, and the implications of this for understanding the ancient economy, became one of the central debates of ancient economic history, to the extent that by the mid-1990s historians were desperately seeking a way 'beyond the consumer city'.[4]

H. approaches the topic in what might at first appear a fairly oblique manner: the bulk of his essay deals with the nature and structure of the Roman economy as a whole, with towns and cities receiving only passing mention until the closing pages. This approach echoes the argument of the sociologist Philip Abrams, co-editor of the volume, that historians need to stop reifying the town and treating it as an independent social variable, and instead see it as one place where wider economic and social processes are expressed and worked through.[5] '[Towns'] contribution to economic change can be understood only in the context of the political system in which they existed, and of the rural hinterland on which they depended' (36 [161]). In other words, we need to understand the ancient economy and its potential for growth and development in order to understand the ancient city, rather than arguing (as Finley tends

[3] Finley 1977; as H. notes (69 n. 71 [197 n. 71]), he saw a copy of this paper prior to publication, and was thus able to engage with its arguments in his essay. Discussions of Finley's approach – often with only minimal reference to H. – include Bruhns 1985; Nippel 1987–9; Osborne 1991; Wallace-Hadrill 1991; Morley 1996: 14–32; D. J. Mattingly 1997. Bruhns 1987–9; Nippel 1991; Capogrossi Colognesi 1995 look back to Weber's original account.

[4] See discussions in Engels 1990; Whittaker 1990; Rich and Wallace-Hadrill 1991; Cornell and Lomas 1995; Parkins 1997.

[5] Abrams 1978.

to) that the pre-modern 'consumer' nature of the city gives us the key to the pre-modern, primitive nature of the ancient economy, or taking it for granted (as some ancient historians and archaeologists still do) that merely identifying an increase in the level of urbanisation is sufficient proof of economic growth and development in the Roman world.[6]

H. thus offers here the most extended summary in his published works of his view of the Roman economy as a whole. In typical manner, he begins with an acknowledgement of the shortage of data and the limitations of our knowledge, and proceeds to offer hypotheses on the basis of what evidence has survived: the diffusion of coined money, the spread of Roman roads, the wide variety of goods consumed across the empire, the division of labour in towns revealed by epigraphy and so forth. His style is, as ever, economical, assertive and supremely self-confident, presenting an argument that rests on inductive reasoning and, implicitly, the comparability of classical antiquity with better documented pre-modern societies, rather than on the accumulation of ancient literary sources.[7] At almost every point, a sceptic could reasonably demand more evidence and more detailed analysis to justify the statements; and indeed H. explored a number of the topics touched upon in this essay in greater depth in other publications.[8] However, what really matters in this style of argument is the coherence and plausibility of the overall interpretation and its underlying assumptions, the extent to which this account is more persuasive than the alternatives; and it is striking how far current approaches to the Roman economy tend to resemble H.'s vision rather than the different perspectives with which he was engaging thirty-five years ago.[9]

[6] Finley 1985: 123–49 and 191–6, 1977 *passim*. For recent examples of historians and archaeologists seeing urbanisation as a more or less unproblematic sign of economic development, see Lo Cascio 2009; A. I. Wilson 2011a with Morley 2011 for a rejoinder.

[7] On H.'s rhetorical style and attitude to literary evidence, see Morley 2006.

[8] E.g. Hopkins 1978b: 1–98, 1980a [essay 6].

[9] See, above all, the papers in Manning and Morris 2005; Scheidel, Morris and Saller 2007.

On the one hand, H.'s account is clearly opposed to the modernising approach of Rostovtzeff and his successors; he is equally creative in showing how fragmentary pieces of evidence, especially material evidence, can reveal the complexity of the ancient economy, but he takes for granted the existence of significant qualitative as well as quantitative differences between antiquity and later periods, especially the modern capitalist economy. H.'s antiquity is thoroughly pre-modern and pre-industrial, with the vast majority of its population occupied in subsistence agriculture; Roman society is dominated by the state and the traditional landed interests rather than by any dynamic new bourgeoisie; and the key historical questions are whether there was any economic growth or development at all, whether aggregate or per capita, and whether there was any significant trade in goods other than luxuries. On the other hand, there are also striking divergences from the 'primitivism' of Finley that was already becoming, as H. suggested, 'the new orthodoxy' in ancient economic history. H. seeks to offer a positive characterisation of classical antiquity, rather than simply insisting on the ways in which it differed from modernity, and he presents it as a world in which there was capacity for some growth and development – indeed, he implicitly questions the idea of a unified and uniform ancient economy, not only by focusing on the special case of the Roman empire, but by grounding his analysis in the contrast, as far as aggregate production and material achievement were concerned, between the world of Rome and that of fifth-century Athens.

However, this is not a lurch back towards the naïve assumption that, because growth occurred and trade became more extensive and substantial, the Roman economy must have been essentially modern. Rather, H. shows how these developments were neither natural nor inevitable, but the product of forces and processes specific to the historical context: above all, the impact of Roman imperialism in diffusing ideas and institutions throughout the empire (especially in the West), in transforming political and social organisation, and in creating new centres of demand, in particular the army and the city of Rome, that changed the conditions under which production and distribution took place and individuals made economic decisions.[10] H. thus anticipates recent approaches that draw upon 'New Institutional Economics', in focusing on the important role of coinage and roads, created by the Roman state for its own non-economic purposes, but nevertheless instrumental in creating conditions favourable to the development of exchange. The stale dichotomies of 'primitivist' and 'modernising' approaches to the ancient economy, in which it is evaluated solely in terms of its resemblance to early modern developments, are circumvented or ignored. H.'s extensive use of comparisons with other historical societies, for example to insist on the importance of textiles and metals in the analysis of any pre-modern economy, emphasises both that the Roman empire was indisputably pre-industrial and pre-modern, and also that there can be significant variations in economic structure and performance between different pre-industrial societies.[11] Establishing the relatively undeveloped nature of the Roman economy by modern standards is simply the beginning of the debate.

This then is the framework, and the logic of the argument, for understanding the role of the Roman city. In terms of the ideal types offered by Sombart, Weber and Finley, the Roman city was clearly a consumer rather than a producer; it was not primarily a centre of trade or industry, nor was it separate from the countryside, economically, politically or socially. However, that is not – as was often assumed in later discussions – the end of the argument. 'The weakness of the ideal type, in spite of the intentions of its creators, is that it replaces complexity with oversimplification' (75 [204]). The Roman city

10 The importance of demand for the development of trade is discussed further in Hopkins 1983a: 90–6 [essay 7: 279–89], and emphasised in Morley 2007: 37–54. The impact of city of Rome is explored further in Hopkins 1995–6: 58–9 and Morley 1996; that of the army as a centre of demand in Erdkamp 1998 and 2002; general discussions of close relation between imperialism, markets and economic activity in Bang 2008 and Morley 2010: 70–101.

11 Metals – both the technology involved in extraction and processing, and their distribution – are increasingly the focus of detailed study; e.g. A. I. Wilson 2002, and the forthcoming publication (ed. A. I. Wilson and A. K. Bowman) of a conference on 'Mining, metal supply and coinage in the Roman world' organised by the Oxford Roman Economy Project in 2010.

was not *essentially* a 'consumer city'; it simply fits that model better than the alternative of the 'producer city'. It was in reality never solely a centre of consumption, but also had administrative, economic and military functions. Just as importantly, the establishment of urban centres, even though this was for entirely non-economic motives, nevertheless promoted economic activity, and the unprecedented level of urbanisation under the Roman empire is one indication that it experienced significant economic growth. None of these ideas is elaborated at any great length, but H.'s essay nevertheless lays the foundation for current understanding of the Roman city: not as an independent social variable, but as one manifestation of the dominant structures of power in the empire, that nevertheless had far-reaching influence on the society that supported it.[12]

12 See e.g. the various new theoretical approaches to urbanisation in Alston 2001; Morley 2008; Zuiderhoek 2016.

6

TAXES AND TRADE IN THE ROMAN EMPIRE (200 BC–AD 400)*

This essay is speculative and tentative, a preliminary attempt at exploring a broad territory of Roman economic history over a long period. For the sake of clarity, I have canvassed several probabilities in the form of propositions, but the evidence is so sparse that it is difficult to *prove* that each proposition is right. It is disappointing to confess at the outset that one's case is unproven and that the generalisations advanced are disproportionately large in relation to the supporting evidence.[1] Even so, the experiments made here with both evidence and methods may stimulate others into refuting or reshaping the propositions. And besides, some of the methods can be usefully applied to other problems in Roman history.

Propositions 1 and 2

The first proposition is that the Romans' imposition of taxes paid in money greatly increased the volume of trade in the Roman empire (200 BC–AD 400). Secondly, in so far as money taxes were levied on conquered provinces and then spent in other provinces or in Italy, then the tax-exporting provinces had to earn money with which to pay their taxes by exporting goods of an equal value.[2]

* First published in *Journal of Roman Studies* 70 (1980) 101–25 (= Hopkins 1980a).

[1] I shall concentrate here on argument and on the economic structure of the Roman empire, rather than on what Romans thought they were doing or on surviving sources. I have adopted this tactic simply because I want to cover a broad canvas in a relatively short article, not because I feel that the Romans' own economic thoughts or writings should be neglected. But it does mean that some of the conventional signposting is missing.

[2] I must stress the correlative form of the second proposition: in so far as …, then … (in so far as …). For the moment, I make no estimate of the volume of taxes, nor of the extent to which they were raised in money.

These two propositions may seem unexceptionable, but their applications are interesting. At the risk of simplification, they lead us to envisage the Roman empire in the central period of the high empire (the first two centuries AD) as comprising three spheres:

(a) an outer ring of frontier provinces in which defensive armies were stationed;
(b) an inner ring of relatively rich tax-exporting provinces, such as Spain, southern Gaul, northern Africa, Asia Minor, Syria and Egypt;
(c) the centre, comprising Italy and the city of Rome, the seat of the court and of the central government, which, like the armies on the frontiers, consumed a large volume of taxes.

The armies on the frontiers (a) and the city of Rome, the court and the central government (c) consumed more taxes than were produced locally. The two propositions imply that in the long run, on average, these tax-importing regions (the frontiers and the city of Rome) imported goods to a value which roughly equalled the imported tax.[3]

The main focus of this paper is on large-scale inter-regional flows of taxes and trade. But large-scale flows were the cumulative result of myriads of local transactions and transformations. Even at local levels, the Roman imposition of money taxes and their expenditure outside the region where they were levied had a serious impact on simple cultivators; they were forced to produce, and to sell, more food in order to pay taxes. The impact was greatest in those regions in which simple cultivators had paid little or no tax in money before the Roman conquest. There, cultivators were forced to produce and sell a surplus which they had not previously produced, or which they had previously consumed themselves (afterwards they simply went without). Some of this surplus was probably shipped direct to tax-consuming regions (for example, Spanish olive oil to the city of Rome). But the costs of transporting staple foods

[3] These two propositions also imply an explanation for the increase of imports into Italy during the high empire. I do not mean that Italy stopped exporting, only that the balance of trade favoured imports; the explanation is to be sought more in economic forces than in an Italian moral decline.

for long distances, especially overland, were high;[4] besides, tax-consuming regions grew some of their own food and in addition drew upon taxes levied in kind (for example, wheat sent to the city of Rome).

The two propositions imply another process, which we can guess at in simple terms. In economically unsophisticated regions, peasant taxpayers increasingly sold some of their primary produce in local markets in order to raise money with which to pay taxes. The food which they sold was consumed locally by artisans, who made goods of higher value and lower volume than staple foods (for example, textiles, leather goods, pots). Again some of these handmade, relatively valuable goods were consumed locally; but others were exported from inner provincial towns, both to the frontier provinces and to the city of Rome.[5]

This simple model implies a whole series of small-scale changes in production, distribution and consumption, whose cumulative impact over time was important. There was a significant increase in agricultural production, an increase in the division of labour, growth in the number of artisans, in the size of towns where many of them lived, development of local markets and of long-distance commerce. Complementarily, there were changes in the pattern of consumption: government employees, soldiers and officials, received tax monies as pay and spent their money on food, services and artisan-made goods, some of which came from the distant provinces

[4] The problem of how much staple food was transported, long-distance overland or by ship, cannot be solved simply by pointing out the high *relative* cost of land transport. That alone did not make it *absolutely* prohibitive. I suspect that availability of transport, information and trader organisation were also important. Comparative evidence illustrates the problems. In Italy in the sixteenth century, staples were occasionally transported from the eastern coast of Italy overland to the city of Rome (Delumeau 1957–9: II 521–649, especially 587–98), but in southern France in the same period, the volume of transport available for carting supplies between towns was too small to even out inter-city variations in price (Baehrel 1961: 530–99).

[5] Archaeological evidence is uncorrectably biased by the survival of pots, which cannot have been so important in the Roman economy. The salvation is that surviving pots can reasonably serve as proxy for perishable goods such as textiles, which have not survived archaeologically, but which probably were important economically. Thus distribution maps of pots illustrate the viability and direction of long-distance trade. For one example, see Peacock 1978: 50 fig. 44.

which paid the original money taxes. There was an increase in the number of people who made it their job to look after the needs of soldiers on the frontiers and of officials in the city of Rome. Thus the model implies an increased monetisation of the Roman economy, the commercialisation of exchange, an elongation of the links between producers and consumers, the growth of specialist intermediaries (traders, shippers, bankers) and an unprecedented level of urbanisation.[6] The model illustrates the close connection between changes on the level of individual action by simple peasants and relatively large-scale changes, such as the growth of towns.

These changes were most dramatic in regions which were economically primitive before their conquest by the Romans. But there were regions, such as Syria and western Asia Minor, which had paid money taxes to local rulers for centuries before the Roman conquest, regions which were already urbanised and had well established networks of intra-regional and inter-regional trade. Other regions lay between these two extremes of economic simplicity and sophistication.[7] Conquest by the Romans disrupted established patterns even in economically advanced regions: the Romans plundered the stored reserves of generations, from towns, temples and from rich individuals' treasure chests. They siphoned off skilled and unskilled labour as slaves; they gave loans to oppressed landowners and then distrained upon their estates when they were unable to pay extortionate rates of interest. The plunder of capital, labour and land, the loans and the debts, were short-term adaptations to the long-term redirection of taxes and trade. The local population had to accommodate the fact that taxes were no longer spent in the regional metropolis, but far away in the city of Rome or in the frontier provinces. In the long term, as we

[6] On the growth of towns, see especially Finley 1977; Hopkins 1978a [essay 5], where several of the issues discussed here are put in a different form.

[7] Once again, I am for the moment concerned more with the logic of the argument than with the evidence by which one could allocate regions conquered by the Romans along a continuum of economic sophistication, or lack of it. I am certainly not assuming that all western provinces were economically primitive before the Roman conquest. I suspect (though how would one prove?) that they did become more sophisticated after conquest by the Romans. Cf. below n. 13.

know, the inner-core provinces were not impoverished by the Roman conquest; indeed, it is plausible to assert (but difficult to prove) that these economically advanced regions adapted to the changed conditions under Roman domination so well that in the high empire they reached a level of general prosperity equal to or higher than any reached previously.[8]

Some Qualifications

Up to now I have concentrated on the reciprocal flows of taxes and trade, their cumulative impact and their contribution to the integration of the economy of the Roman empire. I have stressed the growth in production and consumption, the increasing monetisation of the Roman economy and the commercialisation of exchange. But several qualifications deserve equal emphasis. First, the complex networks of tax-stimulated trade were only gradually established in the wake of Roman conquest, after considerable initial disruption. Secondly, much trade flowed without the stimulus of money taxes. It was based on reciprocal needs and on the location both of supply and of demand. For example, only some districts had a readily available supply of metals, such as gold, silver, copper or lead, for which the demand was widespread. Hence an important export trade all over the Mediterranean basin.

Thirdly, the pattern and volume of demand was also heavily influenced by fluctuations in rainfall. At first sight, the unity of the climate in the Mediterranean basin might suggest a uniformity of crops grown throughout the region and therefore no necessity for long-distance trade in staple foods (wheat, barley, wine, olive oil). But sharp inter-annual fluctuations of rainfall created local gluts and local shortages and stimulated unpredictable flows of surplus staples to unpredicted markets; hence small-scale (but in aggregate large volume) inter-regional trade

[8] The concept, general prosperity, is purposely vague. We know that the rich were rich, and we admire great public buildings, such as the theatre at Aspendus or the temples at Petra and Palmyra. But how can we know about the distribution of wealth and the standard of living of relatively poor townsmen or peasants?

in staples, mostly seaborne.[9] The volume of demand, that is the capacity to pay for food and goods brought over a long distance, was a function both of production over and above the level of minimum subsistence and of inequality. Let me mention, just in passing, that the simple categories, élite/peasantry, luxury trade/trade in staples, cannot do justice to the complexity of demand within the Roman economy. In my view, such simple divisions lead implicitly to a serious underestimate of the sophistication, variety and volume of goods commonly traded in the Roman empire.[10]

Fourthly, many taxes were raised in kind. These taxes in kind, such as wheat from Egypt and North Africa, stand outside my two initial propositions. Taxes in kind do not stimulate trade, because such produce flowed only in one direction from taxpayer to tax-consumer. Indeed, taxes levied in kind limited the sphere of market or monetary transactions; and they tempted the Roman government to have produce transported (such as wheat distributed free of charge to over 200,000 persons in the city of Rome) without consideration of the total cost.[11] The volume of such flows reflected political power; they affected, but they did not depend on, the level of trade.

Finally, the economy of the Roman empire, in spite of its sophistication in some respects, was predominantly a subsistence economy. The monetary economy constituted a thin

[9] 'Traders roam from sea to sea looking for some market which is badly stocked', so Philostr. *VA* 4.32.2. Inter-annual fluctuations of rainfall have been largely ignored by ancient economic historians, perhaps because no ancient source mentions them. See the *International Yearbook of Agricultural Statistics* (International Institute of Agriculture, Rome) for modern national figures. ⟨See Hopkins 1983a: 90–2 [essay 7: 279–82].⟩

[10] The most exciting documents which illustrate the nature of ancient Mediterranean trade are the Genizeh papyri from Cairo, dating from the tenth century AD onwards (see Goitein 1967). Nothing from the classical period can rival them. In spite of their late date, they are useful for Roman historians. ⟨See Hopkins 1978a: 50–2 [essay 5: 177–8].⟩ The long lists of produce in Frank 1933–40 reflect an antiquarian idea of what economic history should be. The main questions should be: which organisations of traders, by what mechanisms (partnership, investment, credit, cash?), sold how much of what to whom? Even the customs lists at Zarai, Numidia (*CIL* VIII 4508) and Palmyra (*OGIS* 629) do not help us reach an answer to these questions.

[11] Augustus, *Res Gestae* 15; van Berchem 1939; cf. the Chinese experience in supplying Peking: H. C. Hinton 1956.

veneer of sophistication, spread over and tied to the subsistence economy by the liens of taxes, trade and rent. The concept, subsistence economy, has important implications. The bulk of the labour force in the Roman empire, perhaps 80–90 per cent, were primarily peasants who produced most of what they themselves consumed and consumed most of what they produced. This solid mass of self-sufficient production always stood outside the money economy. However, this cellular autarky of individual peasant farmers and of most districts was penetrated, but not pervaded, by outside demands. By this I mean that peasants were affected, even burdened, by demands for taxes, for rents and for goods bought in the market (such as knives, or clothes). But the payment of taxes and rents constituted only a minor element out of total production, even if they constituted the major part of peasants' disposable surplus.[12] The term, subsistence economy, also implies that on average levels of consumption were not dramatically above the minimum level of subsistence. Here again, several distinctions should be made. In general, Roman levels of consumption were obviously and significantly higher than pre-Roman levels of consumption, at least in the western provinces.[13] Not only was the Roman élite extremely rich, but the lower strata of the empire's population were differentiated; even among the poor there were differences; hence the high volume of aggregate demand for traded food and goods. That said, the *average* level

[12] Two cautions. First, not all peasants paid rent and the categories rentier/free holder/tenant overlap, since many small landowners in the course of the family cycle supplemented their livelihood by renting out surplus land or by renting it in. This is clear from the evidence of Roman Egypt and is explained theoretically by Chayanov 1966. Secondly, I do not wish to imply that the surplus was fixed in size. Indeed, I argue that the demand for taxes and rent probably increased the size of the surplus produced. Moreover, the concept 'disposable surplus' is an objective account of what was produced over and above minimum subsistence. Peasants themselves may not have thought of it as surplus, although the concept did exist in classical times.

[13] This can be illustrated, but not, I think, proved. Roman levels in excavations reveal more artefacts than pre-Roman levels: more coins, pots, lamps, tools, carved stones and ornaments – in sum, a higher standard of living. Since archaeologists seem very reluctant to write synoptic works, I cite four corroborative illustrations from different regions: Clavel 1970: 331–3; Schulten 1933: 153–5; Morel 1965: 108–11; Kraeling 1962: 8–10, 93–4, 115–16. ⟨See Hopkins 1978a: 71 n. 79 [essay 5: 199 n. 79].⟩

of consumption was not high. Under proposition 6, I shall try, rather rashly, to estimate how much of their total produce the subjects of the Roman empire paid in tax, and to gain some idea about how much on average they lived above the level of minimum subsistence, and finally to gauge, albeit inadequately, the thickness of the monetary veneer.

Proposition 3: Rents and Taxes

Rents, in many respects, functioned in a similar way to taxes. Both were charges on the surplus produced by peasants, which helped support the superstructure of Roman society.[14] Proposition 3 is simply a corollary to propositions 1 and 2: conquest by the Romans brought about an increase in the amount of rent paid, especially in the western provinces. In so far as money rents were levied and then spent away from the farms or districts in which they were levied, to that extent money rent-paying farmers had to earn money with which to pay their rents, by selling crops or labour, equal to the value of the rent. Put formally like that, it sounds innocuous, obvious. But the process was important locally as well as inter-regionally. The imposition of money rents implied an expansion of the market for peasants' crops, both in local towns and beyond. Local landowners resident in towns away from their estates and provincial élites who spent their incomes derived from rents in the chief provincial towns helped create local networks of trade.

The increased wealth of the central Roman élite (senators and some knights) was funded largely by rents drawn from

[14] Were rents paid in money? Wealthy landowners living in the city of Rome clearly needed large amounts of money to spend, as well as produce from nearby estates. Cicero, *Paradoxa Stoicorum* 49 expressed income in money terms, not in wheat, and much later Olympiodorus frag. 44 ⟨= 41.2, ed. Blockley 1983⟩ declared that Roman aristocrats in the fourth century AD received one-quarter of their incomes in kind. Income from large estates given to the Roman church by Constantine (*Lib. Pont.* 34; ⟨trans. R. Davis, Translated Texts for Historians 6, 3rd edn, Liverpool, 2010⟩) was also mostly in money and some of what was to be paid in kind was not grown on the estates but had to be bought in the market. The Igel monument of the third century AD does not show money payments by tenants, but payments made to workers – see the convincing arguments by Drinkwater 1977–8: 116. My fragmentary illustration reflects the neglect of rent by Roman historians.

estates scattered over many districts and regions. Expenditure of rents by absentee landowners in cities distant from their estates had a similar impact, but on a larger scale. Proposition 3 both emphasises the functional similarity of taxes and rents, and directs attention to the competition between them. In order to understand the Roman political economy, we have to take into account the balance between public and private exactions, between taxes and rents. Since production could not easily be increased, taxes and rents competed for a limited surplus. I shall argue tentatively that taxes were kept quite low with the result that private exactions could be correspondingly high. But my main argument is that the impact of money taxes and rents, spent away from the area in which they were raised, was similar in that they contributed to the monetisation and commercialisation of the Roman economy and to the urbanisation of the Roman empire.

Proposition 4: The Growth of Trade 200 BC–AD 200

I have outlined my main arguments. In the rest of this paper, I shall argue four supplementary propositions, which support those already advanced. The fourth proposition is that there was a very considerable rise in inter-regional trade in the period 200 BC–AD 200. This is corroborated by the greater incidence from this period of ships wrecked and recently discovered by underwater archaeologists. Dr A. J. Parker has collected information on 545 dated sea wrecks, mostly from near the coasts of Italy, France and Spain, where underwater archaeology is most developed.[15] The evidence therefore relates predominantly to the western Mediterranean. There is no sorting by size or type of ship (warship, merchantship); the dating is often crude, so the periods are correspondingly long. The results are indeed striking (see figure 6.1), if we can consider discovered shipwrecks as a reasonable index of ship-sailings. Given the large number of finds, this procedure seems reasonable; for

[15] A. J. Parker forthcoming (= 1992); cf. A. J. Parker 1979. I am most grateful to Dr Parker for letting me know about his important findings before their publication.

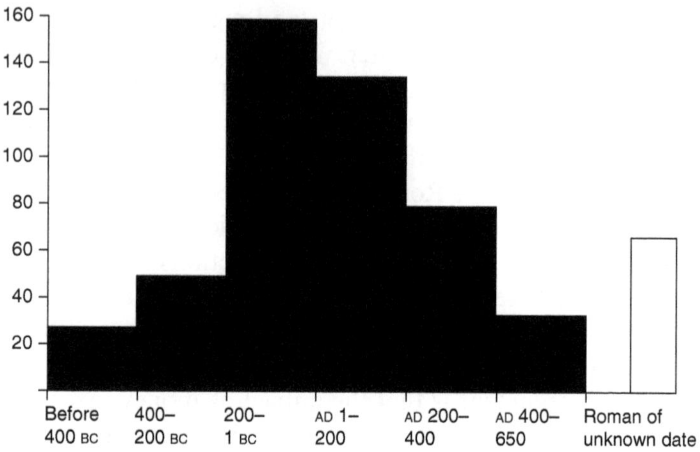

Figure 6.1. Number of dated shipwrecks in Mediterranean waters (A. J. Parker forthcoming ⟨= 1992⟩; cf. A. J. Parker 1979).

example, such evidence surely provides a better basis for generalisation than would statements on this topic, and on this timescale, in a literary source. And besides, it seems likely that the average size of merchantships engaged in long-distance trade increased to reach a peak in the high empire.[16]

Let us take a closer look at figure 6.1. There was a very steep rise in dated wrecks found from the period 200 BC–AD 200. The number of dated wrecks found from the last two centuries BC is three times greater than in the previous two centuries. Surprisingly, it is also higher than the number found from the first two centuries AD. But the difference is absolutely and relatively small; it does not form part of a trend; the last two centuries were more marked by piracy and warfare than the later period; the difference may be due to chance; data do not

[16] See now Pomey and Tchernia 1978, who show that there is now sufficient archaeological and legal evidence (*Dig.* 50.5.3 (Scaevola)) to indicate that ships of about 400 tonnes burden and over were commonly used from the last century BC, a tonnage not reached again until the fifteenth century by Genoa and Venice. I am assuming that average size was influenced by the construction of these large ships, but no direct evidence on average size exists, *pace* Casson 1971: 170–3, 183–90, who relies too heavily on *IG* XII suppl. 348, which has been doubtfully restored in the critical passage – cf. Launey 1933: 394–401. ⟨See Hopkins 1978a: 41–2 n. 13 [essay 5: 167 n. 13], 1983a: 97–102, 108 n. 34 [essay 7: 291–9, 295 n. 34].⟩

always work out exactly as one would like. All these factors taken together persuade me to ignore the difference between the figures for the last two centuries BC and the first two centuries AD. But it is surely significant that the number of dated wrecks found from the first two centuries AD is almost twice as high as from AD 200 to 400. The late empire witnessed a significant downturn in trade, deeper in the third century AD (as it seems from a sub-sample of the evidence) than in the fourth century AD.[17]

Such evidence merely confirms what was commonly believed, but it gives an additional, quantitative dimension to accepted beliefs. The dated shipwrecks show that in the period of Roman imperial expansion and in the high empire (200 BC–AD 200), there was more seaborne trade in the Mediterranean than ever before, and more than there was for the next thousand years.

Proposition 5: The Growth of the Money Supply*

An increase in the volume of inter-regional trade depended upon an increase in the volume of money to finance it. Merchants and their customers needed money in order to buy what was traded. In the modern world, most trade is financed by credit. We know almost nothing of credit in the Roman world; that does not mean that credit played a negligible role in Roman trade, but rather that we cannot estimate its importance. In any case, it is clear that money, predominantly silver coins, was the most important element in financing long-distance trade in the Roman world. Proposition 5 states that the supply of Roman silver coins increased enormously, perhaps tenfold, during a single century of the late Republic (157–50 BC). Proposition 4 and proposition 5 thus support each other.

[17] See A. J. Parker, above n. 15. The unfortunately long time periods used in fig. 6.1 reflect the crudity of dating available. Still, more intervals would create more problems at the boundaries. I imagine there may have been significant variations within each long period. It has been suggested to me that more ships sank in the central period because of the Roman penchant for transporting heavy loads – marble, amphorae – by ship. It may be so, but this argument also illustrates scholarly ingenuity when confronted with a plausible generalisation.

* ⟨See Hopkins 2009: 198–202 [essay 13: 520–6].⟩

Once again, I suspect that this estimate of the growth in the money supply at Rome simply corroborates what is commonly believed by present-day Roman historians, but the method of measurement is novel. Since I am not a numismatist, the arguments may need some corrections.

The evidence which I shall now present is drawn exclusively from Michael Crawford's *catalogue raisonné, Roman Republican Coinage*. His data tell us the amount of silver coins issued in Rome each year in the period 157–50 BC, since coin issues can be distinguished by the types (obverse and reverse) used. The chronological sequence of individual dies (roughly 30,000 obverse dies from this period) is our single best guide to the volume of coinage in circulation.

Modern experiments with ancient techniques for producing coins and estimates of the number of new coins needed for specific purposes in some few years suggest a normal minimum of 30,000 coins struck per obverse die.[18] The acceptance of this minimum estimate (30,000 coins per die) as the average output of all dies is obviously risky. First, the estimate itself is not certain; secondly, we do not know by how much some dies outlasted this minimum; thirdly, we do not know whether some dies were discarded, because of breakage or because of a change in the officials responsible for minting or for any other reason, before this minimum had been reached. Tentatively, I have accepted Crawford's estimate of 30,000 coins minted on average per die as the single best estimate.

However, it is worth stressing that the credibility of figure 6.2 in no way depends upon the acceptance of this average number. Providing we accept that the average number of coins struck per die was roughly stable throughout the period 157–50 BC, then we can regard figure 6.2 as being drawn on a ratio scale, with the exact values on the vertical axis unknown. It is

[18] Crawford 1974: II 694. The evidence supporting the conclusion that 30,000 coins were struck per die, normally, is impressionistic and plausible, but by no means certain. See contra H. B. Mattingly 1977: 206–8, arguing for 15,000 denarii struck per obverse die and for lower military costs. In my judgement, Crawford wins the argument, on points (but see below n. 29).

enough to say that, in this period, the volume of Roman silver coinage in circulation rose over tenfold.

But I have jumped the gun. Acceptance of this growth in money supply and in the monetisation of the Roman economy depends upon two further questionable assumptions: the rate of loss and the initial stock in 157 BC. We know nothing for certain about the rate at which silver coins were lost. That losses were substantial can be gauged from the volume of survivals in modern museums. Individual coins were lost accidentally; other coins were buried in hoards and then for some reason or another were not recovered. Cargoes including coins were lost at sea. Roman coins of this period were almost pure silver, so that they suffered considerably from wear. But their purity also restricted the benefits of reminting, the cost of which fell upon the mint.[19]

Figure 6.2 is based upon a constant loss rate of 2 per cent per year. Tentatively, I have taken this figure as the single best estimate available. It is derived, incongruously, from Patterson's analysis of loss rates of American silver coins in the forty years before 1962; for that period we have accurate data on the size of coin issues and the number of coins recalled and in circulation. The loss rate was 3 per cent per year (more for smaller value coins, less for higher value coins). The differences between the functions of coinage in the USA recently and in Rome 2,000 years ago are too obvious to recount. A loss rate of 2 per cent per year was simply Patterson's best guess about ancient losses in the absence of any obviously reliable ancient evidence.[20] On this point, sophisticated analysis of several ancient coin hoards might help us estimate rates of loss, but we always should bear in mind that the composition of single

[19] Why would the Roman mint systematically take in partly worn old coins, of almost pure silver, and remint to heavier new coins of the same purity? By doing this, the mint would shoulder all the cost of wear and of reminting. The answer depends partly on the fiduciary element in the currency, on how far coins were valued above their silver content and on the availability of silver bullion. According to Polybius (Strabo 3.2.10), the Roman state in the mid-second century BC received 35,000 drachmae per day from the silver mines at New Carthage, Spain, in which 40,000 men worked. This comes to c.35 tonnes per year.

[20] C. C. Patterson 1972: 207–10.

hoards may reflect many factors besides the random availability of coins in the total economy. I should stress that assuming a constant rate of loss is a heuristic device, not a description of reality. In reality, loss rates must have varied considerably, depending for example on the rate of hoarding, the rate at which hoards were recovered and spent, the rate of reminting. The 2 per cent annual loss rate (amounting to a large mass of silver) is simply an attempt to average out these variations. Patterson's main point, and it seems to me convincing, was that the stock of silver diminished sensibly each year, except in so far as it was replenished by fresh production. Alternative rates of loss, 1 per cent or 3 per cent per year, even of 5 per cent per year, do not radically change the shape of the growth curve in figure 6.2.[21] On any reasonable assumption, it seems clear that between 157 and 50 BC the money supply at Rome grew substantially, perhaps tenfold.

The second questionable assumption is the stock of silver coins in circulation in Rome at the beginning of the period in 157 BC. The problem is that we do not know how many silver coins were minted before 157 BC. For the purpose of figure 6.2, I made arbitrary estimates after consultation with Michael Crawford, by the simple process of splitting the difference between a high and a low estimate.[22] The result was a stock of silver coins worth 35 million denarii in 158 BC. This may not be right, but it does not matter too much, since the importance of the initial stock diminishes. With a loss rate of

[21] If we increase the rate of loss to 10 per cent per year, the overall rise in silver coin stock 157–77 BC is still fivefold; the rise during the second century becomes slower, but the fall in the money supply from 77 to 50 BC becomes dramatic – more than 50 per cent. Surely, it is too dramatic to be credible. So is the implied absolute loss of coins.

[22] Both the high and the low estimates were probably on the high side. The high estimate was based on the following assumptions:

200–158 BC: the equivalent of 1 million denarii per annum
220–201 BC: the equivalent of 2 million denarii per annum
240–221 BC: the equivalent of 1 million denarii per annum

The low estimate was half these levels. A loss rate of 2 per cent per year was also assumed. The result was 46 million and 23 million denarii respectively for the stock of silver coins in circulation in 158 BC. The guesswork in these crude calculations hardly needs stressing. Please note that Crawford had already underlined the low volume of silver coins minted in the decade before 157 BC, Crawford 1974: II 625.

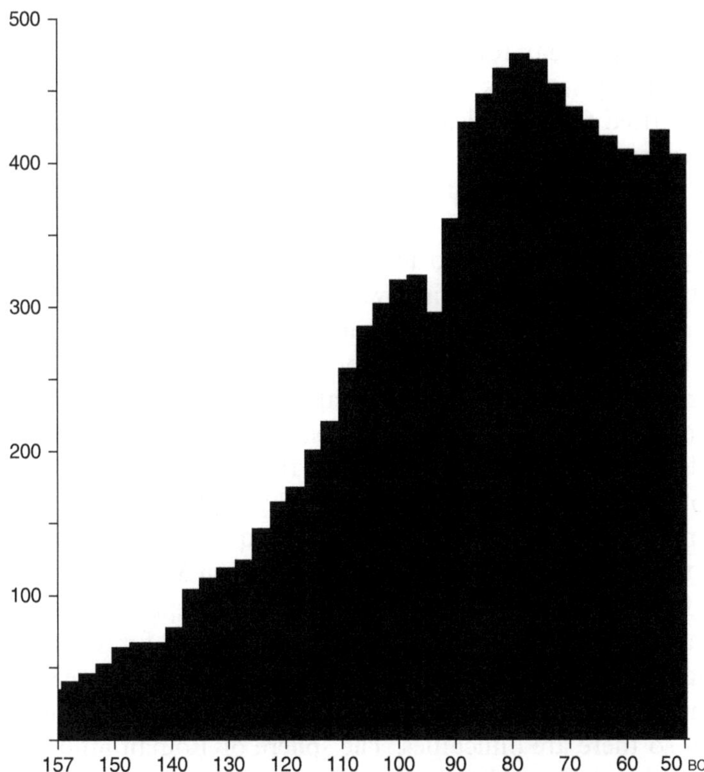

Figure 6.2. Roman silver coins in circulation 157–50 BC (in millions of denarii, by three-year periods).

2 per cent per year, the initial stock (whatever its size) halves in thirty-five years. By 120 BC, the initial stock of 35 million denarii accounted for less than one-tenth of the total money supply; reasonable variation of the initial stock does not change the shape of figure 6.2.[23] In sum, figure 6.2 is based on three or four assumptions: (a) *either* 30,000 coins were on average struck per (obverse) die, *or* the average number of coins struck per die was roughly stable throughout the period 157–50 BC;

[23] If, for example, we began with a stock of 80 million denarii in 158 BC instead of 35 million denarii, again with a loss rate of 2 per cent per year, then the total silver coin stock still rises sixfold to its peak in 77 BC, although the rate of growth in the second century BC is slower. The general trend remains similar.

(b) the rate of loss was significant, and is here set tentatively at 2 per cent per year; (c) the initial stock of silver coins in 158 BC is tentatively set at 35 million denarii. The detailed figures, as I have tried to make clear, are insecure, but the general trend seems firm.

What are the implications of a tenfold increase in money supply? First, some qualifications. Bullion (uncoined silver and gold) is not taken into account; nor is bronze coin, but the relative value of bronze was low. Gold coins are included; their value has been expressed in terms of silver coin. The annual loss rate of 2 per cent is large enough to take account of some hoarding, but in some years, particularly in years of civil disorder and uncertainty, hoarding probably reached much higher levels than normal. Figure 6.2 may therefore exaggerate the amount of money in circulation. Finally, the Roman state had no monopoly of silver coinage. Even conquered states continued to mint silver coins. Indeed, in the eastern Mediterranean, few Roman silver coins are found in hoards deposited before the age of Sulla; that is remarkable and important for the interpretation of figure 6.2.[24] It implies that we are dealing here with money supply only in Italy and in the western Mediterranean. Even so there are difficulties. The sphere of Roman influence widened in the period with which we are concerned. Africa and southern Gaul became Roman provinces. In Spain, large numbers of local silver coins continued to be minted until about 70 BC; then Spain used Roman coins.[25] In other words, some part of the growth in Roman silver coins was simply a replacement for the coinage of the conquered. It seems impossible to measure how much, but archaeological evidence suggests that the volume of pre- and post-conquest provincial coinage was much smaller than subsequent Roman coinage.[26] Whatever the

[24] Crawford 1969a.

[25] Crawford 1969b: 84.

[26] Compare, for example, the fifteen British coins found at Maiden Castle with the several hundred Roman coins found at Verulamium (Wheeler 1943: 329; Wheeler and Wheeler 1936: 227–39). But are the sites comparable? In any such comparison there are some difficulties. And besides there were exceptions: some districts of Britain had come under Roman commercial influence before the conquest. Even so, in spite of the difficulties of illustrating it, the generalisation still holds, I think.

qualifications, there was a real increase in the money supply in the republican period of imperial expansion in the western Mediterranean. The volume of new silver coinage was huge. In the peak period of minting, 119–80 BC, an average production of 14 million denarii a year consumed over 50 tonnes of silver per year, roughly half the average level of silver imported from America into Europe in the sixteenth century.[27]

A steep rise in the money supply is likely to result in an increase in prices, unless there is at the same time a fall in the speed of circulation of money (V) or a rise in the quantity of goods produced (Q).

$$\underset{\text{(P)}}{\text{Price}} = \frac{\overset{\text{(M)}}{\text{Money Supply}} \times \text{Speed of } \overset{\text{(V)}}{\text{Circulation}}}{\text{Quantity of Goods (Q)}}$$

We have no evidence of a substantial rise in the price of goods; the argument from silence is notoriously dangerous. But surely, even our jejune sources might have noted a five- or tenfold increase in prices. It would be reasonable to argue that the speed at which money circulated (V) probably slowed down in this period, for three reasons: the state treasuries must have kept huge sums in reserve and even stored money as treasure; so too did private individuals and professional bankers; thirdly, the greater distance which separated taxpayers and tax-spenders left considerable amounts of cash idle in transit.[28] But above all, and this is the chief implication of the steep rise in money supply, it had little impact on prices, partly because of the substantial rise in the volume of trade in an expanded area and partly because money percolated into a myriad of transactions which had previously been embedded in the subsistence economy. Both M and Q increased. For example, tens of thousands of peasants joined the army and received pay as soldiers, or migrated to the city of Rome where they consumed food and drink, clothing and shelter for which they paid

[27] See G. Parker 1974: 528; on the huge scale of Roman silver mining, see Blázquez 1969; Avery 1974: 419–27; also C. C. Patterson 1972: 225–8; and Hopkins 1978a: 55–7 [essay 5: 182–4].

[28] Ardant 1971: 114; cf. Ardant 1965.

money. The supply of money rose because more people were using it for more activities. Figure 6.2 captures that change in economic activity better than any literary source.

Up to now we have been concerned with the consequences of an increasing money supply for the Roman economic system, without considering the intentions of those who decided to mint more coins. Of course, it is possible that Roman senators, who decided each year how much money should be minted, were in detail and in gross ignorant about the economic implications of their separate decisions and of their cumulative impact. But Crawford has argued that the volume of coins minted was primarily determined by the volume of military expenditure; he postulated a 'remarkable correlation between [military] expenditure and volume of coinage'.[29] This is *prima facie* plausible, as figure 6.3, derived from Crawford's tabulation, shows. Fortunately, Crawford provides us with the data, money minted and army cost for the period 157–97 BC, with which we can test his hypothesis.

Formally, a correlation can be defined as a measure (from 0 low to 1.0 high) of the extent to which a factor x co-varies with or predicts a factor y (such as body weight and height, education and income). The correlation between volume of silver coinage minted and military expenditure between 157 and 97 BC works out at 0.88. It is so high that it is suspect. At this level, military expenditure purportedly explains over 75 per cent of the variance (variance explained is the correlation coefficient squared) in the volume of silver coins minted. One problem with such correlations is that they do not take time sequence into account; the paired observation (x and y) could be rearranged at will; the correlation would stay the same. Moreover, co-variation could be the result of other unnamed factors. For example, coinage and military expenditure may

[29] Crawford 1974: II 694, cf. 617, 633. I cannot agree with Crawford's suggestion that soldiers were typically paid with new coin, even in the second century BC, let alone that minting purposively matched state expenditure on the army. Many soldiers served too far away from the city of Rome to be supplied from there with new coin and besides the annual mintage of new coins constituted only a small proportion of all the coins in circulation. Why pay in new coins only?

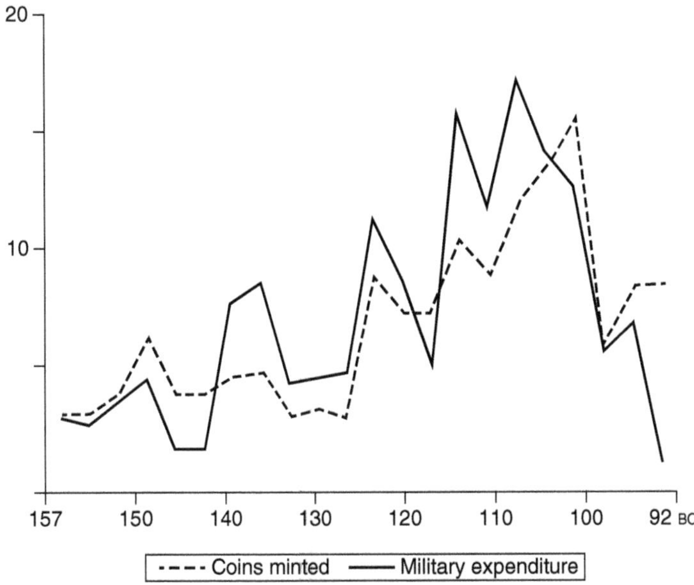

Figure 6.3. Coins minted and military expenditure 157–92 BC (in millions of denarii, annual averages of three-year periods). Based on Crawford 1974: II 696–703.

both have increased in the same period because of imperial expansion; imperial expansion would then be the explanation of both, rather than one being the explanation of the other.

But the real problem is that the simple correlation of silver coins minted and military expenditure is not the best test of Crawford's proposition. In strict logic, his proposition implies that a change in military expenditure brought about a change in the number of coins minted.[30] We can test that hypothesis by correlating the inter-annual percentage change in military expenditure with the inter-annual percentage change in the number of coins minted. Such a test is demanding; the resulting correlation works out at 0.32. The result is still significant,

[30] To be fair, Crawford did not strictly make a proposition; he just drew a conclusion and expressed it sufficiently clearly so that it could be tested. If he had proposed a general relationship between military expenditure and minting which took time to show, then we could have done a lagged correlation: military expenditure in years 1, 2, 3 with minting in years 2, 3, 4, etc. But that is not what he suggested.

but the correlation is much lower than the first correlation, and explains only 9 per cent of the variance in the volume of silver coins minted. The field is left open for other explanatory factors. I do not know what they are.

At this stage, I should like to make only two brief points. First, in some years very large mintages were associated with heavy military expenditure (91–89 BC are obvious examples; but what about 110 and 108 BC?). These exceptionally large mintages had long-term repercussions on the money supply; the large number of coins minted in an emergency stayed in circulation for a long time. In that sense military expenditure was a very important determinant of the volume of silver coins minted. Secondly, the overall pattern was one of steady growth in money supply, as though the senators and their advisers (note Plutarch, *Cato the Younger* 16) had some general idea of the need for money independently of each year's state needs. And besides, as one can see from figure 6.2, by 100 BC the volume of coins in circulation was so large that fluctuations in the supply of new coins in a single year may not have had a significant impact on economic activity. There were two processes at work: large inter-annual fluctuations and a general trend. I wish I knew how they were related.

I would have more confidence in the idea that the Roman senate knew something of what it was doing when it ordered how much silver money was to be minted, but for one significant occurrence. Between 75 and 50 BC, there was a considerable drop in the number of silver coins minted and circulating. For example, the average number of silver coins minted 73–59 BC (at about 4 million denarii per year) was less than one-third of the level of the previous fifteen years. There may have been problems in the supply of new silver from Spain, but no source says so. The drop in the total number of coins circulating was of the order of 15 per cent between 75 and 50 BC, somewhat more if hoarding reduced the annual loss to more than the 2 per cent annual loss assumed.[31] This drop in the total of coins

[31] Crawford 1969c: 79 shows a high frequency of unrecovered hoards in Italy between 75 and 71 BC, but a low frequency 70–50 BC. The evidence is suggestive only. I have

circulating may not seem serious. But the range of activities funded by silver money in the western Mediterranean continued to expand in these years; Roman coins were beginning to be used in the eastern Mediterranean basin also; and some provincial issues, for example Spanish coins, were no longer being minted. Roman silver coins had to take their place. Therefore, the demand for silver coins was increasing at the very same time that supply was falling.

Theoretically, the consequences of a downturn in money supply should be a shortage of money, a crisis in liquidity, a shortage of credit, a rise in interest rates and falling prices. Interestingly enough, we find several of these phenomena attested in 49 BC, in what several scholars have called 'a crisis of credit'.[32] Cicero wrote about the 'shortage of money' (*Letters to Atticus* 9.9.4); Caesar stated that 'credit throughout Italy was tighter and debts were not being repaid' (*Civil War* 3.1.2). I am not claiming that a fall in the money supply alone brought about the crisis of 49 BC. But the downturn in money supply seems to have been an important factor contributing to recurrent domestic crises in Italy during the sixties and fifties BC, which political historians have not known about.

Proposition 6: The Integration of the Monetary Economy in the High Empire

At the beginning of this paper, I proposed a model of the Roman economy, in which the imposition of money taxes and of money rents, and their expenditure at a distance from their source, contributed to the gradual creation of complex networks of trade. The flows of money taxes, of trade and of money rents contributed to the integration of the economy of the whole empire. Proposition 6 states that, in the first two centuries AD, the monetary economy of the Roman empire became integrated into a single system. In the last two sections,

suggested (above n. 21) that the constant loss rate was very probably less than 10 per cent.

32 Cf. Frederiksen 1966: 132; cf. Crawford 1970: 46–7; see also Cic. *Att.* 7.18.4.

I have proposed that there was a huge growth in long-distance seaborne trade in the western Mediterranean in the period 200 BC–AD 200 and a huge growth in the supply of Roman silver coins in the period 157–50 BC, again principally in the western Mediterranean. Evidence on money supply during the first two centuries AD does not allow a similar analysis. The sheer volume of Roman imperial coinage has prevented anyone from counting the number of known silver coin types, let alone dies. And besides, progressive debasement from the middle of the first century AD onwards must have encouraged massive reuse of old coins to mint a larger number of new, debased coins. Estimates of loss rates are therefore extremely problematic, and guessing the total amount of silver coin in circulation would, I think, be unhelpful. We must try another tack.

Perhaps I can best begin by proposing for the sake of argument a counter-hypothesis: the Roman monetary economy was so primitive and localised that state expenditure in one region had no impact in other regions. Money simply piled up and circulated locally.[33] We then face two problems: first, how did inner-core provinces get silver coins with which to trade and pay taxes? As far as we know, the Roman state had no mechanism for distributing coin, other than by state expenditure. Secondly, did heavy expenditure by an emperor in one area, for example by Marcus Aurelius in the Danubian region during his long campaigns there, leave traces in a disproportionately large deposit of his coins? The evidence which I am going to discuss was not designed to test this counter-hypothesis or proposition 6.[34] But I think it suggests that proposition 6 is correct and that the counter-hypothesis is wrong.

Figure 6.4 indicates that the whole Roman empire was integrated into a single monetary economy. At least, that is my

[33] To some extent, this must have happened. And as a result, migrant labourers were attracted to places with high levels of expenditure, such as frontier garrisons (hence the urban development there) and to the city of Rome.

[34] I started by re-analysing Dr Richard Reece's data, published in Reece 1973. I am most grateful to him for discussing his data with me, and particularly for reworking his data from northern Italy for the period AD 69–96 into two sub-periods, 69–81, 81–96. The patterns which emerged enticed me to see what I would find from other regions or coin collections.

interpretation. All the lines of the figure go up, then down, then up and along together. The very fact that it is difficult to distinguish the lines in the figure from each other supports my argument. Let me elaborate. Figure 6.4 is based on the analysis of over 90,000 silver coins found in five regions of the Roman empire: southern Germany, northern Italy, Britain and Gaul, the Balkans and a garrison town in Syria. These regions were chosen arbitrarily, because there were easily accessible catalogues or analyses of coins found there.[35] Each line of the figure represents the coins found in a particular region (where applicable, by type of find – but more of that in a moment). Figure 6.4 shows that, for roughly 150 years (AD 50–200), increases and decreases in the volume of coins, minted by each emperor, were similarly reflected in different and widely separate regions of the empire. Apparently an effective mechanism for distributing silver coins throughout the empire existed, so that several regions (and if these, then surely others also) got roughly the same ratio of coins stamped, for example, with the head of Trajan compared with coins stamped with the head of Domitian. What was this mechanism? We know that state expenditure was concentrated in the city of Rome and on the frontiers. I suggest that it was the flow of money taxes and of tax-stimulated trade which redistributed state-issued silver coins throughout the empire. I cannot prove that this answer is correct. But figure 6.4 poses a problem which deserves an answer.

[35] In addition to Reece's data, I used six volumes of *FMRD* (*Die Fundmünzen der römischen Zeit in Deutschland*): Saar (III), Pfalz (IV.2), Südbaden (II.2), Südwurttemberg (II.3), Schwaben (I.7), Oberbayern (I.1), i.e. a band of adjacent districts in southern Germany. For hoards in the Balkans and in Britain, Gaul and Germany, I used Bolin 1958: 335–57; from this collection, I arbitrarily excluded from consideration one enormous Bulgarian hoard of more than 60,000 silver coins, which overwhelmed the other finds and which seemed different in character from the other hoards. Finally, I used Bellinger 1949. I should note that the museum collections from Britain, northern Gaul (including some from northern Germany) and southern Gaul cover a large area. I checked before compression of the districts, separately analysed by Reece, to make sure that the patterns being compressed were roughly similar, so that the single line drawn from the collections in fig. 6.4 reasonably reflects the individual components. ⟨See Hopkins 1978a: 39–41 n. 11 [essay 5: 165–6 n. 11].⟩

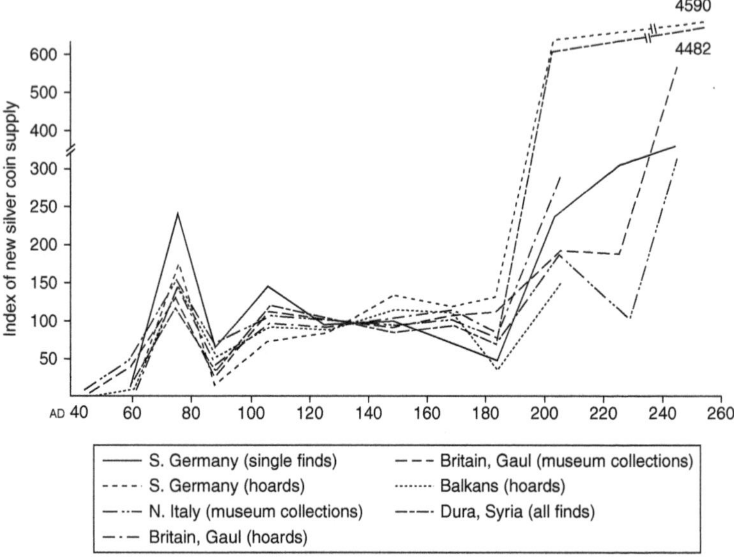

Figure 6.4. Fluctuations in the numbers of silver coins found, by date of minting and by region of find.

Let me now go into the details of figure 6.4's construction. The horizontal axis is divided into reigns of emperors, rather than uniform time periods, because coins are easily and conventionally identified by the emperor's head stamped on each.[36] One then has to divide the number of coins found per reign from each region by the length of the reign, to get a standardised index: coins found per year. The first draft of the figure was based on such raw numbers and it showed what one might have expected (or known), that northern Italy was more monetised than southern Gaul, which in turn was more monetised than northern Gaul …, if one can use relative volume of found coins as an index of monetisation. I then faced two problems, one tactical, one interpretative: first, the differences in the raw numbers were so great that it was difficult to put

[36] In fact, following Reece, I collapsed short reigns with adjacent longer reigns (e.g. Titus with Vespasian, Nerva with Trajan) to form convenient regnal periods.

the evidence in a single figure; secondly, there were more coins found in the Balkans than elsewhere, which was, I suspected, a function more of archaeological activity and the discovery of unrecovered hoards, than of relative monetisation. I therefore decided to concentrate not on relative quantities of coins by regions, but on relative quantities of coins by time of minting, in each region and between regions.

For this purpose, the vertical axis of the graph was converted to a ratio scale, based on an index number 100, like a modern consumer prices index or a wage index. For each region, the base index number, 100, represents the average number of coins found per year of the period AD 96–180. This period was chosen because it was the most stable period of the Roman imperial economy. We can call this base (100) a second-century index number. The average number of coins per year in each reign (or regnal period) was then expressed as a ratio of this second-century index number.[37] Thus each line for each region is drawn by expressing the average number of coins per year from each reign as a ratio of the average number of coins per year from the central index period. What is amazing about figure 6.4 is that data of such varied provenance and composition show such similarities in pattern.

Provenance is a problem which deserves further discussion. In figure 6.4, I have drawn some separate lines for singly found coins, hoards and museum collections. Most silver coins are found in hoards; some silver coins are found singly, dropped by chance in street or home. Many coins are now in modern museum collections with their exact provenance unknown. Although we can make precise, if arbitrary, distinctions between these categories, we cannot assign all coins with certainty to one category. Provenance matters, particularly

[37] For example, there were 3,812 singly found silver coins listed in the six volumes of German coin finds which I analysed. Incidentally, this was by far the smallest number of coins used for any line in fig. 6.4. The average number of coins per year in the period AD 96–180 was 5.3; 5.3 is the second-century index number (100) for south German singly found coins. For the reign of Hadrian, the average number of coins per year was 4.9 which is 92 per cent of the second-century index number, and so on.

because the composition and the incidence of hoards may seriously bias our evidence; fears on this score have hindered the exploitation of coin evidence by ancient economic historians.

The composition of hoards may have been biased because hoards were compiled, sometimes by several collectors, over long periods during which hoarders tended to hoard the better, i.e. the purer, coins and to spend the worse, debased ones. Thus hoards may not correctly represent the coins in people's purses. Secondly, it is well known that the incidence of hoarding is heavily affected by general economic and political conditions. In times of political insecurity, more hoards are stowed away, or more accurately, more hoards are not recovered by hoarders. After all, what we dig up are, rather sadly, hoarders' unrecovered savings. Their loss is our gain. Thus there are many coins now surviving from the third century AD, partly because many hoards were not recovered in that period. Paradoxically, and it is a sobering thought, we may have more coins from the very period in which most coins were withdrawn from circulation.

Luckily, we have a check on these speculations: several thousand singly found silver coins, carefully documented as such in the voluminous catalogue of coin finds in Germany (see n. 35). It is critically important for the conclusions advanced here that the line drawn from singly found coins from southern Germany is similar in shape to the other lines based on hoards or museum collections, both in southern Germany and elsewhere. The singly found coins, casually dropped or lost, do represent what was in people's purses. They represent coins in current use. The striking similarity in the patterns presented in figure 6.4 encouraged me to use the evidence from hoards also.

Let us take a final look at figure 6.4. The general impression, as I have already noted, is that all the lines follow roughly the same path. In the reigns of Vespasian and Titus (AD 69–81), there was a huge rise in the volume of silver coins minted, then during the reign of Domitian (AD 81–96) there was a considerable fall. During the reigns of Nerva and Trajan (AD 96–117) the volume of coins minted rose again significantly, but then levelled out again throughout most of the second century AD. This was a period of economic stability; by some accounts, it was also a period of widespread prosperity. During the reign of Commodus (AD 180–92), five out of the seven lines in figure 6.4 fell, but then during the reign of Septimius Severus (AD 193–211) most lines rose steeply. After that there was confusion; indeed, the lines for southern Germany should be drawn to a completely different scale; and the other lines show no similarity of pattern.[38] The unity of the monetary economy had broken down.

Let me stress again the considerable difference between figure 6.2 and figure 6.4. Figure 6.2 estimated the accumulated volume of silver coins in circulation, deduced from the total number of dies ever used. Figure 6.4 shows the number of silver coins found in each province, by date of minting (expressed as a ratio of the number of coins found per year in the period AD 96–180). Figure 6.4 indicates that there were some very large leaps in new coin supply, for example, at the beginning of the third century AD, which would have had implications for total money supply. But the transformation of the graph into a picture of the accumulated volume of coins in circulation is beset with overwhelming difficulties.[39]

That said, the end of figure 6.4 is of considerable interest. It implies that new money supply from about AD 200 rose, as silver coins were progressively debased. Prices presumably rose, since it seems improbable, even impossible, for a pre-industrial economy to have absorbed such large and sudden increases in valuable coinage without corresponding price increases.[40]

[38] Denarii and so-called antoniniani have been treated equally as silver coins. If we had taken account of the face value of antoniniani (at 2 denarii), which were minted in large quantities only after AD 238, then the lines at the right end of fig. 6.4 would have been higher than shown.

[39] In addition to the problems of debasement, of reminting old coins and of loss rates, which I have already mentioned, coin volume in the high empire is complicated by the operation of several mints in the eastern Mediterranean. Thanks now to the painstaking and impressive work of Walker 1976–8, we can see how Roman provincial mints (e.g. in Syria, Asia Minor and Crete) reflected a central Roman monetary policy. The evidence for this central control (which was directive, not reactive) is that the weight and fineness of provincial silver coins were reduced roughly to the same extent as, and sometimes before, silver coins minted in the city of Rome. This coordination of imperial monetary policy has important historical implications. But it was imperfect, so that measurement is difficult.

[40] The problem is complicated. Fig. 6.4 implies that the volume of debased silver coins rose considerably after AD 193 and that the increase in the volume of coins minted

Our documentary evidence on this point is inadequate; we can prove price rises only much later. But from the analysis of dated shipwrecks (figure 6.1), we have deduced that trade in the third century AD declined. From western archaeological evidence, we can also argue that some towns also declined in the third century.[41] The central government increasingly resorted to taxation in kind and paid its troops and officials in wheat rations (*annona*, *capita*) instead of in money. This complex of changes provides a corollary to my initial propositions: the decline in the exaction of money taxes brought about a decline in trade. The corollary helps corroborate the basic propositions with which I started.

Proposition 7: Taxes in the High Empire were Low

In the last section, I adduced evidence to show that the monetary economy of the Roman empire was integrated into a single system. I proposed, although I could not prove, that taxation in money and the trade which it stimulated were important factors in ensuring the circulation of silver coins throughout the empire. In previous sections, I have proposed

outstripped the rate of debasement. For example, I reckon from Walker's data (see previous note) that the median weight of silver in denarii minted in the city of Rome fell by 43 per cent at most, between AD 180/9 and 211/17 (2.29 g. of silver in 180/9, 1.85 g. in 196/211 and 1.31 g. equivalent in the debased antoniniani minted at the end of Caracalla's reign (face value 2 denarii)). But the proportionate increase in the number of coins found is visibly greater than 43 per cent (see fig. 6.4). Such an increase in money supply might initially have stimulated commerce and production; but the increase in coins was too rapid not to have increased prices also. And in due course there was a downturn in trade; I am not claiming that increased money supply and price rises were alone responsible for the downturn in trade in the third century. Some of these issues are excellently discussed by Corbier 1978; I disagree with Corbier in important detail, while admiring her work in general.

41 The most obvious index of urban decline is the widespread drop during the third century AD in the number of datable inscribed stones, commemorating the erection of new buildings, charitable foundations, statues, gifts, manumissions and deaths. See e.g. the statistical analysis of some evidence by Duncan-Jones 1974: 352 and Laum 1914: I 8–11. Changes in the fashion for inscribing and giving may account for some of this drop, but surely not for all of it. Yet how sensitive are such inscriptions as an index of prosperity, and of whose prosperity? For other illustrative evidence of urban decline see e.g. Duval 1961: 277–82 and, for a fourth-century revival, Patlagean 1977: 232. I cite these isolated illustrations in the absence, as far as I know, of synoptic archaeological reviews.

that seaborne trade increased in the period 200 BC–AD 200 and that the volume of silver coinage minted at Rome and circulating in the western Mediterranean increased, perhaps tenfold, in the period 157–50 BC. It seems likely, to judge by the volume of survivals, that the volume of silver coinage circulating in the high empire was considerably larger than in the late Republic.[42] All these arguments, and the evidence from which they are derived, are partial, but they draw strength from their inter-relationship. They back each other up.[43]

In this section, I want to estimate the level of taxation in the high empire and the importance of taxation in the Roman economy. This is clearly critical for the basic proposition that exacting taxes in money stimulated trade. Unfortunately, no exact evidence of general tax rates in the high empire survives.[44] Some fragments of earlier evidence serve as a first check. According to a possible interpretation of Plutarch (*Pompey* 45), the Roman treasury's income in 62 BC was 340 million sestertii per year. To this we should add income from subsequent conquests, particularly in Gaul and in Egypt. Frank (1933–40: V 4–5, 7) estimated total state revenue in the reign of Augustus at 450 million sestertii, with army expenditure at

[42] The silver coin types listed, by obverse and reverse types, in the several volumes of *BM Coins, Rom. Emp.* are a tenuous index of the volume of coins ever minted, since we do not know how many identical dies of the same type were used. But no one can reasonably doubt the increase in the volume of silver coins minted in the Principate. This absolute growth is important, but once it is divided by the size of the population (coins per head) it becomes less impressive.

[43] This is what I have called a wigwam argument, in which weak arguments prop each other up and circumscribe 'truth'; see Hopkins 1978b: 20.

[44] See particularly A. H. M. Jones 1974b: especially 164–8; Marquardt 1881–5: II is still useful. Much more has been written about taxation in the late empire; see particularly Déléage 1945 and Cerati 1975. But lengthening a bibliography should not disguise our lack of solid information and of real understanding about Roman taxation. Some Romans knew the size of their own state expenditure. Appian (Preface 15) promised that, in his last book, he would outline the size of Roman military forces, the revenues collected from each province, the cost of the navy, etc. Unfortunately, this book does not survive. Augustus, the first emperor, left a will in which he detailed 'the cost of the army, revenues, public expenditure, the amount of money in the treasuries' (Cass. Dio 56.33.2). The conjunction army, revenues, expenditure is suggestive.

275 million sestertii. Both these figures seem serious underestimates.[45] I reckon that an army of 300,000 men (half legionaries, half auxiliaries) cost over 400 million sestertii per year, once we include the cost of retirement bounties for veterans and extra pay for privileged soldiers and officers. But there is a large element of uncertainty in any estimate, since we do not know how much auxiliaries were paid or how much the fleet cost.[46] Several ancient authors state that expenditure on the army constituted by far the largest item in the state budget.[47]

[45] The major problem in estimating Roman state revenues is the quality of the surviving evidence. The following six snippets have been trusted more than they deserve: (a) Julius Caesar imposed a tribute on Gaul of 40 million sestertii (Suet. *Iul.* 25); (b) '[The Gauls] pay almost as much tribute into the treasury as the rest of the world' (Vell. Pat. 2.39.2); (c) 'Augustus made Egypt tributary, thereby contributing nearly as much revenue to the treasury as his father [Caesar] had brought to it from Gaul' (Vell. Pat. 2.39); (d) Herod Agrippa derived from Palestine 'as much revenue as possible, amounting to 12 million drachmae' (= denarii) per year (Joseph. *AJ* 19.352); (e) 'the tribute which [Egypt] yields to Rome in one month surpasses what you [in Palestine] pay in one year; besides money, [Egypt] sends wheat to feed Rome for four months' (Joseph. *BJ* 2.386); (f) 'When the cost had reached 7 million (drachmae), the procurators of Asia wrote to the emperor that it was a scandal for the tribute of five hundred cities [i.e. Asia] to be spent on one city' (Philostr. *VS* 548). There is not much more than this. Frank seeks to make (a) compatible with (b), and (c) compatible with (d) and (e), by claiming that they refer to different periods and that tax rates rose in Gaul and in Egypt between the beginning of the reign of Augustus and the middle of the first century AD. But from 40 million sestertii to half the revenue of the empire in the case of Gaul? And from less than 40 million sestertii to more than 500 million sestertii (12 × 12 million denarii) in the case of Egypt? Yet Asia was reportedly paying less than 30 million sestertii in the second century AD (f)! That is absurd. See Frank 1933–40: V 6–7, 51–4 and below n. 49 on the revenues of Egypt.

[46] It is impracticable to calculate the total cost of the Roman army thoroughly in a footnote. It is a reflection on scholarly concern with detail, rather than with broad problems, that I can cite no standard estimates of how much the Roman army cost. My tentative conclusion is that the total cost of the Roman army at the beginning of the first century AD was 415 million sestertii, plus or minus 50 million sestertii. See appendix I [257–9] for details.

[47] 'Our present revenues are insufficient to provide for the army and everything else'; wrote Cassius Dio (52.6.1) in a speech which he attributed to Agrippa in 29 BC. Another writer (SHA *Prob.* 23) envisaged a dream world in which there would be no soldiers and therefore no tax on land. The jurist Ulpian explained that tax (*tributum*) was what was *attributed to* soldiers (*Dig.* 50.16.27.1: sane appellatur … tributum … ex eo quod militibus tribuatur). The sixth-century anonymous author of *Practical Politics* wrote that 'expenditure on the army is the biggest item of state expenditure each year': Köchly and Rüstow 1853–5: II.2 46 (= 2.4) ⟨= *De re strategica*, ed. G. T. Dennis, *Three Byzantine Military Treatises*, Dumbarton Oaks Texts 9/CFHB 25, Washington, DC, 1985; on this text, see now Rance 2008⟩. None of these sources is earlier than the third century AD; indeed their citation may not be

That is an important observation. It seems intrinsically plausible, and is corroborated by the fact that soldiers, in spite of their political power and participation in civil wars, did not succeed in raising their pay (in terms of silver) above the Augustan level, except for a short period.[48] The state treasury could not afford to pay them much more.

Frank very tentatively estimated total state revenues in AD 70 at about 1,200–1,500 million sestertii; several components of this guess, such as the revenues from Egypt, seem exaggerated.[49] And if the total budget was as high as that, then the cost of the army (at 275 million sestertii by Frank's estimate, or more than 400 million sestertii by my estimate) was not the huge element in the state budget which our sources assumed. In sum, Frank's first estimate of the state budget at 450 million sestertii was too low; but his estimate for AD 70 at 1,200–1,500 million sestertii was too high.

In these circumstances, I thought it would be worthwhile to try a different, somewhat experimental method of overcoming the shortage of direct evidence. Let us deal with relationships between probabilities, rather than with the well documented

convincing. Yet it seems likely that their statements were broadly true and that the cost of the army dominated the state budget during the high empire also.

48 This calculation involves multiplying legionary pay by the average weight of, and by the proportion of silver in, coins minted in the city of Rome under each emperor. According to this calculation, legionary pay was for long periods under the Augustan level, and rose by more than 10 per cent above the Augustan level only briefly, in the reign of Caracalla. See Watson 1969: 91 on soldiers' pay, and Walker 1976–8 for the weight and silver content of coins. To be sure, in so far as coinage was fiduciary, i.e. in so far as its worth did not depend upon its silver content, such a calculation tells us little. I am willing to believe that, in small-scale transactions, the silver currency was substantially fiduciary (since testing coins for exact silver content would have been difficult), but, in gross, I imagine that prices were influenced by the increases in money supply which followed debasement.

49 On the basis of two snippets from Josephus, quoted above in n. 45 (d) and (e), Frank 1933–40: V 51–2 concluded that Egypt yielded 576 million sestertii plus 20 million *modii* of wheat (at say 3 sestertii per *modius* = 636 million sestertii total). The population of Roman Egypt is conventionally regarded as above 7 million (Finley 1973: 97); in K. J. Beloch's view (and I agree completely) that is far too high (Beloch 1886: 258, 507: 5 million); even Beloch's estimate is generous. Seven million people would have been paying 200 kg wheat equivalent per person in tax to yield Frank's estimated total. That is again much too high: the claimed total is five times higher in wheat terms than the total tax levied in Egypt by the Ottomans in the seventeenth century (see S. J. Shaw 1962: 79, 84, 182–3). Cf. the implied tax rate in the fourth century AD (*POxy*. XLVI 3307), which was much lower, and below n. 56 with table 6.1.

'facts' which are the normal building bricks of conventional history. We can move later from abstract to concrete. In the following discussion, three principles apply. First, the range of probability is finite; for example, scholarly estimates of the probable population of the Roman empire at its peak range only between 50 and 120 million.[50] Secondly, the choice of a value for one variable limits the range of probability for cognate variables; for example, the larger we set the size of the taxpaying population, the lower the amount of tax paid by each, if we also think that the Roman government faced difficulty in paying its soldiers. Put another way, and this is my third point, not only do our choices constrain each other, but the final results must also be compatible with whatever else we want to believe.

Tax can be conceived as a proportion of gross product. Can we estimate the gross product of the Roman empire? At first sight, it seems hopeless. But we can make a *minimum* estimate by multiplying the size of the population by the amount of food necessary to keep that population at the minimum level of subsistence. Let us follow the convention of modern agricultural economists and translate consumption needs into terms of basic grain (kg wheat equivalent). In this way, we can easily take account not merely of food, but also of minimum needs for clothing, heat and housing.[51] Obviously, such a calculation poses problems; needs for food depend on climate, age, sex, body weight, height and energy expended. An average of 250 kg wheat equivalent per person/year is low, low enough to take account of the probable age composition of a population suffering high mortality and suffering from recurrent

[50] Russell 1958: 7–8 for literature and for a full discussion of the evidence, and see below n. 52.

[51] Clark and Haswell 1970: 57–73, 175. I once did some fancy calculations allowing for body weight (adult males 60 kg at age 25 years), age structure (e_0 = 20), climate (at Rome), subsistence at 2,000 calories average per person/day. The result coincided with Clark and Haswell's. I added a bit (15 kg wheat equivalent per person/year) for clothing and a similar notional amount for heat and housing. The end result (250 kg wheat equivalent per person/year) is obviously rough and speculative (after all consumption depends on energy expended and vice versa); I thought it best to express the result in a round number (250 kg) to underline its vagueness. But the probable margin of error is not great.

feelings of hunger. Adult males would, normally, have consumed significantly more than this average; children and old people significantly less. Let me stress that the measure is in terms of wheat *equivalent*. It does not mean that people ate only, or indeed any wheat. Wheat equivalent is merely a currency of cross-cultural comparison, such that all consumption is expressed in terms of wheat. Incidentally, one advantage of this convention is that it gives us a key for translating the meaning of Roman money from sestertii, which tells the modern reader very little, into subsistence (e.g. enough to feed a family of four for a month).

To this estimate of minimum consumption, we need to add some allowance for seed, so that we can make a distinction between minimum net product available for consumption and minimum gross product, sufficient to allow farmers to plant for next year's crop. This measure, minimum gross product, does not imply that everyone produces what he/she eats; some people consume food grown by others and some are producing goods in return for which they can buy peasants' surplus food. Our first estimate of minimum gross product (minimum net consumption plus seed) covers all production of food, sufficient to maintain minimum subsistence, but does not include other productive activity, except the production of minimal clothing, housing and heat. It is a minimum estimate of gross product; the actual gross product of the Roman empire was certainly higher. But for the moment a minimum is all we need, because if we add price, we get an impeccable equation:

$$\text{Tax} = \text{Proportion}\left[> \left(\begin{matrix}\text{Minimum}\\ \text{Gross}\\ \text{Product}\end{matrix} = \text{Population} \times \left(\begin{matrix}\text{Minimum}\\ \text{Net}\\ \text{Consumption}\end{matrix} + \text{Seed}\right) \times \text{Price}\right)\right]$$

All we have to do now is to fit values to components of the equation. It is not as difficult as it may appear at first sight. We can do it tentatively, without committing ourselves to the correctness of any estimate, simply to see where it leads us. First, population. Beloch estimated the population of the Roman empire at the beginning of Augustus' reign at 54 million. I think it was a very good estimate, and much better than his revised figure of 100 million for the end of the first century AD.[52] Second, minimum net consumption; we have estimated that at 250 kg wheat equivalent per person/year. Next, seed; to please those who rely on ancient sources, let us follow Columella (*On Agriculture* 3.3.4) and think that the normal yield for wheat in Italy was four times seed. Under cover of ancient authority, we can leave aside the question, how did Columella know the normal yield of a country as large and as varied as Italy.[53] Let us now arbitrarily apply the same average figure to the empire as a whole, again without committing ourselves to its truth. Seed therefore constituted a quarter of the total crop.

Fourth, price. The normal price of wheat in the first century AD is a matter of contention. It obviously varied between seasons, from year to year and from district to district. The city of Rome was much more expensive than a farm deep inland in Asia Minor. But variation in no way precludes the calculation or usefulness of an average. Rostovtzeff considered that, if one had to choose a single price for wheat, which he thought unwise, then 3 sestertii per *modius* (of 6.55 kg) was the single best estimate.[54] Finally, tax rates: no single figure is obviously right. Effective tax rates in Egypt were significantly higher than in Italy, where there was no direct tax on land. In the provinces, tithes on main crops were common, but so were other tax rates;

[52] Beloch 1886: 507 and 1899: 616–20.

[53] Columella wrote: 'We can hardly remember a time when cereals in the greater part of Italy yielded four to one.' On varying yields in one Italian district, see e.g. Rotelli 1968: 121–2 and Aymard 1973.

[54] See M. I. Rostovtzeff, *RE* 7.1: 126–87, s.v. 'frumentum', at 149; cf. Duncan-Jones 1976b: 252, who lists eighteen wheat prices from Lower Egypt in the first century AD; the median and modal price was 8 drachmae per *artaba* of 32 kg, which Duncan-Jones approximates to 2½ sestertii per *modius*. By the end of the second century AD, Lower Egyptian wheat prices had more than doubled to 18–20 drachmae per *artaba,* but only four prices are known and exactly dated AD 191–220. In Asia Minor at the end of the first century AD, in a small town (Antioch in Pisidia), the normal price of wheat was 2¼ sestertii per *modius (AE* 1925, 126b). ⟨See now Wiemer 1997.⟩ In the city of Rome, market prices were obviously higher, perhaps 8–10 sestertii per *modius* (cf. Duncan-Jones 1974: 345–7). Prices fluctuated both within and between years; fluctuations do not preclude an average, but they should induce caution in its use.

and how are we going to take account of indirect taxes such as customs dues, or of taxes on the transfer of property at death, or of tax evasion?[55] Arbitrarily, let us plump for a tax rate of 10 per cent on gross product and see where it leads us.

We are now in a position to calculate:[*]

$$\text{Tax} = 10\%$$

$$\left[> \begin{pmatrix}\text{Minimum}\\ \text{Gross}\\ \text{Product}\end{pmatrix} = \frac{\text{Population}}{54\,\text{million}} \times \begin{pmatrix}\text{Minimum} & 250\text{ kg} & \text{Seed (a}\\ \text{Net} & \text{wheat} + & \text{quarter}\\ \text{Consumption} & \text{equiv.} & \text{of crop)}\end{pmatrix} \times \begin{pmatrix}\text{Price}\\ 3\,\text{HS per}\\ 6.55\,\text{kg}\end{pmatrix} \right]$$

$$= 10\% \quad > \left(54 \times 250 \times \frac{4}{3} \times \frac{3}{6.55}\,\text{million HS} \right) => (8{,}244\text{ million HS})$$

$$\text{Tax} => 824\text{ million HS}$$

All the constituents of this calculation are hypothetical and tentative. But the result is curiously plausible. Given the estimated cost of the army, at over 350 million sestertii per year, and its dominance in the state budget, there is not a great deal of room for manoeuvre. Double the population, and you must halve the effective tax rate or claim that the cost of the army was only a minor element in the state budget. Claim that most

[55] No attempt was made to impose a uniform tax system or a single tax rate on crops and land throughout the empire, though some taxes (inheritance tax on citizens, customs dues) were raised across the empire. Some lands in Roman Germany were called *agri decumates*, tithe lands, and tithes had been raised during the late Republic in Sicily and Asia Minor, by tax farmers. But Hyginus, who wrote in the early second century AD, mentioned tax rates of one-fifth and one-seventh (*De limitibus constituendis* 205L) ⟨= ed. K. Lachmann, *Gromatici veteres/Die Schriften der römischen Feldmesser*, vol. 1, Berlin, 1848, 205; now ed. J.-Y. Guillaumin, *Les arpenteurs romains*, vol. 1, Paris, 2005 (at 20.4); and the further discussion of this text in Hopkins 1995–6: 55⟩; these rates may have been due to local variations or the result of a rise in tax rates (perhaps under Vespasian, see below n. 68). In Syria, the tax rate was 1 per cent of the assessed value of the land (App. *Syr.* 50). These were the main taxes, to which we should add indirect taxes. But for the moment I am taking no account of illegal exactions and squeezes. I am concerned only with what the central government and its agents took officially, in whatever form and wherever spent. I have not touched the problem of how and when a tithe of a main crop, such as wheat, was transformed into money. I can only stress the great difference between a declared tax rate (say 10 per cent) on a main crop and my first estimate of government revenues as 10 per cent of all produce. The survey by Cuinet 1890–5 gives a detailed analysis of taxes raised in Asia Minor and Syria by the Ottomans at the end of the nineteenth century and suggests the different contributions from land taxes, cattle taxes, customs which could be raised in a still undeveloped economy.

[*] ⟨HS = sestertii.⟩

people were producing at twice the level of minimum subsistence, or double the price of wheat, then you must halve the effective tax rate, if the army dominated the state budget. To be sure, this method cannot establish which answers are right, but the matrix of probabilities makes one aware of the implications of choice.

Can we go further? In reality, the gross product of the Roman empire must have exceeded our estimated minimum gross product considerably. Many peasants and non-peasants consumed more than minimum subsistence; many non-peasants produced goods (as did peasants) over and above subsistence needs. But if military expenditure was a very large element in the total state budget – this is the anchor of our calculations – then the budget was probably not much larger than 800 million sestertii in the early first century AD. Therefore, the higher our estimate of gross product, the lower the probable tax rate. Discussion of these variables could be endless. Let me finish with some speculative and tentative conclusions: in my opinion, the population of the empire was never much larger than Beloch's estimated 54 million (I exclude temporary acquisitions); gross product averaged out at less than twice minimum subsistence; the effective tax rate was significantly less than 10 per cent of gross product. My reasons for these conclusions are simply that, if either population or gross product had been much larger than these estimates, then effective tax rates were unbelievably low compared with declared tax rates (such as tithes, fifths). Finally, I conclude that the annual tax exacted by the Roman state was in the region of 33 kg wheat equivalent per person (10 per cent of 250 kg minimum subsistence plus 83 kg seed), about 15 sestertii per head. This is more than was raised in France or in England in the sixteenth century, but much less than these kingdoms raised from about 1700 (see table 6.1).[56] Such measures and comparisons are obviously crude, but they indicate roughly where we should put the Roman state on a scale of social evolution.

[56] In table 6.1 shall first state the results, then the elements in the calculation, then the sources. Needless to say, the results are crude and should be treated with the utmost caution.

Table 6.1. *State budget expenditure per head of population (in kg wheat equivalent).*

Dates	UK	France	Dates
1660–4	12	7	1600
1701–10	64	47	1713
1781	96	122	1815

United Kingdom				France			
Elements: / Dates	Budget (million £ sterling)	Wheat Price (£) (per quarter) (211 kg)	Population (millions)	Dates	Budget (millions)	Wheat Price (per 100 kg)	Population (millions)
1660–4	1.1 (income)	2.24	8.4	1600	5 (ducats)	4.5	16
1701–10	5.1 (expenditure)	1.76	9.5	1713	163 (livres)	18.2	19
1781	13.1 (expenditure)	2.23	13.1	1815	900 (francs)	19.3	25

Sources: United Kingdom: Mitchell 1962: 5, 386–91, 486–8; Chandaman 1975: 207–8; Cipolla 1976: 4. France: Braudel 1966: I 361–83; Baehrel 1961: 535; Sée 1948–51: I 155–72, II 111–22; Cipolla 1976: 4; Wrigley 1969: 153.

Conclusion: Low Taxes and their Consequences

The Roman state was supported by many millions of small contributions. Why were Roman tax rates low? The end of a long article is not the best place to embark on an answer to this question. But a sketch may help place taxes and trade in a wider political context and link this essay to recent discussions of the great debasement of Roman silver coinage in the third century AD. This link is important, because in conclusion I shall suggest that the collapse of taxation in money in the middle of the third century AD and its replacement by taxation in kind were closely connected to the contemporary decline in trade. This is a corollary of the propositions with which I started.

Originally, in the early phase of imperial expansion, there had been a gradual progression from the exacting indemnities to pay for past wars, to levying taxes to pay for current, mostly military expenses. But the concept of empire, and of administration, remained simple, because provinces were originally conceived primarily in terms of military conquest and of exploitation. Provincial governors and their aides had only a limited time in charge of a province in which to recover their previous expenses in their political career at Rome and to get rich. These origins were important because they fixed the framework of the later imperial system. The Roman emperors succeeded in restricting some of the worst abuses in provincial administration, without ever eliminating them.[57]

Tax rates could be low principally because the services offered by the Roman administration were rudimentary. By this I do not mean to underestimate the benefits of Roman peace, prosperity and justice – although they have often been exaggerated. One telling index is the extremely sparse presence of élite administrators in the provinces outside Italy. Contrast, for example, the Roman empire with the Chinese. In the second century AD, to govern a population estimated at 50 to 60 million people, there were only about 150 senatorial and equestrian administrators in the Roman provinces, that

[57] Brunt 1961.

is one élite administrator for every 350,000–400,000 persons. In southern China, in the twelfth century, with a population of a similar size, there were 4,000 gentry officials working in about 1,000 administrative areas outside the capital (compared with forty-five Roman provinces), that is one Chinese élite administrator for roughly every 15,000 people.[58] The scale of difference outweighs any quibbles about the difficulties of comparison. The Chinese government had twenty-five times as many élite administrators at work in the provinces as the Roman government.

The consequence of low penetration by the central government was local autonomy. From one point of view, the Roman administrative system was efficient and cost effective: the ratio of net tax returns to central administrative costs was high. But the ceiling of tax-raising capacity within this system was low and the taxes were maldistributed. These were the costs of local autonomy. Let me elaborate. Because the central government had few representatives of its own in the provinces, it devolved the collection of taxes and the distribution of the tax load onto intermediaries, who were typically prosperous landowners and local town councillors (*decuriones*). The central government in the high empire had no direct relationship with individual taxpayers. As I understand it, the central government simply fixed the total amount of tax which each town and its surrounding area should pay; local town councillors then arranged who should pay what, on the basis of a public declaration of the value of each property.[59] There was ample room for abuse, since political power was concentrated in the hands of those who could benefit most from a maldistribution

[58] McKnight 1971: 7–9; cf. Twitchett 1970: 11, 229.

[59] The system is clear from *IG* V.1 1432–3, convincingly dated by Giovannini 1978: 115–22 to AD 35–44. My interpretation of this important inscription is that the Romans levied a tax of 100,000 denarii on the town of Messene in southern Greece. The town then divided the tax due by the total declared capital value of property including agricultural holdings (which the inscription lists by district totals) and thereby arrived at a tax rate, so much per 100 drachmae or denarii (in fact 8 obols = 1.3 per cent). It is noteworthy that outsiders, *xenoi* explicitly including Romans, had the highest rate of non-payment, at the time the inscription was carved. Cf. Wilhelm 1914: 2–48 for a detailed and interesting commentary with which I reluctantly disagree in part.

of the tax load.[60] The oppressed could and occasionally did appeal successfully to the emperor for help in securing justice.[61] But local leaders must often have had friends in the entourage of the provincial governor or at court, who could be bribed to block an appeal or to present it in an unfavourable light. As a consequence, there was little to stop poorer peasants from paying a disproportionate share of taxes; taxation was regressive. And we should expect there to have been substantial differences between (a) what peasants paid in tax and (b) what rich landowners paid on similar land, and between (c) what tax collectors collected and (d) what they transmitted to the central government.[62] The basic problem was not merely one of injustice, but rather, in the present context, that any attempt to increase taxes threatened the privileges of the prosperous intermediaries upon whom the central government relied.

My general argument is that the Roman state provided a carapace under which relatively low levels of taxation made possible high private profits. The extent to which Roman private individuals grew rich in the conquered provinces (especially during the period of imperial expansion) is *prima facie*

[60] I imagine such techniques as collusively low valuation on the élite's own property, early collection of other people's taxes and late payment of taxes by the rich; loans by the rich to the poor against the surety of their land. My main appeal is to the logic of the situation and to comparable data from other societies (W. Hinton 1966: 39–40; Spence: 43–8; Huang 1974). But Roman evidence also exists; see e.g. A. H. M. Jones 1964: I 467–9.

[61] A famous plea survives from the tenants of an imperial estate in North Africa; they had already appealed to the emperor's local agent (*procurator*), but he was in cahoots with the administrator or lessor (*conductor*) of the estate: 'a collusion which he has practised uninterruptedly not only with Allius Maximus, our oppressor, but also with almost all the lessors, against the law, to the detriment of your treasury. The result is that he has refrained from investigating, for many years, our petitions, supplications and our appeals to your divine rescript; more than that he has yielded to the wiles of the said Allius Maximus, lessor, … to such an extent that he has sent soldiers into (our estate) and given orders that some of us be seized and tortured, and others … be beaten with rods and cudgels although they are Roman citizens' (Frank 1933–40: IV 98 = *CIL* VIII 10570, cf. 25902 and 25943).

[62] The logic of the situation and comparative evidence both suggest what we should expect. The explicit recognition of this tactic in research violates the implicit rule or convention among ancient historians that the surviving testimony provides both the building bricks for our history and its authentication. But by what logic do we decide whether the surviving testimony is true, or representative, and how do we decide between conflicting sources? These are not just problems of historical philosophy; they are recurrent problems of historical interpretation.

evidence of low rates of taxation. The lower the rate of taxation, the greater the private profit which could be exacted from a finite surplus.[63] And the lower the rate of taxation, the less effective was state supervision of private profiteering from public office. One special case of private profit-making was tax farming. The Roman government auctioned the rights to collect taxes in the provinces; in this way, the government secured its revenues in advance and cut out some of the fluctuations caused by bad harvests. It transferred both the risks of tax estimating and the administrative costs of tax collection to private enterprise. Private investors speculated that, in spite of government supervision, they could nevertheless get more out of provincial taxpayers than they had themselves paid to the central government.[64] Tax farming was a mechanism of transferring some of the profits of empire to investors, who belonged to the Roman élite and sub-élites, who were not directly involved in conquest (as soldiers) or in government (as senators).

Two developments deserve special attention. First, at the very end of the Republic and in the early Principate, the dominance of tax farming as a method of tax collection ended; tax farming persisted, but in a subordinate role. This demise of tax farming is almost universally considered as a symptom of moral progress under Roman imperial rule. Ironically, in post-feudal European economic history, the growth of corporate financing and private money-lending to kings is considered a fundamental element in economic growth. The collapse of private finance corporations in Rome meant that there were no institutions which could voluntarily offer private wealth as a buttress for state finances in an emergency. In contrast

63 Not that the surplus was fixed in size. Indeed, the imposition of money taxes and rents probably made peasants increase the size of the surplus produced. But the potential for growth was narrowly finite. Private profit therefore competed with public exactions. I should stress that the concept of surplus is 'objective': what was produced over and above minimum subsistence. Peasants may have wanted to consume it themselves; they probably did not regard it as surplus to their needs.

64 Tax farmers' charges presumably reflected their administrative costs, plus their risks, plus their interest charges on the capital which had been advanced to the Roman government, plus overcharging (loss). Badian 1972, in a sympathetic account, rightly stresses how difficult it would have been for the Roman state to administer its large new empire without private entrepreneurial help.

to post-feudal European economic history, it is worth noting that, as far as we know, the Roman state never borrowed from private individuals or institutions.[65]

A second development of even greater importance was the expansion of landowning in the provinces by the Roman élite. This was a two-way process: Italians owned more land in the provinces, and more provincial landowners entered the Roman élite.[66] One result was that members of the Roman élite in the high empire were typically much richer than they had been in the late Republic, as their average wealth increased to a level commensurate with the aggregate wealth of the enlarged empire.[67] It was a symptom of the integration of the imperial economy that rents, mostly money rents, were transmitted long distances from provinces, principally to the imperial capital where the élite consumed most. Transmitted rents and taxes had a similar impact on trade, but they were competing for a limited surplus. The higher rents were, the lower taxes had to be.

In an emergency, caused by a rebellion or by barbarian invasions or by an emperor's extravagance at court, the government had to meet extra demands on resources by getting more money. Several solutions may seem obvious: spending stored reserves, confiscating the estates of the rich, increasing taxes or debasing the dominant silver coinage. It is striking that Roman emperors in the high empire, as far as we know, either never or only once raised the general rate of taxation.[68] But the silver coinage was repeatedly debased.[69] Recurrent debasement

[65] Early in the reign of Vespasian, the senate voted to accept a loan of 60 million sestertii from individuals, but it was never taken up (Tac. *Hist.* 4.47).

[66] Senators in the early second century AD were formally required to hold one-third of their fortunes in Italian land (Plin. *Ep.* 6.19.4); the proportion was later reduced to one-quarter (SHA *Marc.* 11.9).

[67] According to Pareto's law, the proportion of total wealth held by the wealthy minority in pre-industrial states is constant (see Pareto 1896–7: II §964). Subsequent research has cast some doubt on the strict universality of the law. But it remains suggestive. We should expect the total wealth of Roman senators and knights to grow commensurately with the growth in the size and wealth of the empire.

[68] So A. H. M. Jones 1974b: 177; Suet. *Vesp.* 16.1: 'he increased tribute from the provinces'; and see above n. 55. Silence is of course not proof.

[69] Emperors and their advisers do not seem to have realised the consequences of their repeated decisions to debase coins. But then in post-feudal Europe, when the consequences of debasement were roughly known, debasements still occurred, because of

of the silver coinage was a tactic used to solve a recurrent dilemma: how to meet rising government expenditure, especially expenditure on the army, without a corresponding increase in government revenue. In the middle of the third century AD, barbarian invasions and civil wars induced a headlong reduction in the silver content of coins from about 40 per cent in AD 250 to less than 4 per cent in AD 270 (compared with 97 per cent in the mid-first century AD). The volume of coins minted increased correspondingly. Rapid debasement brought with it a spiral of inflation, which particularly affected soldiers and government officials who were paid salaries in money. The exact sequence of events is obscure since our sources for the period are thin and unreliable. But the main outlines are clear.

The traditional fiscal system broke down. Debasement and inflation had not been matched by an equivalent increase in taxation; indeed, debasement had been used as a method of avoiding an increase in tax rates. As a result, the central government had insufficient money to meet its traditional obligations at current prices. The central government was no longer able to control the empire as a single political system; the spider's web of cash flow was broken (see figure 6.4). Soldiers and government officials, at the local level, increasingly took it upon themselves to secure their own supplies, in kind. The central government, as a result, could no longer control local rates of taxation, although it continued to fulminate against abuses. And finally, as currency became the less valuable part of government revenues, the central government could no longer transfer significant amounts of money (which gave command over distant resources) from one end of the empire to another. The breakdown of central control over taxation, that is over the distribution of a large part of the surplus, was reflected in the formation of separate rival governments under a rapid succession of emperors, generals and kings in France, Britain, Egypt and Syria, as well as in Rome.

their short-term advantages. Cf. Challis 1978: especially 81–112; on Roman debasements see Callu 1969 and A. H. M. Jones 1953.

The collapse of the fiscal system left much economic behaviour untouched. Those with land, peasants and landlords alike, continued to get income from it. Peasants consumed much of their own produce themselves, while landlords could soon adjust rents to current prices, or express them in the more stable forms of wheat or gold or silver (by weight).[70] There was no general reversion from a money economy to what has been called a 'natural' economy. Mostly people traded in local markets in current coins, although we do hear of banks in Egypt more than once closing their doors and refusing to exchange the imperial currency at face value.[71] That said, the mid-third century was almost certainly a period of economic depression. General insecurity probably reduced the volume of inter-regional trade (see figure 6.1); the Persians, for example, captured Antioch, while the Goths (Heruli) sacked Athens. In provincial towns, the number of charitable foundations and of incised tombstones dropped; so too did the number of new public buildings, except for defensive town walls.

In spite of temporary fragmentation, the Roman empire survived as a single political system. The strong government of Diocletian and Constantine (AD 284–337) restored central control; they also institutionalised the changes of the previous half-century, notably, for the present discussion, the predominance of taxation in kind. The imposition of taxes in kind throughout the empire had far-reaching implications. First, food raised as tax cannot easily be transported as far as money; therefore, distances between taxpayers and tax-consumers had to be shortened. In the late empire, the establishment of a strategic military reserve stationed behind the frontiers and the reduction in the size of tactical units so that they were smaller than a legion made it easier to supply the army with taxes in

[70] Mickwitz 1932: 120 shows that the proportion of Egyptian land rents (n = 301) expressed only in natural produce rose considerably in the fourth century AD compared with previous centuries. And in northern Italy ritual fines for violators of graves, threatened on tombstone inscriptions, were in the early fourth century AD expressed in weights of silver and gold, instead of in coin as previously (*CIL* V 8723–80); on which see Pekáry 1959: 462.

[71] *POxy*. XII 1411; cf. Rostovtzeff 1957: I 470–3.

kind raised locally. Secondly, the collection of taxes in kind involves more supervision than the collection of money taxes; there are, for example, more problems over quality, quantity and delivery.[72] We should therefore expect, and we do find, an increase in local bureaucracy, which incidentally helped to consume the taxes without transporting them too far. Thirdly, taxes in kind require no transformation of local surplus of food into goods of lower volume and higher value in nearby towns; so we should expect a lower level of artisan and trader activity in a regime relying on taxes in kind. And that is what we find. In the third century, there was a decline in trade and in towns, and by the fourth century there was a definite drop in the volume of silver currency in circulation. In my view, the changes which occurred in the third century AD help corroborate my hypothesis, that taxation in money in the high empire stimulated trade.[73]

Appendix 1: The Cost of the Roman Army

Frank (1933–40: V 4–5) estimated the total cost of the Roman army in the reign of Augustus, excluding auxiliaries, at 275 million sestertii. Some details, such as the number of praetorians, the total pay of privileged soldiers (*duplicarii*) and of officers

[72] For theoretical and comparative works, see Ardant 1971; Bird 1974; see also Cheung 1968 and Issawi 1957 for similar problems in relation to rent. The most sophisticated ancient discussion of taxation is in the speech attributed to 29 BC but written in the early third century by Cassius Dio (52.28–9). One should also note the early Arabic treatises on taxation, dating from the eighth century AD onwards, which probably in part derived from lost Byzantine texts or from Byzantine practice. See Abū Yūsuf Ya'kūb, *Kitāb al-kharāj* (trans. E. Fagnan, Abou Yousuf Ya'koub, *Le livre de l'impôt foncier*, Paris, 1921, especially 74–7 (= §28) and, in English, Ben Shemesh 1969: 100–2).

[73] An earlier version of this paper was first given in the American Academy at Rome by kind invitation of its then Director, John D'Arms. I am most grateful to him and to the members of his seminar for hospitality and criticism. I want also to thank Sir Henry Phelps Brown and Alan Budd for kindly helping me along with economics; I am very much indebted to Michael Crawford for guidance, and not only on numismatic matters. Finally, I should like to thank Graham Burton, Ronald Mellor, John North and members of seminars in Cambridge, Durham and the Institute of Historical Research in London for their critical thoughts. Inevitably, on this topic, my paper is written in friendly debate with Sir Moses Finley and his *The Ancient Economy* (1973).

(centurions) and the cost of the navy are disputed. But two problems stand out: the pay of auxiliaries and the total cost of retirement bounties.

I am persuaded by Speidel 1973 that auxiliary pay was probably five-sixths of legionary pay. Speidel cautiously reserved his position, and conceded that auxiliary pay was perhaps only two-thirds of legionary pay. But his is the most sensible explanation of two important papyri recording pay to soldiers in Egypt and is compatible with the third (see *Rom. Mil. Rec.* = Fink 1971: nos. 68–70), In general terms, auxiliary pay must have been at a level high enough to secure the recruitment of over 150,000 soldiers under arms, enlisted for twenty-five years' service. This level of recruitment precludes a rate of pay as low as one-third of legionary pay. In the rough calculation below, I have entered auxiliary pay as five-sixths of legionary pay, without making any complicated adjustments to allow for the fact that a large minority of auxiliaries were cavalrymen, paid at premium rates.

Secondly, retirement bounties: I mention them because it is not unknown for scholars to estimate the cost of retirement bounties by dividing the number of legionaries by the normal length of service (sixteen, twenty and later twenty-five years) and multiplying by 12,000 sestertii. Did no Roman soldier die during military service? Did none receive promotion and so extra bounty? If we boldly assume that all soldiers were recruited on their seventeenth birthday, that no more died than would have died naturally (at $e_0 = 25$ years), then in an army of 150,000 men, 8,200 would survive after sixteen years' service, 6,000 after twenty years' service and 4,400 after twenty-five years' service. These figures from UN model life tables can only be rough estimates, but they reveal the fiscal pressure towards lengthening military service. The increase from sixteen years' service to twenty-five years' service almost halved the total cost of retirement bounties. At twenty years' service, with an army of 150,000 legionaries and with retirement bounties at 12,000 sestertii, the total annual cost was 72 million sestertii. Incidentally, are we sure that auxiliaries received no retirement gratuity? No source says so. Was it really possible to recruit equal numbers of troops to each branch of the army (auxiliary and legionary) with marked discrepancies of reward, especially in the second century AD, when many auxiliary recruits were already Roman citizens?

However that may be, on the stated assumptions, in the first century AD the total cost of the army on Frank's estimate, with my two revisions, was:

	million sestertii
140,000 legionaries (126 million sestertii) plus officers, etc. (34 million sestertii)	160
150,000 auxiliaries at five-sixths legionary pay	133
Retirement bounty for 5,600 legionaries per year	67
Praetorians, urban cohorts (including bounties), ordnance, transport, navy	85
	445 (± 50)

AFTERWORD

TAXES AND TRADE IN THE ROMAN EMPIRE (200 BC–AD 400)

WILLEM M. JONGMAN*

Keith Hopkins' 'Taxes and trade' was a brilliant and visionary article. It was brilliant for its innovative intellectual strategies and logic, and it was visionary because it almost single-handedly inaugurated a new paradigm for Roman economic history. The prevailing – so-called 'primitivist' – paradigm had been that of H.'s teacher Moses Finley. In the footsteps of Max Weber, Karl Bücher and Karl Polanyi, Finley had argued that the ancient economy lacked a system of integrated markets, and that trade and manufacturing were largely for local consumption.[1] The economy was under-monetised. Trade and manufacturing remained small-scale, as did the financial system, because the élite despised such activities. Thus the ancient economy was one of many local economies, and not a system of integrated markets. There was no interest in technical innovation, and the economic mentality was acquisitive rather than productive. No economically rational bourgeoisie developed, nor did the state have an economic policy beyond the fiscal. The result was underdevelopment and stagnation. Methodologically, the lack of an economic mentality and the absence of economic policy ostensibly precluded the use of modern economic analysis and quantitative methods – the two cornerstones of modern economic history.[2] As a result, ancient economic history remained a discourse separate from the rest of economic history.

* This essay was written at the Institute for Advanced Study in Princeton, and (once again) I gratefully acknowledge the support from the Andrew W. Mellon Foundation endowment. H. was a member in 1974–5 to work on 'Ancient economic history'.

[1] Finley 1973 (2nd edn, 1985) and the introduction by Ian Morris to the updated edn, 1999; see too Jongman 1988: 15–62.

[2] Jongman 2014a.

'Taxes and trade' was a head-on attack on this primitivist paradigm if there ever was one – even if H. himself called it a friendly debate. Crucially, and in contrast with the prevailing work at the time, H. chose to look at the economy on an empire-wide scale: what difference did it make that Rome was a huge empire (and thus also what differentiated it from classical Greek city-states)? The integrating mechanism that he singled out was that of the regional imbalances between the two counter-flows of taxes and public expenditure. Taxes were not levied everywhere: for much of its history Roman Italy was exempt from most taxes that were paid in the provinces. Public expenditure was distributed similarly unequally: it was spent in Italy (on benefactions and administration) and in the frontier provinces (mostly on the army), but hardly in core (taxpaying) provinces like Spain, Gaul or Asia Minor. The resulting imbalances between these capital flows, H. argued, stimulated export trade from net taxpaying provinces especially to Italy. It stimulated them to commute agricultural surpluses into urban manufactured goods that could be traded over long distances. H. would later add that just like taxes, rents too were not only collected, but also spent.[3] They were spent by the élite, and they were principally spent in the cities, and thus like taxes underwrote the high urbanisation rate typical for the Roman empire, and the growth of the city of Rome in particular. The effect was transformative.

His first empirical evidence for the large scale of such long-distance trade was the graph on dated Roman shipwrecks (106 fig. 1 [222 fig. 6.1]), based on A. J. Parker's unpublished catalogue.[4] It showed 'that in the period of Roman imperial expansion and in the high empire (200 BC–AD 200), there was more seaborne trade in the Mediterranean than ever before, and more than there was for the next thousand years' (105–6 [223]).[5]

[3] Hopkins 1995–6: especially 51–2, 2000b: 256–7, 261–2.

[4] Subsequently published as A. J. Parker 1992.

[5] A. J. Parker 1984: especially 102 for scepticism about the historical interpretation of these data. The graph has since been updated, most recently by A. I. Wilson 2014: 150–4, who also points to the many biases in the data; see also Robinson and Wilson 2011: 3–4.

Methodologically, the graph represents two major innovations. The first is that it introduced ancient historians to the idea of the operational definition of a variable: we cannot measure long-distance shipping directly, but shipwrecks will do as a proxy. Of course, no operational definition will ever cover the original perfectly, but at least we can now measure something that we could otherwise not. The idea was not at all new in the (social) sciences, but unfamiliar in ancient history. The second innovation was the systematic exploitation of a large set of aggregate archaeological time series data. With the explosive growth of archaeological data over the last few decades, this has since become a very promising (and necessary) research strategy. The time series presentation of shipwrecks was unnecessarily crude, with time periods of two hundred years. Subsequent analyses with, for example, fifty-year intervals show an even more marked pattern of expansion and contraction of long-distance trade.[6]

H. then argues, and again in contrast to Finley, that money was the medium that integrated Roman markets: the period of Roman territorial expansion in the second and first centuries BC coincided with a roughly tenfold increase in the money supply. In a subsequent article, H. would extend the argument, using Richard Duncan-Jones' revolutionary and important estimate of the total money supply in the early imperial period.[7] H. observes that this is a very high (but plausible) estimate, thanks largely to the value-based prominence of gold coins. Gold coins may have been too valuable for day-to-day shopping, but because of their high value they still represented a large proportion of the total money supply. Gold coinage was very useful precisely for long-distance transfers of large quantities of money in trade, or as rents from large estates.[8] In addition, H. draws attention to the importance of credit and paper transfers. Between them, the

[6] de Callataÿ 2005; A. I. Wilson 2014: 151–3.

[7] Hopkins 1995–6: 61–3 exploiting Duncan-Jones 1994: 168–70; see Hopkins 2000b: 254–7 for a more concise and more elegant version of the argument; see too 2009: 198–202 [essay 13: 520–6].

[8] Cf Jongman 2003a.

growth of the supply of coinage and the growth of credit money reflected on the one hand the extension of the Roman monetary system and the further monetisation of the economy, but also the growth of trade. In 'Taxes and trade' H. had already argued that during the high empire, fluctuations in coin finds in different regions were highly correlated, suggesting that it was the flow of money taxes and tax-stimulated trade that had redistributed these coins (113 [235]). That correlation began to evaporate after the reign of Septimius Severus. In the turmoil of the third century, the state increasingly levied taxes and paid soldiers in kind: 'the decline in the exaction of money taxes brought about a decline in trade' (116 [240]).

What is remarkable in this analysis is that it was a history with a beginning and an end – and not just an analysis of a static economic structure.[9] The prevailing primitivist orthodoxy had denied that there was any meaningful economic growth: it had been an *histoire immobile* of underdevelopment and life close to the poverty line for all but a small élite. If there was no economic growth, there was no need for a chronological dimension to the analysis. 'Taxes and trade' changed all this in one stroke, with what H. discreetly called the 'mildly developmental' perspective – that for a time the Roman economy was actually doing rather better than before or after.[10] This obviously applied most to previously less developed regions of the empire, but even in the more developed regions 'it is plausible to assert (but difficult to prove) that these economically advanced regions adapted to the changed conditions under Roman domination so well that in the high empire they reached a level of general prosperity equal to or higher than any reached previously' (103 [217]). The new argument required documentation of that growth and subsequent decline – and an explanation. So instead of some juicy anecdotes from literary sources, H. gave us the first of what

[9] Though – curiously enough – more so in 'Taxes and trade' than in the later reworkings (1995–6, 2000b and 2009 [essay 13]).

[10] Hopkins 2000b: 260.

has now become a number of time series graphs of the *conjoncture* of Roman economic history.[11] It was a hammer blow against Finley's primitivist paradigm, both in substance and in method, even if H. himself underplayed the importance of what he did, either (as I think) because at the time he did not quite realise the magnitude of its importance, or out of respect for his admired and beloved teacher and mentor.[12]

The developmental perspective is largely lacking in what then followed in the argument: the first ever reconstructed national accounts for the Roman empire, estimating GDP and state income and expenditure. The reconstruction is based on a (low) estimate for the empire's total population, which is then multiplied by a (low again) estimate for per capita incomes. The methodological weakness of the reconstruction is that there are no obvious constraints on those estimates of population or per capita income, unlike in proper national accounting conventions that look at both the income and the expenditure side of the economy.[13] In a subsequent article, H. defended his model, relying on two related concepts, one of which he had earlier in 'Taxes and trade' teasingly called the 'wigwam argument' (116 n. 43 [241 n. 43]) and the other the 'compatibility theory of truth'.[14] Both are concerned with the challenge of inference from imperfect data. If we use a range of bad data that individually will not stand up to scrutiny, taken together they may still circumscribe the wigwam of truth. A stronger argument for model building is his idea of the necessary compatibility

[11] See e.g. de Callataÿ 2005; Jongman 2014b: 77–86, 2014c; A. I. Wilson 2014.

[12] That H. did not quite realise himself that he was creating a paradigm shift is suggested by the shipwreck graph as he published it: as noted above, it has unnecessarily long time periods of two hundred years, an obvious obstacle to the time series analysis that his data called for. Hopkins 2009: 200 [essay 13: 524] for the use of modern economic theory and 'the ghost of my teacher Moses Finley' (see too Woolf [532–3]).

[13] It was a tactic that is at its best when human behaviour is tightly constrained by, for example, nature, but less successful if the outcome is open and precisely the subject of the investigation. Methodologically, H.'s attempt has been criticised in the subsequent more sophisticated reconstructions by Goldsmith 1984; Temin 2006 and Lo Cascio and Malanima 2009 that are more in line with modern conventions of national income accounting.

[14] Hopkins 1995–6: 42–3, see too 1978b: 19–20. Repeated rewriting had always been part of his self-critical style of working, but this went one step further.

between assumptions. The example H. gives is that of the estimates for population, per capita incomes, taxation and public expenditure. If we assume a larger population, and if we do not change our estimates for taxation or public expenditure, we have to accept a very low taxation rate – too low in his view.[15] In short, what we believe about one variable constrains what we can believe about another, and this only becomes visible if we construct such an explicit model. H. then argues that radically different estimates for specific variables in his reconstruction require deeply implausible estimates for the remainder. I admire the logic, but I do not necessarily agree with the specific outcome. I accept that a larger and more prosperous population *ceteris paribus* implies a surprisingly low tax rate. However, what if the Roman state in fact spent rather more on non-military items, and still taxed its people less than we thought? Even his revised version of the model is surprisingly minimalist by the standards of some recent reconstructions of the Roman economy.[16] I think for once H. was not daring enough.

Inevitably, given the scarcity of data, the reconstruction of national accounts could only offer a static model, amalgamating patchy data from the entire early imperial period.[17] As such it does not sit easily with the earlier dynamic part of H's argument. On the other hand, it serves the useful purpose of underscoring that Rome even at its most successful was squarely located in the pre-industrial world.[18] The Roman state could collect higher per capita taxes than England and France in the sixteenth century, but less than those states raised in the eighteenth century (120 [248 and table 6.1]). This is important because it avoids the simplistic dichotomy of earlier discussions, where the choice had been between

[15] Hopkins 1995–6: 47, 2000b: 253–5.

[16] de Callataÿ 2014; A. I. Wilson 2014; Scheidel, Morris and Saller 2007.

[17] This equally applies to the other more recent reconstructions: Jongman 2014b: 77–8 for criticism.

[18] See now also Allen 2009 for an attempt to locate Roman standard of living in a comparative framework of pre-industrial world history, using data from Diocletian's Price Edict.

'modern' and 'primitive'. Of course, ancient Rome was not like the modern world, but that still leaves a great deal of potential variation between pre-industrial economies. So H. closes with 'such measures and comparisons are obviously crude, but they indicate roughly where we should put the Roman state on a scale of social evolution' (120 [248]). Here was a Roman historian who wanted to once again insert ancient Rome into world history. And that place was not nearly as underdeveloped as Finley had argued – on the contrary.

'Taxes and trade' thus represents a true paradigm shift. The Roman economy was no longer one where nothing ever happened, and where there was no economic growth. H. achieved this by simply sidestepping the preceding cultural discourse on economic mentality and the social status of traders, and replacing it with an analysis of the integration of the economic system as a whole, and its dependence on the growth and subsequent decline of an unprecedented empire.[19] At the same time, H.'s analysis is still bound by what I once called 'the spell of Moses Finley', in that the development of trade and industry are seen as the core parameters to evaluate economic success or failure.[20] Thus, there is no alternative analysis of Rome's remarkable technological advances, nor of the all-important agricultural sector of the economy. And, as in Finley, there is no attempt to measure economic performance and standard of living.

Yet methodologically the difference with previous research is remarkable. First, there is the strongly propositional style of the argument, more akin to a social science paper than to the traditional humanistic discourse. This ruffled some feathers at the time, and also gave him the reputation of a 'model maker', with the implication that his work was 'theoretical' rather than empirical, and not as well grounded in 'the facts'

[19] Hopkins 2009: 200–1 [essay 13: 524–5] for his final statement on the move from a cultural to an economic analysis of the economy.

[20] Jongman 2003b: 32–5.

or 'the texts'. Yet if there is one thing that characterises H.'s work, it is precisely the passion for facts and empirical detail. Sometimes this was in his discovery of revealing passages in obscure and overlooked literary authors. At other times, such as in 'Taxes and trade', it was in his far more systematic and far more critical use of empirical data. H. was acutely aware of the scientific rules for empirical validation, and he tried to invent new ways to implement them in Roman history. Hence the explicit operationalisation of the larger but unknowable concept of long-distance trade into the proxy of shipwrecks, and the subsequent statistical analysis. It was characteristic of the modus operandi in much of H.'s work on economic and social history that rather than come up with a traditional continuous narrative dotted with selective quotations from written sources, he would give a discontinuous analytical account, operationalising variables in such a way that he could measure them, and then create a 'bitty' account from such in-depth, exhaustive analyses, using his incisive rhetoric to glue the bits together. The shipwreck argument set a visionary example of what could be done with large sets of aggregate archaeological data.

The impact of 'Taxes and trade' has been slow. For a long time the article seems to have mainly served to underscore H.'s status as the brilliant maverick in the field, a role he obviously cherished. Initially his tactic of parametric model building was perhaps the most influential part, though even that never influenced more than a small number of scholars. However, this has changed during the last couple of decades. The publication in 2007 of the *Cambridge Economic History of the Greco-Roman World* was a turning point: in a number of chapters there is a clear insistence that there was a measure of economic growth during some periods of antiquity, and an appreciation of the importance of ancient Rome in world history.[21] I think it is fair to say that there are now quite a few scholars who are willing to extend the developmental

[21] Scheidel, Morris and Saller 2007; Morris 2004 for Greece.

perspective well beyond H.'s mild version of a growth that was principally though not exclusively connected with empire.[22] More recently, his innovative use of large archaeological data-sets for time series analysis has equally inspired others. The shipwreck graph was only the first pole of what is now beginning to look like a real wigwam.

[22] Hopkins 2009: 195 [essay 13: 515] for his final words on the subject.

7

MODELS, SHIPS AND STAPLES*

This paper falls into two halves. In the first part, I construct a rough model, in order to show up some probable relationships within the Roman economy, for example, between country and town, trade and taxation, entrepôts and major markets. The main objective is to understand the implications for the Roman economy of staples (wheat, barley, wine, olive oil) transported by farmers usually for sale to, and for consumption by, the inhabitants of towns. In the second part, I concentrate on two issues of detail, the cost of Roman ships and the costs of transport. I argue that Romans commonly used ships of over 350 tonnes burden on the empire's main shipping routes, and that the cost of these large ships was so high that members of the Roman élite were probably involved in their construction and use. I also argue that the surviving Roman testimony on transport prices is untrustworthy. In any case, the importance of transport costs has been over-emphasised in estimates of the volume of trade over land and sea in the Roman world.

A Rough Model

Modern orthodoxy about the ancient economy holds that inter-regional trade was low in volume, because such trade was primarily concerned with luxuries for a small, wealthy élite; it is argued that staples were seldom moved long distances in bulk, except as taxes in kind, partly because of the high cost of transport especially overland and partly because of the low purchasing power of most consumers, who lived near the level

* First published in P. D. A. Garnsey and C. R. Whittaker (eds) *Trade and Famine in Classical Antiquity, Proceedings of the Cambridge Philological Society* supplementary volume 8, Cambridge, 1983, 84–109 (= Hopkins 1983a).

of minimum subsistence; and finally, that traders, even those involved in luxuries, were typically men of small means. Let me stress that this is not, nor is it intended as, a complete description of current orthodoxy.[1] But it is sufficient for my present purposes, because it highlights certain aspects over which I should like to take issue.

I have argued elsewhere that the scale of inter-regional trade in staples and in crafted goods (textiles, leather, pots) was considerable, because of the distance between where money taxes were typically levied and where they were spent. I have also argued that the Finley-Jones model of the ancient economy needs to be modified to accommodate modest but significant economic growth in the Mediterranean basin in ancient times, peaking in the first two centuries AD. I have also argued that by no means all peasants lived at the level of minimum subsistence. Their aggregate demand, for cloth, tools and occasional purchases of minor luxuries, constituted a major dynamic element in Roman trade.[2]

These arguments taken together imply a greater volume of trade than is usually assumed within the dominant orthodoxy. For the sake of convenience, I shall divide trade into three categories: long distance, that is inter-regional trade; medium range, intra-regional, inter-town trade; and short haul, local trade between the countryside and a nearby market town. The term region is unavoidably vague; I am thinking of large areas such as Egypt or Syria or southern Gaul. I should stress that these three types of trade interlocked. The exaction of money taxes and their expenditure predominantly in the city of Rome or in frontier provinces stimulated long-distance, inter-regional trade. To put it crudely, taxpayers had to sell goods in those distant parts in order to earn money with which to pay the next year's taxes. Not that this exchange was a simple, two-way

[1] Finley 1973; A. H. M. Jones 1954: especially 168–70; Garnsey, Hopkins and Whittaker 1983.

[2] Hopkins 1980a [essay 6], 1983c, 1978a [essay 5], 1980b: 342–3; and, for example, on the inequality of landholding in one large Egyptian village, see the data set out in Geremek 1969: 115; the ratio between the mean of the top 6 per cent of village landholdings by size and the mean of the bottom 59 per cent was 13:1.

process between taxpayers on the one hand and tax-spenders (soldiers and courtiers) on the other. The interchange worked through a complex network of trade, in which towns were the intermediate nodes. Local trade fed into medium-range and inter-regional trade and vice versa.

The complexities of the network can best be envisaged by considering the fate of the surplus. Prosperous peasants consumed some of the food surplus themselves.[3] All the rest of the surplus was either (a) transported to a nearby market to be sold, or was delivered in kind (b) as tax or (c) as rent to landlords. Most food, it should be stressed, was consumed on the farm where it was produced. Of the surplus, most was carted or shipped only a short distance. This short-haul transport of the agricultural surplus, typically by farmers themselves to a nearby market town, constituted the greatest proportion of all transport which occurred in the Roman world.[4]

Given the absence of any explicit testimony, it must seem hopeless to estimate the volume of food transported short haul in the Roman empire. But a first fix can be simply made. If the proportion of the empire's total population (>50 million people) living in towns and in urban occupations (i.e. not growing their own food) was 10–15 per cent, and if they lived at the level of minimum subsistence (c. 220 kg wheat equivalent per person/year), then the volume of food was at least 1.1–1.7 million tonnes each year.[5] To this we must add fuel,

3 I define food surplus as all food produced over and above the demands of minimum subsistence and sufficient seed to replace that minimum subsistence. I define minimum subsistence as about 220 kg wheat equivalent per person/year, plus a small allowance of 30 kg wheat equivalent to provide minimal clothing, housing and fuel. This is only a rough approximation: see Clark and Haswell 1970: 62. Careful calculation taking into account the age structure of the population, body weight, temperatures and energies expended is impracticable.

4 Two qualifications are obviously necessary. I take no account here of transport for sale between villages; I do not doubt its significance, but have no way of estimating its value or volume. Secondly, we should take account also of the transport of building materials – timber, stone, cement, bricks and tiles, clay for potteries, mineral ore for smelting and refined metals, timber for fuel. Even so, I suspect that the short-haul transport of food outweighed them all in tonnage and in tonnes/km.

5 The estimate of the empire's population at 50 million is on the low side: see Beloch 1886: 507. The estimate for the urban population at 10 per cent is also on the low side, if we consider that Rome, Alexandria, Antioch and Carthage together had a population of about 2 million. Of course, not all the food was eaten as wheat;

clothing and building materials. In so far as urban dwellers lived above the minimum level of subsistence and consumed other goods imported from towns (metals, artefacts), then the volume of short-haul transport was even greater. Without any commitment as to its truth, let us tentatively estimate short-haul transport of food from farms to towns in the Roman empire in the first two centuries as at least 1,500,000 tonnes each year (table 7.2 [283–4]: A + B + C). I should stress that this is a low estimate, based on the consumption of food alone in towns at the level of minimum subsistence. Even so, we can then use this estimate as a benchmark for the judgement of other figures.

Our next problem is (a) to trace the surplus as it was distributed to consumers and (b) to estimate the volume which was consumed locally or transported further. I shall deal first with food sent on as tax in kind, then with rent in kind, with food sold in the local market and transhipped unconverted to Rome, to other very large cities and to smaller market towns; and finally, I shall deal with the surplus consumed locally in the peasants' nearby market town. My tentative estimates of quantities are set out in table 7.2. Such figures may drive the sober ancient historian to rage, derision or drink. But they are meant to be helpful in two ways. First, these estimates give rough orders of magnitude to dimensions which would otherwise remain nebulous – 'huge', 'very large', 'a small proportion'. Secondly, these figures help establish probabilities and relationships. That has been my own experience in writing this paper. I have been forced to realise, in a way that I had never done before, the huge volume and value of food and goods sold and moved in Roman commerce outside the immediate district of production and the considerable sums of capital involved. The sums were so large that I am now convinced that the upper echelons of Roman society were involved in trade or that there were very rich merchants outside the élite. But more of that later.

although wine and oil weigh less per calorie, their containers are heavy so that 220 kg may not be far out as a measure of the weight of minimum subsistence as transported.

Taxes in Kind

Taxes in kind were delivered primarily in wheat.[6] The biggest target population supported by taxes in kind were citizens living in the city of Rome. They received a free monthly ration of 33 kg wheat, more than enough to feed an adult male, but not enough to feed a whole family. Two hundred thousand adult male recipients would have received 80,000 tonnes of wheat per year.[7] I assume that all the wheat and other foods which they and the other inhabitants of Rome (both free and slave) consumed over and above the free wheat distributed by the state, was bought on the open market.

There is considerable doubt as to whether any other segment of the empire's population was fed directly on taxes raised in kind. The Roman government continued to assess taxes in kind (Hyginus 205L),[*] but we do not know whether these taxes in kind were in fact leased out to private tax farmers, and commuted to money, or exacted as taxes in kind and distributed as such by officials. We do not even know whether Roman soldiers in the first two centuries AD were fed primarily on wheat supplied as tax in kind, or if the Roman authorities bought food for soldiers at fixed prices or on the open market. But we do know that Roman soldiers, legionaries and auxiliaries, were charged for rations *(P.Gen. Lat.* 1, 4).[8] And it seems a bit odd if soldiers were fed out of wheat tax, but charged cash for their rations. I think that provisioning soldiers with food raised as tax (*annona*) first became established from the third century AD. Yet even if we boldly assume that all 300,000 Roman soldiers (legionaries and auxiliaries) were provided with wheat, raised as tax in kind, much earlier and on the same generous scale as given to citizens living in the city of Rome, then their

6 In the fourth century AD, citizens living at Rome received a free ration of pork as well as wheat and olive oil: see *CTh* 14.4; SHA *Sept. Sev.* 18.3, *Aurel.* 35.1–2; Symm. *Relat.* 14.3, 35. And see, in general, A. H. M. Jones 1964: II 696–705.

7 See Augustus, *Res Gestae* 15 for a brief discussion, see Hopkins 1978b: 96–7 and cf. n. 11 below.

* ⟨On this text, see Hopkins 1980a: 119 n. 55 [essay 6: 247 n. 55], 1995–6: 55.⟩

8 On deductions from military pay, see the commentary in *Rom.Mil.Rec.* = Fink 1971: nos. 68–9; Speidel 1973; A. H. M. Jones 1964: I 31, II 626–30. ⟨See too Hopkins 1980a: 124 [essay 6: 258].⟩

total consumption was 120,000 tonnes per year. Two points can be quickly made. First, taxes in kind raised and distributed as such to sizeable target populations in the first two centuries AD totalled a maximum of 200,000 tonnes of wheat (80,000 tonnes to Rome plus 120,000 tonnes to soldiers); this was a small proportion of the total agricultural surplus transported short haul (low estimate: 1,500,000 tonnes wheat equivalent). There was no other large population supported by taxes in kind. Secondly, if soldiers were fed out of tax in kind, much of their wheat was supplied locally from land around the garrisons. They were supplied short haul.

Rents in Kind

The testimony is fragmentary. Most of it comes from Egypt. A very few interesting snippets survive from Italy, but date from the fourth to sixth centuries AD, when the Roman economy was probably less monetised. In Roman Egypt, in the second and third centuries AD, according to one substantial survey of the surviving evidence, approximately half the agricultural tenancies were levied in kind, a third were a mixture of money and kind; less than a fifth were exacted in money. From the fourth century AD, three-quarters of the rents were fixed solely in kind; only a sixth were solely in money.[9] Most of the rents were paid in wheat, but barley, lentils and flax also occurred. The type of rent depended mostly on the crop sown. Most rents in kind were on small-holdings and were for local consumption by local landlords living in nearby villages and towns.

Larger landowners exacted most of their rents in money. This can be illustrated but not proved with a few known examples (e.g. *P.Cair.Goodsp.* 30); and it can be argued theoretically. Large absentee landowners wanted some income in kind: staples for their households, chickens, eggs, ducks, honey, wine and other delicacies for their own table *(P.Ital.*

[9] Based on 300 leases analysed by Mickwitz 1932: 120. ⟨See Hopkins 1980a: 123 n. 70 [essay 6: 256 n. 70].⟩

I 3). But they needed most of their rental income in cash, in order to buy services (slaves, water) and non-farm goods (houses, fuel, clothes, silks, luxuries). Olympiodorus writing in c. AD 400 about the central Roman aristocracy, claimed that three-quarters of their income was in gold and one-quarter was in kind (frag. 44 ⟨= 41.2, ed. Blockley 1983⟩). In the first two centuries AD, I suspect that the proportion paid in kind was even lower. The record of papal estates (*Liber Pontificalis*) lists private estates given to the Church at Rome in the early fourth century; it shows that income from almost all estates was paid exclusively in money.[10] The exceptions are interesting. Some church estates in Egypt were required to deliver considerable quantities of cinnamon, pepper, cloves and nard oil. None of these grow in Egypt. They were imported from India and the East Indies. It seems likely therefore that these estates were forced to buy these precious spices in the open market and send them on to Rome. What happened to them there? It seems likely that they were sold in Rome to yield money for the Church, because they were neither useful for liturgical purposes nor were the clergy numerous enough then to consume such quantities of spices. These rents in kind were closely akin to money rents. In sum, rents in kind were probably only a minor element in long-distance, inter-regional transport, though they may have constituted a significant part of the surplus transported short haul by farmers to local landlords.

Surplus Sold Locally and Transhipped

Next let us discuss what happened to the surplus food which was sold in local market towns. It produced complex patterns which rippled across the Roman economy. But for the sake of simplicity, I should like to isolate four destinations: (a) the city of Rome, (b) the very large cities of Alexandria, Antioch and

[10] See *Lib. Pont.* 34 ⟨trans. R. Davis, Translated Texts for Historians 6, 3rd edn, Liverpool, 2010⟩ with the excellent commentary by Duchesne 1886: p. cl. ⟨See Hopkins 1980a: 104 n. 14 [essay 6: 220 n. 14].⟩

Carthage, (c) other towns, particularly those accessible by river and sea, and (d) local market towns fed on the local surplus.

The City of Rome

The city of Rome in the first century AD had a population of probably 800,000–1,000,000 people.[11] We have calculated that c. 80,000 tonnes of wheat were distributed free of charge to 200,000 adult male citizens. The whole metropolitan population, at the minimum level of subsistence, needed 200,000–220,000 tonnes of wheat equivalent. This makes no allowance for animal fodder, spoilage and consumption above the minimum necessary for subsistence. I should stress that measuring in wheat equivalent is a convenient tactic, not a statement about how much wheat was eaten. There is much debate about that; but Garnsey's recent estimate at 150,000 tonnes seems reasonable. The rest of minimum consumption, and any more on top, was consumed, I reckon, in relatively expensive (denarii per calorie) foods: wine, olive oil, market vegetables, milk, wheat, spices and luxuries. The state provided 80,000 tonnes of wheat equivalent; inhabitants had to buy at least 120,000–140,000 tonnes of wheat equivalent, at a minimum cost of 60–70 million sestertii.[12] This is worked out at farmgate prices, that is, without any transport costs added, at 3 sestertii per *modius* of 6.55 kg. These calculations are inevitably both crude and speculative. My objective here is not accuracy, but a rough order of magnitude to tease out implications which might remain

[11] On the population of Rome, see briefly Hopkins 1978b: 96–8. For wheat consumption, see Garnsey 1983; also Foxhall and Forbes 1982 – the best article on the subject. However, they do not recognise the prescriptive element in FAO minimum standards (which are above actual consumption figures in several poor states); and their hypothetical typical household of six persons over three generations is demographically improbable in ancient conditions.

[12] I calculate total demand as 1,000,000 population × 220 kg wheat equivalent person year. The high population estimate is balanced by the minimal estimate for food consumption, with no allowance for spoilage, waste, above-average consumption and fodder. Transport prices, profit and transaction costs would have more than doubled wheat prices in the capital (6 sestertii per *modius* or even 8 sestertii per *modius*). See the brief discussion by Duncan-Jones 1974: 345–7.

obscured without rough figures. These calculations take absolutely no account of minimum consumption of cloth, fuel and housing, of consumption above the minimum, nor on the other side, of state requisitions to feed soldiers and the emperor's court. But they illustrate a point to which we shall return, that the city of Rome acted as a huge magnet for trade in the Roman economy. It was by far the largest and wealthiest single market. Its supply involved and occasionally made huge fortunes.[13]

The city of Rome had a large population because it was the capital of a large empire. Its population was supported to a considerable extent out of taxation, by the distribution of free wheat and by the expenditure of the emperor, his household and officials of the profits of empire. Rome was thus a consumer city on a large scale, in the sense that its inhabitants depended for their lifestyle not on the production of goods for export, but on the production of goods and services for political overlords and large absentee landlords who spent their taxes and rents within the city.

Alexandria, Antioch, Carthage

The other great cities of the Roman empire, Alexandria, Antioch and Carthage had also once been political capitals of powerful empires. While they remained capital cities, their populations were supported to a considerable extent by the local expenditure of taxes. But after the Roman conquest, that tax expenditure was by and large withdrawn and transferred to Rome. We might have expected them to decline. But decline does not seem to have occurred. In Roman times, each probably had a population in the region of 250,000–500,000 people. The supporting evidence for these figures is flimsy, especially if

[13] See Petron. *Sat.* 76 on the fortune lost and made in trade by his fictional anti-hero Trimalchio, and the comments made by Duncan-Jones 1974: 238–43. D'Arms 1981 tries to trace upper-class involvement in trade from fragile references in the literature and the similarity of names of known ex-slave traders and Roman aristocrats. I agree with him in substance, while regretting that the testimony he cites is far from proving his case. For a suggestive parallel, see Wrigley 1967.

we want precise numbers, but it is sufficient overall, I think, to justify the rough orders of magnitude.[14]

The existence of these very large cities is very important for our picture of the Roman economy. They did not live off the local expenditure of taxes, or not to a significant extent relative to their size. They were each the residences of large provincial grandees and heavily involved in the transmission of taxes from the provinces to Rome; doubtless they derived some of their wealth from rentier expenditure and from entrepôt business. But they were too large to be dependent on rentier business alone. They were too large to be fed from a locally produced surplus, especially because they were surrounded by ancillary settlements. The land in the immediate vicinity of the cities, like land round Rome, must have commanded premium rents, and therefore was devoted to crops of higher value than cereals.[15] Cereal production for these large cities must have been pushed out well beyond the immediate vicinity. In addition, the cities had to buy some of their staples from a distance. It seems reasonable to conclude that they gained a considerable part of their money by manufacture (crafts) and by commerce. These very large cities were not primarily consumer towns, they had to earn money with which to pay for their food by producing and selling their own products.

These very large cities were on or near the sea. That was no accident. The Mediterranean was a Roman lake, and for nearly three hundred years after the accession of Augustus, it was virtually free from pirates. Such security must have encouraged trade.[16] In addition, relatively cheap transport by sea (more about that later) must have made it possible to move sizeable

[14] On the population of Alexandria, see Beloch 1886: 258–9; Fraser 1972: I 90–1, IIa 171–2 n. 358. On Antioch, see Liebeschuetz 1972: 92–6, with the literature cited there. The ancient testimony is fragmentary: see Diod. Sic. 17.52.6; Strabo 16.2.5; Herodian 7.6.1 and 4.3.7. ⟨See Hopkins 1978a: 38 n. 9 [essay 5: 164 n. 9].⟩

[15] I write 'must have' in an appeal to the logic of the situation, based partly on what is known from other large cities. See e.g. Ricardo 1821; J. von Thünen ⟨*Der isolierte Staat in Beziehung auf Landwirtschaft und Nationalökonomie*, Hamburg, 1826 (part I); collected edn, Berlin, 1876⟩ trans. in P. Hall 1966.

[16] Suet. *Aug.* 98.2 records a story of sailors' gratitude to Augustus for the new peace and prosperity from trade: see Rougé 1966: 460–2.

quantities of wheat, wine and olive oil by boat around and across the Mediterranean.

Our problem is to estimate how much was moved and in what directions. So far we have isolated only two (perhaps three) target populations fed to a significant extent from outside their immediate locality. The city of Rome was fed partly by taxation (and rent) in kind, partly by private trade. The frontier armies were perhaps fed in part by taxation in kind. Finally, the very large cities of Alexandria, Antioch and Carthage, which were involved as entrepôts in the transmission of taxes, were too large to be fed by the farmers in their immediate hinterland and were centres of commerce and craft manufacture.

Other Market Towns

What other forces moved staples outside the immediate area of their production? At this point, I want to advance the view that the bulk of Roman staples transported in non-local trade between towns (other than Rome and the very large cities already mentioned) moved because of chance fluctuations in the size of harvests. Table 7.1 illustrates this point. It gives modern national statistics for wheat production from fourteen countries which were once part of the Roman empire.[17] Wheat was the dominant crop. Crops of other grains fluctuated similarly. Wine and olive oil production fluctuated even more. These wheat production figures were the earliest which I could find for such a wide range of countries. The introduction of modern selected seeds, fertilisers and iron ploughs had probably already reduced crop fluctuations in some countries.

Two items in the modern figures deserve special comment: first, in recent times, as in antiquity, Egypt was exceptional, not only for its high fertility, but also for the regularity or low variability of its wheat crop. Secondly, in many countries, especially in the southern and eastern Mediterranean,

[17] Columns *d* and *e* in table 7.1 give two different measures of fluctuations in the size of crops. Column d gives the average percentage deviation around the mean; column e measures the percentage change from each successive year to the next.

Table 7.1. *Annual variations of wheat yields (1921–30) in fourteen Mediterranean countries once part of the Roman empire.**

a	*b*	*c*	*d*	*e*
	Average yield	Range	Mean annual variation around the mean	Average inter-annual variation
Country	kg/ha	(mean = 100)	%	%
Egypt	1,710	92–110	5	12
Spain	904	86–113	8	17
Italy	1,200	79–124	11	21
Cyprus	740	77–124	12	18
Bulgaria	1,005	84–127	13	27
Greece	620	74–123	13	13
France	1,420	89–122	14	19
Tunisia	400	57–122	16	67
Portugal	660	70–127	17	32
Algeria	540	61–143	18	47
Yugoslavia	1,080	70–137	20	34
Syria and Lebanon	750	55–152	20	42
Turkey	840	65–135	21	19
Cyrenaica	269	[0]–279	(two years' crop failure makes this calculation impossible)	

* From the *International Yearbook of Agricultural Statistics, 1922–1938* (International Institute of Agriculture, Rome).
For five countries the figures are from 1925 to 1934, or 1929 to 1938, because earlier figures were not available.
Note that such national statistics are liable to gross error; they are national figures and so disguise much greater regional variations.

where rainfall is lowest, the variation between the size of each crop was considerable. At this point, I should stress that the figures in table 7.1 are national figures from whole states; some of the statistics are probably unreliable (who counted and how?); but above all, national figures cancel out the much larger fluctuations of harvest which occurred in small districts. Peasants coped with these fluctuations, with glut and with shortage, partly through debt and credit, partly by storage in granaries, partly by changes in body-weight. In years of shortage, many of them starved.

The implications of unpredictable local harvests for the trade and transport of staples was considerable. One great difference between modern and Roman marketing systems lay in the absence of any regular routes of large-scale exchange between regions specialising in the production of an agricultural surplus and regions specialising in the production of manufacturers. The lines of ancient trade in staples produced by local glut and famine were unpredictable. The information available about markets must have been scant, distorted by rumour and difficult to trust. If glut occurred, there was no competent organisation of merchant ships, finance or credit, ready waiting to carry the unpredicted surplus away. In times of famine, reciprocally, it was difficult to secure supplies, and the capacity to pay for them was limited by the scale of local bigwigs' generosity and by the poverty of most consumers.[18] Medium-range trade in staples, therefore, was usually carried round in small ships by small-time merchants.

Any estimate is speculative. And the amount of food imported must have differed considerably between landlocked,

[18] On the classical tradition of generosity by local grandees who felt an obligation to give back some of their wealth to the poor, see Veyne 1976: 209–28. Towns often appointed special officers (*sitonai*) to secure wheat for their inhabitants by imports: see A. H. M. Jones 1940: 217–18. But a gift, like the one recorded at Magnesia of 200,000 sestertii (*OGIS* 485) would have provided enough food for only 16,000 people for one month, if the price was 4 sestertii per *modius*; in a general shortage, prices would have been higher, and private generosity usually inadequate relative to the size of the population at risk. Moreover, local landowners often hoarded to make a profit out of the people's misery – see e.g. Philostr. *VA* 1.15. ⟨See Hopkins 1978a: 48–9 [essay 5: 174–5].⟩

riverine and coastal towns. In table 7.2, I have arbitrarily set the level of these middle-range imports at 10 per cent of urban needs. This may seem too high. But the target population, when food was scarce, was not merely the urban population but country folk as well. And some towns may have regularly imported wine and olive oil rather than bulky wheat, from neighbouring market towns without causing a large rise in prices. Once such middle-range intra-regional trade in staples is taken into account, the estimate at 10 per cent of urban minimum consumption seems plausible – even so it may not be right. It is time to desert quantification for qualitative impressions. My impression is that Roman inter-town trade in staples was by and large a topping up operation, the satisfaction of a marginal demand, a transfer of an occasional surplus to places where there was an unpredicted need. 'Traders', wrote Philostratus in his *Life of Apollonius of Tyana* (4.32.2), 'roam from sea to sea looking for some market which is badly stocked'.

Long-Distance and Middle-Range Transport of Staples

In table 7.2, I have attached rough estimates to the arguments advanced. I calculate middle-range and long-distance deliveries of staples alone as at least 460,000 tonnes of wheat equivalent per year. This estimate is based on minimum subsistence, and assumes, for measurement purposes only, that staples were all in wheat. In so far as consumption, particularly in the city of Rome and in the large cities, was above minimum subsistence, or if urban populations were more than 10 per cent of the total population, or if the population of the empire as a whole was more than 50 million, and if towns got more than 10 per cent of their basic food on average from other towns, then these figures would have to be changed upwards. And vice versa. All in all, I think that the estimate of 460,000 tonnes wheat equivalent transported middle and long range is on the low side.

Table 7.2. *Hypothetical minimum estimates of food transport each year in the Roman empire.*

				In tonnes wheat equivalent
A. SHORT HAUL				
Food taken from countryside to nearby market towns and consumed there.				
Assumptions:				
1)	urban population was 10% of empire's total population (50 million), plus metropolitan population of Rome, Alexandria, Antioch and Carthage (say 2 million)			
2)	minimum food intake was 220 kg wheat equivalent per person/year			
A_1	Calculate:	10% × 50,000,000 × 220 kg	=	1,100,000 tonnes
A_2		plus local supply of the four metropolitan cities at say 100,000 for each × 220 kg (see n. 25)	plus	88,000 tonnes
A_3		but see B_1	minus	110,000 tonnes
		Total Short Haul (minimum estimate)		1,078,000 tonnes
B. MEDIUM-RANGE TRANSPORT				
B_1	Transport to other market towns for fluctuating and unpredictable demand; say 10% of minimum urban need (A_1)		=	110,000 tonnes
B_2	Intra-regional food supply of three metropolitan cities (Alexandria, Antioch, Carthage), say 700,000 people × 220 kg (note A_2 above)		=	150,000 tonnes

Table 7.2. (*cont.*)

B_3	Intra-regional, non-local but Italian supply to Rome (see A_2, C_1 and C_2) say 150,000 × 220 kg	=	33,000 tonnes
B_4	Premium trade in wine and oil		Considerable
B_5	Non-local supplies to armies		?
B_6	Rents in kind		negligible?
			>295.000 tonnes
C. LONG-RANGE TRANSPORT			
C_1	Taxes in kind sent to Rome (200,000 recipients of wheat dole × 60 *modii* of 6.55 kg)	=	80,000 tonnes
C_2	Market supply of wheat, wine and oil to Rome, total population say 1,000,000 × 220 kg minus (¼ × A_2), B_3 and C_1	=	85,000 tonnes
C_3	Premium trade all over Mediterranean		?
C_4	Rents in kind		Negligible
			>165,000 tonnes

Its total value, at farmgate prices (i.e. without significant transport costs), say at 3 sestertii per *modius* of 6.55 kg, was 210 million sestertii per year, and much more if we take into account that much of it in fact consisted of higher priced olive oil and wine, not wheat. By this simple base calculation, we can see that, in aggregate, very large sums were involved in the sale and transport of staples outside their immediate district of production. How much of this large sum stuck to the fingers of intermediaries as it passed through the hands of merchants? How much of the large aggregate moved in big chunks through the granaries and storerooms of large merchants?

Trade in goods other than staples is not directly within the purview of this essay. But the division is artificial. The sale and shipment of staples provided the basic framework of shipping, credit and quayside arrangements which could then be used for other foods and goods. Traded goods and fine foods travelled as supplementary cargo or as return cargo on ships carrying staples. Higher value, lower volume goods (textiles, spices, leather) provided merchants with their greatest profits. In addition, bulky goods, such as construction materials (bricks, timber), pots, metals and fuel, could best be moved by boat. Such cargoes were of high volume and low unit value but they increased turnover and the use of harbour facilities. Trade in staples and non-staples were as intimately involved with each other as were short-haul and longer-range trade and transport. We consider this next.

Short-Haul Transport and Local Urban Consumption

Most of the agricultural surplus was transported by farmers to their local market town and consumed there. This conclusion follows from my general argument that there was no large-scale regional specialisation in agricultural production, and no stable lines of inter-town trade in staples, except to Rome and the three other very large cities. All other towns lived mostly off the produce of their immediate hinterland. This follows from my lowish estimate of inter-town trade (tentatively set at 10 per cent of minimum urban demand for food). But even if we double the value of medium-range, inter-town trade in staples, it would not upset the general conclusion. In table 7.2, I estimated that two-thirds of all food transported to local market towns was consumed there (1.1 million out of 1.5 million tonnes wheat equivalent per year).

The economic significance of this short-haul surplus did not stop with its consumption. Most consumers had to pay for their food.[19] In order to earn money, urban consumers typically either provided services to local peasants and townsmen or they made goods. The goods they made went either

(a) back to local peasants, or
(b) to fellow townsmen, or
(c) further afield to other urban markets.

What was the relative size of these three markets? The sheer mass of the agricultural population (>80 per cent of the total) and their differentiation (some lived well above minimum subsistence) means that we should not undervalue peasants' aggregate consumption of urban goods and services (a). Townsmen's capacity to consume (b) and (c) was set by their productivity. In general, I assume that small units of production with negligible capital investment kept urban productivity low, so that townsmen's productivity was roughly similar, on average, to peasants' productivity and consumption, with similar and considerable variation. Except for rentier landowners and their retainers, therefore, there was in general a low ceiling to urban purchasing capacity (*per capita*), and local products (b) presumably competed with imported products (c) for the market.

Three points can be briefly made. First, one of the main stimuli to inter-urban trade was taxation. It created a necessity within each town to sell local food or to produce goods which could either be sent to Rome or sold to frontier garrison towns, where soldiers spent their pay, or to produce goods which could be fed into the network of interconnected middle-range markets. Total state revenues equalled about 800 million sestertii = 1.8 million tonnes wheat equivalent in the mid-first

[19] Absentee landowners and their households living off rents in kind are exceptions.

century AD. Some of this was collected in kind, some no doubt spent near its point of collection. Even if only one-half was spent away from its region of origin and had to be earned back, its impact on trade was considerable.

Secondly, Rome itself and the great cities of Alexandria, Antioch and Carthage were high cost zones within the economy. The population of Rome itself was helped out by state subsidies; otherwise, I imagine, its population would not have been able to earn enough to pay for food, once transport prices and transaction costs had been added. But the populations of the other great cities did earn money with which to pay for imported food. That point has already been made. What I want to stress now is slightly different. The model which I have been developing here is too flat. There were in fact different zones within the Roman economy: fertile zones, arid zones, river accessible and landlocked zones, high cost and low cost zones, mining, pastoral and arable zones. This differentiation in physical endowment, in population densities and in costs, complemented taxation, its exaction and expenditure, in providing the dynamic for trade.

Thirdly, townsmen's capacity to produce goods cheaply and to sell their products outside their locality fixed their capacity to buy other towns' handmade goods and staples. The division of staples from non-staple foods and goods is not merely artificial, it is a definite obstacle to the understanding of the Roman economy.

My objective in the first part of this essay has been to construct a rough model which will show up some probable relationships within the Roman economy. For tactical convenience, I divided the transport of staples into short haul, middle range and long distance. I have tried to show how they tied in with each other, and with the production and sale of goods. I have also touched on some probable relationships between town and country, taxes and trade, entrepôts and major urban markets. One advantage of such a model is that it prevents us from being overwhelmed by the sheer impossibility of coming to any conclusions at all because of the fragmentary character of the surviving testimony.

Two disadvantages need to be stressed. First, the model deals with the main outlines of probability; it does not deal with the complexities of local variations, nor with variations over time. I need hardly emphasise the importance of such variations, to say nothing of the numerous archaeological finds which do not fit in neatly with rational economic expectations. As a tactic of intellectual discovery, my model assumes economic rationality. In fact, I suspect, Romans often behaved economically irrationally or were motivated by factors and prices which we do not know about. Much of the past is irrecoverable. Secondly, I have rather rashly tried to quantify some elements in the discussion. These quantities are experimental. I hope that they are not wildly wrong, but several are closer to guesses than to fact. They should be treated with extreme caution, and if they are cited, they should be cited with some qualification. They are invitations to argument and discussion.

Finally, some comparative evidence may help put these calculations about Roman transport and trade into perspective. Perkins estimated that in fourteenth-century China, about 20–30 per cent of agricultural produce was traded, and that about 7–8 per cent was transported outside its local district of production.[20] At first sight, such calculations may fill the Roman historian with envy. It is obviously impossible to make any such calculations for Roman trade by the traditional techniques of patient, inductive empiricism. We simply cannot build such structures from archaeological finds in scattered sites and from literary or epigraphical fragments. And how, from the evidence available, could we make fine distinctions or measure changes in the volume of Roman transport and trade, say between 6 and 8 per cent of gross agricultural product? Yet such a change, from 6 to 8 per cent, implies growth by one-third. Instead, we have to be content with rough impressions and crude indices, such as the volume of archaeological finds at Roman levels, the number of coins found, the size of ships. We can fit them into competing models of the Roman economy and judge which we find most convincing.

[20] Perkins 1969: 113–24.

Even rough figures may help us in our choice of models. A minimum estimate of gross agricultural product in the Roman empire (Population × Minimum Subsistence + Seed) equals about 18 million tonnes wheat equivalent.[21] 7 per cent of that is 1.3 million tonnes. By contrast, in table 7.2, I have estimated Roman medium-range and long-distance transport of staples at 0.5 million tonnes wheat equivalent. But that calculation took no account of the higher value of some staples (wine, olive oil), and no account of trade in non-staple foods, in luxuries, textiles, construction materials, fuel, leather, metals and pots. Can we estimate the actual total value of Roman middle-range and long-distance trade? I do not think so. And yet, if only one half of the 1.8 million tonnes wheat equivalent raised in taxes was matched by middle-range and long-distance trade, then the total volume of Roman trade approached fourteenth-century Chinese proportions.

The Cost of Ships and of Transport

I turn now to two issues of detail: the cost of cargo ships and of transport in the Roman world. The first is an important element in the rough model. I have argued that the value and volume of long-distance and middle-range transport and trade in staples, non-staple foods and goods in the Roman empire in the first two centuries AD was huge. They must have contributed greatly to the prosperity of the towns through which they passed. I now argue that ships on major trade routes were often large, and that they were so expensive to build, and valuable to own, especially when laden, that members of the Roman social élite were probably involved in their ownership. Ships like mines offered real economies of scale and required a considerable concentration of risk capital.

Roman ships were expensive. We can tell this by comparing their method of construction with that of later ships, both in the Mediterranean and in north-western Europe. Roman

[21] See Hopkins 1980a: 119 [essay 6: 247].

merchant ships were built outer shell first. Each external plank was joined to the next by mortice and tenon joints and by wooden dowels (trenails). Copper bolts were sometimes but not often used in the period 200 BC–AD 100. They were used more often later. The outer shell was then sometimes supplemented by a second internal skin of wooden planks, and the whole shell was finally strengthened by an internal frame. Protection against marine borers was increased by lead sheathing below the waterline, which made ships slower and more expensive. The main tools of construction were the saw, the adze and the plane. There are no known technical improvements in Roman ship construction between 200 BC and AD 400. In summary, Romans built quite large merchant ships with simple tools very carefully, 'like fine pieces of furniture'.[22]

Later Roman ships (increasingly perhaps from about AD 400 onwards), Byzantine ships and northern European ships in medieval times were, by contrast, built up from the internal frame – what is called skeleton construction as against the earlier Roman shell constructions. Once a strong skeleton had been built, outer planks were fixed by iron bolts and nails to the frame to form a waterproof cladding. The gaps between the outer planks were caulked. In the fully developed northern European skeleton-built ship, the outer planks were fastened one over the other, clinker-style. I should stress that the date of the transition is uncertain and probably evolved over a considerable period. But there are distinct signs of a change towards skeleton construction in two wrecks dated about AD 400 and AD 600.

Two differences between the two methods of ship construction deserve emphasis. First, skeleton construction needed far fewer man-hours of skilled carpentry – iron bolts and nails instead of mortice and tenon joints. Secondly, in skeleton construction, the survival of the ship depended more upon the strength of the skeleton than on the condition of the exterior hull. This involved using heavier wood for the frame than in

[22] Unger 1980: 36–7, quoting 36. I am grateful to Mr Robin Craig of University College, London for his generous advice about naval history.

shell construction. Skeleton construction also involved higher repair costs to the outer skin in the course of a ship's life. But overall, the capital costs of skeleton construction should have been significantly less than shell construction.

The Size of Roman Merchant Ships

Let us now consider the size of Roman merchant ships. Our evidence is of four kinds: first, archaeological remains; secondly, occasional comments in ancient Roman histories, in legal texts and literature; thirdly, comparative evidence from other societies at a similar technical level; fourth, analytical thinking. Let us begin with the archaeological finds.

Underwater archaeologists have tracked down perhaps 800 sea wrecks from classical times, of which about 550 can be dated. I have argued elsewhere that these dated wrecks provide a good preliminary index of the relative incidence of ship-sailings in successive periods.[23] The evidence confirms our general supposition that ship-sailing was more frequent between 200 BC and AD 200 than ever before or in the next thousand years. This index is obviously crude; the location of dated wrecks largely depends on the activities of local enthusiasts; the eastern Mediterranean is under-represented; pirates may have sunk some ships; and finally, if ships sailed more in one period across the open sea than along the coast, then their traces are less likely to have been found. These are real problems, but even so I think the correlation roughly holds: the more sailings, the more wrecks, and more wrecks because of more trade.

Only very few of all these wrecks, one or two dozen, have been thoroughly investigated. Clearly, therefore, we cannot deduce from them a typical merchant ship size for Roman times. Nevertheless, I want to draw attention to seven well studied wrecks listed in an excellent synoptic article by P. Pomey and A. Tchernia.[24]

[23] Hopkins 1980a: 105–6 [essay 6: 221–3].

[24] Pomey and Tchernia 1978.

Findspot	Date by Century	Estimated Size (tonnes burden)
Mahdia	early I BC	240
Madrague de Giens	mid I BC	350
Albenga	I BC	450
Saint-Tropez	2 AD	>200
Torre Sgarrata	end 2 AD	210
Marzamemi I	3 AD	>200
Isola delle Correnti	unknown	350

The consistency of this archaeological evidence suggests that Romans commonly built ships in the range 200–350 tonnes burden, from the last century BC onwards.

A legal text, dating from the second century AD seems to bear this out but only in part and ambiguously. Those who built ships and used them to help supply the city of Rome with wheat were freed of other civic obligations, provided that their ships were of at least 325 tonnes burden or that they had several ships of that total, each of at least 65 tonnes burden (*Dig.* 50.5.3 (Scaevola)). The city of Rome by the end of the last century BC had a population of close on 1 million people. Supplying it with food, clothing, fuel and other consumables, to say nothing of building materials, must have generated a huge amount of seaborne traffic. A low estimate, of food alone at 220 kg wheat equivalent per head, is 220,000 tonnes per year.[25]

The demand for wheat in the city of Rome, effectively subsidised by the state, was very stable. If large ships were common, we should have expected them to have been engaged predominantly in bringing wheat to Rome from the regular wheat-exporting provinces, namely Egypt, North Africa and Sicily. Yet this legal text suggests (as does another: *Tit. Ulp.* 3.6 ⟨= Riccobono, *FIRA* II 267⟩) that not enough ships of over

[25] Some of Rome's food supplies must have come from around Rome itself and down the Tiber. I crudely reckon this at enough to feed 100,000 people at minimum subsistence. In the sixteenth century, when Rome's population was about 150,000 people, it relied significantly on imports by sea: see Delumeau 1957–9: II 521–649.

300 tonnes burden could be found; some shipowners engaged in supplying Rome with wheat used small ships of 65 tonnes burden.[26]

At the other extreme, there is some literary evidence for very large ships of 1,000 tonnes burden or more. The three largest ancient merchant ships recorded may have been, by conservative estimates, roughly 1,200–1,900 tonnes burden.[27] Two of these were built by the order of monarchs, and were in no sense ordinary ships. The first was a white elephant, built by a local king of Syracuse before 221 BC, of about 1,900 tonnes burden. It was purportedly a wheat-carrying ship, designed in part by Archimedes. It had more than 700 crew, including marines, but excluding oarsmen; it also had luxurious living quarters for passengers and their horses, and sophisticated armament, including huge catapults. But after it had been built, the king discovered that there were no harbours large enough to take it without damage or risk, so he gave it as a present to the king of Egypt. The ship sailed once to Alexandria, where it was beached (Athenaeus 206–9).

The second was built in the reign of Caligula (in AD 40) to carry an obelisk and its pedestal from Alexandria to Rome. It was of about 1,300 tonnes burden.[28] This ship also sailed only once, and was more useful sunk than afloat, since it served as the foundation for one of the moles of the new harbour at Ostia. 'Nothing', wrote Pliny, 'more amazing than this ship has been seen at sea' (*Natural History* 16.201). His astonishment makes it clear that ships of that size were unusual.

The third large ship has been the subject of much scholarly controversy. It is described at the beginning of a satirical essay about the variety of human wishes by Lucian, who wrote in the second century AD. An 'exceptionally large' wheat ship was

[26] Pomey and Tchernia 1978: 237–43 argue ingeniously (a) that these small ships were engaged primarily in coastal lightering, bringing wheat from the great port at Puteoli to Rome, and (b) that the regulation was the product of a particular crisis in the reign of Claudius (Suet. *Claud.* 18–19; Tac. *Ann.* 12.43), before the harbour at Ostia was built. Maybe. But the regulations persisted until the second century AD.

[27] Pomey and Tchernia 1978: 245–7.

[28] Pomey and Tchernia 1978: 247–8.

on its way from Alexandria to Rome, when it was blown off course. Seventy days after it set sail, it put into the Piraeus, the port of Athens. Lucian described the ship as 120 cubits (*pecheis*) long, 30 cubits broad and 29 cubits at its deepest part (*The Ship* 5). Modern interpretations of these figures vary enormously; its tonnage has been estimated (to cite only six findings) at 1,177, 1,228, 2,157, 2,672, 5,786 and 6,440 tonnes burden.[29] In my opinion, all these estimates seem improbably large. Lucian's statement – 'there's an army of sailors on board, they say. They say that it carries enough wheat to feed all Attica for a year' (*The Ship* 6) – sounds like rhetorical exaggeration, fantasy not fact. It should discourage us from taking the figures cited above as accurate measurements.

I would not have spent so much time on these sea monsters, but for the fact that influential scholars have thought that huge ships of 1,000 tonnes burden were regularly engaged in carrying grain to the city of Rome in the first two centuries AD.[30] On the literary and archaeological evidence cited, such a conclusion seems illegitimate. Nor is it strengthened by comparative evidence. Ships of 1,000 tonnes burden and over were regularly built for the cross Atlantic trade and for northern European trade with India and China only from about 1800. Although ships of over 1,000 tonnes burden were built in Genoa as early as the fifteenth century, they were rare. In the early eighteenth century, the average size of ships trading from England to India was 440 tonnes burden.[31] Ships on these long-distance routes were, of course, selected for size. The average size of all seagoing vessels was significantly lower. For example, in the beginning of the eighteenth century, the average size of all ships entering Boston, Chesapeake and Barbados was only 50, 90 and 57 tons burden.[32] Such evidence, incidentally, casts serious doubt on Casson's much quoted conclusion: 'the smallest craft the ancients reckoned suitable for overseas shipping was

[29] Pomey and Tchernia 1978: 243–50; Rougé 1966: 69–70.
[30] Casson 1971: 172–3, 184–9; Landels 1978: 165–6; Unger 1980: 36.
[31] See Chatterton 1933: 145, 178–9; Morse 1926–9: I 307–13, II 436–51.
[32] Shepherd and Walton 1972: 195–6 tables 8–10.

70 to 80 tons burden'.[33] That is both intrinsically implausible and based as it happens on an inscription (about the harbour regulations at Thasos from the third century BC) which has an unreadable gap where the vital numeral should be.[34]

Let me go back briefly to the comparative evidence, and in particular to those known giants of Mediterranean commerce in early modern times, Genoa and Venice. In the middle of the fifteenth century, the average size of large merchant ships (>380 tonnes) at Genoa was 630 tonnes, and the largest ship was over 1,000 tonnes.[35] By contrast, the largest ships calling in at Marseille and Barcelona in the mid-fifteenth century were less than 500 tonnes burden. Venice, a century later, in 1559 had only thirty-six or thirty-eight ships of more than 240 tonnes burden, of which the largest was 720 tonnes.[36] And in the same period, the average size of ships using the Spanish Mediterranean ports was only about 75 tonnes.[37]

Where does all this lead us? The Romans had the technical capacity to build very large ships (of over 1,000 tonnes burden). There is no evidence that they commonly did so. Understandably, because if they were blown off course, it was difficult to find harbours for them. Large ships were very expensive to build, and even more expensive to lose if they sank with a full cargo. Later evidence and Roman evidence suggest that most Roman merchant ships were small (<200 tonnes and even <80 tonnes). Even on important trade routes, and even if the city of Rome was their market, many ships probably sailed there from small ports in Spain, southern France, Sicily and North Africa. They had to put in at small ports. And yet, the

[33] Casson 1971: 171; cf. Rickman 1980: 123. Incidentally, Rickman (at 10) believes that Romans ate on average 260 kg wheat (not wheat equivalent) per person per year (men, women and children). That's a lot of bread.

[34] The original editor of the inscription, M. Launey 1933: 394–401, restored the gap with 'three thousand' talents (80 tonnes), but commented (at 396) that 4,000, 6,000 or 7,000 could each from an epigraphical viewpoint plausibly fill the gap. The main subsequent edition (*IG* XII suppl. 348) brackets [three] thousand without noting Launey's alternative emendations. ⟨See Hopkins 1978a: 41–2 n. 13 [essay 5: 167 n. 13], 1980a: 105 n. 16 [essay 6: 222 n. 16].⟩

[35] Heers 1961: 273, 639–44.

[36] Aymard 1966: 57–64.

[37] Braudel 1966: I 278.

archaeological evidence from shipwrecks is compelling: ships of 250–450 tonnes burden were built from the last century BC. Shipowners taking wheat to Rome gained tax exemptions only if they owned ships which either in one unit or in several exceeded 330 tonnes.

Can our knowledge of the size of Roman ships, however imperfect, be used to improve our understanding of Roman economic history? I think it can, especially if we can estimate how much Roman ships cost. The main obstacle here is that there is no surviving literary evidence about ship prices. That may not be an insuperable problem. We know that the Romans built some ships of 250–450 tonnes burden by the expensive shell method of construction, with the hull planks fixed one on top of the other by mortice and tenon joints. We know that post-medieval ships were built by the cheaper skeleton method of construction. As a sighting shot, therefore, just to give us a rough order of magnitude, let us look at the price of building 400-tonne ships (a) in Genoa in the mid-fifteenth century and (b) in England in the seventeenth century. I choose these two examples simply because evidence on ship prices there is available.

Needless to say such comparisons pose considerable difficulties. I am not at all sure that I am comparing like with like, and besides the prices of Genoese and English ships varied widely; but then so, I imagine, did the price of Roman ships. Shipbuilders always have to choose between, on the one hand high capital cost plus a long life, and on the other hand lower capital cost and a short life for the ship, and between strength and buoyancy. For the moment, let us ignore variation and take average prices. But prices in Genoese lire and pounds sterling will not help us. So we adopt the standard practice for translating prices between different pre-industrial societies and convert current coin into tonnes of wheat. The justification for this conversion is that the prices of so many goods and wages co-vary broadly with wheat prices. And I must stress again that we are looking for rough orders of magnitude only, not for exact prices. The final jump in what must by now seem an endless series of speculations is to convert tonnes of wheat into Roman currency. I take the standard price to be 3 sestertii per *modius* of 6.55 kg. That price is much too low for the city of Rome and perhaps too high for some regions of the empire. What is the result of all these calculations? The average price of building and fitting out a 400-tonne merchant ship in Genoa in the mid-fifteenth century was 772 tonnes of wheat or 354,000 sestertii ($n = 5$). The equivalent English price in the seventeenth century was 628 tonnes of wheat or 288,000 sestertii ($n = 6$).[38]

Now I have taken the average cost of only eleven ships, and the variation between their costs was considerable. The price of wheat varied, and so did construction costs. Further research is necessary to check that such construction costs were normal. Nonetheless the figures seem striking. A Roman ship of 400 tonnes burden, expensively built by the method of shell construction, probably cost, if my calculations are at all correct, at least 250,000–400,000 sestertii. Its cargo, if it was wheat, was worth, at the same price, another 185,000 sestertii. If wheat was worth more, especially when delivered at Rome, or if the cargo was more valuable, then the total ship's value, including freight, was more than 400,000–600,000 sestertii.

We can go further in an analysis of Roman transport and trade. We have already calculated that Rome's population of about 1 million people consumed at least 220 kg wheat equivalent each (220,000 tonnes). That was a minimum. We must add extra food, luxuries, fodder for animals, building stone and timber, bricks and mortar, paving stones and fuel. The volume of imports to Ostia, Rome's port and to the riverside quays of the city, some 35 km upstream, must have been huge. What volume of shipping was involved? That obviously depends on the

[38] See Heers 1961: 288, 346–8, 621–2; R. Davis 1962: 338–62, 372–6; cf. Albion 1926: 90–3; on wheat prices, see Mitchell 1962: 486. I took the average shipwrights' construction cost of six ships of over 230 measured tons built in England in the second half of the seventeenth century. The cost per measured ton (£6.5) was converted into tonnes burden (4/3), and I reckoned the cost of fitting out to be the same as in the English trade with southern Spain (two-thirds of hull and rigging cost); so R. Davis 1962: 372–3, 378. The average price of wheat 1650–99, I took to be £1.94 per quarter of 211 kg. Each element in this chain of calculation poses difficulties.

number of voyages which each ship made. Two factors deserve particular mention: first, it was customary for Roman cargo ships to stay in port for four months during winter (Vegetius, *On Military Matters* 4.39).[39] Secondly, sailing ships had to stay a considerable time in port, partly because of weather bunching: they tended to arrive all together with a fair wind and wait to leave together when the wind set fair. And this inevitably prolonged average turnaround times.[40] If we allow ships two trips on average to Ostia each year (less from Egypt, more from Sicily), then the capital cost of the merchant fleet provisioning Rome with staples alone (notionally 275 ships of 400 tonnes at say 300,000 sestertii per ship) was 80 million sestertii. Once we include the transport of non-foods and add in the value of river boats bringing the food upstream, 100 million sestertii seems a conservative, minimum estimate.

In sum, supplying the city of Rome involved food and goods of very high aggregate value (enough food for minimum subsistence alone was worth 65 million sestertii per year at farm-gate wheat prices). This food was transported in ships, each of which cost a lot (say 300,000 sestertii per 400 tonnes). The total capital value of ships involved in supplying the city of Rome alone probably equalled over 100 million sestertii, that is the minimum fortunes of one hundred senators. The sums involved, especially in large ships, were so substantial that it was likely to have involved those Romans with substantial capital to invest and to put at risk. They probably split the risk by taking shares in ships (Plutarch, *Cato the Elder* 21.5–6); that enabled Romans of middling means to participate in maritime trade; it did not diminish the total capital involvement. The total risk capital invested in trade and transport to Rome, and in the rest of the Mediterranean, was very large. It did not equal investment in land, either in size or status, but because it

[39] ⟨Trans. N. P. Milner, Translated Texts for Historians 16, 2nd edn, Liverpool, 1996.⟩ Casson 1971: 270–3; Rougé 1966: 32–3. ⟨See now Beresford 2013.⟩

[40] Shepherd and Walton 1972: 198, tables 18 and 20 cite average turnaround times in Boston, Maryland and Virginia in the late seventeenth century as 36, 106 and 94 days. cf. *BGU* 27 = *Sel.Pap.* 113 for delays at Ostia with comments in Casson 1971: 298 n. 5.

was more risky, it was also probably more profitable to those who succeeded.

Transport Prices

Let us now turn to freight charges. Our best evidence, apparently, comes from Diocletian's Edict on Maximum Prices promulgated in Nicomedia in Asia Minor in AD 301. The Edict was widely publicised and set up on stone inscriptions in Greek and Latin; curiously it was often set out in Latin even in Greek-speaking provinces.[41] This is an important point in that it suggests symbolic display rather than effective price control. But more of that later. Well over one thousand prices survive from the Edict including forty-four prices for sea transport. They run like this:

> From Nicomedia to Thessalonika, for one military *modius*, 8 denarii (Price Edict 35.40).
> From Alexandria to Aquileia, for one military *modius,* 24 denarii (Price Edict 35.5).

The price of wheat is also given. Thanks to Duncan-Jones we know that one military *modius* was equal to 1½ Italian *modii,* that is roughly 10 kg of wheat.[42] We can measure the distance between the ports named and work out a price – so many kg of wheat for each tonne/km, that is the price paid to carry one tonne one kilometre. The median price is 0.8 kg wheat per tonne/km, which seems very cheap, though prices vary considerably around that median.[43]

How were the transport prices fixed? It seems to me likely that they were calculated by measuring distances on a map or by taking distances between ports from a nautical gazetteer, similar to but more sophisticated than the local gazetteers which survive from the third and fourth centuries (such as the *Maritime Itinerary* and the *Gazetteer* (*Stadiasmos*) *of the*

[41] Giacchero 1974.
[42] Duncan-Jones 1976a.
[43] The whole list of sea transport prices from Diocletian's Edict and distances between ports is set out in Hopkins 1982: 85–6 table 1.

Great Sea).* Diocletian's Edict was concerned with long voyages between provinces. The map which Diocletian's administrators used was fairly accurate. We can tell this, because, to a significant extent, differences in prices for transport corresponded to actual differences in distances between ports. On the whole, with some notable exceptions, the more you paid, the further your goods could go. The correlation between distances and prices was 0.72; or put another way, distance accounted for just over half (52 per cent) of the variance in prices. Indeed, the calculations which the Roman administrators executed were more subtle; the further your goods went, the lower the unit price of transport (the more km per denarius), although this fit was rougher and there were some serious discrepancies. In other words, there was a discount for very long voyages. The correlation between distance and cost per km was -0.47, a result which it would have been difficult to get by chance. In sum, we can admire the Roman administrators for their general accuracy, and even for subtlety in calculation, while being puzzled by some of their errors.

One contributory explanation of these calculations is that eastern administrators, stationed in Nicomedia, underestimated the length and breadth of the western Mediterranean. This is not the place to go into details. Suffice it to say that the prices given for transport in or through the western Mediterranean were systematically lower than for the eastern Mediterranean. These price differences cannot be explained, either by the volume of shipping travelling along the routes named (e.g. Carthage to Marseille), or by the extra length of the voyages. The easiest explanation is that eastern officials thought that the western Mediterranean was shorter than it was in reality.

* ⟨The *Itinerarium Maritimum* is the second part of the *Itinerarium Antonini*, ed. O. Cuntz, *Itineraria Romana*, Leipzig, 1929; *Stadiasmus Maris Magni* has survived as part of Hippolytus, *Chronicon*, ed. A. Bauer and R. Helm, *GCS* 36, Berlin, 1929 (= *Hippolytus Werke IV: Die Chronik*), 2nd edn, ed. R. Helm, *GCS* 46, Berlin, 1955; on these texts see, very helpfully, Salway 2004: especially 58–67, 77–85.⟩

We find a similar error in the geographies of Eratosthenes and Dicaearchus (reported by Strabo 2.4) in the third century BC. But curiously enough, that error was corrected, overcorrected even, by other later geographers, Polybius, Strabo and by the great Ptolemy. They thought the western Mediterranean was longer (25 per cent longer) than it is in reality and somewhat wider. It would be tempting, therefore, to suppose that the eastern administrators were using a very old map. But more realistically, I suspect the reason is that our surviving geographical sources are only a fraction of what existed. At any one time, several rival guides mixed accurate and misleading information from different traditions. It must have been very difficult for Roman geographers and administrators to decide between competing versions of the truth.

But the administrators' biggest source of error did not arise from the map's distortions, but from using a map, any map, as the basis of calculations for maximum prices of transport. If Diocletian's officials had stepped out of their offices, onto the quayside, they would have discovered, I think, that a wide variety of factors, such as prevalent winds, the time of year and the volume of trade made such a difference to the length, safety and predictability of a voyage that it must have been reflected in differential prices. Yet the maximum prices given in the Edict make no allowance for the possibility that prices on busy routes should be lower than those on less frequented routes and to out of the way ports. Nor was there any separate provision for journeys in summer and autumn, nor for return journeys with or against the wind. And wind made a lot of difference. For example, according to one estimate, the journey from Rome to Alexandria normally took twenty to twenty-five days, but the return voyage against the prevailing winds took fifty-three to seventy-three days.[44] But in the Price Edict, no account was taken of the impact of winds on the cost of a voyage. The Edict as a whole failed because it did not take the complexities of real life into account. For sea transport, it failed because it tried to impose the artificial unidimensional

[44] Casson 1950: 51, 1951: 145.

order of a map on a variegated world. I conclude, reluctantly, that the Edict on Maximum Prices is not a reliable guide to actual transport charges, either in AD 301, or in the previous three centuries.

The same logic can be quickly applied to land transport. The Price Edict (17.3) proposed a maximum price of 20 denarii per Roman mile for a cartload weighing 1,200 Roman pounds. This led A. H. M. Jones to an influential conclusion – 'a wagon load of wheat ... doubled in price by a journey of 300 miles' – and to his famous comparison based on a belief in the Edict's reliability: 'It was cheaper to ship grain from one end of the Mediterranean to the other than to cart it 75 miles.'[45] But once again, it is worth asking how can this price fit all circumstances? Going over a mountain pass cost much more than going over level ground. Jones' dramatic illustration that wheat doubled in price over 300 Roman miles (or rather 200 Roman miles, because the military *modius* measured 1½ ordinary *modii*) is misleading on several counts.[46] First, oxen move at under 3 km per hour and work normally for only five hours a day; let us say that they go 16 km per day. My point is almost made. It would be very surprising if wheat transported by ox-cart only doubled in price in thirty days travel from the point of departure. That is all the way from London to Newcastle, and in the eighteenth century, coal brought by sea from Newcastle to London cost at least five times as much in London as it did at the pithead.[47] Secondly, the oxen and their driver would consume half the load, or its equivalent, on their journey there and back. Put another way, charges for ox-wagon transport increase with distance.

I have tried to show that Diocletian's Edict is an unreliable guide to actual prices. What can be rescued? Perhaps if the

[45] A. H. M. Jones 1964: II 841–2, cited by Finley 1973: 126; Rickman 1980: 14; de Ste. Croix 1981: 11.

[46] A. H. M. Jones 1964: II 841; Jones here apparently forgot that Diocletian's Edict was concerned with military *modii* (*castrenses*), then conventionally (cf. Hultsch 1882: 629–30) equated with two Italic *modii*; so his result should have been 'doubled in price by a journey of 150 [Roman] miles'. A result often cited, but not checked.

[47] Braudel 1979: 317.

details of the Edict are wrong, nevertheless the broad relativities are right. Here we face a common logical difficulty. The test of the acceptability of the ratios between the cost of transport by land, river and sea is comparative evidence. But if we can accept ancient evidence only if it accords with comparative evidence, and reject it if it diverges widely, why bother with the ancient evidence? I leave that methodological doubt on one side. Let us take the mean values of Diocletian's Edict (i.e. let us ignore variation), and add in a few bits of assorted evidence from Egypt. We find the following rough ratios:

10 units of cost per tonne/km for sea transport
60 units of cost per tonne/km for river transport
550 units of cost per tonne/km for land transport

and that roughly accords with comparative evidence on relative transport prices from other societies.[48] This meant of course that no one in his economic right mind normally sent goods overland, if he could send them by river or sea.

On closer inspection, the contrast between sea transport prices and land transport prices is not so persuasive. In reality, most foods sent by sea originated at some distance from the quayside. Wheat had to be carted, unloaded, sold, stored, recarted, loaded into a ship, unloaded, stored, sold and carted again to its destination. In other words, long-distance trade involved a whole series of costs typically including elements of both land transport and sea transport. But they also involved social organisation – collection, distribution, sale, redistribution, the cost of credit and of covering the risk of loss. I am not at all sure that out of all these factors, transport costs were by themselves the largest or the critical element in determining the volume of long-distance and medium-range trade.

In famines, for example, wheat prices rose well above their normal level; to judge from scattered Roman evidence and much comparative data, twice the normal price or more was

[48] See similarly Duncan-Jones 1974: 367–9. ⟨See Hopkins 1978a: 44 n. 21 [essay 5: 169 n. 21].⟩

common in famines. According to Jones' dictum, then, wheat could have been sought overland to relieve a local famine within a radius of 300 Roman miles (444 km). But during a serious famine at Antioch in AD 362/3, this did not happen, or not until the Emperor Julian intervened personally to secure large quantities of wheat from two towns only 50 and 100 km distant by land from Antioch.[49] These supplies had not been tapped previously, I suspect, because the need for them was both sudden and unusual; the organisation of men and animals to trade and transport staples in bulk overland was simply not available. It took an emperor's political power to marshal them.

In this essay, I have argued that the bulk of transport in the Roman empire was short haul. By implication, most of it was overland. I readily acknowledge that transport overland was relatively expensive, and this higher cost was one factor inhibiting the growth of landlocked towns in antiquity. But it was only one factor of several. And as every Roman archaeologist knows, the expense of land transport did not prevent the widespread dispersion of Roman artefacts. Wine and oil were much more widely distributed than wheat, while the distribution of cloth was limited much more, I suspect, by the size of the market, by the capacity to purchase than by the costs of cartage. After all, according to Diocletian's Edict, if I can still use that source, a journey of 300 km overland added only 7 per cent to the cost of medium-quality wool (Prices Edict 17.5 and 25.8).[*] That surely presented no great obstacle to medium-range or to long-distance trade.

Complementarily, cheaper transport by sea was not enough to stimulate the unrestricted growth of coastal towns. That is the critical argument. As far as we know, very few Roman cities, located on riverbank or seacoast, grew in population significantly beyond the supportive capacity of their immediate hinterland. The well-known exceptions, Rome, Alexandria,

[49] A. H. M. Jones 1964: I 445–6. ⟨See Hopkins 1978a: 46–7 [essay 5: 172].⟩
[*] ⟨See the more fully worked out calculation in Hopkins 1978a: 54 [essay 5: 181].⟩

Antioch and Carthage, are all important, and all grew large because they were capitals of empires. The economic growth of large cities in the Roman world was politically inspired. Their survival as cities, after their initial political functions had diminished, was a symptom of the Roman empire's economic sophistication.

AFTERWORD

MODELS, SHIPS AND STAPLES

PETER FIBIGER BANG AND MAMORU IKEGUCHI

'Models, ships and staples' follows through on Keith Hopkins' work modelling and quantifying the Roman economy, and is best read as a sequel to the more famous 'Taxes and trade in the Roman empire, 200 BC–AD 200' [essay no. 6]. It is typical both of the new ancient economic history spearheaded by historians in Cambridge during the 1970s and 1980s, and of H.'s particular take. The first is discernible in the interest shown in social anthropology, development economics and model construction; the other, in a playful, even teasing, insistence on the relevance or crucial importance of hypothetical deductive quantification – given the lack of proper statistical data from the Greco-Roman world. This alternative would inevitably yield cruder results than those obtained from fine-grained statistics, but it could provide a baseline for discussions of the ancient economy by establishing some minimum estimates below which the Roman empire could hardly be believed to have functioned and then attempt to tease out the implications of these findings. 'Models, ships and staples' is a particularly felicitous example of this method. The paper is divided into two parts: Part I focused on quantifying minimum levels of local, regional and long-distance trade and exchange in staples; Part II on the size of ships and the cost of their construction.

Ostensibly, the paper was written against A. H. M. Jones' and Moses Finley's understanding of trade in the ancient economy, setting out to argue that there was more inter-regional trade and that the investment sums required would have resulted in some very rich merchants as well as necessitating the involvement of some aristocratic landowners, even if individual examples of both were hard to document. At a distance of over three decades, it is striking that the paper defies any such easy dichotomy. Perhaps its most notable claim was that in bulk commodities local demand would have outstripped inter-city and long-distance trade by a wide margin. Most trade, in other words, would have taken place in a local context, within city-states. Nonetheless, even if the proportion of the economy which entered more extensive networks of circulation was moderate in relative terms, on an empire-wide basis it still added up to very substantial sums. As such, the argument marks a significant step in the direction of trying to conceptualise the existence of considerable trade flows within an economy which was predominantly agrarian.

One notable advance on this project was Horden and Purcell's attempt, in *The Corrupting Sea*, to ground Mediterranean exchange and economic integration in ecological necessity. Noting, like H. (90–2 [279–82]), that annual rainfall fluctuated strongly across Mediterranean localities and thus impacted the harvest, they argued that communities, by ambition autarchic, would nevertheless have had to import or export grain in years of either shortage or surplus. Offering relatively easy transport, the ancient Mediterranean was characterised by a fundamental 'connectivity' between its many individual locations.[1] Another cluster of studies have put greater emphasis on the element of risk, uncertainty and the relatively moderate scale of ancient trade – which as H. noted in passing would have combined to make supply lines unpredictable and fragile (90 [281]). Classic are Tchernia's discussion of the extensive Italian wine trade – not least the observation that a relatively small territory would have sufficed to produce the wine involved – and Garnsey's analysis, informed by the huge body of work on Mediterranean peasantries, of famine and food-supply around Greco-Roman communities.[2] Both Reger and Erdkamp have pointed to the relative fragmentation of markets and the fragility of integration in the

[1] Horden and Purcell 2000: especially 123–72, 205–9, 342–400.

[2] Tchernia 1983: 87–92, 1986: 108–23; Garnsey 1988: especially 56–8, 70–86. Halstead 2014 for a monumental attempt to synthesise our understanding of peasant agriculture in the pre-industrial Mediterranean based on anthropological observation, personal experience and systematic information about Mediterranean ecology.

ancient Mediterranean, while de Ligt and Bang have explored the character of market institutions fitting such a pattern, the first examining periodic markets and fairs, the latter suggesting the bazaar, with its myriad small agents and asymmetrical distribution of information, as the most plausible model for the functioning of ancient trade.[3] Tchernia adds further to this body of work by insisting both on the great extent of Roman commerce and the need to study trade in its concrete setting of geography and socio-cultural institutions: Roman trade should be analysed as a *commerce imbriqué*.[4]

Bang also attempted to add to H.'s argument that demand generated by the imperial state was a significant spur on, or component of, Roman mid-range and long-distance exchange, by noting that aristocracies around the Mediterranean were able to benefit from state power to build up greater concentrations of wealth, some of which was spent on an increasingly lavish array of consumer goods.[5] Scheidel and Friesen have put more elaborate flesh on the bones of H.'s other suggestion: not to underestimate the aggregate demand of the vast numbers existing below the élite in the Roman empire. Individually their demand for traded items would have been trifling, but the totals would be significant.[6] Several studies over the years have added substance to this view by further attempting to quantify individual trades, notable is Mattingly on oil, a more recent example is Marzano on marine resources, while Mayer makes a powerful case for the economic vibrancy of these sub-élite groups and the significance of investment in urban commercial infrastructure, although his label of 'middle-class'

[3] Reger 1994: 271–6; Erdkamp 2005: 143–205; de Ligt 1993; Bang 2008: 173–201.

[4] Tchernia 2011: 155, and in particular 101–72 (see too 168–72 for a direct and interesting engagement with H.'s 'Taxes and trade' [essay no. 6]). Contrary views, insisting instead on the relatively close integration and lack of fragmentation of Roman markets, are well represented by Temin 2013: especially 1–52, 97–113, with further bibliography. Harris 2011: 155–87 is more measured and historical; Scheidel 2012b: 287–319 ('A forum on trade') usefully assembles a number of different positions on the problem and character of trade in the Roman world.

[5] Bang 2008: 61–127, especially 93–110, 290–306. On the imperial culture of consumption, and the waves of fashion generated by the formation of an aristocratic society and court in Rome and Italy, see Wallace-Hadrill 2008: 315–440.

[6] Scheidel and Friesen 2009: especially 88–91.

is controversial.[7] Finally, Rosenstein has followed up on H.'s attempt to put some quantitative estimates on the trade in consumer staples (grain, wine and oil) in mid- to late republican Italy. Once more, the narrowness of markets and relatively modest scale of demand is brought into focus, making Rosenstein question whether the aristocratic élite in Italy could have maintained its lifestyle on the incomes generated from their agricultural estates. Additional significant sources would have been required; business and commerce is one candidate.[8] Another, perhaps even more important, consequence to draw from these results, is again to call attention to the enormous riches generated for the aristocracy by the acquisition of a Mediterranean empire.[9] These may have enabled the urban élites of Italy to live well above the level of income supported by their agricultural estates. More radical still, Rosenstein's estimates remind us of the fragile basis on which our notions of aristocratic income rest. Perhaps researchers have overestimated the actual size of income enjoyed by this group?

The second part of this essay then moves into a different gear, focusing on the cost of ships and transport. H. first argues that Roman merchant ships, built by the 'shell-first construction' technique, were often as large as 400 tonnes burden: since such ships must have been considerably expensive (at least 250,000–400,000 sestertii), supplying the city of Rome would have involved the Roman élite. Secondly, pointing to the unreliability of Diocletian's Edict on Maximum Prices, H. warns against underestimating land transport based on the costs listed in this text, thereby reinforcing the importance of local networks of trade and exchange.

On the first point, some reconsideration (and some updating of the information) may be helpful. The claimed higher cost of shell-first construction compared to skeleton construction is debatable. H. emphasises the laboriousness of the former technique, including the making of mortice and tenon joints

[7] D. J. Mattingly 1988; Mayer 2012; Marzano 2013.
[8] Rosenstein 2008, 2009: especially 249–50.
[9] Bang 2012.

(96–7 [289–90]) – but this is a flexible method in which the shipwright can constantly check his work and correct mistakes. By contrast, skeleton construction requires precise designs and correctly shaped main timbers in advance.[10] Moreover, since ships constructed shell-first are more resilient, and hence more storm-resistant, than those constructed skeleton-first,[11] annual amortisation costs, rather than the initial capital investments, should be compared – again complicating the problem. At any rate, skeleton construction was already known in the first century BC (the Madrague de Giens shipwreck shows a mixture of the two construction techniques[12]), so the reason why the shell-first method was preferred needs to be explained – even in terms of cost.

Ship sizes are even more problematic. All seven shipwrecks cited by H. (98 [292]) are more than 200 tonnes burden and three are more than 350 tonnes, but according to Parker's data (unpublished when H. wrote this paper), most shipwrecks are under 200 tonnes burden.[13] The most recent combined data on shipwrecks (from the Oxford Roman Economy Project database) shows that only 15 per cent are over 200 tonnes burden, 25 per cent are 100–200 tonnes and as many as 60 per cent are less than 100 tonnes.[14] It may be that larger, especially grain-carrying, ships are under-represented. Most wrecks have been located close to the coast, and most often detected on the basis of amphorae on the seabed. But even taking this factor into account, H.'s suggestion that Roman merchant ships were often of 350–400 tonnes burden still seems – at least archaeologically – in need of some modification. Rathbone, using different kinds of evidence (including ship sales/leasing recorded on papyri and the Rhodian Sea Law) proposed that Roman

[10] Greenhill 1976: 73; Greene 1986: 23.

[11] A. I. Wilson 2011b: 219 (but Wilson himself considers shell-first construction more expensive).

[12] Tchernia et al., 1978: 89–92 and plate 41.

[13] A. J. Parker 1992: 26.

[14] A. I. Wilson 2011b: 212, fig. 14.1; and see helpfully on H.'s approach to data from shipwrecks, Wim Jongman's Afterword to 'Taxes and trade' [261–2].

ships in the first and second centuries AD were 'mostly not very big, and even big ships were not very expensive'.[15]

H. rightly warns against the uncritical use of the transport prices in Diocletian's Price Edict and the consequent underestimate of the importance of land transport.[16] In any case, in practice, as H. points out (105 [303]), sea, river and land transport were combined with each other. A recent and important development in this field is the Standford digital project, initiated by Scheidel, generating a computer-based model of physical transport conditions for the entire Roman world, revealing both intense axes of connectivity and the persistence of (macro)regional fragmentation. The empire at large would not have consitituted a unified market area.[17]

It was sufficient for H.'s purpose to offer a static view of transport prices, but it should be borne in mind that transport costs likely changed with time. The suppression of piracy in the late Republic and the early empire would have reduced costs, especially the *fenus nauticum* or the maritime loan interest-rate (as is suggested by the comparative data from Atlantic Ocean shipping in the seventeenth to the nineteenth centuries).[18] The Claudian and especially Trajanic harbours constructed at Portus near Ostia would have provided safer moorings – again, arguably, resulting in a downward pressure on maritime loans. A recent excavation report from Portus suggests that the aggregate capacity of the warehouses surrounding the harbours in the second century was three times as large as that of Ostia.[19] Supported by a secondary hub port at Centumcellae, this 'port system' facilitated the storing and handling of cargoes transported from the provinces by sea.[20]

[15] Rathbone 2003: 199 with Scheidel 2011a emphasising the fragility of the data.

[16] See Arnaud 2007 and Scheidel 2013 for discussion of the basis of the Edict's price calculations. Laurence 1999: 95–108 argues against the prevailing notion that land transport in Roman times was 'slow or expensive compared with other pre-nineteenth-century economies' (at 95); so too, Adams 2007: especially 3–14 on the importance of land transport to the economy of Roman Egypt. See usefully Campbell 2012: 247–329 on rivers.

[17] Scheidel 2014; http://orbis.standford.edu/.

[18] Ikeguchi 2003–4, 2008: 91–102; see too Scheidel 2011a.

[19] Keay et al. 2005: 310.

[20] Keay 2012.

But the extent to which the imperial peace promoted growth or economic development remains a moot point. Tchernia has recently remarked, 'il n'y a pas ... pour les produits les plus importants, de changements radicaux entre Auguste et Septime Sévère'.[21] While the high empire gives the impression of stability or moderate development, it is by contrast the age of republican conquests that can boast the most dynamic changes.[22] Current debates tend to concentrate on the extent to which the Roman economy resembled that of early modern Europe, but our evidence is unlikely ever to become sufficiently fine-grained to permit the precision that it is possible to achieve for Europe in the sixteenth to eighteenth centuries.[23] From that point of view, H.'s approach in 'Models, ships and staples' still carries an important message for economic historians of the ancient world. Instead of chasing elusive precision, it may be more prudent and profitable to seek to establish some cautious, absolute minimum estimates and then explore the implications of these for our wider understanding of the Roman economy.

[21] Tchernia 2011: 97.
[22] Scheidel 2007b; Bang 2012.
[23] See too Scheidel 2009.

8

FROM VIOLENCE TO BLESSING: SYMBOLS AND RITUALS IN ANCIENT ROME*

Introduction: The Lupercalia

In AD 495, more than a century after the triumph of Christianity, Pope Gelasius I finally forbade Christians to participate in the ancient Roman rites of the Lupercalia.[1] He tried to persuade both Christian traditionalists and pagans of the wickedness of their ways, and of the Lupercalia's inefficacy in protecting the city of Rome against famine and plague. When some Christians objected that previous popes had allowed the Lupercalia to continue, and that they had been celebrated even in the presence of a Christian emperor (Anthemius, r. AD 467–72), Gelasius countered with the argument that it had not been practicable for the Church to dismantle paganism all at once (*Letter against the Lupercalia* 13, 29).[2] The Pope's prohibitions were not immediately successful, even among Christians. But in due course, the Lupercalia disappeared,

* First published in A. Mohlo, K. Raaflaub and J. Emlen (eds) *City States in Classical Antiquity and Medieval Italy: Athens and Rome, Florence and Venice*, Stuttgart: Franz Steiner Verlag, 1991, 479–98 (= Hopkins 1991a).

[1] The title of this chapter is an inversion of Maurice Bloch), *From Blessing to Violence* (1986) a brilliant study of the changing meaning and functions of circumcision rituals among the Merina of Madagascar. I should like to thank Kurt Raaflaub for persistent patience, Glen Bowersock for helpful criticism, and above all Mary Beard and Stephen Hugh-Jones for many intellectual discussions and good advice.

[2] ⟨Gelasius, *Adversum Andromachum contra Lupercalia* = *Coll. Avell.* 100; ed. Pomarès 1959 = (with minor emendations) O. Günther, *CSEL* 35, Vienna, 1895, 453–64; for an elegant English trans. by M. Briel, see now G. E. Demacopoulos, *The Invention of Peter: Apostolic Discourse and Papal Authority in Late Antiquity,* Philadelphia, PA, 2013, 181–9; see too B. Neil and P. Allen, *The Letters of Gelasius I (492–496): Pastor and Micro-Manager of the Church of Rome: Introduction, Translation and Notes*, Turnhout, 2014, 211–21; for a helpful discussion of this text, see McLynn 2008.⟩ The most interesting study of the Lupercalia, from which I have greatly benefited (though I do not always agree with his detailed interpretations), is Holleman 1974, supplemented by Pomarès 1959.

though some of its rituals were transferred to the Feast of the Purification of the Virgin Mary (or Candlemas).[3]

It is easy enough to see why the Pope objected. The Lupercalia celebrated nakedness, sex, bawdy violence, voluntary or forced flagellation, riotous disorder and drunkenness, as well as antique pagan superstitions.[4] Originally, so several Roman intellectuals thought, the Lupercalia had been a rite of purification, derived from Rome's pastoral origins when herds of goats had to be defended from wolves (*lupi* = wolves, hence perhaps, *luperci*, the name given to the runners in the ritual). Apparently, in popular imagination, the symbol of the wolf was associated with the festival, since in the temple of the *Luperci*, discovered at Rome in the seventeenth century, but now destroyed, pictures behind the altar portrayed Rome's founders, Romulus and Remus, being suckled by a wolf, and next to them a *Lupercus*, armed with a whip and ready to run. But in historical times, the main interest of the rites seems to have centred on the fecundity of women.[5]

The core elements of the rites were roughly as follows. Every year, on 15 February, after the sacrifice of a dog and goats (an exceptional sacrifice, since Romans usually killed for the gods the more edible animals: pigs, sheep and bulls), two young men, their foreheads smeared with blood and milk, led teams of young aristocrats and knights, feasted, drunk, garlanded and perfumed, running naked around the ritual centre of the

[3] Gregorovius 1894–1902: I 265; Bede, *De temporum ratione* 12 (*PL* 90: 351C–D) ⟨ed. C. W. Jones, *CCSL* 123B, Turnhout, 1977; trans. F. Wallis, Translated Texts for Historians 29, Liverpool, 1999⟩. See also Schumacher 1968–9 for a very interesting discussion of a third-century Roman tomb probably of a *Lupercus,* depicting the Lupercalia, with candles. It indicates night-time festivities in the Lupercalia, mentioned by Gelasius, and presages the transition to Candlemas.

[4] It is an interesting symptom of the ritual's plasticity and of Christian adaptability that the Lupercalia was celebrated by Christians. But then the Merina circumcision ritual, involving the worship of ancestors among other things, was practised by fervent Christians: see Bloch 1986: 41, 62.

[5] The most detailed ancient accounts of the Lupercalia, apart from Gelasius, are by Ov. *Fast.* 2.267–452 and Plut. *Rom.* 21. These and other accounts, for example, Festus 76 L s.v. 'Februarius' ⟨ed. W. M. Lindsay and J. W. Pirie, *Glossaria Latina IV*, Paris, 1930⟩ and Varro, *Ling.* 6.34, associate the Lupercalia closely with February, from *februa* = a purificatory offering. See helpfully the commentary by Bömer 1957–8: II 82. The painting discovered in Rome in the seventeenth century and now lost, is reproduced from an old drawing by Lanciani 1891: 341 and plate 12.

city. As part of the festivities, they beat anyone they chanced to meet, but especially women, with thongs cut from the sacrificed goats, allegedly in order to render them fertile, or to ease childbirth. In the second and third centuries AD, some Roman senators and knights were so proud of having run as *Luperci* that they boasted about it or had the ceremony portrayed on their tombstones.[6] And in all strata of Roman society, boys and girls were given names which directly recalled the Lupercalia: Lupercus, Luperca, Lupercilla, Lupercianus. The Lupercalia was a ritual which helped Romans identify themselves as Romans.

Pope Gelasius' open letter on the Lupercalia and his polemical prayers, which were especially composed for delivery during mass before and after his prohibition of the Lupercalia, are particularly valuable as sources. Gelasius, a hostile observer, provides us with details about the rites, which earlier and friendlier commentators had merely hinted at. Even so, many details of the Lupercalia rites are uncertain, partly because surviving accounts vary, and partly because it is difficult for us to know how much these variations in description imply differences in perception, or changes in practice. For example, according to Gelasius, men were naked for the flagellation, while earlier sources disagree as to whether men were naked or wore loincloths made of goat skins; Gelasius states that respectable women were stripped naked and flogged, but Plutarch writes that women merely stretched out their hands to be beaten, like children in school (*Julius Caesar* 61).[7] In the

[6] See e.g. *CIL* VI 2160: 'a Roman knight who also ran as a Lupercus'; *CIL* VIII 9405 = 21063: 'awarded a public horse, and who performed at the holy Lupercalia'. For two memorials (one is *CIL* VI 3512 + XIV 3624 = *Inscr. Ital.* IV.1 155), see conveniently Veyne 1960.

[7] The disagreement among ancient authors about the nakedness of the runners and of the beaten women is interesting. Did it reflect contemporary variation (some were, some were not), or a clash of ideals or changes over time? Ov. *Fast.* 2.283–4, Varro, *Ling.* 6.34, Plut. *Caes.* 61 and Gelasius, *Adversum Andromachum* 16 ('respectable women flogged in public with their bodies nude') stress nakedness; Dion. Hal. *Ant. Rom.* 1.80 and Plutarch again (*Quaest. Rom.* 68 = *Mor.* 280B–C) are explicit about the loincloths covering the genitals worn by the *luperci*. Just. *Epit.* 43.1.7 has it both ways: 'naked, clothed in a goat-skin' (ed. O. Seel, Leipzig, 1935, 2nd edn, Stuttgart, 1972). Perhaps the tension was between the nakedness necessary for a

fifth century AD, according to Gelasius, the runners were no longer aristocrats, but despised members of the lower classes. But in the last century BC, aristocratic youths, even magistrates, participated actively in the rites; indeed, Antony was among the runners when he was consul in 44 BC: he turned aside from the ritual, addressed the crowd in the forum naked and offered Julius Caesar a crown (Plutarch, *Antony* 12; Cicero, *Philippics* 2.85–7, 3.12: 'naked, drunk, perfumed'). The carnival spirit had taken on serious political overtones.[8]

The Lupercalian rites involved much more than a brief, half-hearted, symbolic chase by drunken young men through one part of the city.[9] According to Gelasius, they were associated with a charivari, the ritual singing of lewd songs, bawled in rebuke of some wrong-doers' alleged immorality; they involved seductions and even sexual assaults on married women accused of adultery, and finished with ritual flagellations and penance.[10] Perhaps it would be comforting if we could dismiss all this as idle speculation, late accretions, or as the hostile exaggerations of a reforming pope. But centuries earlier, Cicero had hinted that the Lupercalian runners 'had intercourse in a rustic style as was customary before civilisation and law were established' and that they called out accusations against

fertility rite and the difficulty of respectable aristocrats running naked round the city and confronting respectable women who wanted to be fertile.

[8] It is important to stress that some people thought the Lupercalia was fun. The *luperci* were propelled through the streets by collective solidarity, the jollity induced by a banquet and a lot of wine drunk (Cic. *Cael.* 26; Val. Max. 2.2.9).

[9] I used to think that the Lupercalia was perfunctorily ritualistic, mere tokenism, a quick fun run. This common view was a product of our conventional understanding of traditional Roman religion: dull, unemotional and colourless. The latent agenda, I suspect, is to idealise the Romans (masterful and efficient) and to undervalue Roman religion, as a backdrop, soon to be displaced in an evolutionary procession by oriental mystery religions and eventually by Christianity; see e.g. Turcan 1989: 25.

[10] These are the speculative but well argued conclusions of Holleman 1974: 60–87, based principally on Gelasius, *Adversum Andromachum* 2, 5, 16–20, plus *Masses* XVIII–xviii and XVIII–xx ⟨prefaces from the Leonine sacramentary, ed. and trans. Pomarès 1959: 216–25⟩, homilies delivered just after the Lupercalia of AD 495, in which he attacked those who had deserted Christ, were filled with carnal desire, had forcibly entered homes and had taken unfortunate and sinful women captive, not just widows but wives. There seems some colour to Holleman's speculation that the Lupercalia served as a carnival trial, public punishment and penance of wives accused of adultery (cf. Soc. *HE* 5.18).

named people (*Pro Caelio* 26); Cicero's description is at least compatible with that of Gelasius. The centrality of serious flagellation, in the image and so perhaps also in the reality of the Lupercalia, is corroborated by a calendrical mosaic dating from the third century AD. It gives a picture for each month; under the title February, it depicts the Lupercalia and shows two men forcibly holding a naked woman face upwards, while a third man, half naked, whips her thighs.[11] Once again, the festivities have taken a more serious turn. The men's drunken hilarity is matched by the beaten woman's obvious pain. The image of Roman festivals which this mosaic projects (and a third-century sarcophagus from Rome depicts a similar scene) is disturbing.[12] It reminds us, if we needed reminding, not to domesticate Romans into a comfortable familiarity. Romans were dangerously different.

I began with the Lupercalia, because it illustrates the persistence of ritual forms, certainly for six centuries, and perhaps for a thousand years. The rites persisted, in spite of huge changes in the Roman political system, from the early small scale pastoral and agricultural republic, threatened by wolves, through the conquest of a large empire, the growth of the city in size and intellectual sophistication, and in 31 BC the political transformation of the state into a stable monarchy, to the eventual triumph of Christianity in the fourth century AD and the collapse of the western Roman empire in the fifth century. In order to survive so long, the Lupercalian rituals must have occupied a social space which was disassociated both from political government and from religious ideology.[13] The stability of ritual forms must have disguised both radical diversity and radical changes in meaning. For example, it seems likely that the Lupercalian rites had different significance in each period

[11] For the mosaic discovered in El Djem (Roman Thysdrus) in 1961, see conveniently Schumacher 1968–9: 67–8 or Dunbabin 1978: 111–12 and the literature cited there.

[12] On this sarcophagus panel, the woman is being whipped on her buttocks, is naked from the waist down and is depicted as a volunteer sufferer, or so Schumacher deduces from the way she is held; see Schumacher 1968–9: 65.

[13] The best discussion which I have read about how rituals should be interpreted is by Bloch 1986: 157–95; but see also Lane 1981 and A. Cohen 1974.

for different sections of Rome's varied population: spectators, participants, half-naked men and beaten women, full Roman citizens, visiting saints and immigrant traders.[14] And it seems likely that they had different meanings for early Roman peasants, Roman aristocrats in the middle Republic with one eye on the popular electorate, imperial intellectuals thoroughly acquainted with fashionable scepticism, immigrant citizens living in Rome but strangers to Roman traditions, proselytising Christians and late pagan reactionaries. We do not know the secret of the Lupercalia's appeal, but we can speculate. Its central concern was with sexuality and fecundity, with the wild and the civilised, with hierarchical order of men and the humiliation of women. During the cold of February, naked aristocratic men, masked like wolves, hunted for women, but could beat whomever they met in the crowded streets of metropolitan Rome.[15] Respectable women, instead of modestly retreating, stood up to, even offered themselves to, the hunters for a beating. The professed objective was fecundity. But clearly at some stage in the development of the ritual, the focus shifted slightly: the disorderly sexuality of women was symbolically punished by the flagellation of selected wrong-doers or

[14] I doubt the interpretation of Paul Zanker in his rightly influential book, *The Power of Images in the Age of Augustus* (1988): 'To the equites, for example, he [Augustus] assigned the ancient but now meaningless cult of the Lupercalia. In this ritual, which was originally meant to insure the protection and fertility of the flocks, a dog was slaughtered and priests, dressed only in a short skirt, ran a course around the Palatine, incidentally beating women with a whip made of goatskin. It is easy to see how this archaic fertility ritual might have seemed ridiculous in a cosmopolitan environment, and, understandably, Augustus forbade adolescents from being present at this event. … Only recently have honorific statues of *luperci* … been identified, combining a classical seminudity, the short skirt, and goatskin whip into a public image that conforms to classicizing aesthetic standards' (Zanker 1988: 129 and 130 fig. 105). The errors here are multiple: an over-identification with authority, the apparent attribution to all Romans of a single attitude and interpretation, and the imposition of modern art-history categories – which functions as an evasion of analysing the varied meanings of the artefact to its ancient erectors and observers. Why did Roman knights commemorate their participation in the Lupercalia on their tombstones, if the rites were generally considered 'meaningless' or 'ridiculous'?

[15] The idea that *luperci* wore wolf masks is derived from Lactant. *Div. inst.* 1.21.45 ⟨ed. P. Monat, *SC* 326, Paris, 1986; trans. A. J. Bowen and P. Garnsey, Translated Texts for Historians 40, Liverpool, 2003⟩: 'naked, drunk, garlanded, either masked or smeared with dirt', a sequence of words which closely follows Cicero's description of Antony as *lupercus* (*Phil.* 2.85–7, 3.12); and see Holleman 1974: 30–2.

penitents. The Lupercalia became attached to the public punishment of those accused of or confessing to adultery. Some of the runners, as I have said, were proud enough of their participation to have it recorded on their tombstones.

The survival of the Lupercalia for so long was due partly to the confrontation of issues which repeatedly troubled Romans, and partly to the encapsulation of these troublesome emotions in a disorderly dramatisation which bracketed the performance off from the normal world. The sheer unconventionality of the rituals, their barbaric wildness, heightened their appeal; at the same time, they increased the variety and ambiguity of meaning for participants, which in turn helped secure their survival – just as a modern political party survives by meaning many things to different voters. The Lupercalia survived, I suspect, because they were disorderly, without promoting any general disorder.

Participation, as actor or observer, was a symbol of belonging to the community of Rome, which identified itself partly by its religious rites and traditions. Participation also symptomised obedience to the legitimacy of tradition; whether as beater or beaten, the violation of normality was justifiable because the actor was merging his or herself in a collective Roman identity. The naked vulnerability of the male *luperci* was compensated by being masked, drunk and in a gang, wielding whips and asserting the hierarchical privilege of treating whomever they encountered just like slaves. The ritual was insulated by its strangeness into being a special occasion; its violent violation of normality helped contribute to the strenuous self-control of everyday, ordinary Roman life.[16]

A Complex of Rituals

We entered the world of Roman festivals, as outsiders, on a single day. But Romans lived through dozens of religious rituals

[16] I am close here to viewing the Lupercalian rites, functionally, as a safety-valve. This may have been their function, that is, it may have been an unintended result of participation. I acknowledge this as both possible and probable, without committing myself to seeing all Roman rituals as functionally preservative of social order.

and festivals every year, and for year after year throughout their lives.[17] They learned about rituals cumulatively and by assimilation. Consciously or unconsciously, they experienced or intuited Roman rituals and religion, willy-nilly, as a total system, without of course drawing the same boundaries around that knowledge, which we have to, in order to understand it or explain it. Romans, for example, typically intertwined religion and politics; their rituals suffused everyday life, whereas we, in modern industrial societies, typically see religion as separate from politics and, for our own ideological protection, typically consider rituals as non-purposive, non-instrumental, peripheral activities such as sporting occasions or family festivals, disassociated from the serious world of work.

Our understanding of Roman festivals and rituals can best proceed, I think, by pursuing a double strategy. First, we need to use empathetic imagination to help think and feel ourselves back into how different Romans themselves experienced rituals. Secondly, we need to see the totality of Roman festivals and rituals analytically, almost objectively, as a complex system. Both approaches have their dangers and limitations. We can never think like Romans. And yet if we are to understand the power of Roman rituals, their repeated capacity to secure citizens' involvement, then we have to recapture the excitement, the heightened emotions of participants: the cheering, jeering crowds voting death with their thumbs down at the gladiatorial games, the pious prayers of worshippers seeking victory in war or helplessly hoping to escape an epidemic, and the individual anxiety of an 18-year-old recruit who one hot day in July 110 BC stood sweating in his father's armour, borrowed for the occasion, waiting and wondering if he would ever be called out and chosen to serve for the first time as a soldier in a Roman legion. This perspective, as I have said, has its dangers. It is based sometimes on imagination rather than on sources, and so violates the canons of careful scholarship. But it can also serve as a valuable corrective to the unselfconscious élitism of

[17] For a convenient, annotated list of Roman religious festivals, see Scullard 1981: 51–212.

Roman historians, both ancient and modern, who place themselves effortlessly in the very top ranks of Roman society and view rituals only downward, from above.[18]

My second tactic is to consider Roman rituals as a system whose business it was to constitute and reconstitute a Roman sense of identity.[19] This second approach is analytical and comparatively objective, because it is a modern intellectual creation which cannot be attributed to the Romans, who may well have perceived their own institutions quite differently. But all history does violence in some way to actors' perceptions. To be sure, Romans' knowledge of their own ritual world was diverse and probably hierarchical. Some people participated in some festivities actively; in others, they keenly watched their father or mother playing a seemingly complicated part and realised that one day they too would have to go through the same nerve-racking performance. In other festivals perhaps they only watched from a distance, or were puzzled by their complexities or simply slept through. The point I want to make is that Romans' knowledge of ritual was, paradoxically, at the same time systematic, partial and hierarchical. Some people knew a little; only a few knew a lot. Our picture has to cope with this diversity, has to recognise that by no means everyone knew as much as our most knowledgeable sources and so acknowledge that ignorance, and the anxieties which ignorance created, were all part of the Roman ritual system.

In this view, rituals cumulatively, throughout each year and each lifetime, provided Romans with a system of action and knowledge by which they negotiated standardised and repetitive ways of dealing with powerful imponderables, such as

[18] Ronald Syme was the arch-proponent of élitist Roman history; for him explicitly, as for others implicitly, the only history which matters or is possible is the political history of the aristocracy and emperor. This was a prejudice of many, though not of all our surviving sources. Our own prejudices can be different – and there is certainly little justification in a social history for privileging élitist accounts of Roman practice, as though they were true accounts of typical Roman experience.

[19] Viewing Roman rituals as a system implies the complementarity of different rituals. I think they were complementary, but I must stress that rituals can at the same time be expressive, formalist, integrative and subversive. Seeing them as a system is a heuristic device, not a substantive commitment to a particular view; see the path-breaking article by Mary Beard 1987.

sexual appetite, hierarchy and sickness. Rituals also confronted the problematic populations within and surrounding Roman society. Sacrifices, for example, joined humans with their gods, gladiatorial games confirmed Roman superiority over defeated enemies and highlighted the risks of cowardice in battle, the Lupercalia helped delineate the multiple differences between men and women and their mutually problematic sexuality, the Saturnalia dealt with slaves by subverting rank and temporarily giving slaves the power to command, and the Lemuria placated the ghosts of the dead. This whole array of Roman rituals, religious and political, public and private, was like an orchestra, with each ritual standing for a single instrument. None of them can be understood alone, by itself; each ritual depended on the others. To be sure, there was no conductor, no ritual dictator. Each citizen could play or hear different tunes on each instrument. Even so, out of the diversity and apparent cacophony, collective rhythms emerged. Diversity of experience and understanding does not preclude a recognisable score which was identifiably Roman. And besides, one function of the total ritual experience was to help Romans distinguish themselves from outsiders.

Roman rituals confronted yet another anxiety-arousing imponderable, the power of the Roman state. Perhaps all states, but particularly pre-industrial states, because of their limited capacity to enforce widespread obedience among citizens, depend on rituals to enhance their legitimacy. They need to foster a sense of collective identity, in light of the obvious fact that citizens have competing interests. States can do this effectively and economically only by mass rituals. From this perspective, we can somewhat unconventionally envisage some of the central political institutions of the Roman state, such as the census, the military levy, the electoral and legislative assemblies of the people, as rituals. This is not to deny the instrumental and practical importance of these institutions in the republican period (509–31 BC). Far from it. The census regularly listed tens of thousands of citizens by name, recorded their wealth or poverty and fixed their tax liabilities, their status, their entitlement to vote, their obligations to serve in the army. The military levy worked to enlist thousands of soldiers; indeed, during the last century BC, an average of well over a hundred thousand citizen soldiers served in the Roman army every year. The electoral and legislative popular assemblies rejected bills, passed laws, chose between aristocrats competing with each other each year for dozens of prestigious magistracies. We are dealing here with central processes of military and political power. But the processes were also rituals.[20] Whatever the divergence of participants' interests, however bitter their conflicts in elections, their very participation united them under a common cultural flag.

At this stage, it may be useful to try to recombine our two approaches, the empathetic and the analytical. We have to acknowledge the formalism and complexity of constitutional arrangements and at the same time appreciate the subjective anxiety which participation evoked among actors. Each of the rituals which I have just mentioned, the census, the levy and the popular electoral and legislative assemblies, involved large-scale participation, with a cast of many thousands. They also stimulated intense but different reactions. Rituals often work like that. By crowding participants together, they generate strong emotions; and they offer fertile ground for the manipulation of symbols, such as flags, ceremonial clothes or the sounds of music and the smells of a burning sacrifice.[21] Each ritual was a public performance, carried out in front of spectators. The plump knight had to lead his aging horse through the forum in front of the censors. Cold constitutionality had

[20] These central Roman institutions are normally understood constitutionally. Still best is Mommsen 1887–8. In addition, on the census and levy, see Brunt 1971a: parts 1 and 4; on the levy, Hopkins 1978b: 31–7; on the popular assemblies, L. R. Taylor 1966.

[21] Because we rely on surviving written sources for rewriting Roman history, we tend perhaps to undervalue the importance of colour, sounds and smells in Roman rituals. Good modern films, such as *Ben Hur*, *Spartacus* and *I, Claudius* offer interesting supplements. So too do Egyptian mummy cases of Roman citizens, if provincial Romans alive dressed as they were portrayed dead. See the fine pictures of the coffins of Cornelius Pollius (first century AD) and his family, now in the British Museum, reproduced in Neugebauer and Parker 1969: 89–93, plates 46–9. The noise of the crowd in an amphitheatre, such as the Colosseum in Rome, must have been deafening and enhanced the music of trumpet and water-organ which introduced and punctuated gladiatorial fights; see conveniently Hopkins 1983b: 20–7.

a sweating face, set in a potentially jeering crowd. Every head of household had to make a public statement of his wealth for each census, which served as the basis of his taxability, fixed the level and style of his military service and determined his own and his family's social status. Imagine the conflict between under-declaration and exaggeration, between the meanness of the free rider and the boastfulness but expense of social ambition.[22] The Roman census periodically constituted and reconstituted, before a critical audience, hierarchy and social order. It was both a constitutional institution and a mass participation ritual.

Every state has to harness the power of its underclasses. The trick, as Marx saw, was to ensure that peasant potatoes were ordered into sacks, but also to ensure that peasants remained like potatoes, without a consciousness of their collective interest.[23] My argument in the next section of this chapter is that Roman political rituals were organised by complex rules, which worked rather like a stately eighteenth-century dance, such as a gavotte or pavane. The purpose of this metaphor, and it is only a metaphor, is to acknowledge the complexity of constitutional regulations, but also to invest them with the actors' subjective meaning and anxiety.

There were four principles underlying the organisation of Roman rituals. These principles competed and overlapped. First, the populace of citizens was repeatedly divided into mutually competitive strata and sets. Within each set, the citizens were then again subdivided (by regulations so complex that few people could have understood what was going on) into ever-shifting, repeatedly reconstituted groups, like the changing sets of a gavotte. One function of these constitutional rules (by function, I mean here the consequence of the rules envisaged independently of their creators' intentions) was to harness the aggregate power of the Roman masses, without allowing them the repeated possibility of establishing

[22] On the dilemma of the free rider, see D. C. North 1981: 10–12.

[23] Karl Marx, *Der 18. Brumaire des Louis Bonaparte* (1852) §VII (trans. *Karl Marx, Frederick Engels: Collected Works*, vol. 11: *Marx and Engels, 1851–53* (London, 1979), 99–197 at 187–8).

stable internal coalitions, through which they could realise or achieve their collective interests and so undermine the dominance of the senate. The power of the plebs was harnessed, without allowing it to be threatening.

Secondly, the constitutional rules were so complex that few people knew what they or others should be doing. Ignorance about procedures, and the passivity or anxiety which ignorance encouraged, were themselves hierarchical devices, which helped subordinate the ignorant to the knowledgeable.[24] And waiting – waiting for your turn, and especially waiting for your social superiors to have their turn first – was also a device repeatedly used by Romans to reinforce hierarchy.

The third principle of Roman ritual organisation was that affiliations should be differentiated and cross-cutting. Differentiation implies that rituals were organised in such a way that subtle peculiarities of dress, style and self-dramatisation demarcated different social boundaries. Senators, for example, wore tunics and togas with a broad purple stripe as well as distinctive red shoes with black lacing and an ivory buckle. High-ranking senators, as officers of state, were preceded by attendants carrying bundles of rods and axes to signify their powers of corporal punishment and were entitled to sit on special chairs.[25] Similar differentiations suffused all strata of Roman organisation; some divisions, as we shall see, were by birth, others by wealth, others by body armour or physique, still others arbitrarily created by lottery. The important point is that differentiations shifted between rituals, over a year and over each actor's lifetime. Consequently, one function of rituals was to express, and repeatedly to re-express, membership of ever-changing and only partly overlapping sets: senators, knights, a legion, a tribe, a priestly college, a lineage, a

[24] Knowledge is still used as a power base, for example, by governments which withhold or selectively release information and by university professors; see, for example, Bourdieu 1984. As to waiting, it was a well-known aspect of Roman elections; Varro sets one of his dialogues in a period of more than two hours, during which his intellectual and aristocratic conversationalists waited for their election results and whiled away the time discussing birds and bees in some shade near the voting pens (*Rust.* 3.2–17).

[25] Mommsen 1887–8: I 372–414, III 888–92; Talbert 1984: 216–20.

combination of patron with his clients, a social grouping in a morning passeggiata in the forum or an afternoon group at the baths. Rituals are stylised, repetitive social activities, which help express and define social relations. They do their work especially through symbols, just because they combine participants who do not explicitly share common interests.

Finally, rituals and symbols work partly through obscurity and mystery. Symbols and rituals cannot do their symbolic work if all actors are clearly conscious of their functions. In the end, in a stable political system, rituals work because they provide the opportunity for different people to share the illusion that they each belong to a common cultural system. The ritual dramas of publicly declaring one's wealth at the census, joining the army, fighting a battle, running in the Lupercalia, mourning at a young daughter's funeral, losing an election or getting drunk at a public feast, each coalesced a different set of fellows, projected different but yet quintessentially Roman images. Each Roman created his or her own symbolic map; the maps overlapped and so helped create a fluid, but stable, and identifiable cultural system which we call Roman society.[26] This common culture, through its ambiguities, drew together people with different interests and helped propel them toward common actions.

Roman Political Rituals: The Levy, Census and Popular Assemblies

The Levy

These four organising principles of Roman ritual can best be illustrated by taking a closer look at how Roman political rituals worked. Let us begin with the military levy during the Republic. Once again, we owe our best surviving description to an outsider, the Greek historian Polybius, who presumably, unlike the Romans themselves, did not take their traditions for granted. Polybius stayed at Rome for a long time in the mid-second century BC and set himself the task of explaining to

[26] I borrowed the idea of symbolic maps from Smith 1978: especially 289–309.

Greeks why the Romans had succeeded in conquering their cultural superiors. He looked at Roman institutions from inside, but as an outsider. This is how Polybius analysed the ritual dance of the military levy, executed every year, so that a cast of at least 18,000 performers (comprising four legions) were chosen from among the tens of thousands of adult male citizens who had not yet served all the years for which they were eligible. Please note the formalism of the procedural rules, the internal divisiveness of the selection process and of the sets which it produced and, finally, the emphasis on hierarchy and order.

All Roman citizens were eligible for military service between the ages of 17 and 46 years. Up to ten years' service was required from the cavalry, sixteen years from the infantry. The poorest citizens, those with property worth less than 400 denarii, were demoted to service in the navy. On the day of the military levy, previously fixed by the consuls and announced in the popular assembly, all eligible citizens converged on Rome. Needless to say, Polybius' account here is idealistic and ignores population centres outside Rome; but it is quite understandable that his account of a foreign ritual concentrated on the thousands present in the capital city rather than on the absentees.[27]

Let us begin, as Polybius did (6.19), with the officers. Twenty-four military tribunes were elected by the tribal assembly: ten senior tribunes from among the soldiers with at least ten years' service; fourteen junior tribunes from among those with at least five years' service. The twenty-four tribunes were then allocated among the four legions as follows:

Tribunes	*Legions*				*Total*
	I	*II*	*III*	*IV*	
Senior	2	3	2	3	10
Junior	4	3	4	3	14
					24

[27] The classic commentary on Polybius is Walbank 1957–79 (see I 697–703 on the description of the military levy in Polyb. 6.19–21). Polybius' account of the Roman constitution is in book 6.

It is rules like this which remind us of ritual dances. The first soldiers to be selected were the cavalry, three hundred per legion, chosen from among the wealthiest citizens, nominated as such by the censors. The early selection of the cavalry, Polybius noted, was an innovation; it probably reflected the increasing stratification of Roman society, which itself resulted from an expanding empire.

Next came the selection of the infantry. First, the thirty-five tribes were ordered by lot. Then, from the winning tribe (and later from each successive tribe in turn), a tribune chose four young men of similar physique. Next, a tribune from each legion picked one of the quartet, with the order of choice rotating between the legions, so that eventually each legion had soldiers of similar physical standards, but from different tribes. The procedure of enlistment went on, the men being chosen, walking forward, being chosen again, until all four legions, totalling 18,000 thousand men, had been registered and marshalled. Finally, each man singly swore a very brief oath of loyalty. It was a full day's work for those choosing, chosen and rejected: a collective ritual of togetherness and anxiety, repeated each year, and like the periodic census, a public restatement of physique, age and wealth. A few days later, when the soldiers joined their legions for active service, they were once again divided up, by age, poverty and body armour, experience and contiguity, into rows and centuries.

The process of enlisting, choosing, rejecting, marshalling, ordering thousands of Roman citizens every year as soldiers, sailors, infantry, cavalry and officers was both purposive and ritualistic. It was effective but not efficient in time and energy. But its protracted ritual helped Romans realise the might of Rome and the cost at which it was won. The levy celebrated Roman military togetherness and yet, by its repeated subdivisions, it set citizens against or above other citizens. The levy was a collective action, signifying varied meanings and arousing strong emotions, impelling men to conjoint action. The levy was both ritual and institution. I chose to begin with it both because it had a cast of thousands and because it was central to Roman imperial expansion and political identity.

But it was only a start. In order to understand Roman rituals and symbols, we cannot deal with single institutions in isolation. We have to look at the configuration of rites, through which individual Romans in the course of a year, and a lifetime, were socialised and resocialised into their set identities. Of course, in a single essay, that is too large an agenda. But the approach can be illustrated with two further political rites, the census and the electoral and legislative assemblies.

The Census

The periodic census was held on average every six years throughout the late Republic, until the disruptions of the civil wars. The overt purpose of the census was to create lists of citizens, taxpayers, potential soldiers and electors. Citizens had to record their ages, children, slaves and property, and on that basis were allocated to one of seven social categories (knights, five classes and proletarians whose only contribution to the state was their children – *proles*). A sculpture now partly in the Louvre and partly in Munich, dating from the last century BC, shows a census registration in progress.[28] A citizen carrying his own records in a small diptych of wax tablets stands before a seated census official, who is making an entry onto a large record sheet. Behind the census official's left knee we can clearly see a stacked pile of six volumes of census records. At the official's side, another seated census official is taking the oath from the next citizen about to make a declaration, while a saluting soldier looks on. The military and religious elements of census-taking are illustrated in the same relief: the next panel shows soldiers, infantry and cavalry, standing by while preparations are made for the sacrifice of a pig, sheep and bull, the ceremonial and religious termination of the census. The census combined religion, social order, hierarchy and tension.

The Roman census created lists, honour and rank. The mere act of recording the names and property of 300,000, and, in the last century BC, of over a million citizens, should not be

[28] Torelli 1982: 5–25 and the literature cited there.

underestimated. It was a ritual on a large scale. But the census was not just an emotionless head count. It was a social stock-taking, in which each citizen had his social standing confirmed, or changed. The censors reviewed moral behaviour as well as wealth. They reviewed the physique of the upper classes and their horses in the ritual centre of Rome. They demoted even senators for alleged immorality.

In general, the social order was stable. But within this stability, considerable atomic flux occurred; single sons inherited whole estates, while in other families several children split the patrimony between them, with a drop in status for all unless they were lucky and/or married well. The census provided a regular stage for the public declaration of the changing worth of each citizen's property. In a rapidly expanding empire, wealth had to grow for relative status to be maintained. Imagine the added tension at academic conferences, if name badges noted incomes as well as names. The word census came to mean 'declared wealth'; the term equestrian census meant the wealth which qualified a man for the status of a knight. In formal birth certificates, which survive only from a later period, Roman citizens declared the birth of a child. They also stated how much the father was worth, as an open matter of public record:

> I, C. Herennius Geminianus, (census) 375,000 sestertii, have registered (as a Roman citizen) my daughter, Herennia …
>
> (*P.Mich.* III 166 of AD 128, written in Latin)

Census taking in the Republic was an important ingredient in securing the continuity and reproduction of the Roman system of social identity and divisive stratification. It was a recurrent, ritualistic and public fixing of social status. Once again, its emphasis was on order, hierarchy and social divisions by tribe, class and obligations.

Popular Assemblies

The people in Rome had considerable political power. Their power was expressed in the army, in citizens' legal rights and by popular assemblies. This is not to say that Rome was a democracy; far from it. In many respects, it was an ever-changing aristocratic oligarchy. But it had surprisingly strong democratic elements. I say surprising, because conventional scholarly opinion over the last few decades (misled I think by the élitist preoccupations of leading scholars) has assumed the unquestioned dominance of an aristocratic élite.[29] The main reasons for dissent are twofold. First, aristocrats disagreed among themselves, so that popular assemblies often held the balance of power. Secondly, in order to win popular support, competing aristocrats proposed measures which favoured some sectors at least of the broader citizen population. Hence, for example, the distributions of conquered land to citizens, voting by secret ballot and monthly distributions of subsidised (and later free) wheat to citizens resident in Rome itself. Politics is not only about process and who controls the state, but also, even in Rome, about results and who got what share of the cake.

The recurrent tensions in Roman political life, both between competing aristocrats and between competing political objectives (war, peace, expenditure, triumphs) provided the emotional bloodstream for the complicated rituals of legislative and electoral assemblies. The voters had to choose and repeatedly cared about who won. Imagine the conflicting emotions when, for example, laws were debated and passed limiting the amount of state land a rich man could lease (367 BC), displacing the co-option of state priests by popular election (104 BC), allowing secret instead of open voting (137 BC) and establishing a court for trying provincial governors for corruption (149 BC). The issues here are not constitutional niceties, but the lifeblood of Roman political practice.

There were three main popular assemblies in operation during the last centuries of the Republic: the Assembly of the Centuries, which had originally been a military organisation, the Assembly of the Tribes and the Council of the Plebs, which excluded

[29] The best synoptic account of the current debate about the Roman political system in the late Republic is J. North 1990. The classic statements of the élitist view were by Gelzer 1912 and Syme 1939. Revisionist views have been suggested by Hopkins and Burton 1983a: 107–16; Millar 1984, 1986; Brunt 1988.

hereditary nobles and which had been an instrument in the earlier myth-creating struggles of the people against the aristocrats. Each assembly had important electoral, legislative and judicial functions. For example, the Assembly of the Centuries elected senior officers of state (consuls, praetors, censors), the Assembly of the Tribes elected lesser magistrates (aediles, quaestors) and the Council of the Plebs elected tribunes of the people, an office designed to protect ordinary folk against official or senatorial abuse. All laws had to be passed by one of the assemblies. The Assembly of the Centuries made official declarations of war and dealt with crimes punishable by death, at least until the establishment of permanent courts. The Assembly of the Tribes dealt with cases punishable by a fine. Yet, since the membership of all three assemblies was almost identical, the functions of the differences were partly maintenance of tradition, partly mystifying involution (like mazurkas and foxtrots) and partly, like other Roman political rituals, fragmentation of the subordinate classes into constantly changing and therefore never coalescing sets.

The ritual complexities of Roman political practice are well illustrated by the voting procedures of the Assembly of the Centuries or by any modern book on Roman constitutional law. First, I should stress that the voting day was the culmination of prolonged electioneering; in the case of legislation, voting occurred only after due publication of the draft law and open public meetings of citizens, at which rival orators tried to sway public opinion. The elaborate voting rituals which celebrated hierarchy and order followed the controlled disorder of mixed public meetings.[30] On the day appointed for voting, a red flag was hoisted on a hill across the Tiber from the city and a trumpet was sounded from the city walls. The presiding officer said a prayer, then lots were drawn to decide which century from among the younger men in the top social class should vote first.

[30] See the excellent guide by L. R. Taylor 1966: 15–33, 111, on which I lean heavily here. On the procedures for ⟨proposing, approving and⟩ publishing bills, see Mommsen 1887–8: III 369–419.

The first century selected by lot entered the voting pens (as in sheep pens – *ovile*, *saepta*), each man wrote the initials or names of the candidates he favoured (two consuls elected one day, eight praetors elected the next – according to the rules, the names of all candidates were to be written up clearly on white boards in the voting pens), their votes were counted and the result was formally announced.[31] This first result was thought to be influential and predictive, like a modern opinion poll on the eve of an election. On some notorious occasions, an imperious presiding consul who did not like the outcome sent the first century back to vote again (Livy 24.7–9), or suspended proceedings because of a bad omen (Plutarch, *Pompey* 52). Normally, the voting proceeded to the other centuries of the first class. Lots were drawn to decide the order of voting, with the result of each class successively announced until an absolute majority – 97 of the 193 centuries – had been obtained for each consul and praetor. I must stress that results were often unpredictable. Since all candidates had clients, patrons and kinsmen, and since competing aristocrats often had overlapping circles of acquaintance, none of these variables (patronage, clientship or family) is by itself an explanation of success. Votes were therefore usually split and emotions often ran high. We know only of some close decisions, which went to the lowest centuries (Asconius, *Commentary on Cicero, Oratio in senatu in toga candida* 94;[*] Livy 43.16). Voting and counting votes for multiple candidates took a long time and sometimes could not be completed by sunset. We are dealing with a complex, long and important political ritual.

Consider the difficulties, both formal and practical. The 193 centuries were organised by classes, which were based on wealth and on age. From the third century BC, each century also had to be drawn from a different tribe or tribes. This caused some difficult manoeuvring, because members of the thirty-five tribes, younger and older men separately, had to

[31] An excellent account of voting methods is given by L. R. Taylor 1966: 34–58.
[*] ⟨See R. G. Lewis and A. C. Clark, *Asconius: Commentaries on Speeches of Cicero*, Oxford, 2006.⟩

Table 8.1. *Centuries and classes in the Roman Republic.*

	Centuries	
Class 1	70	35 centuries aged 17–45 years, 35 centuries aged 46 years and above
Knights	12	
Aristocratic knights	6	*sex suffragia*
Carpenters	2	
Class 2	20	each 10 centuries aged 17–45 years, 10 centuries aged 46 years and more
Class 3	20	
Class 4	20	
Class 5	40?	20 centuries aged 17–45 years, 20 centuries aged 46 years and more
Musicians	1	
Supernumeraries	1	
Proletarians	1	
	193	

be squeezed into ten or twenty centuries. Table 8.1 illustrates the problem.

In the first class, the thirty-five tribes of younger men (aged 17–45 years) and thirty-five tribes of older men (aged 46 years plus) matched the number of centuries. But in the lower classes, younger and older men from the thirty-five tribes had to be redistributed so as to constitute ten centuries each. The reallocation was done by lot, and we can plausibly reconstruct the procedure from a bronze tablet, the Tabula Hebana, discovered only in 1947 near the ancient town of Heba, which details procedures devised in AD 19 for splitting thirty-three tribes of senators and knights among fifteen centuries, each with its own voting basket. Presumably similar processes of random electoral mixing had regularly occurred previously at the Assembly of the Centuries. The function of the rules was to repeatedly divide up the electors in different ways, so that they did not develop stable alliances or small group identity. It also seems probable that many voters were ignorant about the precise procedures or at least found them confusing.

Ritually, one function of the rules was to develop the voting into a stately and protracted dance, like a pavane. First, balls for each tribe were to be put into a revolving urn. The order in which the balls fell out determined which tribes were to vote in which century:

> The assignment of lots shall be carried out in such a way that for the centuries … (1–10), two tribes shall be allotted for the first, second, third and fourth basket, three for the fifth, two each for the sixth, seventh, eighth and ninth, three for the tenth. And for the centuries … (11–15), the lot shall be carried out in such a way that two tribes shall be allotted to ballot baskets eleven, twelve, thirteen, fourteen, three to fifteen.[32]

It is easy to imagine similar inventiveness in splitting the younger and older voters from thirty-five tribes among ten centuries each in classes 2–4. It is easy to imagine that on a hot day in July voting and counting votes, punctuated by announcements of results from each class, took a long time; sometimes the whole procedure was not finished by sunset and had to be continued on the next day.

Unfortunately, we do not have any figures for attendance at the popular assemblies comparable with those for democratic Athens. But we do have some clues. The stone-walled electoral pens (*saepta*), begun by Julius Caesar and finished in 26 BC, were huge, some 300 metres long and 100 metres wide. They allowed simultaneous voting by all thirty-five tribes in elections by the Assembly of the Tribes. Lily Ross Taylor calculated that the pens could hold seventy thousand voters at a time.[33] Of course, we do not know whether or how often the pens were filled. It is reasonable, albeit risky, to argue that building on so huge a scale simply assumed large-scale voting. The hall where votes were counted, the Diribitorium, was the largest roofed

[32] The translation of the Tabula Hebana is from L. R. Taylor 1966: 90. The full text is printed in Oliver and Palmer 1954; a translation is given in Johnson, Coleman-Norton and Bourne 1961: 131–5 ⟨see now M. H. Crawford, *Roman Statutes*, *BICS* Supplement 64, London, 1996, 2 vols, I no. 37⟩. The voting prescribed by the Tabula Hebana was in order of precedence: senators first, then knights. In Roman political ritual, so it seems, no opportunity was lost to reconfirm status relativities by ordering and waiting.

[33] L. R. Taylor 1966: 113, 47–54.

building in Rome. It seems ironic that both large buildings were erected only after the institution of monarchy, which heralded the death of democratic elements in the Roman constitution. The pens became a site for gladiatorial shows, and suitably a market for antiques (Martial 9.59).[34]

Configurations of a Lifetime: Other Rituals

Up to now I have discussed one religious and three large-scale political rituals: the Lupercalia, the military levy, the periodic census and the popular assemblies. I have argued that it is not sensible to understand them singly, or in cold constitutional terms. Instead, we have to envisage a configuration of varied rites. We have to imagine a Roman citizen, and whole, shifting, permeable sets of citizens, moving from ritual to ritual through the year, through a lifetime of learning, assimilating, being socialised and then teaching others the traditional rites of being Roman. This statement implies neither universal participation, nor equal understanding of what was happening. But the citizens as a body created for themselves, and in some sense shared, a map of rituals, which existed in their minds and on the ground, as well as in learned encyclopaedias. This map constituted an important element in the Roman cultural system.

I have concentrated so far on political rituals, because they were central to the effective running of the Roman state, because they were large-scale, highly formalised rites and because we ourselves are not accustomed (for our own cultural and ideological reasons) to perceiving ritual and symbolic elements in purposive political institutions. Inevitably, I have left much out, even large-scale popular rituals. For example, the free wheat dole involved registering 250,000 citizens who turned up (at least in the system as it developed) once a month, 8,000 per day, at particular outlets ('he received wheat at outlet 39, day 10' ran an epitaph for a 3-year-old: Dessau, *ILS* 6069 ⟨= *CIL* VI 10224b⟩). The whole process of queuing, waiting,

[34] Zanker 1988: 142–3.

revealing one's needs, participating in a lottery for vacant places, carrying, sweating for the privileges of citizenship, was an important ritual of togetherness and social identity. Once again, its organisation fragmented the 250,000 recipient citizens into very much smaller sets, perhaps less than two hundred per outlet per day.[35]

I have said nothing about other civic rituals, such as the triumphal processions, circus races and gladiatorial games which celebrated Roman victories over defeated, captive and plundered enemies; nothing about state religious rituals, which aligned senatorial priests as chief human intermediaries between citizens and the great gods who favoured and protected Rome. I have also not discussed the Vestal Virgins, the extraordinary ritual observances of the priest of Jupiter, the Flamen Dialis, and the strange foreign religions, some of which, like the worship of the Great Mother, Cybele, were officially imported (in 204 BC), while others, like Isis, Dionysus, Judaism and, later, Christianity, came unofficially and were resisted; finally, I have said nothing further about the traditional rituals, such as the Lupercalia with which I began, or the Parentalia and Saturnalia. Obviously, even in a longish paper, I could not discuss all these individually.

Instead, I wondered if it would be profitable to examine this wild profusion of varied, civic and religious rituals by applying the concept of configuration, and by invoking the ancillary ideas of function, the penumbra of moral ambiguity, controlled violence and inversion. My initial intentions can be simply put. I want to envisage how the whole gamut of Roman rituals worked. The central, large-scale political rituals, which we have already discussed – let us call them mass participation rites – implicitly reinforced the virtues of hierarchy and order; they functioned both to harness and to fragment the lower classes. The civic rituals of triumphal processions, gladiatorial

[35] On the wheat dole at Rome, see Rickman 1980: 156–209; for a fascinating parallel at the small market town of Oxyrhynchus in Roman Egypt in the third century AD, see Rea 1972 (= *P.Oxy.* XL). Claimants for the dole there had to attend a public meeting, go through a lottery and have the validity of their status as citizens publicly and administratively approved.

games, the Lupercalia and state sacrifices – perhaps we could call these by contrast, spectator rituals – all presented the citizens who watched, smelt and heard brief but repeated visions of violence: the slaughter of a bull, the hunt of wild animals in the forum or amphitheatre, the murder of captured enemies or convicted criminals, the whipping of women. The Vestal Virgins, the self-mutilating, castrated priests of the Great Mother, and later the ascetic virgins of Christianity, all helped reassert the vigour of normal sexuality by inverting it. So, similarly, the inversion of the Saturnalia reconfirmed the authority of the masters by 'playful' rituals in which masters served slaves and slaves played at being masters. The steeper the hierarchy, the more it both needs and can afford ritual inversions.

The full panoply of rituals at Rome operated as a harmonic configuration, offering citizens antiphony between hierarchic order and encapsulated violence, and securing moral conformity by locating rituals especially in the penumbra of moral ambiguity. As I see it, the core of political mass participation rituals, celebrating hierarchy and order, was held in place by the nimbus of religious and civic spectator rituals, which celebrated violence and the upset of hierarchy and order, albeit in very restricted doses. So too, conventional sexual morality was upheld by worshipping through the medium of priests and priestesses who behaved abnormally. It is as though the margins of normality, what I have called the penumbra of moral ambiguity, provide the ideal staging for the celebration and codification of symbolic values. Spectator rituals concentrate in areas of social strain.

One implication of my argument seems worth exploring briefly. The first emperor, Augustus (31 BC–AD 14), revolutionised Roman political life by superimposing monarchy on traditional republican forms. He and his successors maintained power by demilitarising and depoliticising citizens living at Rome and in Italy, and by cutting the ties which bound the aristocracy to the plebeian electorate. So the annual military levy was effectively abandoned; soldiers served for sixteen or more years and were recruited from all over the Mediterranean basin and beyond. The citizen census, after a brief and intermittent revival, was also abandoned; the political assemblies continued to meet for a while to pass laws, but the area of political debate had shifted from the forum to the Palace. By the end of Augustus' reign, elections to the senate were shifted out of the popular assemblies to an electorate of senators and perhaps knights. In sum, Augustus had degutted the central political rituals of the city of Rome. There was a ritual vacuum. Only bread and circuses remained.

Did it matter?[36] For as long as the empire was effectively defended against barbarian invasions by its professional long-serving armies, and as long as its internal political task was to minimise the combinatory power of its conquered populations, the lack of a centrally controlled symbolic leverage was an advantage. Control over the symbolic map could not fall into the wrong hands. But when the old empire of conquest tried to increase its capacity to mobilise resources against external invaders, the lack of a coordinating ideology of collective interest was critical. The empire as a whole had no effective rituals to give all the inhabitants of the empire a single collective identity. I wonder if this lack of a coordinated set of rituals and symbols at the very centre of empire made the empire as a whole vulnerable to attack across its own symbolic and ritual frontiers. After all, the empire was conquered by the strange sect of Christians a century before the western empire was overrun by barbarians.

[36] I face a problem here which I cannot easily or satisfactorily resolve. The more important I claim political rituals to have been in the political and social life of the Republic, the more problematic their abolition or transformation under the emperors becomes. My claim in this coda that the abolition of ritual created a vacuum, only filled several centuries later by the invasion of Christianity, puts too much weight on a metaphor, and telescopes time uncomfortably. The reader who has got this far deserves comfort; this argument as it stands does not seem entirely convincing; but it seemed too interesting to discard completely; and besides, someone else may improve it out of all recognition.

AFTERWORD

FROM VIOLENCE TO BLESSING: SYMBOLS AND RITUALS IN ANCIENT ROME

JAŚ ELSNER

This essay is characteristic of Keith Hopkins, in his incarnation as a cultural historian, as I knew him when I was a doctoral student in Cambridge in the late 1980s and early 1990s. The paper was written for a conference at Brown University in 1989, and – to judge by its opening footnote thanking the editor for 'persistent patience' – was delivered at the last possible moment before publication in 1991. It is a brilliant and beautifully integrated union of deep classical learning with precise propositional thinking, astutely informed by sociological and anthropological theory. It is cast in H.'s extremely persuasive prose and consistently takes the high ground in calling for methodological self-consciousness in addressing its theme. It is also, simultaneously, an outrageously cavalier dereliction of scholarly duty in that – after the piece very coherently lays out its theoretical and historical ground – it abruptly gives up the ghost on any kind of historical argument or even intellectual cohesion.

The paper ends with a final paragraph, whose opening sentence is: 'Did it matter?' (498 [339]).[1] To this question, in the paper, H. appends this footnote (498 n. 36 [339 n. 36]), which bears quoting in full.

I face a problem here which I cannot easily or satisfactorily resolve. The more important I claim political rituals to have been in the political and social life of the Republic, the more problematic their abolition or transformation under the emperors becomes. My claim in this coda that the abolition of ritual created a vacuum, only filled several centuries later by the invasion of Christianity, puts too much weight on a metaphor, and telescopes time uncomfortably. The reader

[1] This is a version, turned upon himself, of that most brutal of questions which H. would put to the speakers in his ancient history seminar: 'what was the point of that?' But it is a touch kinder (to himself) since it historicises the problem rather than asking why our time has been wasted in the present.

who has got this far deserves comfort; this argument as it stands does not seem entirely convincing; but it seemed too interesting to discard completely; and besides, someone else may improve it out of all recognition.

A historical argument that telescopes time and is based on a metaphor; an argument not entirely convincing, but too interesting to discard completely – some might say that H. was defining his intellectual identity: self-aware and intensely self-critical while at the same time slapdash and downright lazy when bored by doing the necessary work.

From the vantage point of hindsight, some of the paper's very clear merits at the time look more like commonplaces now than when it first came out. It is no longer news that rituals 'helped Romans identify themselves as Romans' (480 [315]), that 'Romans were dangerously different' (482 [317]); that what is 'disorderly, without promoting any general disorder' (483 [319]) might be thought of as a social 'safety-valve' (483 n. 16 [319 n. 16]); that ritual experience helped 'Romans distinguish themselves from outsiders' (485 [322]).[2] More radical remains the 'double strategy' (484 [320]) for which H. calls in the paper's strong and robustly written methodological section. He prescribes a combination of 'empathetic imagination to help think and feel ourselves back into how different Romans themselves experienced rituals' and the 'need to

[2] Work on ritual and antiquity has expanded exponentially since H. published this piece. In one sense, this might suggest that H.'s work is now significantly out of date on several issues of interpretative nuance; but I am struck by how little the vast arena of specialist studies has to offer by way of synoptic or synthetic interpretation, and frankly H.'s broad-brush characterisations remain not only both stylish and penetrating, but arguably ahead of the game. On religion and ritual see e.g. Beard, North and Price 1998a: 450 for 'rituals' in the index and a wide range of discussions within the book referred to there, as well as 1998b: 60–77, 116–47; Scheid 2003: 79–126; Rüpke 2007: 86–116; especially Scheid 2005 with the discussion of Ando 2009. For social and political rituals, see e.g. Graf 2005; Beard 2007: especially 58–61, 257–86; Peachin 2011. In fact, the burgeoning literature of the cultural history of the Roman world might arguably seen as an account of its ritualised activities from such things as walking and laughing to forgetting: on these see e.g. O'Sullivan 2011; Corbeill 1996; Hedrick 2000; Flower 2006. For ritual in the Roman Republic (H.'s ostensible topic), see e.g. Hölkeskamp 2000; Holm Rasmussen and Rasmussen 2008 (in particular, J. North 2008a). For ritual and empire, see especially Benoist 2005. For the ritualising of time at the point of transition between Republic and empire, see Feeney 2007. For scepticism about the usefulness of 'ritual' as it is frequently evoked in the study of material culture, see Elsner 2012.

see the totality of Roman festivals and rituals analytically, almost objectively, as a complex system' (484 [320]). That is, he calls for high levels simultaneously of both subjectivism and objectivity in the historian. Given the paper's genuflection in its title to the work of Maurice Bloch (479 n. 1 [313 n. 1]), its persistent annotation of anthropologists and social theorists (482 n. 13 [317 n. 13]; 487 nn. 22–4 [324–5 nn. 22–4]) – and, particularly its acknowledged debt to the anthropologist Steve Hugh-Jones (479 n. 1 [313 n. 1]) as well as ancient historians – we might see these as the play of the emic and etic strands in anthropological thinking (more popular then than they are today). H.'s objectivism comes down to a model of a structurally differentiated complex of interconnected rituals which together define a system observed, as it were, from an analytic bird's-eye view, and understood in its totality. His subjectivism, proclaiming that intense desire in the ancient historian to have something closer to direct access to ancient culture than our empirical remains allow, comes with acute awareness of some of the dangers his form of empathy may pose (especially the way 'imagination ... violates the canons of careful scholarship' (484 [320])); but he characteristically uses a sketch of the potential benefits for a sideswipe on the Oxford tradition of Ronald Syme as 'the arch-proponent of élitist Roman history' (484 n. 18 [321 n. 18]). It might be added that as an essay on religious history, 'From violence to blessing' anticipates H.'s book, *A World Full of Gods: Pagans, Jews and Christians in the Roman Empire* (1999), which repeats the call for 'empathetic imagination'.[3]

Yet the paper at no point delivers on either part of its double strategy – and one might argue that ultimately both its prongs are impossible. At no stage does H. offer us an empathetic insider's view (despite his call for this), leaving his developed expression of this method to *A World Full of Gods*, which many readers have judged as highly problematic in its attempts

[3] See Hopkins 1999: 2: 'History is, or should be, a subtle combination of empathetic imagination and critical analysis' (with the phrases 'empathetic imagination' and 'empathetic wonder' repeated again in the following paragraphs of the same page).

to combine fantasy with analytic history. At the same time, H. offers accounts only of 'one religious and three large-scale political rituals' (495 [336]) – the Lupercalia, the military levy, the periodic census and the popular assemblies.[4] By no standards can this live up to the promise of a 'totality of Roman festivals and rituals' (484 [320]) or 'the total ritual experience' (485 [322]). Nor is it an analytic or objective account of a complex system. The repeated concessive confessions – 'inevitably I have left much out'; 'I have said nothing about other civic rituals'; 'I have said nothing further about the traditional rituals'; 'obviously, even in a longish paper, I could not discuss all these individually' (496 [336–7]) – point not only to his own awareness of his failure to achieve the methodological task he had set himself, but perhaps also to its virtual impossibility as an ideal ('totality') to which no historical analysis can ever attain. The fissure between the clear theoretical model in the proposed method and its lack of achievement in messy historical reality is perhaps a signal of the idealism of H.'s enterprise in positing (and thinking through) an adequately theorised conceptual model appropriate to a given historical end, but at the same time his lack of empirical zeal (and the woeful inadequacy of the basic empirical data in our sources) when it came to proving the argument. Perhaps, in the end, the sociological theorist in him was always stronger than the empirical historian.

The most fundamental critique of the essay, however, lies in its wilful avoidance of the specific challenges of writing history itself. H. opens in the late fifth century AD with the Christian ban on the Lupercalia. He then doubles back to the Roman Republic to place his analysis of the ritual system in pre-imperial Rome. At this point, where the historical challenge is crystal clear – namely to find a way of linking the sociology of republican ritual culture with the banning of the surviving

[4] How these specific themes have fared as topics of scholarly interest since H. wrote is itself revealing. The Lupercalia remains fashionable – for up-to-date discussion and bibliography see J. North 2008b; McLynn 2008; North and McLynn 2008. The more institutional subjects less so, but e.g. on assemblies, see Millar 1998; on the census, Nicolet 2000 or Unruh, 2001; for military recruitment, de Ligt 2007 or Wesch-Klein 2007.

rituals in the Christian era by means of exploring and defining the changes in the ritual system during the Principate – he simply throws in the towel: 'Augustus had degutted the central political rituals of the city of Rome. There was a ritual vacuum. Only bread and circuses remained' (497 [339]). This is crude (especially by the subtle standards of his methodological arguments for his 'double strategy'). He resorts to the rhetoric of brief Tacitean sentences so that assertion can replace argument; he makes the first emperor stand for the entire imperial system as well as its long and complex history reaching forwards beyond Constantine. H. simply gives up. As his final footnote shows, he was only too acutely aware that none of this could possibly do – in its telescoping of time, its lack of conviction, its reliance on metaphor. Did he get bored? Did he lose the appetite for doing any of the vast and painstaking work needed to assess the ritual system and ritual change across the years of the Principate? Did he see that empirical evidence would never supply a rich enough database to satisfy the needs of the brilliant and challenging theoretical frame of his double strategy?[5]

The question remains, some thirty years after the piece was first published, does it have any value today? For all the paper's weaknesses (and in my account I might be accused of displaying too little *pietas*) I think it does. First, as a coherent theoretical model of how one might do excellent anthropologically informed history of ancient religion, the essay's methodological sections remain sharp and extremely well expressed. Second, despite its failure fully to exemplify its claims, the

[5] H.'s thinking on the Principate, by the time this paper was written, was both post- and anti- the work of Paul Zanker. H. cites Zanker's famous book, Zanker 1988, twice (at 482 n. 14 [318 n. 14] and 495 n. 34 [336 n. 34], the former note with some characteristically penetrating and brutal criticisms). Arguably, the discussion of the transition from Republic to empire has now moved beyond Zanker's model: see Wallace-Hadrill 2008 with the discussion of Osborne and Vout 2010. Oddly, the stress on Augustus – probably the result of the impact of Zanker's account – in the essay's penultimate paragraph, which deals with the entirety of the Principate between the Republic and the Christian empire, is less useful to H.'s argument than his own earlier synchronic account of emperor worship across the empire, that was published as 'Divine emperors and the symbolic unity of the Roman empire' in Hopkins 1978b: 197–242.

paper's characterisation of the Roman ritual nexus (admittedly with too little diachronic texture) is really brilliant. Take this paragraph for example:

> The full panoply of rituals at Rome operated as a harmonic configuration, offering citizens antiphony between hierarchic order and encapsulated violence, and securing moral conformity by locating rituals especially in the penumbra of moral ambiguity. As I see it, the core of political mass participation rituals, celebrating hierarchy and order, was held in place by the nimbus of religious and civic spectator rituals, which celebrated violence and the upset of hierarchy and order, albeit in very restricted doses. So too, conventional sexual morality was upheld by worshipping through the medium of priests and priestesses who behaved abnormally. It is as though the margins of normality, what I have called the penumbra of moral ambiguity, provide the ideal staging for the celebration and codification of symbolic values. Spectator rituals concentrate in areas of social strain (497 [338]).

Now this may fail the test of empirical demonstration. But as a coherent propositional thesis about the fundamental deep structures of (at least, republican) Roman society born from the reflexes of one of its most intelligent and commanding students, it is a superb and incisive formulation that deserves at the very least the honour of attempted disproof. I don't think I know of a better synthetic statement in this area. Third, the acute awareness with which H. signals his discomfort with the paper's weaknesses is itself salutary both as a model of what scholarship may aspire to – and a warning of how much is achievable.

9

SLAVERY IN CLASSICAL ANTIQUITY*

Intellectual interest in the history of slavery has mirrored the modern belief in equality.[1] Research into slavery in the classical world has been all the more piquant because chattel slavery flourished in the city-state of Athens; and it is Athens which has been lauded as the prototype of democracy, as the nursery of political liberty and equality. This paradox has plagued the apologists, and it is only recently that historians have been able to escape from moralising. Of course, they were entitled to moralise and it is difficult not to be shocked by the cruelties of slavery. But the common prejudice in favour of liberty, denied to the slave, has misled historians and sociologists into treating slavery as though it were an isolated method of exploitation.

Slavery as a sociological subject can best be considered in relation to other forms of dependent labour rather than in terms of our own ideologies. Slavery is not only a species of the genus, dependent labour, but wherever it has been found, it has always co-existed with other forms of dependent labour, such as apprenticeship, indenture, concubinage, bondage, debt-bondage, share-cropping, money and/or labour tenancy and wage-labour. Therefore we can fairly ask: why and in what circumstances does slavery flourish rather than, or in addition to, these other forms of dependent labour?

But we must also set slavery in the general context of the 'exploitation' of independent labour. At most periods and in most areas of the classical world, it is probable that

* First published in A. V. S. de Reuck and J. Knight (eds) *Caste and Race: Comparative Approaches*, London: J. & A. Churchill, 1967, 166–77 (= Hopkins 1967).

[1] I have concentrated on Athens in the classical period and on Rome; Sparta is excluded. I should like to thank Dr M. I. Finley for advice and for the sight of his article on slavery to be published in the revised *International Encyclopedia of the Social Sciences* (= Finley 1968); I owe much to it.

self-employed or 'free' workers predominated, especially in agriculture. And it is again probable that about 90 per cent of the labour force was employed in agriculture. Athens was an exception, since it served as the entrepôt for a much larger productive area; the proportion of her population directly engaged in agriculture may have been only 75 per cent in the fifth and fourth centuries BC.[2] As in most pre-industrial societies, the peasantry was very largely self-sufficient. But while they did not consume much which was not produced by themselves, they did produce crops which they did not themselves consume. What is significant for slavery is the size of this 'surplus' and the ways in which it was extracted from the peasants (for example, by market-exchange, clients' gifts to patrons, rent and taxation). Increases in the efficiency and extent of exploitation through tenancy, taxation and bureaucratic corruption laid open new avenues to private wealth, alternative to and to some extent superseding direct exploitation through slavery. Slavery ceased to be a major method of procuring wealth, while it long survived as a method of displaying it.

In spite of the obvious differences between such polar groups as gang-slaves and autarkic citizen-peasantry, there was in the ancient world no clear cut-off point between dependent and independent or between free and slave. There was instead a continuum of status and duties.[3] But on the other hand the distinction independent/dependent does point to very real social differences in self-estimation and in organisation. For example, we have evidence from Athens in the fourth century BC that the independence of self-employment was thought to be worth considerable material sacrifice. We can assume, moreover, that however powerful or wealthy some slaves or ex-slaves became, they were always conscious of their low legal status or origin and of their degradation (*uilitas*). Finally, the distinction implies quite different forms of organisation and cooperation. Dependent labour can be organised into pursuing goals collectively, as set by its rulers, whether owners, masters or

[2] Hasebroek 1933: 96.
[3] Finley 1964.

feudal lords; just as industrialisation rested on the flexible use of wage-labour, hierarchically organised. Societies with large sectors of independent, self-employed peasants have little of this fluidity; and it is only occasionally (for example, in corvées) or for specialised jobs (such as the militia) that the peasantry can be effectively organised to act in concert or to move away from their locality and the well established patterns of agricultural life.

It is in the context of this stability and self-sufficiency, typical of peasant societies, and in the face of the ideology favouring self-employment, that slavery appears as the most efficient pre-industrial method of mobilising labour. In Athens in the fifth century BC there were possibly 60,000–80,000 foreign slaves out of an estimated total population of 250,000; and it has been estimated that the Romans made over 250,000 slaves in the period 200–150 BC alone. Thus huge numbers of men, women and children were transported from conquered lands or distant tribes to Athens and Rome. There they chiefly helped feed the mushrooming cities; but they also serviced the new industries and they symbolised the newly acquired wealth of their captors and purchasers. Such developments would have been possible without slavery, had there been a technical revolution in agricultural production and in the manufacture of power, or if there had been a rapid natural increase in population. But none of these occurred and slavery was used to fill the gap.

For slavery had existed from the earliest times, but apparently on a small scale. In these times male captives were typically ransomed or killed, while women and children were enslaved either because they were more easily supervised or because women's work could be easily and prestigiously extended. Commentators agree that slaves seem then to have been integral members of the household; symptomatically, the masters' children by slave-women were not necessarily slaves, unlike later times. But after debt-bondage of fellow citizens was prohibited at Athens in 594 BC and at Rome in 326 BC, chattel slavery increased greatly; at about the same time coined money became much more common, and both states became involved through trade or conquest with a wider range of foreign states.

Thus, both in Athens and in Rome, it became possible and preferable to purchase aliens as slaves and to exploit them directly rather than, or in addition to, free native citizens. It was possible because the economies of both city-states had become more broadly based. Lands had been conquered and allies made to pay tribute; foreign trade and native industry had expanded and, in the case of Athens, silver mines had been opened. These mines alone employed up to 20,000 men at one time. More labour was required in these international centres of trade and empire than could be met from local sources. A large number of free aliens were attracted, but they valued their independence. Besides, slavery, the institution of trading in humans from other societies, was already well established; there was a system of custom and law sufficiently strong to differentiate citizens from aliens, and slaves from free men, strong enough to provide a barrier against their easy assimilation to each other.

Thus slavery was a product of trade and empire. Rome, for example, after 250 BC became involved in an ever-widening circle of alliance and war. For the first time her peasant soldiers had to fight long campaigns in lands overseas. In the meantime they inevitably neglected their own small-holdings, while those who profited from wars were keen to buy them out; for land was an honourable and profitable investment. Wars provided capital not only for the purchase of land, but also for the purchase of a labour force. And slaves had several advantages over free labour: they were not liable to military service; they could be used in gangs and were often, in contrast to the southern states of America, skilled agricultural workers. Thus large landowners could profitably grow new crops, such as vines and olives, on the former wheat lands of Italy, and with them supply the expanding towns of Rome and south Italy on a capitalistic basis. Yeo has pointed out that these crops, like sugar and rice in the United States, required more labour-intensive attention than wheat; unlike wheat they could be cultivated by gangs of workers who were therefore more easily supervised;

and he suggested that with adequate capital investment these crops gave a higher return on larger units.[4] Thus slavery was a mechanism for transporting and concentrating labour, which was not otherwise available; in all probability cultivation by slaves was profitable, though it is impossible to say whether it was more profitable than free labour would have been. What can be said is that slavery made possible an organisation of labour by which advantage could be taken of the availability of capital, and of new crops and markets.

Weber suggested that slaves were to the Roman economy what coal was to the furnaces of the industrial revolution.[5] In mines and on plantations, certainly, male slaves were kept apart, without families, ruthlessly expended and then replaced. Slaves predominated wherever working conditions were terrible, wherever labour was organised so as to allow the individual little initiative or control over his work or wherever services were required patently at the beck and call of a master (as in domestic service). The subservience of slaves threw the independence of citizens into relief. For the concentration of enslaved aliens in these occupations made the increased range of wealth compatible with the ideology of citizenship and with the equality which that citizenship implied. As Finley has said, slavery and freedom went hand in hand.[6]

Freedom implied not only political and legal rights, but also military duties. Both Athens and Rome were repeatedly involved in wars, and a high proportion of their citizens participated in the fighting. This involved some identification with the defence of the society and its declared interests. This identification was expressed by the ideology of citizenship, the pride of being an Athenian or Roman. The civil wars between plebs and patricians, and the strife (*stasis*) between rich and poor, the few and the many, endemic in most Greek city-states, illustrate the difficulty of maintaining this unity. But for considerable periods the unity was maintained, and in this time

4 Yeo 1951–2.

5 Weber 1896: 66 (= 1924: 298).

6 Finley 1959: 163.

slavery helped the poor citizens to be free while the ideology of citizenship and freedom put some limit to the extent and degree to which citizens could be exploited.

Eventually the Greek and Roman city-states merged into empires (Hellenistic and Roman). Their greater size could support a specialised superstructure of autocratic government, professional army and bureaucracy. In these empires no collective action was required of the peasants. Indeed it was prohibited. They merely had to produce food, pay taxes and remain quiet. There was little ideology of belonging.

In the Roman empire, citizenship, once a prize to be fought for, was given to practically every inhabitant (AD 212). But this did not imply any equality except an equal taxability. The basic social division was no longer conquering Roman citizens, allies and subjects, but *honestiores*, the honourable, and *humiliores*, the humble folk. As this implies, exploitation had hardened into new channels, both indirect, through bribery, taxation and governmental office, and direct, through share-cropping, and money and labour tenancies. For as there was no need, or rather, no possibility of activating the huge population to its own defence, there were fewer structural checks on the extent or degree of exploitation. The peasants' only defence was either rebellion, for which they were too scattered to be effective, religious retreatism, local patronage or flight. In the later empire, under pressure of much higher governmental exactions and general defencelessness against barbarian attacks, many peasants surrendered the last vestiges of independence left to them in return for a local lord's protection. Thus in many respects the distinction between the old slave and the new serf was insignificant.

At the same time the forces which had precipitated the growth of slavery were no longer effective. Wars were less frequent and more often defensive. There was no particular disadvantage in employing indigenous peasants. The towns of south Italy had declined under the twin impact of high transport costs and rudimentary techniques of manufacture, which gave little benefit to quantity production. The oil and wine-producing plantations of the same region had disintegrated in the face of competition from Spain, Gaul and North Africa; they reverted to growing wheat, which was less suited to cultivation by slaves.

Slaves too cost more, whether because they had to be purchased and brought from distant lands outside the empire, or because they were bred. The problems of supervision and enforcement must have made slavery appear more troublesome and no more profitable than money or labour tenancies. Certainly, by the second century AD, mines and former plantations were usually worked by small contractors or tenants. In the overview and in the time-scale of the ancient world, gang-slavery appears a transitory epiphenomenon of empire. It flourished in the heartlands of the Roman empire, but not at the periphery. It required a heavy initial outlay of capital, at risk in the lives and productivity of the slaves. It is possible that gang-slavery was based on, even subsidised by the tremendous influx of treasure, which flooded in as the first profits of empire. As taxation replaced plunder, income was steadier but slower.

How far then can we call classical Athens and Rome *slave societies*? It is meaningless to think of slavery as somehow a basic, or as the basic, moulding institution of classical civilisation. Such claims cannot be validated, and, as we have seen, slavery was itself the product of other forces; it was compatible with, but hardly shaped, aristocratic, democratic and autocratic government. In Athens, slavery was the dominant form of *dependent* labour, but in Rome, where the absolute number of slaves was far greater, it was relatively less important vis-à-vis other forms of dependence; for clientage and tenancy flourished alongside. The major importance of slavery lay in its mobility and in its support of the superior living standards of the well-to-do. But in no sense did either society rest upon the productivity of slaves any more than upon the productivity of other workers. Indeed rather less: first, because the free peasantry was largely self-sufficient and always outnumbered the slaves; and secondly, because such a large proportion of slaves were, in fact, not producers at all, but ostentatious consumers, tokens of their masters' wealth.

Moreover, the concept of slave society is often based on the assumption that slaves were demarcated from free men in all their social roles. This may have been true of gang-slavery. There men were chained, had no family life and no private possessions, and were either worked to death or discarded in old age. It is impossible to deny the significance of this unrestrained exploitation, which seems always to be a feature, perhaps even a distinguishing characteristic of slavery. Yet although gangs were part and parcel of slavery they do not form the whole picture.

Nor is the legal status of slaves a proper basis for discussion. According to Roman law, slaves were in the power and possession (*dominium*) of their masters; they were not humans, but things (*res*, *instrumentum uocale*), without a legal personality of their own. By this definition, slaves may be unambiguously assigned to the lowest social stratum. But we should not mistake such legalistic abstractions for empirical generalisations. Certainly such laws give valuable and often colourful evidence of institutionalised opinion on the degradation of slavery. To some extent the law reflects the low opinion of slaves held by masters, by free men who were not masters, and probably by slaves themselves. Yet the actual life situations of slaves reveal a much greater diversity than their legal status presupposed.

It is this diversity and range of occupations in public service, industry and domestic service, and the absence of any important differences of colour, which distinguish slavery in the classical world from slavery in the British West Indies and the southern states of America. Slaves comprised the Athenian police force and the lower and middle levels of the Roman imperial bureaucratic administration. Among them were numbered craftsmen, whose artistry still survives for us to admire. Slaves acted as overseers, naval captains in the Roman imperial navy, secretaries, scribes, managing agents, bankers and doctors. They worked alongside free men, and earned the same pay. There is no evidence of undercutting, and no anxiety was expressed on that score. Slaves belonged to the same burial clubs and religious societies as free men. Although marriage between slaves was not recognised in law, in fact, as we learn from tombstones, they regarded themselves as married and commemorated their dead. Some slaves lived and worked on their own, and paid their masters only a proportion of their earnings. Still others ran their own business, became wealthy and even bought their own slaves.

One obvious difficulty is that we have next to no idea of numbers. We do not know the numbers of slaves in any particular occupation, nor their chances of prosperity within the framework of slavery. But it is not surprising, given the disadvantages and undertones of servile status, that many slaves used what money they had to purchase their freedom. Others who had not saved enough, borrowed the money from clubs of ex-slaves and repaid it by instalments. Others borrowed the money from a patron, on condition of rendering him services, perhaps until his death or for a certain number of years. The penalty clauses for breaking the agreement were often severe, but often specifically precluded sale back into slavery. Thus slavery was exchanged for indenture. Again we have no figures; but we can at least say that manumission was an accepted feature of classical society, either by purchase or by gift, especially on the owner's death. Here one can get some idea of frequency from a Roman law of 2 BC which prohibited the manumission by testament of more than one-fifth of one's slaves, up to a maximum of one hundred. The ex-slave became a literary stereotype of the *nouveau riche,* and ex-slaves were recognised as a significant social group such that special and quite important municipal priesthoods were reserved for them, as was service in the Roman fire brigade.

The rate of manumission was probably a function of the wide range of slave occupations. But it remains problematical why slaves were given such a wide range of occupations and the opportunity to save and to purchase their freedom, and then accorded a place in society – in Athens as resident aliens, in Rome as citizens. Of course some owners thought that slaves worked harder when given the chance of saving for manumission. Others realised that they stole more. Both are probably true, but owners in other slave systems have not opted for the carrot so much as for the stick. In testamentary manumission there was obviously an element of ostentatious expenditure.

The range of slaves' occupations was wider and manumissions more frequent in Rome. One factor was that Romans recognised the superior culture and skills of some of the nations they conquered. They enslaved doctors and teachers, but it would have been difficult to keep their status at the level of gang slaves. Another factor must have been the weakness of the ideology justifying slavery – not that slavery was ever seriously attacked, certainly not by Christians. But it was recognised as an established institution contrary to nature (*ius gentium contra naturam*). Its incidence was regarded as the work of chance or fate, and masters were warned by philosophers to treat their slaves well, lest they should become slaves themselves one day, by chance. Other Greek philosophers argued for the natural inferiority of barbarians; the implication of this was that the Greeks were superior and should not be enslaved. Unfortunately for the Greek *amour-propre* this opinion was continually neglected, and the power of the Persians and their Great King, as the Greeks called him, was an apparent contradiction. The Romans accepted slavery as an established custom, the product of war, but without moral foundation. And on this basis, they were prepared to accept ex-slaves as Roman citizens, assimilated to the existing status of clients.

I have concentrated on two aspects of slavery – slavery as a method of organising labour and slavery in the context of political organisation. Slavery was only one of the many methods used in the ancient world for extracting surplus production to feed the urban population and to support the distinctive lifestyle of the rich. Our problem has been to assess what determined the choice of buying men's bodies rather than occasionally hiring their labour as it was required, or rather than charging them a rent of money or produce within the framework of property.

I have argued that slavery was an efficient reaction to sudden expansion through trade and conquest. Since the ancient economy was dominated by a self-sufficient peasantry, there was a restricted market in labour and in produce. Wage labour therefore existed only on a small scale and was despised. Slavery had additional advantages in that the powerful could amass wealth through slaves without oppressing those very citizens who composed the conquering armies.

In this respect, then, the growth of slavery was politically determined, and even nurtured, by the egalitarian forces of the city-state. Inversely, the decline of slavery was partially a consequence of the decline in equality. With the creation of a professional army at Rome, the interests of citizens had no longer to be much consulted. The only limits, therefore, to the exploitation of the peasantry by the powerful were the declining tradition of citizen's rights and the emperors' insistence that their subjects should be shorn but not fleeced. In the second century AD, although slavery survived, the profitability of slaves over free peasants must have been marginal. By the fourth and fifth centuries, slavery had diminished in importance not only because their numbers had probably declined, but chiefly because the incipient serfdom of many peasants had closed the gap between free and slave.

AFTERWORD

SLAVERY IN CLASSICAL ANTIQUITY

KEITH BRADLEY

This essay on Greek and Roman slavery was composed as a contribution to an international symposium held in London in April 1966 on 'the general nature of caste segregation and racist ideologies'.[1] The participants were social scientists and social historians, and discussion was by definition comparative. The project was attributable in part, I imagine, to the radical and often violent effects of decolonisation on certain European countries in the 1960s, Britain included, and of the Civil Rights Movement in the United States. Its goal, clearly liberal, was to analyse social forms and practices implicitly understood to be discriminatory with a view to fostering progressive social change.[2] Half a century later, the time-bound character of the proceedings is symbolised by the contributors' use of the term 'American Negro' to refer to African-Americans, which was obviously not intended to cause offence but is striking nonetheless. It is a reminder that in the Western cultural tradition the history of slavery, a necessary component of the symposium, raises images in the first instance of enslaved Africans in the New World, and is almost naturally equated with blackness – Shelley's 'dark slavery' – and the inferiority that blackness has historically presumed.[3] That social and political legacy is still felt.[4]

Keith Hopkins' paper, lucid and, unlike much writing on ancient slavery before and since, refreshingly free of polemic, was meant to provide a statement on the slave-owning character of the ancient Mediterranean world for comparison

[1] de Reuck and Knight 1967: p. vii.
[2] Myrdal 1967: 332 (the concluding remarks to the final discussion of the symposium).
[3] See helpfully Jordan 1968 on white perceptions of black inferiority.
[4] See e.g. Gutman 1976: especially pp. xvii–xviii, 461–75.

with statements on human oppression and prejudice in later ages and other regions. In antiquity, however, as H. emphasised, race and slavery were never intimately connected,[5] and this perhaps explains why he chose as his principal concern to write on the rise and fall of slavery in the two regions where ancient slavery had special significance: classical Athens and Roman Italy. He duly categorised mass slavery as a rare form of dependent labour in economies dominated by the labour of peasants, and he tied mass slavery's exceptionalism to the exceptionalism of Athenian and Roman imperialism: the rise and fall of one was integrally associated with the rise and fall of the other. As he acknowledged, his views owed much to M. I. Finley, but they were views grounded also on a deceptively profound knowledge of ancient sources.[6] His method, typical of the way H. addressed all major historical questions, was to construct a sociologically driven macro-economic model that took proper account of the crucial factor of change over time. The paper has remained relatively unknown.

Given the capacity of slave-owners to coerce labour from those they owned, together with the predominant servile function in modern systems of producing cash crops for sale on world markets, the economic thrust of the paper was both reasonable and predictable. Whether H. was right, however, to say that it is 'meaningless' to 'think of slavery as somehow a basic, or as the basic, moulding institution of classical civilisation' (172 [352]) might depend on how individual historians think of 'basic' and 'moulding'. To the extent, for instance, that Greek and Latin literature embodies general presuppositions about socio-cultural norms,[7] a distinction between slavery and freedom is perceptible from Homer to Augustine and cannot be

[5] Though see Isaac 2004: 170–215 on slavery and 'proto-racism'.

[6] The debt is acknowledged in the first note, where H. refers to access before its publication to Finley's classic article on slavery in the *International Encyclopedia of Social Sciences* (Finley 1968), in which slavery is understood to be above all a species of dependent labour. Other notes cite two celebrated papers, 'Was Greek civilisation based on slave labour?' (Finley 1959), and 'Between slavery and freedom' (Finley 1964).

[7] See e.g. the recent treatments of Hunt 2011 and Joshel 2011 on Greek and Roman literary culture, respectively.

altogether devoid of meaning unless it is assumed that literature and life have no relationship to one another. Artemidorus' procedure in his *Oneirocritica* of interpreting dreams according (in part) to the status of the dreamer, whether free or slave, easily illustrates the point.[8] In order, accordingly, to achieve a historically specific portrait of classical slavery, what is important is to blend the economic with the cultural, a direction in which H.'s later study of slavery in his paper on Aesop was in fact to move [essay 11]. Filling out the portrait remains a priority, especially if classical slavery is to be of interest to, and to be understood by, modern comparativists: for although slavery has existed in many times and places its individual historical forms have shown considerable variation, and comparison is perilous if differences are neglected. At the same time, precision is needed in order to offset the not uncommon tendency, evident for example in the discussion of H.'s paper in the symposium volume, to view 'the Greco-Roman world' as a finite world that never changed.[9] Factors of time and place are important.[10]

The history of classical slavery is bedevilled by the problem of numbers, which H. here did no more than acknowledge. In *Conquerors and Slaves*, however, he suggested that the proportion of slaves in the population of Italy in the period of Roman imperial expansion may have been as high as 35 to 40 per cent.[11] This was significant for the way he thought of a genuine slave society and the number of genuine slave societies there have been in world history. Numbers chiefly determined the category, and his conclusion was that there have been

[8] See the cases from Artemidorus (e.g. 1.45, 2.15, 4.24, 4.69, 5.85) collected and discussed by Annequin 1987, 1989; cf. E. Hall 2011.

[9] de Reuck and Knight 178–91 (H.'s paper was discussed as part of a broader discussion 'Classical and American slavery compared: discussion on the status of slaves in the ancient and modern world'); see also J. C. Miller 2008: 73–81, and contrast D. B. Davis 1966: 62–90.

[10] Observe the sobering remark: 'the entire history of slavery in the United States lasted no more than the period from Augustus to Septimius Severus' (Finley 1980: 80).

[11] Hopkins 1978b: 9, 102; cf. especially 99 n. 1, which sets 20 per cent as an 'arbitrary cut-off point' to qualify as a slave society as opposed to a slave-owning society.

no more than five such societies, two of which were classical Athens and Roman Italy.[12] His thinking is already implicit in this paper. It is self-evident of course that without numerical estimates of some sort the past can scarcely be understood.[13]

Reaction has been severe. Africanists have pointed to Islamic systems in sub-Saharan Africa that were less generally familiar when H. wrote than those of antiquity and the New World;[14] and whether numbers alone should determine definition has been contested.[15] Some in any case now consider H.'s numerical proportions too high, proposing that in Roman Italy slaves were more concentrated in urban centres than the rural regions in which H. (and many others) thought that slave labour was predominantly utilised.[16] Comparable issues arise with Athens.[17]

The Roman case is especially complex: a history extending over a thousand years, through the course of which the extent of territory Rome came to control was enormous, and the number of local cultures subsumed almost limitless. At any moment for which evidence is available, however, Roman social relations appear to have arranged themselves in asymmetrical patterns of authority and deference in which power was exercised by a superior few over an inferior many. The most extreme of these patterns, denying the inferior all legal and moral rights, was that which bound together masters and slaves. Above all, therefore, slavery may be regarded as a manifestation of an immanent propensity in Roman culture.[18]

[12] Hopkins 1978b: 99–100.

[13] See the comments of Brunt 1971a: 3.

[14] Lovejoy 2000: 1–23 with summary at 276–89; see in particular 9–11 and 281–3 where Lovejoy discusses and qualifies ideas drawn from Finley.

[15] For suggestions of broader criteria, see usefully O. Patterson 1982: especially 1–14 for a summary; and 2008: 33 with n. 5 for criticism of H. For the impressionistic quality of numerical estimates see Bradley 2015: 154–5.

[16] Jongman 2003c: 106 (for direct engagement with H.), 116–19 (on slaves and urbanism); Scheidel 2005: especially 64–71, 2011b: 288–9. See also Lo Cascio 2010 who criticises H. (at 24) and puts forward a model of low population and higher reproductivity (at 27–30); Harper 2011: 33–99.

[17] Scheidel 2008 is an explicit attempt to compare the two societies. High estimates are retained for both Athens and Roman Italy by Andreau and Descat 2006: 65–105.

[18] See Bradley 2010 for a survey.

Slavery was an inherently cruel institution, which H. made clear at a time when some were crediting it with a putatively redemptive quality. Cruelty might be thought a historically indeterminate construct, but the wealth of evidence illustrating the severity with which slave-owners treated their slaves in antiquity leaves little doubt.[19] Circumstances varied over time, and allowance can be made for a possible tendency in some places (for example) not to separate families when sales of slaves took place.[20] It is the structural constant, however, that remains important: sale itself was never questioned (any more than slavery itself), and behind every transaction that took place lies a story of human misery, as suggested above all by the deeds of sale that have survived, especially from Greco-Roman Egypt.[21]

The historian's task is to revivify the stories – what H. called 'the actual life situations of slaves' (173 [353]) – one way forward in which might be to ask questions of visual and material evidence,[22] even as abstract discussion continues.[23] What for instance motivated an Athenian artist in the early fifth century BC to portray a slave-owner on a black-figure wine jug apparently threatening to beat a slave with a sandal, and what ideological assumptions might be inferred from the scene? Or why, a little later, was it appropriate to include in an Attic monumental funerary complex sculpted figures of slave women in postures of mourning?[24] Was the sense of what seems to be grief at the loss of their owner their true response? Or is something else discoverable? Much remains to be done to animate classical slavery fully.[25]

Given the importance he attached to 'empathetic imagination'[26] in recovering the past, I suspect that H. would welcome

[19] Seneca's writings are a prime example, see Bradley 1986; and now also Stewart 2012: 80–116, on violence in the comedies of Plautus.

[20] C. P. Jones 2008 analyses one such case.

[21] Straus 2004. For comparable evidence from Italy see Andreau 1974: 104; D. F. Jones 2006: 79, 91, 86–7, 130–1, 137–8.

[22] George 2010; cf. Bradley 2008: 489–96.

[23] For useful surveys of recent approaches, see McKeown 2007; Alston 2011; and from a comparative perspective, Dal Lago and Katsari 2008b.

[24] Both items are in the collections of the Staatliche Museen zu Berlin: Antikensammlung inv. V.1.3230, Pergamonmuseum, inv. sk 498, 499.

[25] For pioneering studies on the Roman side, see now George 2013; Joshel and Petersen 2014.

[26] Hopkins 1993: 26 [essay 11: 423].

the refinements to which new ways of understanding Greek and Roman slavery will lead. The formative value of his own accomplishments would not be diminished, and the particular notion that slavery was an epiphenomenon of empire would still retain value, even as concepts of rise and fall now have to compete with those of transition, continuity and rupture.[27] Further, his realistic recognition, both here and in the subsequent contributions to which his paper led, of slavery's human inhumanity remains indisputable, and he expressed his views with a comparative capacity that few have been able to match. The result was a richness of writing rare in ancient history.

27 For new approaches to the later empire, see Grey 2011; Harper 2011. On the connection between slavery and Rome's ideology of empire, see Lavan 2013: especially 73–155.

10

CONQUEST BY BOOK*

Introduction: Detail, Density and Growth

I start with three scraps of papyrus. One, the size of a credit card, records the payment of customs dues at 3 per cent of the value of six measures of lentils carried by two donkeys out of the gate of a minor Egyptian village along a road into the desert in AD 190. The second is a similar customs receipt from the same village dated to 'the twentieth year of the reign of Aurelius Antoninus and Commodus' (AD 179). This papyrus still has a brownish-grey clay seal attached, stamped with the portraits of the emperor and his son Commodus, and with the words 'imperial' and 'gate' still just legible. The third scrap, not much larger (16 × 10 cm), records that a peasant has duly performed his annual labour by working five days to maintain the field irrigation system. It is certified by four different villagers, each writing in his own hand.[1]

Several hundred similarly trivial receipts and certificates have survived from Roman Egypt, a small fraction of the hundreds of thousands once written.[2] What sense, I wonder,

* First published in *Literacy in the Roman World, Journal of Roman Archaeology* supplementary series 3, Ann Arbor, 1991, 133–58 (= Hopkins 1991a). Particular thanks are due to Dr John Humphrey, General Editor of the *Journal of Roman Archaeology,* for generously granting permission to reprint 'Conquest by book', from *Literacy in the Roman World*, a volume which remains in print.

1 These two customs receipts are both now in Oxford: *P.Grenf.* II 50h (= Bodleian MS Gr. class. e. 62 (P)) and 50e (= Bodleian MS Gr. class. g. 25 (P)). The labour tax certificate is *SB* VI 9567, on which in general see Sijpesteijn 1964: 1–21: only about one-third of surviving complete labour certificates were signed, and usually by only one person. On clay seals attached to papyrus receipts, see Boak 1935: 23–33.

2 The survival ratio, the ratio of texts surviving to those ever produced, is clearly a critical dimension of our historical understanding. It is risky to ignore it. Harris 1989: 218 deduced that prophecies were not written in great numbers, to judge from the three surviving copies of the *Oracle of the Potter* (*P.Oxy.* XXII 2332). But the survival ratio could be lower than 1:10,000. Consider the following: the Romans conducted seventeen censuses of the Egyptian population by households at fourteen-year intervals between AD 19 and 257. If the average household size

did Egyptian donkey-drivers and taxpayers make of their tiny handwritten notes? Why did the Roman government insist on having these trivial and transient actions formally recorded? What sense can we make of them? And where do they fit into the picture of classical literacy, or illiteracy, which William Harris has so vividly portrayed? Was Harris right or wrong in arguing that, even in bureaucratic Egypt, ordinary farmers and artisans probably made little use of writing? And if he was wrong, does it matter?

Harris has written an interesting, important and path-breaking book on a large and important subject. He deals with literacy in the whole of the ancient classical world, covering a large area and well over one thousand years of history, from archaic Greece to the late Roman empire. His main hypothesis is clear, and completely convincing: in all periods of classical antiquity, only a minority of adult males (and a tiny minority of adult females) could read and write. These rates include both sophisticated élite litterateurs and barely functional, semi-illiterate artisans. Given the fragmentary state of the surviving evidence, Harris' statistical estimates can be only very rough orders of magnitude; but even so, they are useful as sighting shots. They centre on less than 10 per cent adult male literates, both in the heyday of democracy in Athens in the fifth century BC (Harris 1989: 61) and in Rome in the second century BC (173), and much less in the western provinces of the Roman empire in the first centuries AD (272); Harris estimates adult male literacy in the city of Rome and in Italy during the same period at well below 20–30 per cent (259). If Harris' figures are anywhere near right, then his minimalist case defeats – even routs – the idealists who apparently believed in mass adult literacy, whether in democratic Athens or in pre-Christian Rome.

was five persons, and the population is deliberately estimated low at 3.5 million, and we have less than one thousand surviving census returns, the survival ratio is c. 1:12,000. Of course, this is only a rough estimate, a cautionary tale – adjustments would have to be made for documents of different value; but three surviving copies of the *Oracle of the Potter* could mean anywhere between three and 35,000+ originals.

About proportions, in my view, Harris is right. But each victory has its costs.[3] And in securing his victory, Harris underplays the impact of absolute number and density. For example, if adult male literacy was about 10 per cent across the Roman empire, then there were roughly 2 million adult males who *could* read and write to some extent in the empire as a whole. In world history, this was an unprecedented number of literates for a single state. The sheer mass of people who could read and write, living in Roman towns (and, as I shall show, in some villages), made a political, economic, social and cultural difference in the experience of living in Roman society. Over time, these literates increased the stored reserves of recorded knowledge and thereby allowed both state and religion unprecedented control over the lives of the illiterate.

Let me reinforce my argument by expanding Harris' long time frame even further, in order to reinterpret his findings. In Pharaonic Egypt, in the third millennium BC, according to one estimate, only ½–1 per cent of the population could write, in hieroglyphs or hieratic; according to the same estimate, the proportion was similar even at the beginning of the last millennium BC. By the first two centuries AD, if the adult male literacy level in Roman Egypt was, say, 10–20 per cent, then the proportion of literates had risen twenty times. And since the ability to read or write was predominantly in Greek rather than, or as well as, in native Egyptian (the ratio of surviving published papyri is 15 to 1 in favour of Greek over demotic), most of that important increase had occurred since the third century BC.[4]

3 Harris' arguments are diverse and sophisticated. In several single sentences, he touches on or covers many of the arguments which I put forward in this essay. But the general impression which I gained from his book was that his minimalist drive led him sometimes to be over-strictly positivist. No surviving evidence for literacy, schools, popular reading, etc., becomes proxy for their non-existence. But then, as here, a single exculpatory footnote (e.g. 245 n. 376) reminds the reader that the author may not be doing full justice in his text.

4 Baines 1983: especially 584. The basis of the calculations seems shaky. See also Baines and Eyre 1983. The ratio of published documents in Greek and demotic can be only a rough guide to the proportions ever existing, since different modern factors affect publication rates.

Literacy as Product and Producer of Changes in the Roman State

The striking growth of literacy in the classical period throughout the Mediterranean basin was not self-generating. It did not have a single identifiable cause. Instead, it was part and parcel of a series of interlinked developments, which reinforced each other. Literacy was not just an inert technical skill, whose level and dispersion can be analysed or measured. Its growth was a product of changes in the political, economic and social culture of the Roman empire. The growth of literacy was a response to a growth of demand for literacy. And its increased use itself then generated further increases in the supply and demand for writing. The mass of writing in existence and the density of its use were, I think, categorically different from what they had ever been before in the Mediterranean basin.[5]

Let us begin our analysis of these interlinked changes with the growth of states and the corresponding growth of state power. The Roman empire was merely one in a long series of even larger conquest states. Its power was based on an expanded economy and on sophisticated instruments of coercion. By 'expanded economy', I mean here both that the economy of the Roman empire was very large and that under Roman rule relatively backward provinces gradually incorporated superior agricultural practices from more advanced regions. Britain, for example, in Roman times imported the practice of growing peas and cabbage, which improved the British diet, even if it ruined British cooking.[6] The productivity of labour grew, as did total population and aggregate product. The surplus grew. There was a greater division of labour, and more and bigger towns. The growth in literacy was both a consumption

[5] My arguments are deductive, hypothetical and impressionistic. For example, I suspect that the growth in literacy induced by Roman rule was greater in the western provinces than in the East, which had previously been governed by centralising monarchies.

[6] Applebaum 1972: 108–21. On improvements in Roman chickens and Danubian horses under Roman rule, *inter* much *alia,* see Sallares 1991: 398.

good – a way of integrating more people within a larger society – and a necessity. A larger scale economy needed (or operated better with) more writing.

A larger economy needed money. One symptom of these changes was coinage. Coinage was a Greek invention of the seventh century BC, used in significant quantities by Romans and Egyptians, perhaps only from the third century BC. And yet at the end of the first century AD, the Roman government was irregularly minting some 20–30 million denarii per year; and in Egypt, it looks as though one emperor refinanced the Egyptian coinage system in a five-year period with a massive injection of 600 million new but debased silver coins. The implications of this huge volume of coinage for the network of taxes and trade, however difficult to interpret, leave us in no doubt that the economy of the Roman empire in the first century AD was on a very different scale from the Mediterranean economy of the eighth or fourth century BC.[7]

The Roman government supplemented taxation with coercion and persuasion. The instruments of coercion, which helped maintain the Roman government and élite in power were, for example, written laws, courts of justice, bureaucratic administration and the army. Once again, the Roman system of laws was not much more sophisticated than its predecessors in the Mediterranean basin (at least until the official codification of Roman laws in the sixth century AD). Nor was the practice of Roman law courts, at least in the conquered provinces, particularly admirable. But the system of justice, the adherence to written law, to the precedents of previous decisions, and the reliance on written petitions all symptomised the spread of the Roman legal system over the whole of the Mediterranean

[7] On the irregularities of Roman minting, see Carradice 1983: 88–9 table K. On the reform of the Egyptian billon coinage, see Christiansen 1988: I 96–106. Christiansen's figures are not exact, but they provide rough orders of magnitude. I once produced a model hypothesising a strong relationship between the volume of taxes in so far as they were levied in money and the volume of interregional trade: Hopkins 1980a [essay 6]. I still think it broadly right. But see the recent criticisms of Duncan-Jones 1990: 30–58, 187–98. He scores a few good points, but, given a little flexibility on both sides, the evidence which he adduces could easily be accommodated in the Hopkins model.

basin.[8] One reason for the growth of literacy was the confrontation of Roman subjects with Roman power. Subjects wrote petitions, and did so in amazing numbers.[9] They learnt the language of the conquerors in order to borrow the conqueror's power and to help protect themselves from exploitation. I am not claiming here that the number of literates exceeded Harris' estimates, but I am trying to explain why the Roman conquest state helped produce more literates than ever before.

The Roman army in the first two centuries AD, with about 300,000 soldiers, was the largest formal organisation in the Roman empire. Harris (254), with unusual idealism, noted the high rate of literacy among legionaries implied by the surviving evidence; and he suggested that this may have been due to soldiers' recruitment from the propertied and educated classes. Soldiers serving in legions were paid an annual salary (before deductions for food, uniform, etc.) roughly equal to twice the subsistence of a peasant family.[10] Education was probably one factor which helped promotion, because the army by its procedures of written rosters, written orders and book-keeping fostered the use of writing. It was not simply that some or many Roman soldiers could write; they were repeatedly asked, ordered or required to write; the Roman army's organisation

[8] On the development of Roman law, Frier 1985, a book much broader in scope than the title implies. Too little has been written on the practice of Roman law in the provinces, but for complicated legal cases, see *P.Oxy.* II 237 and *P.Fam.Tebt.* 24, with associated texts and commentary. See also Katzoff 1972.

[9] The 1,804 petitions received by a governor on tour in 2½ days (*P.Yale* 161) are not as exceptional as Harris implies: see e.g. *P.Oxy.* XVII 2131, which is about petition number 1,009 received by the same governor on tour in a different town. Perhaps he was an exceptional governor? But then, a Chinese description of the Roman empire singles out Roman governors' willingness to receive petitions and to read them as a noteworthy distinguishing feature of Roman government, see Hirth 1885: 71. The governor of Egypt read and answered all 1,804 petitions and publicly posted the replies, as law required, within two months.

[10] This can only be a rough calculation. I am assuming pay in the early first century AD at 900 sestertii per year, wheat at 3 sestertii per *modius* of 6.55 kg = roughly 2 tonnes of wheat equivalent per year. In fact, wheat prices varied unpredictably, and probably systematically increased as one got nearer Rome. Those who believe that a large proportion of legionaries' pay was deducted to pay for food and uniform have to explain why large numbers of educated men voluntarily entered for service in the army. I suspect it was not only the glitter of uniforms but also because net pay was relatively high – but then, that is to privilege deductive thought over fragmentary evidence; see *Rom.Mil.Rec.* = Fink 1971: nos. 68–9 and Speidel 1973.

presupposed that many soldiers could write. We can see this by reconsidering a document of AD 179 which Harris mentions briefly (254) – *P. Hamb.* I 39 = *Rom.Mil.Rec.* = Fink 1971: no. 76. It is a roll (4.33 m long) containing receipts for hay-money paid to eighty-six auxiliary (i.e. non-legionary) cavalry soldiers. To judge by their names, they were mostly native Egyptians; auxiliaries' pay was less than that of legionaries and no one has seriously suggested that auxiliaries were recruited from among the well-to-do. And yet almost one-third of them could write a receipt, which was a paragraph long (and a significant test of literacy), and they could write it in Greek. The sheer, variety of their handwriting, quite visible in the surviving texts, suggests that they learnt how to write not in the army but prior to joining the army, in a variety of schools.[11]

Roman provincial administration was a powerful force in fostering and inculcating literate practice. This may seem surprising, because the Roman bureaucracy was never very large. Even in the fourth century AD, when Roman officialdom had apparently expanded considerably, it numbered only 30,000 regular officials, a small number for such a large empire.[12] And so, compared with the army, the professional bureaucracy was in itself only a minor consumer of literates. Even so, the small size of the bureaucracy and the formality of its procedures induced taxpaying subjects to pay attention to writing and helped persuade at least some of them to write for themselves.

Let me illustrate what I mean. In the Egyptian village of Karanis, male villagers were visited by the local tax inspector on average six times per year to pay instalments of the poll-tax. At each visit, they received a receipt of payment, written on either papyrus or sherd.[13] Many receipts survive, as do extracts from the registers in the village tax office. From these and others, we can see how the village tax office organised its files: there were alphabetically arranged files of taxpayers, so that each

[11] This was pointed out to me by several palaeographers in a medieval history seminar at Berkeley. I would not have spotted it, or thought of it, by myself.

[12] A. H. M. Jones 1964: II 1057.

[13] *P.Mich.* IV 224 is a tax register from Karanis complete for over eleven months of AD 172–3. For small tax receipts, see *O.Mich.* I 116–46; and see similarly *O.Tebt.Pad.*

villager's payment was entered against his or her name; there was a file for each tax: poll-tax, beer tax, weaver's tax, tax on grain; and there was a day-book, which listed each payment in order of receipt or entry, and kept running totals of receipts. Summary accounts, submitted at monthly intervals, had to be sent in multiple copies to the local district capital.[14] All this is well enough known, although the grinding quality of the details and their variations often obscure the significance of the system.

Three implications stand out. First, the system of written tax receipts acquainted many simple villagers with the importance of writing. The ignorant ran the risk of being excessively charged. They needed the help of friendly literates to ensure that they received and knew the meaning of the written receipts. We shall return to this subject in a moment. Their dependence implies that there was public knowledge in the village about exactly who could read or write, and with what degree of proficiency. Social prestige attached to literacy (Harris deals with this very well against the well-known arguments of Youtie); social stigma, however varied, attached to illiteracy.[15] I am not arguing that huge numbers of villagers learnt to read and write as a self-protective measure against Roman taxation. Once again, I agree with Harris' rough orders of magnitude. I am arguing, rather, that significant numbers of villagers learnt how to read and write, in either Greek or demotic or both – and that one of the reasons for learning was self-protection or prestige.[16] In the village of Tebtunis, for example,

[14] For alphabetically ordered tax lists, see conveniently *BGU* IX 1891. For day-books, see e.g. *P.Mich.* IV 223–5 and *P.Cair.Mich.* 359 with the valuable commentary and bibliography by Shelton 1977.

[15] Harris 1989: 144–5, against Youtie 1975 and 1971a. Youtie argued for casual indifference to illiteracy in Greco-Roman Egypt. This formulation assumes a dominant or unified view of literacy, instead of a diverse range of attitudes to it, depending on, say, social class or style.

[16] Why else would many principals in contracts write their own authentication in painfully slow writing, only to be described, derogatively, as slow writers by an attendant literate? This description and their efforts betray ambivalence: the slow writer's pride, the literate's impatience. For much testimony, enlightening discussion, and another conclusion – 'illiteracy carried no stigma in … middle-class life in Graeco-Roman Egypt', see Youtie 1971b (quoting 261).

as I shall show in detail elsewhere, in the middle of the first century AD, certainly over one hundred villagers – and perhaps over two hundred – could write.[17] There was a village schoolmaster and a significant temple library, each of them an index of the production and consumption of knowledge in Roman Egypt.[18] They indicate the density of village literacy and the store of recorded knowledge, which was quite remarkable and unprecedented in human history.

Secondly, because the regular Roman administration was so small, it supplemented its staff by a system of employing temporary administrators drawn from the community. Over time, Roman administration gradually shifted from a system of selling minor administrative offices (such as local tax collectorships) by competitive tender, to a much more far-reaching system of compulsory community service – the so-called liturgy system which allocated a wide variety of posts temporarily, according to importance, and according to taxpayers' declared wealth.[19] One of its functions was to rotate local administrative offices (for example, village secretary, high priest [*prophetes*] of the local temple, village policeman) around a wide circle of villagers and townsmen. Of course, this meant that from time to time, perhaps often, men in putatively literate positions (for example, as village secretary) were barely literate. From a system point of view, that did not matter much (although scholars have occasionally made much of it), since the illiterate boss could always employ a literate subordinate.[20]

[17] See my forthcoming book, tentatively entitled *Crocodile Mummy*, which will review the evidence and the thoughts in this essay in much more detail. ⟨The *Crocodile Mummy* project was never completed; some material on Egypt was reworked in Hopkins 1999.⟩

[18] Many of the papyri from the temple library at Tebtunis have not yet been published. For the list of demotic papyri which have been published, see best Helck, Otto and Westendorf 1975–92: IV 732. For the circumstances of the temple library discovery, see Botti 1936. On Egyptian temple libraries in the Roman period, see Reymond 1976: 23.

[19] On Roman innovations with the liturgical system, see Lewis 1970; Mitteis and Wilcken 1912: I 319–20. For liturgical obligations and liability at the village level, see e.g. *P.Oxy.* XVII 2121 of AD 209/10. For tendering, see e.g. *P.Tebt.* II 295–6; *P.Oxy.* XIV 1633.

[20] See H. C. Youtie's justly celebrated article about a semi-illiterate village tax collector (*komogrammateus*): Youtie 1966.

What did matter was that the system of office-rotation encouraged what I shall call a literate consciousness in village circles. I stress that I am not concerned here with proportions, but simply with consciousness of, and openness to, learning literate forms. Villagers and townsmen had repeatedly to concern themselves with writing.[21]

Thirdly, Roman administrative practice massively increased the stock of information recorded and kept in archives. The very words, library (*bibliotheke*), archive and catalogue, so influential in the later history of literacy, were composite results of Hellenistic intellectualism and Roman administration. Knowledge had to be stored in such a way that it could be effectively recalled. Hence the use of alphabetical files, file numbers, page numbers; to be sure, all of them are dull administrative details, but it was details like these which, for example, enabled Roman tax officials to examine back-files for consistency of taxpayers' reporting and which enabled litigants to search for legal precedents.[22] Writing was used as an instrument of power, by extending the collective memory.[23] My argument is not only that the proportion of literates grew, but that the density of use by literates of writings also grew. And these developments had surprising pay-offs or imitations in other fields. For example, in the magnificent fourth-century Manichaean Psalm Book, each psalm was numbered, each page had a title with the psalm number and first line, and the book was finished with a five-page, two-column index, listing each of the 289 psalms.[24] Religious knowledge, like tax knowledge, had to be ordered so that believers could find their place.

[21] In Tebtunis, in a single year (AD 45–6) 377 men and 84 women acted as principals in a contract, affidavit, memorandum or petition. The number of contracts, affidavits, etc. officially registered in the village scribal office (*grapheion*) totalled about 700 per year, an enormous number for a village. These figures are derived from *P.Mich.* II 123 and V 238, cf. II 121V of AD 42. In the twenty months covered by these contract registers, almost half of all of the adult male villagers were formally involved in making a written contract.

[22] For the constructive use of back-files for checking consistency of reporting, see *P.Panop.Beatty* 2.128–34.

[23] Literacy undermines memory – a view discussed by Harris 1989: 30–3. But libraries and files increased the collective memory.

[24] See Allberry 1938.

Literary culture was both unifying and differentiating. It was unifying in the sense that it provided a set of skills, symbols and values, of which many Romans were aware, even those who could not deploy those skills well. Orators, for example, gave rather long public performances for entertainment, not only at the emperor's court, but also in town theatres, and in front of large audiences.[25] And they exercised their talents in welcoming a visiting emperor, governor or grandee, or at simpler social venues such as wedding feasts or funerals.[26] Rhetoricians, poets, grammarians and teachers were the high-priests, priests and doorkeepers of this cultural system. Literary culture provided a common framework of communications for an upper class which was dispersed over a wide area and several status sets (senators, knights, town councillors of large cities and small towns). Members of the élite quoted snippets of poetry and philosophy to each other at dinner parties (or so the litterateurs tell us), and if they could not they sometimes hired learned slaves to feed them with apposite quotations (or so the satirists tell us).[27] The elaboration of this shared literary culture, in Greek or Latin or both, predated and certainly reinforced the unification of the political élite across the Mediterranean basin.[28] Literary culture provided a thin varnish of community (but not uniformity) among the educated classes, without forging a perceived community of interest. For a monarchy, that was politically advantageous.

Literary culture was differentiating, in that it provided a single set of criteria by which people's performances, and

[25] Heroic lives of professors of rhetoric are celebrated by Philostratus and Eunapius in their *Lives of the Sophists.* For an amusing example, see Eunap. *V. Soph.* 488–90.

[26] See the guide for composing speeches by Menander Rhetor (ed. D. A. Russell and N. G. Wilson, Oxford, 1981).

[27] An idealised style of intellectual, sophisticated conversation is illustrated in Aulus Gellius, *Noctes Atticae;* Macrobius, *Saturnalia;* Athenaeus, *Deipnosophistae.* The position of the intellectual hired for show by the vulgar but pretentious rich man is satirised by Lucian, *De mercede conductis potentium familiaribus* ⟨*On Salaried Posts in Great Houses*⟩, and in Petronius' *Satyricon.*

[28] One index of élite integration is the influx of provincials into the senate of Rome; by the end of the second century AD, just over half of all senators whose origins are known came from the provinces; see Hopkins and Burton 1983b: 144–5. On cultural integration, see best Bowersock 1969, 1965.

therefore their membership in different social strata, could be judged. The diversity of educational attainment ranged from the sophisticated to the superficial, from the economically functional to the marginal, sub-literate, and to the illiterate. This diversity of judgement and attainment was important, because it symptomised the permeability of Roman stratification and underlined the possibility of using education as an effective ladder of social mobility.[29] Becoming educated disguised humble origins. Education was an attainment which could pay off, at many levels of society: among soldiers, as we have seen, or among traders and, at a higher level of society, among minor landowners or intellectuals, who wanted to gain sinecures in the Roman bureaucracy. Education was the currency of a literary culture, which acted as a symbolic glue for a depoliticised upper class.[30] To be sure, there were many other criteria of status and attainment. Modern academics, in particular, have to be wary of exaggerating the importance of bookish knowledge. It also mattered in Rome how you dressed, walked, loved, rode or hunted.[31] But it mattered to a surprising degree *how* you showed, and how much you showed, that you knew something of what was written in books.

The Roman empire was bound together by writing. Literacy was both a social symbol and an integrative by-product of Roman government, economy and culture. The whole experience of living in the Roman empire, of being ruled by Romans, was overdetermined by the existence of texts. I need hardly stress again that I am not arguing for near-universal literacy;

[29] For a whole array of upwardly mobile teachers, see Suetonius, *De illustribus grammaticis* and *De claris rhetoribus*, or Ausonius, *Professores* in the fourth century.

[30] The sheer formal difficulty of many ancient literary products is an indicator of their usefulness as social differentiators. Some authors wrote, still write, not just to be understood but to be appreciated as sophisticated by élite *cognoscenti*. Horace was not meant to be easy; the complex acrostic poems of Optatian Porfyry were presumably meant to be impressively amusing; see Levitan 1985: 262–3. In the school texts published by Goetz 1892 and Dionisotti 1982, conversations turn repeatedly on status differences and on the social advantages of education.

[31] Ancient historians' professional tendency to underrate what many Romans must have rated highly is only partly a function of surviving evidence and of what literate Romans either took for granted or deliberately obscured, by taking their pleasures without describing them. For the importance of pleasures in history, see e.g. the brilliant biography by Spence 1974, or Zeldin 1973.

only a minority of Roman men could read and write. But the mass of literates, the density of their communications and the volumes of their stored knowledge significantly affected the experience of living in the Roman empire. Literacy and writing were active ingredients in promoting cultural and ideological change.

The Birth and Growth of Coptic

This process of cultural change, engineered via the accomplished literacy of provincial sub-élites, can conveniently be illustrated by the birth of Coptic.[32] Towards the end of the first century AD, some Egyptians began to write Egyptian using Greek letters supplemented with a few letters from demotic. The invention of Coptic and its widespread adoption over the next few centuries constituted an intellectually simple, but socially remarkable, technical innovation. Coptic was easier to learn than demotic; it had fewer characters and gave clearer phonetic instructions. Its anonymous inventors succeeded without governmental aid. Contrast the reforms of the Turkish script in the early twentieth century, and of the Korean script in the fifteenth century, both executed by central governmental decree against considerable opposition. In Roman Egypt, groups of nameless men somehow managed to cooperate in creating a new, simplified phonetic script for writing Egyptian. All by themselves they succeeded, without official support or interference, in creating an unofficial script for the Egyptian underclass.[33]

We really do not know how or why they did it. The earliest surviving old Coptic texts are magical spells. But the magical origins of Coptic (if these are not merely a matter of chance

[32] The best introduction to the growth of Coptic which I have found is Kahle 1954: I 193–268.

[33] I use the terms 'underclass' and 'sub-élites' in a woefully loose way. As sub-élites, I have in mind local town councillors and their village equivalents, or leading temple priests, with high-ish local status, enough land to avoid working with their own hands and diverse educational achievements. By underclass, I mean the broad stratum of peasants, artisans and traders, also diverse, below the sub-élites. Note that sub-élites are plural.

survival) do not get us very far in explaining its gradual diffusion, acceptance and standardisation. We know that somewhat later Coptic was in some way tied up with the spread of new religious ideologies (Gnostic, Christian, Hermetic and Manichaean) by sub-élite sectarians. But two points are worth stressing: first, Coptic had developed into a weakly standardised way of writing Egyptian by the middle of the third century, that is, well before the triumph of Christianity. Even then there were different dialects (Fayumic, Achmimic, Bohairic, Sahidic) which in turn probably reflected the pluralist, informal origins of the Coptic script, as well as local phonetic variations. Secondly, Coptic was eventually used for a whole range of writing purposes (just as Greek was) for farm accounts, contracts, tax receipts, private letters, medicine and, of course, magic.

And yet, to judge from surviving manuscripts, Coptic was used particularly to disseminate and to preserve anti-authoritarian ideologies.[34] For example, the famous Nag Hammadi library, discovered in 1945, was a set of a dozen leather-bound codices, containing fifty tracts, mostly Gnostic in character.[35] They are Coptic translations of earlier Greek texts, buried in a jar, perhaps by Christian monks, to preserve them from destruction by orthodox book-burning Christians. The Chester Beatty Library in Dublin has almost as large a collection of Coptic Manichaean texts, many still unpublished, also dating from the fourth century and found in a Fayum village, Medinet Medi.[36] Writing penetrated even villages. Christians, too, used Coptic to help in the conversion and education of the lower-class faithful. The Bible was translated into Coptic by the third century, when Christianity was still a persecuted

[34] I take early Christianity and Manichaeism and probably most forms of Gnosticism as in some sense radical breaks with élite traditions. It is difficult to know how consciously writers used Coptic as a 'religious' script, just as Christians in Egypt apparently used the codex or book form preferentially for religious writings, while the papyrus roll long continued to be used preferentially for traditional pagan literature. See the list of codices and rolls by date compiled by Roberts and Skeat 1983: 37.

[35] Robinson 1977.

[36] See Giversen 1986–8 (four volumes containing over 1,000 pages of text).

sect. And when Christianity triumphed, we know of two interrelated developments.

First, monks in Pachomius' monasteries were taught to read, so that they could study the Holy Scriptures for themselves. And they were taught how to read Coptic, not Greek.[37] However imperfectly executed this general policy was, it serves to remind us that evangelical Christianity was an important stimulus to maintaining and spreading literacy in Coptic among the underprivileged. Secondly, Coptic Christianity helped preserve the sense of struggle by native Egyptian believers against the Roman government, against Greek pagans and Greek-speaking upper-class Christians.[38]

Coptic originated as a script of protest. It was obviously first developed by Egyptians who already knew Greek (hence the Greek letters), but who also wanted to write in Egyptian in order to communicate with Egyptians who did not know Greek. If both parties had known Greek, it presumably would not have been worthwhile inventing the new script. To be sure, at one level the new script represented a cultural fusion between Greek and Egyptian. But on another level Coptic represents a cultural resistance of native Egyptian against the dominance of Greek speakers and writers; by proxy it was, presumably, also aimed against the dominance of Roman rule. It was a development mirrored in other parts of the empire, in the apparent growth of Syriac literature. Coptic was used as a medium of communication among native sub-élites, who knew both Greek and Egyptian but preferred to write in Egyptian, and between them and those Egyptians who did not know Greek.[39] The invention and diffusion of a new script gives us a

[37] Pachomius, *Regulae* 139–40 (*PL* 23: 78B–C) ⟨ed. A. Boon, *Pachomiana Latina*, Bibliothèque de la Revue d'histoire ecclésiastique 7, Louvain, 1932⟩, translated into English by Veilleux 1981. For context, see Rousseau 1985: 70–6. For a good balanced survey of later Roman literacy, see Wipzycka 1984.

[38] See for example the equation repeatedly made by Shenute, abbot of the White Monastery in the fifth century, between Greek (speaker) = rich = pagan: Barns 1964; and Leipoldt 1903: 166–91. Leipoldt's attribution of nationalism seems dated and exaggerated, but Shenute's Christianity is Egyptian rather than Greek.

[39] On Syriac, see the model article by Brock 1980. There seems no similar easy synoptic introduction to Coptic ⟨see now usefully Choate 2009; Boud'hors 2012⟩. In general, see MacMullen 1966.

general insight into the educational level and ideological aspirations of lower social strata in a Roman province, of which we are usually ignorant and which therefore we often choose either to underestimate or to ignore.

The growth of Coptic was complementary in an interesting way with the development of Christianity. Both were social movements which involved interaction, even cooperation, between sub-élites and the underprivileged. Both were movements of protest against Roman dominated conventions. In popular Christian martyr acts, for example, the martyr always wins out, at least spiritually and symbolically, against a repressive representative of Roman power. It is both interesting and revealing that this confrontation between martyr and governor continued to be portrayed in martyr hagiographies written, elaborated and circulated even after the triumph of Christianity.[40] And early Christian writers in their theological treatises repeatedly stressed the primacy of divine power over secular laws and mortal rulers.[41] Christian leaders wanted to subordinate Roman emperors to their own interpretation of God's law.

Christianity, like its competitor religion Manichaeism, was a religion of the written word.[42] It was a religion of the book. To be sure, much religious experience was spiritual, psychic and induced by ritual or the spoken word (cf. Harris 1989: 220). The oral and the written were complementary and in dynamic interaction with each other. But the establishment of Christian orthodoxy and its associated heresies, and their maintenance over centuries and over the whole Mediterranean basin and beyond, were made easier (if not indeed possible) by the existence and

[40] In addition to the well-known martyr acts edited by Musurillo 1972, see Reymond and Barns 1973.

[41] See e.g. *Martyrdom of Polycarp* 9; Justin, *1 Apol.* 13; Athenagoras, *Legatio* 18.2 ⟨ed. and trans. W. R. Schoedel, Oxford, 1972⟩; Tert. *Apol.* 33.1: 'Caesar is appointed by our God'; Origen, *Cels.* 8.73–5 ⟨ed. M. Marcovich, *Vigiliae Christianae* supplement 54, Leiden, 2001⟩.

[42] Mani himself put enormous stress on the importance of the written word; see *Kephalaia* 154, cited by Schmidt and Polotsky 1933: 42: 'The writings and the wisdom … of earlier religions were gathered from everywhere and came to my religion … As water will be added to water…, so were the ancient books added to my writings and became a mighty wisdom …' On context, see Lieu 1985.

repeated use of writings. Sacred texts, exegetical commentaries, letters, written prayers, hymns, sermons and decrees of church councils all helped to integrate Christianity into a coherent if subdivided body; it had a recognisable identity, forged and continually reforged by an argumentative network of writers and readers. The existence of Christian books and readers, emerging from a differentiated set of sub-cultures and disseminated all over the Roman empire, deeply affected the nature of Christian religious teaching and experience.[43] Literacy was not simply a passive technical skill; it was itself a cultural creation and a creator of culture. After all, the Roman empire was conquered by the religious coherence of Christians a century before the western empire was conquered by invading barbarians.

More Details: Literacy in Village and Town

In this final section, I want to analyse some minor texts which illustrate the operation of literacy at the level of village and town. Inevitably, these detailed texts come from Roman Egypt, where almost alone have such texts been preserved in dry sand. I leave aside the question as to how far Romano-Egyptian practice can be used as a valid basis for envisaging customs and attitudes outside Egypt: my own opinion is that, once proper allowance is made for cultural variation and differences in the level of economic development between provinces, much of what we find of governmental practice in Egypt was reflected elsewhere in the Roman empire. I would cite in support the limited number of surviving administrative papyri which originated outside Egypt but were kept there and the rare papyri surviving outside Egypt.[44] They show some striking similarities

[43] The existence of heresies and of orthodoxy itself, as well as of attacks against heresies, rotated around a core of writings. It is interesting to wonder how many pagans, or Christians, in the persecutions of Decius in AD 250 were issued with written certificates of sacrifice (e.g. *P.Ryl.* I 12).

[44] For the most recent discovery of papyri outside Egypt, with a list of previous discoveries, see Feissel and Gascou 1989. The petition included in this archive, dated to AD 245, seems very like those commonly found in Egypt. See similarly the case presented in AD 216 before Caracalla in Syria: a group of farmers against a tax collector. The Syrian court report is structured just like so many court reports from

with Egyptian practice. Those who wish to dismiss Egypt as an idiosyncratic exception at least need to answer that.

I shall look at five topics: (1) bi-partite receipts, (2) authenticators and signatories, (3) village schools, (4) guild rules and secretaries, and (5) tax statistics in the village. Admittedly they are an odd assortment, reflecting adventitious survival and the accidents of my reading. But taken together, they illustrate, I hope, the pervasiveness of writing at levels well below the literary élite and the uses to which writing was put as an instrument of social control and negotiation at several different levels of society.

(1) Bi-partite Receipts, and (2) Authenticators and Signatories

My first data-set illustrates both surprising concentrations of literates and a generalised expectation that illiterates would have a literate friend or patron readily available. I begin with a single papyrus (*P. Oslo* III 111), which records part of a house-to-house census, carried out mostly on a single day in AD 235 in the substantial administrative centre and market town of Oxyrhynchus. As the census officials moved along the streets, they noted the location of each house. They extracted from each house-owner a spoken oath and a written statement that his or her census declaration was complete. The written statement varied; the most common type went along the following lines:

> I, Aurelius Isidorus, also called Harpokration, son of Pauseiris and Sarapias, inhabit the aforementioned house with my son who is a minor, and (confirm) that we are registered in the Cavalry Camp district, or may I be liable under my oath. Year 14, 18th Mecheir (AD 235, 12 February).
>
> (*P. Oslo* III 111 lines 155–60 – 17th hand)

Admittedly a few written statements were more cursory:

> I, Aurelius Ploutarchos, town councillor, have sworn the oath.
>
> (lines 10–11)

Egypt. The text is in Roussel and de Visscher 1942–3. For a now rather old list of papyri surviving in Egypt, but originating outside, see Taubenschlag 1949.

But by and large, these written declarations serve as a reasonable test of literacy.

The readable section of the text covers thirty-one occupied households; of these, twenty-six had at least one literate male in the household. Only five out of the thirty-one households used a literate outsider to write the declaration on their behalf, and each of these households used a different literate subscriber. The proportion of literate householders (84 per cent) is amazingly high. It may simply be a matter of chance – the census tract may derive from a very prosperous sector of the town; but then several houses in the quarter were unoccupied, barred up or confiscated by the Roman government. And several of the declarants wrote in awkward capitals or wrote in a handwriting which reflected a lack of practice, certainly not an educated fluency. In no sense do I wish to generalise from this chance find to the general population of Oxyrhynchus, or of Egypt. But we should note that the very procedure of the census officials presupposed that each householder would either be literate or would have a literate person available to help.

This expectation of pervasive literacy is found elsewhere, and surprisingly even among poor farmers in the Egyptian village of Karanis. I deduce this from a set of 135 tiny receipts for wheat-seed borrowed from a state granary in November AD 158. In antiquity, these receipts had been stored together, presumably by an official at the granary, since when they were rediscovered at the end of the nineteenth century several of them were still tied together with brown thread; still others had a hole in them for the thread to pass through. A typical receipt reads:

> To the grain collectors of Karanis. I have received an advance of seed, contractually acknowledged, in year 22 of the Lord Antoninus Caesar, 44th allotment, Horus, son of Akroes, Karanis, state land, 5½ arourai (= 1½ ha).
>
> (*P.Kar. Goodsp.* 44 = *SB* Beiheft II 44)

These modest receipts for modest loans of wheat-seed allow us to glimpse the percolation of literacy among small farmers in an Egyptian village. Each receipt was normally written by two people. The first part was written by an official in a practised hand. But the second part, beginning in the example quoted above at '44th allotment', was written by someone else. It is not at all easy now to analyse who these writers were, partly because the documents were published almost a century ago by excellent editors neither of whom was interested in statistics on literacy. One of them, Goodspeed, did draw attention to the 'surprising number'* of different handwritings visible in the second part of the receipts, some fine, some crude, many of them apparently written in haste and with abbreviations which were not standardised. We can supplement these editorial impressions with some figures: we can identify twenty-four different writers of the second part of these receipts by name. To be sure, twenty-four literates from a village with over 700 adult male inhabitants is not a large number.[45] But then this is not a complete list of all of the literates in the village, only of those peasants borrowing wheat-seed who could write, out of an undoubtedly incomplete set of receipts. And those were written by village farmers who felt poor enough, or mean enough, to borrow wheat-seed from the state granary.

Literacy, however crude its execution, had percolated down to the level of small Egyptian farmers. And what strikes me as even more interesting than the raw numbers is the bi-partite structure of the documents. As in the census documents, and in the auxiliary soldiers' receipts for hay-money discussed above (at [369]), an official wrote the first part of the document. But there was a built-in expectation that the recipient

* ⟨Goodspeed 1902: 3.⟩

45 The wheat-seed receipts were published in *BGU* I–III, scattered between nos. 31 and 721, with a discussion by their editor in Viereck 1895. Those originally edited by E. J. Goodspeed as *P.Kar.Goodsp.* 1–91 were republished as *SB* Beiheft 2, and a further nine were published as *P.Cair.Goodsp.* 16–24; 135 out of 143 were dated to AD 158. The small sizes of the loans reflected the modest size of the recipients' landholdings. On the population of Karanis, see Boak 1955 and most recently Bagnall 1985, whose findings on falling tax yields are so dramatic that they must either be a fiction (e.g. a function of changing boundaries), or quite exceptional. The more probable multiplier from adult male to total population is about three, not about four (see below n. 50).

would himself write, or get someone else to write, the second part of the document, which identified the size of his obligation to the state. And even if the peasant or soldier himself could not write, there was obviously a wide pool of literates to draw on, not only among auxiliary soldiers but also among peasants at Karanis.

And not at Karanis alone. From Tebtunis also, another village in the Fayum, we have résumés of contracts from one month in the year AD 42 (*P.Mich.* II 121R). In this single month, illiterate villagers, who were participating as principals in contracts, called upon the services of twenty-five different literates to write an authentication or subscription on their behalf. Two points can be made quickly. First, these literate helpers were certainly not professional scribes; most authenticated only one contract in the month.[46] Secondly, the villagers at Tebtunis had a very wide pool of literates from which to draw. From very incomplete data we know of over fifty literate authenticators (*hypographeis* = subscribers) at work in the village in the period from AD 30 to 55. And we know of another fifty literates in the village during the same period who authenticated contracts by writing in Greek or demotic on their own behalf. In one village, therefore, we know that there were over one hundred literate adult males living at the same time. That gives a picture of the density of literacy at the village level, a picture that somehow fails to emerge from Harris' study. Lots of people could write; and there was quite a lot to read, both in private houses and in the library belonging to the temple in the village.[47]

[46] Youtie 1971a argued for the general availability in Roman Egypt of public scribes for hire (cf. Harris 1989: 144). Of course, scribes were available for hire. But the detailed evidence from Tebtunis makes it clear that many other literates were also available, and were used by villagers to help them conduct formal business.

[47] There is no convenient list of literary papyri found at Tebtunis, nor (as far as I know) any reconstruction of what there was available to be read in a village. For the temple library, see above n. 18. For other Tebtunis papyri, see e.g. *P.Tebt.Tait*; *P.Mil.Vogl.* I–II; *P.Tebt.* II. Many more are yet to be published (some have only recently been rediscovered by that productive form of archaeology – looking hard inside a museum); see Avezzù 1977–8.

(3) *Village Schools*

The village of Tebtunis in the mid-first century AD contained certainly more than 100 literates, and probably over 200, however roughly or even generously defined.[48] It was an amazing concentration for a single village, and suggests a literacy rate well above 10 per cent, since there were probably about a thousand adult males living in the village and its associated hamlets. It is difficult to explain these high literacy rates; but several factors should be listed, even though it seems difficult to assess their relative importance: they are, Egyptian religious and cultural traditions, which required at least some temple priests to read demotic and hieratic; the insistence by the Greek, and then by the Roman, administrations that commercial transactions were written down in formal contracts officially registered in the scribal office (*grapheion*); the overt status which literacy gave or enhanced – why else did many people struggle to write their own authentications to a contract, however slowly?[49] Literacy was often a public act of writing before witnesses either on one's own behalf, or to help out a relative, neighbour or client. It gave some protection against exploitation and some power to exploit others, and increased opportunities for employment. I must insist that all of these factors were at work, even at the level of a minor village at the edge of the Fayum.

[48] Very complete records and scattered individual documents certainly attest over 100 literates in Tebtunis in AD 30–55. The actual number of literates was very probably at least double this. How can we tell? There are two arguments: first, a risky, statistical estimate of how many data are missing; secondly, since literates were asked to authenticate contracts only when they had reached social maturity, modally aged 30 or so, there very probably existed younger males aged 15+ who had learnt how to write but had not yet been called upon to exercise their skills as authenticators of contracts. QED.

[49] *P.Tebt.* II 291 of AD 162 illustrates that at least some candidates for the priesthood at the temple to the Crocodile God in Tebtunis were required to show that they could read hieratic and other Egyptian writings. Twenty priests from the temple signed their names in demotic – *P.Mil. Vogl.* III *Dem.* 2 (first century AD). The insistence by Greek rulers of Egypt that contracts written in Egyptian be summarised in Greek and officially registered in order to be legally effective in the second century BC is discussed by Pierce 1972: 183–8.

How were literates produced at Tebtunis? We do not know. But there was a schoolmaster active in the village in the mid-first century (*P.Mich.* II 123R 21.9). A single mention cannot tell us how long the school was active. But a school graduating five literate adolescents each year would, given probable death-rates, produce a pool of well over 100 adult literates.[50] The excavations of 1899–1900 in Tebtunis yielded several wooden writing tablets, including one carefully ruled into squares, and headed with the injunction:

> Good handwriting begins with well formed
> letters and a straight line. Imitate me.

Various schoolchildren then copied the whole of this text several times underneath.[51]

Sometimes instruction apparently had a commercial slant. One papyrus contains an alphabetical list of tradesmen (baker, dyer, fuller) designed presumably to help children with learning Greek (*P.Tebt.* II 278). Another (not from Tebtunis) sets the following arithmetical problems:

a. The freight charge on 100 *artabai* is 5 *artabai.* What is the freight charge on the whole cargo of 1,000 *artabai?*
b. The monthly interest on 100 drachmai is 2 *drachmai* 3 *obols.* In four months, if the principal is 200 *drachmai,* how much is the interest? (*P.Mich.* III 145).

It is a salutary and rare reminder that the village school aimed at the literacy of tradesmen, rather than, or as well as, at teaching the literary Greek which we find so often in other surviving school texts.[52]

[50] Even with high mortality, if we assume an average expectation of life at birth of 23 years for males and a stationary population, the median life expectancy at ages 15–20 is another 30 years. Thus five graduating pupils per year, assuming no emigration, would yield 150 literates. Allow for error in such calculations. I use Coale and Demeny 1966: 4 table Model West, level 3, stationary population.

[51] There are several wooden school tablets from Tebtunis in the Lowie Museum at Berkeley, found by Grenfell and Hunt in 1899–1900. The one cited in the text is inv. no. 6–21416. I am most grateful to Dave Herod and Frank Norick for generously showing me, and sharing their knowledge about, the Tebtunis finds in the Museum.

[52] There is a catalogue of school texts by Zalateo 1961, which may include more than it should; and see also Harrauer and Sijpesteijn 1985 for later additions, commentary and bibliography.

Village schools were not merely training grounds for literates and for the exercise of relative social privilege. They also served as a battleground for cultural conflict. After all, children had to choose between learning Greek or demotic. Some learnt demotic. Demotic texts from Tebtunis in the Roman period set uncommercial arithmetical problems ranging, for example, from the simple 13×17 to the more complex $(^1/_3 + ^1/_{15}) \times (^2/_3 + ^1/_{21})$. The answer, of course, is $^2/_7$. From another Fayum village, Medinet Medi, we have a dump of well over a thousand pottery sherds, once used for school exercises and dating to the second century AD. Roughly equal numbers of the texts were in Egyptian or in Greek, and a slightly smaller number were written in a mixture of both.[53]

Only a few of these texts have been published. They show ancient teachers pressing their pupils to work hard and stressing the value of literacy: 'Your instruction is in your own interest', 'Five days journey on an ass equals one day in which you dedicate yourself to writing' (*O.Narm.Dem.* I 20, 12). But some pupils were not entirely convinced of the value of learning demotic. One demotic sherd reads:

> I shall not write in Greek letters. I am obstinate.
>
> (*O.Narm.Dem.* I 5)

The joke is that the last word, 'obstinate', was written in Greek. My argument here is not statistical, but inevitably impressionistic. The impression that I get – and obviously such fragmentary evidence is open to several, competing interpretations – is that literacy in the Egyptian villages penetrated well below a social élite and reached a variety of levels of competence, dispersed well above and below what one might call 'artisanal' or merely functional literacy.

(4) Guild-Rules and Secretaries

Even in a village, there were jobs and positions which required literacy or in which literacy was an obvious and tempting

[53] Parker 1972: 37–8 on *P.Brit.Mus.* 10520, problem 57 and plate 21. I am grateful to Penny Glare for the reference to *O.Narm.Dem.* I.

advantage. For example, in Tebtunis alone there were about twenty associations of artisans, farmers or traders active in the mid-first century AD.[54] One association, a monthly dining club, with provisions for mutual support and mourning, had a rather high monthly subscription; and nine of its fifteen members were literate (*P.Mich.* V 243, AD 14–37). The guild of saltsellers, like other guilds, had written rules. They behaved as an active trade association: they fixed prices, they fixed penalties for transgressors, they drank together and they allocated a monopoly for selling salt in the outlying villages by lot in return for a fee. Presumably demand there was too small to support competition (*P.Mich.* V 245, AD 47). This was conscious economic rationalism and, on a small scale, economic planning. To be sure, such arrangements could have been fixed orally; the officially registered written rules were perhaps never consulted. But written rules surely defined obligations rather more rigidly and more fixedly than purely oral agreements. One further point: several guilds or groups of farmers had an official secretary (*grammateus*), ranking second after the guild president. The very existence of a guild secretary is a striking index of the importance attached to writing in an Egyptian village, and to recording the decisions of the guild.

(5) *Tax Statistics in the Village*

I began this essay with some tiny individual tax receipts. I would like to end with the transformation of such individual receipts into composite and well organised tax statistics, sent from the Fayum village of Karanis by a marginally literate farmer named Aurelios Isidoros.[55] When it was his turn to be a village tax collector for wheat and barley, he was responsible for compiling and

[54] See conveniently *P.Mich.* V 243–8 and Boak 1937. The price fixing recorded in the rules of the guild of saltsellers defeats the inherently implausible dictat by Finley 1973: 138, that ancient guilds did not fix prices.

[55] See *P.Cair.Isid.* Isidorus was explicitly called illiterate (ἀγράμματος), that is, he did not know how to write his own letters to officials (*P.Cair.Isid.* 8, and Boak and Youtie 1960: 4). But we know several instances in which such categorisation as illiterate was not true (see Youtie 1971a); and I personally agree with Boak's earlier judgement (1946: 42) that Isidorus could probably read; hence his dossier.

transmitting the village tax return for wheat and barley, which involved listing the size of each landholding in the village, the amount of tax due in wheat and barley from each farmer and landowner, the amount so far paid and the arrears (*P. Cair. Isid.* 6, 9, 11). The clarity of the summary statistics is very impressive. Their implications are also, I think, quite interesting.

Aurelios Isidoros was responsible with all of his property for the proper performance of his duty as tax collector. It was only one of several village offices which we know that he held during his life. Knowing how to read, knowing what he was being made responsible for, gave him a clear advantage over those who had to trust a relative, a friend, patron or paid employee. My first point is simple. Even in a village, state intervention and the system of administration stimulated literacy. Literacy was an expedient, an advantage and a public status symbol, possessed by a significant minority.

Secondly, Aurelios Isidoros knew how much tax his village paid every year, in wheat. It was a very sizeable amount. The collective tax return was a form of communication with the governor of Egypt, perhaps even with the emperor. After all, it may well have crossed the peasant's mind that the farmers of the village were paying an awful lot for Roman peace and justice: did they wonder if they were getting good value for their sweated labour? In the dossier of papers which Aurelios Isidoros preserved, there is a preamble to an edict of the Emperor Diocletian (AD 297) reforming taxation and promising a fairer distribution of the tax burden (*P. Cair. Isid.* 1). It is amazing and unexpected that we find an imperial message percolating into the dossier of a modest villager. But from other papers we can also see how very seriously Aurelios Isidoros took the spirit of the imperial message. During the course of his lifetime, he sent twenty petitions to various officials, including two to the governor of the province. And in these petitions, he reflected the government's own message: Roman law was meant to protect the poor against the unjust depredations of the rich.[56]

[56] For example: 'The laws forbid actions aimed at ruining us, the people of modest means, and driving us into flight. Now I myself, who am in every way a man of

In this essay I have tried to argue, at the level of the general and the particular, that literacy and writing helped to integrate the Roman empire into a more unified political, administrative, economic, legal and cultural system. Writing operated, in some ways, for example, like money. Just as money allows sellers and buyers to transcend face-to-face relationships – the seller can use the cash that he gets from the buyer to purchase other goods removed in time and space – so writing allows the writer to communicate with people he cannot see, and with people not yet born. But writing and money are not simply exemplary parallels: their use and operation, which we call literacy and monetisation, were intertwined.

Money stored value, and helped foster the growth of long-distance markets. Writing stored rights and obligations, and helped create a larger store of knowledge, a system of laws and a market in cultural skills and values. Their operation was mutually reinforcing, since both money and writing are systems of impersonal, symbolic exchange. Roman emperors, with their coins and edicts, could try (and they occasionally succeeded in) communicating with simple peasants. Simple peasants could try to communicate via taxes and petitions with the emperor. Writing and money were two powerful agents of communication and control, which helped integrate the Roman empire into a single political system.[57]

Over four centuries, the Roman empire was increasingly integrated in several spheres – political, legal, economic, cultural and religious. But it was in the field of religion that changes in integration were most remarkable. As before, humble believers tried to communicate with god(s) via prayers, dreams and petitions; that was ancient practice. But for the first time in the fourth century, God communicated with all believers in the Roman empire by means of a single book. The empire was hooked into a single religious system, however diverse the interpretations of different sects and churches. The radical and

modest means …' (a self-description which was not completely true) (*P.Cair.Isid.* 68); or 'The laws have repeatedly enjoined that no one be made to suffer oppression or illegal exactions …' (*P.Cair.Isid.* 69, AD 310).

[57] See similar thoughts in von Freyberg 1988: 76–7.

subversive message of primitive Christianity could not have become initially established across the whole empire without significant sub-élite literacy. And it is the pervasiveness and effect of that sub-élite literacy that Harris has underplayed in his book.[58]

[58] I should like to thank Mary Beard, Alan Bowman, Penny Glare, Wim Jongman, John Ray and Dorothy Thompson for help and advice.

AFTERWORD

CONQUEST BY BOOK

WILLIAM HARRIS

Kazan is about 450 miles east of Moscow. Marvin Lyons' book *Russia in Original Photographs, 1860–1920* contains an undated street scene from a village near Kazan in which the principal figures are an army officer and his well-dressed wife.[1] The shops have written labels and advertisements – the officer and his wife were obviously literate. In the background are ordinary soldiers, probably conscripts – evidence of the paper-filled imperial bureaucracy. Further in the background, out of sight (let us suppose that the date is 1880), some of the great masters of the modern novel were writing and being read. How much literacy, and of what kinds, was there in a village outside Kazan, or in the Russian empire more widely? I leave the reader to guess, or to find out.

'Conquest by book' was instigated by my book *Ancient Literacy* (1989), which in turn was considerably influenced by Keith Hopkins' own work. He accepted the main conclusions I reached,[2] but his essay makes a substantial contribution and is not simply a book review. It presents in its author's characteristically limpid way a good deal of material that will have been unfamiliar to many of his readers, and I found the section on the invention and spread of Coptic script especially

[1] Lyons 1977: plate 130.

[2] See also Hopkins 1998: 207–8 [essay 12: 458–9]: 'fluent, sophisticated literacy was concentrated in, but was not the exclusive privilege of, the ruling strata … The Roman empire was a preponderantly agricultural society, with 80 per cent or so of the population engaged in farming and 15 per cent of the population living in towns. The stratification pyramid was very steeply pitched, i.e. there was a huge gap between a small, powerful and rich élite and the mass of rural and urban poor … In between the élite and the mass, there was a sub-élite (inevitably a shadowy, but still a useful concept) of unknown size, which comprised middling landowners, merchants, professionals, such as lawyers, doctors, architects, professors of rhetoric and philosophy, middling and lesser administrators, army officers, scribes, school teachers'. On the concept of a sub-élite see also 145 n. 33 [375 n. 33].

informative.[3] H.'s conclusion, however, is that *Ancient Literacy* 'underplayed ... the pervasiveness and effect of ... sub-élite literacy' (158 [390]), and that is a contention that I shall question in this brief note. It is hateful that H. is not here to answer back, but I have no choice but to defend my point of view.

I could do so by referring to the numerous passages (almost every page) in chapter 7 of that book in which I discussed the actual evidence about the literacy and illiteracy of the 'sub-élite' in H.'s sense of that expression (for which see n. 2).[4] 'Conquest by book' in fact overstates the differences between its author's views about Roman imperial literacy and mine, allowing too much space to his 'general impression' (134 n. 3 [365 n. 3]) about what I was saying and too little to what I actually said. I readily admit that I intended to make a set of forceful – though accurate – statements about ancient literacy and illiteracy, in the hope of disturbing the sleep of certain classical scholars (some sleep on regardless) while making some suggestions about ancient-historical method. But there is little that I disagree with in 'Conquest by book', except on two topics. Topics that are, however, of vital importance in this debate. One is social structure, the other is the typicality of Egypt as a Roman province with respect to the functions and diffusion of writing (for the inhabitants of Egypt are virtually the exclusive subject of H.'s article).[5] Meanwhile the debate about ancient literacy has spread far and wide.[6]

No one perhaps has done more for the understanding of Roman social structure than H., but in this instance there was too much equivocation. What kinds of people in Egypt are

[3] But it is a romantic fancy to say that 'Coptic originated as a script of protest' (146 [377]). Nothing in Kahle 1954, whom H. cites, would justify such a view, unless you want to take magical spells as a form of protest. Coptic script was just easier (Youtie 1975: 203). According to Bagnall and Cribiore 2006: 59, its early development took place in 'privileged' milieux.

[4] That chapter concerns the period 100 BC to AD 250, and this is the only period directly under discussion here.

[5] In discussing the extent to which Egypt can be informative or suggestive about the wider history of the Roman empire, Alan Bowman 2001: 139 speaks of 'the somewhat unhelpful notion of "typicality"', but the notion can, I think, be applied to documentary practice and literacy.

[6] Cf. Harris 2014; Harris and Li forthcoming.

supposed to have been literate, and with what kind of literacy? One slight obscurity in his analysis is that while at times he emphasises the 'sub-élite' such as professionals and merchants, most of his energy goes into arguing that small farmers and artisans were often able to write, a quite different story (I suppose the implication is that if the 'lower-middles' were literate the 'upper-middles' must have been too?).[7] And when H. writes that the inventors of the Coptic alphabet created 'an unofficial script for the Egyptian underclass' (145 [375]), I do not understand what model of Romano-Egyptian society he is employing;[8] certainly a two-class model would be hopelessly simplistic.[9] Admittedly, H. said that I 'underplayed' sub-élite literacy, not that I denied its existence altogether, so let us look at specific social categories and some specific documents.

One social category that is virtually absent from 'Conquest by book' is women, and that has a distorting effect, for while women's literacy was quite widespread by ancient standards in Roman Egypt, as was the propensity of women to make use of writing, women were undoubtedly much less literate than men (historical exceptions to this pattern are extremely rare and always explicable), and any estimate of Egypt's overall literacy must be tempered by that fact. A recently published third-century document, *P.Oxy.* LXXIV 4994, is typical: the husband is literate (in the gymnasial class – that is to say, he was a member of the social élite), the wife is declared to be illiterate. Conspicuously literate individual women do not of course disprove this generalisation. I learned of one such case

7 The expression 'the literary élite' (149 [380]) is mystifying and may be a misprint, since no one in modern times has supposed that literacy in the Roman world was confined to people who read works of literature. 'Conquest by book' does not altogether avoid the subjective language which I attempted in vain to shame scholars into avoiding, phrases such as a 'wide pool of literates' (151 [383]).

8 All the less so, since, as H. points out, the oldest Coptic texts are magical spells, which were probably produced by and for 'religion workers', as I call them, rather than amateur enthusiasts.

9 That is what H. seems to imply when he defines the underclass as 'peasants, artisans and traders'. For an attempt at a more accurate description of Roman class structure see Harris 2011: 15–26 (a revised version of a paper published in 1988). Artisans and traders were demonstrably much more literate in the first/second centuries AD than peasants.

from H. himself, for he first told me of the relief from Rome, now in Dresden, that shows a butcher's shop with a woman – presumably the butcher's wife – keeping the accounts.[10]

I continue to doubt whether small-scale farmers in Roman Egypt, not to mention those who worked on other people's farms, were often literate to any significant extent, and it should not be necessary to point out that these men and their families made up a large majority of the population. No text cited in 'Conquest by book' added anything to the known dossier. As H. himself notes, the *penthemeros* certificate which he cites (133 [363]) (showing that its subject had performed his corvée labour) is atypical of such documents. He seems to imply that when *penthemeros* certificates were signed, it was by the 'villagers' who had completed the work. In fact, as one might logically have expected, they were signed – when they were signed – not by the corvée workers, but by supervising officials called *katasporeis*.[11]

As for the 135 surviving receipts for seed borrowed from a state granary at Karanis in the year 158 (150 [381]), we do not know who wrote them. The borrowers were ordinary farmers, and it is superficially plausible to suppose that the persons who wrote the second half of each receipt (these are not signatures, however) were the individual farmers themselves. But this apparent plausibility depends on a larger and thoroughly implausible picture in which small farmers sent their sons to school or otherwise taught them to read and write. There were always substitute writers available. Twenty-four hands have been detected in these documents: for 'a village with over 700 male inhabitants' that seemed 'not a large number' (151 [382]). In ordinary terminology, however, Karanis was not a village but a town: it extended over some 60 hectares, which made it nearly as large as Pompeii, and in 158 must have had several thousand not several hundred adult male inhabitants.[12] 'Why did the Roman government insist on having these trivial

[10] Illustrated in e.g. D'Ambra 1995: 679; Dixon 2001: plate 9.
[11] Sijpesteijn 1964: 16; on the *katasporeis*, see further Duttenhöffer 2007: 280.
[12] van Minnen 1994.

and transient actions formally recorded?' H. asks (134 [364]). One answer might be that there was just enough literacy in Roman Egypt to make it possible. It is true of course and duly remarked on in *Ancient Literacy* that many papyri and ostraca record economic transactions that seem to us to be fairly trivial.[13] But on the whole, the experts in documentary papyrology seem to be in broad agreement with my estimates of the extent of literacy in Roman Egypt,[14] which were of course much influenced by the research of H. C. Youtie.

The army is an especially intriguing milieu for the study of literacy, since soldiers (legionaries anyway) 'were repeatedly asked, ordered or required to write; the Roman army's organisation presupposed that many soldiers could write' (138 [368–9]). This was quite an old tradition (and it would be interesting to know how well it survived in late antiquity). But H. neglected to make what seems to be a very relevant distinction, between legionaries and *auxilia*. The former were very often literate in some sense.[15] Auxiliaries, even though they were not much worse off materially than legionaries, were very different people. From the scanty evidence,[16] I calculated that perhaps one-third of the cavalrymen in second-century Egypt could write out a set formula, 'an interestingly high figure', as I remarked. I imagine that some of them had learned to do so in the army.

The typicality or otherwise of Egypt within the Roman empire is one of those problems that invites a yes-and-no answer.[17] If the focus is on writing and literacy, then there is considerably more material from other areas than was available twenty-five years ago,[18] or rather, many more documents

[13] E.g. Harris 1989: 201.

[14] Bagnall and Cribiore 2006: 6; Gagos 2009: 199. Others are a little more reluctant, but scarcely differ (e.g. Johnson 2004: 160: 'quite restricted').

[15] For a solitary known exception, see Harris 1989: 253–4 – he was a veteran located, as it happens, in Karanis.

[16] Primarily *Rom.Mil.Rec.* (= Fink 1971) no. 76. When H. writes that 'to judge by their names, they were mostly native Egyptians' (138 [369]), he seems to mean that they were not of Greek descent; in fact roughly two-thirds of the usable names are non-Egyptian.

[17] H. (148 [379–80]) hedges his bets, but tends to see similarity of governmental practice everywhere.

[18] For Syria, Judaea and Arabia, see the catalogue of some 609 papyrological and similar texts in Cotton et al. 1995. There is quite a bit from the West too: for the

are now known (in truth, they do not make a large difference to what needs to be said about literacy). Very briefly: it can be argued on one side that the vast number of Egyptian documents is largely a consequence of the Egyptian environment, that when documents or seals happen to be preserved elsewhere they demonstrate the existence of a deeply documented administrative and economic system, and that there is no good reason to distinguish the realm of the Ptolemies from any other Hellenistic state with respect to the fiscal, commercial or legal use of documents. Roger Bagnall has argued strongly that this set of arguments is broadly applicable to the Hellenistic world,[19] and they can also be applied *mutatis mutandis* to the 'Greek' provinces of the Roman empire (but some, obviously, were more sophisticated than others).

On the other hand, it can be argued that Egypt was at the extreme end of a spectrum of Roman provinces. Rome took over from the Ptolemies a degree of state intervention in economic life (this story has admittedly changed in the last decades), and a complexity of taxation, that is not known to have existed in any other province. Other Middle Eastern and North African provinces have not left comparable evidence – nor did they need to produce nearly as many types of text in order to function as Roman provinces. Roman government and the Roman economy depended on documents, but not on *penthemeros* certificates or state-granary receipts. In particular, we may doubt whether the non-Hellenised or semi-Hellenised provinces (and we must not forget the persistence of local languages) resembled Egypt, as is sometimes very rashly assumed.[20] My view is that Egypt was probably an extreme case in this respect, but that some other provinces (and much of Italy) were also heavily documented. At the other end of the

graffiti from Kaiseraugst, for example, see Féret and Sylvestre 2008, who, however, are entirely out of touch with what historians have written about literacy (and, in truth, their material does not change the picture).

19 Bagnall 2011: 27–53, especially 47–50.

20 This seems to be implied by Johnson 2004: 160. Woolf 2000, in an otherwise excellent summary account of literacy in the high Roman empire (see also Woolf 2009), generalises from Rome and Pompeii to Roman towns everywhere.

spectrum were provinces such as Britain, Lusitania or Moesia, where only a very small proportion of the indigenous population is likely to have acquired literacy of any kind. In between came many other provinces.

Two further points are worth emphasising here. One of the greatest of H.'s achievements as an ancient historian was to introduce quantitative models into the study of Roman society and the Roman economy. A good deal of the confusion about Greek and Roman literacy stems from the persistent unwillingness of classical scholars to think quantitatively about this matter.[21] H., on the other hand, understood the crucial importance of 'rough orders of magnitude' (140 [370]), and it is a pity that this lesson has not been learned more widely. One reason for this is plainly the yearning of some classicists to maintain the myth of mass ancient literacy, even if it means ignoring the overpowering reasons for rejecting it.

A final remark: Bagnall and Cribiore express the need for a study of scribal hands from Egypt 'according to provenance, destination, and type of document'.[22] It is to be hoped that whoever undertakes this study will be ready for mild surprises (not only the scribe who could barely write, but well educated men who wrote negligently[23]), but above all that s/he will be alert to differences of social class.[24]

[21] Harris 1989: especially 7.

[22] Bagnall and Cribiore 2006: 42. See further Bagnall 2011: 79.

[23] Cf. Harris 1989: 249.

[24] I expressed my admiration for H.'s scholarship in a British Academy memoir (Harris 2005), and nothing in this note should be taken as a modification of what I wrote on that occasion.

11

NOVEL EVIDENCE FOR ROMAN SLAVERY*

This is an article about Roman slavery and an experiment with method. Substantively my objective is to sketch the slave's experience of slavery and the fears and anxieties which slavery evoked in Roman masters. I am interested here in thoughts and feelings. Methodologically I am trying a new tack by experimenting at length with lies, whereas most Roman history is purportedly aimed at the discovery of truths, through establishing facts or describing events which are known to have occurred.[1]

This article is built around a single source, which is an inventive fiction, a pack of lies, an anonymous accretive novella, composed and revised, as I suspect, over centuries, as a vehicle for comedy and manners. It is the biography of a slave, the only full-length biography of a slave surviving from classical antiquity; a text which as far as I know has never yet been used as the basis of historical reconstruction, probably because it is so obviously a fiction.[2] But before I get down to discussing

* First published in *Past & Present* 138 (1993) 3–27 (= Hopkins 1993) and reprinted, with a handful of minor changes incorporated here, in Osborne 2004b: 206–25.

1 The dominant convention that history is primarily concerned with 'truth' about events which have occurred hardly needs authentication. See e.g. Veyne 1984: 10–11: 'history is a body of facts … History is the relating of true events'. The tactic of experimenting with conscious fictions as a source of socio-cultural history is not unknown, but still rare in ancient history. It is well known, even fashionable, in early modern history. See e.g. Greenblatt 1988.

2 The text is edited with all its known variants in Perry 1952 (see too G. A. Karla, *Vita Aesopi. Überlieferung, Sprach und Edition einer frühbyzantinischen Fassung des Aesopromans*, Serta Graeca 13, Wiesbaden, 2001). The main manuscripts are very well translated in Daly 1961. I owe a huge amount to Daly's translation, though the translations in this article are my own, except where noted. The *Life of Aesop* is not dealt with, as far as I know, in any modern discussion of ancient slavery; it is not even mentioned, for example by Westermann 1955; Bieżuńska-Malowist 1974–7; Hopkins 1978b; or by M. I. Finley in e.g. Finley 1980, 1981 or 1987. Bradley 1984: 150–3 discusses the fables of Phaedrus, but not Aesop or his *Life*. Levine 1977: especially 81–135 discusses the meaning of slaves' stories – but in an intellectual style quite different from that deployed here.

this biography in detail, I want to dwell a little on a small number of anecdotes, more or less familiar to modern historians of the Roman world, drawn from formal histories and from a medical doctor's observations. My objective here is to illustrate my underlying contention that the social history which can be squeezed from 'real histories' and from fiction may be broadly similar and that, for the interpretation of culture, there is little justification for privileging one above the other.[3]

First, a historian – Tacitus. In AD 61, the senatorial mayor (*praefectus urbi*) of Rome was murdered in his own home by one of his slaves. According to Tacitus, the motive was disputed: was it because the master had promised his slave freedom, and had even agreed the price, only to welch on the deal? Or was it because of some homosexual rivalry between master and slave over a shared lover? Whatever the cause, under strict Roman law, if a slave killed a master in his own house, then all of his slaves living in the household were to be crucified. The murdered mayor was a rich noble, a former consul; in his town house alone, he had 400 slaves. Their imminent execution caused a huge stir. There was a heated debate in the Roman senate. Some senators were for softening the traditional harshness of the law; they pleaded for mercy for the large number of slaves, including women and children, who were undeniably innocent of any complicity in the crime.

But a majority of senators voted to uphold the law as it stood. How else, the traditionalists argued, could a solitary master sleep soundly among a whole gang of slaves, unless it was in the interest of each to protect him against any murderous conspirator? Foreign slaves, worshipping foreign gods or none, could be controlled only by fear. After all the traditional custom of punishing a cowardly legion, by choosing by lot one soldier in ten and then having him cudgeled to death by his former companions, sometimes involved murdering the bravest

[3] In calling fiction 'lies', I am colluding with conventional dichotomies: facts/fictions, truth/lies, evidence/discardable opinions, even though the basic argument of this article is that fiction provides a useable and trustworthy representation of Roman culture. My intention here is not to squeeze fiction for facts, but to interpret fiction as a mirror of Roman thinking and feelings.

men. Making an example benefited the whole community, even if it sacrificed some individuals unjustly. This was the gist of a speech by the triumphant conservative lawyer. The Roman senate was persuaded. The populace was less impressed. A crowd wielding firebrands and stones tried to stop the mass executions, but the Emperor Nero stood firm, had the route lined with soldiers and all 400 slaves were crucified.[4]

Slavery was a cruel and repressive institution, enforced by hatred and fear. 'All slaves are enemies', stated a Roman proverb. The hostility of Roman slave-owners to their slaves, and of slaves to their owners, lay just below the surface of Roman civilisation like an unexploded volcano. To be sure, some slave-owners were probably kind and considerate to some of their slaves, whether out of affection, generosity or the self-interest which was prompted by a desire to safeguard valuable assets. Sometimes owners' kindliness was projected into an idealised image of the grateful and loyal slave, who in an emergency even sacrificed his or her life to save the slave-owner.[5] That favourable image was one side of the coin. The other and dirtier side of slavery rested in slaves' legal powerlessness and in their more or less complete dependence on their owner's favour, which, as far as the slave knew, could turn at any moment from love to hate.

It is not my concern here to describe the varied behaviour of Roman slaves and of their owners, nor to draw up a tentative balance sheet of what was typical. Given the fragmentary state of surviving evidence, that would be impracticable. But the realities of Roman slavery, its scale and pervasiveness throughout the Mediterranean basin, its legal basis and its economic implications, necessarily frame any modern analysis, as they framed all ancient experiences, of slavery.[6] Roman slavery was

[4] Tac. *Ann.* 14.42–5. His account of the senatorial debate may not be accurate and may reflect later political concerns. This is the argument of Wolf 1988.

[5] For the proverb, see Sen. *Ep.* 47.5; Macrob. *Sat.* 1.11.13. On the loyal slave, see Vogt 1972: 83–96; for sharp criticism, see Finley 1980: 93–122. For an equally idealised, but more nuanced view of slave/owner relations within complex households, see Veyne 1991: 16–19.

[6] See Hopkins 1978b: 99–132 for a quasi-objective account of Roman slavery, complementary in intellectual style to this subjective study of relations between masters and slaves, or the other works on slavery cited above in n. 2. We have only

in significant respects distinct from slavery in the American South. For example, Roman slaves were not distinguished by the colour of their skin. Some Roman slaves were educated, sometimes better educated than their masters. Some slaves occupied positions of trust and responsibility, for example, as secretaries, clerks, teachers, physicians and architects, or as administrative agents in business or the management of agricultural estates. Many of these skilled slaves could save up out of profits or pocket money in the hope of buying their freedom. Many thousands of Roman slaves achieved freedom either through purchase or by the master's generosity (or both – the master 'generously' granting the slave the right to buy his freedom). And any male slave, freed in due legal form by a Roman citizen master, himself became a Roman citizen; and a similarly freed female slave could bear free citizen children by a citizen father. The Roman slave system therefore faced a recurrent problem on a scale unknown in the American South: the problem of the clever, talented, educated slave occupying a position of responsibility, who had a realistic prospect of freedom and the constant image before his or her eyes of other slaves who had themselves achieved freedom. At the same time, such slaves were in their owners' power and at the mercy of their whims. The visibility and social prospects of powerful and clever slaves, whose ability owners wanted and needed to harness, intensified the implicit struggle between masters and slaves and the oppressive cruelty of the Roman slave system.

One objective of this essay is to investigate the seamier side of slavery, by analysing some of the stories which slave-owners (and perhaps even slaves) told, at least partly to help themselves delineate and negotiate the boundaries of appropriate behaviour between masters and slaves. These ancient stories are not about normal behaviour, any more than a modern

very sketchy knowledge about how the practice and experience of slavery varied by period and sub-culture in the diverse and vast Roman empire. I use the term 'Roman slavery' rather crudely to refer to slavery in the Roman empire, without implying either uniformity or consistency – just as one might use the term 'bread' to cover bread in France, England, Russia and the USA, in spite of the known variations.

popular newspaper typically reports news of normal conformist behaviour. Stories and news, and perhaps social history, concentrate on the boundaries of morality, or what one can call the penumbra of moral ambiguity, about which even the same reader, let alone different readers, will have had ambivalent feelings and reactions. In some respects what I am doing in this article is like trying to understand conditions in British factories during the depression in the 1930s from an English intellectual's eclectic library, the one surviving copy of Charlie Chaplin's *Modern Times* and a few fragments from British parliamentary papers and *The Times*. The interpretation of comic caricature is necessarily individualistic and error-prone, but it would be dangerous to assume that serious newspapers or the minutes of the Roman senate are more secure guides than creative fiction to the partial recovery of a lost reality.

Roman literature abounds with stories of incidental cruelty to individual domestic slaves, who in the owner's opinion had betrayed a trust, done something wrong or simply had not done something fast enough. Slaves were there to be impatient with. Domestic slaves stood in the front line. They were more privileged and pampered than the tens of thousands of slaves who laboured without realistic hope of freedom in the fields or in the mines. Some domestic slaves, as I have said, could save up in the hope of buying liberty.[7] But domestic slaves also had more contact with their owners and were more often subjected to their despotic whimsy.

Even 'good' masters could be brutish. The Emperor Augustus, for example, who by and large has had a favourable press in history books both ancient and modern, is said to have had the legs of a trusted slave broken because he had taken a bribe and revealed the contents of a letter; and Augustus is also

[7] In the one area of Roman Greece for which testimony is available, a high proportion (63 per cent) of freed slaves were female; the price of bought freedom was significantly high (on average about 3 tonnes of wheat equivalent for an adult slave, enough to provide minimum subsistence for a family of four persons for three years); and the conditions imposed on the newly freed slaves were often onerous, including (in a nearby area) the provision of replacement slave children: Hopkins 1978b: 133–71. For insubstantial quibbles about one of these conclusions, see Duncan-Jones 1984.

said to have had a middle-ranking palace official, a freed slave, nailed to a ship's mast because he had eaten a prize fighting-quail. The court physician Galen records that the Emperor Hadrian once in anger stabbed a slave in the eye with a pen. He later felt remorse and asked the slave to choose a gift in recompense. The slave did not reply. The emperor pressed him for a response. The slave said that all he wanted was his eye back.[8]

Individual stories are difficult to interpret. Some were recorded incidentally, almost casually; or so it appears. Others, perhaps the majority, were told because they marked the frontiers of acceptability. We have to be wary of constructing an image of Roman normality out of what even Romans regarded as exceptional. And yet these individual stories do help us map out Roman attitudes to morality, just as they helped Romans themselves to sort out what was allowable, legitimate and praiseworthy. Individual stories do not tell us directly what was normal, but they do indicate which abnormalities met with overt disapproval, and for these purposes, I should stress, it does not matter so much whether these stories were true. It matters more that they were told and retold.

One striking story dramatised the confrontation of cruel rich man and emperor. An extremely rich man, called Vedius Pollio, himself an ex-slave, but now risen to the status of a knight, had a fishpond stocked with huge lampreys which he fattened on the flesh of slaves who offended him in any way. Once, when Augustus was dining with him, a young slave dropped a precious crystal bowl. His master immediately ordered him to be seized and thrown alive to the lampreys. The boy slipped from his captors' grasp and threw himself at the emperor's feet 'to ask only that he be allowed to die in some other way, not as human bait'. Augustus was so shocked at Vedius' cruelty

[8] Suet. *Aug.* 67; Plut. *Mor.* (*Apophthegmata Romana*) 207B; Gal. *De propriorum animi* 4.8 (ed. D. Kühn, *Opera Omnia*, vol. 5, Leipzig, 1823) ⟨ed. W. de Boer, *CMG* 5.4.1.1, Leipzig, 1937; trans. P. N. Singer, Oxford, 1997⟩. The use of anecdotes here is not to be confused with attempts to use them as authentication of particular actions by individual Romans, a practice rightly criticised by Saller 1980. He shows how stories did the rounds and were amended and then successively attributed to various actors.

that he pardoned the boy and ordered that all Vedius' crystal bowls be smashed there and then and that the fishpond be filled in. Again it does not matter here whether the story is true, or how much it has been embroidered in the telling. It matters that it was told by Romans to each other as a moral story overtly celebrating the evil corruption of non-hereditary riches and the benefits of a benevolent monarch reasserting antique values. At least, that is one interpretation, although ancient readers of the story, or listeners, probably had their own divergent interpretations and sympathies. Such stories circulate, I imagine, partly because their moral messages are problematic and ambiguous (for example, did all slave-owners think that the emperor was right?). However that may be, this moral story has a further twist. When Vedius died, he left most of his property to the emperor, and Augustus had his huge *palazzo* destroyed, converting the site into a public pleasure garden in honour of his mother.[9] Out of vice came virtue and pleasure.

Emperors set the tone, or reflected broadly held values. Galen, for example, also tells us that his mother used to bite her slave maids in fits of rage. He hated her for it. By contrast, he admired and tried to imitate his father's self-control. Neither father nor son, he claimed, had ever whipped one of their slaves with their own hands. But many of his father's friends used to hit their slaves in the face; Galen's father calmly said that these friends deserved to get a dose of boils and seizures and die (rather as fervent early Christians preaching a gospel of peace wished on all heretics and sinners the torments of Hell). After all, Galen's father went on, they could have waited a while and then inflicted as many blows as they wanted with cane or whip, after due consideration.[10] It was not the physical punishment of slaves to which Galen objected, but impulsive, irrational behaviour.

[9] Cass. Dio 54.23.1–6; elaborated by Sen. *De ira* 3.40. See Syme 1961; Zanker 1988: 137.

[10] Gal. *De propriorum animi* 4.6 and 8.1.

Galen recounts another story, which he tells us he often told.[11] He was travelling from Rome to Athens with a friend, who was a simple and friendly fellow, good-natured and open-handed in sharing their daily expenses, but irascible and inclined to strike his slaves with his hands, sometimes even kick them, and quite often hit them with a whip or whatever piece of wood came to hand. When they landed at Corinth, they had sent most of the baggage and slaves on by ship and themselves took the shorter overland route with a carriage they had hired. On the way, Galen's friend asked the slaves who were walking behind for a particular small bag; they replied that they had not brought it with them. 'He was enraged, and because he did not have anything else to beat the young lads with, took his sword in its sheath and hit each of them on the head, not with the flat of the sword, which would not have been serious [!], but with its cutting edge.' The friend hit each of the slaves twice and the sword burst its scabbard, so inflicting serious head wounds. When he saw the huge streams of blood, the friend fled in the direction of Athens, because he did not want to be on the spot when one of the slaves died. Killing a slave under Roman law could count as murder unless death occurred in the course of reasonable punishment.[12] But the excellent doctor Galen looked after the slaves, ensured their recuperation (that, doubtless, was one of the main points of the story) and got them safely to Athens.

Galen's friend was overcome with remorse. One day soon afterwards, he took Galen into a house, stripped off his clothes, handed Galen a whip, went down on his knees and asked to be flogged. The more Galen tried to laugh it off, the more persistent his friend became. Eventually Galen consented, but only if the friend would submit to certain conditions. Willingly the penitent friend agreed. So Galen made him promise to listen to what he had to say and then lectured him on the virtues of self-control and on the possibility of controlling slaves by methods other than the whip. This story would probably evoke

[11] Gal. *De propriorum animi* 4.9–13.

[12] *Dig.* 1.6.1.2 (Gaius); Gai. *Inst.* 1.53; *CTh* 9.12; Buckland 1908: 36–8; ⟨see below n. 20⟩.

different responses in different readers, ancient and modern. In my view, four points emerge: first, beating a slave on the head with the flat of a sword was considered regrettable, but not serious; secondly, even remorse took the form of violence; thirdly, violence and self-control represented an axis of moral strain within polite Roman society – the controlling élite was expected to be self-controlled; and finally, telling stories constituted an instrument of social control, outlining to listeners and subjects the limits and penalties of transgression.[13]

* * *

I too want to tell a story, derived from the only biography of a slave to survive from the ancient world. This slave biography is a satirical fiction, the so-called *Life of Aesop*, written in its finished form in the first century AD in Roman Egypt.[14] It exists in several slightly different versions and in several copies. Most of the surviving copies are in Greek, but a Latin version also survives. The work has no known author; it is a composite text, which was probably frequently revised, anonymously, in order to incorporate the various popular stories circulating in the Greco-Roman world about masters and slaves. The multiple versions and surviving copies of the *Life of Aesop* (several surviving on papyri

[13] I want to stress again that ancient interpretations of such stories were probably pluralistic and conflicting. Even the same person reacts to symbolic messages with a whole range of sometimes conflicting emotions. The story is told again and again, partly just because it strikes a transgressive nerve and precisely because the outcome of a struggle in the imagination between right and wrong is not assured. For an exciting discussion of these issues, see Stallybrass and White 1986.

[14] For the best edition and translation of the *Life of Aesop*, see above n. 2. The two principal manuscripts are denoted by the letters *G* and *W*; I mostly follow *G*, occasionally *W*, and sometimes amalgamate both (for the texts, see Perry 1952). Four papyri fragments of the *Life* found in Egypt and dating from the second to the fifth century AD are listed by Pack 1965: nos. 1614–17. In the opinion of Adrados 1979, the *Life* reached its surviving form by the first century AD. This seems plausible, but I suspect it involves simply working back from the earliest known papyrus fragment. Several passages in the surviving text firmly suggest an Egyptian context for the tale (see below n. 22), but then the mention of Roman money, denarii (*W* 24, *G* 27), the death scene at Delphi (*G* 124–42) and Aesop's visit to the emperor at Babylon (*G* 101), often equated in apocalyptic literature with Rome, and to the legendary king of Egypt at Memphis, whom he also outwits (*G* 112–24) suggest multiple sites, origins and fantasies. There seems mercifully little written in modern times about the *Life of Aesop*, but see Perry 1936; Wiechers 1961; Zeitz 1936.

written in Greek in Roman Egypt from the second to the fifth century AD) indicate its forgotten popularity, and dramatically increase its utility for us; what we have is not a single author's idiosyncratic vision, but a collective, composite work incorporating many different stories told about slaves, and attached here to Aesop. But we can have little or no idea about the audience at whom it was aimed, or by whom it was read or heard. Its survival in Egypt and the occasional adaptation of the text to Egyptian conditions should not mislead us into thinking that it relates primarily to Egypt, any more than its being written first in Greek should make us think that it related primarily to Greek slavery. In my view, the *Life of Aesop* is a generic work, related generally, but not specifically, to slavery in the whole Roman world. To be sure, the *Life* makes jokes about academic pedantry and the respect due from children to their professors, which may indicate its origins or circulation among students.[15] But its simple prose style and unaffected humour suggest that it had a broader appeal among social strata well below the literary and power élites.

Serious historians of the ancient world have often undervalued fiction, if only, as I have said, because by convention history is concerned principally with the recovery of truth about the past.[16] But for social history – for the history of culture, for

[15] Perry 1936: 1 thought the *Life of Aesop* to be 'a naïve, popular, and anonymous book, composed for the entertainment and edification of the common people rather than for educated men'. I think his assumptions about the sophisticated tastes of the educated in the Roman world and the reading capacity of the common people are questionable. Besides, some elements of the intended audience can perhaps be seen towards the end of the novella: Aesop, after he has been freed, becomes tutor at the court in Babylon and the surprising mouthpiece of almost conventional wisdom. He advises his adopted son: 'Above all revere the divine; honour the emperor; since you are human, remember your humanity; God brings the wicked to justice. Honour your professor equally with your parents' (*G* and *W* 109). It seems easy to spot the academic origins of such advice. So also 'When drunk, do not show off your learning by discussing technical points of literature. Someone sometime is bound to outwit you and you'll make a fool of yourself' (*G* 109).

[16] Of course, ancient historians have combed ancient fictions for historical 'facts'. See, for example, the encyclopaedic and to my mind misconceived efforts of Dumont 1987: 309–630, seeking to discover facts and figures about Roman slavery in the comedies of Plautus and Terence. Both do indeed touch often on the issues dealt with at greater length in the *Life of Aesop* and so corroborate the *Life*'s relevance to Roman slavery. See also the more sensitive yet still positivist rendering of Apuleius' novel by Millar 1981a.

the history of people's understanding of their own society – fiction occupies a privileged position. We have here not the 'true' history of a single exceptional slave, who would not be typical.[17] Instead we have an invented, generalised caricature of a slave, whose relations with his master, and his master's wife, guests, friends, other slaves and fellow citizens, reflect the central tensions in the relations between masters and slaves. We see the conflicts of interest, the pressures towards unthinking and therefore unquestioning obedience, towards loyalty and sabotage, seduction and infidelity, hard work, violent punishment and shirking. This fictional biography runs along the raw nerves of slavery, the same raw nerves which Roman comedies repeatedly touched, but never had the time or interest thoroughly to explore.

The hero of the story is the historical Aesop, a slave who, according to tradition, lived in the sixth century BC and who constructed the lively animal fables which are still popular (such as the race between the hare and the tortoise, or the greedy peasant who killed the goose which laid the golden eggs, just to see if its insides were also made of gold). None of these tales survives in its original form. The earliest surviving collection was written in Latin verse by a freed slave, Phaedrus, who claimed that animal fables were invented by slaves as a secret way of talking to each other without being understood by their masters – evidently not with uniform success, since Phaedrus was himself punished by Sejanus, the powerful prefect of the palace guard under the Emperor Tiberius, because of the offence which his fables had caused in court. Perhaps the underlying cause was their pervasive subversiveness. Consider what the ass said to the old shepherd. An anxious old man was grazing an ass in a meadow. Suddenly, he was terrified by the noise of enemy soldiers approaching. He tried to persuade the ass to flee, so that they would not be captured. But the ass,

[17] I am thinking here, enviously, of the difficulties of interpretation posed for the history of slavery in the American South by slave autobiographies: e.g. Douglass 1855; those collected in Osofsky 1969; also of the systematising attempts to overcome the perils of individual reminiscence in Rawick 1972–9, based on faded memories of slavery collected in the 1930s.

unmoved, asked: 'Do you think that the victorious soldiers will load me with two packs?' The old man said no. 'Then', said the ass, 'what difference does it make to me, so long as I carry only one load?' The moral of the fable was clear and explicit: 'A change of emperor brings a change of master for the poor, but not a change in prosperity.'[18] The fables of Aesop were not politically innocent, nor were they written in these versions exclusively or primarily for children.

The real hero or anti-hero of our tale is an Aesop of the imagination: to be sure, a slave, but what a slave! Pot-bellied, weasel-armed, hunchbacked, a squalid, squinting, swarthy midget with crooked legs; a walking disaster, deaf, and what is worse, dumb (*G* and *W* 1). The grotesque repulsiveness of this misshapen body, 'a turnip with teeth' (*W* 24) is consciously deceptive; it hides virtuous generosity, as well as a supremely astute and cunning mind, which is not above teaching his master a sharp lesson. Much of the story turns on the contrast between superficial appearance and unseen capacity, and on the social inversions in which the despised slave repeatedly humbles, even humiliates, his master. His master, Xanthus, is a philosopher, trapped by his status, his academic ambitions and his social pretensions into being both pedantic and reasonable.[19] The slave is both simpler and cleverer. Aesop represents all that a master might despise and fear in a slave. Physically he is a caricature of the alien other and like all slaves an irremediable outsider. And yet the master, in order to exploit his slave to the hilt, has to ask Aesop inside, where he can see all that happens in the house and judge all that he sees. Ideally it would have been more comfortable if the slave had been, or could have been, treated as a machine; just as in Roman tracts on estate management the slave was defined as a talking tool (*instrumentum uocale*), though there was more hope than

[18] Phaedrus 1.15; for the alleged origins of animal fables, see Phaedrus 3.pref.33–44.

[19] The story, inevitably, had many resonances for the ancient listener and reader, which now deserve comment. For example, Xanthus was a common slave name; Aesop, the ugly slave, was also presumably an inversion of the ideal, beautiful slave (*servus formosus*), on whose acquisition rich Roman slave-owners sometimes spent a small fortune.

realism in this persuasive and derogatory definition.[20] In reality, as the master fully realises, the slave does have intelligence, and in order to exploit his domestic slaves thoroughly, the master has to trust the slaves to use that intelligence. He also has to leave the slaves occasionally to act alone, and to be left alone with the master's wife. Hence anxiety, even fear, oppression, cruelty and, perhaps, half-unconscious jealousy.

The master can beat the slave, cheat him of his promised freedom, but only at the cost of showing up his own moral inferiority. And in the end, almost inevitably, since this is a comic satire, the master who teaches his pupils not to trust women unwittingly encourages his own cuckoldry, and is then saved from even deeper, public humiliation in front of his friends by the personal humiliation (which he shares with the reader) of privately depending on the slave Aesop's help. Small wonder then that the story ends with Aesop's liberation and murder by a collectivity of free citizens. Aesop is simply too resourceful and too troubling to be left alive. The irony is that once freed Aesop no longer has the protection of his master. Freedom exposes the ex-slave to fresh dangers.[21] Slavery here is not just a tool for telling a story, but a category for thinking with, a way of understanding the tensions of Roman society. The appeal of the story for Romans depended, I think, on its nightmarish understanding of all that might go wrong in a master's control over his slaves.

[20] See Varro, *Rust.* 1.17.1; presumably, it was convenient for owners of large slave gangs to think of slaves as non-human. In Roman law, the slave was repeatedly defined as a thing (*res*), though of course the slave's utility to his/her owner depended largely on not being a thing. See *Dig.* 1.6.2 (Ulpian); Gai. *Inst.* 1.53, for qualifications; see also the classic Buckland 1908, in which part 1 is divided into eight chapters, called 'The Slave as *Res* [Thing]' (chs 2–3), and 'The Slave as Man' (*sic*) (chs 4–9).

[21] The idea that freedom would be problematic for some slaves is touched on by Epictetus (*Discourses* 4.1.35: the freed slave has to earn a living and has no one who automatically feeds him) and in Phaedrus' version of Aesop's tales (Phaedrus, appendix 20). Here an old slave complains that he has earned his freedom. His hair has turned grey, he gets beaten too much and is given too little food. When the master dines at home, he stands by all night. When his master is invited out, the slave waits outside the host's house in the street till dawn. He decides to run away. The wise slave reminds him that then his life would be much worse. To be sure, the issue here may be an amalgamation of the risks of freedom and of running away. But it is interesting that even a modest slave attendant was thought to have some chance of being freed.

But let us get down to the story. The *Life of Aesop* begins, as Greek novels often did, with the religious. Aesop shares his simple food and shows the way to a lost priestess of Isis, and in response to her prayer, Isis appears to Aesop while he is asleep, exhausted from his work in the fields, and gives him back the gift of speech and the capacity to weave tales in Greek.[22] Aesop immediately uses his newfound tongue to rebuke the overseer, himself a slave, for his cruelty, and unsettles him to such an extent that he rushes to their master in the town and reports Aesop's recovery of speech, not as a miracle, but as an ill omen. The overseer receives permission, because Aesop is so ugly, 'like a dog-faced baboon', to give him away, or, if that fails, to flay him alive (*G* 11). Masters, in real life in the Roman empire as well as in fiction, had effective power of life and death over slaves. Physical punishment, the fact of it and the threat of it, threads through the whole story, like the shouts of small children at play; even silence is ominous.[23]

As often happens in short stories, a slave trader is passing by. The overseer sees his chance of a tidy profit, and has Aesop summoned from the fields. Aesop complains bitterly about the hardships of serving and obeying another slave, instead of his true master – this recalls the fiction of the good king, which resurfaces in the tales of Robin Hood: if only the good King

[22] Here is one hint among several that the *Life of Aesop* in its surviving form was adapted to an Egyptian context, where Isis (but not Greek) was thoroughly at home. Later on (*G* 65), the local district magistrate is called *strategos*, a term used in this sense as far as I know only in Egypt under Greek and Roman rule. For the texts of Greek novels in English, see conveniently Reardon 1989; for recent bibliography and discussion, see Bartsch 1989; see also the imaginative Heiserman 1977.

[23] Slavery involved being whipped, either in actuality or in fearful anxiety. That is the image which emerges repeatedly from ancient authors. The working conditions for slaves in mines and factories were particularly harsh. Apuleius, again in a novel (written in Latin in the second century AD) about a man turned into an ass, which is also a symbol for a slave, describes the physical conditions of slaves in a bakehouse with a surprising sympathy: 'Their skins were seamed all over with the marks of old floggings, as you could easily see through the holes in their ragged shirts, which shaded rather than covered their scarred backs; some wore only loincloths. They had letters tattooed on their foreheads and their heads were half-shaved and they had irons on their legs. Their complexions were frighteningly yellow. Their eyelids were caked with the smoke of their baking ovens, their eyes so bleary and inflamed they could hardly see out of them. Like athletes in the arena, they were powdered, not with dust but with dirty flour': Apul. *Met.* 9.12.

Richard knew, he would stop the misdeeds of the wicked sheriff of Nottingham. Aesop gives a brief picture of what he is required to do, from laying the table to feeding the livestock, drawing the water and heating the bath, as well as working in the fields. Whatever Roman lawyers said, this is a salutary warning against dividing slaves too readily into separate categories, agricultural and domestic.[24] Many slaves performed a whole range of jobs and services.

When the slave trader, who is a specialist in fancy boys, sees 'what a piece of human garbage' (*G* 14) Aesop appears to be, he at first refuses to buy. But Aesop appeals to Isis and to the trader's sense of profit and is soon proving his worth to his new master by his ingenuity, much to the indignation of the other slaves; one of them says: 'That fellow deserves to be crucified' (*G* 19). The symbol of the cross and the terrifying threat of crucifixion overshadowed the lives of slaves for centuries, before Christians converted it into a sign of religious devotion and eternal salvation.[25]

At last the slave trader is left with only three slaves to sell, Aesop and two quite good-looking, skilled slaves, one a musician, the other a teacher. He stands them on the slave block as a trio. The philosopher's wife passing by in her litter hears the herald advertising the sale. She goes home and persuades her husband to buy a nice-looking male slave. He goes to the slave market, is too mean to buy one of the expensive slaves and buys Aesop instead. When he gets home, he tells Aesop to wait outside and goes inside the house to tell his wife the good news. She immediately thanks Aphrodite, the goddess of love, for realising her dreams, and starts fantasising about the new slave's charms. The female slaves of the household all start

[24] *Dig.* 33.7. Dividing slaves into categories and into hierarchical sets, commanded by slaves and by freed slaves, was a device for controlling slaves.

[25] Based on an emendation of the text in *G* to *staurou*. The image of the cross, a symbol of punishment for slaves and bandits, reminds us of early Christianity's appeal to the oppressed and its promotion of a heaven which would be a world upside down: the poor would be privileged and the rich would be refused entrance. Needless to say, this radical vision receded as Christianity triumphed and forged alliances with the state. For other ancient restricted Utopian visions, see Diod. Sic. 34.2; Athenaeus 6.265–6; Vogt 1972: 25–8.

squabbling, and even come to blows, each imagining to herself that the new slave will be her husband.[26] 'The master bought him for me', says one; 'No, he's mine', says another, 'because I saw him in my dream.' 'Where is this idyll?' asks the mistress. 'Outside', replies the philosopher Xanthus, 'waiting to be asked inside' (*G* 20–30). And so the stage is set for master and mistress, and the rest of the household, to welcome inside the house their own undoing. Comedy takes on the trappings of tragedy.

Once inside the philosopher's house, the new slave Aesop succeeds in turning everything upside down.[27] Unlike a real slave, Aesop speaks his mind and so uncovers what is in the mind of others. The comedy lies in the shocking recognition of the truth behind the pretensions; the comedy's cruelty lies in the revelation of what everyone would prefer to keep hidden. The husband loves his wife, but the wife, as so often in Greek thought, is portrayed as a 'sex-crazed slut', on the lascivious lookout for a 'young, handsome, athletic, good-looking blond slave', desired, as Aesop says openly to the wife, in order to shame her: 'so that this fine slave can escort you to the baths and there take your clothes from you, and when you come out of the bath, the same good-looking slave will put your wrap around you and will kneel at your feet and put your sandals on, and then he'll play games with you and look into your eyes as though you were one of his slave playmates he had just taken a fancy to, and you'd smile back and try to look young and feel excited, and [then later] you'd call him into your bedroom to

26 The wife's litter, presumably carried by male slaves, and the quarrelling female slaves suggest a considerable slave establishment in the philosopher's household. That was what the story demanded; it is difficult to know how typical that was for philosophy professors in the Roman provinces. I suspect it depended on how much teaching philosophy was the primary means of support and how much the philosopher could rely on inherited wealth. Assistants to a famous professor of rhetoric at Antioch in the fourth century AD (Libanius) had only two to three slaves each, or not even that: see Lib. *Or.* 31.11 (trans. A. F. Norman, Translated Texts for Historians 34, Liverpool, 2000).

27 The polarity upright world/world upside down is to be sure only one of several polarities played against each other in the novel: slave/free, male/female, insider/outsider, educated philosopher/uneducated peasant. The reader can shuttle his identification from one to another as speedily as a modern filmgoer. See Henderson 1989 for a speedy introduction to multiple meanings.

have your feet rubbed and in a fit of excitement you would pull him towards you and kiss him and do with him what suits your shameful impudence' (*G* 32).

The baths, cleanliness, heat and lust were a heady mixture; and the close association between powerful female mistresses and their male slave attendants in public and in private stimulated the anxieties of husbands, the malicious gossip of envious observers and of later Christian moralisers.[28] And besides, Aesop himself, who begins by severely rebuking his new mistress for immorality, ends up by seducing her, in revenge for his master's ingratitude and broken promises. Admittedly it is a dangerous game to have sex with a tempestuous mistress, but Aesop's revenge is all the sweeter, because when the lovers quarrel, as lovers inevitably do, Aesop inventively appeals to his master for arbitration and so gets him unwittingly to foster his own wife's further infidelity (*W* 74–6).

Some of the original manuscript has been lost in antiquity, so that we cannot follow the story through all its ramifications. But at one stage, clearly, both master and mistress have been completely infuriated by Aesop's wilful misunderstanding of their instructions. I imagine it was a common enough problem with slaves, as later with servants.[29] In the modern industrial world, this sense of impatient outrage is perhaps best paralleled by the consumer's frustration or fury at not being able to understand or follow the instructions which accompany a self-assembly kit for a piece of household equipment. I suggest the comparison because I want to stress that the conflict between Aesop and his owner is structural and symptomatic, not personal and idiosyncratic. To be sure, the respected professor is constrained by his philosophy to be, as I have said, both reasonable and pedantic. He is the Goliath of the story, but more a figure of fun, at least outside the academic profession, where

[28] E.g. Clement of Alexandria, *Paedagogos* 3.5 (ed. M. Marcovich, *Vigiliae Christianae* supplement 61, Leiden, 2002), launched a viciously colourful attack on the loose morals of women who stripped naked in front of male slaves in the baths.

[29] For the corrupting dependency of masters on their slaves, see Seneca, *Ep.* 47, who argues that human nature transcends slave or free status. Did awareness of his view help slaves tolerate slavery better?

the obsession with formal definitions and verbal precision has rarely caught on. Almost against his will, the philosopher is trapped by his profession into being stolidly reasonable, into not punishing his slave without good reason. Driven to despair, he tries to control his slave by giving very precise instructions: 'do nothing more or less than you are told', under threat of a beating (*G* 38). But the slave, as of course the plot demands, determines to teach his master a lesson. He says to himself: 'Masters who are overdemanding with regard to the services they want have only themselves to blame for what goes wrong' (*G* 38). What is so remarkable surely about this story, designed I must stress to be read in a slave society (and perhaps even, as often happened, designed to be read aloud by a slave reader to his listening master and family), is that we are asked and expected in a slave society to side with the slave against the master.[30] If the midget Aesop is David to Xanthus' Goliath, it is as though the story was destined to be told not among Jews, but among Philistines.

Humour camouflages, but does not fully hide, the lines of battle in the unceasing guerrilla warfare between master and slave. The master says: 'Take the oil flask in your hands, and the towels, and let's go to the baths.' So Aesop picks them up and, without putting any oil in the flask, follows his master. The comedy lies in the predictability of conflict, in our knowledge of whom the fictional victor will be, in the unrealistic patience of the master, who is by inversion the fall guy.

Xanthus gets undressed, hands his clothes to Aesop and says: 'Give me the oil flask.' Aesop gave it to him. Xanthus took the oil flask, turned it upside down, found that there was nothing in it and said: 'Aesop, where is the oil?' Aesop said: 'At home.' Xanthus said: 'Why?' And Aesop said: 'Because you said to me "bring the oil flask and the towels", but you didn't say anything about oil. You

[30] Various Roman slave-owners are known to have had their slaves read to them, during meals, in the bath or while they went to sleep; the mere fact that some slaves were explicitly called 'reader' (*lector*, *anagnostes*) strongly suggests that such functions were common in grand households. See Marquardt 1879–82: I 148 for collected references. The implicit picture of a master, mistress, children and slaves all hearing the *Life of Aesop* read aloud reinforces my claim that hearers interpreted what they heard diversely.

had told me not to do anything more than I was told, or else, if I broke that rule, I was likely to be beaten.' And then he kept his peace (*G* 38).[31]

End of Round 1.

In the next round, Xanthus tries to be even more careful and precise. He meets some friends at the bath and plans to invite them to dinner, so he sends Aesop back home: 'Aesop, go on back home … and cook lentil [*sic*][32] for us. Put it in the pot, put some water in with it, set it on the cooking range, put wood under [the pot], light it; if it goes out, blow on it. Now, do exactly as I say.' Aesop says: 'I will.' And he goes back to the house, into the kitchen, tosses one lentil into the cooking pot and cooks it. Meanwhile back at the baths, Xanthus (as befits a stereotypical philosopher) is making a parade of his simplicity and asks his friends back home to eat a modest snack. They accept. Xanthus brings his friends to the house and says to Aesop: 'Give us something to drink for men straight from the bath.' So Aesop runs to the baths with a pitcher and fills it up from the outlet, handing it with a flourish to Xanthus, who is overcome by the stench of it and asks, 'Phew, what's this?' And Aesop says 'Something to drink straight from the bath' (*G* and *W* 39–40). End of Round 2.

Eventually, when Xanthus and his friends have been drinking wine for a time, Xanthus asks Aesop whether the 'lentil' is cooked. Aesop replies that it is ready. Xanthus, just to make

[31] Plutarch, a Greek commentator on Roman life, writing mostly towards the end of the first century AD, noted that Roman slave-owners were trapped by the very strict discipline which they themselves imposed on their slaves. He tells a story nowhere else recorded, about a Roman consul of 61 BC, M. Pupius Piso. He invited another magistrate, Clodius, to dinner and prepared a sumptuous feast. The other guests came, but not Clodius. So he sent the same slave who had carried the original invitation to see if Clodius was coming. After another long wait, Pupius asked the slave if he had really invited Clodius. 'Yes', said the slave. Master: 'Why then has he not arrived?' Slave: 'Because he did not accept the invitation.' Master: 'Why did you not tell me immediately?' Slave: 'Because you did not ask me that' (Plut. *De garrulitate* 18 = *Mor.* 511D–E). The story has the same point, or so it seems, as this section of the *Life of Aesop*: that is reassuring. What the *Life of Aesop* tells us is not so much new, as unparalleled in its richness and in its perspective.

[32] The Greek word for 'lentil' used here, *phakos*, like the English 'sheep', has unusually the same form for singular and plural.

sure, asks to try it. So Aesop brings him the one lentil on a spoon. Xanthus eats the lentil, and says: 'That's fine; it's well cooked. Bring in the food and serve it.' So Aesop gets a large dish, pours in the boiling water, and says: '*Bon appetit*; it's well cooked.' When his master expostulates, Aesop explains that he has eaten the one cooked lentil and that he had originally ordered 'lentil', not 'lentils'; 'the one is singular, the other plural' (*G* 41). So the pedantry is volleyed back, the master is mastered. The slave relents and says: 'You shouldn't have laid down the law so literally, or I would have served you as best I could. But don't mind, master ... you've learnt not to make similar errors in lectures.' And since Xanthus can find no proper reason for flogging Aesop, he says nothing (*G* 43).

The hard-nosed realist may well object that all this is mere comic fantasy. In 'real life', no slave had such licence or such a self-controlled, philosophical master. But real life consists of fantasies and feelings as well as of external realities. We think, we laugh and dream, as well as behave; our thoughts and feelings shape our behaviour and mould its meanings. And each of us thinks, both idiosyncratically and by orchestrating a standard repertoire of culturally specific stereotypes. The slave of Aesop's story, as a stereotypical outsider, invited inside, was good to think with; his story served as a social mirror which helped insiders to define themselves and their relations with each other.

Stories about *au pairs* in modern British families serve similar functions; so perhaps do stories about summer camps or college in the USA, where children and post-adolescents learn about being insiders, by being exported *en masse*, of course 'for their own good', into the outside. What matters here is not just the master's experience of the slave, or the slave's experience of slavery, or the child's experience of summer camp, or the parents' ideas about what a college education achieves. The experience and ideas about the experience are orchestrated and enhanced partly by the stories which we tell about our experiences with outsiders. And what is fascinating is that these stories repeatedly reveal the dependency of the insiders on outsiders for the delineation of their identity. So too

Roman masters needed slaves in order to be masters, and they needed stories about slaves in order to work through and recreate some of the problems which their own social superiority inevitably caused.[33]

In these stories, the anti-hero, the ugly hunchback dwarf slave, rather like Rumpelstiltskin, is a representative of the other, who is allowed to express what cannot easily be attributed to a free insider. He is socially despised, but symbolically central. He is created from a repertoire of social images, whose appeal lies in the tension they generate between underpinning and undermining the dominant culture.[34] Aesop is a projection of repressed emotions; he is potent, cunning and vengeful. He is what we desire, envy and fear.

The appropriate question is not, 'Did slaves really talk like that to their masters?', but rather, 'Did many slave-owners in some way fear that they might?' The passing recognition of that common fear, set in a disconcerting, but reassuringly untrue story, bound masters together as masters. The story allowed repressed fears and erotic attributions to rise briefly to the surface, gave fantasy a short airing and then blocked off the imaginary transgressions (for example, the slave's wit, wisdom and seductive virility) by mocking them away as comic fictions. To be sure this is only one interpretation of a story. I cannot be sure that it is right. But interpretative history flourishes on precisely those ambiguities which the substantivist (conservative) historian of objective truth finds least comfortable, or most objectionable.[35]

[33] The stories were not merely reflections of problems, or part of their easy resolution, but became themselves part of the process by which the multiplicity of meanings which slavery generated were negotiated by masters and slaves – just as stories about footballers and football hooligans are part of the experience of football.

[34] The ideas of interdependence between the despised and the despiser, and the common repertoire of images which they may share, are fruitfully explored in Stallybrass and White 1986.

[35] In ancient history, at least, the lines of this particular intellectual battle are not clearly drawn. The protagonists, conservative positivists and interpretative pluralists, prefer, I suspect, to ignore or to undervalue each other's work, rather than to discuss each other's methodological advantages and shortcomings. There may be something to be said for divergent practice over naïve epistemology, as in Veyne 1984 or Alföldy 1986: 30: 'History as created by scholars is not identical with the

The hostility between master and slave runs like a sore throughout the story.[36] One pungent scene illustrates this. The master, after a hot bath and a few drinks, feels the 'call of nature' and goes to the privy, with Aesop in attendance holding a towel and a pail of water; they discuss why men after defecating often inspect their shit (*G* 67). This episode reminds us of what our own cultural prudery (not about looking, but perhaps about telling) tempts us to forget. Roman domestic slaves, especially in small 'bourgeois' households, were body slaves. To their repeated degradation, they knew their master inside out. They knew him in all his vulnerability, with his trousers down – rather as a wife does, but without the tender feelings or the commitment of a lifetime. The master understandably hated the slaves who knew his weaknesses and projected the anxiety which that hatred aroused on to the slaves themselves. At least, that is my interpretation of why the master repeatedly in the *Life of Aesop* calls the slave 'refuse' (*katharma*). It reflects, by denial, the master's fear that the slave is really human. Indeed each of the other common ways of addressing slaves – 'boy', 'whipling', 'runaway' – also reflected by denial a different aspect of the master's anxieties.[37] Calling him 'boy', for example, both expressed and repressed the fear that the slave was a responsible adult, just like the master; 'whipling' expressed the idea that the master was fully entitled to beat the slave as he wished, but repressed the idea that the beaten slave might take revenge if or unless beaten; 'runaway' tempted, teased and dared the oppressed slave to do just that, and so leave the master with one slave less to exploit. On both sides, hatred was based in fear.

actual past' (!) ('Geschichte als Produkt der Wissenschaft, ist nie voll identisch mit jener Geschichte').

36 I think the polarity master/slave is dominant in the text, but as I have said (see above n. 27) other polarities, male/female, educated/uneducated, transect and enrich the comedy of the conflict between master and slaves.

37 Slaves were variously called boy (*puer*, *pais*), whipling (*uerbero*), which was particularly common in Latin comedies, and runaway (*drapeta*). Such derogatory forms of address were matched by the common Greek word for a slave, *andropedon*, which is neuter rather than masculine or feminine in form, and by the practice in Greece and Rome of denying that a slave could have a legal father or a legal spouse. Slaves were effectively rightless, powerless and neutered.

The slaves knew of the discrepancy between private weakness and public show. The comedy in many of the scenes in the *Life of Aesop* turns on Aesop's audacious willingness to show his master up in public. The master wants an intelligent slave, but not that intelligent; he therefore is repeatedly torn between a desire to exploit his slave's intelligence and the desire to flog him into senseless submission. The slave reciprocally is torn between the desire to serve loyally by identification with the master, the hope of freedom, dumb insolence and revenge. The novel explores the whole range of these options; and makes its explorations of conflict between master and slave, seen from the slave's point of view, tolerable by cloaking them in comedy. Only modern historians need to take them seriously.

In the remainder of the story, Aesop works through all the permutations of relationships inside and outside the household. He takes revenge on his mistress by driving a wedge between her and her husband. He demonstrates that the bitch (dog) loves her master more than his wife does, and when the wife, understandably indignant, withdraws in dudgeon to her parents' house, Aesop devises a simple stratagem for getting her back home (*G* 44–50). Here, as elsewhere, the novella is pointedly misogynist. Next Aesop, by outwitting the students, as well as the professor in front of his students, to say nothing of his scholarly friends, illustrates, at least to the reader, the superiority of native intelligence over learned folly (*G* 48, 51–4, *W* 50a, 77b).

The same point, the superiority of simplicity over contrived sophistication, is driven home in the next scene. The master makes a desperate attempt with his wife's help to find a good reason for thrashing Aesop. The term used for thrashing here in the Greek literally means 'teach him a lesson'; but of course, it is the master and the reader who are taught the lesson. Aesop is challenged to find a dinner guest who really can mind his own business. He duly succeeds in finding, not a sophisticated, self-controlled philosopher, but a taciturn peasant, who simply tolerates all the provocations put in his way by his host and hostess, who humiliate only themselves by their offensively unconventional behaviour. In the end, the professor, Xanthus, is inevitably forced to admit defeat to his own slave. But the topsy-turvy world is put partly to rights when Aesop in return reaffirms his loyalty to his master (*G* 64). The real lesson is that good service from a high-quality slave cannot be based on explicit instructions or fear of punishment. It has to be based on trust.

In this new phase of loyal service, Aesop tries to save his master from a drunken folly. He is rebuffed. Even so, with typical cunning resourcefulness, he saves his master from the social death of bankruptcy and from public humiliation in front of his fellow citizens.[38] In return, Aesop asks for his freedom; his master ungratefully refuses. Aesop swears revenge and sets about seducing his mistress.[39] One morning, Aesop stands outside the house holding his cock in his hand 'like a shepherd' to stimulate it and to give himself comfort from the cold. When Xanthus' wife came outside and suddenly sees how long and thick it is, her lust is aroused and she says to Aesop: 'If you do what I want, I'll give you more pleasure than your master gets.' Aesop demurs, like a shy young maiden feigning reluctance, and reminds her of the risks which he runs, if he is found out. But she, in hot pursuit, says: 'Have sex with me ten times and I'll give you a shirt.' He says: 'Swear on it.' She is so excited that she swears the oath. Aesop takes her word. He wants vengeance on his master. He has sex with her nine times. And then he says: 'Lady, I can't do it any more.' She is burning with desire and says: 'If you don't do it ten times, then you'll get nothing from me.' So he tries a tenth time, but fails to satisfy her. He says: 'Give me the shirt or I'll appeal to the master.' She says: 'Do it once more and you can have the shirt.' He cannot, but her petulance hardens his resolve. So naturally,

[38] The humiliation and dishonour of slaves in different slave cultures is a central argument of O. Patterson 1982: 10–13.

[39] The following section also owes something to the Latin version of the *Life of Aesop* (Perry 1952: 127). The episode reminds us that we should not domesticate the Romans to be cosy, idealised mirror-images of our civilised selves. They told and presumably some of them enjoyed stories which are more vulgar than most modern histories of Rome. But should Roman history be as nice as we might like to be ourselves?

when the master comes home, Aesop goes up to him and says: 'Master judge between me and my mistress.' And as is to be expected, he tells Xanthus the whole story, in the form of a fable, which Xanthus the philosopher fails to understand. So the master adjudges Aesop the winner, but, to make the peace, says with the wisdom of Solomon that, when they have been to the marketplace, Aesop should try the tenth time again. So the wife is satisfied and promises once more to give Aesop the shirt (*W* 75–6).

Eventually, to cut a longish story short, Aesop is flogged, saves his master from suicide and finally tricks him into giving him freedom irrevocably in a public assembly. He then outwits the collective citizens, the governor (here called *strategos*, which is a good clue that these versions derive in part from Egypt*) and various kings, but is finally forced to die by an unholy alliance between a jealous god (Apollo), local dignitaries and the free citizens. Aesop, the wise man, like Socrates, is put to death, because he is too free with his thinking.

The murder of the scapegoat is not just a convenient end to the story. It also reflects, I think, the endemic hostility to the clever slave in Roman society. From the masters' point of view, Aesop is too clever by half and finally, like the villain in a western, gets what he richly deserves; the hostility of the god Apollo helps legitimate his execution.

This novel about Aesop is a rebellion of the mind, and none the less potent for that. Like much comedy, it works by the inversion of normality and by the suspension of probability. But the rebellion is soon put down. And in the end, the anti-hero, the dwarf slave, the fall guy, is forced to his death and jumps over a cliff. Society has exacted its revenge and normality has been restored. Indeed the plot may have been only a ruse, just as authoritarian governments, from ancient Sparta to modern China, sometimes encourage displays of initiative, and so foster the hope and the illusion of freedom among the oppressed, all the better subsequently to reinforce repression.

* See above n. 22.

The very tactic of inversion implies its opposite. Disorder implies order.

I shall finish, as I began, by commenting very briefly on method. Inevitably, when I write a piece like this, I wonder what type of history it is, how I can show that I am right, how anyone else can show that I am wrong. I suppose the first point to be made is that the categories right/wrong are not so much irrelevant here as broadly unhelpful when applied to this type of history. So what type of history is it?

In this article I have tried to create an evocative history out of fiction, not by describing a single reality, but by delineating one set of realities out of the many probably available and used by different Roman slaves and masters. I have tried by the conservative method of reading a text and by empathetic imagination to reconstruct how a master and a slave, and by implication how many masters and many slaves, struggled to negotiate their competing interests.[40] The *Life of Aesop* taught me to perceive the relationships between masters and slaves not just as a hierarchy governed by the external structures of law and economy. To be sure, these external structures visibly impinged in the stories I have told and set broad limits to what a master and slave typically did; but they left each master and each slave some degree of freedom to find their own paths within the broad avenues of convention. Each master and slave had some freedom of manoeuvre to act in accord with his or her capacities, opportunities and interests. By implication, I have argued that this type of social history, which deals with what we could call 'the considered experience', deserves more care and attention than it has received – at least when compared with the public time-ordered history of external structures and élite politics. By implication, I think I have also argued that empathy, rhetoric, psychological insight and story-telling are appropriate techniques for a historian trying to recapture not

40 Giddens 1984 has created the concept structuration, awkwardly named, to capture the idea that actors are not simply the passive victims of external pressures, but themselves repeatedly reinterpret conventional social values and mores, and so by their actions reproduce the social order. Action here includes both behaviour and thoughts.

all the evidence, but some of the past. Put less grandly, the *Life of Aesop* has taught me to understand aspects of Roman slavery more fully than I ever had, and it is that experience which in this article I have tried to share.[41]

[41] I should like to thank Mary Beard, Simon Goldhill, John Henderson and Richard Saller for conversations and criticisms, and audiences at Berkeley, Cambridge, Copenhagen, Eton, Los Angeles, Oxford, Princeton and Victoria for indicating where I failed to be persuasive. In some, the text produced the same reactions as its hero, Aesop; out of respect, I have changed it little.

AFTERWORD

NOVEL EVIDENCE FOR ROMAN SLAVERY

CATHARINE EDWARDS

'Novel evidence for Roman slavery', first published in 1993, advertises a new approach, as well as a particular genre of subject matter; the contrast in method with 'Slavery in classical antiquity' first published in 1967 [essay 9], perceptively discussed by Keith Bradley earlier in this volume, is notable. 'Novel evidence' exemplifies Hopkins' fascination with the relationship between social structures and emotional life. Taking as its principal focus the satirical *Life of Aesop* (which has more in common with the ancient novel than with most ancient biographies), H.'s essay pushes the reader to engage with material generally neglected by ancient historians, in order to look at ancient slavery through fresh eyes.[1] The only known biography of a slave to survive from antiquity, this text is made to reveal with disturbing power the routine humiliations of servile life – and to cast light on their broader significance.

Our hero Aesop begins as a slave, hideously ugly and without the power of speech. Rewarded by the goddess Isis (after he shows kindness to her priestess) not merely with speech but with the ability to tell compelling stories, Aesop is sold on to a professor of philosophy, Xanthus, to whom he, despite (or because of?) his status, teaches a variety of important lessons. Eventually he secures his freedom, rescues the island of Samos with his sage advice from falling into the hands of King Croesus

[1] H. criticises, among other scholars, his earlier self – the author of *Conquerors and Slaves* (1978) – for failing to engage with Aesop, though, he notes, a few earlier studies did exploit some aspects of fictional works, for example (in a more positivistic vein), Millar 1981a. The innovative nature of H.'s approach is noted by Bowersock 1994: p. ix and Potter 1999: 20 n. 1. McKeown 2007: especially 97–8, 107–8, 121–2, explores a range of approaches to the use of literary texts to throw light on slavery, taking H.'s essay as his starting point.

of Lydia and goes off to Babylon for further, increasingly fantastical, adventures, before meeting an unfortunate end at the hands of the inhabitants of Delphi. The figure of Aesop first appears in literature and art of the fifth century BC.[2] However the *Life* as we have it (though it is evidently a collective, composite work) apparently dates from first-century AD Egypt.[3]

What is the value of this kind of fiction for history? Alert to the fictive qualities of *all* ancient texts, H. rightly warns, for instance, against the use of anecdotes to authenticate particular actions by individual Romans. Did Vedius Pollio really feed his offending slaves to his pet lampreys – as Seneca claims (*Clem.* 1.18.2, *De ira* 3.40)? How could we ever be sure? Yet this does not mean such stories should be ignored. 'It does not matter so much whether these stories were true. It matters more that they were told and retold' (8 [403]). Stories, whether factual (allegedly) or fictional, can be hugely valuable as a reflection of Roman thinking and feelings. H. urges his reader to consider *why* these stories were told, and the purposes they served.

In his analysis of the collection of anecdotes associated with Aesop as a slave, H. induces us to confront some of the disturbing cultural and psychological consequences for Greco-Roman slave-owners of living cheek by jowl with slaves, to imagine the complex feelings which must have been associated with status dissonance in the context of physical intimacy: Xanthus and Aesop discuss the contents of a chamber pot; Aesop's overliteral interpretation of instructions leaves Xanthus publicly humiliated at the baths. The frictions of daily life bring continual reminders of the master's dependency on another who has good reason to hate him. Legally powerless, a human

[2] The historical Aesop was traditionally thought to have lived in the sixth century BC. Herodotus (2.134) refers to Aesop as the slave of a Samian master who meets an unjust end at the hands of the Delphians.

[3] Leslie Kurke's recent study (2011) offers a rich and perceptive analysis of the traditions associated with Aesop, which follows H.'s lead in 'reading for ideology' (at 25), though her primary focus is the archaic and classical Greek world. There are, as she argues, good reasons for seeing the figure of Aesop as already by the fifth century 'available as a mask or alibi for critique, parody, or cunning resistance' from below (at 12). The work of Pavlos Avlamis (2011) considers Aesop in later urban contexts. Mary Beard (2014: 137–40) analyses the humour of the *Life of Aesop* in relation to Roman traditions of humour more generally.

possession, a slave might nevertheless exploit his knowledge of the household's dirty secrets, of the master's innermost anxieties, to improve his own position, at least temporarily – while always running the risk of experiencing grievous punishment if he went too far. H. persuades us to empathise with both slave and master in this most alien of relationships. This is a compelling invitation to think hard about the full emotional implications of living with slaves.[4]

H. makes a persuasive case for seeing these stories as appealing to masters and slaves alike.[5] A particular virtue of his essay is its emphasis on the multiple meanings of the Aesop anecdotes. For H., these stories explore 'the penumbra of moral ambiguity, about which even the same reader, let alone different readers, will have had ambivalent feelings and reactions' (6–7 [402]). While others (often directly influenced by H.[6]) have subsequently written with perhaps greater subtlety on engagements with slavery in literature from the Roman world, this landmark article illuminates with characteristic bravura the power of story-telling to mediate profound social tensions, to help readers – both free and slave – process the anxieties inevitably aroused by their asymmetric mutual dependency.

The conflict between Aesop and his master is, as H. demonstrates, both 'structural and symptomatic' (18 [414]). H. was alert to the potential of anthropological approaches to offer insights into the social structures of antiquity.[7] Written in the early 1990s, 'Novel evidence' also shows the productive

[4] H.'s insights continue to inform much work on attitudes to slavery in antiquity, for example Toner 2009: 162–84 (= ch. 5: 'Popular resistance').

[5] Richlin's otherwise compelling study of Plautine humour as a channel for slave anger underestimates this aspect of H.'s work: see Richlin 2014: 200 n. 27.

[6] Important here are Fitzgerald 2000 (who cites H. repeatedly); McCarthy 2000; Beard 2002 (who also pays tribute to 'Novel evidence' at 135 n. 99) in her discussion of relations between Cicero and Tiro. A suggestive overview from a cultural history perspective is offered by Joshel 2011, to which should be added a number of recent studies: Alston, Hall and Proffitt 2011; Stewart 2012; Richlin 2014.

[7] H. exhorted ancient historians to aspire to a 'thick description' of ancient practices, with Clifford Geertz's classic account of the Balinese cock-fight a key model (Geertz 1972). See e.g. Hopkins 1983b: 1 n. 1: 'in some respects this chapter is written in direct imitation of that essay'. H.'s early interest in anthropology (especially in relation to kinship structures) was further stimulated during his years at King's College, Cambridge, where his colleagues included Ernest Gellner.

influence of Stallybrass and White's classic literary-theoretical study, *The Politics and Poetics of Transgression* (1986), which focused on exploring the unstable polarity between high and low in early modern representations of the grotesque body and the carnivalesque. For these scholars, representations of the low, disclosing both repugnance and fascination, serve as an arena for the negotiation of unresolved ideological conflict. H., evoking their analysis, characterises the hideous outcast Aesop as 'socially despised, but symbolically central' (21 [418]).[8]

'Novel evidence' highlights some aspects of the sexual politics of slavery and alludes, too, to the gender polarity at work in the *Life of Aesop*. H. offers a brief analysis, for instance, of the stereotypical image of the philosopher's wife as 'sex-crazed slut' and her dreams, later detailed by Aesop, of a beautiful young male slave to serve her sexual pleasure (17–18 [413–14]).[9] Recent work, especially among more 'textualist' ancient historians, has put gender as a category under more sustained interrogation.[10] Revisiting the *Life of Aesop* in the early twenty-first century, we might want to scrutinise more closely the impact of slavery on the sexual and gender dynamics of the family. It is hard not to detect a strongly misogynistic streak in the *Life* (though this is not the only text from the Greco-Roman world to air concerns about élite wives indulging their lusts with slaves).[11]

Xanthus, the philosopher, is devoted to his wife.[12] The *Life* makes much, however, of the wife's interest in acquiring a handsome young male slave for her own pleasure. When Xanthus'

[8] This essay, in its assumption of the mutual permeability of literature and history, also reflects the influence of New Historicism (3 n. 1 [398 n. 1]), whose chief exponent Stephen Greenblatt characteristically exploits the potential of apparently trivial anecdotes to cast a revealing light on the social context which generates them.

[9] *Life of Aesop (Vita G)* 29, 32 (ed. Perry [1952]). On slavery in ancient accounts of dreams, including those in the *Life of Aesop*, see now E. Hall 2011.

[10] On the constructed nature of masculinity (and the relationship between masculinity and social status) in the Roman world, see now Santoro L'Hoir 1992; Edwards 1993: 63–97; Gleason 1995; Walters 1997; Murnaghan and Joshel 1998; Williams 2010.

[11] See e.g. Cic. *Cael.* 31, 36, 38; Juv. 6.76–81; Mart. 8.31; Petron. *Sat.* 69.3, 75.11, 126.5–11; Edwards 1993: 52–4.

[12] Interestingly, there is no reference to his sexual interest in his female slaves – unless this is reflected in his wife's justification for the acquisition of a new male slave (*G* 22). He also has no sexual interest in Aesop (unlike his wife).

wife criticises her husband for buying the ugly Aesop, she is rebuked by Aesop himself for bringing shame on her husband through her lascivious desires; Aesop reprimands her with an apt quotation from Euripides (vastly impressing his new master) (*G* 32). Later, when Xanthus sends Aesop home from a party with a parcel of food 'for her who loves me' (*G* 44), Aesop feeds this to the dog on the grounds that while Xanthus' wife threatens to leave if he does not treat her well (so cannot truly love him) the dog will put up with any number of beatings and still remain faithful (*G* 49–50).[13] Aesop protects Xanthus from the consequences of his own uxoriousness. Some of the most important 'lessons' the slave teaches the philosopher are about how Xanthus can better keep his wife in her place.[14]

Later, Aesop is persuaded to have sex with his mistress (whose initial revulsion at his ugly appearance is overcome when she catches sight of his impressive genitalia). But the *Life* does not suggest he feels any desire for her; he goes along with her proposition, doing his best to satisfy her excessive desires, both to gain the shirt she promises, and to get his own back on his master for failing to reward him justly for his earlier services (*W* 75). In this sense, the *Life* offers (the free male reader) a paradoxically reassuring picture of a slave who (even while having sex with his wife!) still works to protect his master's interests – though, for his own good, he teaches him some lessons along the way. This slave has more than a passing resemblance to the *servus callidus* of Roman comedy – even if, unlike him, Aesop both aspires to freedom and succeeds in winning it.[15]

13 Sympathy for/identification with animals is a key characteristic of the fables associated with Aesop. On the potential of the animal to stand for the slave in relation to Apuleius' *Metamorphoses*, see the (significantly differing) interpretations of Fitzgerald 2000: especially 94–9 and Bradley 2000 (who alludes fleetingly to 'Novel evidence' at 114 n. 9).

14 For the scenario of the slave teaching his master a philosophically informed lesson, compare Hor. *Sat.* 2.7 and the discussion by Fitzgerald 2000: 17–24. For recent work on the more general philosophical resonances of the *Life of Aesop*, see Holzberg 1999 and Kurke 2011: 41–2.

15 On the appeal of the figure of the *servus callidus* to masters as well as slaves, see McCarthy 2000. For contrasting views of the extent to which Plautine comedy is complicit with the perspective of the master, or channels the anger of the slave, see further Stewart 2012 and Richlin 2014.

Xanthus and his household retreat from the limelight in the latter sections of the *Life*, when Aesop finally secures his freedom (having rescued Xanthus from public embarrassment yet again) and goes off to Babylon. The last scene in Xanthus' household is revealing in more ways than one, however. Aesop has been asked to prepare a good dinner by Xanthus, who has invited some of his students. Aesop puts some dishes on the table, then asks his mistress to keep an eye on the food (in case the dog comes in) while he is busy in the kitchen. 'I'll keep a look-out', says she, 'Even my behind has eyes.' Lying on the couch, however, she falls asleep, her back to the table. When Aesop comes in, he leaves her sleeping – but pulls up her robe, exposing her buttocks to view. Xanthus and his students enter the dining room and are filled with shame, seeing her asleep and exposed (*W* 77a).[16] This is a text, I would suggest, with limited appeal to a female audience. While the reader may be invited to sympathise at times with Aesop the trickster hero, at times with Xanthus, or indeed with his students, there is little to make us want to identify with Xanthus' wife (who, unlike his dog, does not even have a name in the story).

In Petronius' *Satyricon,* the freedman Trimalchio, though now liberated and unimaginably wealthy, himself owner of many slaves, declares that he was once the *puer delicatus*, the sexual favourite of his master, and indeed his mistress (*Sat.* 69).[17] Is this, perhaps, another reason (an especially potent one even) for the educated reader to think of him as beyond the pale? Aesop, by contrast, is never treated as an object of male desire and never subjected to sexual penetration. We may speculate that the ancient male reader will, perhaps, have found

[16] A humiliating situation intriguingly resonant with the exposure of Trimalchio's wife Fortunata – to her great embarrassment – by one of his dinner guests (Petron. *Sat.* 67).

[17] As seems to have been the fate of many young male slaves. On the *puer delicatus*, see Dupont and Éloi 2001: 207–12. On sexual relations between masters and slaves more generally, see Kolendo 1981; Fitzgerald 2000: 51–5. A master's masculinity was not, it seems, significantly compromised by using male slaves for sexual pleasure, provided that he took a penetrative role and maintained a degree of control over his appetite (Williams 2010: 20–9).

it less troubling to identify with a slave whose masculinity is, to this extent, uncompromised.[18]

In his essay, H. weaves evocative history out of the flagrantly fictional.[19] The hero of the *Life*, the mischievous trickster Aesop, was himself a celebrated teller of stories. H. was drawn to fiction not only as a source but also as a model for history-writing. Though he was never very interested in the structural rhetoric of history in the manner of Hayden White, H.'s final book, *A World Full of Gods: Pagans, Jews and Christians in the Roman Empire* (1999), offered a series of bold experiments in self-conscious fiction as a way to engage with aspects of history (in this case religious practice and belief) less susceptible to traditional analytic methods. Aesop's relentless provocation of his master also appealed to H.'s more subversive streak. He enjoyed retelling the stories of sexual misbehaviour.[20] He also took pleasure in the fact that the master was a professor whose pedantry functions as a source of amusement to the reader. If humour and lubricious subject matter could have a social and psychological function in the slave-owning societies of the first century AD, they might also have a function in late twentieth-century Western academia – as the always self-reflexive H. was well aware.

[18] Walters' discussion (1997) of the relationship between Roman ideals of manhood and penetrability is illuminating here.

[19] For one critic, 'it probably underestimates – oddly enough – the distorting effects of story-telling, but it is nonetheless remarkable, for it shows the historian thinking his way into the life of a Roman slave' (Harris 2005: 99).

[20] Causing something of a stir when a version of this essay was presented to school-age students at Eton (I am grateful to Ian McAuslan for sharing his recollections of this occasion).

12

CHRISTIAN NUMBER AND ITS IMPLICATIONS*

This paper is an experiment in both method and substance. Substantively, I want to show that, in all probability, there were very few Christians in the Roman world, at least until the end of the second century. I then explore the implications of small number, both absolutely and as a proportion of the empire's total population.[1]

One tentative but radical conclusion is that Christianity was for a century after Jesus' death the intellectual property at any one time of scarcely a few dozen, perhaps rising to two hundred, literate adult males, dispersed throughout the Mediterranean basin. A complementary conclusion (of course, well known in principle, but not often explored for its implications) is that by far the greatest growth in Christian numbers took place in two distinct phases: first, during the third century, when Christians and their leaders were the victims of empire-wide and centrally organised persecutions; and then in the fourth century, after the conversion of Constantine and the alliance of the Church with the Roman state under successive emperors. The tiny size of the early Church and the scale and speed of its later growth each had important implications for Christianity's character and organisation.

My methods are frankly speculative and exploratory. For the moment, I am interested more in competing probabilities, and in their logical implications, than in established or establishable facts. That may not be as problematic as it at first appears. Facts require interpretation. Only the naïve still believe that

* First published in *Journal of Early Christian Studies* 6 (1998) 185–226 (= Hopkins 1998).

[1] A similar tactic is used by Stark 1996: 4–13. I found his book suggestive, helpful and provocative. My debt to his thinking pervades this article, though I differ from him in emphases and interpretation.

facts or 'evidence' are the only, or even the most important, ingredients of history. What matters at least as much is who is writing or reading the history, with what prejudices or questions in mind and how those questions can best be answered. Facts and evidence provide not the framework, but the decoration to those answers.[2]

One of my main objectives in this paper is to show how the same 'facts', differently perceived, generate competing but complementary understandings. For example, leading Christians were highly conscious of their sect's rapid growth and understandably proud of their 'large numbers'. But many Romans, both leaders and ordinary folk, long remained ignorant of and unworried by Christians, probably because of their 'objectively' small numbers and relative social insignificance. Such differential perceptions often occur, then and now. Perhaps these discrepancies were all the more pervasive in a huge and culturally complex empire, with very slow communications. So, the Roman or religious historian has the delicate job of understanding and analysing these networks of complementary but conflicting meanings – and at the same time, the exciting task of finding, inventing or borrowing best methods for constructing critical paths through or round our patchy knowledge of what inevitably remains an alien society.

My first task is to calculate the size and growth in the number of Christians during the first four centuries AD. But before I do that, a word of caution. The term *Christian* is itself more a persuasive than an objective category. By this, I mean that ancient Christian writers may often have counted as 'Christian' a number of people who would not have thought of themselves as Christian or who would not have taken Christianity as their primary self-identifier. As I imagine it, ambiguity of religious identity was particularly pervasive in a polytheistic

2 This opposition between what we could call interpretative or reflexive understanding and critical path analysis is sometimes conceptualised as being between soft history and hard sociology. But history and sociology are each immensely diverse. Besides, I prefer to think of them as complementary, with many overlaps of concept and practice. That said, I should stress that my arguments in this article are predominantly of the 'suppose if'/parametric probability kind.

society, because polytheists were accustomed to seek the help of strange gods occasionally, or in a crisis, or on a wave of fashion. Or put another way, it was only in a limited number of cases or contexts in ancient society that religious affinity was a critical indicator of cultural identity. But monotheistic Christians, whether out of hope or the delusion of enthusiasm, chose gratefully to perceive Jewish or pagan interest as indicative of a commitment, which Christians idealised as exclusive. It is this exclusivism, idealised or practised, which marks Christianity off from most other religious groups in the ancient world.

So ancient Christian leaders (and modern historians) may have chosen to consider as Christian a whole range of ambiguous cases, such as occasional visitors to meetings, pious Jewish godfearers who also attended synagogue or ambivalent hypocrites who continued to participate in pagan sacrifices and saw nothing particularly wrong in the combination of paganism and Christianity, or rich patrons, whose help early Christian communities wanted and whose membership they claimed. In my view then, the term Christian in the early Church is a persuasive, hopeful and often porous category, used optimistically to describe volunteers in a volatile and widely dispersed, though very successful, set of small cult-groups.[3] And of course, as is now commonly agreed, there were always in the early Church a fairly large number of different Christianities, gnostic, docetist, heretical; Epiphanius lists eighty, Augustine eighty-eight, Filastrius of Brescia more than a hundred and fifty varieties of heretic, some of them claiming to be, and thinking of themselves as, the true Christians.[4] Now that I have made this point

[3] I take it for granted that membership of voluntary associations fluctuates; how could it not? For historical illustration, see the excellent analysis of Shakers, Mormons and the Oneida community by Foster 1981.

[4] Epiphanius, *Panarion* ⟨ed. K. Holl, *GCS* 25, Leipzig, 1915, 2nd edn, ed. C.-F. Collatz and M. Bergermann, *GCS* (NF) 10/1–2, Berlin, 2013 (*Haer.* 1–33); K. Holl, *GCS* 31, Leipzig, 1922, 2nd edn, ed. J. Dummer, *GCS*, Berlin, 1980 (*Haer.* 34–64); K. Holl, GCS 37, Leipzig, 1933, 2nd edn, ed. J. Dummer, *GCS*, Berlin, 1985 (*Haer.* 65–80); trans. F. Williams, Nag Hammadi and Manichaean Studies 63 and 79, 2nd edn, Leiden, 2009 and 2013⟩; Augustine, *De haeresibus* ⟨ed. R. Vander Plaetse and C. Beukers, *CCSL* 46, Turnhout, 1969; trans. R. J. Teske, *Arianism and Other Heresies*, The Works of St Augustine: A Translation for the 21st Century

about the porosity and fluidity of Christianity at its periphery and the diversity of its core, in the rest of this paper I shall, for the sake of argument, treat the category 'Christian' as broadly unproblematic.

The Limitations of Induction

And now to number. The conventional method is heavily inductive. Scholars string together snippets of testimony from surviving sources. This has been done with exemplary skill and intelligence by Adolph von Harnack in successive editions of *Die Mission und Ausbreitung des Christentums*.[5] The basic difficulty here is that ancient writers, whether pagan, Jewish or Christian, did not think statistically, and confused cool observation with hope, despair and polemic. As a result, to put it bluntly, most ancient observations about Christian numbers, whether by Christian or pagan authors, should be taken as sentimental opinions or metaphors, excellently expressive of attitudes, but not providing accurate information about numbers.

There would be no profit in going through all the same testimony in detail and *seriatim* again. But even at the risk of going over well-worn ground, let me illustrate the difficulties of interpretation, and my preferred path, by briefly running through five well-known examples. First, St Paul (Romans 1:8), writing before AD 60: 'your faith is proclaimed *in the whole world*'. Secondly, the Acts of the Apostles, written towards the end of the first century, recounts a speech to Paul in Jerusalem by James the brother of Jesus: 'you see, brother, how many *tens of thousands* of the Jews have believed' in Christ (21:20). The RSV translation perceives and gets over the difficulty of exaggeration here, by translating the Greek *muriades* (i.e. tens of thousands) by *thousands*. It is widely accepted that we should

I/18, New York, 1995); Filastrius, *Diversarum hereseon liber* (ed. F. Marx, *CSEL* 38, Vienna, 1898); to say nothing of the other heresiologists, such as Irenaeus and Hippolytus, who celebrated Christian centripetality and diversity.

5 Harnack 1924 is the 4th edition; Harnack 1908 is an English translation of the 2nd edition. This is still an indispensable discussion of the surviving testimony.

not take such statements about the extent and number of early Christians literally.[6]

Next, the famous exchange of letters in 112 between the Roman Emperor Trajan and a provincial governor Pliny, who consulted him about what to do with Christians in northern Asia Minor (Pontus). This is the oldest surviving account by a pagan writer about the practices of early Christians and an official Roman reaction to them.[7] It is, outside the New Testament, the most frequently cited authentication of early Christian success and persecution in their struggle with pagans. The Roman governor, then just in the second year of his governorship, asked the emperor whether all Christians were to be executed, irrespective of age, except of course for the Roman citizens, who – like St Paul – were sent for trial to Rome. If those discovered to be Christian foreswore their faith, should they be pardoned? Pliny himself had devised successive tests for those who claimed not to be, or to be no longer, Christian. They were required to pray to the gods, to burn incense, pour a libation of wine and supplicate a statue of the emperor, specially brought by Pliny into court, along with other statues of gods, and to curse Christ.

Pliny clearly indicated that merely being a Christian was in itself sufficient grounds for execution, though the obstinacy with which some Christians clung to their perverse superstition (*superstitionem prauam et immodicam*) afforded additional justification.[8] But reports by some repentant apostates and

[6] In a similar vein, the British Princess Margaret, returning from a holiday in the West Indies, is reported to have said that she had had a wonderful time: 'Absolutely no one was there.'

[7] Plin. *Ep.* 10.96–7, dated about AD 112. For a glimpse into the enormous literature on this correspondence, see Sherwin-White 1966: 691–712. Tacitus' account of the persecution of Christians under Nero was written a few years later.

[8] de Ste. Croix 1963, a justly famous article, argued that being called a Christian (technically the *nomen christianum*) was a sufficient criminal charge against early Christians. Sherwin-White 1964 argued less convincingly that it was the early Christians' *obstinacy*, mentioned in Pliny's letter (10.96), which ensured their persecution. In my opinion, de Ste. Croix's superior advocacy (see de Ste. Croix 1964) has unjustly obscured the nature of the problem. Both were partly right, though answering different questions. The first answer is to the question: on what formal charge were Christians prosecuted? The second is an incomplete answer to the more general social question: why were Christians prosecuted/condemned?

confessions wrung by torture from two slave women revealed no criminal activities (such as infanticide or incest), only regular prayer meetings and simple meals eaten together.

According to Pliny, the publicity surrounding the cases which he had already tried stimulated further accusations and, in particular, an anonymous accuser's list of alleged Christians. Pliny was uneasy about the implications of further action; so he wrote his letter to the emperor, finishing with a polite suggestion of a way out. Actually, since these are highly edited letters, Pliny may have changed his ending in the light of Trajan's reply. Pliny wrote:

> *many of all ages and ranks, and of both sexes*, have been or will be summoned on a capital charge. The infection of this superstition has *spread not only to the towns but also to the villages and countryside*. But it does seem possible to stop it and put matters right. At any rate it is absolutely certain that *temples previously deserted* have begun to be frequented again. Sacred rites long neglected are being revived and fodder for victims is once again being sold. Previously buyers were very scarce. So I conclude that a *multitude of* men could be reformed, if opportunity were given them for repentance. (*Letters* 10.96, with my italics)

The emperor replied briefly that he would not make a general rule about procedure; Christians should not be sought out, anonymous accusations should not be admitted, those who said and proved that they were not Christian by worshipping the gods were to be set free and those who admitted that they were Christians should be executed. Trajan may have been thinking that anonymous denunciations were what marred the reign of his tyrannical predecessor, Domitian. Trajan's reign was to be more civil. So Rome's central political concerns influenced how even peripheral Christians were treated. But later Christian writers waxed indignant that merely being a Christian was sufficient grounds for execution, whereas real criminals were punished only after they had been proved guilty of crimes committed.[9] They had a good point in equity, but the emperor was being practical.

[9] Justin, *1 Apol.* 3–4; Athenagoras, *Legatio* 1–2 ⟨ed. and trans. W. R. Schoedel, Oxford, 1972⟩; Tert. *Apol.* 1–2.

I read Trajan's letter as recommending an almost benign neglect: don't get too worked up, don't look for trouble, ignore it if you can; confront it if you have to; it's not a serious problem. A Christian apologist would probably interpret Pliny's letter quite differently. Here we have a high-level pagan administrator, disinterestedly reporting that, even in this insignificant corner of northern Asia Minor, Christianity had already succeeded on such a scale that it had been emptying pagan temples and was widespread in towns, villages, countryside. It was already well launched on its voyage to eventual success.

This interpretation is possible, but I think suspect. The sequence – many Christians, everywhere, can be cured, I've taken effective action, once deserted temples now filled, long-neglected rites now restored – seems disproportionate to the care with which Pliny claimed to have proceeded at the initial trials (more care, less throughput) and the subsequent single anonymous set of accusations described in the first part of Pliny's letter; pagan rites neglected seems more a literary cliché than precise reporting; Paul, according to the notoriously unreliable Acts (19:23–7), had exactly the same impact in the large city of Ephesus in the mid-fifties. If the temples were deserted (and in a polytheistic culture, temples have, and claim, fluctuating fortunes), it was probably not because of Christianity, nor were they recently frequented just because Pliny's show trials had made new Christians lose their faith. In short, I suspect (but it is a matter of judgement) that Pliny's Christians were numbered in dozens rather than in hundreds. And even if his account is more accurate than I think, the situation was not typical. Pagan temples elsewhere in the Roman empire flourished, or fluctuated in their popularity, for the next two centuries. In my view, Pliny's account is either inaccurate and/or describing something atypical.

Finally, three brief quotations from somewhat later Christian writers, Justin, Tertullian and Origen – I cite them to illustrate an important point of method. Since some writers lie consciously, others unconsciously mislead, some are factually correct and others are misinformed, the criteria of usefulness, acceptance or rejection cannot be the source itself, but must be the nature of the problem at issue and the critical intelligence and relevant knowledge, in the light of which modern historians understand and interpret the sources.[10] History should not be, *pace* the practice or presenting style of many colleagues, an amalgam of sources. Or perhaps rather, it depends what you want, a pre-packed meal from a factory (*Listenwissenschaft*) or a crafted confection from a chef. The ingredients are partly the same, the results significantly different.

Justin, in the middle of the second century, wrote that 'more Christians were ex-pagans than ex-Jews' (*First Apology* 53), and I think (for reasons to be discussed) that during his lifetime this had probably come to be true, though he cannot have had enough information to know so accurately. Tertullian in the beginning of the third century wrote of Christians: 'In spite of *our huge numbers, almost a majority in every city*, we conduct our lives in silence and modesty' (*To Scapula* 2.10). I doubt if either claim can have been true; and I doubt if anyone ever accused Tertullian of modesty. Origen, in the middle of the third century, wrote: 'It is obvious that in the beginning Christians were small in number' (*Against Celsus* 3.10).[*] But even a hundred passages of this quality do not allow us to trace the pattern of Christianity's growth with any confidence.

Harnack made the best possible use of such impressionistic sources. He was very reluctant to plumb for a single overall estimate of the number of Christians in the Roman empire as a whole. He thought that at the beginning of the fourth century, on the eve of the Constantinian revolution, the density of Christianity varied so much between different provinces as to make an overall estimate useless. In Asia Minor, Harnack reckoned that almost half the population was Christian, while the proportion of Christians, for example, in France or Germany was insubstantial or negligible. But then, in a footnote, he surrendered and declared that between 250 and 312,

[10] See R. G. Collingwood's brilliant autobiography (1939: 79–81) for a long-unheeded but still all too relevant criticism of ancient history's 'scissors-and-paste men' and the criteria for using evidence.

[*] ⟨Tert. *Scap.*, ed. V. Bulhart, *CSEL* 76, Vienna, 1957; Origen, *C. Cels.*, ed. M. Marcovich, *Vigiliae Christianae* supplement 54, Leiden, 2001.⟩

the Christian population probably increased from 7 to 10 per cent of the empire's total population.[11] But any such estimate, however well informed, can inevitably be only that, on a guess.

Seduction by Probability

Other scholars have not been so cautious as Harnack, but have generally more or less followed his lead. Their general opinions seem to hover around a gross estimate that in 300 about 10 per cent of the total population of the Roman empire was Christian.[12] With Harnack's qualification about variation in mind, let's tentatively, and without any commitment as to its truth, take this overall estimate (that in 300, 10 per cent of the population of the Roman empire, i.e. roughly 6 million people, were Christian) as a benchmark and see where it leads us. We can call it arguing by parametric probability, that is, by setting an arbitrary boundary against which to test other conclusions.[13] It is as though we set about estimating the weight of an elephant by first imagining it to be a solid cube.

We have an end point. Now we need a beginning. It is obvious that Christianity began small. And Origen says so (*Against Celsus* 3.10)! Let us make an arbitrary estimate that in AD 40 about one thousand people were Christians[14] – though of course at this stage of Christian evolution it is probable that they would have envisaged themselves as Jews who also believed in the divinity of Jesus. Actually, not a lot hangs on the exact numbers either at the beginning or the end, as will become clear when we consider figure 12.1 and table 12.1. Our primary purpose overall in this article is to think through the

[11] Harnack 1924: II 946–58, 1908: II 324–37. The influential footnote which contains a confusing misprint is found at II 806 and II 248, respectively.

[12] See Stark 1996: 6 for several modern estimates.

[13] On the tactics of model-construction in Roman history, see Hopkins 1995–6: 41–4.

[14] Following Stark 1996: 5.

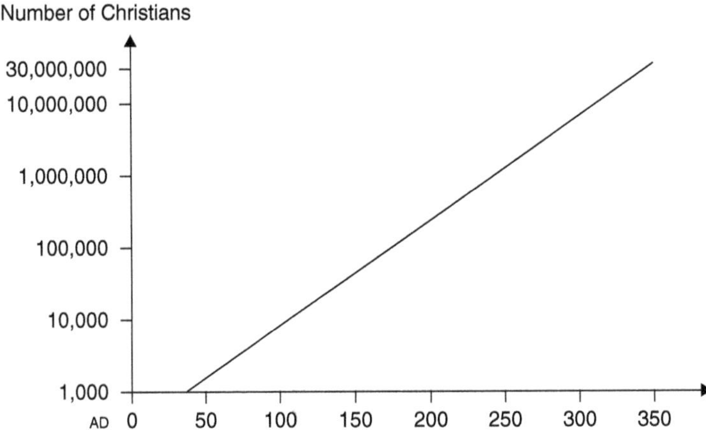

Figure 12.1. A speculative graph showing the growth of Christianity at a constant growth rate from AD 40–350 (3.35 per cent per annum) (semi-log scale).

implications of Christian growth, not to measure it precisely (that is impossible), nor even to explain it.[15]

Figure 12.1 sets out a constant growth line implied by simple intrapolation between our starting number, 1,000 Christians in AD 40, and our end number, 6 million Christians in AD 300. I have plotted the growth in Christian numbers on a semi-log scale, because that allows us to envisage huge growth from 1,000 to 6 million at a glance.[16] But to avoid misunderstanding, let me stress that my initial acceptance of these estimates is only a heuristic device. Initial acceptance implies no final commitment to the estimates' truth. To help matters along, I have also set out the implications of this consistent growth-line, by reading across the graph to specify the

[15] It is quite possible to think of implications without knowing the exact size of the Christian population. But that is why so many of my arguments here have the form 'if x then y' or 'the more x the more (or less) probable y is'. For example, if Christians usually met in private houses and if regular attendance was a condition of being Christian, then the more Christians there were, the more house cult-groups there were.

[16] This graph is a re-expression of the illustrative figures given by Stark 1996: 7 table 1.1. One advantage of a graph is that it is easy to see the crudity of the linear assumption and to read off interstitial numbers.

Table 12.1. *Some interstitial numbers of Christians, AD 40 to 178.*

AD 40	1,000	AD 200	210,000
AD 50	1,400	AD 246	1,000,000
AD 100	7,400	AD 250	1,100,000
AD 109	10,000	AD 300	6,000,000
AD 150	40,000	AD 315	10,000,000
AD 178	100,000	AD 350	32,000,000

Christian numbers implied at successive intervals between AD 50 and 350 (table 12.1).[17]

Of course, in reality, Christian membership probably fluctuated. It probably grew faster in some periods, while in others, for example, during persecutions, it even reduced in numbers.[18] In reality, growth was probably not consistent. We can easily imagine three competing probabilities:

(a) perhaps in the beginning growth was faster and then slower later (i.e. above the first part of the line in figure 12.1); or
(b) perhaps it was slower at the beginning and even faster later (below the first part of the line in figure 12.1); or
(c) perhaps growth fluctuated at different periods (above and below the line in figure 12.1). Drawing a single path of consistent growth is merely an intellectual economy in the face of competing probabilities and in the absence of reliable data.

My general procedure here is obviously experimental. Instead of being inductive, moving from the evidence to a conclusion, I start with a parametric pattern, which is like a limiting case, against which the fragments of evidence can be tested, or around which they can be fitted. I then wonder what the implications of this parametric pattern are for understanding early Christianity. I hope you will be persuaded that this experimental and unashamedly speculative method is a useful

[17] These are rounded up versions of the precise numbers given by Stark 1996: 7 table 1.1 with a couple of additions. Note: they are guesstimates, not facts.

[18] See, e.g., on mass desertions from Christianity in the persecutions under Decius, Cyprian, *De lapsis* 7–9 (ed. M. Bévenot, *CCSL* 3, Turnhout, 1972 = *SC* 547, Paris, 2012) and Dionysius of Alexandria in Eus. *HE* 6.41.11–12; on sacrifice by the bishop of Smyrna, see *Acta Pionii* 15 (ed. and trans. H. Musurillo, *The Acts of the Christian Martyrs*, Oxford, 1972). Even so, the overall number of Christians increased in the same general period.

supplement to, though of course not a replacement for, common inductive practices. And it will not have escaped you that I am behaving rather like an early Christian in pagan society, trying to upset fellow scholars by non-conformity.

But what is the use of so speculative a line, so arbitrarily drawn? What is its epistemological status? These questions are completely reasonable. My answer is that the straight line in figure 12.1 is like a set of goal posts in a game of football; arbitrarily placed, but good to measure the game against. So let's play. Five gambits deserve attention: (1) absolute numbers and proportions over time, (2) community numbers and size, (3) distribution by sex and age, (4) literacy and (5) comparison with Jews. Let us deal with each in turn.

Absolute Numbers, Proportions and Persecutions

According to figure 12.1, in AD 100, there were only about 7,000 or so Christians, equal to barely 0.01 per cent of the empire's population (roughly say 60 million). And in 200, there were only just over 200,000 Christians, barely 0.35 per cent of the total population.[19] Let me stress once again that these are not truth statements; they are crude probabilities attached to very rough orders of magnitude. They are numerical metaphors, good for thinking about Christians with.

Such estimates imply that, practically speaking, for the whole of this period, Christians were statistically insignificant. Of course, an objector might say, numbers by themselves do not necessarily equate with importance. Perhaps not, but the number of members in a religious movement is one measure of its importance; or rather it is one factor in the discrepancy between self-importance and importance as perceived by

[19] Cf. Stark 1996: 7 table 1.1. It's worth emphasising that no one knows the size of the population of the Roman empire. Estimates vary, though most scholars by convention use 50–60 million as plausible middling figures, following in the track of Beloch 1886: 507, who estimated the total population in AD 14 as 54 million. For a modern view, see Frier in the *Cambridge Ancient History*, vol. 11 (2nd edn) ⟨= Frier 2000⟩. He argues plausibly that the population of the Roman empire grew in the first and second centuries AD. If so, then all my proportional arguments hold *a fortiori*.

others. Even if we accommodate all Christians in 200 in the urban population of the central and eastern Mediterranean (a very strong and probably incorrect assumption), they still constituted only about one-thirtieth of the probable urban and metropolitan population.[20]

The statistical insignificance of Christians, in relation to the rest of the empire's population, allows us to complement and correct the perspective of surviving Christian writers. Christians themselves could properly see that their religion was expanding successfully and very fast. And they sometimes, as we have seen, made exaggerated and self-inflating claims to that effect.[21] But their absolute numbers long remained small. The same facts, differently perceived, generated variant accounts. From an official, upper-class Roman point of view, Christians did not matter, except as occasional individual or local nuisances, or as scapegoats, sacrificed to placate unruly crowds.[22] For example, Herodian's political history of the Roman empire, written in the early third century and covering the period from 180 to 238, does not mention Christians at all. From a Roman government point of view, it was not worthwhile persecuting Christians systematically. And from a Jewish

[20] This calculation is based on a very rough estimate. Let us say that the population of the eastern half of the Roman empire, more urbanised than the West, was 35 million out of the 60 million total population. Let us say that the urbanised population was 15 per cent or 5.25 million, which includes the large cities of Antioch and Alexandria. And as our present problem is the visibility of Christians in towns and cities, we should include Carthage and Rome in our calculations. So in total, we have to reckon say 220,000 Christians in AD 200 as a proportion of (urbanites in the eastern Mediterranean, plus Rome and Carthage) say 6.4 million = 3.4 per cent. But according to Dionysius of Alexandria in Eus. *HE* 7.24.6, Christianity did spread to villages in Egypt.

[21] E.g. 2 *Clement* 2.3 ⟨ed. and trans. C. Tuckett, Oxford, 2012, with commentary at 142–4⟩ states that Christians were more numerous than Jews (but see below [465–8]); Tertullian claims that Christianity has spread widely geographically and socially upwards: 'we have filled cities … villages, towns … town councils, palace, senate, forum, leaving only the temples to you' (*Apol.* 37.4).

[22] It is obviously risky to use Christian apologetics or martyr acts to portray relations between Roman provincial governors and Christian leaders, since what we have are Christian self-representations, not official accounts of trials. For the considerable difference between surviving court records of trials from Roman Egypt and martyr acts, see the convincing account by Bisbee 1988: especially 33–64. That said, Roman irritation with, rather than anger against, Christians comes out e.g. in Tert. *Scap.* 4–5.

perspective, as we shall see in a moment, Christians were only a minor annoyance.

But what of Christian stories about being persecuted, repeatedly and from the earliest days, by Romans, Jews and pagans, everywhere?[23] As I see it, the image of persistent persecution which Christians manufactured for themselves was more a mode of self-representation or a tactic of self-unification than an objective description of reality. I am not saying that persecutions did not happen. Sure they did, occasionally and sporadically. And the fear of persecution probably sat like a huge cloud over Christian prayer meetings. It may even have kept many Christians from openly professing their faith. But persecutions were also useful. Fear of them pulled Christians together, sorted the sheep from the goats, decreased the risk of insincere hangers-on and helped enthuse the survivors that being a Christian was really worthwhile. Being persecuted was collective proof of Christian radicality and an instrument of togetherness. Besides, martyrdom was a special, Christian type of heroism. Mostly, you didn't actually have to die for your faith, though you could parade your willingness – if the need arose. But you had to admire those who, like Christ, were willing to, or had died, for their faith.[24]

So the traditional question: 'Why were the Christians persecuted?' with all its implications of unjust repression and eventual triumph, should be rephrased: 'Why were the Christians persecuted so little and so late?' Our answer should recognise

[23] On persecutions, see the full but credulous account by Frend 1965 and, with flair, Droge and Tabor 1992. On Jews as an alleged source of persecution, see e.g. Justin, *Dialogus cum Tryphone* 16.4 ⟨ed. P. Bobichon, Paradosis 47, 2 vols, Fribourg, 2003⟩: 'You are powerless to lay hands on us, because of our overlords [the Romans], but you have done so whenever the opportunity arose', and Tertullian: 'the synagogues of the Jews are the cause of our persecution' (*Scorpiace* 10) ⟨ed. A. Reifferscheid and G. Wissowa, *CSEL* 20, Vienna, 1890 = *CCSL* 2, Turnhout, 1954⟩.

[24] Individual martyrs became a special Christian type of hero, with power, so some believed, to forgive sins, even in this world (much to the controlled indignation of bishop Cyprian, *Ep.* 15–20 ⟨ed. S. Deléani, Collection des Études augustiniennes, Série Antiquité 182, Paris, 2007⟩). Contrarily, though it was not the winning position, some Christians thought that voluntary martyrdom was as futile as the suicide of an Indian fakir and that real martyrdom was to be sought in daily life (Clem. Al. *Strom.* 4.4.17 ⟨ed. A. van den Hoek and trans. C. Mondésert, *SC* 463, Paris, 2001⟩, 2.20.104 ⟨ed. C. Mondésert, *SC* 38, Paris, 1954⟩).

that, for most of the first three centuries AD, Christians were protected from persistent persecution, both by the Roman government's failure to perceive that Christianity, mattered and by its punctilious legalism, which prohibited anonymous denunciation through the courts. At a formal level, Roman legalism protected Christianity against large-scale persecution for well over a century. Informally, in unofficial assaults and mass disturbances, Christians were persecuted, but, as I have said, only occasionally and sporadically. So too were Jews.[25]

In these unofficial attacks, it was, I suspect, pagan perception of Christians' behaviour as idiosyncratic (their refusal to attend traditional public festivals, their private meetings, their rigid morality and secret gestures), more than their beliefs, which provoked repression.[26] In a publicly committed, polytheistic society, Christians seemed, to those who noticed them, a new-fangled and oddball group of monotheists. Besides, Christianity could expand so fast only by winning adherents from old-established practices/gods and by drawing attention to how very different Christians were from everybody else.[27] Small wonder if this combination of ostentatious difference and successful proselytism provoked occasional outbursts of hostility.

In the first two centuries after Jesus' death, Christians needed Roman persecutors, or at least stories about Roman persecutors, rather more than Romans saw the need to persecute Christians. Christianity survived and prospered, partly

[25] By modern scholarly convention, Jews rebelled, but Christians were persecuted. Statistically, Jews for a long time had more to complain about. For oppression in Antioch, see Joseph. *BJ* 7.46–62, 103–4; in Alexandria, Philo, *In Flacc.* 53–96. On the long anti-Jewish prejudice in Alexandria, see Musurillo 1954.

[26] For example, repeatedly making the sign of the cross on the forehead and not wearing or decorating doorposts with wreaths during festivals (in so far as Christians actually behaved openly as their leaders told them) must have set them apart (Tert. *De corona* 3, 10) ⟨ed. E. Kroymann, *CSEL* 70, Vienna, 1942 = *CCSL* 2, Turnhout, 1954⟩.

[27] Christian apologists in the second and third centuries from Justin to Minucius Felix and Origen) preserve Christian versions of the (powerful) attacks which pagans made against them. It would be foolish to assume that these rationalised arguments were the only criticisms popularly made against the Christians. For all their overt appearance as documents addressed to emperors and educated pagans, it would take a very patient pagan to read them. They are aimed at Christians, and celebrate Christian difference.

because of its intrinsic virtues, but partly also because Roman persecutions allowed Christians to nurture a sense of danger and victimisation, without there ever having been a real danger of collective extirpation. Christianity was also often protected by Roman officials' insistence on a legalism which effectively shielded Christians against arbitrary prosecutions. And that protectivism itself persisted, because the Roman government long failed to realise that it needed to protect itself against religious subversion as much as, or more than, against barbarian invasions. The religious frontier was largely undefended, because well organised attacks along it were unexpected.

But it is only when we play this game of numbers and proportions that we see most clearly that the third century was the critical period of Christian growth. According to the figures tentatively projected in figure 12.1, Christian numbers grew in the third century from about 200,000 to over 6 million. Or put another way, it was only in the third century that Christianity gained the prominence that made it worthwhile persecuting on an empire-wide scale. But by the time the Roman government finally began to realise that Christianity posed a significant threat and started systematic persecution of Christian leaders and their property (in 250–1 under Decius, in 257–60 under Valerian, after 303 under Diocletian), Christianity was too embedded to be stamped out easily. And it was particularly in this period of persecutions, in spite of temporary losses, that Christianity grew fastest in absolute terms. In other words, in terms of number, persecution was good for Christianity.

Communities: Number, Size and Dispersion

First a word of caution, 'community', like the term 'Christian', is a persuasive and porous category. In modern histories of the early Church, *community* is often used as a category of expansion and idealism. For example, when we have a text, it is understandably tempting to assume that the author and his immediate audience constituted a 'community'. Hence the commonly touted concept of Pauline communities, Johannine communities, Gnostic communities; each text is assumed to have had a matching set of the faithful, who formed solidary communities, and these communities putatively used particular texts as their foundation or charter myths.

In fact, we have very little information about how early Christian followers organised themselves or how these so-called communities used early Christian writings. We can argue quite plausibly that successive changes in reporting Jesus stories in the gospel texts (e.g. from Mark to Matthew/Luke to John) reflected the new and varying needs/interests of successive communities. But plausibility does not equal truth. All we have are the texts. The invention of communities is a defensible, but abusable, tactic of inflating the text into social history.

But there is more to it than that – early Christian communities are often imaged in modern pious thought, and in much scholarly literature, as models for modern believers. In the beginning, the myth seems to go, early Christians faithfully followed the prescriptions of Jesus and the apostles; the earliest Christian communities were close-knit, pious, mutually supportive and devoted; in short, the earliest Christians were 'true Christians'. And, of course, early Christian writers themselves idealised the community/ies (*koinonia*, *ekklesia*) of Christians. The concept community plays a crucial role in the self-representations of early Christian collectivities.

Needless to say, practice diverged from the ideal, even if ideals of community played a significant role in influencing practice. Paul's letters to the Corinthians, for example, amply indicate the internal tensions which affected and divided groups of early Christians.[28] Inevitably, some early communities were riven by internal differences (social and doctrinal) and partly so, exactly because they contained fervent idealists. Some individuals thought that they had already been saved, so that they were free from ethical strictures. Others differed in their practice, commitment and teachings. Some teachers

[28] On the internal divisions within Paul's group at Corinth (1 Cor. 11.17–34), see e.g. Theißen 1982: 145–74.

even were greedy and exploitative.[29] In sum, the concept community is used to disguise these internal divisions and shifting boundaries and to project the legitimacy and effectiveness of Christianity's exclusive claims over its members, as though all early Christians must have been full members of a community of Christians.

But the concept still has its uses. Let us proceed by trying to estimate how many Christian communities there were. The normal procedure is of course inductive. Harnack listed as the location of a Christian community any place mentioned in early Christian texts as having had Christians. This procedure yields estimates of about fifty Christian communities in AD 100 and about one hundred Christian communities in 180. But this inductive procedure is suspect. Such listings are liable to be seriously incomplete, as Harnack himself fully realised.[30] Surviving sources are only a small fraction of what was once written.

Once again we can play with probabilities in a scissor argument. As a heuristic device, without commitment to its truth, let us assume that these fifty Christian communities wrote/received on average two letters per year during the period 50–150. That is surely a low level of inter-community correspondence; less and there was little hope of securing inter-community coherence; more, then my argument holds *a fortiori*. But if the average inter-community correspondence was only two letters per year, then in this period 10,000 letters were written, of which barely fifty survive. I do this calculation, *exempli causa*, merely to illustrate how hazardous conventional inductive procedures are when scholars so carefully reconstruct church history only from surviving sources. Or put another way, those who think, as I do, that the earliest Christian communities corresponded about their religion quite frequently, i.e. more than twice a year

29 For warnings against false teachers, who want to stay in a house cult-group for more than three days without working and who ask for money as well as food, see *Didache* 11–12. The notion of false prophets haunts the dispersed early Christian groups. How can they tell?

30 Harnack 1924: II 618–28, 1908: II 89–96. See also Aharoni and Avi-Yonah 1977: 166–7.

on average, must also recognise the appalling unrepresentativeness of their sources and the limitations of induction.

My own guess is that in 100 and 180 respectively, there were significantly more than the fifty/hundred Christian communities listed by Harnack. I have two principal reasons for increasing his numbers. First, I see no reason in principle why Christian success was limited to those towns mentioned in the scarce surviving sources. Secondly, early Christian groups (through lack of resources and fear of persecution) typically met in private houses.[31] So in larger towns, there were probably several distinct Christian gatherings, by which I mean groups of Christians who regularly worshipped together, but who may or may not have thought of themselves as linked with all other local or regional Christian groups.

I prefer to think of these early Christian nodules as 'house cult-groups', rather than as communities. The term captures the image of enthusiasm, radicality and fear of persecution which perhaps characterised some early Christian gatherings. Ideally, of course, these house cult-groups may have been loosely coordinated, by cooperation or hierarchically under a priest or bishop, into a community. However, I suspect that in the conditions of early Christianity, close coordination of dispersed house cult-groups would have been difficult to achieve. The different house cult-groups within each town were more likely to reflect Christian diversity than homogeneity. Some Jewish evidence, though not strictly comparable, illustrates the dispersion of the faithful among groups inside towns. In Sepphoris and Tiberias, each of them middle-size Palestinian towns, there were eighteen and thirteen synagogues respectively.[32] A principle is easily deducible: the larger the number of

[31] White 1990: especially 105–6; he notes that there were in Paul's time six houses in Corinth used for meetings by Christians.

[32] Jerusalem Talmud, *Kilayim* 9.4, 32b, *Shabbat* 6, 8a (for Sepphoris; Babylonian Talmud, *Berakhot* 8a for Tiberias; and on these texts see, usefully, S. S. Miller 2005). These passages may reflect fourth-century, not second-century, conditions; but for my current purposes that does not matter. The principle I want to establish is that if attendance was a condition of membership in a religion, then the larger the town, the more meeting places you needed, even for a licit religion, *a fortiori* for an illicit one.

Christians within any town and the larger the town, the greater the probable number of house cult-groups.

How big were these communities or house cult-groups? We do not know. So, once again, I think the most sensible procedure is to play probabilities with a scissor argument. Three preliminary considerations seem important. First, we should take into account the diversity of primitive Christianity, its incapacity to control fragmentation and the probability that there were several separate house cult-groups in larger towns. Secondly, the larger the community in each town, the more separate house cult-groups there probably were, since, at least up to the end of the second century, Christians usually met in private houses and not in dedicated, stand-apart religious buildings. Thirdly, above a certain size (perhaps a few dozen), the larger the house cult-group, the less possible it was for all members to meet together regularly in a private house. Larger size involved a diminution of attendance or commitment.

If we follow Harnack, then in 100, there were about fifty Christian communities; each Christian community therefore (according to the numbers set out in figure 12.1), had a membership on average of one hundred and forty people (7,000/50 = 140).[33] But if we follow the arguments outlined above, there were significantly more than fifty communities and/or house cult-groups. I suspect that even by 100, there were probably more than one hundred Christian house cult-groups dispersed over the eastern Mediterranean basin, with an average size of less than seventy people. This reconstruction surely fits better with the idea of early Christian radical commitment and the probable size of houses used by a non-élite sect (see below).

Let us move ahead in time. By 180, according to Harnack, there were a hundred or so Christian communities recorded in surviving sources.[34] As before, it seems reasonable to think, because of the accidents of loss and survival in the sources, that this is an underestimate; and if only because of

[33] Harnack 1924: II 621–6, 1908: II 89–94. I may seem to be being a bit unfair to Harnack, since his agenda was to establish what can be known/proved about Christian expansion. The trouble is that positivist followers translate *known* into *all*.

[34] Harnack 1924: II 626–8, 1908: II 94–6.

intermittent persecutions, meetings were still held in houses or house-churches, so that there were many more house cult-groups than communities. And of course, by this time there was more heaping in the density of Christian membership. In the huge cities of Rome and Alexandria, and in Antioch and Carthage, each with a population of above 100,000, Christian communities were probably substantial. Each metropolitan church (considered as a single collective or community) probably had several (e.g. five to ten) thousand members, enough to support a hierarchy of professional and dependent clergy and a visible programme of support for the poor.[35] But in many other towns, Christian communities and their associated house cult-groups must have remained still quite small. The house cult-group, even towards the end of the second century, was still the norm.

We could, as before, simply and arbitrarily double Harnack's estimate and say that there were Christian communities (and many more house cult-groups) in say 200 towns, with an average membership of 500 people (figure 12.1: 100,000/200 = 500). But according to this reconstruction, the vast majority of the 2,000-odd cities of the Roman empire, 1,800 out of 2,000, had no Christian community at all.[36] If the historical reconstructor has to choose between, on the one hand, relative concentration and larger average community size and, on the other hand, dispersed smallness, with a handful of exceptionally large metropolitan communities, I myself favour the second choice. As I see it, Christianity towards the end of the second century was more pervasive; i.e. it had more small cells in more towns, say 200–400 of the 2,000 towns in the Roman empire. This

[35] According to Eusebius (*HE* 6.43.11 ⟨quoting a letter of Cornelius, bishop of Rome⟩), the Church at Rome in AD 251 supported forty-six priests, over a hundred lesser clergy and employees, plus 1,500 widows and beggars. Harnack (1924: II 806, 1908: II 247–8) guessed that there needed to be at least 30,000 Christians at Rome to support that number of clergy and dependants.

[36] This is and can be only a very rough order of magnitude. There are two problems, our ignorance and the arbitrariness of the boundary which divides a town from a village, not notionally (town council, baths, acknowledged status), but in fact. All that said, I think 2,000 is about right. For the testimony on which this is based, see A. H. M. Jones 1964: II 712–18.

dispersion was a significant factor in the character of early Christianity, both because it considerably increased the difficulties of controlling diversity, but at the same time stimulated attempts among Christian leaders to control it.

Christianity was still probably concentrated in towns in the central and eastern Mediterranean basin, although there were some Christian communities in southern Gaul. And by this period, Christianity had begun to attract some, though very limited numbers, from among influential provincial supporters and contributors, including knights and town councillors. It now had some well educated members and sponsors (but see below [475–65]). Its liability to sporadic persecution, its general shortage of funds and the recurrent need to keep discreetly quiet about its activities kept its normal cell size still within the bounds of house meetings. It seems no accident therefore that the earliest dated church building to survive comes from the mid-third century and that very few ostensibly Christian burial inscriptions date from the third century or earlier.[37] Christianity in the early third century still had the aroma of a once secret society. In the third and fourth centuries, as Christianity expanded, Christians came more out into the open, built large churches, but inevitably many of them became actually, though not ideally, more like other Romans.[38]

Age, Sex and the Role of Women

According to modern historical demographers, ancient populations were usually made up, roughly speaking, of 30 per cent adult males, 40 per cent adult females and 30 per cent children

[37] On the relatively late coming out of Christians (at the end of the second, early third century), see e.g. Lampe 1989: 13–26. On the earliest, archaeologically known church, an unobtrusive, mud-brick refurbished house, no longer used as a residence, built in about 230, converted to church use about ten years before its destruction in 256 (its assembly hall held sixty-five to seventy-five people), see Kraeling 1967: especially 3, 19, 37–9.

[38] On the building of large churches, see Porphyry (died c.305) cited by Macarius Magnes, *Apocriticus* 4.21b.5 ⟨ed. and trans. R. Goulet, *Macarios de Magnésie. Le Monogénès*, 2 vols, Paris, 2003⟩.

of both sexes under age 17.[39] Mortality was particularly high among infants and children under 5, but by modern standards continued to be very high in adult populations. For example, roughly speaking, half of those surviving to the age of 15 died by the age of 50. Sickness and death, and presumably the fear of death, were pervasive. Hence, crudely speaking, the significance and appeal of immortality.

These basic figures are fundamental for understanding the structure and growth of early Christian communities and house cult-groups. So, for example, if by AD 100 there were one hundred Christian communities, then the average community consisted of seventy people (figure 12.1: 7000/100 = 70) with perhaps twenty adult males, twenty adult females (or twenty families) and thirty children. Of course, early Christian house cult-groups were probably more numerous, and correspondingly smaller (perhaps averaging a dozen or so families?), depending as they did on the sizes of houses owned by Christians and available for meetings.

But some ancient critics of Christianity and modern scholars have argued that women were particularly prone to conversion to Christianity; and it is clear from the earliest Christian writings that women played an important role in primitive Christian house cult-groups.[40] Of course, it is arguable that women, marginalised in a male-dominated Roman society, were more likely to join a marginal religion, such as Christianity, as a covert form of rebellion. But to my eyes,

[39] See Coale and Demeny 1966: 4 table Model West, level 3, stationary population. To be unnecessarily precise, children aged 0–17 constituted 31.9 per cent of the total population, adult males 28.6 per cent and adult females 39.5 per cent. Mortality of adult females was lower than of males. The sex ratio from Roman Egyptian census returns is in the region of 108:100, m.:f.; see Bagnall and Frier 1994: 95.

[40] On the appeal of Christianity to women and children, see Celsus in Origen, *C. Cels.* 3.55; on the preponderance of women among Christians, see *C. Ilib.* (*Council of Elvira*) canon 15, and for a collection of testimony, Harnack 1924: II 589–611; 1908: II 64–84. Stark 1996: 95–128 in his chapter on Christian women indicates that, in modern proselytising religious movements, women are primary converts. But in treating ancient evidence, I think he too readily equates prescription with performance, and single instances with general patterns of behaviour. See also Bremmer 1989; the answer must surely be that before the fourth century, it did not attract many (proportionately) and the stress on their membership which we find in Christian sources arises precisely from women's social visibility and rarity.

the homology (marginal women, marginal religion) seems more rhetorical than descriptive. And ancient pagan criticisms that Christianity was particularly attractive to women and slaves were a literary cliché, expressing a depreciatory attitude towards women and Christianity more than cool observation.

Modern evidence on conversion to religious cults also suggests that young adults (sometimes of both sexes, sometimes females primarily, with males as secondary converts through the female converts) are prime customers for conversion, through personal social contacts. It seems likely that the pattern of religious recruitment to Christianity in the Roman empire was similar, if only because young adults could and sometimes did feel they wanted to break away from what they perceived as repressive familial norms. So in a rapidly growing cult, there may be a tendency to over-recruit young adults (and arguably more women than men).[41]

But a religion growing as fast as Christianity is supposed to have done (according to figure 12.1, 3.4 per cent compound increase per year) needed both men and women. Demographically, the new religion can be understood as being like a colony, which receives lots of young immigrants. It benefits from the fresh converts' higher (age-specific) fertility, compared with the general population, and providing that the converts' children themselves continue as Christians, this age imbalance among Christians may account for some (though it

[41] See Iannaccone 1990: 301–2; Stark 1996 15–21. In my view, preferential female recruitment in Roman conditions was probably more a rhetorical figment than a statement of general fact. And its impact was less in an ancient society, suffering high mortality, than it would be in a modern society, enjoying lower mortality. In the Roman world, if, *exempli causa*, all recruitment was among young adults, of whom 75 per cent were female and prior to the birth of their first surviving child, and 25 per cent male at a similar age, then, if all the children of Christians became Christian, the sex ratio in the total body of Christians, growing at a constant 3.4 per cent per year, would be 40 per cent male, 60 per cent female (Stark 1996: 101, miscalculated by omitting children). But among adults, because of the high constant rate of recruitment, the ratio would be 33 per cent male, 67 per cent female. In a typical community, therefore, in AD 100 there would be only thirteen adult males and twenty-seven adult females, plus thirty children. This would have caused difficulties. I conclude therefore that differential recruitment was not as great as 25:75, m.:f. Do other people argue like this?

cannot account for all) the growth in Christian numbers.[42] But the greater the degree that the religion depends on children of Christians as recruits (and how else could a cult grow so rapidly?), the smaller the probability of persistent sexual imbalance. Or put another way, the larger the number of Christians, the more likely that their demographic and social composition reflects that of the larger population.

Once we take all the considerations which we have discussed together (sex and age composition, dispersion, variety of belief and practice, fission, the fear of persecution, the need for secrecy, the prevalence of house cult-groups and the availability of houses for meetings), we can plot a plausible path of Christian evolution. In 100, there were perhaps about one hundred Christian communities, dispersed in towns, mostly in the eastern and central Mediterranean basin; and many of these communities were further split into house cult-groups. On average, each community had seventy members, and many of these were children. House cult-groups were, by definition, even smaller, with an average size of a dozen or so families. By 200, Christian numbers had grown to over 200,000, spread in several hundred (say 200–400) towns out of the 2,000-odd towns in the Roman empire. So the average size of each community was in the range of 500 to 1,000. But some metropolitan communities were very large (several thousand strong) and hierarchically organised. Even there and elsewhere, house cult-groups were still the dominant norm.

What are the implications of the small average size of early Christian house cult-groups and communities? First, in small groups it is easier to enforce discipline, to foster internal collusion about the benefits of belief, to give mutual reassurance and to diminish the role of free riders, i.e. those who undermine collective commitment by seeking the benefits without

[42] Natural increase (excluding migration) in a pre-industrial population before the demographic revolution is unlikely to persist for a long period at above 1 per cent per annum. The growth of Christians posited at 3.4 per cent per annum compounded by the numbers in fig. 12.1 may therefore be made up by c.1 per cent per annum natural increase (allowing for the extra fertility of young adult recruits), plus c.2.4 perent per annum increase via conversions.

paying the costs of membership. In other words, small groups can more easily maintain a collusive sense of the superiority of their own vision and of the benefits of their own beliefs and lifestyle. Secondly, the relative importance of women in the workings of the primitive Church, albeit disputed, may have been a function of the small numbers in each cult-group, as well as of differential recruitment.

But, *per contra*, it is extremely difficult for dispersed and prohibited house cult-groups and communities to maintain and enforce common beliefs and common liturgical practices across space and time in pre-industrial conditions of communications.[43] The frequent claims that scattered Christian communities constituted a single Church was not a description of reality in the first two centuries AD, but a blatant yet forceful denial of reality. What was amazing was the persistence and power of the ideal in the face of its unachievability, even in the fourth century. On a local level, it is also unlikely that twenty households in a typical community, let alone a dozen households in a house cult-group, could maintain even one full-time, non-earning priest. Perhaps a group of forty households could, especially if they had a wealthy patron. But for most Christian communities of this size, a hierarchy of bishop and lesser clergy seems completely inappropriate.

Literacy and Stratification

The concepts literacy/illiteracy cover a broad range of techniques (from inability to read or write, barely reading, or writing slowly and with difficulty, artisanal/instrumental reading or writing of a limited range of words, reading and writing fluently, to reading/writing poetry or theology) and

[43] Augustine tells the story of how Manichees at Rome, a prohibited sect in the late fourth century, were reluctant to enforce discipline against miscreant *electi*, because of the fear that any disgruntled member might report them to the Roman authorities (*De moribus Manichaeorum* 69) ⟨ed. J. B. Bauer, *CSEL* 90, Vienna, 1992; trans. R. J. Teske, *The Manichean Debate*, The Works of St Augustine: A Translation for the 21st Century I/19, New York, 2006⟩. Similar forces must have been at work in the early Christian Church.

correspondingly different levels of competence and understanding. William Harris, in his ground-breaking and synoptic survey of ancient literacy, cautiously estimated that ancient literacy rates after about 100 BC in the Roman world were on average no more than 10–20 per cent among males (much less for females). The general literacy rate in the Roman empire as a whole was kept down by the gap between various native languages (Egyptian, Aramaic, Punic, etc.) and the administrative and upper-culture language of the Roman conquerors, Greek and Latin. Urban literacy rates were in all probability significantly higher than rural rates; and there was considerable regional variation (the eastern Mediterranean was more literate than the western Mediterranean). Most literacy was at the basic, slow and functional end of the literacy range.[44] Fluent, sophisticated literacy was concentrated in, but was not the exclusive privilege of, the ruling strata.

A brief analysis of Roman stratification might be helpful here. The Roman empire was a preponderantly agricultural society, with 80 per cent or so of the population engaged in farming and 15 per cent of the population living in towns.[45] The stratification pyramid was very steeply pitched, i.e. there was a huge gap between a small, powerful and rich élite and the mass of rural and urban poor. For example, a middling senator at the end of the first century AD had an income sufficient to support 2,000 families at subsistence level.[46] In between the élite and the mass, there was a sub-élite (inevitably a shadowy, but still a useful concept) of unknown size, which comprised middling landowners, merchants, professionals, such as lawyers, doctors, architects, professors of rhetoric and philosophy, middling and lesser administrators, army officers,

[44] Harris 1989: 175–284, especially 272, 323–37.

[45] There was some crossover between urban and rural populations, in the sense that some people living in towns worked in fields outside towns and some (a significant minority) of those living in villages were artisans, either full- or part-time, or engaged in other non-agricultural occupations (e.g. priests, scribes, tax collectors, traders).

[46] The income of Pliny the Younger is estimated at 1.1 million sestertii by Duncan-Jones 1982: 21. Subsistence is crudely reckoned at about 250 kg wheat equivalent per person/year, so that an average family of four persons would need one metric ton wheat equivalent, roughly 150 *modii* at 3 sestertii per *modius*.

scribes, school teachers and eventually Christian ideologues. These sub-élites were probably particularly concentrated in the metropolitan centres (Rome, Alexandria, Antioch, Carthage), in the larger cities (such as Ephesus, Corinth or Milan) and in merchant ports (Puteoli, Ostia, Cadiz) and the university town of Athens.

The steepness of the stratification pyramid and the relatively small size of the Roman middle class meant that people in intermediate positions could both be despised by their superiors and appear privileged to those beneath them. It is also worth stressing that sophisticated literacy correlated significantly with wealth and high social status, but high status, literacy and wealth did not completely coincide. There were some slaves and ex-slaves, for example, who were low in status, but who were literary sophisticates, just as there were rich landowners who were, or were thought to be, cultural boors. It is sometimes argued that Christianity particularly appealed to people with high status inconsistency; it may be correct, and particularly important for the first phase of Christian expansion, but cannot account for the rate of expansion in the empire as a whole.[47]

Now for proportions and numbers. As usual in Roman history, little is known for sure. But the ruling élite of senators, knights and town councillors (*decuriones*) can be estimated at just over 1 per cent of the adult population, comprising some 210,000 adult males.[48] There is no particular advantage in estimating the size of the sub-élite, since its bottom boundaries are necessarily fuzzy. But I speculate that it constituted say another 2 per cent of the total population, of whom at most half (another 200,000 adult males and far fewer females) possessed a sophisticated and fluent literacy.

[47] Meeks 1983: 72–3.

[48] Any such calculation must be vague, since there was/is no single valid definition of Roman ruling strata. But if we combine senators, knights and town councillors (100 for each of 2,000 towns), we get a total of say 210,000 adult males (i.e. 1.2 per cent) out of 17 million adult males in the empire. I use adult males as a unit of calculation for convenience. In fact, some towns did not have as many as 100 town councillors, and their wealth differed dramatically according to the size and wealth of the town.

This relatively low percentage of literary sophisticates, compared with the modern industrial world, reflects the level of Roman social evolution (the percentage of literates at any level in the Mediterranean basin as a whole had been near zero a thousand years earlier) and the relative absence from Roman society of a middle class.[49] That said, the proportion of sophisticated literates may seem low, at <2 per cent of adult males, but it is also, I think, a generous estimate, if they constituted between a fifth and a tenth of all literates at whatever level (and if literates constituted 10–20 per cent of the male population). By this tentative reckoning, there were about 400,000 literary sophisticates (of different levels) in the Roman empire.[50]

Let's now apply these general, albeit hypothetical, literacy rates to Christians. The basic problem is that we know very little about the social standing of early Christians. But we can follow several clues. It seems generally agreed that Christianity did not initially attract converts from among the ruling strata of senators, knights and town councillors, or not in significant numbers, at least until the third century. Complementarily, the self-presenting profile of primitive Christianity is repeatedly anti-rich (Luke 6:24: 'Woe to you that are rich'), anti-ruling powers (e.g. Revelation 17, in which Rome is portrayed as 'Babylon the great, mother of harlots and of earth's abominations' (17:5)), and artisanal.[51] Jesus himself is represented as the son of a carpenter, a simple man at home in the villages of Galilee, Paul is proud of earning his living as a tent-maker, the apostles are drawn from a set of illiterate fishermen and tax collectors. Pagan critics of Christianity accused them of avoiding the educated (a charge which the third-century Origen

[49] In the third millennium BC in Egypt, less than 1 per cent of adult males had been literate, according to Baines and Eyre 1983. In the rest of the Mediterranean basin, presumably, literacy rates were as low or lower until very much later.

[50] Since not all town councillors (or even bishops) could write, let alone rank as sophisticated literates, this estimate seems overgenerous.

[51] Cf. James 2:5–6: 'Listen, my beloved brethren. Has not God chosen those who are poor in the world to be rich in faith and heirs of the kingdom which he has promised to those who love him? … Is it not the rich who oppress you, is it not they who drag you to court?'

denied strenuously) and of recruiting particularly among tradesmen, illiterates, women and children. Or, put briefly, in this view primitive Christianity was aimed at the poor and was led by the underprivileged.[52] It was, and was seen as, a religion of opposition.

These arguments have both strengths and weaknesses. To be sure, as Christianity grew, it had to recruit from among the poor; and Christian writers themselves acknowledged that the bulk of the faithful were illiterate.[53] How could it have been otherwise, if the sect was to grow so fast? But two counter-arguments also seem compelling. First, the texts of the New Testament itself, the New Testament apocrypha and early Apostolic Fathers must have been written by members of that small stratum, within the top 2 per cent of Roman society, who could write Greek fluently. The New Testament writings are of course not part of high classical culture; they do not match the careful court writings of essayists like Seneca, historians like Tacitus or rhetoricians such as Dio Chrysostom. The Gospels are written in ostensibly, one might even say ostentatiously, simpler, instrumental prose; but Matthew and John, at least, are consciously artful, while Paul is idiosyncratically inventive.

Complementarily, the rhetoric of simplicity and the appeal to the foolish and poor was just that, a rhetorical play. It made the best of Jesus' humble background in the urban world of Hellenised culture in which the gospel message was sold. But why was the message so successful, how could it remain virtually unchanged in its primary focus, as Christianity went socially up-market?[54] I wonder if the answer lies partly in the

52 Origen, *C. Cels.* 3.44, 55. This traditional view has been criticised e.g. by Judge 1960: 52–61 and Meeks 1983: 51–73.

53 Origen, *C. Cels.* 1.27: 'among the great number of people' converted to Christianity, 'because there are many more vulgar illiterates than educated rational thinkers, it is inevitable that the uneducated should outnumber the more intelligent'. Needless to say I cite this extract, not as proof, but as illustration. So too Tertullian's dictum that most Christians were simple and uneducated (*Adversus Praxean* 3.1) (ed. G. Scarpat, Corona Patrum 12, Turin, 1985).

54 Of course, Justin, Tertullian, Clement and Origen are dressing Christian arguments in increasingly well-educated clothes, but the appeal to simplicity, poverty and charity remains and persists as a rhetorical figure and as a spur to action. See Brown 1992.

steepness of the social pyramid and in the tiny size of its middle class. Roman society demanded an uncomfortable mixture of pervasive deference to superiors and openly aggressive brutishness to inferiors, not just slaves. It was a world of deference and condescension, of curt commands and pervasive threats. It was in this world that nearly everyone, even a middling senator with an income which could support thousands, could imagine himself to be poor. Poverty is best seen as a subjective, not an objective category.

Two subsidiary points need to be dealt with briefly. It might be argued that early Christians were disproportionately literate, partly because sacred texts were central to Christian religious practice and partly because they inherited a commitment to education and reading from Jewish tradition and practice. But the centrality of sacred texts to liturgical practice is no proof of widespread or disproportionate literacy; believers can participate by listening, as well as by reading. The development of the post of *lector* (i.e. reader) in the early Christian Church indeed suggests that most believers could not read and had the text read to them. Besides, the Greek translation of the Hebrew Bible, which was the exemplary Christian sacred text well into the second century (or even of selected passages from it) would have been too expensive for most people to afford. And as to the New Testament, it is doubtful if many/most Christian communities had a full set even of the core texts (Gospels, Acts, Letters) before the second half of the second century.[55]

As to the Jewish tradition of widespread literacy, I suspect assessment of it is often apologetic and idealistic. Prescription was conflated with practice. Ideally, of course, Jewish fathers

[55] The (later to be) canonical Gospels long circulated separately, not as a set of four, and since they were not canonical, nor regularly cited by Christian writers until the middle of the second century, there was no particular reason why Christian communities should get copies, indeed if they knew of their collective existence. A case in point are the Marcionite prefaces to the Pauline epistles, written in the mid-second century, but found in a major set of Latin vulgate manuscripts; their adoption indicates that western Christian communities did not receive a text of the Pauline letters until after the mid-second century and/or were indifferent to their heretical introductions. See de Bruyne 1907: especially 11–16.

had a duty to teach their sons to read. Rabbinical sources emphasise how many schools there had been in the old days, in first-century Palestine: for example, 480 schools in Jerusalem and 500 in the undistinguished town of Beitar, each with 500 students. Even if we grant that Jews in the first century were exceptionally educated, compared with pagans, and that this tradition had some initial effect on primitive Christianity (after all, it too became a religion of the book), the characteristic was not central to Christian self-identity. Early Christians did not establish their own specifically Christian elementary or secondary schools.[56] Therefore, it seems reasonable to conclude that Christians were, roughly speaking, no more literate or only marginally more literate than the sub-populations from which they were recruited.

In sum, let us suppose, generously, that 20 per cent of Christian adult males were literate at some level or other and that 2 per cent of Christian adult males were sophisticated, fluent literates. Female literacy was, I assume, very significantly lower, even, from a statistical point of view, negligible. The estimate for sophisticated literacy is especially generous, if our argument is granted that almost no Christians, in the first two centuries AD, were recruited from the ruling élite of senators, knights and town councillors (though obviously some came from the sub-élites). The consequences of these proportions can be analysed for Christians as a whole and for typical communities and house cult-groups, at different periods.

The implications of these literacy rates are quite startling. In 100, there were, according to the numbers estimated in figure 12.1, about 7,000 Christians, of whom about 30 per cent = 2,100 were adult males. Of these, say 20 per cent = 420 could read and write at varying levels of literacy. But only 2 per cent, that is 42 adult Christian males, were fluent and skilled literates. Of course, the reasoning is too speculative to be trusted in detail; the number 42 is here a symbol for a small

[56] On parental obligations, see Joseph. *Ap.* 2.204, *AJ* 4.211. On ubiquitous schools, see Jerusalem Talmud, *Megillah* 3.1, 73d, *Ketubot* 13.1, 35c, *Taanith* 4.8, 69a. See the good discussion on these points by Gamble 1995: 2–10.

number of unknown size. But even if we double or treble it, in order to flatter the social composition or literary skills of primitive Christianity, and add in some female skilled literates, we can still see that intellectual Christianity, that is, the part of Christianity which is preserved and transmitted in the sacred texts, was composed, explained and developed by a tiny group of specialists, very thinly spread across the eastern and central Mediterranean basin.[57]

If we split these 7,000 Christians of AD 100 among one hundred or so communities (and more house cult-groups), each on average with seventy members, the implications are striking. Each community had, on average, twenty adult male members, of whom two were literate at some level. But many or most Christian communities (and *a fortiori* even more house cult-groups) simply did not have among them a single sophisticated reader or writer. After all, sophisticated literate Christians were likely to concentrate in the bigger towns.

By 178, according to the numbers posited in figure 12.1, there were about 100,000 Christians, of whom 30,000 were adult males, split among say 200 or more town communities and significantly more house cult-groups. By this time, the total number of sophisticated literate adult males who were Christian had burgeoned to 600. And by the end of the second century, it was, by these calculations, well over 1,000. Indeed, we can see in the surviving literature that Christian writers were now trying to assimilate their writings to classical upper-class pagan culture.[58] And there were enough Christian sophisticated literates overall, even with bunching in larger towns, for us to imagine that each community had one sophisticated literate leader. I think the imaging of Christian growth proposed

[57] Now that we know the implications of the reasoning, some critical or precommitted readers may want to question it again. But as I see it, the room for manoeuvre is constricted. Either primitive Christians were recruited more than anyone has suspected from the sophisticated literate sub-élites, or these sub-élites constituted a much larger proportion of the Roman urban population than anyone has suspected, or there were many more Christians than the 7,000 estimated for AD 100.

[58] With Tertullian, Clement and Origen, Christian writing showed overt ambition and some success in clothing itself like pagan classical culture. See e.g. Bigg 1913; Chadwick 1966; Clark 1977.

here has some implications for the evolution of the episcopacy. Only towards the end of the second century was it possible to find an educated leader for each Christian community.

Christians and Jews

Before we desert number, let us take a brief look at the Jews. Modern scholars, from hopelessly inadequate data, customarily guess that Jews in the early first century AD constituted about 7–8 per cent of the population of the Roman empire. According to these guesses, which may be inflated, there were about 4.2–4.8 million Jews in the Roman empire in the mid-first century AD.[59] The great majority of these Jews lived outside Palestine, because the carrying capacity of Palestine in ancient economic conditions (and by no means all the inhabitants there were Jews) was about a million people.[60] I myself would be happier with a much lower estimate of 3 million Jews than with the higher estimate, but with either there is a high probable margin of error. However, numerical precision is not important here; for the moment, we are concerned only with very rough orders of comparative magnitude.

Jews outside Palestine but in the Roman empire, like Christians initially, were concentrated in towns in the eastern and central Mediterranean basin. For all the differences between Jews and Christians, Jews constituted the most obvious target customers for evangelical Christians, particularly after the destruction of the temple, and three disastrously unsuccessful rebellions against Rome (AD 66–74, 117–18, 132–5). By then, many Jews must have been disenchanted, disaffected and despondent, ready to receive alternative messages or even to desert their Judaism.[61] Some Jews must have been

[59] Reported by Simon 1986: 33–4, who in turn depended mainly on Juster 1914: I 180–209.

[60] Broshi 1979.

[61] *2 Baruch* (like *4 Ezra*) celebrates the despair felt by some Jews after the destruction of Jerusalem; although the author finishes by reaffirming his trust in God and the Law, and the hope of eventual revenge, he also acknowledged that some Jews had deserted (41.3: 'Behold, I see many of your people who separated themselves from your Law'; 85.3–4: 'we have nothing now apart from the Mighty One and his Law. Therefore,

tempted, as the original followers of Jesus were, to join a radical renewal movement. After all, Jews knew half the Christian story, some expected or hoped for a messiah and believed in an interventionist God; they largely shared Christian ethics and thought that religious piety involved religious control over private life.

If I had been a hungry, wandering Christian beggar-missionary in search of success and food in the first hundred years after Jesus' death, I, like Paul, perhaps even at the risk of a beating, would have made for a synagogue or house of a pious god-fearer in preference to the market square or the temple of Jupiter.[62] In sum, it seems reasonable to suppose that Jewish-Christians, who awkwardly straddled both Judaism and Christianity, to the eventual indignation of both, probably for a significant period constituted the central, numerical core of Christians.

Three arguments of unequal weight support this claim. First, modern studies of cult-group conversions in North America show that conversion flows principally along lines of social networks.[63] Relatives and friends are primary targets as converts. Few conversions are made cold, for example, on doorsteps or by telephone. Of course, the social conditions of ancient and modern cultures are different. The New Testament and early Christian writings dwell on mass or exemplary conversions after miracles and healings.[64] But for me these sound like stories told to bolster the faith of the

if we direct and dispose our hearts, we shall receive everything which we lost again by many times') (trans. A. F. J. Klijn in J. H. Charlesworth, *The Old Testament Pseudepigrapha*, 2 vols, London, 1983–5, I 615–52). In the rebellion of Bar Kokhba, Jews who had had their foreskins surgically restored, presumably in order to take part nude in Hellenistic civic life, were forcibly recircumcised (Tosefta, *Shabbat* 15.9). To not much avail, at the end of the second century, the Jewish cities of Sepphoris and Lydda, for example, changed their names to Diocaesarea and Diospolis (Zeustown).

[62] Luke/Acts records repeated visits by Paul to synagogues in different towns, where he taught his message to Jews and persuaded many of them. Of course, Acts is not a work of accurate history (whatever that is), but a doctrinal tract with a message. Even when it was written, towards the end of the first century, the appeal of Christianity to Jews, and the break from Judaism, was central to Luke's perception of Christian evolution and, I suspect, of contemporary Christian preoccupations. See, very helpfully on Acts' historicity, Pervo 1987.

[63] Stark 1996: 16.

[64] See e.g. Acts 3–4.4; *Acts of Andrew* 1–8; *Acts of John* 18–25, 37–47; *Acts of Peter* 27–9; *Acts of Thomas* 23–6, 30–8 (trans. J. K. Elliott, *The Apocryphal New*

faithful, not descriptions of reality. Since the first Christians were Jews, then ethnic Jews and their associates at synagogues, the god-fearers, were the most probable clients for early Christian missionaries in towns throughout the eastern Mediterranean and beyond.

Secondly, Justin (*First Apology* 53) wrote in the mid-second century that by then the number of ex-gentile Christians outnumbered ex-Jewish Christians. I am not concerned here with the statistical element in Justin's formulation, but with the historical process to which he alludes. In all probability, he did not know the proportion of ex-Jews and ex-gentiles in dispersed Christian groups, but did think that ex-Jews formed a substantial portion of Christians, even in the mid-second century. And to me, that seems highly probable. It makes sense.

Finally, I cite, *exempli causa*, the preoccupations of the Gospels with things Jewish, the great body of pseudepigraphic writings of Jewish origin preserved by Christians and the early Christian ethical writings like the *Didache* and the *Epistle of Barnabas*, which illustrate the continuity and overlap between Judaism and early Christianity. In this view, Christianity was to a large extent ethical Judaism, without circumcision and detailed rules of observance, plus a belief in Jesus as Messiah. It was a religion which in its early form was more likely to appeal to Jews than pagans. Indeed, Christian preoccupation with the wickedness of the Jews, from Pharisees to High Priest, and with establishing their moral inferiority illustrates the urgency of Christian leaders' needs to differentiate themselves from their prime rivals.

Back, once again, to parametric (im)probabilities. My general argument here is that Christianity should have appealed particularly to Jews rather than to pagans. But according to the figures which I have cited, if only 3.3 per cent, or one in thirty Jews (i.e. according to my low estimate, 3,000,000/

Testament: A Collection of Apocryphal Christian Literature in English Translation, Oxford, 1993). MacMullen 1984 considers miracles central to Christian expansion. But I'm not sure that Romans 'took miracles quite for granted. That was the general starting point' (22).

30 = 100,000) embraced Christianity before AD 175 (and some could have done that as Judaeo-Christians without necessarily thinking that they were deserting Judaism), then ex-Jews and their descendants constituted all Christians existing in 175 (see figure 12.1). Let me stress immediately that I am not claiming as a fact that 3 per cent of Jews did convert to Christianity or that all Christians in 175 were ex-Jews or their descendants. To me, each of these two estimates appears far too high.

What I am arguing instead is that these exemplary speculations can be useful as exploratory devices. They illustrate the boundaries of probability and the reasonable derivation of radically divergent interpretations. For example, whatever the associative affinities between Judaism and Christianity, and whatever the sympathetic appeal of monotheism to both and however distressed Jews were after AD 70 at the apparent failure of God's special relationship with Israel, we can now easily say that most Jews stayed Jewish, or at least they did not embrace Christianity. So Jews and their leaders could have sensibly considered Christians as only a minor irritation. To be sure, in some Jewish prayers, heretics (including by implication Christians) were routinely cursed every day; but it is by no means clear (although mentioned by Justin) that such curses were universally practised by all Jewish groups in the second century.[65] Much more striking is the absence of explicit mention of Christians in the mass of rabbinical writings. Or put another way, most Jews did not become Christians and most Jews before 300 did not obviously care about Christianity. But complementarily, in the early period, I suspect until about 150, most Christians were ex-Jews or their descendants, and that is one reason why Christians fixated on the Judaeo-Christian boundary as a major problem. Or put crisply, Jews mattered much more for Christians until the fourth century than Christians did for Jews.

[65] I take seriously Justin's clear and repeated statement that Jews cursed Christians (*Dialogus cum Tryphone* 16.4, 93.4, 95.4, 96.2, 108.3, 123.6, 133.6, 137.2). But the issue is complicated; see Horbury 1982; van der Horst 1993–4.

On the Social Production of Religious Ideology

At this point I want to change tack and investigate the social production of religious ideology. My argument is that the number of Christians and the number and size of Christian cult-groups or communities materially influenced the style of Christian ideology. By ideology, I mean here a system of ideas which seeks to justify the power and authority of a set of ethical prescriptions and metaphysical explanations and also, of course, to justify the power and authority of a particular set of interpreters of these ideas. Let me proceed by crudely contrasting Judaism and Christianity.

Christianity was different from all religions of the Roman world. Like Judaism, it was (or claimed to be) monotheistic. Like Judaism, it was exclusivist, in the sense that its leaders claimed that believers in the one true god could not, or should not, pay homage to any other god. Unlike Judaism after the destruction of the Temple, Christianity was dogmatic and hierarchical; dogmatic, in the sense that Christian leaders from early on claimed that their own interpretation of Christian faith was the only true interpretation of the faith, and hierarchical in that leaders claimed legitimacy for the authority of their interpretation from their office as priests or bishops. 'Obey your bishop', Ignatius of Antioch ordered (allegedly in the early second century), 'so that God may heed you.'[66]

Admittedly, individual Jewish leaders claimed that their own individual interpretation of the law was right and that other interpretations were wrong. But systemically, at some unknown date, Jewish rabbis seem to have come to the conclusion, however reluctantly, that they were bound to disagree and that disagreement was endemic. Truth for them (as for Roman jurists) came to lie in, or was represented as, a balance of competing opinions. Now, of course, this systemic property of sceptical balance is a characteristic of the system. Each individual rabbi in his own group could be, and probably was, as dogmatic as he dared be. But each lacked power over a large, pluralistic, dispersed and ethnically embedded set of followers.

[66] Ignatius, *Polyc.* 6, cf. *Smyrn.* 8, *Philad.* 7.

The balanced incapacity to enforce a single interpretative view and a broad acceptance of that incapacity became a characteristic of Judaism, considered as a system, not a characteristic necessarily of each member of the system.[67]

Christianity, by contrast, never accepted tolerance of diverse belief as an ideal, though of course Christians too as individuals were often inclined or forced to accept variety in practice. And it was this very intolerance as a defining characteristic of Christianity which eventually made it such a useful, if expensive, tool of state control. Christian ideologues, from Paul onwards, repeatedly attempted to lay down the law. Each claimed that his own interpretation of Christian belief was right, and that anyone who disagreed was wrong and should be excommunicated.[68]

In the beginning, leaders of the primitive Church had little (or insufficient) power to enforce their views. But the very idea that correct belief identified the true Christian and that incorrect belief pushed the believer who wanted to be a Christian beyond the pale became entrenched as a core defining characteristic of early Christianity. By the end of the second century, leaders tried to enhance their authority by claiming that the catholic Church had held constant and unified beliefs since apostolic times. There was a direct line of legitimacy stretching from God to Jesus to the apostles and from them to bishops of the 'united' orthodox Church. Christians invented, or gave unprecedented force to, the idea of orthodoxy and heresy. And as soon as the Church gained extra power from its alliance with the state in the fourth century, Christian leaders persecuted those Christians whom they considered deviant (and

[67] My favourite text, illustrating (to me) the balance of disagreements among rabbis and describing the excommunication of Eliezer ben Hyrcanus, is Babylonian Talmud, *Baba Mezia* 59a–b; the structure of the text is made more evident in the translation in Neusner 1990: 154–6. The same story, but with important variants, is told in the Jerusalem Talmud, *Mo'ed Qatan* 3.1.

[68] Perhaps this is overdramatic and overstated; perhaps reconciliation and tolerance of differences, which certainly occurred, leave less trace in the sources or are less remarkable. All that said, the hostility between early Christian sectarians is notable, a symptom of their commitment. Examples are 2 Cor. 6:14 (interpolated?); Col. 2:8; Eph. 4:14; 1 Jn 2:18; 2 Jn 7–8; Rev. 2:6.

the boundaries shifted unpredictably) more assiduously than pagan Romans had usually persecuted Christians.

The centrality of correct dogma, as a defining characteristic of Christian praxis, was a religious innovation. It arose, I think, from the circumstances in which Christianity evolved. Two factors seem important: first, number and dispersion, and second, the continuously rapid rate of growth. Let us deal with each factor in turn. Members of the Christian Church were spread in small groups all over the Mediterranean basin. Numbers, as we have seen, are necessarily speculative; but it seems reasonable to imagine that, in the first century or more after its birth, Christianity was typified by having more than one hundred smallish house cult-groups or cells, each with less than a handful of fluent literates. Indeed, on the figures crudely proposed in the first part of my paper, it is possible to think that in AD 100 Christian ideology was the intellectual possession of barely fifty fluent literates. It was the tiny size of this creative body and the small cult-groups within and between which they worked which together account for the exclusivist and dogmatic character of their self-representation.[69]

In its early stages, say during the first century and a half of its existence, Christianity was a set of small and vulnerably fissile cult-groups. Internally, each group may have been held together by a demanding ethic, communal worship and an encouraging message of hope. And all the groups, as a set, may have been held together by shared oral traditions and a thin stream of beggar-missionaries. But if Christianity was to survive over time as a recognisable entity, some mechanism had to be found to unify these small, scattered and volatile communities. Writing and belief, or rather writing about belief, became the prime instrument of unification. And the dogmatic

[69] I hope this does not sound too reductionist. I am thinking here not that the small size of house cult-groups, their dispersion and the scarcity of sophisticated literates in the early Church created the importance of dogma, rather that perhaps these were the main factors which preserved and enhanced the importance of dogma. Perhaps also the importance of dogma, or of explicit belief statements, as a criterion of sect membership is itself a figment of the surviving literary sources: sophisticated literates stressed belief, stalwart practising Christians stressed practice. I suspect truth lies in their combination.

style of exclusivism (only my version of the truth is acceptable) was, I argue, partly a function of the small average size of each cell and the rarity value of literate leaders within each. In these circumstances, single teachers might feel encouraged to be dogmatic.

Of course, the drive towards unification did not succeed completely, ever. The house cult-groups and communities were too diverse and too diffused over different regions with their own cultural traditions, and individual Christian believers were too passionate and inventive for unity ever to be achieved in reality. But the ideal and illusion of unity as a church and as a grand (apostolic) tradition persisted and had a powerful effect on Christian organisation and self-representation. Christian church leaders repeatedly tried, at least from the middle of the third century onwards, to achieve unity of belief and practice.

The continuous, rapid rate of growth of Christianity, envisaged in figure 12.1 (3.4 per cent cumulative per year), implies that at any one time about two-fifths of all adult Christians had become converts, and so new members of house cult-groups or communities, during the previous ten years.[70] This rate of continuous growth put a tremendous strain on the absorptive and instructional capacity of older members. And it helps us understand the idea, which so differentiated Christians from pagans and Jews, that Christians were made, not born. At any one time in the first three centuries of Christianity, if the numbers in table 12.1 are anywhere near right, a significantly large proportion of the adult members of the Christian Church were new members, pupils, volunteers.

But volunteers could both join and leave, or be ejected. So Christianity shared with devotees of a polytheistic cult (but not with Judaism) the possibility of temporary attendance.

[70] This is a bit complex to work out and depends on several assumptions, such as the age of the new converts, whether before or after marriage, and the age distribution of pre-existing members, as well as on their respective fertility. On reasonable (but not necessarily true) assumptions, *exempli causa*, if all converts were young adults, and older and new converts had similar fertility, then those converted within the previous ten years constituted about 40 per cent of adult Christians, but only a quarter of all Christians including children.

But membership of pagan cult was by and large a function of locality and performance, not belief. Pagans performed local cult, as a matter of course, by living in a city or village, by growing up as polytheists. They could voluntarily opt into extra religious performances, as the desire or need took them. In saying this, I do not want to collude with a Christianising distinction between belief and behaviour. Inevitably, religious behaviour consciously or unconsciously involves mental attitudes. Jewish thinkers and pagan ideologues expected religious performances to be accompanied by appropriate thoughts, such as pious reverence or purity of heart (or at least the absence of hate).[71]

Christian leaders too expected this internal piety from their followers. But, in addition, they expected and exacted formal commitment to specific beliefs about Jesus' godhead and redeemership, and their own hopes of salvific redemption and immortality. This demand constituted a radical break from both Judaism and polytheism. Why? Two explanations seem important, one genetic (in the Genesis sense), the other functional.

Genetically, Christian leaders' fixation on their common beliefs arose from their extraordinary nature: Jesus was both human and divine, he suffered death to save humanity; by believing in him as the son of God, we will be saved. By both Jewish and pagan standards, this message was extraordinary. No wonder it played a crucial role in Christians' self-definition. Functionally, concentration on formal statements of belief made it much easier to join communities spread around the Mediterranean. A simple test (do you believe x and y?) could be administered and their justifications could be elaborated, by letter. The dispersed and vagrant leadership of the primitive Church could maintain the illusion of homogeneity through writing about their beliefs. Of course, it took some time to decide exactly what the identifying beliefs were (the creed was not formalised until the fourth century) and what the test of belonging should be or how it should be administered. But

[71] S. J. D. Cohen 1987: especially 66–9.

the innovative principle that their religion was founded on a shared belief (rather than, or as well as, on a shared practice) remained constant for centuries.

Concentration on belief rather than on practice originated in part as a device for differentiating Christians from Jews, just as Sunday and Sabbath differentiated them (though both sects remained similarly distinctive in the Roman world, by having a weekly holy day). But functionally speaking, belief statements were an economy travel package, so much more easily transportable between widely dispersed, fast growing and freshly established cult-groups than detailed rules of legal observance which needed a solid body of long-time practitioners to socialise new adherents. Simple capsules of Christian belief statements could be so much more easily absorbed by a constant flood of new recruits than complex rules of daily life or even of liturgical practice. Or, put another way, it was much simpler to learn how to be a Christian than to learn how to be a Jew. And we must remember that according to the crude numbers outlined in figure 12.1, 40 per cent of the adult members of any Christian community had become new members in the previous decade. Christianity was a religion which, because of the rapidity of its expansion, always had to be questioning its members about the nature and degree of their adherence.

This strategy of privileging belief over practice carried high risks. The high risks arose from the need to maintain coherence by expelling (or threatening to expel) deviants. Expulsion or the threat of expulsion seriously increased the risk and incidence of heresy and schism. I don't think that anyone in the middle of the second century could have reasonably predicted that the policy of dogmatic exclusivism would end up with a triumphant monopoly. The success of the strategy was discovered only over time; it was not purposively invented as a marketing device. Yet, in balance, the costs of maintaining orthodoxy were mitigated, especially in small groups, by the advantages of inculcating a heightened sense among the survivors that they were the sole inheritors and the correct propagators of the one true Christian message. And in the medium term, concentration on belief allowed a constant elaboration and sophistication of what these beliefs implied and how they fitted in with each other. This elaboration of belief, which we call theology, allowed a gradual rapprochement between Christian leaders and pagan philosophy. And this gradual rapprochement gave the Christian message a socially acceptable veneer. Sophisticated elaboration of Christian ideology also allowed or even encouraged an internal differentiation among the Christian faithful, so that ideological specialists could gain symbolic capital, material rewards and ecclesiastical power from their intellectual proficiencies. For all its pretentions at universality, Christianity particularly rewarded its élite; indeed, such differential rewards were a necessary part in Christianity's political success and influence.

The Implications of Mass Conversion

Rapid growth in the absolute numbers of Christians occurred only in the third and fourth centuries. According to the estimated numbers in table 12.1, there was an increase of about 1 million Christians in the first half of the third century, 5 million new Christians in the second half of the third century and 30 million plus in the fourth century. From such figures, it becomes easier to judge the scale of what church historians often claim for the growth of Christianity. The problems of internal adjustment, and the cumulative impact of paganism on Christian practice, must have been tremendous. But for the moment, let us put scepticism aside. Let us assume that the straight growth line is roughly right.[72]

Now we can see that it was only in the third century, when the number of Christians grew from say 220,000 to over 6 million, that the Church gained the resources and numbers to justify building churches devoted to meetings. And in most towns, it was only then that internal differentiation evolved to a degree which could maintain a hierarchy of bishops and

[72] Of course, I do not mean by this that straight-line growth is an accurate description of what happened; it is merely the easiest? best? most economical way of thinking about Christian growth; it is a first approximation, which elicits correspondingly simple, structural implications and further thought.

priests, working exclusively as priests and supported by the contributions of the faithful.

But the increase in numbers brought its own troubles. Visibility and bulk provoked the first serious attempts by the central Roman government to destroy Christianity in 250–1, 257–60 and after 303. And amazingly, if these growth figures are anywhere near right, then the persecutions or contemporary conditions (civil wars, barbarian invasions, rampant inflation, repeated plagues, urban decline), or their combination, encouraged an unprecedented growth in the numbers of Christians. Success in achieving growth also prompted a battle royal among Christians themselves, between the traditional rigorists, who wanted to maintain the old ways of the devoted small community, and the laxists, who wanted growth in numbers, even if that meant sacrificing moral standards.

The conversion of the Emperor Constantine, the continued Christianity of his successors and the alliance of the church triumphant with the Roman state brought about a still more dramatic increase, of say 30 million people, in the membership of the Church during the fourth century. But by then, for most people being a Christian must have meant something quite different from what it had meant in the first three centuries AD and the nature of some conversions may have been, must have been, superficial.

The utility of the Christian Church to the state was, I imagine, discovered only over time, by Constantine and his successors. It was not necessarily foreseen by any one of them. But it is worth noting that successive Sasanian kings towards the end of the third century moved the Iranian empire towards religious (Mazdaean) exclusivism and the systematic persecution of religious 'deviants'.[73] It seems that the two rival and hostile empires, Iran and Rome, were moving along a similar path at roughly the same time. Was it because both empires

[73] The (attempted) religious unification of Iran by the high priest Kartir under four successive third-century Iranian kings is recorded in four autobiographical inscriptions, three of which are transcribed and translated with learned commentary by Sprengling 1953. The fourth Kartir text is given in Gignoux 1968.

needed a greater degree of symbolic unity in order to squeeze greater resources from their subjects?

In the long run, Christianity gave to the Roman state a degree of symbolic unity and exploitable loyalty which it had previously lacked. Christianity had more combinatory power and more power to demand self-sacrifice than the previous combination of localised polytheisms, vague henotheism and emperor cult. Christian rulers and their henchmen now had the legitimacy and authority of a powerful and interventionist God to support their authority and the enforcement of state regulations. The Roman state endorsed and then borrowed Christian intolerance.

In the medium term, a unified religion helped the Roman state to secure the self-sacrifice required of both soldiers and taxpayers. Sacrifice, so their leaders said, was demanded by God. The Christian religion became, in other words, a supplementary weapon of political and social control, used alongside law, violence and taxation. Christianity also helped provide a cohesiveness of religious discourse among enthusiasts, which, rather like political discourse in modern developed states, bound competitors together via their minor differences. One advantage of religious over political discourse was that, at least overtly, enthusiasts were not discussing the redistribution of resources (always a tricky issue in a pre-industrial society with a limited disposable surplus), but the irresolvable issues of the nature of God or of life after death.

One significant short-term advantage of switching to Christianity as the state religion lay in the possibility it opened up to pillage the stored reserves of pagan temples. Only one source, the fifth-century church historian Sozomen, states that Constantine took money from pagan temples.[74] But it is difficult to envisage how Constantine managed to find the huge sums needed to found the new capital of Constantinople without using the funds of the temples, which increasingly over the next sixty years were destroyed. Christianity also allowed successive emperors to switch patronage from an over-privileged

[74] Soz. *HE* 2.5.3 (see now, usefully, Lenski 2016: 168–70).

traditional aristocracy to fresh swathes of often newly Christianised supporters.

The disadvantages of Christianity, from a political point of view, lay mainly in transition costs, in the alienation of the conservative and pagan upper classes and in the difficulty of effecting a thoroughgoing mass conversion. The superficiality of Christianisation in broad areas of the Roman world was revealed only three centuries later, when Islam swept triumphantly through exactly those regions where it is alleged Christianity first took deepest root. The Church was also prone to zealous schism and dissent. The combination of alienation, superficiality and division meant that the Church could not always deliver to the state the political loyalty of its putative believers. It has also been argued that the Christian Church was itself expensive to the state in tax immunities, diversion of ability and non-productive lifestyles, particularly at a time when the empire was desperately trying to defend itself against barbarian incursions. There may be something in these arguments, but the survival of the eastern empire, for close on a thousand years after the conversion of Constantine, indicates that the internal costs of religion were not excessive.

Summary

In this paper, I have experimented with estimating the number of Christians at successive stages of Christian evolution. The figures are necessarily speculative, but nevertheless can usefully serve as a framework against which to test alternatives and implications. I have come to five main conclusions. First, the number of Christians expanded fast, but for a long time remained tiny relative to the total population of the empire. The disparity between number and proportion helped produce two different but complementary accounts; Christians thought of themselves as successful but persecuted, while leading Romans long remained ignorant of their activities. Stories about persecution, rather more than persecution itself, were an important factor in Christian self-representation and togetherness.

Secondly, Christian house cult-groups in the first century after Jesus' death were on average both small and dispersed. The small size of the groups helped maintain enthusiastic vigour and ethical rigour among converts. The rapid growth and expansion of the religion depended upon the creation of an easily administrable test of membership, encapsulated in brief statements of belief. This emphasis on belief combined with ethical practice was a significant religious innovation. It was, I argue, a function of dispersion, small numbers and rapid growth.

Thirdly, given general rates of literacy among the Roman population, and even allowing for somewhat higher rates among Christian converts, it seems likely that the development and maintenance of Christian religious ideology in the first century after Jesus' death was at any one time the intellectual property of only a few dozen men, scattered throughout the Mediterranean basin. The maintenance of identity between groups depended therefore upon writing, and particularly upon the writing of letters. The smallness of the group of educated devotees helped give early Christianity its intense internalised character.

Fourthly, the number of Jews was very large compared with the number of Christians, at least until the late third century. Because enthusiastic cult-groups, according to modern evidence, expand usually along family and social networks, i.e. among relatives and friends, it seems likely that Jews were the main early customers for conversion to Christianity. But differences in experience between Christians and Jews (as between Christians and Romans) helped generate complementary, but contrasting, accounts. In the early days, most Christians were ex-Jews or their descendants. So Christians, at least until the completion of the New Testament texts (roughly speaking, the middle of the second century), were preoccupied with their relationship to Judaism. But Jews, the vast mass of whom remained immune to Christianity, for a long time largely ignored the existence of what was for them a marginal group. This discrepancy of experience helps explain why Christians continued to use the Jewish Bible as their main authenticating text. The main focus of Christian expansion moved to the gentiles only during the second century. This change of focus perhaps helps explain why the letters of Paul and the Acts of the Apostles, both of which celebrate the mission to the gentiles, were finally included in the canonical New Testament.

Finally, the greatest surge in Christian numbers (in absolute terms) occurred in two stages, in the third century and fourth centuries. Surprisingly, the first mass, centrally organised and reputedly severe persecutions coincided with considerable Christian growth. In terms of number, persecutions helped Christianity. And then the mass of Christian conversions, which followed the alliance of the Christian Church with the Roman state under Constantine and his Christian successors, was on a huge scale and was sufficient significantly to change the nature of Christian practice. It is customary to consider Constantine's conversion and adoption of Christianity as a state-favoured religion in terms of his personal sincerity or his perception of Roman interests. It is extremely interesting that Iran, Rome's most powerful enemy, had gone along the same road of trying to create an exclusive monopoly of state religion barely thirty years before Constantine's conversion.[75]

[75] My warm thanks for encouragement, help and advice to Jaime Alvar, Mary Beard, Keith Carne, Elizabeth Clark, Simon Goldhill, Christopher Kelly, Seth Schwartz and to this journal's anonymous reader.

AFTERWORD

CHRISTIAN NUMBER AND ITS IMPLICATIONS

KATE COOPER

'Christian number and its implications' formed part of a special issue of the *Journal of Early Christian Studies* published in 1998 – an issue dedicated to the then controversial study, *The Rise of Christianity: A Sociologist Re-considers History* published in 1996 by Rodney Stark. Challenging a framework of thought about the growth of early Christian communities that had lain more or less undisturbed since Adolf von Harnack, *Mission und Ausbreitung des frühen Christentums* (4th edn, 1924), Stark proposed that in order to explain the ever-multiplying Christian numbers of the first centuries AD, scholars ought to divert their attention away from providence, miracle-working and compelling theological arguments,[1] and consider social factors instead. In the early 1980s, Ramsay MacMullen had shifted the balance away from theological argument among élites toward the effect of miraculous displays on popular audiences as the key factor explaining the speed of Christian growth.[2] But the emphasis on events involving large crowds was simply not necessary, Stark suggested, if early Christianity was set alongside the modern high-growth religions in America, such as Mormonism and the Unification Church of the Reverend Sun Myung Moon, the models derived from modern fieldwork studies would make it possible to account for growth on the basis of an entirely different kind of missionary encounter.[3]

[1] For an overview of twentieth-century approaches to religious conversion, see Praet 1992–3, supplemented by Cooper 2005.

[2] MacMullen 1983 and 1984: 25–34.

[3] Stark 1996: 13–21, 39–44.

The central discovery of Stark's own fieldwork, conducted in the 1960s with his colleague John Lofland, was that the religious groups who sustain high growth tend not do so thanks to large-scale events at which dozens or hundreds are converted at a time. Rather, the numbers begin to multiply when missionaries tap into pre-existing friendship and family networks. What effects the social magic of high growth is not the cumulative effect of one-off large-scale events such as tent gatherings, but rather the geometric progression of one-on-one conversations in social settings, low-key encounters in which an individual invites a friend or family member to attend an event or socialise with other members of the group. The usefulness of large-scale events is not in directly generating new converts, but in providing a point of focus for the social networks of the already converted. 'In effect, conversion is not about seeking or embracing an ideology; it is about bringing one's religious behavior into alignment with that of one's friends and family members.'[4]

Stark's early fieldwork with Lofland also reassessed the role of preaching in the success of missionaries who routinely attracted high numbers of converts. Instead of simply interviewing converts after the fact, as previous studies had done, Stark and Lofland followed selected missionaries and systematically interviewed their listeners directly following the initial encounter without knowing whether or not they would convert. Then, a year later, they interviewed the much smaller number who had remained with the movement as converts. The intention was twofold: first, to find out whether an initially positive view of the group's ideas was a predictor of conversion, and second, to test how retrospective accounts given after individuals had invested time and energy in the group would compare to the comparatively spontaneous accounts given at the time of first contact. What they found was that those who stayed were not necessarily listeners who initially found the new group's ideas attractive. Rather, the joiners tended to be those who felt some sort of social affinity with the preacher and his

[4] Stark 1996: 16–17; see too Lofland and Stark 1965: 871–2; Lofland 1977.

or her colleagues. If the chemistry was there, even those who initially characterised the group as peddlers of nonsense sometimes stayed on to learn more. But when asked in the follow-up interviews to explain why they had joined, even the sceptics now emphasised the attractiveness of the group's teaching, claiming to remember it as the factor that had caused them to want to become involved. Stark and Lofland had uncovered a kind of positive false-memory syndrome: recruits managed not only to become interested in the ideas espoused by their new friends, but also to forget that they had ever found those ideas unappealing.[5]

In *The Rise of Christianity*, Stark offered a view of early Christianity informed by this work, challenging the traditional emphasis on preaching and miracles as the factors in early Christian missionary success and suggesting that early Christian expansion followed a pattern of growth not so very different from that of the modern Mormons. Since he could make no claim of commanding the ancient sources, Stark let his analysis rest on the empirical work of others, framing his study as a provocation rather than a conclusive intervention. If there was ever a scholarly debate crying out for the distinctive Hopkins mix of source-critical and social-science mastery, this was it.

At the outset of his essay, H. pronounces himself reasonably happy with Stark's suggestions (185 n. 1 [432 n. 1]). Agreeing that the numbers tell a story very different to the one told by the ancient sources and accepted by modern historians, he offers an independent assessment of the numbers along with a caveat about the (vast) margin for error, and then moves swiftly on to the question of why the numbers matter. For all its number-crunching, 'Christian number and its implications' is not really an essay about the numerical growth of the Christian movement. It is the implications, not the numbers, that interest H. most.

First of all, H. avers, the emergence of an audible Christian voice within the cultural mix of the Roman provinces took

[5] Stark 1996: 19–20.

quite some time. It took more than two centuries before Christians became statistically significant, And then, quite swiftly, between the mid-third century and the early fourth, things picked up speed. The now not-so-new faith would prove a powerful tool when it came into the hands of Roman emperors. Critical here was the age and gender profile of the faithful. In modern environments, Stark had noted, women play a key role in networks as brokers of family connectedness. Similarly influential are young adults, a segment of the population unusually receptive to change, and characteristically interested in building social networks. In other words, it is not adult males but their wives and children who tend to be most active in emerging religious networks, an insight that dovetails surprisingly well with the story told by the ancient sources.[6]

Others, notably Elizabeth Castelli, have hesitated to accept Stark's arguments on gender,[7] but H. took them in an unexpected direction. If adult men were comparatively rare in the early Church, he noted, even rarer were adult men who could read and write. H. was a key player in the ongoing conversation about ancient literacy, and in a characteristic lateral move, he showed how the traditional focus on literate adult males had distorted historians' view of the early Christian polity. What, he asked, would happen if the early Christian numbers were seen in light of a post-Harris approach to ancient literacy?[8] A Roman world where few could read and even fewer could write with moderate competence made for an early Church populated by children and other illiterates, not theologians. Even allowing for an unusually high emphasis on literacy within Christian communities, the number of participants literate enough to participate in, say, theological controversies dropped to a handful. In the year 100, for example, H. posited the existence, empire-wide, of a mere

[6] Stark 1996: especially 111–15; Cooper 2005 and 2014: especially 13–16.
[7] Castelli 1998: 249–54.
[8] Harris 1989, with Hopkins 1991b [essay 10].

42 Christian males who could be classed as 'fluent and skilled literates' (212 [463]).

The point to be taken here was not the precise number. H. was as aware as anyone of the limits of statistical projections involving ancient data: 'the number 42', he clarified, 'is here a symbol for a small number of unknown size' (212 [463–4]). The emphasis, simply, was on the word 'small'. With a single stroke, H. uncovered an entirely different picture from the brotherhood of theologically minded literates imagined by Eusebius and accepted by most historians ever since. It was because of the rarity value of literacy, H. suggested, that dogma – and writing about it – became so important to the churches of the second and third centuries. 'Simple capsules of Christian belief statements' were the tool by which a tiny literate élite could control and encourage the constantly renewing pool of recruits (221 [474]). The implication of Stark's slowly building pyramid of one-on-one conversions was that at any given time around two-fifths of all adult members of a given community were comparatively recent converts – and this, H. suggested, would contribute to their sense that they ought to listen to their betters.

Here, perhaps, H. opened a door he did not whole-heartedly want to walk through. 'Christian number' outlines H.'s hypothesis about the role of dogma (and truth claims more generally) in a few evocative paragraphs, moving swiftly toward a concluding section in which the Christian élite allowed – perhaps even encouraged – representatives of the Roman state to redevelop their tradition as 'a supplementary weapon of political and social control', a tool which the state could use 'alongside law, violence and taxation' in managing its subjects (224 [477]). In Hume and Gibbon's 'two-tiered' vision of fourth-century Christianity, men of reason made doomed efforts to wrestle the illiterate and half-converted rabble into some appreciation of the finer points of Christian wisdom,[9] but here, in a surprise inversion, H. took the view that cultural distance allowed literate élites to play fast and

[9] Brown 1981: 12–22 with Cooper 2005.

loose with the social and symbolic capital built up across generations by their cultural inferiors. During and after the age of Constantine, they would hand over the inheritance to be appropriated by the politically powerful.

One of the larger – and to this reader most interesting – items of unfinished business in the wider H. portfolio remains the suggestion, made toward the end of 'Christian number', that in Christianity the Roman state finally discovered the source of 'symbolic unity and exploitable loyalty' (223 [477]) that it had previously lacked but perhaps always needed. The social (and political) value of symbolic unity was a theme to which H. returned repeatedly in his later work. Perhaps most famously in 'Murderous games', his much-cited essay on gladiatorial competitions, H. clarified the value of ritual and spectacle as mechanisms by which existing hierarchies could be both reinforced and challenged. With Fronto (the second-century rhetor and imperial tutor), H. averred that 'Control is secured as much by amusements as by serious things'.[10] But at the same time, public ritual could offer an escape valve for unresolved tensions: 'Under the emperors, as citizens' rights to engage in politics diminished, gladiatorial shows, games and theatre together provided repeated opportunities for the dramatic confrontation of rulers and ruled'.[11] Less well developed, but utterly evocative was the hint of where Christianity might fit in. In 'Christian number', H. returns glancingly to a suggestion mooted in an earlier essay ('From violence to blessing' [essay 8]), that 'the abolition of ritual [at the end of the Republic] created a vacuum, only filled several centuries later by the invasion of Christianity'.[12] If the proposal was never fully elaborated, the idea nonetheless remains worthy of attention.

In many ways, 'Christian number' remains a provocation – a collection of propositions to be tested, rather than of fully worked-out conclusions. But this, perhaps, is as it should be.

[10] Fronto 2.216, cited in Hopkins 1983b: 17.

[11] Hopkins 1983b: 15.

[12] 1991a: 498 n. 36 [essay 8: 339 n. 36]; see too Introduction [17–18] and Elsner [340–5].

H. had no interest in offering certainties, and it is striking how well the approaches outlined here have maintained their heuristic value over time. And it is noticeable, too, how many of the issues whose significance H. flagged in his study of early Christian numbers – gender, educational level, parent–child conflict – are increasingly central to scholarship not only on ancient religion but also on the religious tensions of the contemporary English-speaking world. H. found the balance between imaginative reach and clear-headed common sense in a way that remains all too rare – even as it is ever more urgently needed.

13

THE POLITICAL ECONOMY OF THE ROMAN EMPIRE*

1 Introduction**

The Roman empire lasted as a single political system for five centuries and more. At its height, it stretched from the Black Sea to the Red Sea to the Atlantic Ocean. This essay explores how the empire was governed, how its wealth was created and how that wealth was distributed among competing elements of the population: the central government, the emperor, the aristocracy, the army, the city of Rome, municipal élites, peasants and slaves.

2 Origins and Evolution

By origin, the Roman empire was an empire of conquest, one of a handful of empires which developed throughout the world in the golden millennium of empire formation and religious innovation (c.550 BC–AD 650). This worldwide evolution of large pre-industrial states depended crucially on three material innovations: the effective use of iron weapons and tools, writing and money. Iron was used to conquer and plough. Writing was used to organise collectives of humans toward common objectives, both instrumentally and symbolically in spite of distances in space and time (for example, via written religious

* First published in I. Morris and W. Scheidel (eds) *The Dynamics of Ancient Empires: State Power from Assyria to Byzantium*, Oxford Studies in Early Empires, Oxford/New York: Oxford University Press, 2009, 178–204 (= Hopkins 2009).

** Keith Hopkins died in March 2004, before he was able to revise this chapter for publication. With very minor adjustments, the text of this chapter represents the final version of his manuscript, dated 13 August 2002. Walter Scheidel supplied almost all of the footnotes and bibliographical references in April 2006. Only the references in the main text and elements of footnotes 21, 47–9, 57, 66–7, 71, 76–8, 83, 87 and 89 are derived from Hopkins' own manuscript. We are grateful to Christopher Kelly for helpful comments on these editorial revisions.

texts and law codes). Coinage (first introduced in large quantities into Rome in the third century BC) was used to store value and to reward, motivate and exploit subjects.

In this perspective, the Roman empire represented only one further stage in the gradual evolution of states from tribes to kingdoms and from kingdoms to larger and larger empires. Rome was thus the grandchild of Mycenae and Troy and the heir of countless and now unknown warring tribes, which have left no epics or histories. Rome was also the immediate heir and beneficiary of important empires, such as Carthage (conquered in 202 BC), Macedon (conquered in 168 BC), Syria (63 BC) and Egypt (30 BC). Symptomatically, the first Roman emperor, Augustus (31 BC–AD 14), wore the image of that other great empire-builder Alexander on his signet ring but then later changed his seal to his own image.[1]

One secret of successful empire lay in frequent and sometimes radical innovations. Politically, for example, Rome changed from an early monarchy of allegedly Etruscan kings (traditional dates 753–509 BC) to a native oligarchic aristocracy. And then, much later, Rome changed again, from a primarily aristocratic form of government back to monarchy (31 BC–AD 476 in the West, and for much longer in the eastern empire). But even this oligarchic aristocracy (509–31 BC, in a period conventionally labelled the Republic) was itself significantly restrained by a powerful combination of participatory democracy and the widespread obligation of citizens to military service. So aristocratic leaders had to solicit election to high political office from their social inferiors. And laws were passed by a mass electorate. In disputed votes on the passage of laws and in disputed elections for high office – and most elections were disputed – the plebs had effective political power, even though the collective power of the people was constitutionally manipulated in an elaborate block-voting system, which repeatedly gave disproportionate weight to the more prosperous citizens.[2]

[1] Suet. *Aug.* 50.

[2] The role of the people in the political system of the Republic continues to be much debated: see most recently Millar 1998; Mouritsen 2001; Morstein-Marx 2004.

Aristocratic exploitation of the poor was also limited by the collective power of the Roman citizen army. Once drawn up in military formation, the armed citizens had irresistible power; their repeated withdrawal from cooperation with the rich was celebrated in historical myth, as the 'secessions of the Plebs'. The aristocracy had little choice but to give way and concede privileges to the people. These populist movements, enshrined constitutionally in the prestige and powers of the ten Tribunes of the People and in the Roman sense of collective identity, were historically and symbolically important. They performed perhaps the same function in Roman cultural self-perception as the English charter myth of the Magna Carta or the American individualistic dream of Abraham Lincoln or the self-made millionaire, from rags to riches.

The threat of using military force to resolve political issues recurred and civil wars broke out toward the end of the period of rapid imperial expansion (225–30 BC).[3] Social tensions were exacerbated because the rewards of empire were very unequally distributed. For example, in this period, a huge number, well over 1 million, perhaps even 2 million slaves were imported from conquered provinces into Italy. And these imported slaves displaced even larger numbers of free peasants in central and southern Italy. Tens of thousands of these slaves were subsequently freed and absorbed into the Roman citizen body. The ejected peasants, in their turn, created wave upon wave of migrants to different areas. Many of them were recruited into the Roman army; others went to the city of Rome, where they were tempted by the prospect of state-subsidised and later free wheat doles; others migrated to other growing Italian towns. Yet more peasants and ex-peasant soldiers emigrated to colonies, where they were granted land by victorious generals, at first in southern and northern Italy and later also in the conquered provinces.[4]

[3] See Brunt 1971b: 74–147 for an overview of the period of instability from 133 to 27 BC.

[4] This model has been developed in detail in Hopkins 1978b: 1–98, especially 1–74. For recent qualifications, cf. Jongman 2003c. For the scale of colonisation, see Brunt 1971a: 190–8, 234–65, 294–344. For a higher estimate of slave imports in the last two centuries BC (2–4 million), cf. Scheidel 2005.

This process of overseas colonisation (49–13 BC), especially during and in the aftermath of bitter civil wars, served multiple functions. It removed literally tens of thousands of Italian peasants from the crowded Italian land market and gave them bigger individual plots overseas, which were useful as bulwarks of Roman power in the conquered provinces. So imported slaves and Roman colonists moved in opposite and complementary directions: slaves to Italy and free Romans to the provinces. And, at the same time, the mass emigration of free citizens from Italy freed more land for ownership by the newly enriched and land-hungry aristocrats, who in this period of expansion and insecurity wanted their large estates in Italy worked by imported slaves. There was no other investment opportunity that offered the same security and status. Together, mass overseas colonisation and the regular provision of free wheat doles to a large number of citizens (more than 200,000 adult males) in the city of Rome provided the economic underpinning of Augustus' political settlement.

Augustus was the victorious leader of one faction in the long civil wars that followed Julius Caesar's assassination, in 44 BC. He successfully turned his military power into a quasi-constitutional but autocratic monarchy (the so-called Principate or high empire (31 BC–AD 235)). Augustus and his immediate successors transformed the governance of the Roman state. Familiarity with their long-lasting success should not blind us to the brilliant inventiveness of their reforms.[5]

First, the army was recruited decreasingly from among Roman citizens living in Italy and increasingly from among citizens living in the provinces and from provincials (see section 6.3). The army was no longer recruited ad hoc for particular campaigns but was recruited long-term for from sixteen to twenty-five years, with a very large terminal bonus (equal to almost thirteen years' pay), which helped ensure loyalty. The army (except for the small élite palace guard and metropolitan police force) was not stationed in Italy but strung out

5 On Augustus' regime and reforms, see e.g. Zanker 1988; Raaflaub and Toher 1990; and most recently Eck 2003; Galinsky 2005.

defensively along the distant frontiers. In short, the citizen army that had so threatened the central polity during the last century of the Republic was demilitarised and disempowered. The army was well paid but dispersed so that it could not easily unite to rebel. Few modern third-world countries have managed to control their military so effectively. (Admittedly, the palace guard played a hand in choosing and dismissing emperors – but the selection of emperors rarely had consequences for the efficiency of government.)

Second, under the emperors, the old aristocrats who had survived the murderous civil wars of the late Republic were apparently seduced by their individual chances of success in a superficially restored oligarchy. But now there was an emperor in charge to ensure that all the traditional oligarchic rules about power-sharing were strictly enforced (such as short tenure of offices and long gaps between offices). So, politically successful aristocrats spent about fifteen or twenty long years competing with one another, under the sceptical and supervisory eyes of a less than generous emperor (or his heir), who repeatedly used capricious cruelty (if we are to believe aristocratic commentaries), confiscations and executions as techniques of control. The end result was that the Roman aristocracy became, much more than it had ever been before, an aristocracy of office with extremely low rates of hereditary succession (see section 6.1 for more details). As in the army, élite vacancies were increasingly filled by provincials. So the élite of the conquerors merged with the élite of the conquered.

Third, the emperors at Rome effectively changed the nature of Roman citizenship. The plebs at Rome were disfranchised and no longer constituted the electorate for competing aristocrats; for that task the emperors probably considered that they were too volatile and corruptible. So the emperors enlarged on republican tradition and bought off the plebs with bread and circuses. Not that the metropolitan crowd was completely depoliticised. After all, it still remained each emperor's biggest captive audience. That was where he knew he was king and god; the people in circus or amphitheatre were his personal claque, mostly conned into servile flattery, bought by lavish gifts and shows, but from time to time, as both sides must have known, the crowd could turn nasty and bayed for blood.

The disfranchisement and demilitarisation of the citizens at Rome allowed citizenship itself to become a status symbol. Here the emperors built on what had long been a radical Roman tradition. After all, Rome had begun as a city-state. It had conquered the surrounding towns and tribes and, as it expanded, had incorporated its successive neighbours into partial and then full citizenship.[6] It was a stroke of generous and self-interested genius. Julius Caesar, Augustus and their successors followed this absorptive tradition and increasingly rewarded first Italians, then leading provincials with the symbolic status of citizens. In the reign of Augustus, citizens numbered about 4–5 million people (about 7–10 per cent of the empire's population).[7] Thereafter, the number of citizens steadily increased, until in AD 212 practically all the inhabitants of the empire were awarded full citizenship. It was now time, the emperors apparently considered, for the traditional divide between conquerors and conquered to be forgotten. All inhabitants of the empire were now both citizens and subjects. But they were by no means all equal. A new empire-wide stratification of respectables (*honestiores*) and mean folk (*humiliores*) now separated the privileged from the exploited.[8] And, needless to say, several exquisite gradings (e.g. 'most perfect', 'most egregious', 'illustrious') differentiated the élite.[9]

3 The Fiscal System

Early Rome was, and for long remained, a warrior state. In order to survive and flourish, Rome had to exploit not only its enemies and allies but also its own citizens. Initially, it exploited its own citizens primarily by exacting military service, civil

[6] See Cornell 1995: 293–398 for a full survey.

[7] Augustus, *Res Gestae* 8. Brunt 1971a: 116 reckons with 5 to 6 million, allowing for some under-registration.

[8] Garnsey 1970; Rilinger 1988.

[9] Eck 2000: 262.

obedience and a small proportional tax on property (0.1 per cent of capital value each year).[10] All citizens (adult males) were liable to military service, up to ten years in the cavalry and sixteen years in the infantry, although even in the infantry obligations were graded according to wealth. For example, the very poorest citizens (*proletarii*) were considered capable of contributing only children (*proles*) to the state. At the very least, this rudimentary system implied that the Roman state from early times kept lists of all its citizens and recorded the value of each citizen's property so that each could be allocated with rough justice to one of seven classes (knights, classes I–V, proletarians). Seen another way, the Roman system of obligation, whether to fight or pay taxes, differentiated and reinforced various layers of the status pyramid. But overall the state did not require much money, because most administrative jobs, even the highest, were undertaken by volunteers, that is, by those who could afford them. This ancient parsimony moulded the Roman state's expectations for centuries.

In retrospect, one central problem of the Roman state during this period of rapid growth was how to reward the beneficiaries of empire differentially (e.g. how to let the rich and powerful get richer and more powerful) without alienating the support and compliance of the various strata at the bottom of the social pile. Even the richest Romans needed the obedience of the Roman free poor, slaves, allies and conquered subjects. And that dependency of the rich on the poor constrained exploitation. The problem was all the more intractable because, as the empire expanded, relative positions, even at the bottom of the social scale, shifted.

The allies provide a neat case in point. As Rome defeated its neighbours, they were successively embraced as Latins or allies, as almost like Romans. The sole obligation of the allies in return was to provide Rome with soldiers, annually or as requested. The more Rome expanded territorially within Italy, the more generous Rome became in extending allied status to its defeated Italian enemies. Again, in retrospect, it seems that

[10] Cf. Frank 1933–40: I 75, 79.

Rome's continuous drive to territorial expansion derived partly from Romans' own warrior ambitions and greed and partly from the repeated need to reinforce the allies' military obligations by getting them once again to provide troops. By the end of the second century BC, allies were regularly contributing perhaps two-thirds of the Roman field armies without sharing significantly in the profits of empire.[11] Small wonder, then, that the allies eventually rebelled. Surprisingly, their dominant collective objective (at least in the Roman records) was not secession but overt equality with full Roman citizens. Rome, after a considerable struggle, adroitly surrendered.[12] At one stroke, then, in the 80s BC, the number of adult male Roman citizens trebled to close to one million.[13] Once again, the Roman state had managed to restore the delicate balance between beneficiaries of empire and its exploited subjects.

Defeated enemies understandably paid most of the costs of empire. At first, Roman conquerors compensated themselves handsomely for the trouble of overcoming resistance, with booty, comprising stored treasure in gold and silver, or captured humans, who were either ransomed or sold as slaves. Ideally, this booty was originally handed over to the Roman state, though victorious generals occasionally dedicated a portion to a god to whom they had made a solemn vow in the heat of the battle in return for securing victory. Gradually, generals also took an increasing share for themselves and their lieutenants and distributed relatively modest sums to their lesser officers and soldiers. By the end of the period of rapid imperial expansion, conquering generals and administrators of pacified provinces routinely expected to make substantial personal profits with which to cover the costs of their political careers and their social ostentation at Rome. They shared some of these profits of office with their entourage and occasionally secured land grants for their retiring veterans. Also in the growing empire, defeated enemies paid huge indemnities to

[11] Velleius 2.15.2, with Brunt 1971a: 677–86.

[12] Cf. Mouritsen 1998 for a revisionist account.

[13] Brunt 1971a: 91–9.

recompense Rome for the costs of defeating them. Carthage, for example, paid an indemnity over fifty years after its second defeat, in 202 BC. But gradually these indemnities were transformed into routine taxation, only some of which went to pay and feed occupying troops. The substantial rest was remitted to Rome.

4 Taxation and the Central Government

The Roman empire began as an empire of conquest, which gradually and disjointedly moved along an axis from booty to indemnities to taxation. Some sense of the scale of Roman taxation would be helpful. Unfortunately, reliable statistics are scarce. In the third century BC, before its expansion overseas, the Roman state subsisted on low and fluctuating taxation, which reflected its own unpredictable needs and its reliance on the voluntary services of its citizens. A generous estimate puts its revenues then at 4–8 million sestertii per year. By 150 BC state revenues had risen sevenfold to 50–60 million sestertii per year (at roughly constant prices); before the middle of the last century BC, revenues had risen again sixfold, to 340 million sestertii, as Rome conquered the wealthiest kingdoms accessible. By the middle of the first century AD, again at near constant prices, revenues had more than doubled to about 800 million sestertii per year.[14] In sum, tax revenues had risen at least one hundredfold in three centuries.

But Roman taxes were low as a proportion of probable gross product. Per capita taxes amounted to only 13 sestertii per person per year, or, at a standard (and arbitrary) farmgate price (3 sestertii per *modius* of 6.55 kg), 28 kg wheat equivalent per person/year, 11 per cent of minimum subsistence.[15] This tax load in wheat terms was more than the English or French governments raised regularly in the seventeenth century but very much less than they raised in the eighteenth century.[16]

[14] Frank 1933–40: I 66–8, 126–41, 322–4; Hopkins 1980a: 119 [essay 6: 247], with Duncan-Jones 1994: 45–6 and Hopkins 1995–6: 46.

[15] Hopkins 1995–6: 45–6, slightly modifying earlier estimates in 1980a: 120 [essay 6: 248].

[16] Hopkins 1980a: 120 n. 56 [essay 6: 248 n. 56 and table 6.1].

Since many inhabitants of the Roman empire produced and consumed significantly more than minimum subsistence, the actual rate of taxation was significantly less than 10 per cent, probably closer to 5 per cent of gross product.[17] Of course, the tax burden was probably not evenly distributed. And taxes transmitted to the central government were probably less than the total of taxes exacted by greedy and corrupt tax collectors. It seems clear that, at least in Egypt, the Roman state operated a pervasive and invasive apparatus, even at these levels of tax extraction.[18] When I say that taxes were low, I do not mean to imply that Roman peasants, paying for benefits they could not see, typically experienced them as low. Indeed, there is significant evidence that many Egyptian peasants struggled to pay their poll-tax in cash by splitting it into several instalments.[19]

Why were Roman taxes so low? Two immediate answers come to mind: one genetic (in the Genesis sense), the other structural. Genetically, the Roman state had set its tax targets only by the need to recover the costs of war and defence. Since it was an empire of conquest, taxpayers were defeated subjects (after 167 BC until the fourth century AD, the citizen inhabitants of Italy paid no land tax). And, since it was an empire of conquest, the state did not offer its subjects much service: rudimentary justice to prevent violence, roads for speedy military communications and defence. Tax collection was the main job of provincial governors. But even by the second century AD, there was only one Roman élite administrator for every 400,000 inhabitants of empire, whereas in twelfth-century China there was one élite administrator per 15,000 people.[20] Roman administrators levied their taxes and by and large provided only peace in return.[21]

[17] cf. Hopkins 1995–6: 47, for taxes at 5–7 per cent of actual GDP.

[18] Wallace 1938.

[19] Wallace 1938: 116–34.

[20] Hopkins and Burton 1983b: 186. Even if we allow for perhaps up to 10,000 support staff (slaves and seconded soldiers) in this period, total numbers increased several times in the following centuries: Kelly 2004: 111.

[21] This may be a misleading generalisation. One mid-second-century administrator in Egypt received nearly 2,000 petitions submitted in fewer than three days (*P. Yale* I 61). He had answers publicly posted for the petitioners to read ⟨Hopkins 1991b: 137 n. 9 [essay 10: 368 n. 9]⟩.

Structurally, the Roman state always operated a binary system of beneficiaries. The state shared the profits from conquest with its leaders and, to a lesser extent, with its soldiers. Public taxes were low so that private incomes of the rich, primarily rents from estates, could be higher. Rents and taxes were in competition for a limited surplus. And, at the same time, they were complementary. The profits of the rich bound them into supporting the state, of which they were the prime beneficiaries. The aggregate wealth and income of the aristocracy, broadly understood, was probably as great as, or greater than, the tax income of the central government.[22] That is why emperors in need repeatedly confiscated the estates of the super-rich, both as an expression of their autocratic power and because these were the biggest assets available in the Roman economy. But, even if these stolen estates were incorporated into the private property of the emperors, their management had to be delegated back to an aristocrat (in the broad definition of the term). In sum, aristocratic wealth seriously constrained the central government's tax-raising powers. And, in the later empire, rich landowners' capacity to resist the central government's attempts to raise taxes was the rock on which the western empire foundered.

5 The Steady State

The Roman empire was one of the largest political systems ever created, and one of the longest lasting. Only the Chinese empire lasted longer. At its height, in the second century AD, the Roman empire stretched from the Atlantic coast of North Africa to the Black Sea and from Hadrian's Wall, in the north of England, to the Red Sea. Its land mass was equal to more than half that of the continental United States. The territory once occupied by the Roman empire is now split among forty different countries. Its population totalled perhaps 60 million people, or between one-fourth and one-sixth of the whole world's population at the time.[23]

[22] Hopkins 1995–6: 50. See now also Jongman 2007: 615–17.
[23] Frier 2000: 814 (Roman empire); J. E. Cohen 1995: 400 (world).

Size matters; it was an important source and index of the power that Rome exercised. In a pre-industrial economy, land and labour are the two primary ingredients of wealth. The larger the Roman empire became, the more people it subjected and the more taxes it exacted. The more wealth the Roman state controlled, the more territory it was able to acquire and defend. For example, between 225 and 25 BC, the period of Rome's striking imperial expansion, the population subject to Roman rule increased perhaps fifteenfold, from about 4 to 60 million people. But the government's tax revenues rose by at least a hundredfold (from about 4–8 million sestertii in 250 BC to more than 800 million sestertii in 25 BC, at roughly constant prices: see section 4). Rome had conquered and absorbed several mini-empires (Macedon, Syria, Egypt) and numerous tribes. It had total control of the Mediterranean basin and beyond.

The huge size of the Roman empire was a symptom of the fanatical dedication at all levels of Roman society to fighting wars and to military discipline and of the desire both for immediate victory and for long-term conquest. 'No human force could resist Roman might' (Livy 1.16.7). Some Romans even imagined that they could, if they wished, rule or had already 'subjugated the whole world' (Augustus, *Res Gestae,* Preface). As it was, they absorbed all that (or more than what) was then worth conquering, with the giant exception of the Parthian empire, on its eastern borders. Further expansion, as the first emperor, Augustus, was reported to have said, would have been like fishing with a golden hook (Suet. *Aug.* 25.4). The prize was not worth the risk. A Roman historian in the second century, looking back over more than a century of 'long and stable peace and the empire's secure prosperity', wrote:

> Since they [the emperors] control the best regions of the earth and sea, they wisely wish to preserve what they have rather than to extend the empire endlessly by including barbarian tribes, which are poor and unprofitable. (Appian, Preface 7)

Appian commented that he had himself seen some of these barbarian ambassadors at court in Rome, offering themselves up as subjects. But their petitions had been refused, as they would have been 'of no use'.

The empire's persistence was a symptom of the thoroughness with which Romans destroyed previous political systems and overrode the separate cultural identities of the kingdoms and tribes which they had conquered. Or, rather, the Romans, particularly in areas of already established polities and high culture, left their victims with a semi-transparent veil of self-respect that allowed them an illusion of local autonomy. This partial autonomy was limited to individual towns (not groups of towns). And it was restricted by Roman provincial governors' expectation of subservience and, reciprocally, by the local élites' own desire for assimilation – whether that meant assuming Roman culture and Roman-style rank or borrowing Roman power in order to resolve local power struggles. Either way, as élite and sub-élite provincials became more like Romans, and filled Roman administrative posts, local independence was systematically undermined. And provincial cultures all over the empire, at least in outward veneer, became ostensibly Romanised.[24]

For example, by the end of the second century, half of the central Roman senate was of provincial origin.[25] In western Europe, the language of the conquerors percolated to all levels and effectively displaced native local languages as the *lingua franca*. Latin became the common root of modern Romance languages. But, in the eastern half of the empire, Greek remained the accepted language of Roman government. Even there, it was an instrument of change; for example, in the ancient culture of Egypt, writing in Greek letters (Coptic) displaced native Egyptian demotic script.[26] And many Romans, to establish their credentials as people of high culture, learned Greek. Assimilation was a two-way process, by which the ideal of what it meant to be Roman itself gradually changed. That

[24] For recent perspectives on the complex process of culture change in the Roman empire, see Woolf 1998; MacMullen 2000; Keay and Terrenato 2001; Cooley 2002; Hingley 2005.

[25] Hopkins and Burton 1983b: 144–5, 200 table 3.15, based on Hammond 1957: 77.

[26] Hopkins 1991b: 144–8 [essay 10: 375–9].

said, the impact of Roman rule is still visible in the ruins of Roman towns from all over the empire: temples to Roman Jupiter and to the Capitoline gods, statues of emperors (in some towns by the dozen), triumphal arches, colonnaded town squares and steam baths. To be Roman was to be sweaty and clean. The Roman empire was an empire of conquest but also a unitary symbolic system.

A modern map gives only a slight indication of Roman achievements. Rome's huge empire was created when the fastest means of land transport was the horse-drawn chariot, the pack-donkey and the ox-cart. So the Roman empire was in effect several months wide – and larger in winter than in summer. But the modern map shows up the empire's single salient feature: the centrality of the Mediterranean Sea. The Mediterranean Sea was at the centre of Roman power, if only because transport by land, in Roman conditions, cost fifty or sixty times as much (per ton/km) as transport by sea and about ten times as much as transport by river.[27]

So the Roman empire was at heart a fusion of coastal cultures, bound together by cheap sea transport, except in winter, when ships usually did not sail. The suppression of piracy during the last century BC made the Mediterranean into the empire's internal sea. Cheap transport gave the Roman empire a geopolitical advantage, which in its economic impact was the equivalent of the highly productive irrigation agriculture at the core of other pre-industrial empires. The city of Rome could profit from and enjoy the surplus produce imported from all its coastal provinces. Rome stood at the centre of a network of major cities (Alexandria, Antioch, Carthage, Cadiz, Ephesus, Aquileia), all of which were on the seacoast or rivers.

The city of Rome was by far the richest market in the whole empire, by volume and by value. Prices there were highest. It was there that merchants could make (or lose) their fortunes. It was there that the emperor and high aristocrats had their palaces. Rome was where emperors and aristocrats spent a large part of their taxes and rents. Rome was the prime engine of

[27] Hopkins 1983a: 104–5 [essay 7: 302–4].

long-distance trade. The principle behind this assertion is simple. Whatever was imported into Rome from the provinces as money taxes and money rents, provincial towns had to earn back (taking one year with another) by the manufacture and sale of goods. In order to be able to pay money taxes again in subsequent years, provincial towns (villages, peasants) had to earn back the money that they had paid and sent overseas in taxes and rents. This simple equation – taxes plus rents exported roughly equalled in value exported and traded goods – however oversimplified it is, highlights the lines of trade and the volume of traffic that criss-crossed the Mediterranean, through a network of coastal or riverine towns centred on, and fuelled primarily by, consumption in the city of Rome.[28]

The centrality of the Mediterranean should not blind us to the huge landmass of Roman conquests. Julius Caesar, in pursuit of military glory, advanced Roman power to Gaul and Britain. Under Augustus, armies and administrators incorporated large territories in north-western Spain, western Germany, Switzerland and the Balkans. In sum, the Romans had advanced the boundaries of empire as far as the ocean in the west and the Sahara desert in the south. To the north-west, the rivers Rhine and Danube (eventually supplemented by a long line of forts) roughly demarcated the comfortable limits of Roman power and also served as convenient lines of supply to the frontier armies.[29]

The considerable distance between the city of Rome and its land frontiers had far-reaching but diverse, even contradictory, implications. Distance and slow travel overland effectively insulated Rome and its political leaders from attack by marauding barbarians (until AD 410) or by rebellious generals, whose collaboration was in any case hindered by fragmented commands split along an extended frontier and among rival aristocrats. Frontier armies intervened effectively only twice in central politics (in AD 69 and 193) in more than two centuries.

[28] This model was first developed in Hopkins 1980a [essay 6] and revised in Hopkins 1995–6.

[29] On the imperial frontiers, see especially Dyson 1985; Whittaker 1994.

The Roman military was depoliticised – an achievement all the more remarkable if we compare it with the frequency of coups d'état in contemporary third-world states. Complementarily, sheer size and slowness of communications also prevented close control and swift reaction by the central government to crises on the periphery. Even in an emergency, for example, it took nine days for a messenger on a series of horses to ride from Mainz, Germany, to Rome.[30] Routine messages about the death of rulers took very much longer and the time of their arrival was unpredictable.[31] In the late third century AD, in an effort to resolve these problems, emperors split the empire into four parts, each with its capital closer to the frontiers. But there was another and seemingly insuperable problem. The northern territories were economically less developed, less urbanised and less densely populated than the southern coastal regions of the Mediterranean. These northern regions could only with difficulty in Roman (as against post-medieval) times produce sufficient taxes to pay for their own extensive defence.

6 Configurations of Power

6.1 *Emperors and Aristocrats*

For emperors, too, the maintenance of control was (it seems reasonable to imagine) a central objective. If it was, they were not very good at it. Of the first eleven emperors, only four died (or were reputed to have died) naturally. The basic problem was the founding ideology of the Principate. Monarchy was made more acceptable to the traditional senatorial aristocracy by the fiction that the emperor was only first among equals (*princeps*). The clear implication was, therefore, that any Roman aristocrat of distinguished descent could himself become emperor. Hence, there was a long-term structural tension between emperors and aristocrats. That was a basic feature of Roman

[30] Tac. *Hist.* 1.12, 1.56 with Ramsay 1925: 63–5; cf. Plut. *Caes.* 17.4 (from Rome to the Rhone in seven days).

[31] Duncan-Jones 1990: 7–29.

politics. Emperors in the first century killed dozens of aristocrats. They repeatedly created a reign of terror that would have made Ivan the Terrible seem mild.

The Roman aristocracy was remarkably different from any feudal or post-feudal European aristocracy. At its core was a political élite of 600 senators. They were chosen in each generation both from among the sons of senators and from a politically inactive, much larger landowning élite, originally based in Italy but increasingly derived from all over the empire. Ideologically, the image usually represented by Roman élite writers (and by modern historians suckered to think that ideology represents reality instead of disguising it) is that the Roman senatorial aristocracy was hereditary. But, in fact, intergenerational succession rates in the Roman aristocracy were remarkably low. The basic reason was that, unlike European feudal and post-feudal aristocracies, which were aristocracies based on land ownership and hereditary title, the Roman senatorial aristocracy was a competitive aristocracy of office. And, in order to be a top official (ordinary consul or supplementary/suffect consul), the successful contestant had to have held a whole series of administrative posts; this demand was sometimes relaxed for claimants of very distinguished descent, who were promoted quickly without any qualifying military experience. In short, the successful Roman political aristocrat had to have been a successful administrator and to remain in favour for years, sometimes under different emperors or influential advisers at court.

The net effect, as I have indicated, was an extraordinarily low rate of succession in the Roman political élite. Roughly speaking, in the first two centuries AD and beyond, far fewer than half of top consuls had a consular son(s); among the second rank of supplementary consuls, overall far fewer than a quarter had a consular son, grandson or great-grandson. The number of consuls after AD 70 varied between eight and ten per year, far fewer than the usual cohort of twenty entrants to the senate at age about 25; allowing for death, between half and two-thirds of entrants to the senate achieved a consulship. By extension, it is reasonable to assume that among the third-ranking senators who never became consul, succession rates were even lower than for first- or second-ranking consuls. Overall, the succession rate among all known senators in the second century was less than half that of British barons in the fourteenth or fifteenth centuries.[32]

The great majority of senators were newcomers to the political aristocracy. Looked at from another perspective, and as in modern political élites, most Roman politicians came from families that sent representatives into politics for only one generation. Complementarily, and this for our present purposes is most important, there was a rather large pool of rich landowners spread across the empire, some of whom occasionally sent a son as its representative into central politics. These provincial families subsequently profited for generations in their home localities from the hereditary honorary status that their exceptional representative's political success had secured through senatorial membership or consular status, without incurring, again, the huge expense, risk – or profits – that a political career involved. The Roman aristocracy, broadly understood, had a small semi-hereditary core, a fluid and porous outer ring of politically and administratively active representatives (albeit with no explicit representative functions) and a broader pool of potential senators who were politically active, if at all, only at the local level.

By tradition, senatorial aristocrats were the wealthiest men at Rome. Under the Republic (until 31 BC), they were the generals and governors who benefited most from the booty and plunder of wars and provincial administration.[33] Under the Principate, emperors controlled senatorial aristocrats (at least according to history books written by senators and their allies) by a whole array of divisive tactics. I list them without being able to assign them relative weights:

- capricious and terrorising persecution, imprisonment, murder
- strict adherence to the old-fashioned rules of oligarchic power sharing (short tenure of office, collegiality, gaps between offices, age-related promotion, prosecutions for corruption)

[32] Hopkins and Burton 1983b.
[33] Shatzman 1975.

- cutting of the ties between political careers and popular election (the Roman plebs were disfranchised early in the first century AD)
- supplementing of collective senatorial decisions (*senatus consulta*) with individual decisions made by the emperor himself (*decreta*), sometimes in consultation with friends (*consilium*)
- denial of military experience to the most prestigious aristocrats – an increase in the status costs of being an aristocrat at court in Rome (many were bankrupted)
- promotion of provincial newcomers to senatorial rank (which diluted hereditary hold)

The cumulative impact of all these devices was to weaken the collective and institutional power of the senate as a consultative, policy-making body. The court, and its corridors, displaced the senate as the powerhouse of the Roman state.[34]

Nevertheless, the monarchy, for all the aristocratic complaints, provided a carapace for aristocratic enrichment. The landowning aristocracy, broadly understood, increased in aggregate prosperity.[35] The basic reason for this is clear. In republican times, nearly all senatorial wealth was concentrated in Italian landholdings and investment in in-town housing, supplemented by investment through agents in collective enterprises, such as overseas trade and tax collection. Expert scholars will know the slender evidential base for generalisations of this type, but my reasoning is simple enough. The larger the investment needed (for example, in Roman housing or in overseas trade), the more likely was senatorial involvement. After all, a single 400-ton ship laden with wheat arriving in a port near Rome was worth up to 1 million sestertii, the minimum qualifying fortune for a senator; one luxury cargo arriving in Alexandria from India is known from a recently discovered papyrus fragment to have been valued at 7 million sestertii.[36] If no senators were involved in such ventures (to say nothing of silver mines, of which more later), we have to posit the existence of a class of equally wealthy non-senators. These were presumably the ascendants

34 Winterling 1999.

35 Mratschek-Halfmann 1993.

36 Rome: Hopkins 1983a: 101 [essay 7: 297] (for a value of 400,000–600,000 sestertii, which must be adjusted upwards to account for higher wheat prices in the capital). Alexandria: Hopkins 1995–6: 59 with 73 n. 75.

of future senators. And I have already argued for the existence of a wider group of basically landowning 'senatorands' – that is, families capable of sending a representative into aristocratic politics occasionally. Under the emperors, aristocratic wealth was no longer concentrated in Italy.

Under the emperors, aristocrats increasingly owned estates spread over the whole empire. In the second century, they were legally required to own first one-third, later reduced to one-quarter, of their estates in Italy – in itself an index of their continuing provincialisation.[37] Over time, aristocrats collectively owned a significant share not just of Italy but of the whole Mediterranean basin. In the middle of the first century AD, six senators were reputed (of course it was an exaggeration, but a straw in the right wind) to own all Tunisia.[38] Aristocrats' aggregate wealth increased, as did the fortunes of individual aristocrats. A few illustrative figures will suffice. Cicero in the middle of the last century BC wrote that a rich Roman needed an annual income of 100,000 to 600,000 sestertii; in the late first century, Pliny, a middling senator, had an annual income of about 1.1 million sestertii per year. In the fourth century, middling senators in the city of Rome were said to enjoy incomes of 1,333 to 2,000 Roman pounds of gold a year, equivalent to 6–9 million sestertii per year.[39] In sum, aristocratic fortunes, on these, admittedly vulnerable figures, had doubled or trebled in the first century of the Principate and had again risen more than sixfold between AD 100 and 400. Monarchy and the politico-economic integration of the whole empire, however superficial, had enabled aristocrats to become very much richer.

6.2 The City of Rome

The city of Rome was by far the largest city in the Roman world. By the end of the first century BC, it had a population

[37] Plin. *Ep.* 6.19.4; SHA *Marc.* 11.
[38] Plin. *HN* 18.35.
[39] Hopkins 1995–6: 50 with 69 n. 37.

of about 1 million people.[40] It was as large as London in 1800, when London was the largest city in the West. Rome could be so large because it was the capital not just of Italy (population c.7 million) but of a Mediterranean empire. Rome's population had grown rapidly by more than six times from an estimated 150,000 in 225 BC.[41] The capital's growth was fed by three streams of immigrants:

- free citizens and allied rural emigrants from Italy (as small peasant families were displaced by fewer slaves working on larger farms);
- slaves, adult males particularly, who were forced to migrate by Rome's conquest of the Mediterranean basin in the last two centuries BC;
- free craftsmen and traders, particularly from coastal towns in the Mediterranean.

The city of Rome grew, and its huge size was maintained only by a steady stream of immigrants.

Rome could be so large, partly because the Roman state (from 58 BC) continually subvented and guaranteed (with occasional glitches) a basic supply of wheat to its registered free citizen population. The reported number of recipients varied, but in the reign of Augustus seems to have stabilised at around 200,000–250,000 adult males. Each received 33 kg wheat (5 *modii* of 6.55 kg) per month, which was more than enough for one adult (if he did not live on bread alone), but not enough for a family. In the fourth century AD, state handouts were supplemented by rations of wine and pork.[42]

The state supply of free wheat to a fixed number of adult male citizens had significant political, economic and demographic implications. Free distributions symbolised citizens' right to benefit collectively from the fruits of conquest. Romans were now the chosen people. The first emperor, Augustus, reportedly wondered whether to abolish the wheat dole but wisely decided against it, allegedly on the grounds that the issue might become a political football and others might seek or

[40] Hopkins 1978b: 96–8.
[41] Cf. Morley 1996: 39 (?200,000 in 200 BC).
[42] Rickman 1980: 156–209.

gain kudos from the dole's restoration.[43] Augustus' successor, Tiberius (AD 14–37), preserved the dole but abolished the people's participation in elections. Citizens at Rome had become state pensioners, bribed into quiescent dependence by bread and circuses. The emperors' generosity underwrote their continued popularity. Rome was, after all, the main stage on which emperors acted their role as rulers of the world.

Economically, the exaction, storage, transport and distribution of 100,000 tons of wheat per year to Rome was a sizeable task. The wheat came primarily from southern Sicily, North Africa and Egypt.[44] The volume itself was not the problem, though at peak periods Rome's port at Ostia and the short stretch of the Tiber (21 km) along which barges were hauled must have been jammed. Egypt alone yielded in wheat tax more than the city of Rome and the frontier armies needed together.[45] It was more a problem of organisation, consistency of supply and price. On the private market (since state supplies had to be supplemented), wheat prices in Rome were four times higher than they were in Egypt and two to three times as high as they were in Sicily and the rest of Italy.[46] The city of Rome stood at the peak of a pyramid of rising prices. The total cost of supplying state wheat to Rome amounted to more than 15 per cent of state revenues (100,000 tons at 9 sestertii per *modius* = 135 million sestertii). But the supply of free wheat to citizens at Rome presumably also helped the labour force buy wine and oil produced on the estates of the rich and/or held down the price of labour in the capital. The free wheat dole subsidised the rich as well as the poor.

Demographically, the attractions of the free wheat dole and the huge consumer market that Rome constituted must have helped stimulate a continuous flow of immigrants to the city of Rome. In outsiders' imagination, the streets of Rome were paved with gold. For the Christian writer of Revelation,

[43] Suet. *Aug.* 42.
[44] Garnsey 1988: 231–2.
[45] Hopkins 1995–6: 55–6.
[46] Hopkins 1995–6: 58 with 73 n. 68. On the grain market in the Roman empire in general, see now Erdkamp 2005.

Rome was a scarlet harlot adorned with gold and jewels, sitting astride its seven hills, sucking the blood of countless nations and drinking from a golden cup full of abominations and the impurities of fornication; Rome was the 'great city that holds sway over the kings of the earth'.[47] In a Jewish writer's imagination, Rome had 365 streets; in each street there were 365 palaces; each palace had 365 storeys; and each storey contained enough food to feed the whole world.[48] Rome, with its huge baths, its temple roofs glistening with gilded bronze, beckoned as a city of opportunity even to those who had little chance of ever going there.

But in pre-industrial societies, larger cities have higher deathrates than smaller cities, and smaller cities have higher deathrates than the surrounding countryside. The city of Rome was a deathtrap, which sucked people in and killed them off with infectious diseases. Even the baths, which cleansed the relatively prosperous, may have helped concentrate diseases (like modern hospitals); Roman doctors recommended baths for people suffering from malaria, cholera, dysentery, infestation by worms, diarrhoea and gonorrhoea, and the emperor Hadrian allowed the sick to use baths in the morning before the healthy.[49]

So Rome could maintain its huge population only by constant influx of immigrants, both from its Italian hinterland and from overseas. If deathrates in Rome were only ten per thousand higher than in the rest of Italy – and Wrigley thinks that in London in the eighteenth century, the difference may have been significantly greater than that – then Rome, with a population of 1 million people, needed 10,000 migrants a year.[50] If the difference in mortality between metropolis and countryside was fifteen per thousand, then just to maintain its population, Rome needed 15,000 fresh migrants per year.[51] Immigration to

47 Revelation 17.

48 Babylonian Talmud, *Pesahim* 118b.

49 Celsus, *Med.* 4.2–28; SHA *Had.* 22. On disease in the city of Rome in particular, see Scheidel 2003.

50 Wrigley 1967: 46; cf. Morley 1996: 44.

51 Cf. Scheidel 2003: 175 (?20 per 1,000).

Rome took place at double the rate of migration to the army (see section 6.3). It must have prevented any natural increase in Italian population and/or contributed, like military recruitment, to Italy's depopulation.[52] On the other hand, migration had a triply beneficial impact. It allowed an effective increase in agricultural productivity (the remaining peasants, fewer in number, could each work more land); it provided migrants who were lucky enough to return to their hometown or village an image of metropolitan lifestyles (classy pots and silk underwear); and it either increased or maintained the market for agricultural and manufactured (handmade) exports.

6.3 The Army

The army was the biggest (typically 300,000 soldiers) and by far the most effectively organised power grouping in Roman politics. It combined hierarchy, training, a clear command structure, discipline, regular pay, flexibility in unit size (from small maniple to army-size groups of several legions) and aggressive persistence in the pursuit of fixed objectives. It had no similarly effective rival or imitator in civilian politics. During the late republican period, soldiers, in search of bounty and security, had repeatedly intervened in central Italian politics. But, under the emperors, as part of the Augustan settlement, the army was effectively depoliticised. This was an amazing political achievement.

After 31 BC, frontier armies intervened directly in central politics only twice in more than two centuries: in AD 69 (after the death of Nero) and in AD 193 (after the assassination of Commodus and the auctioning of the imperial throne by the palace guards). The Roman peace meant both an end to imperial expansion – with the exception of Britain and Dacia (modern Romania) and the absorption of marginal client kingdoms such as Mauretania (modern Morocco) – and the internal pacification of conquered provinces. As a result, for

[52] See also Morley 1996: 33–54.

almost two centuries, most inhabitants of the Roman empire never or rarely saw a soldier. Rome had become a civil society.

This radical shift toward depoliticising the military was (?purposefully) engineered by a whole series of evolutionary changes.[53] The great bulk of the army was eventually dispersed along distant frontiers, in garrisons that usually held only one legion (of 5,000–6,000 soldiers), so that cooperation between rival commanders that might threaten the centre became very difficult to achieve. Governors of provinces in which legions were stationed were typically chosen only after years of loyal service and almost never from among the top echelons of the senatorial élite; that is, army commanders by social rank were not regarded as potential claimants to the throne.[54] They held office for only shortish terms (typically three years). Under-officers – tribunes, prefects and centurions – also either held office for short terms and/or were shifted to different legions on promotion so that no long-term loyalty could build up between under-officers and men.[55]

Soldiers serving in legions (about 150,000 men), on the expiry of their service of twenty-five to twenty-six years, were paid a loyalty bonus equal to thirteen years' pay. The length of soldiers' service was increased from an unsustainable sixteen years, first to twenty and then to twenty-five years; this extension of military service both reduced costs, because a large proportion of soldiers died during these extra years, and mitigated problems of recruitment. This new system of cash bonuses to veterans on retirement, inaugurated in AD 6, helped divert Roman legionaries from their traditional ambition to end their days owning Italian land – a process that had contributed so much to land seizures and the consequent political instability of the late Republic. Instead, veterans, increasingly of provincial origin, typically settled in the provinces, along the frontiers where they had already lived the bulk of their lives.[56]

[53] See especially Campbell 1984, 2002: 106–19.
[54] Hopkins and Burton 1983b: 173.
[55] Domaszewski 1967: 97 and n. 2.
[56] E.g. Mann 1983.

The depoliticisation of the army under the emperors was based on long service along distant frontiers, on the regular grant of a large bounty on retirement, on the increasingly provincial origin of the army and on the severance of the link between citizens at Rome (soon disfranchised) and their empowerment by military service. There were fewer citizen soldiers and effectively no citizen voters.

Locating the new imperial army along the distant frontiers contributed significantly to the rural depopulation of Italy, even though the imperial army was necessarily, substantially and increasingly of provincial (i.e. not Italian) origin. A simple calculation illustrates probabilities. At twenty years of service, a legionary (i.e. citizen) army of 150,000 soldiers needs on average 9,500 recruits per year; it may seem, as it has seemed to some scholars, a smallish number from a free population of 5 million people. But if soldiers were recruited at age 20, they would have equalled 20 per cent of all Italian citizen 20-year-olds (if Italy's free citizen population equalled 5 million, then, in ancient conditions of mortality ($e_0 \sim 25$), there were only 47,500 male survivors to age 20).[57] If the soldiers then spent their army service in the provinces and settled there, Italy would be rapidly depopulated by emigration at this rate. I must stress that this calculation is a statement not of fact but of parametric probability. Fertility obviously depends on the females left behind as much as on the soldiers who emigrated, and about that we know nothing. But at first sight it seems that an unforeseen consequence of Augustus' and his successors' policy of locating citizen troops along the frontiers was an immediate and significant depopulation of Italy.

Surviving evidence of burial inscriptions, which may or may not be statistically representative, suggests that during the reign of Augustus, 68 per cent of legionaries were of Italian

[57] Accurate calculation is more complex than this. Crucially, we do not know what happened to the fertility of the women whom the soldiers would have married if they had stayed in Italy. The estimate for annual recruitment has been extrapolated from Scheidel 1996b: 122 table 3.15. For similar intake requirements (15–20 per cent of Italian 20-year-old males) under the early emperors, cf. Scheidel 1996b: 93–4, 95 n. 18.

origin. By the middle of the first century, this proportion had fallen to less than half (48 per cent) and by the end of the century to 22 per cent; in the second century, apparently, only 2 per cent of citizen soldiers were of Italian origin.[58] No wonder that in AD 9, after the crushing defeat of a Roman army (three legions each nominally of 6,000 soldiers were killed in north Germany), Augustus, who feared that the Germans would invade Italy, had great difficulty in raising recruits and resorted against all tradition to recruiting ex-slaves.[59]

Military costs remained by far the largest element in the Roman state budget; in the first century AD, they accounted for more than half the total (c.450? out of a budget of more than 800 million sestertii).[60] And, although, with hindsight, we know that the Roman army did not often intervene in central politics, Roman emperors must always have feared that it might. The army had to be placated. What is surprising, then, is that, given the army's potential for disruption, soldiers' pay in terms of silver never surpassed the level reached in the reign of Augustus. Put another way, every time that the nominal pay of soldiers was subsequently raised (in c. AD 83?, 193 and 212), the silver coinage was soon debased so that the cost in precious metal to the treasury was held roughly constant.[61] Soldiers collectively did not exercise their armed might to increase their sector share of total wealth. For whatever reason, it looks as though total army costs had reached the limit of what Roman financial administrators could raise or allocate to the army within the state budget.

The dispersion of the legionary armies and their auxiliary (non-citizen) counterparts, hundreds of miles from Rome along the frontiers, left a power vacuum at the centre. It was filled partially by the palace (praetorian) guard. This palace guard was a small élite troop, a few thousand strong, of highly paid soldiers, garrisoned in Rome. It was commanded by usually two prefects, each of whose powers were designed to balance

[58] Derived from Forni 1953: 159–212,with 1974: 366–80.
[59] Suet. *Aug.* 25.
[60] Hopkins 1995–6: 46 (see 1980a: 119 [essay 6: 247]).
[61] Duncan-Jones 1994: 227 table 15.6 summarises the data on silver fineness.

those of the other. They were considered to be extremely influential within palace politics, but they were also only knights (albeit with the rank of consuls) and so socially disbarred from becoming emperor (until Macrinus in AD 217, but he reigned for only one year). On several occasions, the palace guard played a key role in securing the throne for a particular candidate. And, for historians of Rome, ancient and modern, individual successions to the throne have often seemed to be the very stuff of politics.

7 Economic Growth

Over the past few years, there have been several attempts to locate economic growth in antiquity.[62] Of course, some scholars have denied that it occurred. Certainly, there was never in antiquity the steep curve of economic growth that marks the modern world.[63] Perhaps the very search is an attempt to find the roots of modern experience in classical antiquity, which forged so many aspects of western culture.

All that said, I still think the Roman empire provided conditions for modest economic growth (a growth that was minuscule by modern standards but significant for the experience of some Romans):

- by extending the area of cultivated land, especially in north-western Europe and the Balkans;
- by increasing the size of agricultural units to achieve economies of scale;
- by using systematic accounting methods to control costs or measure relative rates of return from different crops;
- by allowing and encouraging the growth or persistence of towns, with their relatively sophisticated division of labour;
- by achieving significant increases in productivity, but only in very limited spheres, which had only a superficial impact on the total economy.

[62] E.g. Millett 2001; Saller 2002; Morris 2004, 2005; Hitchner 2005; Jongman 2007; Scheidel 2007b.

[63] Cf. Saller 2002: 259 fig. 12.1.

Under Roman rule, the northern provinces adopted some of the superior farming techniques, first tried out in the south-east, such as crop rotation, selective breeding (for example, to produce larger oxen) and new crops (for example, peas and cabbage were first introduced into Britain under Roman rule – with long-term effects on British cooking). Even if some of the extra land brought into cultivation was marginal, with lower productivity, nevertheless the total impact of Roman conquest was both to increase average agricultural productivity and aggregate product.[64]

We have exiguous but significant evidence in Roman agricultural handbooks that at least some landowners were thinking (however inexpertly) about relative rates of return from different crops and the most effective use of labour and draught animals. The Heroninus archive from Roman Egypt in the third century AD shows systematic attempts to control draught-animal costs by the unified management of the scattered farms that made up a large estate.[65] Perhaps what is most surprising is that the central Roman government, at the end of the third century and in the fourth, actually tried to increase agricultural productivity (and its own tax returns) by encouraging farmers to cultivate extra land (emphyteutic leases) and to use innovative techniques.[66] Alas, we have no idea how successful or isolated these initiatives were. But at least Roman rulers tried, and that is quite unexpected.

Successive empires that came under Roman control, and the Roman empire in particular, encouraged the growth of towns and so of non-agricultural occupations. Towns, even pre-industrial towns, make possible a relatively sophisticated division of labour and concentrate higher value production. There are eighty-five different occupations recorded in stone inscriptions and painted slogans on the street walls of the small town of Pompeii (population c.12,000?), 110 in the small town

64 Extension: e.g. Drexhage, Konen and Ruffing 2002: 72–84. Intensification: e.g. Kron 2000, 2002.

65 Rathbone 1991.

66 ⟨Bagnall 1993: 311–12⟩; see too *P.Panop.Beatty* 2.211–14, discussed in Kelly 2004: 118.

of Kōrykos in southern Turkey and 268 occupations named on stone inscriptions found in the city of Rome.[67] All these lists are likely to be incomplete, and besides, having separate names for slightly different occupations or hierarchical gradings within occupations may reflect cultural differences as well as differences in occupational specialisation. That said, relative numbers can serve as a crude index of economic development. Compare, for example, the Roman number with the more than 350 occupations found in London in the eighteenth century.[68]

What is particularly striking about the towns of the Roman empire is their number, their location mainly in the coastal regions around the Mediterranean Sea and the size of the largest cities. Rome, as we have seen, had a population (if our ancient evidence is to be trusted) of about 1 million people; Alexandria is thought to have had a population of half a million people.[69] Antioch and Carthage had populations of well over 100,000. Although each of these secondary but major cities began as the capital of a mini-empire later conquered by Romans, they maintained or even expanded their populations even after they ceased to be the seats of kings. Unlike Rome, their populations were not subsidised by free distributions of basic food. They had to support themselves by the services that they provided, by manufacture and by trade. Only to a limited extent can they be envisaged as 'consumer' cities, that is, unproductive cities, living off the expenditure of agricultural rents by their richest inhabitants.[70] That said, it seems doubtful that the population of all the towns in the Roman empire exceeded 20 per cent of the total population.[71]

The Roman empire was huge, and large enough to effect important economies of scale. One obvious saving was in

[67] Hopkins 1978a: 72 [essay 5: 200]; Joshel 1992: 176–82.
[68] Hopkins 1978a: 71 [essay 5: 199].
[69] Rome: see n. 40. Alexandria: Delia 1988: especially 284.
[70] On this concept, see most recently Erdkamp 2001.
[71] The major cities (Rome, Alexandria, Antioch and Carthage) had a total population of less than 2 million, or 3 per cent of the empire's total population. I suspect the rest of the urban population in the empire totalled more than 10 per cent but less than 15 per cent of the total. At the moment, I have no idea how to calculate the proportion of villagers engaged primarily in non-agricultural occupations.

military expenditure. The Roman army at about 300,000 soldiers in the first century AD, and fewer than 400,000 in the second century, was significantly smaller than the aggregate armies of the mini-empires, kingdoms and tribes that the Roman empire conquered. The Roman imperial army in the first century constituted barely 2 per cent of all adult males in the empire, whereas average military participation among Romans in the last two centuries BC was 13 per cent of adult males. That was one part of the peace dividend. But the cut in overall military expenditure (Ptolemaic Egypt alone had been credited with an army of 240,000 soldiers[72]) indicates that the apparent wealth of Rome in the first two centuries AD was not so much the product of economic growth as it was the product of piling up into Rome (and, to a lesser extent, other cities) the transferred savings from the taxes previously spent in the conquered kingdoms.

Another arena for massive growth was in the production of coinage. Duncan-Jones reckoned that by the middle of the second century AD there were 7,000 million sestertii of silver coins in circulation, which is roughly four times my estimate of the volume of Roman coins in circulation in the middle of the last century BC.[73] And the volume of Roman coinage had already grown ten times in the century before that.[74] But more of that in a moment. Confirmation of the huge volume of Roman silver-lead mining (silver was produced by cupellation as a by-product of lead mining) comes impressively from an apparently incontrovertible source.

I refer to the Greenland icecap and the peat bogs or lake sediments of France, Germany, Ireland, Spain, Sweden and Switzerland. A whole series of recent studies from a variety of sites has shown with remarkable concordance that the volume of wind-borne contaminants from smelting mineral ores reached a significant peak in the Roman period.[75] Hong and

[72] Appian, Preface 10.

[73] Duncan-Jones 1994: 170 (mid-second century AD); Hopkins 1980a: 109 fig. 2 [essay 6: 227 fig. 6.2] (mid-first century BC).

[74] Hopkins 1980a: 106–7 [essay 6: 223–6]. See now also Backendorf 1998 and Lockyear 1999, for a five- to tenfold increase in that period.

[75] Hong et al. 1994, 1996a, 1996b; Renberg, Persson and Emteryd 1994; Martínez Cortizas et al. 1997, 2002; Rosman et al. 1997; Weiss et al. 1997; Shotyk et al.

associates showed that lead pollution from systematic samples of the Greenland icecap, datable to between 500 BC and AD 300, reached densities four times the natural (i.e. prehistoric) levels. Renberg and associates showed that lead contamination in a wide assortment of sediments from southern Swedish lakes reached a peak in or around the first century AD. Shotyk and associates showed, in a study of a Swiss peat bog, that there was a huge upsurge in lead pollution from the first century BC to the third century AD, when pollution (and presumably production) began to decline.[76]

There seems little doubt among these investigators that the main source of contamination in this period was lead smelting and cupellation for silver and copper in the Roman empire, and particularly Spain. Hong and associates showed that copper production in the world rose sevenfold in the last five centuries BC, continued at a high but reducing level in the first five centuries AD and then fell sevenfold to reach a trough in the thirteenth century. Once again, they are convinced that classical civilisations, and in particular the Roman empire, were the major source of this wind-borne pollution.[77]

Ancient methods of smelting were so inefficient that in the period 500 BC to AD 500, according to these estimates, some 800 metric tons of copper were carried in the high atmosphere to Greenland. Lead pollution in antiquity reached levels not reached again until the eighteenth century. And lead production in the Roman period averaged at least three times the level reached in the first half of the last millennium BC.[78] If air-borne pollutants constituted 10 per cent of lead smelted, total production in the Roman period can be estimated as on average 32,000 tons per year, reaching a peak of about 50,000

1998; Brännvall et al. 1999, 2001; Renberg et al. 2000; Kempter and Frenzel 2000; Alfonso et al. 2001; Boutron et al. 2004; Kylander et al. 2005; Schettler and Romer 2006. For surveys of some of these case studies, see Weiss, Shotyk and Kempf 1999 and Makra and Brimblecombe 2004; cf. also Nriagu 1998. Among ancient historians, a few of these findings have been utilised by A. I. Wilson 2002: 25–7 and de Callataÿ 2005.

[76] Hong et al. 1994; Renberg, Persson and Emteryd 1994; Shotyk et al. 1998: 1637.

[77] Hong et al. 1996a.

[78] Hong et al. 1994; Nriagu 1998.

tons. This may be compared with an average world production of only about 4,000–7,000 tons per year in the period AD 1000–1500. In sum, Roman levels of metal production (lead, copper, silver) were very much higher than the levels in either earlier or immediately subsequent periods.

These scientific estimates of ancient pollution and total production give us an unprecedented vision of economic growth and inefficiency in classical antiquity. Of course, the scientific conclusions may be both speculative and subsequently disputed. And they do relate to only one small sector of the Roman economy. Perhaps tens of thousands of Roman miners, woodcutters, charcoal burners and donkey-drivers slaved in harsh conditions to produce these metals for consumption as coins and divine statues. And, perhaps, their mining activity was made possible by rich men (or emperors) investing fortunes in some mines that burrowed deep underground.[79] But the basic productivity of each worker was probably low, and tens of thousands of miners is but a tiny fraction of the millions of peasants working in agriculture. As so often in Roman economic history, we confront a Janus image: on the one hand mass low productivity and on the other hand seemingly impressive advance, but in a narrow sector.

We can approach the implications of a massive growth in money supply more conservatively. The most important product of the Spanish mines was silver, which was used from the third century BC onward principally for minting coins. As the Roman empire grew in size, the money supply increased dramatically. And the money supply grew, even more dramatically, once peace had been established throughout the empire under successive emperors (31 BC– AD 235). Peace and stable government helped mould the whole of the Mediterranean basin and beyond into a single (relatively) integrated monetary economy. Table 13.1 illustrates this process of growth in the money supply.

In the mid-second century BC, when the Roman empire included parts of Spain, southern France, Italy, northern

[79] On the scale of the imperial mining economy, see now A. I. Wilson 2002: 17–29.

Table 13.1. *Crude estimates of growth in the Roman money supply (total amount in circulation, in millions of denarii).*

Date	Gold	Silver	Tax Revenues	Price Index
150 BC	v. low	50	13	33
100 BC	v. low	320	–	–
50 BC	low	410	85	100
27 BC–AD 14	?1,000	750	?200	–
c. AD 160	3,000[a]	1,716[b]	?250	200
c. AD 230	–	–	–	300/400

Dash indicates data not available. [a]120 million gold coins (aurei) weighing c.880 tons. [b]Total weight 5,766 tons.

Africa and Greece, according to a crude and inevitably fallible estimate, the gross number of Roman silver coins in circulation was only 50 million denarii. A century later, in about 50 BC, when the Roman empire included virtually the whole of the Mediterranean basin (except Egypt), the volume of silver money in circulation had increased eightfold, to about 410 million denarii.[80] The biggest known stimulus to this growth was increased expenditure on paying soldiers and on fighting wars and the correspondingly increased income from taxation. Soldiers and taxpaying subjects needed coins. In the same period, taxes rose more than sixfold, from about 13 million denarii per year in the mid-second century BC to 85 million denarii per year in 62 BC.[81] Please note that money supply (as estimated here) was several times (much more than five times, if we include the silver coinage minted in the cities of the eastern Mediterranean) as large as the tax flow. Does this indicate that money transactions were servicing much more than the payment of taxes and the reciprocal flow of trade that taxes stimulated?

[80] Hopkins 1980a: 106–9, especially 108 and n. 23 [essay 6: 223–8, especially 226–8 and n. 23].

[81] See n. 14.

By the mid-second century AD, when the Roman empire was at its greatest territorial extent, the volume of silver coinage in circulation had again grown. By a similarly fallible estimate, the volume of silver coinage in circulation was roughly four times greater than it had been in 50 BC (1,716,000,000 instead of 410,000,000 denarii, excluding Egypt).[82] The earlier figures cover only the silver coins minted in Rome and circulating principally in the western half of the empire (including Italy). The later figures comprise silver coins circulating in the whole of the Mediterranean basin and beyond. But it is doubtful that the whole increase in the number of silver coins circulating can be attributed to this extension of the geographical area covered.[83] It seems more probable that this huge increase in the volume and value of silver coins circulating throughout the whole Roman empire reflected a rise in the volume and value of goods bought and sold for money.

The huge growth in the Roman money supply under the emperors is corroborated by the radical restructuring and unification of the coinage system that the Roman emperors instituted and maintained. Julius Caesar, Augustus and their successors minted huge volumes of gold coins (well over 1 million gold coins a year on average).[84] By the middle of the second century AD, according to Duncan-Jones' admittedly speculative estimates, the value of gold coins amounted to twice the value of all silver coins in circulation.[85] The whole configuration of the Roman monetary economy had been revolutionised. The total value of the coinage system (gold plus silver) had, by these estimates, grown twelve times since the middle of the last century BC. But prices had perhaps only doubled (table 13.1).

Of course, gold coins constituted only the top tier of the money market. A single gold coin perhaps supported a poor

[82] See n. 73.

[83] Duncan-Jones reckons that the volume of silver coinage minted in the eastern towns totalled 'perhaps not more than one-third' of all the silver coinage in circulation (1994: 170).

[84] Duncan-Jones 1994: 167. Note that 1 gold coin (aureus) = 25 denarii = 100 sestertii.

[85] Duncan-Jones 1994: 168–70.

citizen family in the city of Rome for a month. Even so, gold coins were not out-of-reach rarities. Young soldiers, for example, typically received three gold coins when they were recruited.[86] Emperors gave regular, though smaller, bonuses in gold to their troops and to the citizens registered for the free wheat dole in the city of Rome on accession, on announcing an heir or to commemorate an anniversary. Complementarily, subjects paid a special tax in gold (*aurum coronarium*) on precisely the same occasions. The emperors had diversified the Roman monetary system out of silver and bronze into a three-tiered system of gold, silver and bronze.

By the mid-second century AD, the Roman monetary system (outside Egypt, which had its own rather inferior coinage but again one that expanded enormously under Roman rule),[87] again according to Duncan-Jones' innovative and speculative estimates, consisted of 120 million gold coins (aurei struck at forty-five to the Roman pound) worth 3,000,000,000 denarii and about 1,700,000,000 silver denarii.[88] All the gold coins and the great majority of the silver coins (perhaps three-quarters of the total) were minted at Rome itself; the rest were minted in Syria and Asia Minor, but to a compatible standard and purity.[89] Bronze coinage (with perhaps more than 5,000,000,000 coins in circulation) was mostly produced locally and circulated locally. It represented only about 5 to 10 per cent of total value.[90]

By these estimates, in the mid-second century, Roman gold coinage in total weighed 880 tons and by recent values (c. US$400–600 per troy oz. in 2005–6) was worth $11,000,000,000–17,000,000,000, not much for a modern industrial economy but a huge investment for a pre-industrial state. The silver coinage also constituted a huge investment. It weighed in total something over 5,000 tons at a time when producing a ton of silver

[86] R. W. Davies 1969: 225.
[87] See Christiansen 1988.
[88] Duncan-Jones 1994: 168–70.
[89] For the latter, see Harl 1996: 97–124. Eastern silver coins were tariffed at 3 or 4 denarii. Under Nero, debasement was tried out on Egyptian, then on other eastern coins before being introduced at Rome. Similarly, in the second century AD, eastern silver coins were debased sooner than central Roman coins.
[90] Duncan-Jones 1994: 169.

cost up to one thousand man-years of labour (mining, draining, carting, felling timber, making charcoal, smelting, refining, guarding, transporting, minting).[91] From 1530 to 1630, by comparison, on average Europe imported from America about 140 tons of silver a year.[92] The Roman silver coinage system would have absorbed only about 50 tons per year for more than a century.

How was it possible for the Roman coinage system to grow so much without hyperinflation? I assume here that classical economic principles, and in particular Fisher's price equation,

$$\overset{(P)}{\text{Price}} = \frac{\overset{(M)}{\text{Money Supply}} \times \overset{(V)}{\text{Speed of Circulation}}}{\text{Quantity of Goods (Q)}}$$

holds where P = the price level, M = the money supply, V = the speed of circulation and Q = the quantity of goods bought and sold. We know nothing or very little about the speed at which money circulated in Roman conditions. For the moment, let us assume that V was constant. So if money supply increased twelvefold (albeit over a considerably greater geographical area) and if prices only doubled (though the database for any such conclusion is dangerously, even recklessly, thin), then it must be that the quantity of goods traded in the market increased hugely between 50 BC and AD 150.

But does Fisher's price equation apply in Roman conditions? I am inclined to think that this is a nonsensical question. But I do still have colleagues (as well as the ghost of my teacher Moses Finley in my conscience) who believe that it is impossible or at least unprofitable to use modern economic concepts in order to analyse a pre-industrial embedded economy. For them, the ancient economy was a cultural system, which was dominated by non-rational considerations of status and ritual and so was immune to cold rational analysis or reconstruction. So let us pursue the question for a minute. At the end of the second century and at the beginning of the third century AD,

[91] C. C. Patterson 1972: 231.
[92] D. H. Fischer 1996: 336 n. 37.

Table 13.2. *Growth in military expenditure (in millions of denarii).*

Date	Actual	Standardised to 50 BC prices
218–201 BC	31	10
200–188 BC	14	5
187–168 BC	9	3
AD 6–70	123	92
AD 83–170	179	90
AD 195	287	?200
AD 215–30	434	217

successive emperors raised soldiers' pay significantly, so total annual military expenditure over forty years (AD 190–230) more than doubled (the increase was 142 per cent: see table 13.2). The average volume of silver coins minted per year rose in roughly the same period (AD 180–235) by 40 per cent and the silver content of the dominant coin the denarius was almost halved (from 71 per cent to 37 per cent) (table 13.3). Prices (again, unfortunately, on exiguous evidence) apparently rose in the same period by 50 or 100 per cent (table 13.3). This chain of cause and consequence does make it seem that the Roman monetary economy is analysable in terms of classic price theory.

It may seem tempting to regard such a massive increase in the money supply and in the probable volume of traded goods as an unequivocal index of economic growth. But I suspect that the huge volume of money minted is explicable only if a large proportion was exported in return for eastern luxuries or if a large proportion, especially of gold coins, were kept inert as treasure, with practically nil velocity. As I reconstruct it, Roman emperors competitively produced silver and gold as a virtual state monopoly, without much regard for the costs of production. They produced coins as economic objects for the facilitation of trade and taxation but above all as symbolic objects of ostentation and political authority. In short, Roman money did not match completely its modern equivalents. Roman money was part real money and part a monument to political ambition. It cannot therefore be readily used as an index of growth.

Table 13.3. *Annual rates of coin production, purity index and price index.*

	Coins produced per year in millions of denarii		Purity Index (27 BC = 100)		
Date	Gold	Silver	Gold[a]	Silver[b]	Price Index (50 BC = 100)
200–158 BC	–	1	–	–	–
119–80 BC	–	14	–	–	33
73–59 BC	–	4	–	–	–
50 BC	–	–	–	–	100 (base)
43 BC	>7	–	103	–	–
27 BC	>14	–	100 (base)	100 (base)	–
AD 64–8	202	8	93	84	133
AD 69–79	90	38	–	82	–
AD 88–96	–	23	97	88	–
AD 98–117	31	19	93	83	–
AD 117–38	28	16	–	81	–
AD 138–61	35	19	–	79	–
AD 161–80	31	16	–	71	200
AD 193–211	–	30	–	50	–
AD 215	–	20	82	44	–
AD 222–35	–	22	–	37	300/400

Dash indicates data not available. [a] Gold content in percentage. [b] Denarii per pound of silver.
Sources: Hopkins 1980a [essay 6]; Duncan-Jones 1994; Harl 1996.

AFTERWORD

THE POLITICAL ECONOMY OF THE ROMAN EMPIRE

GREG WOOLF

This posthumous publication is due largely to the diligence of Walter Scheidel who retyped the manuscript and supplied much of the annotation (202 n.* [488 n.**]).[1] Had Keith completed the revision himself, the result would certainly have been different. Those supervised by him remember he was as critical of his own first drafts as he was of others', and that he was a meticulous stylist. We may be confident that he would have removed some repetition, and perhaps rounded the essay off with a flourish. Most of all we miss the jokes with which he peppered his polished publications.

This account of the political economy of Rome may be his final published work, but it also represents a return to some of his earliest interests. It is also very different from most of the work he produced in the latter stage of his career. During the early 1980s, H. drew for inspiration eclectically on thinkers as diverse as Clifford Geertz, Maurice Bloch and Jonathan Z. Smith and became preoccupied with the thought world of the ancient Romans. Yet in this piece the experience of individuals is subsumed into analysis of their interests and behaviour as members of broad social groups. Nor does the analysis of the structure of the empire reflect his growing interest in Roman symbolic systems, and in the ways ceremonial and ritualised violence described and sustained the Roman political order. Instead, what we have here is Keith Hopkins' last (or

[1] This essay originated in a paper given in 2000, and lightly revised by H. in 2002. Walter Scheidel revised it in 2006, relying on H.'s published work and on discussion at the three conferences held in 2000–2. I have also been able to consult an earlier draft of the paper. I am grateful to Christopher Kelly and Walter Scheidel for discussion and information.

better his latest) take on a set of interconnected problems that had fascinated him since the late 1970s.

It was characteristic of H.'s working methods that he returned again and again to certain historical problems, in an attempt improve on his previous conclusions and formulations. This was true, for example, of his work on the relation between taxation and trade (most notably the paper reprinted in this volume as essay 6) and also of his work on brother-sister marriage in Roman Egypt.[2] In the same way, the first essay in *Conquerors and Slaves* (1978) underpins parts of what appear here as sections 2 and 6.2;[3] the two central chapters of *Death and Renewal* (1983) (written with Graham Burton) are the prototypes of another part of section 2 and also for section 6.1,[4] which, in addition, summarises the argument of 'Models, ships and staples' (1983) [essay 7]; section 4 draws on various versions of 'Taxes and trade in the Roman empire (200 BC–AD 400)' (1980) [essay 6];[5] while section 7 draws on both those discussions and on 'Economic growth and towns in classical antiquity' (1978) [essay 5].

Reading this chapter alongside those earlier essays is a revealing exercise. In particular, it draws attention to the robustly empirical dimension of H.'s research. Those earlier versions had attracted some trenchant criticism as well as much admiration and imitation, and other views of both the ancient economy and Roman political life had naturally emerged in the interim. Yet what H. engages with most consistently was not the synthetic view or broad argument of other historians so much as new calculations and new data. The new calculations here are those of Richard Duncan-Jones, Walter Scheidel and David Hackett Fischer. The new data include both the mounting evidence for high levels of heavy-metal pollutants from the Greenland ice-cores and other sites and also Sandra Joshel's (1992) study of professions attested on Roman epitaphs. The few notes left on H.'s original version relate almost entirely

[2] Hopkins 1980b, 1994b.
[3] Hopkins 1978b: 1–98.
[4] Hopkins and Burton 1983a and b.
[5] See also Hopkins 1995–6, condensed with some revisions in 2000b.

to such empirical matters. They reflect his faith in quantification, whether this meant actual data-sets – such as might be extracted from the study of Roman coinage, from shipwrecks or the papyri – or hypothetical/proxy data that allowed parametric modelling, the process of establishing acceptable limits for values that could not be established precisely. Herein lay the greatest difference between H.'s economic history and that of A. H. M. Jones and Moses Finley. This was an argument that H. won decisively, at least in the Anglophone world, where quantitative analysis is now central to the study of the ancient economy whether by historians or archaeologists.[6]

Yet perhaps the most original feature of this chapter is now the least visible, that is H.'s use of the concept of 'political economy'. As a generalising concept – one that allowed the specifics of the Roman case to be compared to those of other ancient empires – it is completely appropriate for the conference series for which it was written. H. was often invited to address conferences with a comparativist flavour, and some of his best work originated from those invitations.[7] Yet H.'s interest in political economy was long-standing: the term features in the title of the first chapter of *Conquerors and Slaves.* It reflects the way social science informed his own brand of ancient history, offering a total approach to the subject, rather than the tactical borrowing of a method here and an analogy there to answer a particular problem, the usage of social theory that is still the dominant form of interdisciplinarity encountered among ancient historians. Even after his move to the chair of ancient history in Cambridge in 1985, following more than twenty years teaching sociology, H.'s membership of the editorial boards of *Past & Present* and *Comparative Studies in Society and History* kept him involved with the social sciences. Besides, King's College, Cambridge offered the possibility for further collaboration with Ernest Gellner, Anthony Giddens and others with whom he had worked in London, first at the

6 For instance, Scheidel, Morris and Saller 2007; Bowman and Wilson 2009; Harris 2011.

7 See e.g. 1978a [essay 5] and 1991a [essay 8].

LSE and then at Brunel where he was Dean of the Faculty of Social Sciences between 1981 and 1985. H. remained, to the last, a sociologist among the classicists.

Consider the opening of this paper. By characterising Rome as 'one of a handful of empires which developed throughout the world in the golden millennium of empire formation and religious innovation' (178 [488]), H. referred not only to the comparative approach characteristic of Max Weber but also to Karl Jaspers' notion of an Axial Age, and particularly to its sociological reception by Shmuel Eisenstadt, whose work is cited in *Conquerors and Slaves.*[8] In conversation, H. credited the influence of John Kautsky, a political scientist and comparativist particularly interested in the division of functions within ancient empires. Similarly, 'Taxes and trade' [essay 6] seems to show the influence of Immanuel Wallerstein's influential *Modern World-System* which contained within it a Marxist characterisation of pre-modern 'world-empires' as extensive exchange systems organised by political power rather than markets.[9] Thinking of the Roman empire as a system – one in which different interest groups competed for control of limited resources – was not an ancient historical issue until H. put it on the agenda. Indeed, H.'s opening remarks on the significance of writing, money and iron technology have become such commonplaces that it is almost necessary to open up issues of journals published in the 1970s to remind oneself how unusual it then was to start by standing *outside the frame* of Greco-Roman antiquity, and by deliberately adopting a perspective alien to the minds of the classical authors through whom it was most often studied. H. was much more radical in this respect than Moses Finley, whose reconstructions of ancient society remained firmly based on classical texts, who devoted great attention to the ideas and explicit statements of Demosthenes and Cicero *inter alios*, and who generally made only anecdotal use of epigraphic and archaeological data. Finley was certainly inspired by some strands in sociological

8 Jaspers 1949; Eisenstadt 1963 in Hopkins 1978b: 8 n. 15, 74 n. 96.

9 Kautsky 1982; Wallerstein 1974 with Rowlands 1987: 8–11.

thought, at first Polanyi's notions of embedded economies and ports-of-trade,[10] and then Weber's notion of the *Idealtypus* which as 'model' provided the basis for his own work on the ancient city.[11] But these insights were generally used to generate new readings of ancient texts. Almost every chapter in *The Ancient Economy* begins with a passage of classical literature. H. was much more likely to begin from establishing a research question, and he then sought data and methods with which to answer it. The difference was particularly marked in their diverging attitudes to archaeological data, to which Finley was increasingly hostile, and H. increasingly open.[12]

H.'s approach may be characterised as an eclectic historical sociology. It drew most strongly on the founding figures of classical economics and sociology, on the work of Adam Smith, Pareto, Engels and Durkheim as well as Marx and Weber. It was also engaged with certain varieties of current Marxist scholarship, but not (interestingly enough, and again quite unlike Finley) with archaeologists and ancient historians of Marxist inclinations such as Andrea Carandini, Jean-Pierre Vernant and Geoffrey de Ste. Croix, so much as with Marxist historians of other periods. Works by Perry Anderson, Barry Hindess and Paul Hirst feature in the supplementary bibliography at the end of *Conquerors and Slaves* which was designed largely as a starting point for Roman historians who might want to explore historical sociology further. While some ancient historians found the language of 'modelling' unfamiliar and uncomfortable, H. was not a theorist and focused on applications of sociology. For instance this essay is careful to avoid the great debates about the applicability of class analysis to pre-capitalist societies, and the discussion of slavery sidesteps the ferocious discussions raging across the Iron Curtain (although H. was well aware of them). Again unlike Finley, he was much more interested in antiquity than in its historiography. This

[10] Polanyi, Arensberg and Pearson 1957 with Humphreys 1969.

[11] Finley 1977; and especially Finley 1985, with Morley's Afterword to 1978a [essay 5] at [207–8 and 211–12].

[12] Contrast the polemic in the second chapter (7–26) of Finley 1985, to H.'s use of shipwreck evidence as one of the central planks of 1980a [essay 6].

essay presents a thoroughly materialist account of the workings of the empire, one in which the key variables are the system of government, social structure and economic growth, linked by the means by which revenue was extracted and force controlled, all constrained by the conditions under which production took place. Ancient ideals feature not at all, and when comparison is employed it is with other ancient empires, not with the economies of medieval or capitalist Europe. Nothing could be more different from Finley's *The Ancient Economy*, which weaves discussions of a century of debate together with discussions of key passages of ancient testimony in a series of mutually supporting thematic essays, but as Finley states in his preface 'it is not a book one would call an "economic history"'.[13]

Despite these differences, H. was correct to evoke 'the ghost of my teacher Moses Finley' in the closing pages of this essay (200 [524]). Not only did Finley encourage and facilitate H.'s original transformation from classicist into sociologist, reputedly arranging his appointment at Leicester during a dinner party which Finley had H. host for Ilya Neustadt on the eve of the job interview. It was also Finley's influence that led H. (cautiously) to approach the issue of economic growth first of all as a possible consequence of taxation. Finley's austere minimalist vision of the ancient economy was in some respects a reaction to the modernising accounts presented by Rostovtzeff, Tenney Frank and before them Eduard Meyer.[14] Today evidence for exchange is found in empirical observations of quantitative changes in material evidence; from an appreciation of the uneven distribution of the raw material consumed right across the empire (from marble quarries to olive trees, and human population to fish stocks); from an understanding of the volatility of Mediterranean micro-ecologies that could deliver bumper crops or crop failures in successive years – meaning that even modest settlements relied

[13] Finley 1973 (quoting 9), revised but without major changes of direction in 1985. An updated edition with a useful interpretative essay by Ian Morris was published in 1999.

[14] See Morley's Afterword to 1978a [essay 5] at [208–9 and 210–11].

on exchange to survive in hard times; and from demographic modelling that indicates the huge demand for food, slaves and water in the cities of the empire.[15] H. was well aware of these arguments, especially the archaeological ones, many of which he had heard rehearsed in London seminars. This essay gathers together environmental evidence for increased level of mining, numismatic evidence for a growth in the money supply, some suggestions of agricultural intensification in northern Europe and the corollaries of the urbanisation processes that reached an apogee in the second century AD. Less explicit (yet still present in this essay) are the facilitating roles H. saw were played by common systems of money, weights and measures, law and language, and by the peace and communications infrastructure generated by the empire. But it was Finley's influence that required that H. deduce a growth in trade as an effect of overwhelming power of the imperial state which dominated the accounts of ancient economics offered both by substantivists like Polanyi and Marxists like Wallerstein. Political economy was acceptable, in other words, where market economics were not. Moses Finley died in 1985, just months after H. took up the Cambridge chair. It would have been perfectly possible then for H. to abandon his more tactful formulations of the late 1970s and early 1980s. That Finley's ghost still hangs over H.'s final words of the subject is a sign of his enduring *pietas* towards the admired teacher whose work he had surpassed, and from whom he was in many ways a very different advocate of the social sciences.

15 See Bang and Ikeguchi's Afterword to 1983a [essay 7] at [306–12]. The documentation of archaeological evidence for economic activity has now taken a great leap forward with the work of the Oxford Roman Economy Project www.romaneconomy.ox.ac.uk/ led by Alan Bowman and Andrew Wilson.

14

HOW TO BE A ROMAN EMPEROR: AN AUTOBIOGRAPHY*

Editor's Foreword

In Cambridge, our communications with Heaven are still subject to irritating delays and prohibitions, so the text which follows is less complete than I would have wished, and I am not at liberty to disclose its provenance. However, I assure you that my own part in it is confined to the addition of section headings and a translation of the original Latin, which is fluent, with just a trace of an African accent. My translation is intentionally somewhat free, and you may suspect that it has been unconsciously influenced by certain modern parallels such as K. A. Wittfogel, *Oriental Despotism* (1957), Jonathan Spence, *Emperor of China: Self-Portrait of K'ang-hsi* (1974) and Perry Anderson, *Lineages of the Absolutist State* (1974), all of them thrilling reads. I cheerfully admit that it counterpoints Ronald Syme, *The Roman Revolution* (1939) and Fergus Millar, *The Emperor in the Roman World* (1977), both of whom may dislike it intensely.

The author, for his own reasons, wishes to remain anonymous; but it can be deduced that he is a dead Roman emperor, deified and living splendidly in Heaven. Time in Heaven defies mortal understanding, but it does not seem to have prevented him from learning about events subsequent to his arrival there. Internal evidence suggests that he lived towards the end of the second century, and by elimination the likely candidate is Septimius Severus (reigned AD 193–211). But over eighteen centuries he has absorbed some of the characteristics of the other emperors with whom he has been in close contact, and

* First published in R. Tomlin (ed) *History and Fiction: Six Essays Celebrating the Centenary of Sir Ronald Syme (1903–89)*, London: Grime & Selwood, 2005, 72–85 (= Hopkins 2005).

in consequence he has an attenuated sense of individuality; in other words, he seems quite unlike what he probably was in fact. This may be a source of error, but since this is only the first draft of my edition, I will spare you the commentary in which such questions are discussed.

An Introduction to Heaven

Mortals often wonder what Heaven is like. I can tell you one thing: those Christian writers got it very wrong. There are no massed choirs of angels, at least not in any part of Heaven that I have visited. The main difference between your world and mine is metaphysical. Mine is difficult to describe, just as it is difficult to reduce a dream to words. In fact, this is not like a dream world. We exist as recognisable entities, personalities even, but without bodies, without sickness, without physical symptoms. Here there are no bodies, no physical functions; just floating spirits and personalities. We still have emotions, but it is hunger without food, greed without fat, satisfaction without satiety, lust without an erection. I suppose that is what wretched Augustine was on about.

Anyhow, I am male but without a body; and to tell you the truth, notions of gender, like notions of age here, are more symbolic than real. Young Caligula took ages to adapt. Without his normal twice-daily physical reinforcement, he almost wasted away. He lost his self-respect. Even worse, he lost his identity. Heaven does not suit everybody; even for divinity you pay a price. What matters here still is rank and status, culture and language. I know it sounds funny, but these are the inescapable elements of the divine order; so I inhabit – 'live in' would be too strong a term – a splendid pleasure park, a pavilion of the Roman emperors, with hundreds of grovelling attendants. It is their pleasure to please us, just as it was so many centuries ago.

There is nothing to stop us travelling to other heavenly spheres. Theoretically, I could go and visit David or Abraham, or even the emperors of China, just to compare notes, as it were, but you never know what sort of reception you would get, or whether they would be able to understand my sort of questions. Or even whether you would be able to get back; and wandering in limbo would be hell, or at least hellish. So, for better or worse, we tend to stay with each other in ancient Rome, as it were. After almost two thousand years, even with the attenuated sense of time, that is a bit claustrophobic, so I decided to write my memoirs. Perhaps I should have done it ages ago when memories were sharper, fresher, but there is some advantage in distance and selection. I can see much more clearly now what mattered most, or what mattered most to me; and now I know something of what happened later, and that certainly is an advantage.

Most of the old histories of Rome were written by aristocrats or bureaucrats – like waspish Tacitus, long-winded Cassius Dio or gossipy Suetonius. They all were, consciously or unconsciously, anti-emperor. For them history is an impotent form of *post mortem* revenge on dead emperors, and there is little to correct their imbalance. Among previous emperors only Augustus, Claudius and Marcus Aurelius put pen to paper constructively, except, of course, for the inevitable official documents and correspondence. But Augustus was too intent on self-aggrandisement and putting a smooth gloss on his ghastly record. Claudius was an old-fashioned antiquarian, so no one bothered to preserve his long-winded meanderings. And as for Marcus, well, he was a good man, but he found living difficult, had a wayward son, found consolation in his mistress and writing boring philosophy. So what I want to do here and now is to correct the balance, to give the emperor's view, to say how it was, or how it seemed to me when I controlled Rome and its empire.

Holding onto Power

Of course, you do not have to be emperor for long to realise the huge gap between apparent omnipotence and real power. You are omnipotent only in subjects' imagination, only so long as you do not put it to the test. To take a trivial example: when you were feeling peckish and ordered a hot snack, it took simply ages for anything to arrive, and when it did it was usually cold. Okay, you can take it out on the slaves. One of my predecessors, Hadrian, was so provoked once that he petulantly poked a slave in the eye with his pen, but then he was filled with remorse, and offered to compensate the slave for being blind. No way. My attitude was quite different. Like any slave-owner, I ruled partly through fear and unpredictability, and that applies not just to slaves. You had to be rough with aristocrats as well. It all really goes back to Augustus' troublesome constitutional settlement of which he was so unreasonably proud, though admittedly it worked quite well for him; but it left the rest of us who succeeded him with recurrent problems. He was scared of getting it in the back – and front – like Julius Caesar, so he pussyfooted around, and pretended to be just first among equals. That gave all sorts of overbred aristocrats the fantasy they could fill my shoes and become emperor, just by getting a favourable horoscope from some cheapskate astrologer, or by teaming up secretly with the Prefect of the Guard.

Now, I had to make sure that they knew who was boss, and I had certain weapons on my side. I personally used selective promotion, time and flattery. Most of them were such egoists, they thought they were promoted for ability and, in a sense, they were. I would not send a congenital idiot to govern Germany where the legions are. He might attack some tribes and get our legions murdered. Even worse, he might win and I would have to deal with his inflated ego and ambition. But then, I would not send a blue-blooded aristocrat there either. I kept them at home and got them to squander their inheritance on entertaining each other – and me – lavishly.

And why put a good general in charge of an army? He would want to use it either against me or in some wasteful war. True, we needed a stock of experienced men in reserve in case of emergency, but most soldiers, let me tell you, are best employed polishing uniforms and building roads as monuments to the emperor's power. Promotion should be arbitrary, to keep people guessing, waiting, kicking their heels and hoping. Modern prosopographers, those wretched bores who treat history as though it is one of your railway timetables, have never guessed my sheer sense of fun in picking people for promotion. Virius

Lupus goes off to ghastly Britain for three years – and I know personally from experience what Britain is like. I went there; it killed me. Anyhow, he goes off, proud as punch, and we all sigh with relief that he has gone. 'How good to see you back', I say, when eventually I give him a private audience before I go hunting. 'I hear you've done a splendid job.' You should see him puff up with pleasure. Does he not see that he is not the only one to smarm his way around? Does he not realise that his every step has been tracked by one of the palace officials who write a monthly report? Not that I specially trusted the special agents' reports. Those guys are notoriously susceptible to bribes, but if things go really wrong, the local notables are always ready to complain and send a boring delegation full of hot air and flattery, and the agents do not want to be found out too easily. After all, they can be done away with by a simple flick of a stylus. Checks and balances: that is one secret of staying in power.

Okay, I can hear you say, if you're so smart, how come so few emperors have died in bed? Well, it is a delicate subject up here, not easy to bring up in casual conversation. I do not think that old buffer Claudius knows even now that his fourth and last wife bumped him off with a dish of mushrooms, but then he always was blind to their faults. Fancy the third one getting married to her lover while Claudius was off on a trip to the beach at Ostia! Perhaps that is just a story, but it is a good one; and at least it illustrates the heat of secret passions that a court whips up, and the licence it allows, within limits.

Anyhow, I once did have a heart-to-heart with Nero and Domitian, not both together, to find out what they thought had gone wrong. Galba and Otho were always trying to set the record straight and say how much they had been misunderstood. I will tell you what they said another time, but personally I think you have to plan carefully, step by step, and keep eyes in the back of your head. In the end, of course, it is up to Fate; but even Fate, I am convinced, responds to whip and bridle.

Every emperor needs friends, confidants, people he can trust, chat to, listen to, without feeling got at. One obvious recourse is chamberlains, trusty slaves who can be useful without being powerful. Some emperors have even gone for eunuchs, though I personally find them repulsive – high-voiced, oily skinned, over-sensitive and volatile – but the great risk is that they want to feather their own nests and those of their friends. They cannot have children, but they sure club together to protect each other, and they are so unpopular. You have to execute some of them every couple of years just to keep the mob in the Colosseum, or the aristos, happy. By the way, I faced up to some angry demonstrations in the Colosseum occasionally. Sometimes I just let them shout out what they wanted; other times, I simply sent in the soldiers and killed the ringleaders.

At the other extreme are wives and concubines – and by the way, if anyone tries to pretend that sexual licence is not a perk of power, they are retarded. What is the point of being omnipotent if you are not potent? Of course, it is offensive to throw *ius primae noctis* in the face of all your courtiers. Caligula buggering his sister on her wedding altar was certainly going too far. As for Tiberius and his small boys on Capri, or Augustus and his penchant for virgins pandered by his wife, what can I say? Of course, *you* can say that those are just stories, journalistic inventions or fantasies spun by tittle-tattlers infantilely preoccupied with their rulers' sexuality; but there is no smoke without fire, and from my own experience I could tell you some things I have known happen at court. It makes me quite sweetly nostalgic.

But the real point is that emperors have wives, wives have children, and emperors have mothers, princes have ambitions and greedy courtiers. Each coterie is a party – it's like a traffic jam outside the Colosseum with no one to direct the traffic; it's a mess, and the mess is made much worse if the emperor has had more than one wife, and children by each. Who is going to succeed? Who is this month's favourite? Just look at it from the poor emperor's point of view; how would *you* like it if every sneeze was thought of as a symptom of imminent death? The only hope is to play it cool, switch horses, break up factions, play one against the other and hide your true feelings; but I simply could not do that with my own wife. She was far too cunning and, besides, I loved her. And, of course, I really wanted my sons to succeed me and make a line of kings; but they were still so young, so headstrong.

In the end, since death came a little unexpectedly, I left it to chance, to Fate and to both of my sons. That was my one big mistake. Within months one was dead, killed in his mother's arms by his brother. The curse of Romulus, that is what I call it. I really should have seen it coming; but even if I had, what could I have done? Should Marcus Aurelius have disinherited his beautiful Commodus? Fathers love sons and exaggerate their virtues. Court politics require a special type of behaviour. Out in the real world you can say what you feel, unless, of course, one of the imperial agents happens to be listening; but that is rare, and anxiety about them is exaggerated. Still, they are occasionally useful.

The court is quite different; even the walls have ears. Business is conducted in whispers behind curtains. Rumour rules. At court what matters is that you say what is appropriate and express what is expected. You need to wear a mask of smooth politeness. That is the great contribution of emperors to Roman politics: hypocrisy. Think of all those courtiers listening to Nero sing, or that glorious moment when Britannicus dropped dead at Nero's dinner party. Everyone knew it was in young Nero's interest to get rid of his step-brother, three years younger and twice as popular. He was poisoned, fell down, went into contortions; no one knew how to react. Everyone watched Nero, who calmly said it must be an epileptic fit and carried on with his dinner. Even the boy's sister who was there – she was married to Nero, by the way – even she had to contain her grief as the body was taken away. That is what you learn at court: steely self-control.

One real trouble about being emperor is the feeling that you are trapped – trapped by other people's expectations, flattery, ambitions and lies. If someone tells a joke, the courtiers are too scared to laugh until they see you laugh. The court attendants feel that laughter is intrinsically outrageous; it offends their exaggerated sense of propriety. Their leverage increases, and their income, if everyone is scared and asks them how they should behave. The only way to keep them actively controlled is to kill one of them occasionally, but I always had the sneaking feeling that one day one of them would get his own back. Look what happened to Commodus. *He* was killed by his wife, in cahoots with the commander of the palace guard, after being betrayed unwittingly by a bejewelled boy lover.

Everyone knows that the emperor needs real friends, but whom can he trust? I did trust a friend once, someone from my own city and province. I made him commander of the palace guard, gave him wealth and immense authority. I even arranged for his daughter to marry my wilful son in the vain hope that she would calm him down a bit, but he just hated her. Quite unreasonably my wife always thought that marriage was a bad idea: he was too young, she said, and she always sided with her son. Okay, the Prefect abused his power and took huge bribes and went about pretending to be Caesar. He calmed down a bit after I had dressed him down, but then one night a captain of the palace guard came to get the evening password and told me privately that he had had orders from the Prefect to assassinate me. I did not believe him at first: how could a long-standing, loyal friend turn traitor? But we laid a trap for him: he came to the palace with full armour hidden under his clothes. It was true: he really had planned to kill me. For old times' sake I had mercy on the daughter and sent her into exile. The father I killed, of course, and had his corpse thrown out with the rubbish. But the whole episode nearly broke my heart.

A Brief Escapade

I did break free once; it was delicious but risky. I crept out of the palace one night with only one slave, both of us simply dressed. We went into some smoky taverns and watched the people enjoying themselves, hookers flirting, covert glances, drunken gamblers. I suppose I had half hoped for praise or criticism, you know the sort of thing – 'that emperor, he's not bad' – but not a murmur spoken out loud. I suppose they all knew that walls have ears. What they talked about instead was the races upcoming in the circus. I suppose I should have been delighted. After all, giving the people in Rome wheat and games has proved a master stroke of state policy or – should I say? – policing. It effectively abolished popular participation in politics except for the occasional knee-jerk reaction by the crowd in the Colosseum, and that is easily enough controlled: seduce them with gifts thrown to the crowd, or kill a few.

I should say, by the way, that the really dangerous part of my escape trip was getting back into the palace. I stupidly, and uncharacteristically, had not thought about it carefully enough. Palace security was surprisingly tight: we were challenged, I did not want to say who I was and, at first, it looked as though, if I had persisted, we would both have been beaten up or locked away, dismissed as fraudsters. Luckily my smart slave ingeniously thought of pretending that I was his lover, and we made it to his humble quarters. We never tried that again. Too risky.

Getting There

You may be wondering how I became emperor. Well, I was provincial governor in Pannonia. I was at my headquarters at Carnuntum, just near modern Vienna, when I heard that the palace guardsmen, spoilt by luxury, had murdered the good Pertinax. He was a worthy emperor. I was not just going to let those softies stuffed with pomp and ceremony govern the empire in their own interests. They gave me no choice. I made inquiries: fifteen legions in the north, pretty well all except for those in Britain and Spain, supported me. I summoned the troops, made honeyed speeches, promised the earth, issued coins of gold and silver, flattered a few key people with hints about their prospects under me and marched on Italy.

All the auspices were good, all the sacrifices were favourable and I had a tremendous dream. Pertinax was riding in Rome but his horse bucked and threw him off. I was watching, and the horse came up to me and sort of invited me to get up on him. I did, and he carried me with the crowds cheering, right into the middle of the forum. What an omen! Later, when

I was emperor, I put up a great bronze statue, horse and all, right on the spot where we stopped.

The only resistance I met was the occasional messenger from that upstart Julianus who had bought his throne from the palace guard in an auction. What a farce! He never paid them what he promised, or not all of it, and too late. No wonder they turned against him. No loyalty. Anyhow, he sent these messengers with secret instructions to kill me, but they all saw it was more profitable and less dangerous to come clean, so his dirty tricks were useless. My spies indicated that he had very little support. I sent off small fast mobile units from my army with instructions to infiltrate Rome. Then that pathetic old man Julianus tried to make peace, and offered to share his empire with me. What a laugh! Anyhow, he was assassinated himself, and by a common soldier. I had gained supreme power, in a couple of months.

I thought a lot about my next steps. The senators had marched out to meet me and greet me as emperor. It did them good to walk a few miles down the road. I summoned the palace guard and instructed them to come in ceremonial dress, as they normally would for an imperial parade, and that is what the suckers did. They gathered around to hear me speak, and were immediately surrounded by my soldiers armed to the teeth. I did not kill them, though they fully deserved it for murdering Pertinax and for deserting the new emperor who had bought them. The whole of Roman history is peppered with the palace guard's treacheries. They have the fantasy that they can make or break emperors. Well, this put the boot on the other foot. I told them straight that they deserved death, but I let them go, disarmed, dishonoured, stripped of their insignia and their useless show daggers chased in silver and gold. If they put their faces within a hundred miles of Rome – death. They did not like it, but had no choice. Now, *that* is being a real emperor.

Of course, reality is more complex. I made a few promises to the senate: respect for the aristocracy, no death without trial, no informers – routine stuff, but most of them looked pleased. A few, no doubt, had read enough history to know that is what every emperor promises. I gathered in the children of all the governors of the provinces. It's good to have a lever for their loyalty. Okay, it's not cuddly behaviour, but holding on to power in the early stages is a risk-business. I paid off the troops, not as much as I had promised, but as much as I could afford. I attended a few gladiatorial shows, just to show willing, and decided to settle Niger's hash. Niger was governor of Syria. He had also had himself declared emperor by his effete legions. They suited each other. From the news I had got he was living a life of idle luxury. For me the only way to win the throne was to fight. You do not get to be emperor without effort, and while I was beating him – and I felt convinced I would – I had to secure my back. Albinus, governor of Britain, was a danger: he was rich, noble and simple-minded. I just offered him a share of power, the title of Caesar, a few statues and coins with his head on. He bought it all, and I would deal with him later.

I beat Niger and his army easily enough in a huge battle at Issus, just where Alexander the Great beat Darius centuries before. Niger escaped on a fast horse, but my men caught up with him and cut off his head on the banks of the Euphrates. The traitor was probably thinking he could escape to the Parthian empire. Needless to say, I rewarded the cities which had stood up for me, and punished my enemies. You need to show people that there are risks in opposition. I also executed quite a few senators, then and later, partly *pour encourager les autres.* The only way to stay in control is to keep tabs on your potential enemies. It helped a lot getting hold of my rivals' private letters – very revealing. Confiscations helped too: they keep aristocratic wealth circulating.

There is no point here in detailing my campaigns or my victories in Mesopotamia, and my long march at the head of my soldiers all the way from Mesopotamia to Gaul, or the detour to Rome. They are in the history books. What *is* important is that I shared in my soldiers' hardships. I marched with them. That is why they always fought so hard for me. Look after the soldiers, and you stay in power. That is the best advice I gave my son, and that is why I increased the soldiers' pay.

In the final battle against Albinus just outside Lyons, Albinus stayed in town, like the over-educated coward that he was. I was in the heat of battle. When I was knocked off my horse, I tore off my riding cloak and pitched in with the infantry. *That* is how to win wars. And when it was all over, Albinus committed suicide. The rumours that I executed him are plain wrong, but I sent his head to Rome as a warning to the hoity-toity senators who had sided with him and had his children thrown into the River Rhône. I had won, fair and square. All three of my rival claimants to the supreme power were dead.

There is no good point in my going through my reign bit by bit: I think you can see how I came to power and how I stayed in power for over seventeen years. One point I would like to clear up is my dying words. Not as funny as Vespasian's 'Alas, I think I'm becoming a god'. Not as shameful as Claudius': 'Oh dear, I've crapped myself', but proud and conscious of all I had achieved: 'I've done everything', I said, 'but it doesn't help.'

Editor's Afterword

When I had finished translating this and tidying it up a bit, I sent it to a couple of friends, as I always do, to see what they thought of it. Michael wrote back immediately, saying he was very busy, and would get to it as soon as he could.

Martha replied as follows:

Dear Keith,

Thank you for sending me your text. I read it with interest. For the moment I will leave aside all questions of provenance and authenticity, though I am sure the generality of ancient historians would think that crucial. We have quite enough genuine sources to work on, thank you, without worrying about cheap fakes; though, as I said, I will take it at face value and concentrate initially on two aspects: rhetoric and perspective.

Rhetorically your text works by the simple trick of combining shock tactics with frank naïvety. Your emperor – like you, I prefer for the moment not to call him Septimius Severus, though incidentally I thought that was surprisingly restrained of you. Your emperor speaks simply, without affectation, in short sentences of educated but colloquial English. In this way, he or you gains credence. He is apparently telling the true, insider story: he was there, he should know. But of course, we all know from countless autobiographies that being there is no guarantee of truth. He may be trying to deceive, or simply have deceived himself, and he might even not have known the truth. In short, even if we accept the veracity of the tale to the teller, it still might not be what we need to know. And simply because it's all a huge ego-trip – whether yours or his, doesn't matter – the text constantly revolves around one man; there are simply too many 'I's in your text.

Rhetorically that presents a huge difficulty because the audience may not warm to your 'I'. And since it is not a romance, but a quasi-serious history – or at least I suppose that is what you want it to be – you have no plausible tactic to make us like your chief character. At least when we read a conventional autobiography we begin with the parents, childhood, adolescence, romance. In other words, we establish the basic human characteristics of the hero. Your hero, who by his own admission has 'done everything', never becomes human, because you don't allow us to see his emotions. He is still, in spite of your attempts at cosy familiarity, made of papier mâché varnished with selected factoids.

Now to perspective. Inevitably, because your vision is blinkered by scholarly conventions, you stick by and large to the sources – Herodian, Dio, with bits of Tacitus and Philo – and you gain considerably by taking a fresh look and inverting their perspective. Instead of seeing the emperor objectively from the outside, we are forced to wonder with you what it all seemed like to him from the inside. Excellent, but it is a single tactic ploy, say, like playing Beethoven backwards. You get the idea quite quickly; I am not sure that it is worthwhile playing a whole symphony.

So what we don't get – I admit this is a catalogue of faults of omission as well as commission – is the empire viewed retrospectively as a complex system. Because you are stuck on one man – and it wouldn't help from this point of view even if you dealt with a whole series of different emperors – what we can't get is the sheer variety of perspectives which make up the richness of Roman history. To understand the emperor, we need to know how a whole slew of diverse people – senators, administrators, provincials, slaves, women – perceived, idolised, criticised and even fantasised about him or simply, as Kafka saw, lived their arduous lives in arduous miscognition of him.

It's amusing to think, Keith, that what I am really saying is that you have committed exactly the same mistake as Fergus Millar. You have taken what the emperor did as the central element of his importance, but it is what he didn't do, as well as what he was thought to have done or not done, which mattered just as much. His image was a vital part of his reality. I know you know that, but why did you let it slip?

Hope this helps. Don't hesitate to let me see the revised version.

Love, Martha

I thought deeply how best to reply. I took a bit of time to get over my mild resentment: how could she have been so critical?

After all, it was not a book; it was a lecture, a *pièce d'occasion*. I could not include everything. But eventually I wrote as follows:

Dear Martha,

Thank you very much for taking the time and trouble to send me such thoughtful and constructive criticisms. [You see it is not only emperors who are hypocritical.] You must be right, and I will work on it, but for the moment can I feebly say in defence that this piece is called 'How to be an Emperor', so it is based on the emperor's own records and is understandably focused on what the emperor saw, on his sense of what the world was like? It's not my fault if he was an egomaniac, though I suspect that any successful emperor had to have a very thick skin and blinkered perception.

His insensitivity to other people's needs and sufferings was a job requirement. He won the throne and survived on it, at least that is what he apparently thought, by repeatedly having his enemies executed. He ruled through fear, though there must have been numerous other active ingredients in his apparent success: character, charisma and even religious enthusiasm, to name but three.

But actually, I am not really interested in his emotions. I know that some people are, and that biographies are very popular. TV directors always want us to say what heroes' and villains' motives were: why did the assassins kill Julius Caesar, what was Nero really like?

But there is a huge gap between post-Freudian western culture and ancient Rome. We are interested in emotions. They weren't. So we never, or rarely, know the emotions and motives of ancient characters. All that ancient sources tell us about this emperor is that he worked hard, was very energetic, brave and prone to anger. That doesn't get you very far psycho-wise, and he doesn't reveal much in this piece either. He seems to suffer from the delusion which I would call 'voluntaristic individualism'. By this I mean that he sees his world as though it were under his personal control, and he is free to act as he chooses. Whereas I see him as bounded by a complex social and governmental system which largely determines his decisions and actions. So it's the system which is more interesting than the intentions of self-deluding actors. I am interested in Septimius Severus as an archetypal emperor more than as an individual. That is why I made so little of who he actually was.

What I did think you would criticise me for was the tightness of my timeframe. Septimius Severus' policies had serious mid-term repercussions. His huge increase in army pay started a spiral of coin debasement and inflation. His predatory raid on Mesopotamia and capture of the Parthian capital, Ctesiphon, were irresponsible. They soured relations with another empire which potentially was Rome's most powerful enemy, without yielding any long-term return.

And Septimius stops his story and with it, apparently, his responsibility, with his own death, even though he now knows what happened afterwards.

All that he really seems bothered about was the rapid death of his two sons and the end of his imperial line. He was interested in power only as a personal prop, not in the great empire he ruled for over seventeen years. That was self-indulgent. Even his dying words were self-deceptive: 'I have done everything, but it doesn't help.'

Still, I will certainly rewrite this before I publish it.

Thanks, as ever, Keith.

AFTERWORD

HOW TO BE A ROMAN EMPEROR: AN AUTOBIOGRAPHY

MARY BEARD

This fictional autobiography of a Roman emperor – Septimius Severus we are led to assume – is a classic example of 'late Hopkins' and, to be honest, of some of the more irritating features of that period of H.'s work. 'How to be a Roman emperor' pretends to include the first publication of a recently discovered text and is full of rather inelegant attempts to capture the authentic voice of a Roman emperor, complete with his moans about 'hoity-toity senators' (81 [545]) and unconvincing attempts at local colour: 'like a traffic jam outside the Colosseum' (77 [539]). It also includes a spoof letter from one of H.'s colleagues and playful insults at old sparring partners (Fergus Millar gets the usual rap over the knuckles). The whole essay is driven by concerns about the contested boundary between fiction and history. This is the world of *A World Full of Gods*.[1] The particularly clunky style is almost certainly the result of just how late 'How to be a Roman emperor' came in H.'s working life. It was originally delivered as a lecture in February 2003, just a year before he died – and, although in *his* spoof letter at the very end of the essay (84–5 [547–8]), H. promises, 'I will certainly rewrite this before I publish it', he did not get the chance. A lightly edited version of the text of the lecture, which he had approved, appeared after his death.

In this case, the theme of 'History and Fiction' was not only the result of H.'s own preoccupations at the time. The lecture had been written for a series on exactly that topic sponsored by Wolfson College, Oxford, to celebrate the centenary of the birth of Ronald Syme, Camden Professor of Roman History from 1949 to

[1] Hopkins 1999.

1970 – and now best remembered as a supremely cynical analyst of Roman politics and literature, and master of the art of 'prosopography', the detailed study of the relationships between members of the Roman élite, as well as their individual careers and career patterns.[2] A collection of essays, based on the lecture series, was published in 2005. There were six essays in all, two others on classical themes: Miriam Griffin's investigation of Syme's own (and less well-known) fascination with 'fictional history', both ancient and modern; and Kathleen Coleman's exploration of the interface between reality and illusion in the Roman imagination.[3] As I recall from conversations then, H. was rather boyishly excited at being asked to deliver a lecture in honour of a man whose historical approach he had long criticised.[4] And he had mischievous fun in anachronistically conscripting his Septimius Severus into the project. The emperor, we discover in the 'autobiography', when reflecting on his own promotions' policy, deplored the likes of Syme: 'Modern prosopographers, those wretched bores who treat history as though it is one of your railway timetables, have never guessed my sheer sense of fun in picking people for promotion' (75 [537]). H. had always wanted to use the careers of the Roman aristocracy as part of a broad structural picture: who got promoted and why, and how did that sustain the emperor's position? Syme had not been unaware of the importance of that, but for him the issues of individual personal connections, of the clubs and cabals of Roman 'oligarchs' (where the power, he claimed, *really* lay), and of the micro-systems of patronage and back-scratching (or -stabbing) often took centre stage.[5]

2 Among his many books, *The Roman Revolution* (= Syme 1939) and *Tacitus* (= Syme 1958) remain classics. For a warm discussion of Syme's achievement, see Millar 1981b; for a similarly warm discussion of prosopography as a method, see Barnes 2007.

3 Tomlin 2005a: M. Griffin '"Lifting the mask": Syme on fictional history' (16–39) (= Griffin 2005); K. Coleman '"Truth severe, by fairy fiction drest": reality and the Roman imagination' (40–70). The other essays are on modern themes: N. A. M. Rodger on the historicity of the novels of Patrick O'Brien; Richard Holmes on accounts of the Great War; and screen-writer and historian Julian Mitchell on how history is dramatised. It is a collection that deserves to be better known.

4 Sideswipes at Syme in Hopkins 1991a: 484 n. 18 [essay 8: 321 n. 18]; Hopkins and Burton 1983a: 38 n. 12, 48 n. 26, 52 n. 33.

5 Particularly influential examples of his prosopographical method can be found in Syme 1939: on the working of Augustus' regime: ch. 24 'The party of Augustus' (349–68) and ch. 25 'The working of patronage' (369–86).

The truth is that H. had an ideological blindspot for Syme. He saw only the narrow prosopographer, the Syme of such technical studies as 'Governors of Pannonia Inferior' or 'The wrong Marcius Turbo'.[6] But Griffin's essay in the same commemorative volume shows that – whatever our views of prosopography – there was much more overlap between Syme and Hopkins than H. would have liked to think. H. certainly missed the range and imagination of Syme: the man who could celebrate the fourth-century *Historia Augusta* as an extravagant and instructive fiction and who could puzzle about the historiography of Marguerite Yourcenar's *Memoirs of Hadrian* (1951).[7]

But, in a way, the pot shots at Syme were a game, and a nostalgic throw-back to some traditional version of Oxford vs Cambridge antagonism. It is, I suspect, no coincidence that the essay starts, 'In *Cambridge* …' (72 [534]); unlike *Oxford*, we must assume. And underneath the casual jibes, there were much bigger questions about the role of the Roman emperor as the 'ruler' of the biggest European empire ever. H. had long been an admirer of Jonathan Spence's *Emperor of China: Self-Portrait of K'ang-hsi* (1974), which was effectively a montage autobiography of the Chinese emperor who ruled from 1661 to 1722 – a book that pieced together and expanded the emperor's original testimony.[8] This was H.'s attempt to do something similar for Rome. How could you ever understand the role of the emperor and his attempts to run the Roman world, from the emperor's point of view?

'How to be a Roman emperor' tries to capture the impossibility of the role of the man at the heart of the Roman power structure. On whom could the emperor depend? How did he diffuse the opposition to his own rule? How did he deal with a difficult and recalcitrant aristocracy? H. ventriloquises his Septimius Severus, to make some powerful points about the

[6] Syme 1965, 1962.

[7] Griffin 2005: especially 25–30, with special reference to Syme's A. James Bryce Memorial Lecture given at Somerville College, Oxford in May 1984 (a lecture much concerned with Yourcenar) = Syme 1986.

[8] Spence 1974 is cited approvingly at 72 [534].

position of the emperor: the lack of trust between emperor and courtiers; the ambivalent role of the court eunuchs; or the rigid protocols of life at the top of Roman society – when Octavia didn't bat an eyelid as her brother Britannicus was killed in front of her, she was of course playing the perfect role of imperial princess (77 [540]). In many ways this is familiar H. territory, even if less elegantly expressed than in some of his other work. His ability to write winning analytic prose was second to none (the first chapter of *Conquerors and Slaves* rightly still remains an *exemplum* of rigorous and engaging academic argument[9]). What the 'emperor' has to say here is conveyed in the uncomfortably bloke-ish, almost boy-scoutish, language of a fictionalising H., impersonating an emperor. The reader probably needs to retranslate it back into academic 'Hopkins-speak', to appreciate how important his points are: amongst other things, we see the emperor both as controller and prisoner of his own court; and we see him as victim as well as beneficiary of the contested pattern of Roman imperial inheritance. What gave an emperor the right to claim the throne and how did he keep it? The dilemmas and anxieties that lie just under the surface of the ghost-written memoir of Septimius Severus are probably not far off the mark.

It remains, however, a flawed, and more or less unfinished, essay. So why still read it? In fact, it is precisely because of its raw state that it is so revealing and so vividly opens up some of the themes with which H. was most concerned in the last ten years of his life – and more. We tend now to think that the main strengths of H.'s academic career were his skills as a consummate statistician, theorist and hard-headed analyst, exposing the half-truths and sloppy thinking with which most of the rest of us bumbled along. And that in many ways is true. But he had been concerned with the lived experience of the Romans, and how we might ever access that, long before *A World Full of Gods*. 'Novel evidence for Roman slavery' [essay 11], which appeared in 1993 was part of this project. But already in 1983, he had introduced the chapter on 'Death

[9] Hopkins 1978b: 1–98.

in Rome' in *Death and Renewal* by heralding his aim 'to evoke and recapture some of the feelings which Romans experienced in accommodating death. I wondered, and still wonder what it was like to be there'.[10] H. could be both tenacious and slippery in defending these efforts at historical imagination. I suspect (indeed, I know) that his response to the objection that no Roman emperor would have written like a watered-down Keith Hopkins would have been to argue, correctly in a way, just how conventionalised our assumptions about imperial style are – and far too influenced by the 'boring philosophy', as H.'s Septimius puts it (74 [536]), of Marcus Aurelius. But at the same time, H. was intensely self critical, not only of these imaginative essays but of much else he wrote, often saying that the acutest reviewer of a book would always be the author himself (*sic*); for the author was the one person who really knew what its faults were.

That, of course, was the point of the spoof letters included here, and famously in *A World Full of Gods*, apparently sent to H. by an array of critical colleagues (including me, appearing both as 'Mary' and thinly disguised as 'Martha', as time-traveller in *A World Full of Gods* and slightly crotchety correspondent in 'How to be a Roman emperor').[11] These letters have often fascinated H.'s readers, partly because it has been so difficult to pin down just how 'authentic' they were. Did their 'signatories' have anything at all to do with them, or not? James Davidson puzzled about exactly that in his review of *A World Full of Gods* in the *London Review of Books*. 'The letters are supposed to be real', he wrote, '(if not, they are remarkably convincing ventriloquies) and offer thoughtful criticisms and substantial arguments in favour of alternative interpretations'. Yet he also spots many of the contrary clues: 'Mary's' letter, for example, is sent from the 'wrong' college (New Hall, not Newnham) and she recommends a book (her own!) that had not been published at the date the letter was supposed to have been written. There is a sense, he suggests, that the 'authors' of

[10] Hopkins 1983b: 203.
[11] Hopkins 1999: 7–45.

all these letters are the 'textual twins' of those who they are supposed to be, a vicarious device at the heart of H's argument.[12]

The truth is, so far as I know, that the letters were written entirely by H. himself, even if attempting in part to ape the style of their 'writers' (unsurprisingly, perhaps, I find that aspect less 'remarkably convincing' than Davidson did). They were indeed a vicarious device, for introducing alternative perspectives, disagreement and uncertainty into the heart of the arguments. In 'How to be a Roman emperor', the letter from 'Martha' underlines the teasing quality of Septimius' memoir: she treats it *both* as a potentially genuine item, with her worries about provenance and authenticity, *and* as an unsatisfactory confection of H. himself, 'papier mâché varnished with selected factoids' (83 [546]). But she also raises the big questions that troubled H. about the value of autobiography ('there are simply too many "I"s in your text' (82 [546]) and what the limitations of any such project would be, even if it were what it purported to be. 'It's amusing to think, Keith, that what I am really saying is that you have committed exactly the same mistake as Fergus Millar. You have taken what the emperor did as the central element of his importance, but it is what he didn't do, as well as what he was thought to have done or not done, which mattered just as much. … I know you know that, but why did you let it slip?' (83 [546]). For H., a spoof letter, on the subject of a spoof document, clunky or not, captured better than more conventional forms of historiography, some of his own dilemmas in writing the history of ancient Rome, and in wondering 'what it was like to be there'.

'How to be a Roman emperor' remains with me as a reminder of that other H., that had always been in tension with the confident number-cruncher, the sometimes destructive interlocutor ('so what?'; 'I have two reactions to your paper and the first is boredom'; and so on), and the one-man ginger group determined to reveal to the ancient historical profession its own hopeless lack of rigour and sophistication. This is the H. whose vision of the historian's task was impossibly

[12] Davidson 2000: 28.

diffracted, the H. plagued by uncertainty about what good history was and whether he met the exacting standards he trailed before everyone else; the H. 'in' (not 'doing') analysis. In that sense too – and perhaps more than any other – 'How to be a Roman emperor' makes usefully uncomfortable reading.

ORIGINAL PUBLICATION DETAILS

1 ‘Contraception in the Roman empire’, *Comparative Studies in Society and History* 8 (1965) 124–51.
2 ‘A textual emendation in a fragment of Musonius Rufus: a note on contraception’, *Classical Quarterly* 15 (1965) 72–4.
3 ‘On the probable age structure of the Roman population’, *Population Studies* 20 (1966): 245–64.
4 ‘Graveyards for historians’, in F. Hinard (ed.) *La mort, les morts et l’au-delà dans le monde romain. Actes du colloque de Caen, 20–22 novembre 1985*, Caen: Centre des Publications de l’Université de Caen, 1987, 113–26.
5 ‘Economic growth and towns in classical antiquity’, in P. Abrams and E. A. Wrigley (eds) *Towns in Societies: Essays in Economic History and Historical Sociology*, Cambridge: Cambridge University Press, 1978, 35–77.
6 ‘Taxes and trade in the Roman empire, 200 BC–AD 200’, *Journal of Roman Studies* 70 (1980) 101–25.
7 ‘Models, ships and staples’, in P. D. A. Garnsey and C. R. Whittaker (eds) *Trade and Famine in Classical Antiquity, Proceedings of the Cambridge Philological Society* supplementary volume 8, 1983, 84–109.
8 ‘From violence to blessing: symbols and rituals in ancient Rome’, in A. Molho, K. Raaflaub and J. Emlen (eds) *City States in Classical Antiquity and Medieval Italy: Athens and Rome, Florence and Venice*, Stuttgart: Franz Steiner Verlag, 1991, 479–98.
9 ‘Slavery in classical antiquity’, in A. V. S. de Reuck and J. Knight (eds) *Caste and Race: Comparative Approaches*, London: J. & A. Churchill, 1967, 166–77.
10 ‘Conquest by book’, in *Literacy in the Roman World, Journal of Roman Archaeology*, supplementary series 3, Ann Arbor MI, 1991, 133–58 (and see [363 n. *]).
11 ‘Novel evidence for Roman slavery’, *Past & Present* 138 (1993) 3–27, reprinted with minor corrections in R. Osborne (ed) *Studies in Ancient Greek and Roman Society*, Cambridge: Cambridge University Press, 2004, 206–25.
12 ‘Christian number and its implications’, *Journal of Early Christian Studies* 6 (1998) 185–226.

13 'The political economy of the Roman empire', in I. Morris and W. Scheidel (eds) *The Dynamics of Ancient Empires: State Power from Assyria to Byzantium*, Oxford Studies in Early Empires, New York/Oxford: Oxford University Press, 2009, 178–204.

14 'How to be a Roman emperor: an autobiography', in R. Tomlin (ed.) *History and Fiction: Six Essays Celebrating the Centenary of Sir Ronald Syme (1903–89)*, London: Grime & Selwood, 2005, 72–85.

BIBLIOGRAPHY

⟨This bibliography serves two simultaneous purposes. It gathers together all the items cited by H. in thirteen of the essays collected in this volume (the exception is the posthumously published 'The political economy of the Roman empire') – offering some impression of H.'s library. It also includes items cited in the Introduction, Afterwords and the ⟨bracketed⟩ additions to the footnotes. Save for H.'s own works, these latter are, in each case, marked by an asterisk (*). See above [p. xviii].⟩

Abrams, P. (1978) 'Towns and economic growth: some theories and problems', in Abrams and Wrigley, 9–33.

Abrams, P. and Wrigley, E. A. (eds) (1978) *Towns in Societies: Essays in Economic History and Historical Sociology*, Cambridge.

Acsádi, G. and Nemeskéri, J. (1970) *History of Human Life Span and Mortality*, trans. K. Balás, Budapest.

*Adams, C. (2007) *Land Transport in Roman Egypt: A Study of Economics and Administration in a Roman Province*, Oxford.

Adrados, F. R. (1979) 'The "Life of Aesop" and the Origins of Novel in Antiquity', *Quaderni urbinati di cultura classica* 30: 93–112.

Aharoni, Y. and Avi-Yonah, M. (1977) *The Macmillan Bible Atlas*, rev. edn, New York (3rd edn, 1993; 4th edn as *The Carta Bible Atlas*, Jerusalem, 2002).

Albion, R. G. (1926) *Forests and Sea Power: The Timber Problem of the Royal Navy, 1652–1862*, Harvard Economic Studies 29, Cambridge, MA.

Alföldy, G. (1986) *Die römische Gesellschaft. Ausgewählte Beiträge*, Heidelberger althistorische Beiträge und epigraphische Studien 1, Stuttgart.

*Alfonso, S., Grousset, F., Massé, L. and Tastet, J.-P. (2001) 'A European lead isotope signal recorded from 6000 to 300 years BP in coastal marshes (SW France)', *Atmospheric Environment* 35: 3595–605.

Allberry, C. R. C. (1938) *A Manichaean Psalm-Book: Part II*, Manichaean Manuscripts in the Chester Beatty Collection 2, Stuttgart.

Allbutt, T. C. (1921) *Greek Medicine in Rome: The Fitzpatrick Lectures on the History of Medicine Delivered at the Royal College of Physicians of London in 1909–1910, with Other Historical Essays*, London.

*Allen, R. (2009) 'How prosperous were the Romans? Evidence from Diocletian's Price Edict (AD 301)', in Bowman and Wilson, 327–45.

*Alston, R. (2001) *The City in Roman and Byzantine Egypt*, London.

*(2011) 'Introduction: rereading ancient slavery', in Alston, Hall and Proffitt, 1–33.

*Alston, R., Hall, E. and Proffitt, L. (eds) (2011) *Reading Ancient Slavery*, London.

Anderson, P. (1974) *Lineages of the Absolutist State*, London.

*Ando, C. (2009) 'Evidence and orthopraxy', *JRS* 99: 171–81.

*Andreau, J. (1974) *Les affaires de Monsieur Jucundus*, Collection de l'École française de Rome 19, Rome.

*Andreau, J. and Descat, R. (2006) *Esclave en Grèce et à Rome*, Paris (trans. M. Leopold, *The Slave in Greece and Rome*, Madison, WI, 2011).

*Annequin, J. (1987) 'Les esclaves rêvent aussi .... Remarques sur *La clé des songes* d'Artémidore', *Dialogues d'histoire ancienne* 13: 71–113.

*(1989) 'Rêver c'est vivre. Du songe de l'esclave à la réalité de l'esclavage chez Artémidore', *Index. Quaderni camerti di studi romanistici/International Survey of Roman Law* 17: 139–54.

Applebaum, S. (1972) 'Roman Britain', in H. P. R. Finberg (ed.) *The Agrarian History of England and Wales*, I.2: *A.D. 43–1042*, Cambridge, 3–277.

Ardant, G. (1965) *Théorie sociologique de l'impôt*, 2 vols, Paris.

(1971) *Histoire de l'impôt I. De l'antiquité au XVII*[e] *siècle*. Paris.

Ariès, P. (1948) *Histoire des populations françaises et de leurs attitudes devant la vie depuis le XVIII*[e] *siècle*, Paris (2nd edn, 1971).

(1949) 'Attitudes devant la vie et devant la mort du XVIIe au XIXe siècle. Quelques aspects de leurs variations', *Population* 4: 463–70.

(1953) 'Sur les origines de la contraception en France', *Population* 8: 465–72.

*(1960) *L'enfant et la vie familiale sous l'ancien régime*, Paris.

Armini, H. (1916) *Sepulcralia Latina*, Gothenburg.

*Arnaud, P. (2007) 'Diocletian's Prices Edict: the prices of seaborne transport and the average duration of maritime travel', *JRA* 20: 321–36.

Avery, D. (1974) *Not on Queen Victoria's Birthday: The Story of the Rio Tinto Mines*, London.

Avezzù, G. (1977–8) 'Nuovi papiri della missione archeologica Anti-Bagnani a Umm el Breighât (Tebtynis)', *Bollettino dell'Istituto di filologia greca, Università di Padova* 4: 192–6.

*Avlamis, P. (2011) 'Isis and the people in the *Life of Aesop*', in P. Townsend and M. Vidas (eds) *Revelation, Literature and Community in Late Antiquity*, Texts and Studies in Ancient Judaism 146, Tübingen, 65–101.

Aymard, M. (1966) *Venise, Raguse et le commerce du blé pendant la seconde moitié du XVI*[e] *siècle*, Ports, routes, trafics 20, Paris.

(1973) 'Rendements et productivité agricole dans l'Italie moderne', *Annales* 28: 475–98.

*Backendorf, D. (1998) *Römische Münzschätze des zweiten und ersten Jahrhunderts v. Chr. vom italienischen Festland*, Studien zu Fundmünzen der Antike 13, Berlin.

Badian, E. (1972) *Publicans and Sinners: Private Enterprise in the Service of the Roman Republic*, Oxford (rev. edn, 1983, Ithaca, NY).

Baehrel, R. (1961) *Une croissance. La Basse-Provence rurale (fin XVI*[e] *siècle–1789). Essai d'économie historique statistique*, Démographie et sociétés 6, Paris.

Bagnall, R. S. (1985) 'Agricultural productivity and taxation in later Roman Egypt', *TAPA* 115: 289–308 (repr. in his *Later Roman Egypt: Society, Religion, Economy and Administration*, Aldershot, 2003, no. 17).

(1993) *Egypt in Late Antiquity*, Princeton.

*(2011) *Everyday Writing in the Graeco-Roman East*, Sather Classical Lectures 69, Berkeley, CA.

*Bagnall, R. S. and Cribiore, R. (2006) *Women's Letters from Ancient Egypt, 300 BC–AD 800*, Ann Arbor.

Bagnall, R. S. and Frier, B. W. (1994) *The Demography of Roman Egypt*, Cambridge Studies in Population, Economy and Society in Past Time 23, Cambridge (rev. edn, 2006).

Baines, J. (1983) 'Literacy and ancient Egyptian society', *Man* (NS) 18: 572–99 (repr. in his *Visual and Written Culture in Ancient Egypt*, Oxford, 2007, 33–62).

Baines, J. and Eyre, C. J. (1983) 'Four notes on literacy', *Göttinger Miszellen* 61: 65–96 (rev. in J. Baines, *Visual and Written Culture in Ancient Egypt*, Oxford, 2007, 63–94).

*Bang, P. F. (2008) *The Roman Bazaar: A Comparative Study of Trade and Markets in a Tributary Empire*, Cambridge.

*(2012) 'Predation', in Scheidel 2012b: 197–217.

*Barnes, T. D. (2007) 'Prosopography and Roman history', in K. S. B. Keats-Rohan (ed.) *Prosopography, Approaches and Applications: A Handbook*, Prosopographia et Genealogica 13, Oxford, 83–93.

Barns, J. (1964) 'Shenute as a historical source', in J. Wolski (ed.) *Actes du X*[e] *congrès international de papyrologues, Varsovie–Cracovie 3–9 septembre 1961*, Wrocław, 150–9.

Bartsch, S. (1989) *Decoding the Ancient Novel: The Reader and the Role of Description in Heliodorus and Achilles Tatius*, Princeton.

Beard, M. (1987) 'A complex of times: no more sheep on Romulus' birthday', *PCPS* 33/213: 1–15 (repr. in C. Ando (ed.) *Roman Religion*, Edinburgh, 2003, 273–88).

*(2002) 'Ciceronian correspondences: making a book out of letters', in T. P. Wiseman (ed.) *Classics in Progress: Essays on Ancient Greece and Rome*, Oxford, 103–44.

*(2007) *The Roman Triumph*, Cambridge, MA.

*(2014) *Laughter in Ancient Rome: On Joking, Tickling, and Cracking up*, Sather Classical Lectures 71, Berkeley, CA.

*Beard, M., North, J. and Price, S. (1998a) *Religions of Rome*, vol. 1: *A History*, Cambridge.

*(1998b) *Religions of Rome*, vol. 2: *A Sourcebook*, Cambridge.

Bellinger, A. R. (1949) *The Excavations at Dura-Europos Conducted by Yale University and the French Academy of Inscriptions and Letters, Final Report 6: The Coins*, New Haven.

Beloch, K. J. (1886) *Die Bevölkerung der griechisch-römischen Welt*, Historische Beiträge zur Bevölkerungslehre 1, Leipzig.

(1899) 'Die Bevölkerung im Altertum', *Zeitschrift für Sozialwissenschaft* 2: 505–14, 600–21.

*Benoist, S. (2005) *Rome, le prince et la cité. Pouvoir impérial et cérémonies publiques: 1er siècle av.–début du IV siècle apr. J.-C.*, Paris.

Ben Shemesh, A. (1969) (trans.) *Taxation in Islam*, vol. 3: *Abū Yūsuf's Kitāb al-kharāj*, Leiden.

Beresford, J. (2013) *The Ancient Sailing Season, Mnemosyne* supplement 351, Leiden.

Bieżuńska-Malowist, I. (1974–7) *L'esclavage dans l'Égypte gréco-romaine*, trans. J. Wolf and J. Kasińska, 2 vols, Archiwum filologiczne 30 and 35, Wrocław.

Bigg, C. (1913) *The Christian Platonists of Alexandria, being the Brampton Lecture of the year 1886*, rev. edn (ed. F. E. Brightman), Oxford.

Biondi, B. (1952–4) *Il diritto romano cristiano*, 3 vols, Milan.

Bird, R. M. (1974) *Taxing Agricultural Land in Developing Countries*, Cambridge, MA.

Bisbee, G. A. (1988) *Pre-Decian Acts of Martyrs and Commentarii*, Harvard Dissertations in Religion 22, Philadelphia.

Blázquez, J. M. (1969) 'Explotaciones mineras en Hispania durante la República y el Alto Imperio romano. Problemas económicos, sociales y técnicos', *Anuario de Historia Económica y Social de España* 2: 9–68.

Bloch, M. (1986) *From Blessing to Violence: History and Ideology in the Circumcision Ritual of the Merina of Madagascar*, Cambridge Studies in Social Anthropology 61, Cambridge.

*Blockley, R. C. (1983) *The Fragmentary Classicising Historians of the Later Roman Empire: Eunapius, Olympiodorus, Priscus and Malchus*, vol. 2: *Text, Translation and Historiographical Notes*, ARCA Classical and Medieval Texts, Papers and Monographs, 10, Liverpool.

Boak, A. E. R. (1935) *Soknopaiou Nesos: The University of Michigan Excavations at Dimê in 1931–32*, University of Michigan Studies, Humanistic Series 39, Ann Arbor.

(1937) 'The organization of gilds in Greco-Roman Egypt', *TAPA* 68: 212–20.

(1946) 'An Egyptian farmer of the age of Diocletian and Constantine', *Byzantina-Metabyzantina* 1: 39–53.

(1955) 'The population of Roman and Byzantine Karanis', *Historia* 4: 157–62.

Boak, A. E. R. and Youtie, H. C. (1960) *The Archive of Aurelius Isidorus in the Egyptian Museum, Cairo, and the University of Michigan*, Ann Arbor.

Bolin, S. (1958) *State and Currency in the Roman Empire to 300 A.D.*, Stockholm.

Bömer, F. (ed.) (1957–8) *P. Ovidius Naso. Die Fasten*, 2 vols, Heidelberg.

Botti, G. (1936) 'I papiri ieratici e demotici degli scavi italiani di Tebtynis', in *Atti del IV congresso internazionale di papirologia, Firenze, 28 aprile–2 maggio 1935/XIII*, Milan, 217–23.

*Boud'hors, A. (2012) 'The Coptic tradition', in S. F. Johnson (ed.) *The Oxford Handbook of Late Antiquity*, Oxford, 224–46.

Bourdieu, P. (1988) *Homo academicus*, trans. P. Collier, Cambridge (first published as *Homo academicus*, Paris, 1984).

*Boutron, C., Rosman, K., Barbante, C., Bolshov, M., Adams, F., Hong, S. and Ferrari, C. (2004) 'L'archivage des activités humaines par les neiges et glaces polaires: le cas du plomb', *Comptes Rendus Geoscience* 336: 847–67.

Bowersock, G. W. (1965) *Augustus and the Greek World*, Oxford.

(1969) *Greek Sophists in the Roman Empire*, Oxford.

*(1994) *Fiction as History: From Nero to Julian*, Sather Classical Lectures 58, Berkeley, CA.

*Bowman, A. K. (2001) 'Documentary papyrology and ancient history', in I. Andorlini, G. Bastianini et al. (eds) *Atti del XXII congresso internazionale di papirologia, Firenze, 23–29 agosto 1998,* Florence, 2 vols, I 137–45.

Bowman, A. K., Garnsey, P. D. A. and Rathbone, D. (eds) (2000) *The Cambridge Ancient History*, vol. 11: *The High Empire, A.D. 70–192*, 2nd edn, Cambridge.

*Bowman, A. K. and Wilson A. (eds) (2009) *Quantifying the Roman Economy: Methods and Problems*, Oxford.

*(2011) *Settlement, Urbanization, and Population*, Oxford.

*Boyaval, B. (1976) 'Remarques sur les indications d'âges de l'épigraphie funéraire grecque d'Égypte', *ZPE* 21: 217–43.

Bradley, K. R. (1984) *Slaves and Masters in the Roman Empire: A Study in Social Control*, Collection Latomus 185, Brussels.

*(1986) 'Seneca and slavery', *Classica et Mediaevalia* 37: 161–72 (repr. with additions in J. G. Fitch (ed.) *Seneca*, Oxford, 2008, 335–47).

*(2000) 'Animalizing the slave: the truth of fiction', *JRS* 90: 110–25 (repr. in his *Apuleius and Antonine Rome: Historical Essays, Phoenix* supplementary vol. 50, Toronto, 2012, 59–78).

*(2008) 'Roman slavery: retrospect and prospect', *Canadian Journal of History* 43: 477–500.

*(2010) 'Freedom and slavery', in A. Barchiesi and W. Scheidel (eds) *The Oxford Handbook of Roman Studies*, Oxford, 624–36.

*(2015) 'The bitter chain of slavery', *Dialogues d'histoire ancienne* 41: 149–76.

*Bradley, K. R. and Cartledge, P. (eds) (2011) *The Cambridge World History of Slavery*, vol. 1: *The Ancient Mediterranean World*, Cambridge.

Bram, J. R. (1975) *Ancient Astrology: Theory and Practice = Matheseos libri VIII by Firmicus Maternus*, Park Ridge, NJ.

*Brännvall, M.-L., Bindler, R., Renberg, I., Emteryd, O., Bartnicki, J. and Billström, K. (1999) 'The medieval metal industry was the cradle of modern large-scale atmospheric lead pollution in northern Europe', *Environmental Science and Technology* 33: 4391–5.

*Brännvall, M.-L., Bindler, R., Emteryd, O. and Renberg, I. (2001) 'Four thousand years of atmospheric lead pollution in northern Europe: a summary from Swedish lake sediments', *Journal of Paleolimnology* 25: 421–35.

Braudel, F. (1966) *La Méditerranée et le monde méditerranéen à l'époque de Philippe II*, 2 vols, 2nd edn, Paris (trans. S. Reynolds, *The Mediterranean and the Mediterranean World in the Age of Philip II*, 2 vols, London, 1972–3).

(1979) *Civilisation matérielle, économie et capitalisme, XV*[e]*–XVIII*[e] *siècle*, vol. 2: *Les jeux de l'échange*, Paris (trans. S. Reynolds, *Civilization and Capitalism, 15th–18th Century*, vol. 2: *The Wheels of Commerce*, London, 1982).

Bremmer, J. (1989) 'Why did early Christainity attract upper-class women?', in A. A. R. Bastiaensen, A. Hilhorst and C. H. Kneepkens (eds) *Fructus centesimus. Mélanges offerts à Gerard J. M. Bartelink à l'occasion de son soixante-cinquième anniversaire*, Instrumenta Patristica 19, Dordrecht, 37–47.

Brock, S. (1980) 'An introduction to Syriac studies', in J. H. Eaton (ed.) *Horizons in Semitic Studies: Articles for the Student*, University Semitic Study Aids 8, Birmingham, 1–33.

Broshi, M. (1979) 'The population of western Palestine in the Roman-Byzantine period', *Bulletin of the American Schools of Oriental Research* 236: 1–10.

*Brown, P. R. L. (1981) *The Cult of the Saints: Its Rise and Function in Latin Christianity*, Chicago (2nd edn, 2015).

(1992) *Power and Persuasion in Late Antiquity: Towards a Christian Empire*, Madison, WI.

*Bruhns, H. (1985) 'De Werner Sombart à Max Weber et Moses I. Finley. La typologie de la ville antique et la question de la ville de consommation', in P. Leveau (ed.) *L'origine des richesses dépensées dans la ville antique. Actes du colloque organisé à Aix-en-Provence par l'U.E.R. d'histoire, les 11 et 12 mai 1984*, Aix-en-Provence, 255–73.

*(1987–9) 'La cité antique de Max Weber', *Opus* 6–8 (*La città anticà? La cité antique?*): 29–42.

Brunt, P. A. (1961) 'Charges of provincial maladministration under the early Principate', *Historia* 10: 189–227 (repr. in Brunt 1990: 53–95).

(1971a) *Italian Manpower 225 B.C.–A.D. 14*, Oxford (repr. with new postscript, 1987).

*(1971b) *Social Conflicts in the Roman Republic*, London (rev. edn, 1986).
(1976) 'The Romanization of the local ruling classes in the Roman empire', in D. M. Pippidi (ed.) *Assimilation et résistance à la culture gréco-romaine dans le monde ancien. Travaux du VI*[e] *congrès international d'etudes classiques (Madrid, Septembre 1974)*, Bucharest/Paris, 161–73 (repr. in Brunt 1990: 267–81).
(1981) 'The revenues of Rome', *JRS* 71: 161–72 (repr. in Brunt 1990: 324–46).
(1988) *The Fall of the Roman Republic and Related Essays*, Oxford.
*(1990) *Roman Imperial Themes*, Oxford.
Bücher, K. (1904) *Die Entstehung der Volkswirtschaft. Vorträge und Versuche*, 4th edn, Tübingen (9th edn, 1913).
Buckland, W. W. (1908) *The Roman Law of Slavery: The Condition of the Slave in Private Law from Augustus to Justinian*, Cambridge.
Burn, A. R. (1953) 'Hic breve vivitur: a study of the expectation of life in the Roman empire', *Past & Present* 4: 2–31.
(1965) review of Nordberg 1963, *JRS* 55: 253–7.
Burns, C. M. (1942) *Infant and Maternal Mortality in Relation to Size of Family and Rapidity of Breeding: A Study in Human Responsibility*, Newcastle upon Tyne.
*Caldwell, J. C. (2004) 'Fertility control in the classical world: was there an ancient fertility transition?', *Journal of Population Research* 21: 1–17.
Callu, J.-P. (1969) *La politique monétaire des empereurs romains de 238 à 311*, Bibliothèque des Écoles françaises d'Athènes et de Rome 214, Paris.
Calza, G. (1940) *La necropoli del porto di Roma nell'Isola Sacra*, Rome.
*Campbell, J. B. (1984) *The Emperor and the Roman Army 31 BC–AD 235*, Oxford.
*(2002) *War and Society in Imperial Rome 31 BC–AD 284*, London.
*(2012) *Rivers and the Power of Ancient Rome*, Chapel Hill, NC.
Capitanio, M. (1974) 'La necropoli romana di Portorecanati', *Not. scav.* (ser. 8) 28: 142–445.
*Capogrossi Colognesi, L. (1995) 'The limits of the ancient city and the evolution of the medieval city in the thought of Max Weber', in T. J. Cornell and K. Lomas (eds) *Urban Society in Roman Italy*, London, 27–37.
Carlile, R. (1828) *Every Woman's Book; or, What is Love? Containing Most Important Instructions for the Prudent Regulation of the Principle of Love, and the Number of a Family*, London.
Carradice, I. (1983) *Coinage and Finances in the Reign of Domitian, A.D. 81–96*, British Archaeological Reports: International Series 178, Oxford.
Casson, L. (1950) 'The Isis and her voyage', *TAPA* 81: 43–56.
(1951) 'Speed under sail of ancient ships', *TAPA* 82: 136–48.
(1957) 'New light on maritime loans', *Eos* 48.2 (= *Symbolae Raphaeli Taubenschlag dedicatae* II): 89–93.

(1971) *Ships and Seamanship in the Ancient World*, Princeton (2nd edn, 1995, Baltimore).

*(1986) 'New light on maritime loans: *P. Vindob. G* 19792 (= *SB* VI 9571)', in R. S. Bagnall and W. V. Harris (eds) *Studies in Roman Law in Memory of A. Arthur Schiller*, Columbia Studies in the Classical Tradition 13, Leiden, 11–17.

*Castelli, E. (1998) 'Gender, theory, and *The Rise of Christianity*: a response to Rodney Stark', *Journal of Early Christian Studies* 6: 227–57.

Cerati, A. (1975) *Caractère annonaire et assiette de l'impôt foncier au Bas-Empire*, Bibliothèque d'histoire du droit et droit romain 20, Paris.

Chadwick, H. (1966) *Early Christian Thought and the Classical Tradition: Studies in Justin, Clement, and Origen*, Oxford.

Challis, C. E. (1978) *The Tudor Coinage*, Manchester.

Chandaman, C. D. (1975) *The English Public Revenue, 1660–1688*, Oxford.

*Chandrasekhar, S. (1981) *'A Dirty Filthy Book': The Writings of Charles Knowlton and Annie Besant on Reproductive Physiology and Birth Control and an Account of the Bradlaugh-Besant Trial*, Berkeley, CA.

Chatterton, E. K. (1933) *The Old East Indiamen*, London.

Chayanov, A. V. (1966) *The Theory of Peasant Economy* (ed. D. Thorner, B. H. Kerblay and R. E. F. Smith), Homewood, IL (new edn, Manchester, 1986).

Cheung, S. N. S. (1968) 'Private property rights and sharecropping', *Journal of Political Economy* 76: 1107–22.

*Choat, M. (2009) 'Language and culture in late antique Egypt', in P. Rousseau (ed.) *A Companion to Late Antiquity*, Blackwell Companions to the Ancient World, Chichester, 342–56.

Christiansen, E. (1988) *The Roman Coins of Alexandria: Quantitative Studies*, 2 vols, Aarhus.

Cipolla, C. M. (1976) *Before the Industrial Revolution: European Society and Economy, 1000–1700*, London (3rd edn, 1993).

Clark, C. and Haswell, M. (1970) *The Economics of Subsistence Agriculture*, 4th edn, London.

Clark, E. A. (1977) *Clement's Use of Aristotle: The Aristotelian Contribution to Clement of Alexandria's Refutation of Gnosticism*, Texts and Studies in Religion 1, New York.

*Clauss, M. (1973) 'Probleme der Lebensalterstatistiken aufgrund römischer Grabinschriften', *Chiron* 3: 395–417.

Clavel, M. (1970) *Béziers et son territoire dans l'antiquité*, Annales littéraires de l'Université de Besançon 112, Paris.

Cleere, H. (1976) 'Some operating parameters for Roman ironworks', *Bulletin of the Institute of Archaeology* 13: 233–46.

Coale, A. J. and Demeny, P. (1966) *Regional Model Life Tables and Stable Populations*, Princeton.

(1983) *Regional Model Life Tables and Stable Populations*, 2nd edn, New York.

Cohen, A. (1974) *Two-Dimensional Man: An Essay on the Anthropology of Power and Symbolism in Complex Society*, London.

*Cohen, J. E. (1995) *How Many People Can the Earth Support?*, New York.

Cohen, S. J. D. (1987) *From the Maccabees to the Mishnah*, Library of Early Christianity 7, Philadelphia (3rd edn, Louisville, KY, 2014).

Collingwood, R. G. (1939) *An Autobiography*, Oxford.

*Cooley, A. (ed.) (2002) *Becoming Roman, Writing Latin? Literacy and Epigraphy in the Roman West*, *JRA* supplementary series 48, Portsmouth, RI.

*Cooper, K. (2005) 'Ventriloquism and the miraculous: conversion: preaching, and the martyr exemplum in late antiquity', in K. Cooper and J. Gregory (eds) *Signs, Wonders, Miracles: Representations of Divine Power in the Life of the Church*, Studies in Church History 41, Woodbridge, 22–45.

*(2010) 'Family, dynasty, and conversion in the Roman *Gesta Martyrum*', in R. Corradini, M. Diesenberger and M. Niederkorn-Bruck (eds) *Zwischen Niederschrift und Wiederschrift. Hagiographie und Historiographie im Spannungsfeld von Kompendienüberlieferung und Editionstechnik*, Österreichische Akademie der Wissenschaften, Denkschriften der philosophisch-historischen Klasse 405, Vienna, 273–81.

*(2014) 'Relationships, resistance and religious change in the early Christian household', in J. Doran, C. Methuen and A. Walsham (eds) *Religion and the Household*, Studies in Church History 50, Woodbridge, 5–22.

*Corbeill, A. (1996) *Controlling Laughter: Political Humour in the Late Roman Republic*, Princeton.

Corbier, M. (1978) 'Dévaluations et fiscalité (161–235)', in *Les "dévaluations" à Rome. Époque républicaine et impériale I (Rome, 13–15 novembre 1975)*, Collection de l'École française de Rome 37, Rome, 273–309.

*Cornell, T. J. (1995) *The Beginnings of Rome: Italy and Rome from the Bronze Age to the Punic Wars (c. 1000–264 B.C.)*, London.

*Cornell, T. J. and Lomas, K. (eds) (1995) *Urban Society in Roman Italy*, London.

*Cotton, H. M., Cockle, W. E. H. and Millar, F. (1985) 'The papyrology of the Roman Near East: a survey', *JRS* 85: 214–35.

*Craik, E. M. (2015) *The 'Hippocratic' Corpus: Content and Context*, London.

Crawford, M. H. (1969a) *Roman Republican Coin Hoards*, Royal Numismatic Society Special Publications 4, London.

(1969b) 'The financial organization of republican Spain', *Numismatic Chronicle* (7th ser.) 9: 79–93.

(1969c) 'Coin hoards and the pattern of violence in the late Republic', *PBSR* 37: 76–81.

(1970) 'Money and exchange in the Roman world', *JRS* 60: 40–8.

(1974) *Roman Republican Coinage*, 2 vols, London.

Cuinet, V. (1890–5) *La Turquie d'Asie. Géographie administrative, statistique descriptive et raisonée de chaque province de l'Asie-Mineure*, 4 vols, Paris.

*Dal Lago, E. and Katsari, C. (eds) (2008a) *Slave Systems: Ancient and Modern*, Cambridge.

*(2008b) 'The study of ancient and modern slave systems: setting an agenda for comparison', in Dal Lago and Katsari, 3–31.

Daly, L. W. (1961) *Aesop without Morals: The Famous Fables, and a Life of Aesop*, New York.

*D'Ambra, E. (1995) 'Mourning and the making of ancestors in the Testamentum relief', *AJA* 99: 667–81.

Dandekar, K. (1962) 'Family planning studies conducted by the Gokhale Institute of Politics and Economics, Poona', in Kiser, 3–16.

D'Arms, J. (1981) *Commerce and Social Standing in Ancient Rome*, Cambridge, MA.

*Davidson, J. (2000) 'Feel what it's like', review of Hopkins 1999, *London Review of Books* 22.5, 2 March, 28–9.

Davies, O. (1935) *Roman Mines in Europe*, Oxford.

*Davies, R. W. (1969) 'Joining the Roman army', *Bonner Jahrbücher* 169: 208–32 (repr. in his *Service in the Roman Army*, ed. D. Breeze and V. A. Maxfield, Edinburgh, 1989, 3–30).

*Davis, D. B. (1966) *The Problem of Slavery in Western Culture*, Ithaca, NY (rev. edn, 1988).

Davis, R. (1962) *The Rise of the English Shipping Industry in the Seventeenth and Eighteenth Centuries*, London.

de Bruyne, D. (1907) 'Prologues bibliques d'origine marcionite', *Revue bénédictine* 24: 1–16.

*de Callataÿ, F. (2005) 'The Graeco-Roman economy in the super long-run: lead, copper, and shipwrecks', *JRA* 18: 361–72.

*(ed.) (2014) *Quantifying the Greco-Roman Economy and Beyond,* Pragmateiai 27, Bari.

Déchelette, J. (1913) *La collection Millon. Antiquités préhistoriques et gallo-romaines*, Paris.

Degrassi, A. (1964) 'L'indicazione dell'età nelle iscrizioni sepolcrali latine', in *Akte des IV. Internationalen Kongresses für griechische und lateinische Epigraphik (Wien, 17. bis 22. September 1962)*, Vienna, 72–98 (repr. in his *Scritti vari di antichità III*, Trieste, 1967, 211–41).

de Laszlo, H. and Henshaw, P. S. (1954) 'Plant materials used by primitive peoples to affect fertility', *Science* 119: 626–31.

Déléage, A. (1945) *La capitation du Bas-Empire,* Annales de l'Est. Mémoire 14, Nancy.

Delia, D. (1988) 'The population of Roman Alexandria', *TAPA* 118: 275–92.

*de Ligt, L. (1993) *Fairs and Markets in the Roman Empire: Economic and Social Aspects of Periodic Trade in a Pre-Industrial Society*, Dutch Monographs on Ancient History and Archaeology 11, Amsterdam.

*(2007) 'Roman manpower and recruitment during the middle Republic', in P. Erdkamp (ed.) *A Companion to the Roman Army*, Blackwell Companions to the Ancient World, Oxford, 114–31.

della Corte, M. (1954) *Case ed abitanti di Pompei*, 2nd edn, Pompeii (3rd edn, ed. P. Soprano, Naples, 1965).

Del Panta, L. and Livi Bacci, M. (1980) 'Le componenti naturali dell'evoluzione demografica nell'Italia del Settecento', in *La popolazione italiana nel Settecento. Relazioni e comunicazioni presentate al convegno su 'La ripresa demografica del Settecento', Bologna, 26–28 aprile 1979*, Bologna, 71–139.

Delumeau, J. (1957–9) *Vie économique et sociale de Rome dans la seconde moitié du XVI*[e] *siècle*, 2 vols, Bibliothèque des Écoles françaises d'Athènes et de Rome 184, Paris.

de Marchi, A. (1903) 'Cifre di mortalità nelle iscrizioni romane', *Rendiconti del Reale Istituto Lombardo di scienze e lettere* 36: 1025–34.

de Reuck, A. V. S. and Knight, J. (eds) (1967) *Caste and Race: Comparative Approaches*, London.

de Robertis, F. M. (1963) *Lavoro e lavoratori nel mondo romano*, Bari.

de Ste. Croix, G. E. M. (1963) 'Why were the early Christian persecuted?', *Past & Present* 26: 6–38 (repr. in Finley 1974: 210–49, and in de Ste. Croix 2006: 105–45).

(1964) 'Why were the early Christian persecuted? – a rejoinder', *Past and Present* 27: 28–33 (repr. in Finley 1974: 256–62, and in de Ste. Croix 2006: 145–52).

(1981) *The Class Struggle in the Ancient Greek World: From the Archaic Age to the Arab Conquests*, London.

*(2006) *Christian Persecution, Martyrdom, and Orthodoxy*, ed. M. Whitby and J. Streeter, Oxford.

Diepgen, P. (1937) *Die Frauenheilkunde der alten Welt*, Handbuch der Gynäkologie 12.1, Munich.

(1949) *Geschichte der Medizin. Die historische Entwicklung der Heilkunde und des ärztlichen Lebens*, vol. 1. *Von den Anfängen der Medizin bis zur Mitte des 18. Jahrhunderts*, Berlin.

Dionisotti, A. C. (1982) 'From Ausonius' schooldays? A schoolbook and its relatives', *JRS* 72: 83–125.

*Dixon, S. (2001) *Reading Roman Women: Sources, Genres and Real Life*, London.

*Domaszewski, A. von (1967) *Die Rangordnung des römischen Heeres*, 2nd edn, Beihefte der *Bonner Jahrbücher* 14, Cologne.

Douglass, F. (1855) *My Bondage and my Freedom*, New York (revised and expanded as *Life and Times of Frederick Douglass*, Hartford, CT, 1882).

Drabkin, I. E. (1944) 'On medical education in Greece and Rome', *Bulletin of the History of Medicine* 15: 333–51.

Drabkin, M. F. and Drabkin, I. E. (1951) *Caelius Aurelianus, Gynaecia: Fragments of a Latin Version of Soranus' Gynaecia from a Thirteenth Century Manuscript, Bulletin of the History of Medicine* supplement 13, Baltimore.

*Drexhage, H.-J., Konen, H. and Ruffing, K. (2002) *Die Wirtschaft des römischen Reiches (1.–3. Jahrhundert). Eine Einführung*, Berlin.

Drinkwater, J. F. (1977–1978) 'Die Secundinier von Igel und die Woll- und Textilindustrie in Gallica Belgica. Fragen und Hypothesen', *Trierer Zeitschrift* 40–1: 107–25.

Droge, A. J. and Tabor, J. D. (1992) *A Noble Death: Suicide and Martyrdom among Christians and Jews in Antiquity*, San Francisco.

Duchesne, L. (1886) *Le liber pontificalis. Texte, introduction et commentaire I*, Paris.

Dumont, J. C. (1987) *Servus. Rome et l'esclavage sous la République*, Collection de l'École française de Rome 103, Rome.

Dunbabin, K. M. D. (1978) *The Mosaics of Roman North Africa: Studies in Iconography and Patronage*, Oxford.

Duncan-Jones, R. P. (1962) 'Costs, outlays and summae honorariae from Roman Africa', *PBSR* 30: 47–115.

(1963) 'Wealth and munificence in Roman Africa', *PBSR* 31: 159–77.

(1974) *The Economy of the Roman Empire: Quantitative Studies*, Cambridge (2nd edn, 1982).

(1976a) 'The size of the modius castrensis', *ZPE* 21: 53–62.

(1976b) 'The price of wheat in Roman Egypt under the Principate', *Chiron* 6: 241–62.

(1982) *The Economy of the Roman Empire: Quantitative Studies*, 2nd edn, Cambridge.

(1984) 'Problems of the Delphic manumission payments 200–1 B.C.', *ZPE* 57: 203–9.

(1990) *Structure and Scale in the Roman Economy*, Cambridge.

(1994) *Money and Government in the Roman Empire*, Cambridge.

*Dupont, F. and Éloi, T. (2001) *L'érotisme masculin dans la Rome antique*, Paris.

Durand, J. D. (1959–60) 'Mortality estimates from Roman tombstone inscriptions', *American Journal of Sociology* 65: 365–73.

*Duttenhöffer, R. (2007) 'Neue *Penthemeros*-Quittungen aus der Beinecke Library', in A. J. B. Sirks and K. A. Worp (eds) *Papyri in memory of P. J. Sijpesteijn (P.Sijp.)*, American Studies in Papyrology 40, Oakville, CT, 278–86.

Duval, P.-M. (1961) *Paris antique, des origins au troisième siècle*, Paris.

*Dwyer, D. J. (ed.) (1972a) *The City as a Centre of Change in Asia*, Centre of Asian Studies Series 4, Hong Kong.

*(1972b) 'Attitudes towards spontaneous settlement in third world cities', in Dwyer, 166–78.

*Dyson, S. L. (1985) *The Creation of the Roman Frontier*, Princeton.
*Eck, W. (2000) 'The growth of administrative posts', in Bowman, Garnsey and Rathbone, 238–65.
*(2003) *The Age of Augustus*, trans. D. L. Schneider, Oxford (2nd edn, 2007) (first published as *Augustus und seine Zeit*, Munich, 1998).
*Edwards, C. (1993) *The Politics of Immorality in Ancient Rome*, Cambridge.
*Edwards, C. and Woolf, G. D. (eds) (2003a) *Rome the Cosmopolis*, Cambridge.
*(2003b) 'Cosmopolis: Rome as world city', in Edwards and Woolf, 1–21.
*Eisenstadt, S. (1963) *The Political Systems of Empires*, London (repr. with new introduction, New Brunswick, NJ, 1993).
Elias, N. (1939) *Über den Prozess der Zivilisation. Soziogenetische und psychogenetische Untersuchungen*, 2 vols, Basel (2nd edn, 1969, Bern) (trans. E. Jephcott, *The Civilizing Process*, 2 vols, Oxford, 1978–82).
*Elsner, J. (2012) 'Material culture and ritual: state of the question', in B. D. Wescoat and R. G. Ousterhout (eds) *Architecture of the Sacred: Space, Ritual, and Experience from Classical Greece to Byzantium*, Cambridge, 1–26.
*Engel, D. M. (2003) 'Women's role in the home and the state: Stoic theory reconsidered', *HSCP* 101: 267–88.
*Engels, D. (1990) *Roman Corinth: An Alternative Model for the Classical City*, Chicago.
*Erdkamp, P. (1998) *Hunger and the Sword: Warfare and Food Supply in Roman Republican Wars (264–30 BC)*, Dutch Monographs on Ancient History and Archaeology 20, Amsterdam.
*(2001) 'Beyond the limits of the "consumer city": a model of the urban and rural economy in the Roman world', *Historia* 50: 332–56.
*(ed.) (2002) *The Roman Army and the Economy*, Amsterdam.
*(2005) *The Grain Market in the Roman Empire: A Social, Political and Economic Study*, Cambridge.
*(ed.) (2007) *A Companion to the Roman Army*, Blackwell Companions to the Ancient World, Oxford.
Éry, K. K. (1969) 'Investigations on the demographic source value of tombstones originating from the Roman period', *Alba Regia* 10: 51–67.
Esperandieu, É. (1907–28) *Recueil général des bas-reliefs [statues et bustes] de la Gaule romaine*, 10 vols, Paris.
Étienne, R. (1959) 'Démographie et épigraphie', in *Atti del terzo congresso internazionale di epigrafia greca e latina (Roma 4–8 settembre 1957)*, Rome, 415–24.
Fagnan, E. (1921) (trans.) *Le livre de l'impôt foncier (Kitâb el-Kharâdj), Abou Yousof Ya'koub*, Bibliothèque archéologique et historique 1, Paris.
*Feeney, D. C. (2007) *Caesar's Calendar: Ancient Time and the Beginnings of History*, Sather Classical Lectures 65, Berkeley, CA.

Feissel, D. and Gascou, J. (1989) 'Documents d'archives romains inédits du Moyen Euphrate (IIIe siècle après J.-C.)', *CRAI* 133: 535–61.
*Féret, G. and Sylvestre, R. (2008) *Les graffiti sur céramique d'Augusta Raurica,* Forschungen in Augst 40, Augst.
Fink, R. O. (1971) *Roman Military Records on Papyrus*, Philological monographs of the American Philological Association 26, Cleveland, OH.
Finley, M. I. (1959) 'Was Greek civilisation based on slave labour?', *Historia* 8: 145–64 (repr. in M. I. Finley (ed.) *Slavery in Classical Antiquity: Views and Controversies*, Cambridge, 1960, 53–72 and in Finley 1981: 96–115).
(1964) 'Between slavery and freedom', *Comparative Studies in Society and History* 6: 233–49 (repr. in Finley 1981: 116–32).
(1968) 'Slavery', *International Encyclopaedia of the Social Sciences*, vol. 14, New York, 307–13.
(1973) *The Ancient Economy*, Sather Classical Lectures 43, Berkeley, CA (2nd edn, London, 1985; updated edn with foreword by I. Morris, Berkeley, CA, 1999).
(ed.) (1974) *Studies in Ancient Society*, London.
(1977) 'The ancient city: from Fustel de Coulanges to Max Weber and beyond', *Comparative Studies in Society and History* 19: 305–27 (repr. in Finley 1981: 3–23).
(1980) *Ancient Slavery and Modern Ideology*, London (expanded edn, ed. B. D. Shaw, Princeton, 1998).
(1981) *Economy and Society in Ancient Greece*, ed. B. D. Shaw and R. Saller, London.
*(1985) *Ancient History: Evidence and Models*, London.
(1987) *Classical Slavery*, London.
*Fischer, D. H. (1996) *The Great Wave: Price Revolutions and the Rhythm of History*, Oxford.
Fischer, I. (1927) *Die Gynäkologie bei Dioskurides und Plinius*, Vienna.
Fisher, R. A. (1930) *The Genetical Theory of Natural Selection*, Oxford (2nd rev. edn, 1958).
*Fitzgerald, W. (2000) *Slavery and the Roman Literary Imagination*, Cambridge.
*Flemming, R. (1999) review of Riddle 1997, *Isis* 90: 102–3.
*(2000) *Medicine and the Making of Roman Women: Gender, Nature, and Authority from Celsus to Galen,* Oxford.
*Flower, H. I. (2006) *The Art of Forgetting: Disgrace and Oblivion in Roman Political Culture*, Chapel Hill, NC.
Forbes, R. J. (1934) *Notes on the History of Ancient Roads and their Construction*, Archaeologisch-historische bijdragen 3, Amsterdam.
(1955–64) *Studies in Ancient Technology*, 9 vols, Leiden (2nd edn, 1964–72).
*Forni, G. (1953) *Il reclutamento delle legioni da Augusto a Diocleziano*, Pubblicazioni della Facoltà di lettere e filosofia dell'Università di Pavia 5, Milan.

*(1974) 'Estrazione etnica e sociale dei soldati delle legioni nei primi tre secoli dell'impero', in *ANRW* II.1, ed. H. Temporini, Berlin, 339–91.

Foster, L. (1981) *Religion and Sexuality: Three American Communal Experiments of the Nineteenth Century*, Oxford.

*Foucault, M. (1976–84) *Histoire de la sexualité*, vol. 1. *La volonté de savoir* (1976); vol. 2. *L'usage des plaisirs* (1984); vol. 3. *Le souci de soi* (1984), Paris (trans. R. Hurley, *The History of Sexuality*, vol. 1: *The Will to Knowledge*; vol. 2: *The Use of Pleasure*; vol. 3: *The Care of the Self*, London, 1979–88).

Foxhall, L. and Forbes, H. A. (1982) 'Σιτομετρεία: the role of grain as a staple food in classical antiquity', *Chiron* 12: 41–90.

Frank, T. (ed.) (1933–40) *An Economic Survey of Ancient Rome*, 6 vols, Baltimore.

Fraser, P. M. (1972) *Ptolemaic Alexandria*, 3 vols, Oxford.

Frederiksen, M. W. (1966) 'Caesar, Cicero and the problem of debt', *JRS* 56: 128–41.

Frend, W. H. C. (1965) *Martyrdom and Persecution in the Early Church: A Study of a Conflict from the Maccabees to Donatus*, Oxford.

Friedländer, L. and Wissowa, G. (eds) (1921–3) *Darstellungen aus der Sittengeschichte Roms in der Zeit von Augustus bis zum Ausgang der Antonine*, 10th edn, 4 vols, Leipzig (trans. of 7th edn by L. B. Magnus, J. H. Freeze and A. B. Gough, *Roman Life and Manners under the Early Empire*, 4 vols, London, 1908–13).

Frier, B. (1982) 'Roman life expectancy: Ulpian's evidence', *HSCP* 86: 213–51.

(1983) 'Roman life expectancy: the Pannonian evidence', *Phoenix* 37: 328–44.

(1985) *The Rise of the Roman Jurists: Studies in Cicero's Pro Caecina*, Princeton.

*(1994) 'Natural fertility and family limitation in Roman marriage', *CPh* 89: 318–33.

(2000) 'Demography', in Bowman, Garnsey and Rathbone, 787–816.

Gabba, E. (1972) 'Urbanizzazione e rinnovamenti urbanistici nell'Italia centro-meridionale del I secolo a.C.', *Studi classici e orientali* 21: 73–112 (repr. in his *Italia romana*, Biblioteca di Athenaeum 25, Como, 1994, 63–103).

*Gagos, T. (2009) '4967: Work contract of public herald', in D. Obbink, N. Gonis et al. (eds) *The Oxyrhynchus Papyri LXXIII: In Honour of Peter Parsons and John Rea,* London, 199–202.

*Galinsky, K. (ed.) (2005) *The Cambridge Companion to the Age of Augustus*, Cambridge.

Galton, F. (1869) *Hereditary Genius: An Enquiry into its Laws and Consequences*, London.

Gamble, H. Y. (1995) *Books and Readers in the Early Church: A History of Early Christian Texts*, New Haven.

*Garnsey, P. D. A. (1970) *Social Status and Legal Privilege in the Roman Empire*, Oxford.

(1983) 'Grain for Rome', in Garnsey, Hopkins and Whittaker, 118–30.

*(1988) *Famine and Food Supply in the Graeco-Roman World: Responses to Risk and Crisis*, Cambridge.

Garnsey, P. D. A., Hopkins, K. and Whittaker, C. R. (eds) (1983) *Trade in the Ancient Economy*, London.

*Geertz, C. (1972) 'Deep play: notes on the Balinese cockfight', *Daedalus* 101: 1–37 (repr. in his *The Interpretation of Cultures: Selected Essays*, New York, 1973, 412–53).

*(1977) 'Centers, kings and charisma: reflections on the symbolics of power', in J. Ben-David and T. N. Clark (eds) *Culture and its Creators: Essays in Honor of Edward Shils*, Chicago, 150–71 (repr. in his *Local Knowledge: Further Essays in Social Anthropology*, New York, 1983, 121–46).

Gelzer, M. (1912) *Die Nobilität der römischen Republik*, Leipzig (trans. R. Seager, *The Roman Nobility*, Oxford, 1969).

*George, M. (2010) 'Archaeology and Roman slavery: problems and potential', in H. Heinen (ed.) *Antike Sklaverei, Rückblick und Ausblick. Neue Beiträge zur Forschungsgeschichte und zur Erschließung der archäologischen Zeugnisse*, Forschungen zur antiken Sklaverei 38, Stuttgart, 141–60.

*(2013) *Roman Slavery and Roman Material Culture*, *Phoenix* supplementary vol. 52, Toronto.

Geremek, H. (1969) *Karanis, communauté rurale de l'Égypte romaine au IIe–IIIe siècle de notre ère*, Archiwum filologiczne 17, Wrocław.

Gerschenkron, A. (1962) *Economic Backwardness in Historical Perspective: A Book of Essays*, Cambridge, MA.

Giacchero, M. (1974) *Edictum Diocletiani et collegarum de pretiis rerum venalium in integrum fere restitutum e Latinis Graecisque fragmentis*, Pubblicazioni dell'Istituto di storia antica e scienze ausiliarie dell'Università di Genova 8, 2 vols, Genoa.

Giddens, A. (1984) *The Constitution of Society: Outline of the Theory of Structuration*, Cambridge.

Gignoux, P. (1968) 'L'inscription de Kartir à Sar Mašhad', *Journal Asiatique* 256: 387–418.

Giovannini, A. (1978) *Rome et la circulation monétaire en Grèce au IIe siècle avant Jésus-Christ*, Schweizerische Beiträge zur Altertumswissenschaft 15, Basel.

Giversen, S. (ed.) (1986–8) *The Manichaean Coptic Papyri in the Chester Beatty Library*, Cahiers d'orientalisme 14–17, 4 vols, Geneva.

Glass, D. V. (1965) 'Population growth and population policy', *Journal of Chronic Diseases* 18: 1079–94.

*Gleason, M. (1995) *Making Men: Sophists and Self-Presentation in Ancient Rome*, Princeton.

Goetz, G. (ed.) (1892) *Corpus Glossariorum Latinorum*, vol. 3: *Hermeneumata Pseudodositheana*, Leipzig.

Goitein, S. D. (1967) *A Mediterranean Society: The Jewish Communities of the Arab World as Portrayed in the Documents of the Cairo Geniza*, vol. 1: *Economic Foundations*, Berkeley, CA.

*Goldsmith, R. W. (1984) 'An estimate of the size and structure of the national product of the early Roman empire', *Review of Income and Wealth* 30: 263–88.

Goodchild, R. G. and Forbes, R. J. (1956) 'Roads and land travel, with a section on harbours, docks, and lighthouses', in C. Singer, E. J. Holmyard et al. (eds) *A History of Technology*, vol. 2: *The Mediterranean Civilizations and the Middle Ages, c. 700 BC to c. AD 1500*, Oxford, 493–536.

Goodchild, R. G. and Reynolds, J. M. (1962) 'Some military inscriptions from Cyrenaica', *PBSR* 30: 37–46.

Goodspeed, E. J. (1902) 'Papyri from Karanis', *Studies in Classical Philology* 3: 1–66.

*Goody, J. (1983) *The Development of the Family and Marriage in Europe*, Cambridge.

Gould, J. D. (1972) *Economic Growth in History: Survey and Analysis*, London.

*Graf, F. (2005) 'Satire in a ritual context', in K. Freudenburg (ed.) *The Cambridge Companion to Roman Satire*, Cambridge, 192–206.

Greenblatt, S. (1988) *Shakespearean Negotiations: The Circulation of Social Energy in Renaissance England*, Oxford.

Greene, K. T. (1973) 'The pottery from Usk', in A. Detsicas (ed.) *Current Research in Romano-British Coarse Pottery: Papers Given at a C.B.A. Conference Held at New College, Oxford, March 24 to 26, 1972*, Council for British Archaeology Research Report 10, London, 25–37.

*(1986) *The Archaeology of the Roman Economy*, London.

*Greenhill, B. (1976) *Archaeology of the Boat: A New Introductory Study*, London.

Greenwood, M. (1940) 'A statistical mare's nest?', *Journal of the Royal Statistical Society* 103: 246–8.

Gregorovius, F. (1894–1902) *History of Rome in the Middle Ages*, 8 vols, trans. A. Hamilton, London (first published as *Geschichte der Stadt Rom im Mittelalter. Vom V. bis zum XVI. Jahrhundert*, 4th edn, 8 vols, Stuttgart, 1886–96).

Grenier, A. (1934) *Manuel d'archéologie gallo-romaine. Deuxième partie: l'archéologie du sol*, Manuel d'archéologie préhistorique, celtique et gallo-romaine 6, 2 vols, Paris.

*Grey, C. (2011) 'Slavery in the late Roman world', in Bradley and Cartledge, 482–509.

*Griffin, M. (2005) '"Lifting the mask": Syme on fictional history', in Tomlin 2005a: 16–39.

Gunther, R. T. (1934) *The Greek Herbal of Dioscorides*, Oxford.

Gutierrez, H. and Houdaille, J. (1983) 'La mortalité maternelle en France au XVIIIe siècle', *Population* 38: 975–94.

*Gutman, H. G. (1976) *The Black Family in Slavery and Freedom, 1750–1925*, New York.

Hähnel, R. (1936) 'Der künstliche Abortus im Altertum', *Sudhoffs Archiv für Geschichte der Medizin und der Naturwissenschaften* 29: 224–55.

*Hall, E. (2011) 'Playing ball with Zeus: strategies in reading ancient slavery through dreams', in Alston, Hall and Proffitt, 204–28.

Hall, P. (ed.) (1966) *Von Thünen's 'Isolated State': An English Edition of Der isolierte Staat by Johann Heinrich von Thünen*, trans. C. M. Wartenberg, Oxford.

*Hallett, J. P. and Skinner, M. B. (eds) (1997) *Roman Sexualities*, Princeton.

*Halstead, P. (2014) *Two Oxen Ahead: Pre-Mechanized Farming in the Mediterranean*, Chichester.

*Hammond, M. (1957) 'Composition of the senate, A.D. 68–235', *JRS* 47: 74–81.

Harkness, A. G. (1896) 'Age at marriage and at death in the Roman empire', *TAPA* 27: 35–72.

Harl, K. W. (1996) *Coinage in the Roman Economy, 300 BC to AD 700*, Baltimore.

Harnack, A. von (1908) *The Mission and Expansion of Christianity in the First Three Centuries*, trans. J. Moffatt, 2nd edn, 2 vols, Theological Translation Library 19–20, London.

(1924) *Die Mission und Ausbreitung des Christentums in den ersten drei Jahrhunderten*, 4th edn, 2 vols, Leipzig.

*Harper, K. (2011) *Slavery in the Late Roman World, AD 275–425*, Cambridge.

Harrauer, H. and Sijpesteijn, P. J. (1985) *Neue Texte aus dem antiken Unterricht*, Mitteilungen aus der Papyrussammlung der Österreichischen Nationalbibliothek (NS) 15, 2 vols, Vienna.

Harris, W. V. (1989) *Ancient Literacy*, Cambridge, MA.

*(2005) 'Morris Keith Hopkins, 1934–2004', *Proceedings of the British Academy* 130: 81–105.

*(2011) *Rome's Imperial Economy: Twelve Essays*, Oxford.

*(2014) 'Literacy and epigraphy II', in C. Apicella, M.-L. Haack and F. Lerouxel (eds) *Les affaires de Monsieur Andreau. Économie et société du monde romain*, Scripta antiqua 61, Bordeaux, 280–9.

*Harris, W. V. and Iara, K. (eds) (2011) *Maritime Technology in the Ancient Economy: Ship-Design and Navigation*, *JRA* supplement 84, Portsmouth, RI.

*Harris, W. V. and Li, F. (forthcoming) 'Ancient literacy: parallels and divergences between the Mediterranean world and China'.

Hasanat, A. (1945) *Controlled Parenthood: Voluntary Limitation and Promotion of Birth*, Dacca.

Hasebroek, J. (1933) *Trade and Politics in Ancient Greece*, trans. L. M. Fraser and D. C. Macgregor, London (first published as *Staat und Handel im alten Griechenland. Untersuchungen zur antiken Wirtschaftsgeschichte*, Tübingen, 1928).

*Hedrick, C. W. (2000) *History and Silence: Purge and Rehabilitation of Memory in Late Antiquity*, Austin, TX.

Heer, D. M. (1968) *Society and Population*, Englewood Cliffs, NJ.

(1975) *Society and Population*, 2nd edn, Englewood Cliffs, NJ.

Heers, J. (1961) *Gênes au XVe siècle. Activité économique et problèmes sociaux*, Affaires et gens d'affaires 24, Paris.

Heiserman, A. (1977) *The Novel Before the Novel: Essays and Discussions about the Beginnings of Prose Fiction in the West*, Chicago.

Helck, W., Otto, E. and Westendorf, W. (eds) (1975–92) *Lexikon der Ägyptologie*, 7 vols, Wiesbaden.

Henderson, J. (1989) 'Satire writes "women": *Gendersong*', *PCPS* 35: 50–80 (rev. in his *Writing Down Rome: Satire, Comedy, and Other Offences in Latin Poetry*, Oxford, 1999, 173–201).

Henry, L. (1957) 'La mortalité d'après les inscriptions funéraires', *Population* 12: 149–52.

(1959) 'L'âge au décès d'après les inscriptions funéraires', *Population* 14: 327–9.

Hermet, F. (1934) *La Graufesenque (Condatomago)*, 2 vols, Paris.

Herter, H. (1960) 'Die Soziologie der antiken Prostitution im Lichte des heidnischen und christlichen Schrifttums', *Jahrbuch für Antike und Christentum* 3: 70–111.

Hicks, J. (1969) *A Theory of Economic History*, Oxford.

Himes, N. E. (1936) *Medical History of Contraception*, London.

*Hin, S. (2011) 'Family matters: fertility and its constraints in Roman Italy', in C. Holleran and A. Pudsey (eds) *Demography and the Graeco-Roman World: New Insights and Approaches*, Cambridge, 99–116.

Hinard, F. (ed.) (1987) *La mort, les morts et l'au-delà dans le monde romain. Actes du colloque de Caen, 20–22 novembre 1985*, Caen.

*Hingley, R. (2005) *Globalizing Roman Culture: Unity, Diversity and Empire*, London.

Hinton, H. C. (1956) *The Grain Tribute System of China, 1845–1911*, Cambridge, MA.

Hinton, W. (1966) *Fanshen: A Documentary of Revolution in a Chinese Village*, New York.

Hirth, F. (1885) *China and the Roman Orient: Researches into their Ancient and Mediaeval Relations as Represented in Old Chinese Records*, Leipzig.

*Hitchner, R. B. (2005) '"The advantages of wealth and luxury": the case for economic growth in the Roman empire', in Manning and Morris, 207–22.

*Hölkeskamp, K.-J. (2000) '*Fides – deditio in fidem – dexta data et accepta*. Recht, Religion und Ritual in Rom', in C. Brunn (ed.) *The Roman*

Middle Republic: Politics, Religion, and Historiography, c. 400–133 BC: Papers from a Conference at the Institutum Romanum Finlandiae, September 11–12, 1998, Acta Instituti Romani Finlandiae 23, Rome, 223–50 (repr. in his *Senatus Populusque Romanus. Die politische Kultur der Republik: Dimensionen und Deutungen*, Wiesbaden, 2004, 105–35).

Holleman, A. W. J. (1974) *Pope Gelasius I and the Lupercalia*, Amsterdam.

Hollingsworth, T. H. (1957–8) 'A demographic study of the British ducal families', *Population Studies* 11: 4–26.

*Holm Rasmussen, A. and Rasmussen, S. W. (eds) (2008) *Religion and Society: Rituals, Resources and Identity in the Ancient Graeco-Roman World. The BOMOS-Conferences 2002–2005*, Analecta Romana Instituti Danici supplement 40, Rome.

*Holzberg, N. (1999) 'The fabulist, the scholars and the discourse: Aesop studies today', *IJCT* 6: 236–42.

Hombert, M. and Préaux, C. (1945) 'Note sur la durée de la vie dans l'Égypte gréco-romaine', *Chronique d'Égypte* 20: 139–46.

(1952) *Recherches sur le recensement dans l'Egypte romaine (P. Bruxelles inv. E. 7616)*, Papyrologica Lugduno-Batava 5, Leiden.

Hong, S. M., Candelone, J.-P., Patterson, C. C. and Boutron, C. F. (1994) 'Greenland ice evidence of hemispheric lead pollution two millennia ago by Greek and Roman civilizations', *Science* 265: 1841–3.

(1996a) 'History of ancient copper smelting pollution during Roman and medieval times recorded in Greenland ice', *Science* 272: 246–9.

*(1996b) 'A reconstruction of changes in copper production and copper emissions to the atmosphere during the past 7000 years', *Science of the Total Environment* 188: 183–93.

Hopkins, K. (1961) 'Social mobility in the later Roman empire: the evidence of Ausonius', *CQ* (NS) 11: 239–48.

(1963a) 'Eunuchs in politics in the later Roman empire', *PCPS* 189 (NS 9): 62–80 (rev. in 1978b: 172–96).

(1963b) 'The later Roman aristocracy: a demographic profile', unpublished fellowship dissertation, King's College, Cambridge.

(1964–5) 'The age of Roman girls at marriage', *Population Studies* 18: 309–27.

(1965a) 'Contraception in the Roman empire', *Comparative Studies in Society and History* 8: 124–51 [= essay no. 1].

(1965b) 'A textual emendation in a fragment of Musonius Rufus: a note on contraception', *CQ* 15: 72–4 [= essay no. 2].

(1965c) 'Élite mobility in the Roman empire', *Past & Present* 32: 12–26 (repr. in Finley 1974: 103–20).

(1965d) review of R. Bendix, *Nation-Building and Citizenship: Studies of our Changing Social Order*, New York, 1964, *Social Sciences Information/Information sur les sciences sociales* 4.4: 196–7.

(1966a) 'On the probable age structure of the Roman population', *Population Studies* 20: 245–64 [= essay no. 3].

(1966b) review of S. N. Eisenstadt, *Essays on Comparative Institutions*, New York, 1965, *British Journal of Sociology* 17: 325–26.

(1966c) 'Civil-military relations in developing countries', *British Journal of Sociology* 17: 165–82.

(1967) 'Slavery in classical antiquity', in A. V. S. de Reuck and J. Knight (eds) *Caste and Race: Comparative Approaches*, London, 166–77 [= essay no. 9].

(1968) 'Structural differentiation in Rome (200–31 BC): the genesis of an historical bureaucratic society', in I. M. Lewis (ed.) *History and Social Anthropology*, London, 63–79.

(1969a) 'Public housing policy in Hong Kong: an inaugural lecture from the Chair of Sociology', Supplement to the *University of Hong Kong Gazette* 16.5, 21 May, 1–17.

(1969b) 'Squatters here to stay', *Far Eastern Economic Review*, 64.18, 1 May: 308–10.

(ed.) (1971a) *Hong Kong: The Industrial Colony: A Political, Social and Economic Survey*, Hong Kong/London.

(1971b) 'Housing the poor', in 1971a: 271–335.

(1971c) 'Preface', in 1971a: xi–xvi.

(1972a) 'Classicists and sociologists', *Times Literary Supplement*, 3657, 31 March, 355–6.

(1972b) 'Public and private housing in Hong Kong', in Dwyer, 200–15.

(1973) 'Overcrowding in Hong Kong', *UNICEF News* 77: 16–19.

(1974a) 'Some sociological approaches to Roman history', seminar given in January in Oxford (unpublished MS).

(1974b) 'Demography in Roman history', *Mnemosyne* 27: 77–8.

(1978a) 'Economic growth and towns in classical antiquity', in Abrams and Wrigley, 35–77 [= essay no. 5].

(1978b) *Conquerors and Slaves*, Sociological Studies in Roman History 1, Cambridge.

(1978c) 'Rules of evidence', review of Millar 1977, *JRS* 68: 178–86.

(1980a) 'Taxes and trade in the Roman empire (200 BC–AD 400)', *JRS* 70: 101–25 [= essay no. 6].

(1980b) 'Brother-sister marriage in Roman Egypt', *Comparative Studies in Society and History* 22: 303–54.

(1982) 'The transport of staples in the Roman empire', in *Eighth International Economic History Congress Budapest 1982*, Budapest [Section B12: Trade in Staples in Antiquity (Greece and Rome)], 80–7.

(1983a) 'Models, ships and staples', in P. D. A. Garnsey and C. R. Whittaker (eds) *Trade and Famine in Classical Antiquity, PCPS* supplementary vol. 8, Cambridge, 84–109 [= essay no. 7].

(1983b) *Death and Renewal*, Sociological Studies in Roman History 2, Cambridge.

(1983c) 'Introduction', in Garnsey, Hopkins and Whittaker, ix–xxv.

(1983d) 'Chromatic harmony', review of F. M. Snowden, *Before Color Prejudice: The Ancient Views of Blacks*, Cambridge, MA, 1983, *Times Literary Supplement*, 4203, 21 October, 1152.

(1987) 'Graveyards for historians', in Hinard, 113–26 [= essay no. 4].

(1990) 'Seven missing papers', in J. Andreau and H. Bruhns (eds) *Parenté et stratégies familiales dans l'antiquité romaine. Actes de la table ronde des 2–4 octobre 1986*, Collection de l'École française de Rome 129, Rome, 623–30.

(1991a) 'From violence to blessing: symbols and rituals in ancient Rome', in A. Molho, K. Raaflaub and J. Emlen (eds) *City States in Classical Antiquity and Medieval Italy: Athens and Rome, Florence and Venice*, Stuttgart, 479–98 [= essay no. 8].

(1991b) 'Conquest by book', in *Literacy in the Roman World*, *JRA* supplementary series 3, Ann Arbor, 133–58 [= essay no. 10].

(1991c) 'Know thyself and see God: a religion for the lovers of lost causes', review of G. Filoramo, *A History of Gnosticism*, trans. A. Alcock, Oxford, 1990, *Times Literary Supplement*, 4586, 22 February, 3–4.

(1993) 'Novel evidence for Roman slavery', *Past & Present* 138: 3–27 (repr. with minor corrections in Osborne 2004b: 206–25) [= essay no. 11].

(1994a) 'The truly Roman?: soft and hard versions of the empire', review of A. Giardina (ed.) *The Romans*, trans. L. G. Cochrane, Chicago, 1993; A. Lintott, *Imperium Romanum: Politics and Administration*, London, 1993 and Averil Cameron, *The Later Roman Empire: AD 284–430*, London, 1993, *Times Literary Supplement*, 4750, 15 April, 4.

(1994b) 'Le mariage frère-sœur en Égypte romaine', in P. Bonte (ed.) *Épouser au plus proche. Inceste, prohibitions et stratégies matrimoniales autour de la Méditerranée*, Civilisations et sociétés 89, Paris, 79–95.

(1995–6) 'Rome, taxes, rents and trade', *Kodai* 6/7: 41–75 (repr. in W. Scheidel and S. von Reden (eds) *The Ancient Economy*, Edinburgh, 2002, 190–230).

(1996a) 'Centro e periferia. L'economia politica dell'Imperio Romano', trans. R. Cittadini in V. Castronovo (ed.) *Storia dell'economia mondiale,* vol. 1. *Permanenze e mutamenti dall'antichità al medioevo*, Rome, 1996, 213–32.

(1996b) 'The numbers game: erotic play in a Roman bath-house', review of Jacobelli 1995 and D. Montserrat, *Sex and Society in Graeco-Roman Egypt,* London, 1996, *Times Literary Supplement*, 4881, 18 October, 5.

(1997a) 'Half-resurrection man', review of J. Murphy-O'Connor, *Paul: A Critical Life*, Oxford, 1996 and A. N. Wilson 1997, *London Review of Books*, 19.12, 19 June, 14–15.

(1997b) 'Who cares about Corax?', review of S. Hornblower and A. Spawforth (eds) *The Oxford Classical Dictionary*, 3rd edn, 1996, *Times Literary Supplement,* 4898, 14 February, 6.

(1998) 'Christian number and its implications', *Journal of Early Christian Studies* 6: 185–226 [= essay no. 12].

(1999) *A World Full of Gods: Pagans, Jews and Christians in the Roman Empire*, London.

(2000a) 'The Temple replaced: Jewish rebellion and renewal through the rabbinate', review of W. Horbury, W. D. Davies and J. Sturdy (eds) *The Cambridge History of Judaism*, vol. 3: *The Early Roman Period*, Cambridge, 1999, *Times Literary Supplement*, 5064, 21 April, 4–5.

(2000b) 'Rent, taxes, trade and the city of Rome', in E. Lo Cascio (ed.) *Mercati permanenti e mercati periodici nel mondo romano. Atti degli incontri capresi di storia dell'economia antica (Capri 13–15 ottobre 1997),* Pragmateiai 2, Bari, 253–67.

(2001) 'Mind the gap', review of Hedrick 2000, *Times Literary Supplement*, 5105, 2 February, 7.

(2004) 'Introduction', to J. Carcopino, *Daily Life in Ancient Rome: The People and City at the Height of the Empire*, trans. E. O. Lorimer (first published as *La vie quotidienne à Rome à l'apogée de l'Empire*, Paris, 1939), Folio Society reprint, London, xi–xx.

(2005) 'How to be a Roman emperor: an autobiography', in Tomlin 2005a: 72–85 [= essay no. 14].

(2009) 'The political economy of the Roman empire', in I. Morris and W. Scheidel (eds) *The Dynamics of Ancient Empires: State Power from Assyria to Byzantium*, Oxford, 178–204 [= essay no. 13].

*Hopkins K. and Beard M. (2005) *The Colosseum*, London.

Hopkins, K. and Burton, G. (1983a) 'Political succession in the late Republic (249–50 BC)', in Hopkins 1983b: 31–119.

(1983b) 'Ambition and withdrawal: the senatorial aristocracy under the emperors', in Hopkins 1983b: 120–200.

Horbury, W. (1982) 'The benediction of the *minim* and early Jewish-Christian controversy', *JTS* (NS) 33: 19–61.

*Horden, P. and Purcell, N. (2000) *The Corrupting Sea: A Study of Mediterranean History,* Oxford.

Huang, R. (1974) *Taxation and Governmental Finance in Sixteenth-Century Ming China*, London.

*Huebner, S. R. (2007) '"Brother-sister" marriage in Roman Egypt: a curiosity of humankind or a widespread family strategy?', *JRS* 97: 21–49.

*(2011) 'Household composition in the ancient Mediterranean – what do we really know?', in B. Rawson (ed.) *A Companion to Families in the Greek and Roman Worlds*, Blackwell Companions to the Ancient World, Chichester, 73–91.

*(2013) *The Family in Roman Egypt: A Comparative Approach to Intergenerational Solidarity and Conflict*, Cambridge.

Hultsch, F. (1882) *Griechische und römische Metrologie*, 2nd edn, Berlin.

*Humphreys, S. C. (1969) 'History, economics, and anthropology: the work of Karl Polanyi', *History and Theory* 8: 165–212.

*Hunt, P. (2011) 'Slaves in Greek literary culture', in Bradley and Cartledge, 22–47.

*Hui, E. and Wong, F. (2003) 'Financial arrangement', in Y. M. Yeung and T. K. Y. Wong (eds) *Fifty Years of Public Housing in Hong Kong: A Golden Jubilee Review and Appraisal*, Hong Kong, 155–78.

Iannaccone, L. R. (1990) 'Religious practice: a human capital approach', *Journal for the Scientific Study of Religion* 29: 297–314.

*Ikeguchi, M. (2003–4) 'Settlement patterns in Italy and transport costs in the Mediterranean', *Kodai* 13/14: 239–49.

*(2008) 'The dynamics of agricultural locations in Roman Italy', unpublished Ph.D. thesis (University of Cambridge).

Ilberg, J. (1910) *Die Überlieferung der Gynäkologie des Soranos von Ephesos*, Abhandlungen der Sächsischen Akademie der Wissenschaften zu Leipzig, philologisch-historische Klasse 28.2, Leipzig.

Inwood, B. and Gerson, L. P. (2008) *The Stoics Reader: Selected Writings and Testimonia*, Indianapolis, IN.

*Isaac, B. (2004) *The Invention of Racism in Classical Antiquity*, Princeton.

Issawi, C. (1957) 'Farm output under fixed rents and share tenancy', *Land Economics* 33: 74–7.

Jackson, H. (1959) 'Antifertility substances', *Pharmacological Reviews* 11: 135–72.

*Jacobelli, L. (1995), *Le pitture erotiche delle Terme Suburbane di Pompei*, Ministero per i beni culturali ambientali, Soprintendenza archaeologica di Pompei, Monografie 10, Rome.

*Jaspers, K. (1949) *Vom Ursprung und Ziel der Geschichte*, Munich (trans. M. Bullock, *The Origin and Goal of History*, London, 1953).

Johnson, A. C., Coleman-Norton, P. R. and Bourne, F. C. (1961) *Ancient Roman Statutes*, Austin, TX.

*Johnson, W. A. (2004) *Bookrolls and Scribes in Oxyrhynchus*, Toronto.

Jones, A. H. M. (1940) *The Greek City: From Alexander to Justinian*, Oxford.

(1953) 'Inflation under the Roman empire', *Economic History Review* (2nd ser.) 5: 293–318 (repr. with additions in A. H. M. Jones 1974a: 187–227).

(1954) 'The cities of the Roman empire: political, administrative and judicial institutions', in *La ville. Première partie: institutions administratives et judiciaires*, Recueils de la Société Jean Bodin 6, Brussels, 135–73 (repr. in A. H. M. Jones 1974a: 1–34).

(1956) 'Slavery in the ancient world', *Economic History Review* (2nd s.) 9: 185–99 (repr. in M. I. Finley (ed.) *Slavery in Classical Antiquity: Views and Controversies*, Cambridge, 1960, 1–15).

(1957) *Athenian Democracy*, Oxford.

(1960) 'The cloth industry under the Roman empire', *Economic History Review* (2nd ser.) 13: 183–92 (repr. in A. H. M. Jones 1974a: 350–64).

(1964) *The Later Roman Empire, 284–602: A Social, Economic, and Administrative Survey*, 3 vols, Oxford.

(1971) *The Cities of the Eastern Roman Provinces*, 2nd edn, rev. M. Avi-Yonah, Oxford.

(1974a) *The Roman Economy: Studies in Ancient Economic and Administrative History*, ed. P. A. Brunt, Oxford.

(1974b) 'Taxation in antiquity', in A. H. M. Jones 1974a: 151–85.

*Jones, C. P. (2008) 'Hyperides and the sale of slave-families', *ZPE* 164: 19–20.

Jones, D. F. (2006) *The Bankers of Puteoli: Finance, Trade and Industry in the Roman World*, Stroud, Glos.

Jones, W. H. S. (1956) (trans.) *Pliny: Natural History, Books XXIV–XXVII*, Loeb Classical Library 393, Cambridge, MA.

Jones, R. F. J. and Bird, D. G. (1972) 'Roman gold-mining in north-west Spain, II: workings on the Rio Duerna', *JRS* 62: 59–74.

*Jongman, W. M. (1988) *The Economy and Society of Pompeii*, Dutch Monographs on Ancient History and Archaeology 4, Amsterdam.

*(2003a) 'A golden age: death, money supply and social succession in the Roman empire', in E. Lo Cascio (ed.) *Credito e moneta nel mondo romano. Atti degli incontri capresi di storia dell'economia antica (Capri 12–14 ottobre 2000)*, Pragmateiai 8, Bari, 181–96.

*(2003b) 'The Roman economy: from cities to empire', in L. de Blois and J. Rich (eds) *The Transformation of Economic Life under the Roman Empire: Proceedings of the Second Workshop of the International Network Impact of Empire (Roman Empire, c. 200 BC–AD 476), Nottingham, July 4–7, 2001*, Leiden, 28–47.

*(2003c) 'Slavery and the growth of Rome: the transformation of Italy in the second and first centuries BCE', in Edwards and Woolf, 100–22.

*(2007) 'The early Roman empire: consumption', in Scheidel, Morris and Saller, 592–618.

*(2014a) 'Why modern economic theory applies, even to the distant Roman past', *TRAC (Theoretical Roman Archaeology Conference) Proceedings 2013*, 27–36.

*(2014b) 'Re-constructing the Roman economy', in L. Neal and J. G. Williamson (eds) *The Cambridge History of Capitalism*, vol. 1: *The Rise of Capitalism: From Ancient Origins to 1848*, Cambridge, 75–100.

*(2014c) 'The new economic history of the Roman empire', in de Callataÿ, 169–88.

*Jordan, W. D. (1968) *White over Black: American Attitudes towards the Negro, 1550–1812*, Chapel Hill, NC.

Joshel, S. R. (1992) *Work, Identity and Legal Status at Rome: A Study of the Occupational Inscriptions*, Oklahoma Series in Classical Culture 11, Norman, OK.

*(2011) 'Slavery and Roman literary culture', in Bradley and Cartledge, 214–40.

*Joshel, S. R. and Petersen, L. H. (2014) *The Material Life of Roman Slaves*, Cambridge.

Judge, E. A. (1960) *The Social Pattern of the Christian Groups in the First Century: Some Prolegomena to the Study of New Testament Ideas of Social Obligation*, London.

Juster, J. (1914) *Les Juifs dans l'empire romain. Leur condition juridique, économique et sociale*, 2 vols, Paris.

Kahle, P. E. (1954) *Bala'izah: Coptic Texts from Deir el-Bala'izah in Upper Egypt*, 2 vols, London.

Kahrstedt, U. (1921) 'Über die Bevölkerung Roms', in Friedländer and Wissowa 1921–3: IV 11–21.

Kajanto, I. (1968) *On the Problem of the Average Duration of Life in the Roman Empire*, Annales academiae scientiarum fennicae series B 153.2, Helsinki.

Kaser, K. (1955–9) *Das römische Privatrecht*, 2 vols, Handbuch der Altertumswissenschaft 10.3.3, Munich (2nd edn, 1971–5).

Katzoff, R. (1972) 'Precedents in the courts of Roman Egypt', *ZRG (Rom)* 89: 256–92.

*Kautsky, J. H. (1982) *The Politics of Aristocratic Empires*, Chapel Hill, NC (repr. with new introduction, New Brunswick, NJ, 1997).

*Keay, S. (2012) 'The port system of imperial Rome', in his (ed.) *Rome, Portus and the Mediterranean*, Archaeological Monographs of the British School at Rome 21, London, 33–67.

*Keay, S., Millett, M., Paroli, L. and Strutt, K. (2005) *Portus: An Archaeological Survey of the Port of Imperial Rome*, Archaeological Monographs of the British School at Rome 15, London.

*Keay, S. and Terrenato, N. (eds) (2001) *Italy and the West: Comparative Issues in Romanization*, Oxford.

Keil, J. (1930) 'XV. Vorläufiger Bericht über die Ausgrabungen in Ephesos', *Jahreshefte des Österreichischen Archäologischen Institutes in Wien, Beiblatt* 26: 5–66.

*Kelly, C. M. (2004) *Ruling the Later Roman Empire*, Cambridge, MA.

*Kempter, H. and Frenzel, B. (2000) 'The impact of early mining and smelting on the local tropospheric aerosol detected in ombrotrophic peat bogs in the Harz, Germany', *Water, Air, and Soil Pollution* 121: 93–108.

Keyfitz, N. and Flieger, W. (1968) *World Population: An Analysis of Vital Data*, Chicago.

Kiechle, F. (1969) *Sklavenarbeit und technischer Fortschritt im römischen Reich*, Forschungen zur antiken Sklaverei 3, Wiesbaden.

*King, C. (2011) *Musonius Rufus: Lectures and Sayings*, CreateSpace.

*King, H. (1998) *Hippocrates' Woman: Reading the Female Body in Ancient Greece,* London.

Kiser, C. V. (1950) 'L'enquête d'Indianapolis sur la fécondité', *Population* 5: 271–90.

(ed.) (1962) *Research in Family Planning*, Princeton.

Knowlton, C. (1880) *Fruits of Philosophy: An Essay on the Population Question*, 2nd edn, London (first published anonymously in January 1832 in New York as *Fruits of Philosophy: The Private Companion of Young Married People* and under the author's name the following year in London).

Köchly, H. A. T. and Rüstow, W. (eds) (1853–5) *Griechische Kriegsschriftsteller*, 2 vols, Leipzig.

*Kolendo, J. (1981) 'L'esclavage et la vie sexuelle des hommes libres à Rome', *Index. Quaderni camerti di studi romanistici/International Survey of Roman Law* 10: 288–97.

Koos, E. L. (1947) 'Class differences in the employment of contraceptive measures', *Human Fertility* 12: 97–101.

Körte, A. (1939) 'Literarische Texte mit Ausschluß der christlichen', *Archiv für Papyrusforschung und verwandte Gebiete* 13: 78–132.

Kraeling, C. H. (1962) *Ptolemais: City of the Libyan Pentapolis*, University of Chicago, Oriental Institute publications 90, Chicago.

(1967) *The Excavations at Dura-Europos Conducted by Yale University and the French Academy of Inscriptions and Letters, Final Report 8, Part 2: The Christian Building*, New Haven.

*Kron, G. (2000) 'Roman ley-farming', *JRA* 13: 277–87.

*(2002) 'Archaeozoological evidence for the productivity of Roman livestock farming', *Münstersche Beiträge zur Antiken Handelsgeschichte* 21.2: 53–73.

*Kurke, L. (2011) *Aesopic Conversations: Popular Tradition, Cultural Dialogue and the Invention of Greek Prose*, Martin Classical Lectures, Princeton.

*Kylander, M. E., Weiss, D. J., Martínez Cortízas, A., Spiro, B., Garcia-Sanchez, R. and Coles, B. J. (2005) 'Refining the pre-industrial atmospheric Pb isotope evolution curve in Europe using an 8000 year old peat core from NW Spain', *Earth and Planetary Science Letters* 240: 467–85.

Lachs, J. (1949) *Ginekologia u Dioskuridesa*, Krakow.

Lampe, P. (1989) *Die stadtrömischen Christen in den ersten beiden Jahrhunderten. Untersuchungen zur Sozialgeschichte*, Wissenschaftliche Untersuchungen zum Neuen Testament. Reihe 2.18, 2nd edn, Tübingen (trans. M. Steinhauser, *From Paul to Valentinus: Christians at Rome in the First Two Centuries*, London, 2003).

Lanciani, R. (1888) *Ancient Rome, in the Light of Recent Discoveries*, London.

(1891) 'Miscellanea topografica', *Bull. Comm. Arch.* 19: 305–29 and 341.

Landels, J. G. (1978) *Engineering in the Ancient World*, London (rev. edn, 2000).

Lane, C. (1981) *The Rites of Rulers: Ritual in Industrial Society – The Soviet Case*, Cambridge.

*Laqueur, T. (1990) *Making Sex: Body and Gender from the Greeks to Freud*, Cambridge, MA.

Lassère, J.-M. (1977) *Ubique Populus. Peuplement et mouvements de population dans l'Afrique romaine de la chute de Carthage à la fin de la dynastie des Sévères (146 a.C.–235 p.C.)*, Paris.

Last, H. (1947) 'Letter to N. H. Baynes', *JRS* 37: 152–6.

Lauffer, S. (ed.) (1971) *Diokletians Preisedikt*, Texte und Kommentare 5, Berlin.

Laum, B. (1914) *Stiftungen in der griechischen und römischen Antike. Ein Beitrag zur antiken Kulturgeschichte*, 2 vols, Leipzig.

Launey, M. (1933) 'Inscriptions de Thasos', *Bulletin de correspondance hellénique* 57: 394–415.

*Laurence, R. (1999) *The Roads of Roman Italy: Mobility and Cultural Change*, London.

*Lavan, M. (2013) *Slaves to Rome: Paradigms of Empire in Roman Culture*, Cambridge.

Ledermann, S. (1969) *Nouvelles tables-types de mortalité*, Institut national d'études démographiques, travaux et documents 53, Paris.

Leipoldt, J. (1903) *Schenute von Atripe und die Entstehung des national ägyptischen Christentums*, Texte und Untersuchungen zur Geschichte der altchristlichen Literatur 25, Leipzig.

*Lenski, N. (2016) *Constantine and the Cities: Imperial Authority and Civic Politics*, Philadelphia, PA.

Levine, L. W. (1977) *Black Culture and Black Consciousness: Afro-American Folk Thought from Slavery to Freedom*, Oxford (30th anniversary edn, 2007).

Levison, W. (1898) 'Die Beurkundung des Civilstandes im Altertum. Ein Beitrag zur Geschichte der Bevölkerungsstatistik', *Bonner Jahrbücher* 102: 1–82.

Levitan, W. (1985) 'Dancing at the end of the rope: Optatian Porfyry and the field of Roman verse', *TAPA* 115: 245–69.

Lewis, N. (1970) '"Greco-Roman Egypt": fact or fiction?', in D. H. Samuel (ed.) *Proceedings of the 12th International Congress of Papyrology*, American Studies in Papyrology 7, Toronto, 3–14 (repr. in his *On Government and Law in Roman Egypt: Collected Papers of Naphtali Lewis*, American Studies in Papyrology 33, Atlanta, GA, 1995, 138–49).

Lewis, P. R. and Jones, G. D. B. (1970) 'Roman gold-mining in north-west Spain', *JRS* 60: 169–85.

Lewis-Faning, E. (1949) *Report on an Enquiry into Family Limitation and its Influence on Human Fertility during the Past Fifty Years*, Papers of the Royal Commission on Population 1, London.

Liebeschuetz, J. H. W. G. (1972) *Antioch: City and Imperial Administration in the Later Roman Empire*, Oxford.

Lieu, S. N. C. (1985) *Manichaeism in the Later Roman Empire and Medieval China: A Historical Survey*, Manchester (2nd edn, Wissenschaftliche Untersuchungen zum Neuen Testament 63, Tübingen, 1992).

Livi Bacci, M. (1968) 'Fertility and nuptiality changes in Spain from the late 18th to the early 20th century: part I', *Population Studies* 22: 83–102.

*Lo Cascio, E. (ed.) (2003) *Credito e moneta nel mondo romano. Atti degli incontri capresi di storia dell'economia antica (Capri 12–14 ottobre 2000)*, Pragmateiai 8, Bari.

*(2007) 'The early Roman empire: the state and the economy', in Scheidel, Morris and Saller, 619–47.

*(2009) 'Urbanization as a proxy of demographic and economic growth', in Bowman and Wilson, 87–106.

*(2010) 'Thinking slave and free in coordinates', in U. Roth (ed.) *By the Sweat of your Brow: Roman Slavery in its Socio-Economic Setting*, *BICS* supplement 109, London, 21–30.

*Lo Cascio, E. and Malanima, P. (2009) 'GDP in pre-modern agrarian economies (1–1820 AD): a revision of the estimates', *Rivista di Storia Economica* (NS) 25: 391–419.

*Lockyear, K. (1999) 'Hoard structure and coin production in antiquity – an empirical investigation', *Numismatic Chronicle* 159: 215–43.

*Lofland, J. (1977) '"Becoming a world-saver": revisited', *American Behavioral Scientist* 20: 805–18.

*Lofland, J. and Stark, R. (1965) 'Becoming a world-saver: a theory of conversion to a deviant perspective', *American Sociological Review* 30: 862–75.

*Lovejoy, P. (2000) *Transformations in Slavery: A History of Slavery in Africa*, 2nd edn, African Studies 36, Cambridge.

*Lyons, M. (1977) *Russia in Original Photographs, 1860–1920*, London.

*McCann, A. M. (1968) *The Portraits of Septimius Severus, AD 193–211*, Memoirs of the American Academy in Rome 30, Rome.

*McCarthy, K. (2000) *Slaves, Masters, and the Art of Authority in Plautine Comedy*, Princeton.

Macdonell, W. R. (1913) 'On the expectation of life in ancient Rome, and in the provinces of Hispania and Lusitania, and Africa', *Biometrika* 9: 366–80.

*McKeown, N. (2007) *The Invention of Ancient Slavery?*, London.

McKnight, B. E. (1971) *Village and Bureaucracy in Southern Sung China*, Chicago.

*McLynn, N. B. (2008) 'Crying wolf: the Pope and the Lupercalia', *JRS* 98: 161–75.

MacMullen, R. (1966) 'Provincial languages in the Roman empire', *AJP* 87: 1–17 (repr. in MacMullen 1990: 32–40).
(1974) *Roman Social Relations, 50 B.C. to A.D. 284*, New Haven.
*(1983) 'Two types of conversion to early Christianity', *Vigiliae Christianae* 37: 174–92 (repr. in MacMullen 1990: 130–41).
(1984) *Christianizing the Roman Empire, A.D. 100–400*, New Haven.
*(1990) *Changes in the Roman Empire: Essays in the Ordinary*, Princeton.
*(2000) *Romanization in the Time of Augustus*, New Haven.
McWhirter, N. D. and McWhirter, A. R. (1964) *The Guinness Book of Records*, 11th edn, London.
*Makra, L. and Brimblecombe, P. (2004) 'Selections from the history of environmental pollution, with special attention to air pollution. Part 1', *International Journal of Environment and Pollution* 22: 641–56.
*Mann, J. C. (1983) *Legionary Recruitment and Veteran Settlement during the Principate*, University of London Institute of Archaeology Occasional Publications 7, London.
*Manning, J. G. and Morris, I. (eds) (2005) *The Ancient Economy: Evidence and Models*, Stanford, CA.
Margary, I. D. (1955–7) *Roman Roads in Britain*, 2 vols, London (3rd edn, 1973).
Marquardt, J. (1879–82) *Das Privatleben der Römer*, Handbuch der römischen Alterthümer 7, 2 vols, Leipzig (2nd edn, 1886).
(1881–5) *Römische Staatsverwaltung*, Handbuch der römischen Alterthümer 4–6, 2nd edn, 3 vols, Leipzig.
Mathen, K. K. (1962) 'Preliminary lessons learned from the rural population control study of Singur', in Kiser, 33–49.
*Martínez Cortizas, A., Pontevedra Pombal, X., Nóvoa Muñoz, J. C. and García-Rodeja, E. (1997) 'Four thousand years of atmospheric Pb, Cd and Zn deposition recorded by the ombrotrophic peat bog of Penido Vello (northwestern Spain), *Water, Air, and Soil Pollution* 100: 387–403.
*Martínez Cortizas, A., García-Rodeja, E., Pontevedra Pombal, X., Nóvoa Muñoz, J. C., Weiss, D. and Cheburkin, A. (2002) 'Atmospheric Pb deposition in Spain during the last 4600 years recorded by two ombrotrophic peat bogs and implications for the use of peat as archive', *Science of the Total Environment* 292: 33–44.
*Marzano, A. (2013) *Harvesting the Sea: The Exploitation of Marine Resources in the Roman Mediterranean,* Oxford.
*Mattingly, D. J. (1988) 'Oil for export? A comparison of Libyan, Spanish and Tunisian olive oil production in the Roman empire', *JRA* 1: 33–56.
*(1997) 'Beyond belief? Drawing a line under the consumer city', in H. M. Parkins (ed.) *Roman Urbanism: Beyond the Consumer City*, London, 210–18.
Mattingly, H. B. (1977) 'Coinage and the Roman state', *Numismatic Chronicle* 137 (7th ser. 17): 199–215.
Mau, A. (1899) *Pompeii, its Life and Art*, trans. F. W. Kelsey, London (new edn, 1902).

*Mayer, E. E. (2012) *The Ancient Middle Classes: Urban Life and Aesthetics in the Roman Empire, 100 BCE–250 CE*, Cambridge, MA.

Meeks, W. A. (1983) *The First Urban Christians: The Social World of the Apostle Paul*, New Haven.

Meyer, H. (ed.) (1835) *Anthologia veterum Latinorum epigrammatum et poematum*, 2 vols, Leipzig.

Mickwitz, G. (1932) *Geld und Wirtschaft im römischen Reich des vierten Jahrhunderts n. Chr.*, Commentationes humanarum litterarum 4.2, Helsinki.

Millar, F. (1977) *The Emperor in the Roman World (31 BC–AD 337)*, London (2nd edn, 1992).

*Millar, F. (1979) 'Putting figures on the Romans', review of Hopkins 1978b, *Times Literary Supplement*, 4005, 21 December, 170–1.

Millar, F. (1981a) 'The world of the *Golden Ass*', *JRS* 71: 63–75 (repr. in S. J. Harrison (ed.) *Oxford Readings in the Roman Novel*, Oxford, 1999, 247–68 and in Millar 2004: 313–35).

*(1981b) 'Style abides', *JRS* 71: 144–52 (repr. in Millar 2004: 399–416).

(1984) 'The political character of the classical Roman Republic, 200–151 B.C.', *JRS* 74: 1–19 (repr. in Millar 2002: 109–42).

(1986) 'Politics, persuasion, and the people before the Social War (150–90 B.C.)', *JRS* 76: 1–11 (repr. in Millar 2002: 143–61).

*(1998) *The Crowd in Rome in the Late Republic*, Jerome lectures 22, Ann Arbor.

*(2002) *Rome, the Greek world, and the East*, vol. 1: *The Roman Republic and the Augustan Revolution*, ed. H. M. Cotton and G. M. Rogers, Chapel Hill, NC.

*(2004) *Rome, the Greek World, and the East*, vol. 2: *Government, Society, and Culture in the Roman Empire,* ed. H. M. Cotton and G. M. Rogers, Chapel Hill, NC.

*Miller, J. C. (2008) 'Slaving as historical process: examples from the ancient Mediterranean and the modern Atlantic', in Dal Lago and Katsari, 70–102.

*Miller, S. S. (2005) 'The rabbis and the non-existant monolithic synagogue', in S. Fine (ed.) *Jews, Christians and Polytheists in the Ancient Synagogue: Cultural Interaction during the Greco-Roman Period*, London, 57–70.

*Millett, P. (2001) 'Productive to some purpose? The problem of ancient economic growth', in D. J. Mattingly and J. Salmon (eds) *Economies Beyond Agriculture in the Classical World*, Leicester-Nottingham Studies in Ancient Society 9, London, 17–48.

Mitchell, B. R. (1962) *Abstract of British Historical Statistics*, Cambridge.

Mitteis, L. and Wilcken, U. (1912) *Grundzüge und Chrestomathie der Papyruskunde*, 2 vols, Leipzig.

Moeller, W. O. (1976) *The Wool Trade of Ancient Pompeii*, Studies of the Dutch Archaeological and Historical Society 3, Leiden.

Mommsen, T. (1887) *Römisches Staatsrecht*, 3rd edn, 3 vols, Handbuch der römischen Alterthümer 1–3, Leipzig.

(1899) *Römisches Strafrecht*, Systematisches Handbuch der deutschen Rechtswissenschaft 1.4, Leipzig.

Morel, J.-P. (1965) 'Les niveaux préromaines', in J.-P. Callu, J.-P. Morel, R. Rebuffat and G. Hallier (eds) *Thamusida. Fouilles du Service des antiquités du Maroc I,* École française de Rome. Mélanges d'archéologie et d'histoire 2, Paris, 61–111.

Moretti, L. (1959) 'Statistica demografica ed epigrafia: durata media della vita in Roma imperiale', *Epigraphica* 21: 60–78.

*Morley, N. (1996) *Metropolis and Hinterland: The City of Rome and the Italian Economy, 200 BC–AD 200*, Cambridge.

*(2006) 'Narrative economy', in P. F. Bang, M. Ikeguchi and H. G. Ziche (eds) *Ancient Economies, Modern Methodologies: Archaeology, Comparative History, Models and Institutions*, Pragmateiai 12, Bari, 27–47.

*(2007) *Trade in Classical Antiquity*, Cambridge.

*(2008) 'Urbanisation and development in Italy in the late Republic', in L. de Ligt and S. Northwood (eds) *People, Land, and Politics: Demographic Developments and the Transformation of Roman Italy, 300 BC–AD 14, Mnemosyne* supplement 303, Leiden, 121–37.

*(2010) *The Roman Empire: Roots of Imperialism*, London.

*(2011) 'Cities and economic development in the Roman empire', in Bowman and Wilson, 143–60.

*Morris, I. (2004) 'Economic growth in ancient Greece', *Journal of Institutional and Theoretical Economics/Zeitschrift für die gesamte Staatswissenschaft* 160: 709–42.

*(2005) 'Archaeology, standards of living, and Greek economic history', in Manning and Morris, 91–126.

Morse, H. B. (1926–9) *The Chronicles of the East India Company, Trading to China 1635–1834*, 5 vols, Oxford.

*Morstein-Marx, R. (2004) *Mass Oratory and Political Power in the Late Roman Republic*, Cambridge.

*Mouritsen, H. (1998) *Italian Unification: A Study in Ancient and Modern Historiography, BICS* supplement 70, London.

*Mouritsen, H. (2001) *Plebs and Politics in the Late Roman Republic*, Cambridge.

*Mratschek-Halfmann, S. (1993) *Divites et praepotentes. Reichtum und soziale Stellung in der Literatur der Prinzipatszeit*, *Historia* Einzelschriften 70, Stuttgart.

*Murnaghan, S. and Joshel, S. R. (eds) (1998) *Women and Slaves in Greco-Roman Culture: Differential Equations*, London.

Musurillo, H. (1954) *The Acts of the Pagan Martyrs*, Oxford.

(1972) *The Acts of the Christian Martyrs*, Oxford.

*Myrdal, G. (1967) 'A comparative approach to caste and race', in A. V. S. de Reuck and J. Knight (eds) *Caste and Race: Comparative Approaches*, London, 327–32.

Nag, M. (1956) *Factors Affecting Human Fertility in the Nonindustrial Societies: A Cross-Cultural Study*, Yale University Publications in Anthropology 66, New Haven.

Nash, W. G. (1904) *The Rio Tinto Mine: Its History and Romance*, London.

Neugebauer, O. and Parker, R. A. (eds) (1969) *Egyptian Astronomical Texts*, vol. 3: *Decans, Planets, Constellations and Zodiacs*, Brown Egyptological Studies 6i, Providence, RI.

Neusner, J. (1990) *The Talmud of Babylonia: An American Translation, XXIB: Tractate Bava Mesia, Chapters 3–4*, Brown Judaic Studies 214, Atlanta, GA.

*Nicolet, C. (2000), *Censeurs et publicains. Économie et fiscalité dans la Rome antique*, Paris.

*Nippel, W. (1987–9) 'Finley and Weber: some comments and theses', *Opus* 6–8: 43–50.

*(1991) 'Introductory remarks: Max Weber's "The City" revisited', in A. Molho, K. Raaflaub and J. Emlen (eds) *City States in Classical Antiquity and Medieval Italy: Athens and Rome, Florence and Venice*, Stuttgart, 19–30.

*Nissen, H. (1902) *Italische Landeskunde*, vol. 2: *Die Staedte*, Berlin.

*Nixon, C. E. V. and Rodgers, B. S. (1994) *In Praise of Later Roman Emperors: The Panegyrici Latini*, Transformation of the Classical Heritage 21, Berkeley, CA.

Noonan, J. T. (1965) *Contraception: A History of its Treatment by the Catholic Theologians and Canonists*, Cambridge, MA (rev. edn, 1986).

Nordberg, H. (1963) *Biometrical Notes: The Information on Ancient Christian Inscriptions from Rome Concerning the Duration of Life and the Dates of Birth and Death*, Acta Instituti Romani Finlandiae 2.2, Helsinki.

Nörr, D. (1965) 'Zur sozialen und rechtlichen Bewertung der freien Arbeit in Rom', *ZRG (Rom)* 82: 67–105.

North, D. C. (1981) *Structure and Change in Economic History*, New York.

North, J. (1990) 'Democratic politics in republican Rome', *Past & Present* 126: 3–21 (repr. in Osborne 2004b: 140–58).

*(2008a) 'Action and ritual in Roman historians: or how Horatius held the door-post', in Holm Rasmussen and Rasmussen, 23–36.

*(2008b) 'Caesar at the Lupercalia', *JRS* 98: 144–60.

*North, J. and McLynn, N. B. (2008) 'Postscript to the Lupercalia: from Caesar to Andromachus', *JRS* 98: 176–81.

Nriagu, J. O. (1998) 'Tales told in lead', *Science* 281: 1622–3.

*Nussbaum, M. C. (2002) 'The incomplete feminism of Musonius Rufus, Platonist, Stoic, and Roman', in M. C. Nussbaum and J. Sihvola (eds)

The Sleep of Reason: Erotic Experience and Sexual Ethics in Ancient Greece and Rome, Chicago, 283–326.

Oehler, J. (1909) 'Epigraphische Beiträge zur Geschichte des Aerztestandes', *Janus* 14: 4–20, 111–23.

Oliver, J. H. and Palmer, R. E. A. (1954) 'Text of the Tabula Hebana', *AJP* 75: 225–49.

Orelli, J. C. von (1828–56) *Inscriptionum Latinarum selectarum amplissima collectio ad illustrandam Romanae antiquitatis disciplinam accommodata, ac magnarum collectionum supplementa complura emendationesque exhibens*, 3 vols, Zurich.

*Osborne, R. (1991) 'Pride and prejudice, sense and subsistence: exchange and society in the Greek city', in Rich and Wallace-Hadrill, 119–45.

*(2004a) 'Keith Hopkins', *Past & Present* 185: 3–7.

*(ed.) (2004b) *Studies in Ancient Greek and Roman Society*, Cambridge.

*Osborne, R. and Vout, C. (2010) 'A revolution in Roman history?', review of Wallace-Hadrill 2008, *JRS* 100: 233–45.

Osofsky, G. (ed.) (1969) *Puttin' on Ole Massa: The Slave Narratives of Henry Bibb, William Wells Brown, and Solomon Northup*, New York.

*O'Sullivan, T. M. (2011) *Walking in Roman Culture*, Cambridge.

Owen, R. D. (1831) *Moral Physiology: or, a Brief and Plain Treatise on the Population Question*, 3rd edn, New York.

Pack, R. A. (1965) *The Greek and Latin Literary Texts from Greco-Roman Egypt*, 2nd edn, Ann Arbor.

Panella, C. (1981) 'La distribuzione e i mercati', in A. Giardina and A. Schiavone (eds) *Società romana e produzione schiavistica*, vol. 2. *Merci, mercati e scambi nel Mediterraneo*, Rome, 55–80.

Pareto, V. (1896–7) *Cours d'économie politique, professé à l'Université de Lausanne*, 2 vols, Lausanne (new edn, Geneva, 1964).

Parker, A. J. (1979) 'Method and madness: wreck hunting in shallow water', *Progress in Underwater Science* 4: 7–27.

(1992) *Ancient Shipwrecks of the Mediterranean and the Roman Provinces*, British Archaeological Reports: International Series 580, Oxford.

*(1984) 'Shipwrecks and ancient trade in the Mediterranean', *Archaeological Review from Cambridge* 3.2: 101–11.

Parker, G. (1974) 'The emergence of modern finance in Europe, 1500–1730', in C. M. Cipolla (ed.) *The Fontana Economic History of Europe*, vol. 2: *The Sixteenth and Seventeenth Centuries*, London, 527–94.

Parker, R. A. (1972) *Demotic Mathematical Papyri*, Brown University Egyptological Studies 7, Providence, RI.

*Parkin, T. G. (1992) *Demography and Roman Society*, Baltimore.

*Parkins, H. M. (ed.) (1997) *Roman Urbanism: Beyond the Consumer City*, London.

Patlagean, E. (1977) *Pauvreté économique et pauvreté sociale à Byzance, 4e–7e siècles*, Civilisations et sociétés 48, Paris.

Patterson, C. C. (1972) 'Silver stocks and losses in ancient and medieval times', *Economic History Review* (2nd ser.) 25: 205–35.

Patterson, O. (1982) *Slavery and Social Death: A Comparative Study*, Cambridge, MA (new edn, 1990).

*(2008) 'Slavery, gender, and work in the pre-modern world and early Greece: a cross-cultural analysis', in Dal Lago and Katsari, 32–69.

*Peachin, M. (ed.) (2011) *The Oxford Handbook of Social Relations in the Roman World*, Oxford.

Peacock, D. P. S. (1978) 'The Rhine and the problem of Gaulish wine in Roman Britain', in J. du Plat Taylor and H. Cleere (eds) *Roman Shipping and Trade: Britain and the Rhine Provinces*, Council for British Archaeology Research Report 24, London, 49–51.

Peel, J. (1964) 'Contraception and the medical profession', *Population Studies* 18: 133–45.

Pekáry, T. (1959) 'Studien zur römischen Währungs- und Finanzgeschichte von 161 bis 235 n. Chr.', *Historia* 8: 443–89.

Perkins, D. H. (1969) *Agricultural Development in China, 1368–1968*, Chicago.

Perry, B. E. (1936) *Studies in the Text History of the Life and Fables of Aesop*, American Philological Society Philological Monographs 7, Haverford, PA.

(1952) *Aesopica: A Series of Texts Related to Aesop or Ascribed to Him or Closely Connected with the Literary Tradition that Bears his Name*, vol. 1: *Greek and Latin Texts*, Urbana, IL (new edn, 2007).

Pervo, R. I. (1987) *Profit with Delight: The Literary Genre of the Acts of the Apostles*, Philadelphia.

Pierce, R. H. (1972) *Three Demotic Papyri in the Brooklyn Museum: A Contribution to the Study of Contracts and their Instruments in Ptolemaic Egypt, Symbolae Osloenses* supplement 24, Oslo.

*Polanyi, K., Arensberg, C. M. and Pearson, H. W. (eds) (1957) *Trade and Market in the Early Empires: Economies in History and Theory*, New York.

Pomarès, G. (ed.) (1959) *Gélase Ier. Lettre contre les Lupercales et dix-huit messes du Sacramentaire léonien, SC* 65, Paris.

Pomey, P. and Tchernia, A. (1978) 'Le tonnage maximum des navires de commerce romains', *Archaeonautica* 2: 233–51.

Poti, S. J., Chakraborti, B. and Malaker, C. R. (1962) 'Reliability of data relating to contraceptive practices', in Kiser, 51–65.

*Potter, D. S. (1999) *Literary Texts and the Roman Historian*, London.

Pounds, N. J. G. (1969) 'The urbanization of the classical world', *Annals of the Association of American Geographers* 59: 135–57.

Powell, J. E. (1937) 'Musonius Rufus: εἰ πάντα τὰ γινόμενα τέκνα θρεπτέον', *Archiv für Papyrusforschung und verwandte Gebiete* 12: 175–8.

*Praet, D. (1992–3) 'Explaining the Christianization of the Roman empire: older theories and recent developments', *Sacris erudiri: jaarboek voor Godsdienstwetenschappen* 33: 7–119.

*Raaflaub, K. A. and Toher, M. (eds) (1990) *Between Republic and Empire: Interpretations of Augustus and his Principate*, Berkeley, CA.

*Ramsay, A. M. (1925) 'The speed of the Roman imperial post', *JRS* 15: 60–74.

*Rance, P. (2008) 'The date of the military compendium of Syrianus Magister (formerly the sixth-century anonymus Byzantinus)', *BZ* 100: 701–37.

Rathbone, D. (1991) *Economic Rationalism and Rural Society in Third-Century A.D. Egypt: The Heroninos Archive and the Appianus Estate*, Cambridge.

*(2003) 'The financing of maritime commerce in the Roman empire, I–II AD', in E. Lo Cascio (ed.) *Credito e moneta nel mondo romano. Atti degli incontri capresi di storia dell'economia antica (Capri 12–14 ottobre 2000)*, Pragmateiai 8, Bari, 197–229.

Rawick, G. P. (1972–9) *The American Slave: A Composite Autobiography*, 19 vols, Westport, CT.

Rea, J. R. (1972) *The Oxyrhynchus Papyri*, vol. 40, Egypt Exploration Society, Graeco-Roman Memoirs 56, London.

Reardon, B. P. (ed.) (1989) *Collected Ancient Greek Novels*, Berkeley, CA (new edn, 2008).

Rebuffat, R. (1965) 'Le camp', in J.-P. Callu, J.-P. Morel, R. Rebuffat and G. Hallier (eds), *Thamusida. Fouilles du Service des antiquités du Maroc*, vol. 1, École française de Rome, Mélanges d'archéologie et d'histoire 2, Paris, 135–233.

Reece, R. (1973) 'Roman coinage in the western empire', *Britannia* 4: 227–51.

*Reger, G. (1994) *Regionalism and Change in the Economy of Independent Delos, 314–167 BC*, Hellenistic Culture and Society 14, Berkeley, CA.

*Remijsen, S. and Clarysse, W. (2008) 'Incest or adoption? Brother-sister marriage in Roman Egypt revisited', *JRS* 98: 53–61.

Renberg, I., Persson, M. W. and Emteryd, O. (1994) 'Pre-industrial atmospheric lead contamination detected in Swedish lake sediments', *Nature* 368: 323–6.

*Renberg, I., Brännvall, M.-L., Bindler, R. and Emteryd, O. (2000) 'Atmospheric lead pollution history during four millennia (2000 BC to 2000 AD) in Sweden', *Ambio* 29: 150–6.

*Reydams-Schils, G. J. (2004) 'Musonius Rufus, Porphyry, and Christians in Counter-Point on Marriage and the Good', in A. Kijewska (ed.) *Being or Good? Metamorphoses of Neoplatonism*, Lublin, 153–68.

Reymond, E. A. E. (1976) *A Medical Book from Crocodilopolis: P. Vindob. D. 6257*, Mitteilungen aus der Papyrussammlung der Österreichischen Nationalbibliothek (NS) 10, Vienna.

Reymond, E. A. E. and Barns, J. W. B. (1973) *Four Martyrdoms from the Pierpoint Morgan Coptic Codices*, Oxford.

Ricardo, D. (1821) *On the Principles of Political Economy and Taxation*, 3rd edn, London.

*Rich, J. and Wallace-Hadrill, A. (eds) (1991) *City and Country in the Ancient World*, Leicester-Nottingham Studies in Ancient Society 2, London.

*Richlin, A. (2014) 'Talking to slaves in the Plautine audience', *Cl. Ant.* 33: 174–226.

Richter, P. (1911) 'Beiträge zur Geschichte des Kondoms', *Zeitschrift für Bekämpfung der Geschlechtskrankheiten* 12: 35–8.

Rickard, T. A. (1932) *Man and Metals: A History of Mining in Relation to the Development of Civilization*, 2 vols, New York.

Rickman, G. (1980) *The Corn Supply of Ancient Rome*, Oxford.

*Riddle, J. M. (1992) *Contraception and Abortion from the Ancient World to the Renaissance,* Cambridge, MA.

*(1997) *Eve's Herbs: A History of Contraception and Abortion in the West,* Cambridge, MA.

*Rilinger, R. (1988) *Humiliores – Honestiores. Zu einer sozialen Dichotomie im Strafrecht der römischen Kaiserzeit*, Munich.

Rivet, A. L. F. (1964) *Town and Country in Roman Britain*, 2nd edn, London.

Roberts, C. H. and Skeat, T. C. (1983) *The Birth of the Codex*, London (2nd edn, 1987).

*Robinson, D. and Wilson, A. I. (2011) 'Introduction: maritime archaeology and the ancient economy', in D. Robinson and A. I. Wilson (eds) *Maritime Archaeology and Ancient Trade in the Mediterranean*, Oxford Centre for Maritime Archaeology monograph 6, Oxford, 1–11.

Robinson, J. M. (1977) *The Nag Hammadi Library in English*, Leiden (4th edn, 1996).

*Rosenstein, N. (2008) 'Aristocrats and agriculture in the middle and late Republic', *JRS* 98: 1–26.

*(2009) 'Aristocrats and agriculture in the late Republic: the "high count"', in J. Carlsen and E. Lo Cascio (eds) *Agricoltura e scambi nell'Italia tardo-repubblicana*, Pragmateiai 16, 243–57.

*Rosman, K. J. R., Chisholm, W., Hong, S., Candelone, J.-P. and Boutron, C. F. (1997) 'Lead from Carthaginian and Roman Spanish mines isotopically identified in Greenland ice dated from 600 BC to 300 AD', *Environmental Science and Technology* 31: 3413–16.

*Rostovtzeff, M. I. (1941) *The Social and Economic History of the Hellenistic World*, 3 vols, Oxford.

(1957) *The Social and Economic History of the Roman Empire*, 2nd rev. edn, ed. P. M. Fraser, 2 vols, Oxford.

Rotelli, C. (1968) 'Rendimenti e produzione agricola nell'Imolese dal XVI al XIX secolo', *Rivista storica italiana* 80: 107–29.

Rougé, J. (1966) *Recherches sur l'organisation du commerce maritime en Méditerranée sous l'empire romain*, Ports, routes, trafics 21, Paris.

Rousseau, P. (1985) *Pachomius: The Making of a Community in Fourth-Century Egypt*, Transformation of the Classical Heritage 6, Berkeley, CA (rev. edn, 1999).

Roussel, P. and de Visscher, F. (1942–3) 'Les inscriptions du temple de Dmeir', *Syria* 23: 173–200.

*Rowlands, M. (1987) 'Centre and periphery: a review of a concept', in M. Rowlands, M. Larsen and K. Kristiansen (eds) *Centre and Periphery in the Ancient World*, Cambridge, 1–11.

*Rowlandson, J. and Takahashi, R. (2009) 'Brother-sister marriage and inheritance strategies in Greco-Roman Egypt', *JRS* 99: 104–39.

*Rüpke, J. (2007) *Religion of the Romans*, ed. and trans. R. Gordon, Cambridge (first published as *Die Religion der Römer*, Munich, 2001).

Russell, J. C. (1958) 'Late ancient and medieval population', *Transactions of the American Philosophical Society* 48.3: 1–152.

(1972) *Medieval Regions and their Cities*, Newton Abbot.

(1985) *The Control of Late Ancient and Medieval Population*, Memoirs of the American Philosophical Society 160, Philadelphia.

Saller, R. P. (1980) 'Anecdotes as historical evidence for the Principate', *G&R* (2nd ser.) 27: 69–83.

*(1987) 'Men's age at marriage and its consequences in the Roman family', *CPh* 82: 21–34.

*(1994) *Patriarchy, Property and Death in the Roman Family*, Cambridge Studies in Population, Economy and Society in Past Time 25, Cambridge.

*(2002) 'Framing the debate over growth in the ancient economy', in W. Scheidel and S. von Reden (eds) *The Ancient Economy*, Edinburgh, 251–69 (repr. in Manning and Morris, 223–38).

Saller, R. P. and Shaw, B. D. (1984) 'Tombstones and Roman family relations in the Principate: civilians, soldiers and slaves', *JRS* 74: 124–56.

Sallares, J. R. (1991) *The Ecology of the Ancient Greek World*, London.

*Salmon, P. (1987) 'Les insuffisances du matériel épigraphique sur la mortalité dans l'antiquité romaine', in Hinard, 99–112.

*Salway, B. (2004) 'Sea and river travel in the Roman itinerary literature', in R. J. A. Talbert and K. Brodersen (eds) *Space in the Roman World: Its Perception and Presentation*, Antike Kultur und Geschichte 5, Münster, 43–96.

*Santoro L'Hoir, F. (1992) *The Rhetoric of Gender Terms: 'Man', 'Woman', and the Portrayal of Character in Latin Prose*, *Mnemosyne* supplement 120, Leiden.

*Scarborough, J. (2013) 'Theodora, Aetius of Amida, and Procopius: some possible connections', *GRBS* 53: 742–62.

*Scheid, J. (2003) *An Introduction to Roman Religion*, trans. J. Lloyd, Edinburgh (first published as *La religion des Romains*, Paris, 1998).

*(2005) *Quand faire, c'est croire. Les rites sacrificiels des Romains*, Paris.

*Scheidel, W. (1996a) 'What's in an age? A comparative view of bias in the census returns of Roman Egypt', *BASP* 33: 25–59.

*(1996b) *Measuring Sex, Age and Death in the Roman Empire: Explorations in Ancient Demography*, *JRA* supplementary series 21, Ann Arbor.

*(1999) 'Emperors, aristocrats, and the grim reaper: towards a demographic profile of the Roman élite', *CQ* 49: 254–81.

*(ed.) (2001a) *Debating Roman Demography, Mnemosyne* supplement 211, Leiden.

*(2001b) 'Progress and problems in Roman demography' in Scheidel 2001a: 1–81.

*(2001c) *Death on the Nile: Disease and the Demography of Roman Egypt, Mnemosyne* supplement 228, Leiden.

*(2001d) 'Roman age structure: evidence and models', *JRS* 91: 1–26.

*(2003) 'Germs for Rome', in Edwards and Woolf, 158–76.

*(2005) 'Human mobility in Roman Italy, II: the slave population', *JRS* 95: 64–79.

*(2007a) 'Roman funerary commemoration and the age at first marriage', *CPh* 102: 389–402.

*(2007b) 'A model of real income growth in Roman Italy', *Historia* 56: 322–46.

*(2008) 'The comparative economics of slavery in the Greco-Roman world', in Dal Lago and Katsari, 105–26.

*(2009) 'In search of Roman economic growth', *JRA* 22: 46–70.

*(2011a) 'A comparative perspective on the determinants of scale and productivity of Roman maritime trade in the Mediteranean', in Harris and Iara, 21–37.

*(2011b) 'The Roman slave supply', in Bradley and Cartledge, 287–310.

*(2012a) 'Epigraphy and demography: birth, marriage, family, and death', in J. Davies and J. Wilkes (eds) *Epigraphy and the Historical Sciences, Proceedings of the British Academy* 177, Oxford, 101–29.

*(2012b) *The Cambridge Companion to the Roman Economy*, Cambridge.

*(2012c) 'Physical well-being', in Scheidel 2012b: 321–33.

*(2013) 'Explaining the maritime freight charges in Diocletian's Prices Edict', *JRA* 26: 464–8.

*(2014) 'The shape of the Roman world: modelling imperial connectivity', *JRA* 27: 7–32.

*(2015) 'State revenue and expenditure in the Han and Roman empires', in W. Scheidel (ed.) *State Power in Ancient China and Rome*, Oxford, 150–80.

*Scheidel, W. and Friesen, S. J. (2009) 'The size of the economy and the distribution of income in the Roman empire', *JRS* 99: 61–91.

*Scheidel, W., Morris, I. and Saller, R. P. (eds) (2007) *The Cambridge Economic History of the Greco-Roman World*, Cambridge.

*Schettler, G. and Romer, R. L. (2006) 'Atmospheric Pb-pollution by pre-medieval mining detected in the sediments of the brackish karst lake An Loch Mór, western Ireland', *Applied Geochemistry* 21: 58–82.

Schmidt, C. and Polotsky, H. J. (1933) 'Ein Mani-Fund in Ägypten. Originalschriften des Mani und seiner Schüler', *Sitzungsberichte der preussischen Akademie der Wissenschaften, philosophisch-historische Klasse* 1933: 4–90.

Schoff, W. H. (1912) (trans.) *The Periplus of the Erythraean Sea: Travel and Trade in the Indian Ocean, by a Merchant of the First Century*, London.

Schofield, R. S. (1986) 'Did the mothers really die? Three centuries of maternal mortality in "the world we have lost"', in L. Bonfield, R. M. Smith and K. Wrightson (eds) *The World we have Gained: Histories of Population and Social Structure. Essays Presented to Peter Laslett on his Seventieth Birthday*, Oxford, 231–60.

Schulten, A. (1933) *Geschichte von Numantia*, Munich.

Schumacher, W. N. (1968–9) 'Antikes und Christliches zur Auspeitschung der Elia Afanacia', *Jahrbuch für Antike und Christentum* 11–12: 65–75.

Scullard, H. H. (1981) *Festivals and Ceremonies of the Roman Republic*, London.

Sée, H. (1948–51) *Histoire économique de la France*, 2nd edn, 2 vols, Paris.

Seeck, O. (1920–2) *Geschichte des Untergangs der antiken Welt*, 4th/2nd/1st edn, 6 vols, Stuttgart.

*Seiler, F. (1992) *Casa degli amorini dorati (IV 16,7.38)*, Häuser in Pompeji 5, Munich.

*Shatzman, I. (1975) *Senatorial Wealth and Roman Politics*, Collection Latomus 142, Brussels.

*Shaw, B. D. (1982) 'Social science and ancient history: Keith Hopkins *in partibus infidelium*', *Helios* 9: 17–57.

*(1984) 'Latin funerary epigraphy and family life in the later Roman empire', *Historia* 33: 457–97.

*(1987) 'The age of Roman girls at marriage: some reconsiderations', *JRS* 77: 30–46.

*(2001) 'The seasonal birthing cycle of Roman women', in Scheidel 2001a: 83–110.

Shaw, S. J. (1962) *The Financial and Administrative Organization and Development of Ottoman Egypt, 1517–1798*, Princeton Oriental Studies 19, Princeton.

Shelton, J. C. (1977) *A Tax List from Karanis (P.Cair.Mich. 359): Part 2, Commentary and Indexes*, Papyrologische Texte und Abhandlungen 18, Bonn.

Shepherd, J. F. and Walton, G. M. (1972) *Shipping, Maritime Trade, and the Economic Development of Colonial North America*, Cambridge.

Sherwin-White, A. N. (1964) 'Why were the early Christians persecuted? – an amendment', *Past & Present* 27: 23–7 (repr. in Finley 1974: 250–5).

(1966) *The Letters of Pliny: A Historical and Social Commentary*, Oxford.

Shils, E. A. and Finch H. A. (1949) (trans.) *Max Weber on the Methodology of the Social Sciences*, Glencoe, IL.

Shotyk, W., Weiss, D., Appleby, P. G., Cheburkin, A. K., Frei, R., Gloor, M., Kramers, J. D., Reese, S. and Van Der Knaap, W. O. (1998) 'History of atmospheric lead deposition since 12,370 ^{14}C yr BP from a peat bog, Jura Mountains, Switzerland', *Science* 281: 1635–40.

Sijpesteijn, P. J. (1964) *Penthemeros-Certificates in Graeco-Roman Egypt*, Papyrologica Lugduno-Batava 12, Leiden.

Simon, M. (1986) *Verus Israel: A Study of the Relations between Christians and Jews in the Roman Empire AD 135–425*, trans. H. McKeating, London (first published as *Verus Israel. Étude sur les relations entre Chrétiens et Juifs dans l'empire romain, 135–425*, 2nd edn, Paris, 1964).

*Smart, A. (2006) *The Shek Kip Mei Myth: Squatters, Fires and Colonial Rule in Hong Kong, 1950–1963*, Hong Kong.

Smith, J. Z. (1978) *Map is Not Territory: Studies in the History of Religions*, Studies in Judaism in Late Antiquity 23, Leiden.

Snodgrass, A. M. (1965) 'Barbaric Europe and early Iron Age Greece', *Proc. Prehist. Soc.* 31: 229–40.

*Soechting, D. (1972) *Die Porträts des Septimius Severus*, Habelts Dissertationsdrucke, Reihe klassische Archäologie 4, Bonn.

Sombart, W. (1916–27) *Der moderne Kapitalismus. Historisch-systematische Darstellung des gesamteuropäischen Wirtschaftslebens von seinen Anfängen bis zur Gegenwart*, 2nd edn, 3 vols, Munich.

Speidel, M. (1973) 'The pay of the auxilia', *JRS* 63: 141–7 (repr. in his *Roman Army Studies*, vol. 1, Amsterdam, 1984, 83–9).

Spence, J. D. (1974) *Emperor of China: Self-Portrait of K'ang-hsi*, London.

(1978) *The Death of Woman Wang*, London.

Sprengling, M. (1953) *Third Century Iran, Sapor and Kartir*, Chicago.

Stallybrass, P. and White, A. (1986) *The Politics and Poetics of Transgression*, London.

Stanfield, J. A. and Simpson, G. (1958) *Central Gaulish Potters*, London.

Stark, R. (1996) *The Rise of Christianity: A Sociologist Reconsiders History*, Princeton.

*Stewart, R. L. (2012) *Plautus and Roman Slavery*, Malden, MA.

Stopes, M. C. (1927) *Contraception (Birth Control): Its Theory, History and Practice: A Manual for the Medical and Legal Profession*, new edn, London (first edn, 1923).

(1931) 'Positive and negative control of conception in its various technical aspects', *Journal of State Medicine* 39: 354–60.

*Straus, J. A. (2004) *L'achat et la vente des esclaves dans l'Égypte romaine. Contribution papyrologique à l'étude de l'esclavage dans une province orientale de l'empire romain*, Archiv für Papyrusforschung und verwandte Gebiete 14, Munich.

Syme, R. (1939) *The Roman Revolution*, Oxford.

*(1958) *Tacitus*, 2 vols, Oxford.

(1960) 'Bastards in the Roman aristocracy', *Proceedings of the American Philosophical Society* 104: 323–7 (repr. in his *Roman Papers II*, ed. E. Badian, Oxford, 1979, 510–17).

(1961) 'Who was Vedius Pollio?', *JRS* 51: 23–30 (repr. in his *Roman Papers II*, ed. E. Badian, Oxford, 1979, 518–29).

*(1962) 'The wrong Marcius Turbo', *JRS* 52: 87–96 (repr. in his *Roman Papers II*, ed. E. Badian, Oxford, 1979, 541–56).

*(1965) 'Governors of Pannonia Inferior', *Historia* 14: 342–61 (repr. in his *Danubian Papers*, Bucharest, 1971, 225–44).

*(1986) *Fictional History Old and New: Hadrian* (A. James Bryce Memorial Lecture, 10 May 1984), Somerville College, Oxford (repr. in his *Roman Papers VI*, ed. A. R. Birley, Oxford, 1991, 157–81).

Szilágyi, J. (1961) 'Beiträge zur Statistik der Sterblichkeit in den westeuropäischen Provinzen des römischen Imperiums', *Acta Archaeologica Academiae Scientiarum Hungaricae* 13: 125–55.

(1963a) 'Prices and wages in the western provinces of the Roman empire', *Acta Antiqua Academiae Scientiarum Hungaricae* 11: 325–89.

(1963b) 'Die Sterblichkeit in den Städten Mittel- und Süd-Italiens sowie in Hispanien (in der römischen Kaiserzeit)', *Acta Archaeologica Academiae Scientiarum Hungaricae* 15: 129–224.

(1965) 'Die Sterblichkeit in den nordafrikanischen Provinzen I', *Acta Archaeologica Academiae Scientiarum Hungaricae* 17: 302–34.

(1967) 'Die Sterblichkeit in den nordafrikanischen Provinzen III', *Acta Archaeologica Academiae Scientiarum Hungaricae* 19: 25–59.

Taeuber, I. B. (1958) *The Population of Japan*, Princeton.

Talbert, R. J. A. (1984) *The Senate of Imperial Rome*, Princeton.

Taubenschlag, P. (1949) 'Papyri and parchments from the eastern provinces of the Roman empire outside Egypt', *Journal of Juristic Papyri* 3: 49–61 (repr. in his *Opera minora*, 2 vols, Warsaw, 1959, vol. 2, 29–43).

Taylor, E. G. R. (1956) *The Haven-Finding Art: A History of Navigation from Odysseus to Captain Cook*, London (new edn, 1971).

Taylor, L. R. (1966) *Roman Voting Assemblies from the Hannibalic War to the Dictatorship of Caesar*, Jerome Lectures 8, Ann Arbor.

*Tchernia, A. (1983) 'Italian wine in Gaul at the end of the Republic', in Garnsey, Hopkins and Whittaker, 87–104.

*(1986) *Le vin de l'Italie romaine. Essai d'historie économique d'après les amphores,* Bibliothèque des Écoles françaises d'Athènes et de Rome 261, Paris.

*(2011) *Les Romains et le commerce,* Centre Jean Bérand: Études 8, Naples (trans. J. Grieve, *Romans and Trade*, Oxford, 2016).

*Tchernia, A., Pomey, P., Hesnard A. et al. (1978) *L'Épave romaine de la Madrague de Giens (Var), campagnes 1972–1975. Fouilles de l'Institut d'archéologie méditerranéenne*, *Gallia* supplément 34, Paris.

*Temin, P. (2006) 'Estimating GDP in the early Roman empire', in E. Lo Cascio (ed.) *Innovazione tecnica e progresso economico nel mondo romano. Atti degli incontri capresi di storia dell'economia antica (Capri 13–16 aprile 2003)*, Pragmateiai 10, Bari, 31–54.

*(2013) *The Roman Market Economy*, Princeton.

Temkin, O. (1956) (trans.) *Soranus' Gynecology*, Publications of the Institute of the History of Medicine, Johns Hopkins University, series 2, vol. 3, Baltimore.

Theißen, G. (1982) *The Social Setting of Pauline Christianity: Essays on Corinth*, trans. J. H. Schütz, Edinburgh (first published as *Studien zur Soziologie des Urchristentums*, Wissenschaftliche Untersuchungen zum Neuen Testament 19, Tübingen, 1979, 3rd edn, 1989).

*(1986) *Der Schatten des Galiläers. Historische Jesusforschung in erzählender Form*, Munich (trans. J. Bowden, *The Shadow of the Galilean: The Quest of the Historical Jesus in Narrative Form*, London, 1987).

Thomson, J. O. (1948) *History of Ancient Geography*, Cambridge.

Thorndike, L. (ed.) (1946) *The Herbal of Rufinus*, Chicago.

Tietze, C. (1962) 'The use-effectiveness of contraceptive methods', in Kiser, 357–69.

*Tomlin, R. (ed.) (2005a) *History and Fiction: Six Essays Celebrating the Centenary of Sir Ronald Syme (1903–89)*, London.

*(2005b) 'Preface and introduction' in Tomlin, 6–13.

*Toner, J. P. (2009) *Popular Culture in Ancient Rome*, Cambridge.

Torelli, M. (1982) *Typology and Structure of Roman Historical Reliefs*, Jerome Lectures 14, Ann Arbor.

Turcan, R. (1989) *Les cultes orientaux dans le monde romain*, Paris.

Twitchett, D. C. (1970) *Financial Administration under the T'ang Dynasty*, University of Cambridge Oriental Publications 8, 2nd edn, Cambridge (first edn, 1963).

Tylecote, R. F. (1962) *Metallurgy in Archaeology: A Prehistory of Metallurgy in the British Isles*, London.

Ubelaker, D. H. (1978) *Human Skeletal Remains: Excavations, Analysis, Interpretation*, Chicago (3rd edn, 1999).

Unger, R. W. (1980) *The Ship in the Medieval Economy, 600–1600*, London.

United Nations (1953) *The Determinants and Consequences of Population Trends: A Summary of the Findings of Studies on the Relationships between Population Changes and Economic and Social Conditions*, United Nations Population Studies 17, New York.

(1956) *Methods for Population Projections by Sex and Age*, United Nations Population Studies 25, New York.

*Unruh, F. (2001) '... *Dass alle Welt geschätzt würde'. Volkszählung im römischen Reich*, Schriften des Limesmuseums Aalen 54, Stuttgart.

van Berchem, D. (1939) *Les distributions de blé et d'argent à la plèbe romaine sous l'empire*, Geneva.

van der Horst, P. W. (1993–4) 'The Birkat ha-minim in recent research', *Expository Times* 105: 363–8 (repr. in his *Hellenism – Judaism – Christianity: Essays on their Interaction,* Contributions to Biblical Exegesis and Theology 8, 2nd edn, Leuven, 1998, 113–24).

*van Minnen, P. (1994) 'House-to-House enquiries: an interdisciplinary approach to Roman Karanis', *ZPE* 100: 227–51.

Veilleux, A. (1981) *Pachomian Koinonia*, vol. 2: *Pachomian Chronicles and Rules*, Cistercian Studies 46, Kalamazoo, MI.

Veyne, P. (1960) 'Iconographie de la «transvectio equitum» et des Lupercales', *Rev. Ét. Anc.* 62: 100–12.

(1976) *Le pain et le cirque. Sociologie historique d'un pluralisme politique*, Paris (abridged as *Bread and Circuses: Historical Sociology and Political Pluralism*, trans. B. Pearce, London, 1990).

(1984) *Writing History: Essay on Epistemology*, trans. M. Moore-Rinvolucri, Manchester (first published as *Comment on écrit l'histoire. Essai d'épistémologie*, Paris, 1971).

(1991) *La société romaine*, Paris.

Viereck, P. (1895) 'Quittungen aus dem Dorfe Karanis ueber Lieferung von Saatkorn', *Hermes* 30: 107–23.

Vogt, J. (1972) *Sklaverei und Humanität. Studien zur antiken Sklaverei und ihrer Erforschung*, 2nd edn, *Historia* Einzelschriften 44, Wiesbaden (trans. T. Wiedemann, *Ancient Slavery and the Ideal of Man*, Oxford, 1974).

von Freyberg, H.-U. (1988) *Kapitalverkehr und Handel im römischen Kaiserreich (27 v. Chr.–235 n. Chr.)*, Schriftenreihe des Instituts für Allgemeine Wirtschaftsforschung der Albert-Ludwigs-Universität Freiburg im Breisgau 32, Freiburg im Breisgau.

Walbank, F. W. (1957–79) *A Historical Commentary on Polybius*, 3 vols, Oxford.

Walker, D. R. (1976–8) *The Metrology of the Roman Silver Coinage*, 3 vols, British Archaeological Reports: supplemetary series 5, 22, 40, Oxford.

*Wallace, S. L. (1938) *Taxation in Egypt from Augustus to Diocletian*, Princeton University Studies in Papyrology 2, Princeton.

*Wallace-Hadrill, A. (1991) 'Elites and trade in the Roman town', in J. Rich and A. Wallace-Hadrill (eds) *City and Country in the Ancient World*, Leicester-Nottingham Studies in Ancient Society 2, London, 241–72.

*(2008) *Rome's Cultural Revolution*, Cambridge (corrected edn, 2010).

*Wallerstein, I. (1974) *The Modern World-System,* vol. 1: *Capitalist Agriculture and the Origins of the European World-Economy in the Sixteenth Century,* London.

*Walters, J. (1997) 'Invading the Roman body: manliness and impenetrability in Roman thought', in J. P. Hallett and M. B. Skinner (eds) *Roman Sexualities*, Princeton, 29–43.

Watson, G. R. (1969) *The Roman Soldier*, London.

Weber, M. (1896) 'Die sozialen Gründe des Untergangs der antiken Kultur', in *Die Wahrheit. Halbmonatsschrift zur Vertiefung in die Fragen und Aufgaben des Menschenlebens*, ed. C. Schrempf, Stuttgart, 3.63: 57–77 = Weber 1924: 289–311 = *Max-Weber-Gesamtausgabe*, vol. 1/6. *Zur Sozial- und Wirtschaftsgeschichte des Altertums. Schriften und Reden 1893–1908*, ed. J. Deininger, Tübingen, 2006, 82–127 (trans. C. Mackauer, *The Journal of General Education* 5 (1950) 75–88, repr. in J. E. T. Eldridge, *Max Weber: The Interpretation of Social Reality*, London, 1972, 254–75 and R. I. Frank, *The Agrarian Sociology of Ancient Civilizations*, London, 1976, 389–411).

(1904) 'Die "Objectivität" sozialwissenschaftlicher und sozialpolitischer Erkenntnis', *Archiv für Sozialwissenschaft und Sozialpolitik* 19: 22–87 (repr. in his *Gesammelte Aufsätze zur Wissenschaftslehre*, Tübingen, 1922, 146–214).

*(1909) 'Agrarverhälnisse im Altertum', in J. E. Conrad, L. Elster, W. Lexis and E. Loening (eds) *Handwörterbuch der Staatswissenschaften*, 3rd edn, Jena, vol. 1, 52–188 = Weber 1924: 1–288 = *Max-Weber-Gesamtausgabe,* vol. 1/6. *Zur Sozial- und Wirtschaftsgeschichte des Altertums. Schriften und Reden 1893–1908,* ed. J. Deininger, Tübingen, 2006, 320–747 (trans. R. I. Frank, *The Agrarian Sociology of Ancient Civilizations*, London, 1976, 37–747).

(1924) *Gesammelte Aufsätze zur Soziologie und Sozialpolitik*, ed. Marianne Weber, Tübingen.

*Weiss, D., Shotyk, W., Cheburkin, A. K., Gloor, M. and Reese, S. (1997) 'Atmospheric lead deposition from 12,400 to ca. 2,000 yrs BP in a peat bog profile, Jura Mountains, Switzerland', *Water, Air, and Soil Pollution* 100: 311–24.

*Weiss, D., Shotyk, W. and Kempf, O. (1999) 'Archives of atmospheric lead pollution', *Naturwissenschaften* 86: 262–75.

Weiss, K. M. (1973) *Demographic Models for Anthropology*, Memoirs of the Society for American Archaeology 27, Washington, DC.

*Wesch-Klein, G. (2007) 'Recruits and veterans', in P. Erdkamp (ed.) *A Companion to the Roman Army*, Blackwell Companions to the Ancient World, Oxford, 435–50.

Westermann, W. L. (1955) *The Slave Systems of Greek and Roman Antiquity*, Memoirs of the American Philosophical Society 40, Philadelphia.

Wheeler, R. E. M. (1943) *Maiden Castle, Dorset*, Reports of the Research Committee of the Society of Antiquaries of London 12, Oxford.

Wheeler, R. E. M. and Wheeler, T. V. (1936) *Verulamium: A Belgic and Two Roman Cities*, Reports of the Research Committee of the Society of Antiquaries of London 11, Oxford.

White, L. M. (1990) *Building God's House in the Roman World: Architectural Adaptation among Pagans, Jews, and Christians*, Baltimore.

Whittaker, C. R. (1985) 'Trade and the aristocracy in the Roman empire', *Opus* 4: 49–75 (repr. in his *Land, City and Trade in the Roman Empire*, Aldershot, 1993, no. 12).

*(1990) 'The consumer city revisited: the *vicus* and the city', *JRA* 3: 110–18 (repr. in his *Land, City and Trade in the Roman Empire*, Aldershot, 1993, no. 8).

*(1994) *Frontiers of the Roman Empire: A Social and Economic Study*, Baltimore.

Wiechers, A. (1961) *Aesop in Delphi*, Beiträge zur klassischen Philologie 2, Meisenheim.

*Wiemer, H.-U. (1997) 'Das Edikt des L. Antistius Rusticus. Eine Preisregulierung als Antwort auf eine überregionale Versorgungskrise?', *Anatolian Studies* 47: 195–215.

Wilhelm, A. (1914) 'Urkunden aus Messene', *JÖAI* 17: 1–120.

Willcox, W. F. (1938) 'The length of life in the early Roman empire: a methodological note', *Congrès international de la population, Paris, 1937*, vol. 2. *Démographie historique*, Actualités scientifiques et industrielles 711, Paris, 14–22.

*Williams, C. A. (2010) *Roman Homosexuality*, 2nd edn, Oxford.

*Wilson, A. I. (2002) 'Machines, power and the ancient economy', *JRS* 92: 1–32.

*(2011a) 'City sizes and urbanization in the Roman empire', in Bowman and Wilson, 161–95.

*(2011b) 'The economic influence of developments in maritime technology in antiquity', in Harris and Iara, 211–33.

*(2014) 'Quantifying Roman economic performance by means of proxies: pitfalls and potential', in de Callataÿ, 147–67.

*Wilson, A. N. (1997) *Paul: The Mind of the Apostle*, London.

*Winterling, A. (1999) *Aula Caesaris. Studien zur Institutionalisierung des römischen Kaiserhofes in der Zeit von Augustus bis Commodus (31 v. Chr.–192 n. Chr.)*, Munich.

Wipszycka, E. (1961) 'The Δωρεά of Apollonios the Dioeketes in the Memphite Nome', *Klio* 39: 153–90.

(1965) *L'industrie textile dans l'Égypte romaine*, Archiwum filologiczne 9, Wrocław.

(1984) 'Le degrée d'alphabétisation en Égypte byzantine', *REAug* 30: 279–96 (repr. in her *Études sur le Christianisme dans l'Égypte de l'Antiquité tardive*, Studia Ephemeridis Augustinianum 52, Rome, 1996, 107–26).

Wittfogel, K. A. (1957) *Oriental Despotism: A Comparative Study of Total Power*, New Haven.

Wolf, J. G. (1988) *Das Senatusconsultum Silanianum und die Senatsrede des C. Cassius Longinus aus dem Jahre 61 n. Chr.*, Sitzungsberichte der

Heidelberger Akademie der Wissenschaften, philologisch-historische Klasse 1988/2, Heidelberg.

*Wong, L. S. K. (1978) 'The squatter problem', in his (ed.) *Housing in Hong Kong: A Multi-Disciplinary Study*, Hong Kong, 204–32.

*Woods, R. (2007) 'Ancient and early modern mortality: experience and understanding', *Economic History Review* 60: 373–99.

*Woolf, G. D. (1998) *Becoming Roman: The Origins of Provincial Civilization in Gaul*, Cambridge.

*(2000) 'Literacy', in Bowman, Garnsey and Rathbone, 875–97.

*(2009) 'Literacy or literacies in Rome?', in W. A. Johnson and H. N. Parker (eds) *Ancient Literacies: The Culture of Reading in Greece and Rome*, Oxford, 46–68.

Wrigley, E. A. (1967) 'A simple model of London's importance in changing English society and economy 1650–1750', *Past & Present* 37: 44–70 (repr. in Abrams and Wrigley, 215–43, and in his *People, Cities and Wealth: The Transformation of Traditional Society*, Oxford, 1987, 133–56).

(1969) *Population and History*, London.

Wrigley, E. A. and Schofield, R. S. (1981) *The Population History of England, 1541–1871: A Reconstruction*, London.

Yeo, C. A. (1951–2) 'The economics of Roman and American slavery', *Finanzarchiv* (NS) 13: 455–85.

*Yourcenar, M. (1951) *Mémoires d'Hadrien*, Paris (trans. G. Frick, *Memoirs of Hadrian,* London, 1955).

Youtie, H. C. (1966) 'Pétaus, fils de Pétaus, ou le scribe qui ne savait pas écrire', *Chronique d'Égypte* 41: 127–43 (repr. in Youtie 1973–5: II 677–95).

(1971a) 'ΑΓΡΑΜΜΑΤΟΣ: an aspect of Greek society in Egypt', *HSCP* 75: 161–76 (repr. in Youtie, 1973–5: II 611–27).

(1971b) 'Βραδέως γράφων, between literacy and illiteracy', *GRBS* 12: 239–61 (repr. in Youtie, 1973–5: II 629–51).

(1973–5) *Scriptiunculae*, 3 vols, Amsterdam.

(1975) 'ὑπογραφεύς: the social impact of illiteracy in Graeco-Roman Egypt', *ZPE* 17: 201–21 (repr. in his *Scriptiunculae posteriores*, 2 vols, Bonn, 1981–2, vol. 1, 179–99).

*Yung, B. R. (2008) *Hong Kong's Housing Policy: A Case Study in Social Justice*, Hong Kong.

Zalateo, G. (1961) 'Papiri scolastici', *Aegyptus* 41: 160–235.

Zanker P. (1988) *The Power of Images in the Age of Augustus*, trans. A. Shapiro, Ann Arbor (first published as *Augustus und die Macht der Bilder,* Munich, 1987).

Zeitz, H. (1936) 'Der Aesoproman und seine Geschichte. Eine Untersuchung im Anschluss an die neugefundenen Papyri', *Aegyptus* 16: 225–56.

Zeldin, T. (1973) *France 1848–1945*, vol. 1: *Ambition, Love and Politics*, Oxford.
*Zhao, Z. (1997) 'Long-term mortality patterns in Chinese history: evidence from a recorded clan population', *Population Studies* 51: 117–27.
*Zuiderhoek, A. (2016) *The Ancient City*, Cambridge.

INDEX

For EU product safety concerns, contact us at Calle de José Abascal, 56–1°, 28003 Madrid, Spain or eugpsr@cambridge.org.

www.ingramcontent.com/pod-product-compliance
Ingram Content Group UK Ltd.
Pitfield, Milton Keynes, MK11 3LW, UK
UKHW020321140625
459647UK00018B/1960

* 9 7 8 1 0 0 9 3 5 3 7 8 6 *